Practical Research
PLANNING AND DESIGN

ELEVENTH EDITION

Paul D. Leedy
Late of American University

and

Jeanne Ellis Ormrod
University of Northern Colorado (Emerita)

PEARSON

Boston   Columbus   Indianapolis   New York   San Francisco   Hoboken
Amsterdam   Cape Town   Dubai   London   Madrid   Milan   Munich   Paris   Montréal   Toronto
Delhi   Mexico City   São Paulo   Sydney   Hong Kong   Seoul   Singapore   Taipei   Tokyo

Vice President and Editorial Director: Jeffery W. Johnston
Vice President and Publisher: Kevin Davis
Editorial Assistant: Caitlin Griscom
Development Editor: Gail Gottfried
Executive Field Marketing Manager: Krista Clark
Vice President, Director of Marketing: Margaret Waples
Senior Product Marketing Manager: Christopher Barry
Project Manager: Lauren Carlson
Procurement Specialist: Carol Melville
Senior Art Director: Diane Lorenzo
Cover Designer: Jennifer Hart
Full-Service Project Management: Mary Tindle, S4Carlisle Publishing Services
Composition: S4Carlisle Publishing Services
Printer/Binder: Courier Kendallville
Cover Printer: Courier Kendallville
Text Font: Garamond 3 LT Std

Credits and acknowledgments for materials borrowed from other sources and reproduced, with permission, in this textbook appear on the appropriate page within text.

Every effort has been made to provide accurate and current Internet information in this book. However, the Internet and information posted on it are constantly changing, so it is inevitable that some of the Internet addresses listed in this textbook will change.

Library of Congress Cataloging-in-Publication Data
Leedy, Paul D.
  Practical research: planning and design/Paul D. Leedy, Jeanne Ellis Ormrod, University of Northern
    Colorado (Emerita).—Eleventh edition.
    pages cm.
  Includes bibliographical references and index.
  ISBN-13: 978-0-13-374132-2
  ISBN-10: 0-13-374132-X
  1. Research—Methodology.   I. Ormrod, Jeanne Ellis.   II. Title.
  Q180.55.M4L43 2015
  001.4—dc23
                                                        2014023060

10 9 8 7 6 5 4 3 2 1

ISBN 10:   0-13-374132-X
ISBN 13: 978-0-13-374132-2

Preface

Every year brings exciting new strategies in research methodologies, making any updated edition of *Practical Research* a joy to write. With this eleventh edition, the book has been revised in numerous ways. As always, every page has been revisited—every word, in fact—and many minor changes have been made to tighten the prose or enhance its clarity. Also, discussions of technology-based strategies have been updated to reflect not only new software options but also the increasing technological sophistication of most of our readers.

Probably the two most noteworthy changes in this edition are the addition of a new chapter and a reorganization of some of the other chapters. In response to reviewers' requests, the tenth edition's chapter "Qualitative Research" has been expanded into two chapters, "Qualitative Research Methods" and "Analyzing Qualitative Data." Discussions of quantitative research methods now precede (rather than follow) discussions of qualitative methodologies, and the chapter on analyzing quantitative data now immediately follows the two chapters on quantitative methodologies.

Other significant changes in the eleventh edition are these:

Chapter 1. Revision of Figure 1.1 and accompanying text to include seven (rather than six) steps in order to better align with discussions that follow in the chapter; new section on philosophical underpinnings of various methodologies; new discussion of quantitative vs. qualitative vs. mixed-methods research (moved from its previous location in Chapter 4); discussion of the iterative nature of research; expansion of Table 1.1; revision of the guidelines for using word processing software to focus on features that readers may not routinely use in their day-to-day writing.

Chapter 2. Introduction of the idea of *a priori* hypotheses (to distinguish them from hypotheses that researchers might form midway through a study); new discussion about identifying the limitations (as well as delimitations) of a proposed study.

Chapter 3. Elimination of outdated sections "Using Indexes and Abstracts" and "Locating Relevant Government Documents," with electronically based strategies in those sections being incorporated into the sections "Using Online Databases" and "Surfing the Internet"; relocation of the discussion of database creation to the Practical Application "Planning a Literature Search."

Chapter 4. Better balance between discussions of quantitative and qualitative approaches; addition of design-based research to what is now Table 4.2 (previously Table 4.5).

Chapter 6 (formerly Chapter 8). New discussion of rubrics; omission of a random numbers table (because such tables are widely available on the Internet); expanded discussion of possible biases in descriptive research; new Guidelines feature ("Identifying Possible Sampling Bias in Questionnaire Research"); new Checklist feature ("Identifying Potential Sources of Bias in a Descriptive Study").

- **Chapter 7 (formerly Chapter 9).** New section on possible biases in quantitative research; new Checklist ("Identifying Potential Sources of Bias and Potential Threats to External Validity in an Experimental, Quasi-Experimental, or Ex Post Facto Study").
- **Chapter 8 (formerly Chapter 11).** New example (regarding a cancer prognosis) as an illustration of the limitations of a median as a predictor; addition of the five-number summary as a possible indicator of variability in ordinal data.
- **Chapter 9 (formerly Chapter 6).** Focus now on general design, planning, and data collection in qualitative research, with data analysis being moved to the new Chapter 11; new section on validity and reliability; expanded discussion of how cultural differences can influence interviews; relocation of the extensive example in international relations (formerly in the chapter "Descriptive Research") to this chapter, where it is more appropriately placed.
- **Chapter 10 (formerly Chapter 7).** Expanded discussion of possible biases in primary and secondary sources; updated and expanded list of online databases.
- **Chapter 11 (new chapter).** Greatly expanded discussion of qualitative data analysis; new Checklist ("Pinning Down the Data Analysis in a Qualitative Study"); new Sample Dissertation (by Society for Research in Child Development award winner Christy Leung).
- **Chapter 12 (formerly Chapter 10).** Expanded discussion of mixed-methods designs, with a new fifth category, *multiphase iterative designs*; new Conceptual Analysis Exercise ("Identifying Mixed-Methods Research Designs"); new section on sampling; expanded discussion of data analysis strategies; new Practical Application section discussing helpful software for analyzing mixed-methods data; new section on systematic reviews.
- **Chapter 13 (formerly Chapter 12).** Better balance between quantitative and qualitative research reports; reorganization and revision of the section "Essential Elements of a Research Report" (formerly titled "Planning a Research Report"); updated discussion of APA style for electronic resources; new Guidelines feature ("Writing a Clear, Coherent Report").

THE PURPOSE OF THIS BOOK

Practical Research: Planning and Design is a broad-spectrum, cross-disciplinary book suitable for a wide variety of courses in basic research methodology. Many basic concepts and strategies in research transcend the boundaries of specific academic areas, and such concepts and strategies are at the heart of this book. To some degree, certainly, research methods do vary from one subject area to another: A biologist might gather data by looking through a microscope, a historian by examining written documents from an earlier time period, and a psychologist by administering certain tests or systematically observing people's behavior. Otherwise, the basic approach to research is the same. Regardless of the discipline, the researcher identifies a question in need of an answer, collects data potentially relevant to the answer, analyzes and interprets the data, and draws conclusions that the data seem to warrant.

Students in the social sciences, the natural sciences, education, medicine, business administration, landscape architecture, and other academic disciplines have used this text as a guide to the successful completion of their research projects. *Practical Research* guides students from problem selection to completed research report with many concrete examples and practical, how-to suggestions. Students come to understand that research needs planning and design, and they discover how they can effectively and professionally conduct their own research projects. Essentially, this is a do-it-yourself, understand-it-yourself manual. From that standpoint, it can be a guide for students who are left largely to their own resources in carrying out their research projects. The book, supplemented by occasional counseling by an academic advisor, can guide the student to the completion of a successful research project.

LEARNING ABOUT THE RESEARCH PROCESS IS AN ESSENTIAL COMPONENT OF ACADEMIC TRAINING

All too often, students mistakenly believe that conducting research involves nothing more than amassing a large number of facts and incorporating them into a lengthy, footnoted paper. They reach the threshold of a master's thesis or doctoral dissertation only to learn that simply assembling previously known information is insufficient and unacceptable. Instead, they must do something radically different: They must answer a question that has never been answered before and, in the process, must discover something that no one else has ever discovered. Something has gone tragically wrong in the education of students who have, for so many years of their schooling, entirely misunderstood the true nature of research.

Research has one end: the discovery of some sort of "truth." Its purpose is to learn what has never before been known; to ask a significant question for which no conclusive answer has previously been found; and, by collecting and interpreting relevant data, to find an answer to that question.

Learning about and doing research are of value far beyond that of merely satisfying a program requirement. Research methods and their application to real-world problems are skills that will serve you for the rest of your life. The world is full of problems that beg for solutions; consequently, it is full of research activity! The media continually bring us news of previously unknown biological and physical phenomena, life-saving medical interventions, and ground-breaking technological innovations—all the outcomes of research. Research is not an academic banality; it is a vital and dynamic force that is indispensable to the health and well-being of Planet Earth and its human and nonhuman inhabitants.

More immediate, however, is the need to apply research methodology to those lesser daily problems that nonetheless demand a thoughtful resolution. Those who have learned how to analyze problems systematically and dispassionately will live with greater confidence and success than those who have shortsightedly dismissed research as nothing more than a necessary hurdle on the way to a degree. Given the advantages that a researcher's viewpoint provides, considering an academic research requirement as annoying and irrelevant to one's education is simply an untenable position.

Many students have found *Practical Research* quite helpful in their efforts both to understand the nature of the research process and to complete their research projects. Its simplification of research concepts and its readability make it especially suitable for those undergraduate and graduate students who are introduced, perhaps for the first time, to genuine research methodology.

We hope we have convinced you that a course on research methodology is not a temporary hurdle on the way to a degree but, instead, an unparalleled opportunity to learn how you might better tackle any problem for which you do not have a ready solution. In a few years you will undoubtedly look back on your research methods course as one of the most rewarding and practical courses in your entire educational experience.

Acknowledgments

No man is an iland, entire of it selfe; every man is a peece of the Continent, a part of the maine . . .

So wrote John Donne, the great dean of St. Paul's Cathedral in the 17th century. And so do we authors write in the 21st century.

Those who have had a part in the making of this book, known and unknown, friends and colleagues, gentle critics and able editors—all—are far too many to salute individually. Those of you who have written in journals and textbooks about research methods and strategies, the generations of graduate and undergraduate students whom we authors have taught and who have also taught *us,* the kindly letters and e-mail messages that so many of you have written to describe how this book has helped you in your own research endeavors—to all of you, I extend my acknowledgment and appreciation wherever you may be. You have had the greater part in bringing this book through its previous ten editions. I am especially grateful to the reviewers of the eleventh edition, who recently offered many good suggestions for strengthening the book so that it can better assist novice researchers in the 21st century: Brian Belland, Utah State University; Robert Hayden, Michigan State University; Walter Nekrosius, Wright State University; Lloyd Rieber, University of Georgia; and Susan Twombly, University of Kansas.

I am also indebted to the students whose research proposals, doctoral dissertations, and master's theses have enabled me to illustrate some of the research and writing strategies described in the book. In particular, I extend my gratitude to Rosenna Bakari, Arthur Benton, Jennifer Chandler, Kay Corbett, Dinah Jackson, Ginny Kinnick, Laura Lara-Brady, Peter Leavenworth, Christy Leung, Matthew McKenzie, Kimberly Mitchell, Richard Ormrod, Luis Ramirez, Janie Shaklee, Nancy Thrailkill, and Debby Zambo. Pete Leavenworth and Matt McKenzie gave me their time as well as their research reports, and their recommendations for the chapter on historical research were superb.

Equally important is to say "Thank you, thank you, thank you" to many folks at Pearson and S4Carlisle who have been key players in bringing this book to fruition. In particular, I extend my deepest gratitude to Gail Gottfried, who has lined up helpful multimedia supplements to the book and, in general, has been a regular and reliable sounding board and source of support throughout my writing endeavors in recent years. Thanks also to Lauren Carlson and Mary Tindle, both of whom have expertly coordinated what has become an ever-evolving and increasingly complex textbook-production process in the electronic age. A shout-out to Chris Feldman, whose close attention to nitty-gritty details during copy edits has consistently warmed the cockles of my obsessive-compulsive heart. And several people have worked diligently outside my range of sight to make the whole project come together; hearty thanks to Kate Wadsworth for the interactive quizzes and end-of-chapter activities, as well as to Carrie Mollette, Caroline Fenton, and Caitlin Griscom for the many behind-the-scenes contributions I can only begin to fathom.

Finally, I must thank our editor, Kevin Davis, for his guidance throughout this and preceding editions. Throughout its many editions, Kevin has shared Paul's and my vision for the book and struck the ever-so-important balance between providing guidance to help us improve it while also trusting our instincts about how best to explain and illustrate the complex, multifaceted nature of research planning and design.

No author is an island, entire of itself. Paul and I have had many hands guiding our pens and many minds adding richness and depth to our thoughts. All of you have been exceedingly helpful, all of you have been "a peece of the Continent, a part of the maine." For that, I offer my humble and hearty thanks.

Jeanne Ellis Ormrod

Brief Contents

Contents

PART II   Focusing Your Research Efforts

USING TECHNOLOGY

USING TECHNOLOGY

Chapter 4

Chapter 5

PART III   Quantitative Research

Chapter 6

Descriptive Research. 136

Chapter 7

Experimental, Quasi-Experimental, and Ex Post Facto Designs 178

Chapter 8

PART IV   Qualitative Research

Chapter 9

Chapter 10

Historical Research 278

Chapter 11

Analyzing Qualitative Data 291

PART V   Mixed-Methods Research

PART VI   Research Reports

Interpretation of the Data 333
Identification of Possible Weaknesses of the Study 335
Summary and Connections to a Broader Context 335
Maintaining Your Academic Integrity 335
Front Matter and End Matter 336
Preliminary Pages 336
Endnotes and Footnotes 337
USING TECHNOLOGY *Reference List* 337
Appendix Content 340
Organizing a Research Report 340
Writing—and Finishing!—A Report 342
PRACTICAL APPLICATION: Writing Your Final Report 342
GUIDELINES: Writing a Clear, Coherent Report 343
PRACTICAL APPLICATION: Developing a Writing Schedule 344
GUIDELINES: Pinning Down and Adhering to a Workable Schedule 345
PRACTICAL APPLICATION: Critiquing a Final Research Report 346
CHECKLIST: Criteria for Critiquing a Research Report 346
Beyond the Unpublished Research Report: Presenting and Publishing 348
Conference Presentations 348
PRACTICAL APPLICATION: Presenting Your Research at a Professional Conference 349
GUIDELINES: Presenting an Effective Paper or Poster 349
Journal Articles 350
Sharing Authorship 351
Responding to Reviewers' Critiques 351
A Closing Thought 352
For Further Reading 352

APPENDICES

Appendix A Using a Spreadsheet: Microsoft Excel 354
USING TECHNOLOGY Using Excel to Keep Track of Literature Resources 354
Using Excel to Record and Recode Data 356
Reorganizing Data in Excel 359
Using Excel to Perform Simple Statistical Analyses 359

Appendix B Using SPSS 361
USING TECHNOLOGY Creating a Data Set 361
Computing Basic Descriptive Statistics 363
Computing Inferential Statistics 364

Glossary 367

References 373

Index 378

The Nature and Tools of Research

In virtually every subject area, our collective knowledge about the world is incomplete: Certain questions remain unanswered, and certain problems remain unsolved. Systematic research provides many powerful tools—not only physical tools but also mental and social tools—that can help us discover possible answers and identify possible solutions.

Learning Outcomes

1.1 Distinguish between (a) common uses of the term *research* that reflect misconceptions about what research involves and (b) the true nature of research in academic settings.

1.2 Describe the cyclical, iterative nature of research, including the steps that a genuine research project involves.

1.3 Distinguish among positivism, postpositivism, constructivism, and pragmatism/realism as philosophical underpinnings of a research project.

1.4 Identify examples of how six general research tools can play significant roles in a research project: (a) the library and its resources, (b) computer technology, (c) measurement, (d) statistics, (e) language, and (f) the human mind.

1.5 Describe steps you might take to explore research in your field.

In everyday speech, the word *research* is often used loosely to refer to a variety of activities. In some situations the word connotes simply finding a piece of information or taking notes and then writing a so-called "research paper." In other situations it refers to the act of informing oneself about what one does not know, perhaps by rummaging through available sources to locate a few tidbits of information. Such uses of the term can create considerable confusion for university students, who must learn to use it in a narrower, more precise sense.

Yet when used in its true sense—as a systematic process that leads to new knowledge and understandings—the word *research* can suggest a mystical activity that is somehow removed from everyday life. Many people imagine researchers to be aloof individuals who seclude themselves in laboratories, scholarly libraries, or the ivory towers of large universities. In fact, research is often a practical enterprise that—given appropriate tools—*any* rational, conscientious individual can conduct. In this chapter we lay out the nature of true research and describe the general tools that make it possible.

WHAT RESEARCH IS NOT

Following are three statements that describe what research is not. Accompanying each statement is an example that illustrates a common misconception about research.

1. ***Research is not merely gathering information.*** A sixth grader comes home from school and tells her parents, "The teacher sent us to the library today to do research, and I learned a lot

about black holes." For this student, research means going to the library to find a few facts. This might be *information discovery,* or it might be learning *reference skills.* But it certainly is not, as the teacher labeled it, research.

2. ***Research is not merely rummaging around for hard-to-locate information.***   The house across the street is for sale. You consider buying it and call your realtor to find out how much someone else might pay you for your current home. "I'll have to do some research to determine the fair market value of your property," the realtor tells you. What the realtor calls doing "some research" means, of course, reviewing information about recent sales of properties comparable to yours; this information will help the realtor zero in on a reasonable asking price for your own home. Such an activity involves little more than searching through various files or websites to discover what the realtor previously did not know. Rummaging—whether through records in one's own office, at a library, or on the Internet—is not research. It is more accurately called an *exercise in self-enlightenment.*

3. ***Research is not merely transporting facts from one location to another.***   A college student reads several articles about the mysterious Dark Lady in William Shakespeare's sonnets and then writes a "research paper" describing various scholars' suggestions of who the lady might have been. Although the student does, indeed, go through certain activities associated with formal research—such as collecting information, organizing it in a certain way for presentation to others, supporting statements with documentation, and referencing statements properly— these activities do not add up to true research. The student has missed the essence of research: the *interpretation* of data. Nowhere in the paper does the student say, in effect, "These facts I have gathered seem to indicate such-and-such about the Dark Lady." Nowhere does the student interpret and draw conclusions from the facts. This student is approaching genuine research; however, the mere compilation of facts, presented with reference citations and arranged in a logical sequence—no matter how polished and appealing the format—misses genuine research by a hair. Such activity might more realistically be called *fact transcription, fact documentation, fact organization,* or *fact summarization.*

Going a little further, this student would have traveled from one world to another: from the world of mere transportation of facts to the world of interpretation of facts. The difference between the two worlds is the distinction between transference of information and genuine research—a distinction that is critical for novice researchers to understand.

WHAT RESEARCH IS

Research is a systematic process of collecting, analyzing, and interpreting information—*data*— in order to increase our understanding of a phenomenon about which we are interested or concerned.[1] People often use a systematic approach when they collect and interpret information to solve the small problems of daily living. Here, however, we focus on *formal research,* research in which we intentionally set out to enhance our understanding of a phenomenon and expect to communicate what we discover to the larger scientific community.

Although research projects vary in complexity and duration, in general research involves seven distinct steps, shown in Figure 1.1. We now look at each of these steps more closely.

1. ***The researcher begins with a problem—an unanswered question.***   Everywhere we look, we see things that cause us to wonder, to speculate, to ask questions. And by asking questions, we strike a spark that ignites a chain reaction leading to the research process.

---

[1]Some people in academia use the term *research* more broadly to include deriving new equations or abstract principles from existing equations or principles through a sequence of mathematically logical and valid steps. Such an activity can be quite intellectually challenging, of course, and is often at the heart of doctoral dissertations and scholarly journal articles in mathematics, physics, and related disciplines. In this book, however, we use the term *research* more narrowly to refer to *empirical* research—research that involves the collection and analysis of new data.

FIGURE 1.1
The Research Cycle

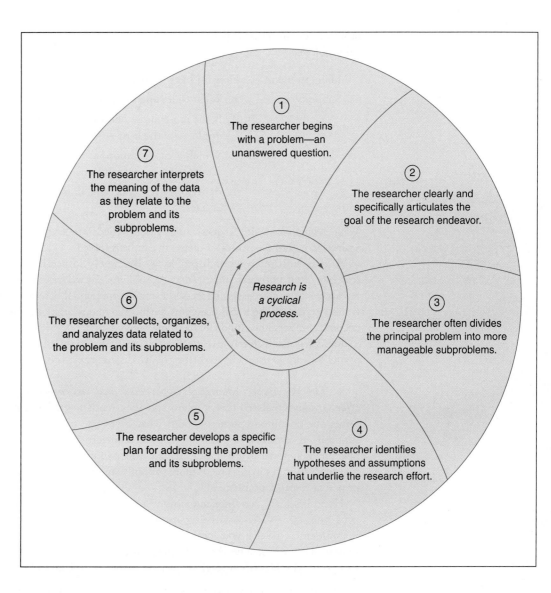

An inquisitive mind is the beginning impetus for research; as one popular tabloid puts it, "Inquiring minds want to know!"

Look around you. Consider unresolved situations that evoke these questions: What is such-and-such a situation like? Why does such-and-such a phenomenon occur? What does it all mean? With questions like these, research begins.

2. *The researcher clearly and specifically articulates the goal of the research endeavor.* A clear, unambiguous statement of the problem one will address is critical. This statement is an exercise in intellectual honesty: The ultimate goal of the research must be set forth in a grammatically complete sentence that specifically and precisely answers the question, "What problem do you intend to solve?" When you describe your objective in clear, concrete terms, you have a good idea of what you need to accomplish and can direct your efforts accordingly.

3. *The researcher often divides the principal problem into more manageable subproblems.* From a design standpoint, it is often helpful to break a main research problem into several subproblems that, when solved, can resolve the main problem.

Breaking down principal problems into small, easily solvable subproblems is a strategy we use in everyday living. For example, suppose you want to drive from your hometown to a town many miles or kilometers away. Your principal goal is to get from one location to the other as expeditiously as possible. You soon realize, however, that the problem involves several subproblems:

Main problem:	How do I get from Town A to Town B?
Subproblems:	1. What route appears to be the most direct one?
	2. Is the most direct one also the quickest one? If not, what route might take the least amount of time?
	3. Which is more important to me: minimizing my travel time or minimizing my energy consumption?
	4. At what critical junctions in my chosen route must I turn right or left?

What seems like a single question can be divided into several smaller questions that must be addressed before the principal question can be resolved.

So it is with most research problems. By closely inspecting the principal problem, the researcher often uncovers important subproblems. By addressing each of the subproblems, the researcher can more easily address the main problem. If a researcher doesn't take the time or trouble to isolate the lesser problems within the major problem, the overall research project can become cumbersome and difficult to manage.

Identifying and clearly articulating the problem and its subproblems are the essential starting points for formal research. Accordingly, we discuss these processes in depth in Chapter 2.

4. *The researcher identifies hypotheses and assumptions that underlie the research effort.*   Having stated the problem and its attendant subproblems, the researcher sometimes forms one or more hypotheses about what he or she may discover. A hypothesis is a logical supposition, a reasonable guess, an educated conjecture. It provides a tentative explanation for a phenomenon under investigation. It may direct your thinking to possible sources of information that will aid in resolving one or more subproblems and, as a result, may also help you resolve the principal research problem.

Hypotheses are certainly not unique to research. In your everyday life, if something happens, you immediately try to account for its cause by making some reasonable conjectures. For example, imagine that you come home after dark, open your front door, and reach inside for the switch that turns on a nearby table lamp. Your fingers find the switch. You flip it. No light. At this point, you identify several hypotheses regarding the lamp's failure:

Hypothesis 1: A recent storm has disrupted your access to electrical power.
Hypothesis 2: The bulb has burned out.
Hypothesis 3: The lamp isn't securely plugged into the wall outlet.
Hypothesis 4: The wire from the lamp to the wall outlet is defective.
Hypothesis 5: You forgot to pay your electric bill.

Each of these hypotheses hints at a strategy for acquiring information that may resolve the nonfunctioning-lamp problem. For instance, to test Hypothesis 1, you might look outside to see whether your neighbors have lights, and to test Hypothesis 2, you might replace the current light bulb with a new one.

Hypotheses in a research project are as tentative as those for a nonfunctioning table lamp. For example, a biologist might speculate that certain human-made chemical compounds increase the frequency of birth defects in frogs. A psychologist might speculate that certain personality traits lead people to show predominantly liberal or conservative voting patterns. A marketing researcher might speculate that humor in a television commercial will capture viewers' attention and thereby will increase the odds that viewers buy the advertised product. Notice the word *speculate* in all of these examples. Good researchers always begin a project with open minds about what they may—or may *not*—discover in their data.

Hypotheses—predictions—are an essential ingredient in certain kinds of research, especially experimental research (see Chapter 7). To a lesser degree, they might guide other forms of research as well, but they are intentionally *not* identified in the early stages of some kinds of qualitative research (e.g., see the discussion of grounded theory studies in Chapter 9).

Whereas a hypothesis involves a prediction that may or may not be supported by the data, an assumption is a condition that is taken for granted, without which the research project would be pointless. Careful researchers—certainly those conducting research in an academic environment—set forth a statement of their assumptions as the bedrock upon which their study rests. For example, imagine that your problem is to investigate whether students learn the unique grammatical structures of a language more quickly by studying only one foreign language at a time or by studying two foreign languages concurrently. What assumptions would underlie such a problem? At a minimum, you must assume that

- The teachers used in the study are competent to teach the language or languages in question and have mastered the grammatical structures of the language(s) they are teaching.
- The students taking part in the research are capable of mastering the unique grammatical structures of any language(s) they are studying.
- The languages selected for the study have sufficiently different grammatical structures that students might reasonably learn to distinguish between them.

Aside from such basic ideas as these, however, careful researchers state their assumptions, so that other people inspecting the research project can evaluate it in accordance with *their own* assumptions. For the beginning researcher, it is better to be overly explicit than to take too much for granted.

5. *The researcher develops a specific plan for addressing the problem and its subproblems.* Research is not a blind excursion into the unknown, with the hope that the data necessary to address the research problem will magically emerge. It is, instead, a carefully planned itinerary of the route you intend to take in order to reach your final destination—your research goal. Consider the title of this text: *Practical Research: Planning and Design.* The last three words—*Planning and Design*—are especially important ones. Researchers plan their overall research design and specific research methods in a purposeful way so that they can acquire data relevant to their research problem and subproblems. Depending on the research question, different designs and methods are more or less appropriate.

In the formative stages of a research project, much can be decided: Are any existing data directly relevant to the research problem? If so, where are they, and are you likely to have access to them? If the needed data *don't* currently exist, how might you generate them? And later, after you have acquired the data you need, what will you do with them?[2] Such questions merely hint at the fact that planning and design cannot be postponed. Each of the questions just listed—and many more—must have an answer early in the research process. In Chapter 4, we discuss several general issues related to research planning. Then, beginning in Chapter 6, we describe strategies related to various research methodologies.

6. *The researcher collects, organizes, and analyzes data related to the problem and its subproblems.* After a researcher has isolated the problem, divided it into appropriate subproblems, identified hypotheses and assumptions, and chosen a suitable design and methodology, the next step is to collect whatever data might be relevant to the problem and to organize and analyze them in meaningful ways.

The data collected in research studies take one of two general forms. Quantitative research involves looking at amounts, or *quantities,* of one or more variables of interest. A quantitative researcher typically tries to measure variables in some numerical way, perhaps by using

---

[2]As should be apparent in the questions posed in this paragraph, we are using the word *data* as a plural noun; for instance, we ask "Where *are* the data?" rather than "Where *is* the data?" Contrary to popular usage of the term as a singular noun, *data* (which has its origins in Latin) refers to two or more pieces of information. A single piece of information is known as a *datum,* or sometimes as a *data point.*

commonly accepted measures of the physical world (e.g., rulers, thermometers, oscilloscopes) or carefully designed measures of psychological characteristics or behaviors (e.g., tests, questionnaires, rating scales).

In contrast, qualitative research involves looking at characteristics, or *qualities,* that cannot be entirely reduced to numerical values. A qualitative researcher typically aims to examine the many nuances and complexities of a particular phenomenon. You are most likely to see qualitative research in studies of complex human situations (e.g., people's in-depth perspectives about a particular issue, the behaviors and values of a particular cultural group) or complex human creations (e.g., television commercials, works of art). Qualitative research is not limited to research problems involving human beings, however. For instance, some biologists study, in a distinctly qualitative manner, the complex social behaviors of other animal species; Dian Fossey's work with gorillas and Jane Goodall's studies of chimpanzees are two well-known examples (e.g., see Fossey, 1983; Goodall, 1986).

The two kinds of data—quantitative and qualitative—often require distinctly different research methods and data analysis strategies. Accordingly, three of the book's subsequent chapters focus predominantly on quantitative techniques (see Chapters 6, 7, and 8) and three others focus largely on qualitative techniques (see Chapters 9, 10, and 11). Nevertheless, we urge you *not* to think of the quantitative–qualitative distinction as a mutually exclusive, *it-has-to-be-one-thing-or-the-other* dichotomy. Many researchers collect both quantitative and qualitative data in a single research project—an approach sometimes known as mixed-methods research (see Chapter 12). Good researchers tend to be *eclectic* researchers who draw from diverse methodologies and data sources in order to best address their research problems and questions (e.g., see Gorard, 2010; Onwuegbuzie & Leech, 2005).

7. *The researcher interprets the meaning of the data as they relate to the problem and its subproblems.*   Quantitative and qualitative data are, in and of themselves, *only* data—nothing more. The significance of the data depends on how the researcher extracts *meaning* from them. In research, uninterpreted data are worthless: They can never help us answer the questions we have posed.

Yet researchers must recognize and come to terms with the subjective and dynamic nature of interpretation. Consider, for example, the many books written on the assassination of U.S. President John F. Kennedy. Different historians have studied the same events: One may interpret them one way, and another may arrive at a very different conclusion. Which one is right? Perhaps they both are; perhaps neither is. Both may have merely posed new problems for other historians to try to resolve. Different minds often find different meanings in the same set of facts.

Once we believed that clocks measured time and that yardsticks measured space. In one sense, they still do. We further assumed that time and space were two different entities. Then along came Einstein's theory of relativity, and time and space became locked into one concept: the time–space continuum. What's the difference between the old perspective and the new one? It's the way we think about, or interpret, the same information. The realities of time and space have not changed; the way we interpret them has.

Data demand interpretation. But no rule, formula, or algorithm can lead the researcher unerringly to a correct interpretation. Interpretation is inevitably a somewhat subjective process that depends on the researcher's hypotheses, assumptions, and logical reasoning processes.

Now think about how we began this chapter. We suggested that certain activities cannot accurately be called research. At this point you can understand why. None of those activities demands that the researcher draw any conclusions or make any interpretations of the data.

We must emphasize two important points related to the seven-step process just described. First, *the process is **iterative***: A researcher sometimes needs to move back and forth between two or more steps along the way. For example, while developing a specific plan for a project (Step 5), a researcher might realize that a genuine resolution of the research problem requires addressing a subproblem not previously identified (Step 3). And while interpreting the collected data (Step 7), a researcher may decide that additional data are needed to fully resolve the problem (Step 6).

Second, *the process is **cyclical**.* The final step in the process depicted in Figure 1.1—interpretation of the data—is not *really* the final step at all. Only rarely is a research project a one-shot effort that completely resolves a problem. For instance, even with the best of data, hypotheses in a research project are rarely proved or disproved—and thus research questions are rarely answered—beyond a shadow of a doubt. Instead, hypotheses are either *supported* or *not supported* by the data. If the data are consistent with a particular hypothesis, the researcher can make a case that the hypothesis probably has some merit and should be taken seriously. In contrast, if the data run contrary to a hypothesis, the researcher *rejects* the hypothesis and turns to other hypotheses as being more likely explanations of the phenomenon in question. In either case, one or more additional, follow-up studies are called for.

Ultimately, then, most research studies don't bring total closure to a research problem. There is no obvious end point—no point at which a researcher can say *"Voila!* I've completely answered the question about which I'm concerned." Instead, research typically involves a cycle—or more accurately, a *helix* (spiral)—in which one study spawns additional, follow-up studies. In exploring a topic, one comes across additional problems that need resolving, and so the process must begin anew. Research begets more research.

To view research in this way is to invest it with a dynamic quality that is its true nature—a far cry from the conventional view, which sees research as a one-time undertaking that is static, self-contained, an end in itself. Here we see another difference between true research and the nonexamples of research presented earlier in the chapter. Every researcher soon learns that genuine research is likely to yield as many problems as it resolves. Such is the nature of the acquisition of knowledge.

PHILOSOPHICAL ASSUMPTIONS UNDERLYING RESEARCH METHODOLOGIES

Let's return to Step 4 in the research process: *The researcher identifies hypotheses and assumptions that underlie the research effort.* The assumptions underlying a research project are sometimes so seemingly self-evident that a researcher may think it unnecessary to mention them. In fact, the researcher may not even be consciously aware of them! For example, two general assumptions underlie many research studies:

- The phenomenon under investigation is somewhat lawful and predictable; it is *not* comprised of completely random events.
- Cause-and-effect relationships can account for certain patterns observed in the phenomenon.

But are such assumptions justified? Is the world a lawful place, with some things definitely causing or influencing others? Or are definitive laws and cause-and-effect relationships nothing more than figments of our fertile human imaginations?

As we consider such questions, it is helpful to distinguish among different philosophical orientations[3] that point researchers in somewhat different directions in their quests to make sense of our physical, social, and psychological worlds. Historically, a good deal of research in the natural sciences has been driven by a perspective known as positivism. Positivists believe that, with appropriate measurement tools, scientists can objectively uncover absolute, undeniable *truths* about cause-and-effect relationships within the physical world and human experience.

In the social sciences, most researchers have been less self-assured and more tentative, especially within the past few decades. Some social scientists take a perspective known as postpositivism, believing that true objectivity in seeking absolute truths can be an elusive goal. Although researchers might strive for objectivity in their collection and interpretation

---

[3]Some writers use terms such as *worldviews, epistemologies,* or *paradigms* instead of the term *philosophical orientations.*

of data, they inevitably bring certain *biases* to their investigations—perhaps biases regarding the best ways to measure certain variables or the most logical inferences to draw from patterns within the data. From a postpositivist perspective, progress toward genuine understandings of physical, social, and psychological phenomena tends to be gradual and probabilistic. For example, recall the earlier discussion of hypotheses being either *supported* or *not supported* by data. Postpositivists don't say, "I've just proven such-and-such." Rather, they're more likely to say, "This increases the probability that such-and-such is true."

Still other researchers have abandoned any idea that absolute truths are somewhere "out there" in the world, waiting to be discovered. In this perspective, known as constructivism, the "realities" researchers identify are nothing more than human *creations* that can be helpful in finding subjective meanings within the data collected. Constructivists not only acknowledge that they bring certain biases to their research endeavors but also try to be as upfront as possible about these biases. The emphasis on subjectivity and bias—rather than objectivity—applies to the phenomena that constructivist researchers study as well. By and large, constructivists focus their inquiries on people's *perceptions* and *interpretations* of various phenomena, including individuals' behaviors, group processes, and cultural practices.

Many of the quantitative methodologies described in this book have postpositivist, probabilistic underpinnings—a fact that becomes especially evident in the discussion of statistics in Chapter 8. In contrast, some qualitative methodologies have a distinctly constructivist bent, with a focus on ascertaining people's *beliefs* about truth, rather than trying to pin down absolute, objective truths that might not exist at all.

Yet once again we urge you *not* to think of quantitative research and qualitative research as reflecting a mutually exclusive, *either-this-or-that* dichotomy. For instance, some quantitative researchers approach a research problem from a constructivist framework, and some qualitative researchers tend to think in a postpositivist manner. Many researchers acknowledge *both* that (a) absolute truths regarding various phenomena may actually exist—even if they are exceedingly difficult to discover—and (b) human beings' self-constructed beliefs about those phenomena are legitimate objects of study in their own right. You might see the labels pragmatism and realism used in reference to such a philosophical orientation (e.g., see R. B. Johnson & Onwuegbuzie, 2004; Maxwell & Mittapalli, 2010).

TOOLS OF RESEARCH

Every professional needs specialized tools in order to work effectively. Without hammer and saw, the carpenter is out of business; without scalpel or forceps, the surgeon cannot practice. Researchers, likewise, have their own set of tools to carry out their plans.

The tools that researchers use to achieve their research goals can vary considerably depending on the discipline. A microbiologist needs a microscope and culture media; an attorney needs a library of legal decisions and statute law. By and large, we do not discuss such discipline-specific tools in this book. Rather, our concern here is with general tools of research that the great majority of researchers of all disciplines need in order to collect data and derive meaningful conclusions.

We should be careful not to equate the *tools* of research with the *methodology* of research. A research tool is a specific mechanism or strategy the researcher uses to collect, manipulate, or interpret data. The research methodology is the general approach the researcher takes in carrying out the research project; to some extent, this approach dictates the particular tools the researcher selects.

Confusion between the tool and the research method is immediately recognizable. Such phrases as "library research" and "statistical research" are telltale signs and largely meaningless terms. They suggest a failure to understand the nature of formal research, as well as a failure to differentiate between tool and method. The library is merely a place for locating or discovering certain data that will be analyzed and interpreted at some point in the research process. Likewise, statistics merely provide ways to summarize and analyze data, thereby allowing us to see patterns within the data more clearly.

Six general tools of research are these:

1. The library and its resources
2. Computer technology
3. Measurement
4. Statistics
5. Language
6. The human mind

In the following sections, we look more closely at each of these general tools.

The Library and Its Resources

Historically, many literate human societies used libraries to assemble and store their collective knowledge. For example, in the seventh century B.C., the ancient Assyrians' Library of Nineveh contained 20,000 to 30,000 tablets, and in the second century A.D., the Romans' Library of Celsus in Ephesus housed more than 12,000 papyrus scrolls and, in later years, parchment books as well.[4]

Until the past few decades, libraries were primarily repositories of concrete, physical representations of knowledge—clay tablets, scrolls, manuscripts, books, journals, films, and the like. For the most part, any society's collective knowledge expanded rather slowly and could seemingly be contained within masonry walls. But by the latter half of the 20th century, people's knowledge about their physical and social worlds began to increase many times over, and at the present time it continues to increase at an astounding rate. In response, libraries have evolved in important ways. First, they have made use of many emerging technologies (e.g., microforms, CDs, DVDs, online databases) to store information in more compact forms. Second, they have provided increasingly fast and efficient means of locating and accessing information on virtually any topic. And third, many of them have made catalogs of their holdings available on the Internet. The libraries of today—especially university libraries—extend far beyond their local, physical boundaries.

We explore efficient use of a library and its resources in depth in Chapter 3. For now, we simply want to stress that the library is—and must be—one of the most valuable tools in any researcher's toolbox.

Computer Technology

USING TECHNOLOGY

As a research tool, the personal computer is now commonplace. Personal computers have become increasingly compact and portable—first in the form of laptops and more recently in the forms of iPads, other tablet computers, and smartphones. In addition, computer software packages and applications have become increasingly user friendly, such that novice researchers can easily take advantage of them. But like any tool—no matter how powerful—computer technology has its limitations. Yes, computers can certainly calculate, compare, search, retrieve, sort, and organize data more efficiently and accurately than you can. But in their present stage of development, they depend largely on people to give them directions about what to do.

A computer is not a miracle worker—it cannot do your thinking for you. It can, however, be a fast and faithful assistant. When told exactly what to do, it is one of the researcher's best friends. Table 1.1 provides suggestions for how you might use computer technology as a research tool.

Measurement

Especially when conducting quantitative research, a researcher needs a systematic way of *measuring* the phenomena under investigation. Some common, everyday measurement instruments—rulers, scales, stopwatches—can occasionally be helpful for measuring easily observable variables,

---

[4]Many academic scholars would instead say "seventh century BCE" and "second century CE" in this sentence, referring to the more religiously neutral terms *Before Common Era* and *Common Era*. However, we suspect that some of our readers are unfamiliar with these terms, hence our use of the more traditional ones.

TABLE 1.1 ▣ The Computer as a Research Tool

Part of the Study	Relevant Technological Support Tools
Planning the study	• Brainstorming assistance—software used to help generate and organize ideas related to the research problem, research strategies, or both. • Outlining assistance—software used to help structure various aspects of the study and focus work efforts. • Project management assistance—software used to schedule and coordinate varied tasks that must occur in a timely manner. • Budget assistance—spreadsheet software used to help in outlining, estimating, and monitoring the potential costs involved in the research effort.
Literature review	• Literature identification assistance—online databases used to help identify relevant research studies to be considered during the formative stages of the research endeavor. • Communication assistance—computer technology used to communicate with other researchers who are pursuing similar topics (e.g., e-mail, Skype, electronic bulletin boards, list servers). • Writing assistance—software used to facilitate the writing, editing, formatting, and citation management of the literature review.
Study implementation and data gathering	• Materials production assistance—software used to develop instructional materials, visual displays, simulations, or other stimuli to be used in experimental interventions. • Experimental control assistance—software used to physically control the effects of specific variables and to minimize the influence of potentially confounding variables. • Survey distribution assistance—databases and word processing software used in combination to send specific communications to a targeted population. • Online data collection assistance—websites used to conduct surveys and certain other types of studies on the Internet. • Data collection assistance—software used to take field notes or to monitor specific types of responses given by participants in a study.
Analysis and interpretation	• Organizational assistance—software used to assemble, categorize, code, integrate, and search potentially huge data sets (such as qualitative interview data or open-ended responses to survey questions). • Conceptual assistance—software used to write and store ongoing reflections about data or to construct theories that integrate research findings. • Statistical assistance—statistical and spreadsheet software packages used to categorize and analyze various types of data sets. • Graphic production assistance—software used to depict data in graphic form to facilitate interpretation.
Reporting	• Communication assistance—telecommunication software used to distribute and discuss research findings and initial interpretations with colleagues and to receive their comments and feedback. • Writing and editing assistance—word processing software used to write and edit successive drafts of the final report. • Dissemination assistance—desktop publishing software and poster creation software used to produce professional-looking documents and posters that can be displayed or distributed at conferences and elsewhere. • Presentation graphics assistance—presentation software used to create static and animated slides for conference presentations. • Networking assistance—blogs, social networking sites, and other Internet-based mechanisms used to communicate one's findings to a wider audience and to generate discussion for follow-up studies by others in the field.

such as length, weight, or time. But in most cases, a researcher needs one or more specialized instruments. For example, an astronomer might need a high-powered telescope to detect patterns of light in the night sky, and a neurophysiologist might need a magnetic resonance imaging (MRI) machine to detect and measure neural activity in the brain.

In quantitative research, social and psychological phenomena require measurement as well, even though they have no concrete, easily observable basis in the physical world. For example, an economist might use the Dow-Jones Industrial Average or NASDAQ index to track economic growth over time, a sociologist might use a questionnaire to assess people's attitudes about marriage and divorce, and an educational researcher might use an achievement test to measure the extent to which school children have learned something. Finding or developing appropriate measurement instruments for social and psychological phenomena can sometimes be quite a challenge. Thus, we explore measurement strategies in some depth when we discuss the research planning process in Chapter 4.

Statistics

Statistics tend to be more useful in some academic disciplines than in others. For instance, researchers use them quite often in such fields as psychology, medicine, and business; they use statistics less frequently in such fields as history, musicology, and literature.

Statistics have two principal functions: to help a researcher (a) describe quantitative data and (b) draw inferences from these data. Descriptive statistics summarize the general nature of the data obtained—for instance, how certain measured characteristics appear to be "on average," how much variability exists within a data set, and how closely two or more characteristics are associated with one another. In contrast, inferential statistics help the researcher make decisions about the data. For example, they might help a researcher decide whether the differences observed between two experimental groups are large enough to be attributed to the differing experimental interventions rather than to a once-in-a-blue-moon fluke. Both of these functions of statistics ultimately involve summarizing the data in some way.

In the process of summarizing data, statistical analyses often create entities that have no counterpart in reality. Let's take a simple example: Four students have part-time jobs on campus. One student works 24 hours a week in the library, a second works 22 hours a week in the campus bookstore, a third works 12 hours a week in the parking lot, and the fourth works 16 hours a week in the cafeteria. One way of summarizing the students' work hours is to calculate the arithmetic mean.[5] By doing so, we find that the students work, "on average," 18.5 hours a week. Although we have learned something about these four students and their working hours, to some extent we have learned a myth: None of these students has worked exactly 18.5 hours a week. That figure represents absolutely no fact in the real world.

If statistics offer only an unreality, then why use them? Why create myth out of hard, demonstrable data? The answer lies in the nature of the human mind. Human beings can cognitively think about only a very limited amount of information at any single point in time.[6] Statistics help condense an overwhelming body of data into an amount of information that the mind can more readily comprehend and deal with. In the process, they can help a researcher detect patterns and relationships in the data that might otherwise go unnoticed. More generally, statistics *help the human mind comprehend disparate data as an organized whole.*

Any researcher who uses statistics must remember that calculating statistical values is not—and must not be—the final step in a research endeavor. The ultimate question in research is, *What do the data indicate?* Statistics yield *information* about data, but conscientious researchers are not satisfied until they determine the *meaning* of this information.

Although a book such as this one cannot provide all of the nitty-gritty details of statistical analysis, we give you an overview of potentially useful statistical techniques in Chapter 8.

Language

One of humankind's greatest achievements is language. Not only does it allow us to communicate with one another but it also enables us to think more effectively. People can often think more clearly and efficiently about a topic when they can represent their thoughts in their heads with specific words and phrases.

---

[5]When the word *arithmetic* is used as an adjective, as it is here, it is pronounced with emphasis on the third syllable ("ar-ith-MET-ic").
[6]If you have some background in human memory and cognition, you may realize that we are talking about the limited capacity of *working memory* here (e.g., see Cowan, 2010; G. A. Miller, 1956).

For example, imagine that you're driving along a country road. In a field to your left, you see an object with the following characteristics:

- Black and white in color, in a splotchy pattern
- Covered with a short, bristly substance
- Appended at one end by something similar in appearance to a paintbrush
- Appended at the other end by a lumpy thing with four smaller things coming out of its top (two soft and floppy; two hard, curved, and pointed)
- Held up from the ground by four spindly sticks, two at each end

Unless you have spent most of your life living under a rock, you would almost certainly identify this object as a *cow.*

Words—even those as simple as *cow*—and the concepts that the words represent enhance our thinking in several ways (J. E. Ormrod, 2012; also see Jaccard & Jacoby, 2010):

1. *Words reduce the world's complexity.*   Classifying similar objects and events into categories and assigning specific words to those categories can make our experiences easier to make sense of. For instance, it's much easier to think to yourself, "I see a herd of cows," than to think, "There is a brown object, covered with bristly stuff, appended by a paintbrush and a lumpy thing, and held up by four sticks. Ah, yes, and I also see a black-and-white spotted object, covered with bristly stuff, appended by a paintbrush and a lumpy thing, and held up by four sticks. And over there is a brown-and-white object . . . ."

2. *Words allow abstraction of the environment.*   An object that has bristly stuff, a paintbrush at one end, a lumpy thing at the other, and four spindly sticks at the bottom is a concrete entity. The concept *cow,* however, is more abstract: It connotes such characteristics as *female, supplier of milk,* and, to the farmer or rancher, *economic asset.* Concepts and the labels associated with them allow us to think about our experiences without necessarily having to consider all of their discrete, concrete characteristics.

3. *Words enhance the power of thought.*   When you are thinking about an object covered with bristly stuff, appended by a paintbrush and a lumpy thing, held up by four sticks, and so on, you can think of little else (as mentioned earlier, human beings can think about only a very limited amount of information at any one time). In contrast, when you simply think *cow,* you can easily think about other ideas at the same time and perhaps form connections and interrelationships among them in ways you hadn't previously considered.

4. *Words facilitate generalization and inference drawing in new situations.*   When we learn a new concept, we associate certain characteristics with it. Then, when we encounter a new instance of the concept, we can draw on our knowledge of associated characteristics to make assumptions and inferences about the new instance. For instance, if you see a herd of cattle as you drive through the countryside, you can infer that you are passing through either dairy or beef country, depending on whether you see large udders hanging down between two of the spindly sticks.

Just as *cow* helps us categorize certain experiences into a single idea, so, too, does the terminology of your discipline help you interpret and understand your observations. The words *tempo, timbre,* and *perfect pitch* are useful to the musicologist. Such terms as *central business district, folded mountain,* and *distance to k* have special meaning for the geographer. The terms *lesson plan, portfolio,* and *charter school* communicate a great deal to the educator. Learning the specialized terminology of your field is indispensable to conducting a research study, grounding it in prior theories and research, and communicating your results to others.

Two outward manifestations of language usage are also helpful to the researcher: (a) knowing two or more languages and (b) writing one's thoughts either on paper or in electronic form.

The Benefits of Knowing Two or More Languages   It should go without saying that not all important research is reported in a researcher's native tongue. Accordingly, many doctoral programs require that students demonstrate reading competency in one or two foreign languages in addition to their own language. The choice of these languages is usually linked to the area of proposed research.

The language requirement is a reasonable one. Research is and always has been a worldwide endeavor. For example, researchers in Japan have made gigantic strides in electronics and robotics. And two of the most influential theorists in child development today—Jean Piaget and Lev Vygotsky—wrote in French and Russian, respectively. Many new discoveries are first reported in a researcher's native language.

Knowing two or more languages has a second benefit as well: Words in a second language may capture the *meaning* of certain phenomenon in ways that one's native tongue may not. For example, the German word *Gestalt*—which roughly means "organized whole"—has no direct equivalent in English. Thus, many English-speaking psychologists use this word when describing the nature of human perception, because people often perceive organized patterns and structures in visual data that, in the objective physical world, are *not* organized. Likewise, the Zulu word *ubuntu* defies an easy translation into English. This word—which reflects the belief that people become fully human largely through regularly caring for others and contributing to the common good—can help anthropologists and other social scientists capture a cultural worldview quite different from the more self-centered perspective so prevalent in mainstream Western culture.

The Importance of Writing

To be generally accessible to the larger scientific community and ultimately to society as a whole, all research must eventually be presented as a written document—a *research report*—either on paper or in electronic form. A basic requirement for writing such a report is the ability to use language in a clear, coherent manner.

Although a good deal of conventional wisdom tells us that clear thinking *precedes* clear writing, in fact writing can be a productive form of thinking in and of itself. When you write your ideas down on paper, you do several things:

- You must identify the specific ideas you do and do not know about your topic.
- You must clarify and organize your thoughts sufficiently to communicate them to your readers.
- You may detect gaps and logical flaws in your thinking.

Perhaps it isn't surprising, then, that writing about a topic actually enhances the writer's understanding of the topic (e.g., Kellogg, 1994; Shanahan, 2004).

If you wait until all your thoughts are clear before you start writing, you may never begin. Thus, we recommend that you start writing parts of your research proposal or report as soon as possible. Begin with a title and a purpose statement for your study. Commit your title to paper; keep it in plain sight as you focus your ideas. Although you may very well change the title later as your research proceeds, creating a working title in the early stages can provide both focus and direction. And when you can draft a clear and concise statement that begins, "The purpose of this study is . . .," you are well on your way to planning a focused research study.

PRACTICAL APPLICATION Communicating Effectively Through Writing

In our own experiences, we authors have found that most students have a great deal to learn about what good writing entails. Yet we also know that with effort, practice, mentoring, and regular feedback, students *can* learn to write more effectively. Subsequent chapters present specific strategies for writing literature reviews (Chapter 3), research proposals (Chapter 5), and research reports (Chapter 13). Here we offer general strategies for writing in ways that can help you clearly communicate your ideas and reasoning to others. We also offer suggestions for making the best use of word processing software.

GUIDELINES   Writing to Communicate

The following guidelines are based on techniques often seen in effective writing. Furthermore, such techniques have consistently been shown to facilitate readers' comprehension of what people have written (e.g., see J. E. Ormrod, 2012).

1. *Be specific and precise.*   Precision is of utmost importance in all aspects of a research endeavor, including writing. Choose your words and phrases carefully so that you communicate your *exact* meaning, not some vague approximation. Many books and online resources offer suggestions for writing clear, concise sentences and combining them into unified and coherent paragraphs (e.g., see the sources in the "For Further Reading" list at the end of the chapter).

2. *Continually keep in mind your primary objective in writing your paper, and focus your discussion accordingly.*   All too often, novice researchers try to include everything they have learned—both from their literature review and from their data analysis—in their research reports. But ultimately, everything you say should relate either directly or indirectly to your research problem. If you can't think of how something relates, leave it out! You will undoubtedly have enough things to write about as it is.

3. *Provide an overview of what you will be talking about in upcoming pages.*   Your readers can more effectively read your work when they know what to expect as they read. Providing an overview of what topics you will discuss and in what order—and possibly also showing how the various topics interrelate—is known as an **advance organizer**. As an example, Dinah Jackson, a doctoral student in educational psychology, was interested in the possible effects of *self-questioning*—asking oneself questions about material one is studying—on college students' note taking. Jackson began her dissertation's "Review of the Literature" with the following advance organizer:

> The first part of this review will examine the theories, frameworks, and experimental research behind the research on adjunct questioning. Part two will investigate the transition of adjunct questioning to self-generated questioning. Specific models of self-generated questioning will be explored, starting with the historical research on question position [and progressing] to the more contemporary research on individual differences in self-questioning. Part three will explore some basic research on note taking and tie note taking theory with the research on self-generated questioning. (Jackson, 1996, p. 17)

4. *Organize your ideas into general and more specific categories, and use headings and subheadings to guide your readers through your discussion of these categories.*   We authors have read many student research reports that seem to wander aimlessly and unpredictably from one thought to another, without any obvious organizational structure directing the flow of ideas. Using headings and subheadings is one simple way to provide an organizational structure for your writing *and* to make that structure crystal clear to others.

5. *Use concrete examples to make abstract ideas more understandable.*   There's a fine line between being abstract and being vague. Even as scholars who have worked in our respective academic disciplines for many years, we authors still find that we can more easily understand something when the writer gives us a concrete example to illustrate an abstract idea. As an example, we return to Jackson's dissertation on self-questioning and class note taking. Jackson made the point that how a researcher evaluates, or *codes,* the content of students' class notes will affect what the researcher discovers about those notes. More specifically, she argued that only a superficial coding scheme (e.g., counting the number of main ideas included in notes) would fail to capture the true quality of the notes. She clarified her point with a concrete example:

> For example, while listening to the same lecture, Student A may record only an outline of the lecture, whereas Student B may record an outline, examples, definitions, and mnemonics. If a researcher only considered the number of main ideas that students included in their notes, then both sets of notes might be considered equivalent, despite the fact that the two sets differ considerably in the *type* of material recorded. (Jackson, 1996, p. 9)

6. *Use figures and tables to help you more effectively present or organize your ideas and findings.* Although the bulk of your research proposal or report will almost certainly be prose, in many cases it might be helpful to present some information in figure or table form. For example, as you read this book, look at the variety of mechanisms we use to accompany our prose, including art, diagrams, graphs, and summarizing tables. We hope you will agree that these mechanisms help you understand and organize some of the ideas we present.

7. *At the conclusion of a chapter or major section, summarize what you have said.* You will probably be presenting a great deal of information in any research proposal or report that you write. Summarizing what you have said in preceding paragraphs or pages helps your readers identify the things that are, in your mind, the most important things for them to remember. For example, in a dissertation that examined children's beliefs about the mental processes involved in reading, Debby Zambo summarized a lengthy discussion about the children's understanding of what it means to pay attention:

> In sum, the students understand attention to be a mental process. They know their attention is inconsistent and affected by emotions and interest. They also realize that the right level of material, amount of information, and length of time helps their attention. The stillness of reading is difficult for some of the students but calming for others, and they appear to know this, and to know when reading will be difficult and when it will be calming. This idea is contrary to what has been written in the literature about struggling readers. (Zambo, 2003, p. 68)

8. *Anticipate that you will almost certainly have to write multiple drafts.* All too often, we authors have had students submit research proposals, theses, or dissertations with the assumption that they have finished their task. Such students have invariably been disappointed—sometimes even outraged—when we have asked them to revise their work, usually several times. The need to write multiple drafts applies not only to novice researchers but to experienced scholars as well. For instance, we would hate to count the number of times this book has undergone revision—certainly far more often than the label "eleventh edition" indicates! Multiple revisions enable you to reflect on and critically evaluate your own writing, revise and refocus awkward passages, get feedback from peers and advisors who can point out where a manuscript has gaps or lacks clarity, and in other ways ensure that the final version is as clear and precise as possible.

9. *Fastidiously check to be sure that your final draft uses appropriate grammar and punctuation, and check your spelling.* Appropriate grammar, punctuation, and spelling are not just bothersome formalities. On the contrary, they help you better communicate your meanings. For example, a colon announces that what follows it explains the immediately preceding statement; a semicolon communicates that a sentence includes two independent clauses (as the semicolon in this sentence does!).

Correct grammar, punctuation, and spelling are important for another reason as well: They communicate to others that you are a careful and disciplined scholar whose thoughts and work are worth reading about. If, instead, you mispel menny of yur words—as we our doing in this sentence—your reeders may quikly discredit you as a sloppy reyearcher who shuldn't be taken seriusly!

Many style manuals, such as those in the "For Further Reading" list at the end of this chapter, have sections dealing with correct punctuation and grammar. In addition, dictionaries and word processing spell-check functions can obviously assist you in your spelling.

GUIDELINES Using the Tools in Word Processing Software

USING TECHNOLOGY

Most of our readers know the basics of using word processing software—for instance, how to "copy," "paste," and "save"; how to choose a particular font and font size; and how to format text as *italicized,* underlined, or **boldface**. Following are specific features and tools that you may not have routinely used in previous writing projects but that can be quite useful in writing research reports:

- *Outlining.*   An "outlining" feature lets you create bullets and subbullets to organize your thoughts. (In Microsoft Word, you can find this tool under the "View" pull-down menu at the top of the screen.)
- *Setting headers and footers.*   A "header" is a line or two at the top of the page that appears on every page; a "footer" appears at the bottom of each page. For example, using the "insert date" function, you might create a header that includes the specific date on which you are writing a particular draft. And using an "insert page number" function will add appropriate numbers to the tops or bottoms of successive pages.
- *Creating tables.*   Using a "table" feature, you can create a table with the number of rows and columns you need. You can easily adjust the widths of various columns; format the text within each table cell; add new rows or tables; and merge two or more cells into a single, larger cell. Usually an "autoformat" option will give you many possible table formats from which to choose.
- *Inserting graphics.*   You are likely to find a variety of options under an "Insert" pull-down menu. Some of these options enable you to insert diagrams, photographs, charts, and other visuals you have created elsewhere. (For instance, in Microsoft Word, you might explore the possibilities within the "insert picture" and "insert object" options.)
- *Creating footnotes.*   Footnotes are easy to create using an "insert footnote" feature. Typically you can choose the symbols to be used in designating footnotes—perhaps *1, 2, 3, . . ., a, b, c, . . .,* or special symbols such as * and †.
- *Using international alphabets and characters.*   Computers and computer software sold in English-speaking countries have the English alphabet as the default alphabet, but often either your word processing software or your "system preferences" on your computer's operating system will let you choose a different alphabet (e.g., Turkish, as in the surname Kağitçibaşi) or certain characters (e.g., in Chinese or Japanese) for particular words or sections of text.
- *Tracking changes.*   A "track changes" feature enables you to keep a running record of specific edits you have made to a document; you can later go back and either "accept" or "reject" each change. This feature is especially useful when two or more researchers are coauthoring a report: It keeps track of who made which changes and the date on which each change was made.

We offer three general recommendations for using a word processor effectively.

1. *Save and back up your document frequently.*   We authors can recall a number of personal horror stories we have heard (and in some cases experienced ourselves) about losing data, research materials, and other valuable information. Every computer user eventually encounters some type of glitch that causes problems in information retrieval. Whether the electricity goes out before you can save a file, a misguided keystroke leads to a system error, or your personal computer inexplicably crashes, things you have written sometimes get lost. It's imperative that you get in the habit of regularly saving your work. Save multiple copies so that if something goes awry in one place, you will always have a backup in a safe location. Here are a few things to think about:

- Save your work-in-progress frequently, perhaps every 5 to 10 minutes. Many software programs will do this for you automatically if you give them instructions about whether and how often to do it.
- Save at least two copies of important files, and save them in different places—perhaps one file at home and another at the office, at a relative's house, in a safe deposit box, or somewhere in cyberspace. One option is to save documents on a flash drive or external hard drive. Another is to copy them to an electronic dropbox, iCloud (for Macintosh), or other Internet-based storage mechanism. One of us authors uses a flash drive to back up much of her past work (including several book manuscripts) and any in-progress work; she keeps this flash drive in her purse and takes it everywhere she goes. Also, she occasionally sends

herself in-progress documents as attachments to self-addressed e-mail messages—giving her an almost-current backup version of the documents in the event that an unintended keystroke somehow wreaks havoc on what she has written.

- Save various versions of your work with titles that help you identify each version—for instance, by including the date on which you completed each file.
- If your computer completely dies—seemingly beyond resuscitation—some software programs (e.g., Norton Utilities) may be able to fix the damage and retrieve some or all of the lost material. And service departments at computer retailers can often retrieve documents from the hard drives of otherwise "dead" machines.

2. *Use such features as the spell checker and grammar checker to look for errors, but do NOT rely on them exclusively.* Although computers are marvelous machines, their "thinking" capabilities have not yet begun to approach those of the human mind. For instance, although a computer can detect spelling errors, it does so by comparing each word against its internal "dictionary" of correctly-spelled words. Not every word in the English language will be included in the dictionary; for instance, proper nouns (e.g., surnames like Leedy and Ormrod) will *not* be. Furthermore, it may assume that *abut* is spelled correctly when the word you really had in mind was *about,* and it may very well not know that *there* should actually be *their* or *they're.*

3. *Print out a paper copy for final proofreading and editing.* One of us authors once had a student who turned in a dissertation draft chock-full of spelling and grammatical errors—and this from a student who was, ironically, teaching a college-level English composition course at the time. A critical and chastising e-mail message to the student made her irate; she had checked her document quite thoroughly before submitting it, she replied, and was convinced that it was virtually error-free. When her paper draft was returned to her almost bloodshot with spelling and grammatical corrections, she was quite contrite. "I don't know how I missed them all!" she said. When asked if she had ever edited a printed copy of the draft, she replied that she had not, figuring that she could read her work just as easily on her computer monitor and thereby save a tree or two. But in our own experience, it is *always* a good idea to read a printed version of what you have written. For some reason, reading a paper copy often alerts us to errors we have previously overlooked on the computer screen.

The Human Mind

The research tools discussed so far—the library, computer technology, measurement, statistics, and language—are effective only to the extent that another critical tool also comes into play. The human mind is undoubtedly the most important tool in the researcher's toolbox. Nothing equals its powers of comprehension, integrative reasoning, and insight.

Over the past few millennia, human beings have developed several general strategies through which they can more effectively reason about and better understand worldly phenomena. Key among these strategies are critical thinking, deductive logic, inductive reasoning, scientific method, theory building, and collaboration with *other* minds.

Critical Thinking

Before beginning a research project, effective researchers typically look at research reports and theoretical discussions related to their topic of interest. But they don't just accept research findings and theories at face value; instead, they scrutinize those findings and theories for faulty assumptions, questionable logic, weaknesses in methodologies, and unwarranted conclusions. And, of course, effective researchers scrutinize their *own* work for the same kinds of flaws. In other words, good researchers engage in critical thinking.

In general, **critical thinking** involves evaluating the accuracy, credibility, and worth of information and lines of reasoning. Critical thinking is reflective, logical, and evidence-based. It also has a purposeful quality to it—that is, the researcher thinks critically in order to achieve a particular goal.

Critical thinking can take a variety of forms, depending on the context. For instance, it may involve any one or more of the following (Halpern, 1998, 2008; Nussbaum, 2008):

▨ *Verbal reasoning.*   Understanding and evaluating persuasive techniques found in oral and written language.
▨ *Argument analysis.*   Discriminating between reasons that do and do not support a particular conclusion.
▨ *Probabilistic reasoning.*   Determining the likelihood and uncertainties associated with various events.
▨ *Decision making.*   Identifying and evaluating several alternatives and selecting the alternative most likely to lead to a successful outcome.
▨ *Hypothesis testing.*   Judging the value of data and research results in terms of the methods used to obtain them and their potential relevance to certain conclusions. When hypothesis testing includes critical thinking, it involves considering questions such as these:
  • Was an appropriate method used to measure a particular outcome?
  • Are the data and results derived from a relatively large number of people, objects, or events?
  • Have other possible explanations or conclusions been eliminated?
  • Can the results obtained in one situation be reasonably generalized to other situations?

To some degree, different fields of study require different kinds of critical thinking. In history, critical thinking might involve scrutinizing various historical documents and looking for clues as to whether things *definitely* happened a particular way or only *maybe* happened that way. In psychology, it might involve critically evaluating the way in which a particular psychological characteristic (e.g., intelligence, personality) is being measured. In anthropology, it might involve observing people's behaviors over an extended period of time and speculating about what those behaviors indicate about the cultural group being studied.

Deductive Logic

Deductive logic begins with one or more *premises.* These premises are statements or assumptions that the researcher initially takes to be true. Reasoning then proceeds logically from these premises toward conclusions that—if the premises are indeed true—must *also* be true. For example,

> If all tulips are plants, (Premise 1)
> And if all plants produce energy through photosynthesis, (Premise 2)
> Then all tulips must produce energy through photosynthesis. (Conclusion)

To the extent that the premises are false, the conclusions may also be false. For example, .

> If all tulips are platypuses, (Premise 1)
> And if all platypuses produce energy through spontaneous combustion, (Premise 2)
> Then all tulips must produce energy through spontaneous combustion. (Conclusion)

The if-this-then-that logic is the same in both examples. We reach an erroneous conclusion in the second example—we conclude that tulips are apt to burst into flames at unpredictable times—only because both of our premises are erroneous.

Let's look back more than 500 years to Christopher Columbus's first voyage to the New World. At the time, people held many beliefs about the world that, to them, were irrefutable facts: People are mortal, the Earth is flat, the universe is finite and relatively small. The terror that gripped Columbus's sailors as they crossed the Atlantic was a fear supported by deductive logic. If the Earth is flat (premise) and the universe finite and small (premise), the Earth's flat surface must stop at some point. Therefore, a ship that continues to travel into uncharted territory must eventually come to the Earth's edge and fall off, and its passengers (who are mortal—another premise) will meet their deaths. The logic was sound; the conclusions were valid. Where the reasoning fell short was in two faulty premises: that the Earth is flat and relatively small.

Deductive logic provides the basis for mathematical proofs in mathematics, physics, and related disciplines. It is also extremely valuable for generating research hypotheses and testing theories. As an example, let's look one more time at doctoral student Dinah Jackson's dissertation project about the possible effects of self-questioning during studying. Jackson knew from well-established theories about human learning that forming mental associations among two or more pieces of information results in more effective learning than does trying to learn each piece of information separately from the others. She also found a body of research literature indicating that the kinds of questions students ask themselves (mentally) and try to answer as they listen to a lecture or read a textbook influence both what they learn and how effectively they remember it. (For instance, a student who is trying to answer the question, "What do I need to remember for the test?" might learn very differently from the student who is considering the question, "How might I apply this information to my own life?") From such findings, Jackson generated several key premises and drew a logical conclusion from them:

> If learning information in an associative, integrative manner is more effective than learning information in a fact-by-fact, piecemeal manner, (Premise 1)
>
> If the kinds of questions students ask themselves during a learning activity influence how they learn, (Premise 2)
>
> If training in self-questioning techniques influences the kinds of questions that students ask themselves, (Premise 3)
>
> And if learning is reflected in the kinds of notes that students take during class, (Premise 4)
>
> Then teaching students to ask themselves integrative questions as they study class material should lead to better-integrated class notes and higher-quality learning. (Conclusion)

Such reasoning led Jackson to form and test several hypotheses, including this one:

> Students who have formal training in integrative self-questioning will take more integrative notes than students who have not had any formal training. (Jackson, 1996, p. 12)

The data Jackson collected in her dissertation research supported this hypothesis.

Inductive Reasoning

Inductive reasoning begins not with a preestablished truth or assumption but instead with an observation. For instance, as a baby in a high chair many years ago, you may have observed that if you held a cracker in front of you and then let go of it, it fell to the floor. "Hmmm," you may have thought, "what happens if I do that again?" So you grabbed another cracker, held it out, and released it. It, too, fell to the floor. You followed the same procedure with several more crackers, and the result was always the same: The cracker traveled in a downward direction. Eventually you may have performed the same actions on other things—blocks, rattles, peas, milk—and invariably observed the same result. Eventually you drew the conclusion that all things fall when dropped—your first inkling about a force called *gravity*. (You may also have concluded that dropping things from your high chair greatly annoyed your parents, but that is another matter.)

In inductive reasoning, people use specific instances or occurrences to draw conclusions about entire classes of objects or events. In other words, they observe a *sample* and then draw conclusions about the larger *population* from which the sample has been taken. For instance, an anthropologist might draw conclusions about a certain culture after studying a certain community within that culture. A professor of special education might use a few case studies in which a particular instructional approach is effective with students who have dyslexia to recommend that teachers use the instructional approach with other students with dyslexia. A sociologist might conduct three surveys (one each in 1995, 2005, and 2015) asking 1,000 people to describe their beliefs about AIDS and then drawing conclusions about how society's attitudes toward AIDS have changed over the 20-year period.

Figure 1.2 graphically depicts the nature of inductive reasoning. Let's look at an example of how this representation applies to an actual research project. Neurologists Silverman, Masland, Saunders, and Schwab (1970) sought the answer to a problem in medicine: How long can a

FIGURE 1.2 ■ The Inductive Process

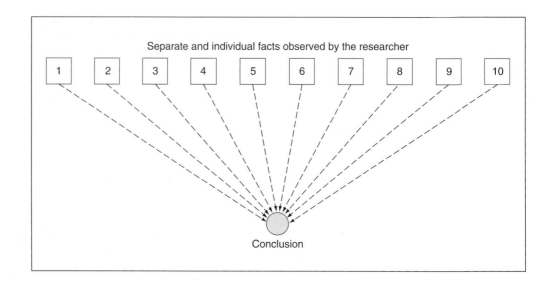

person have a "flat EEG" (i.e., an absence of measurable electrical activity in the brain, typically indicative of cerebral death) and still recover? Silverman and his colleagues observed 2,650 actual cases. They noted that, in all cases in which the flat EEG persisted for 24 hours or more, not a single recovery occurred. All of the data pointed to the same conclusion: *People who exhibit flat EEGs for 24 hours or longer will not recover.* We cannot, of course, rule out the unexplored cases, but *from the data observed,* the conclusion reached was that recovery is impossible. The EEG line from *every* case led to that *one* conclusion.

Scientific Method

During the Renaissance, people found that when they systematically collected and analyzed data, new insights and understandings might emerge. Thus was the scientific method born; the words literally mean "the method that searches after knowledge" (*scientia* is Latin for "knowledge" and derives from *scire,* "to know"). The scientific method gained momentum during the 16th century with such men as Paracelsus, Copernicus, Vesalius, and Galileo.

Traditionally, the term scientific method has referred to an approach in which a researcher (a) identifies a problem that defines the goal of one's quest; (b) posits a hypothesis that, if confirmed, resolves the problem; (c) gathers data relevant to the hypothesis; and (d) analyzes and interprets the data to see whether they support the hypothesis and resolve the question that instigated the research. In recent years, however, the term has been a controversial one, because not all researchers follow the steps just listed in a rigid, lock-step manner; in fact, as noted earlier, some researchers shy away from forming any hypotheses about what they might find. Some of the controversy revolves around which article to use in front of the term—more specifically, whether to say "*the* scientific method" or "*a* scientific method." If we are speaking generally about the importance of collecting and analyzing data systematically rather than haphazardly, then saying "*the* scientific method" makes sense. If, instead, we are speaking about a specific methodology—say, experimental research or ethnographic research (described in Chapter 7 and Chapter 9, respectively), it is probably better to say "*a* scientific method." In any event, we are talking about a somewhat flexible—although certainly also rigorous—process.

As you may already have realized, application of a scientific method usually involves both deductive logic and inductive reasoning. Researchers might develop a hypothesis either from a theory (deductive logic) or from observations of specific events (inductive reasoning). Using deductive logic, they might make predictions about the patterns they are likely to see in their data *if* a hypothesis is true. And they often use inductive reasoning to generalize about a large population from which they have drawn a small sample.

Theory Building

Psychologists are increasingly realizing that the human mind is a very *constructive* mind. People don't just passively absorb and remember a large body of unorganized facts about the world. Instead, they pull together the things they see and hear to form well-organized and integrated understandings about a wide variety of physical and social events. Human beings, then, seem to have a natural tendency to develop *theories* about the world around them (e.g., see Bransford, Brown, & Cocking, 2000; J. E. Ormrod, 2012).

In general, a theory is an organized body of concepts and principles intended to explain a particular phenomenon. Even as young children, human beings are inclined to form their own, personal theories about various physical and social phenomena—for instance, why the sun "goes down" at night, where babies come from, and why certain individuals behave in particular ways. People's everyday, informal theories about the world aren't always accurate. For example, imagine that an airplane drops a large metal ball as it travels forward through the air. What kind of path will the ball take as it falls downward? The answer, of course, is that it will fall downward at an increasingly fast rate (thanks to gravity) but will also continue to travel forward (thanks to inertia). Thus, its path will have the shape of a parabolic arc. Yet many college students erroneously believe that the ball (a) will fall straight down, (b) will take a straight diagonal path downward, or (c) will actually move *backward* from the airplane as it falls down (McCloskey, 1983).

What characterizes the theory building of a good researcher is the fact that it is supported by well-documented findings—rather than by naive beliefs and subjective impressions of the world—and by logically defensible reasoning. Thus, the theory-building process involves thinking *actively* and *intentionally* about a phenomenon under investigation. Beginning with the facts known about the phenomenon, the researcher brainstorms ideas about plausible and, ideally, *best* explanations—a process that is sometimes called abduction (e.g., Jaccard & Jacoby, 2010; Walton, 2003). Such explanations are apt to involve an interrelated set of concepts and propositions that, taken together, can reasonably account for the phenomenon being studied.

After one or more researchers have developed a theory to explain a phenomenon of interest, the theory is apt to drive further research, in part by posing new questions that require answers and in part by suggesting hypotheses about the likely outcomes of particular investigations. For example, one common way of testing a theory is to use deductive reasoning to make a prediction (hypothesis) about what should occur *if the theory is a viable explanation of the phenomenon being examined.* As an example, let's consider Albert Einstein's theory of relativity, first proposed in 1915. Within the context of his theory, Einstein hypothesized that light passes through space as photons—tiny masses of spectral energy. If light has mass, Einstein reasoned, it should be subject to the pull of a gravitational field. A year later, Karl Schwarzschild predicted that, based on Einstein's reasoning, the gravitational field of the sun should bend light rays considerably more than Isaac Newton had predicted many years earlier. In 1919 a group of English astronomers traveled to Brazil and North Africa to observe how the sun's gravity distorted the light of a distant star now visible due to a solar eclipse. After the data were analyzed and interpreted, the results clearly supported the Einstein–Schwarzschild hypothesis—and therefore also supported Einstein's theory of relativity.

As new data emerge that either do or do not support particular hypotheses, a researcher may continue to revise a theory, reworking parts to better account for research findings, filling in gaps with additional concepts or propositions, extending the theory to apply to additional situations, and relating the theory to other theories regarding overlapping phenomena (Steiner, 1988; K. R. Thompson, 2006). Occasionally, when an existing theory cannot adequately account for a growing body of evidence, a good researcher casts it aside and begins to formulate an alternative theory that better explains the data.

Theory building tends to be a relatively slow process, with any particular theory continuing to evolve over a period of years, decades, or centuries. Often, many researchers contribute to the theory-building effort, testing hypotheses that the theory suggests, suggesting additional concepts and propositions to include in the theory, and conducting additional investigations to test one or more aspects of the theory in its current state. This last point brings us to yet another strategy for effectively using the human mind: collaborating with *other* minds.

Collaboration with Other Minds

As an old saying goes, two heads are better than one. Three or more heads can be even better. Any single researcher is apt to have certain perspectives, assumptions, and theoretical biases—not to mention gaps in his or her knowledge about the subject matter—that will limit how he or she approaches a research project. By bringing one or more professional colleagues into a research project—ideally, colleagues who have perspectives, backgrounds, and areas of expertise somewhat different from the researcher's own—the researcher brings many more cognitive resources to bear on how to tackle the research problem and how to find meaning in the data obtained (e.g., see Nichols, 1998).

Sometimes these colleagues enter the picture as equal partners. At other times they may simply offer suggestions and advice. For example, when a graduate student conducts research for a master's thesis or doctoral dissertation, the student is, of course, the key player in the endeavor. Yet the student typically has considerable guidance from an advisor and, especially in the case of a doctoral dissertation, from a faculty committee. The prudent student selects an advisor and committee members who have the expertise to help shape the research project into a form that will truly address the research question and—more importantly—will make a genuine contribution to the student's topic of study.

USING TECHNOLOGY

As a general rule, productive researchers keep in regular communication with others who conduct similar research in their field, exchanging ideas, critiquing one another's work, and directing one another to potentially helpful resources. Such ongoing communication is also a form of collaboration—albeit a less systematic one—in that everyone can benefit from and build on what others are thinking and finding. Increasingly, computer technology is playing a central role in this cross-communication and cross-fertilization. For example, some researchers maintain professional web pages that describe their research programs and include links to relevant research reports; often you can find these web pages by going to the websites of the researchers' universities or other home institutions. Also of value are list servers, which provide a mechanism for electronic discussion groups. A list server is essentially a mailing list, and any e-mail message sent to it is distributed to everyone who has subscribed to the list.

As the preceding sections should make clear, we human beings are—or at least have the potential to be—*logical, reasoning* beings. But despite our incredible intellectual capabilities—which almost certainly surpass those of all other species on the planet—we don't always reason as logically or objectively as we might. For example, sometimes we "discover" what we *expect* to discover, to the point where we don't look objectively at the data we collect. And sometimes we are so emotionally attached to particular perspectives or theories about a phenomenon that we can't abandon them when mountains of evidence indicate that we should. Figure 1.3 describes some common pitfalls in human reasoning—pitfalls we urge you to be on the lookout for and try to overcome. Good researchers are *reflective* researchers who regularly and critically examine not only their research designs and data but also their own thinking processes.

REFLECTIONS ON NOTEWORTHY RESEARCH

The time: February 13, 1929. The place: St. Mary's Hospital, London. The occasion: the reading of a paper before the Medical Research Club. The speaker: a member of the hospital staff in the Department of Microbiology. Such was the setting for the presentation of one of the most significant research reports of the early 20th century. The report was about a discovery that has transformed the practice of medicine. Dr. Alexander Fleming presented to his colleagues his research on penicillin. The group was apathetic. No one showed any enthusiasm for Fleming's paper. Great research has frequently been presented to those who are imaginatively both blind and deaf.

Despite the lukewarm reception, Fleming knew the value of what he had done. The first public announcement of the discovery of penicillin appeared in the *British Journal of Experimental Pathology* in 1929. It is a readable report—one that André Maurois (1959) called "a triumph of clarity, sobriety, and precision." Get it; read it. You will be reliving one of the great moments in 20th-century medical research.

We human beings often fall short of the reasoning capacities with which Mother Nature has endowed us. Following are seven common pitfalls to watch for in your own thinking as a researcher.

1. *Confusing what must logically be true with what seems to be true in the world as we know it—a potential pitfall in deductive reasoning.* Our usual downfall in deductive reasoning is failing to separate logic from everyday experience. For example, consider Isaac Newton's second law of motion: Force equals mass times acceleration $(F = ma)$. According to this basic principle of Newtonian physics, any force applied to an object results in acceleration of the object. Using simple algebra—deductive reasoning at its finest—we can conclude that $a = F \div m$ and therefore that if there is no acceleration $(a = 0)$, then there is no force $(F = 0)$. This deduction makes no sense to anyone who has ever tried to push a heavy object across the floor: The object may not move at all, let alone accelerate. What explains the object's stubbornness, of course, is that other forces, especially friction with and resistance from the floor, are counteracting any force that the pusher may be applying.

2. *Making generalizations about members of a category after having encountered only a restricted subset of that category—a potential pitfall in inductive reasoning.* The main weakness of inductive reasoning is that, even if all of our specific observations about a particular set of objects or events are correct, our generalizations about the category as a whole may *not* be correct. For example, if the only tulips we ever see are red ones, we may erroneously conclude that tulips can *only* be red. And if we conduct research about the political or religious beliefs of people who live in a particular location—say, people who live in Chicago—we may draw conclusions that don't necessarily apply to the human race as a whole. Inductive reasoning, then, is most likely to fall short when we gather data from only a small, limited sample.

3. *Looking only for evidence that supports our hypotheses, without also looking for evidence that would disconfirm our hypotheses.* We humans seem to be predisposed to look for confirming evidence rather than disconfirming evidence—a phenomenon known as **confirmation bias**. For many everyday practical matters, this approach serves us well. For example, if we flip a light switch and fail to get any light, we might immediately think, "The light bulb probably burned out." We unscrew the existing light bulb and replace it with a new one—and *voila!* We now have light. Hypothesis confirmed, problem solved, case closed. However, truly objective researchers don't just look for evidence that confirms what they believe to be true. They also look for evidence that might *disprove* their hypotheses. They hope that they don't find such evidence, of course, but they look for it nevertheless.

4. *Confirming expectations even in the face of contradictory evidence.* Another aspect of our confirmation bias is that we tend to ignore or discredit any contradictory evidence that comes our way. For example, consider the topic of global climate change. Convincing evidence continues to mount to support the ideas that (a) the Earth's average temperature is gradually rising and (b) this temperature rise is at least partly the result of carbon emissions and other human activities. Yet some folks have great difficulty looking at the evidence objectively—perhaps the researchers incorrectly analyzed the data, they say, or perhaps the scientific community has a hidden agenda and so is not giving us the straight scoop.

5. *Mistaking dogma for fact.* Although we might be inclined to view some sources of information with a skeptical, critical eye, we might accept others without question. For example, many of us willingly accept whatever an esteemed researcher, scholarly book, or other authority source says to be true. In general, we may uncritically accept anything said or written by individuals or groups we hold in high esteem. Not all authority figures and works of literature are reliable sources of information and guidance, however, and blind, unquestioning acceptance of them can be worrisome.

6. *Letting emotion override logic and objectivity.* We humans are emotional beings, and our emotions often infiltrate our efforts to reason and think critically. We are apt to think quite rationally and objectively when dealing with topics we don't feel strongly about and yet think in decidedly irrational ways about emotionally charged issues—issues we find upsetting, infuriating, or personally threatening.

7. *Mistaking correlation for causation.* In our efforts to make sense of our world, we human beings are often eager to figure out what causes what. But in our eagerness to identify cause-and-effect relationships, we sometimes "see" them when all we really have is two events that just happen to occur at the same time and place. Even when the two events are *consistently* observed together—in other words, when they are *correlated*—one of them does not necessarily cause the other. The ability for a researcher to distinguish between causation and correlation is a critical one, as you will discover in Chapter 6.

FIGURE 1.3 ■ Common Pitfalls in Human Reasoning

List of pitfalls based on Chapter 8, "Common Sense Isn't Always Sensible: Reasoning and Critical Thinking" in *Our Minds, Our Memories* by J. E. Ormrod, 2011, pp. 151–183. Copyright by Pearson Education, Inc. Used by permission.

Soon after the publication of Fleming's paper, two other names became associated with the development of penicillin: Ernst B. Chain and Howard W. Florey (Chain et al., 1940; also see Abraham et al., 1941). Together they developed a pure strain of penicillin. Florey was especially instrumental in initiating its mass production and its use as an antibiotic for wounded soldiers in World War II (Coghill, 1944; also see Coghill & Koch, 1945). Reading these reports takes you back to the days when the medical urgency of dying people called for a massive research effort to make a newly discovered antibiotic available for immediate use.

On October 25, 1945, the Nobel Prize in medicine was awarded to Fleming, Chain, and Florey.

If you want to learn more about the discovery of penicillin, read André Maurois's *The Life of Sir Alexander Fleming* (1959), the definitive biography done at the behest of Fleming's widow. The book will give you an insight into the way great research comes into being.

The procedures used in groundbreaking research are identical to those every student follows in completing a dissertation, thesis, or other research project. All research begins with a problem, an observation, a question. Curiosity is the germinal seed. Assumptions are made. Hypotheses might be formulated. Data are gathered. Conclusions are reached. What *you* do in a research project is the same as what many others have done before you, including those who have pushed back the barriers of ignorance and made discoveries that have greatly benefited humankind.

EXPLORING RESEARCH IN YOUR FIELD

Early in the chapter we mentioned that academic research is popularly seen as an activity far removed from everyday living. Even graduate students working on theses or dissertations may consider their task to be meaningless busywork that has little or no relevance to the world beyond the university campus. This "busywork" conception of an academic program's research requirement is simply not accurate. Conducting the research required to write an acceptable thesis or dissertation is one of the most valuable educational experiences a person can have. Furthermore, a good research project adds to our knowledge about our physical and social worlds and so can ultimately promote the welfare and well-being of ourselves as a species and of the planet as a whole.

Even if you plan to become a practitioner rather than a researcher—say, a nurse, social worker, or school principal—knowledge of strong research methodologies and legitimate ways to collect and analyze data is essential for keeping up with advances in your field. The alternative— *not* being well versed in sound research practices—can lead you to base important professional decisions on faulty data, inappropriate interpretations and conclusions, or unsubstantiated personal intuitions. Truly competent and effective practitioners base their day-to-day decisions and long-term priorities on solid research findings in their field.

As a way of getting your feet wet in the world of research, take some time to read articles in research journals in your academic discipline. You can do so by spending an hour or two in the *periodicals* section of your local college or university library or, alternatively, making use of your library website's online databases to download and read a number of articles at home.

Your professors should have suggestions about journals that are especially relevant to your discipline. Reference librarians can be helpful as well. If you are shy about asking other people for advice, you can get insights about important journals by scanning the reference lists in some of your textbooks.

Keep in mind that the quality of research you find in your explorations may vary considerably. One rough indicator of the quality of a research study is whether the research report has been juried or nonjuried. A juried (or *refereed*) research report has been judged by respected colleagues in one's field and deemed to be of sufficient quality and importance to warrant publication. For instance, the editors of many academic journals send submitted manuscripts to one or more reviewers who pass judgment on the manuscripts, and only manuscripts that meet certain criteria are published in the journal. A nonjuried (or *nonrefereed*) report is one that appears in a journal or on the Internet without first being screened by one or more experts. Some nonjuried reports are excellent, but others may not be.

PRACTICAL APPLICATION Identifying Important Tools in Your Discipline

We have introduced several key research tools in the preceding pages, and we describe many more specific ones in subsequent chapters. Some of the tools you learn about in this book may be somewhat new to you. How will you learn when, how, and why you should use them? One effective means of learning about important tools in your discipline is to work closely with an expert researcher in your field.

Take the time to find a person who has completed a few research projects—perhaps someone who teaches a research methods class, someone who has published in prestigious journals, someone who has successfully obtained research grants, or even someone who has recently finished a dissertation. Ideally this individual should be someone in your own field of study. Ask the questions listed in the following checklist and, if possible, observe the person as he or she goes about research work. If you can't locate anyone locally, it may be possible to recruit one or more willing individuals through e-mail.

✔ CHECKLIST

Interviewing an Expert Researcher

_____ 1. How do you start a research project?

_____

_____

_____ 2. What specific tools do you use (e.g., library resources, computer software, forms of measurement, statistics)?

_____

_____

_____ 3. How did you gain your expertise with the various tools you use?

_____

_____

_____ 4. What are some important experiences you suggest for a novice researcher?

_____

_____

_____ 5. If I wanted to learn how to become a competent researcher, what specific tools would you suggest I work with?

_____

_____

✔ Check Your Understanding in the Pearson etext

Practice Thinking Like a Researcher

Practice Thinking Like a Researcher Activity 1.1: Identifying Hypotheses and Assumptions
Practice Thinking Like a Researcher Activity 1.2: Communicating Effectively about Research

FOR FURTHER READING

General Research Design

Bouma, G. D., & Ling, R. (2004). *The research process* (5th ed.). New York: Oxford University Press.

Creswell, J. W. (2014). *Research design: Qualitative, quantitative, and mixed methods approaches* (4th ed.). Los Angeles: Sage.

Goodwin, C. J. (2013). *Research in psychology: Methods and design* (7th ed.). New York: Wiley.

Johnson, R. B., & Onwuegbuzie, A. J. (2004). Mixed methods research: A research paradigm whose time has come. *Educational Researcher, 33*(7), 14–26.

McMillan, J. H., & Wergin, J. F. (2010). *Understanding and evaluating educational research* (4th ed.). Upper Saddle River, NJ: Pearson.

Nieswiadomy, R. M. (2012). *Foundations in nursing research* (6th ed.). Upper Saddle River, NJ: Prentice Hall.

Niglas, K. (2010). The multidimensional model of research methodology: An integrated set of criteria. In A. Tashakkori & C. Teddlie (Eds.), *Mixed methods in social & behavioral research* (2nd ed., pp. 215–236). Thousand Oaks, CA: Sage.

Repko, A. F. (2008). *Interdisciplinary research: Process and theory.* Thousand Oaks, CA: Sage.

Rosnow, R. L., & Rosenthal, R. (2013). *Beginning behavioral research: A conceptual primer* (7th ed.). Upper Saddle River, NJ: Pearson.

Effective Writing

American Psychological Association. (2010). *Concise rules of APA style* (6th ed.). Washington, DC: Author.

American Psychological Association (APA). (2010). *Publication manual of the American Psychological Association* (6th ed.). Washington, DC: Author.

Beebe, L. (Ed.). (1992). *Professional writing for the human services.* Washington, DC: National Association of Social Workers Press.

Chicago manual of style (16th ed.). (2010). Chicago: University of Chicago Press.

Council of Science Editors. (2006). *Scientific style and format: The CSE manual for authors, editors, and publishers* (7th ed.). Reston, VA: Author.

Flesch, R. (1974). *The art of readable writing.* New York: Harper & Row.

Glicken, M. D. (2007). *A guide to writing for human service professionals.* New York: Rowman and Littlefield.

Mitchell, M. L., Jolley, J. M., & O'Shea, R. P. (2013). *Writing for psychology* (4th ed.). Belmont, CA: Wadsworth/Cengage.

Modern Language Association. (2008). *MLA style manual and guide to scholarly publishing* (3rd ed.). New York: Author.

Strunk, W. (1920). *The elements of style.* New York: Harcourt, Brace. [This classic book has since been reprinted and/or updated by several publishers.]

Williams, J. M., & Bizup, J. (2014). *Style: Lessons in clarity and grace* (11th ed.). Upper Saddle River, NJ: Pearson.

Reasoning, the Scientific Method, and Theory Building

Bicak, L. J., & Bicak, C. J. (1988). Scientific method: Historical and contemporary perspectives. *American Biology Teacher, 50,* 348–353.

Bickle, J., Mauldin, R., & Giere, R. N. (2005). *Understanding scientific reasoning* (5th ed.). New York: Wadsworth.

Carey, S. S. (2012). *A beginner's guide to scientific method* (4th ed.). Florence, KY: Cengage.

Jaccard, J., & Jacoby, J. (2010). *Theory construction and model-building skills.* New York: Guilford Press.

Jung, S. (1995). *The logic of discovery: An interrogative approach to scientific inquiry.* New York: Peter Lang.

Poplin, M. S. (1987). Self-imposed blindness: The scientific method in education. *Remedial and Special Education, 8*(6), 31–37.

Popper, K. (2002). *The logic of scientific discovery.* New York: Routledge.

Shank, G. D. (2006). *Qualitative research: A personal skills approach* (2nd ed.). Upper Saddle River, NJ: Pearson. [See Chapter 7.]

Chapter 2

The Problem: The Heart of the Research Process

The main research problem or question is the axis around which the whole research effort revolves. It clarifies the goals of the research project and can keep the researcher from wandering in tangential, unproductive directions.

Learning Outcomes

2.1 Identify strategies for choosing and refining a research problem.

2.2 Subdivide a main research problem into useful subproblems.

2.3 Recognize examples of independent, dependent, mediating, and moderating variables.

2.4 Pin down a proposed research study by (a) stating one or more hypotheses, (b) identifying variables to be examined, (c) defining terms, (d) stating assumptions, (e) identifying delimitations and limitations, and (f) explaining the study's importance.

The heart of every research project—the axis around which the entire research endeavor revolves—is the problem or question the researcher wants to address. The first step in the research process, then, is to identify this problem or question with clarity and precision.

FINDING RESEARCH PROJECTS

Problems in need of research are everywhere. Some research projects can enhance our general knowledge about our physical, biological, psychological, or social world or shed light on historical, cultural, or aesthetic phenomena. For example, an ornithologist might study the mating habits of a particular species of birds, and a psychologist might study the nature of people's logical reasoning processes. Such projects, which can advance theoretical conceptualizations about a particular topic, are known as basic research.

Other research projects address issues that have immediate relevance to current practices, procedures, and policies. For example, a nursing educator might compare the effectiveness of different instructional techniques for training future nurses, and an agronomist might study the effects of various fertilizers on the growth of sunflowers. Such projects, which can inform human decision making about practical problems, are known as applied research. Occasionally, applied research involves addressing questions in one's immediate work environment, with the goal of solving an ongoing problem in that environment; such research is known as *action research*.

Keep in mind, however, that the line between basic research and applied research is, at best, a blurry one. Answering questions about basic theoretical issues can often inform current practices in the everyday world; for example, by studying the mating habits of a particular species of birds, an ornithologist might lead the way in saving the species from extinction. Similarly, answering questions about practical problems may enhance theoretical understandings of particular phenomena; for example, the nursing educator who finds that one approach to training nurses is more effective than another may enhance psychologists' understanding of how, in general, people acquire new knowledge and skills.

To get an online sample of recently published research studies in your area of interest, go to Google Scholar at scholar.google.com; type a topic in the search box and then click on some of the titles that pique your curiosity. As you scan the results of your Google search, especially look for items labeled as pdf, referring to portable document format; these items are often electronic photocopies of articles that have appeared in academic journals and similar sources.

You might also want to look at typical research projects for doctoral dissertations. For example, your university library probably has a section that houses the completed dissertations of students who have gone before you. Alternatively, you might go to the electronic databases in your library's catalog. Among those databases you are likely to find ProQuest Dissertations & Theses, which includes abstracts—and in many cases, the complete texts—for millions of dissertations and theses from around the world.

Regardless of whether you conduct basic or applied research, a research project is likely to take a significant amount of your time and energy, so whatever problem you study should be *worth* your time and energy. As you begin the process of identifying a suitable research problem to tackle, keep two criteria in mind. First, your problem should address an important question, such that the answer can actually *make a difference* in some way. And second, it should advance the frontiers of knowledge, perhaps by leading to new ways of thinking, suggesting possible applications, or paving the way for further research in the field. To accomplish both of these ends, your research project must involve not only the collection of data but also the *interpretation* of those data.

Some problems are not suitable for research because they lack the interpretation-of-data component; they don't require the researcher to go beyond the data themselves and reveal their meaning. Following are four situations to avoid when considering a problem for research purposes.

1. ***Research projects should not be simply a ruse for achieving self-enlightenment.*** All of us have large gaps in our education that we may want to fill. But mere self-enlightenment should not be the primary purpose of a research project (see Chapter 1). Gathering information to know more about a certain area of knowledge is entirely different from looking at a body of data to discern how it contributes to the solution of the problem.

A student once submitted the following as the statement of a research problem:

> The problem of this research is to learn more about the way in which the Panama Canal was built.

For this student, the information-finding effort would provide the satisfaction of having gained more knowledge about a particular topic, but it would *not* have led to *new* knowledge.

2. ***A problem whose sole purpose is to compare two sets of data is not a suitable research problem.*** Take this proposed problem for research:

> This research project will compare the increase in the number of women employed over 100 years—from 1870 to 1970—with the employment of men over the same time span.

A simple table completes the project.

	1870	*1970*
Women employed	13,970,000	72,744,000
Men employed	12,506,000	85,903,000

This "research" project involves nothing more than a quick trip to a government website to reveal what is already known.

3. ***Simply calculating a correlation coefficient between two related sets of data is not acceptable as a problem for research.*** Why? Because a key ingredient in true research—*making sense* of the data—is missing. A correlation coefficient is nothing more than a statistic that expresses how closely two characteristics or other variables are associated with each other. It tells us nothing about *why* the association might exist.

Some novice researchers think that after they have collected data and performed a simple statistical procedure, their work is done. In fact, their work is *not* done at this point; it has only begun. For example, many researchers have found a correlation between the IQ scores of children and those of their parents. In and of itself, this fact is of little use. It does, however, suggest a problem for research: What is the underlying *cause* of the correlation between children's and parents' intelligence test scores? Is it genetic? Is it environmental? Does it reflect some combination of genetic heritage and environment?

4. ***Problems that result only in a yes-or-no answer are not suitable problems for research.*** Why? For the same reason that merely calculating a correlation coefficient is unsatisfactory. Both situations simply skim the surface of the phenomenon under investigation, without exploring the mechanisms underlying it.

"Is homework beneficial to children?" That is no problem for research, at least not in the form in which it is stated. The researchable issue is not whether homework is beneficial, but wherein the benefit of homework—if there is one—lies. Which components of homework are beneficial? Which ones, if any, are counterproductive? If we knew the answers to these questions, then teachers could better structure homework assignments to enhance students' learning and classroom achievement.

There is so much to learn—there are so many important questions unanswered—that we should look for significant problems and not dwell on those that will make little or no contribution. When asked about conducting research, Peter Medawar, recipient of a Nobel Prize for his research on organ transplantation, gave wise advice to young scientists:

> It can be said with complete confidence that any scientist of any age who wants to make important discoveries must study important problems. Dull or piffling problems yield dull or piffling answers. It is not enough that a problem should be "interesting"—almost any problem is interesting if it is studied in sufficient depth. (Medawar, 1979, p. 13)

Good research, then, begins with identifying a good question to ask—ideally a question that no one has ever thought to ask before. Researchers who contribute the most to our understanding of our physical, biological, psychological, and social worlds are those who pose questions that lead us into entirely new lines of inquiry. To illustrate, let's return to that correlation between the IQ scores of children and those of their parents. For many years, psychologists bickered about the relative influences of heredity and environment on intelligence and other human characteristics. They now know not only that heredity and environment *both* influence virtually every aspect of human functioning but also that they *influence each other's influences* (for a good, down-to-earth discussion of this point, see Lippa, 2002). Rather than ask the question, "How much do heredity and environment each influence human behavior?" a more fruitful question—one that is relatively new on the scene—is, "How do heredity and environment *interact* in their influences on behavior?"

PRACTICAL APPLICATION Identifying and Describing the Research Problem

How can a beginning researcher formulate an important and useful research problem? Here we offer guidelines both for choosing an appropriate problem and for describing it sufficiently to focus the research effort.

GUIDELINES Choosing an Appropriate Problem

Choosing a good research problem requires genuine curiosity about unanswered questions. But it also requires enough knowledge about a topic to identify the kinds of investigations that are likely to make important contributions to one's field. Following are several strategies that are often helpful for novice and expert researchers alike.

1. ***Look around you.***   In many disciplines, questions that need answers—phenomena that need explanation—are everywhere. For example, let's look back to the early 17th century, when Galileo was trying to make sense of a variety of earthly and celestial phenomena. Why did large bodies of water (but not small ones) rise and fall in the form of tides twice a day? Why did sunspots consistently move across the sun's surface from right to left, gradually disappear, and then, about 2 weeks later, reappear on the right edge? Furthermore, why did sunspots usually move in an upward or downward path as they traversed the sun's surface, while only occasionally moving in a direct, horizontal fashion? Galileo correctly deduced that the various "paths" of sunspots could be explained by the facts that both the Earth and sun were spinning on tilted axes and that—contrary to popular opinion at the time—the Earth revolved around the sun, rather than vice versa. Galileo was less successful in explaining tides, mistakenly attributing them to natural "sloshing" as a result of the Earth's movement through space, rather than to the moon's gravitational pull.

We do not mean to suggest that novice researchers should take on such monumental questions as the nature of the solar system or oceanic tides. But smaller problems suitable for research exist everywhere. Perhaps you might see them in your professional practice or in everyday events. Continually ask yourself questions about what you see and hear: Why does such-and-such happen? What makes such-and-such tick? What are people thinking when they do such-and-such?

2. ***Read the existing research literature about a topic.***   One essential strategy is to find out what things are already known and believed about your topic of interest—a topic we address in more detail in Chapter 3. Little can be gained by reinventing the wheel. In addition to telling you what is already known, the existing literature about a topic is likely to tell you what is *not* known in the area—in other words, what still needs to be done. For instance, your research project might

- Address the suggestions for future research that another researcher has identified
- Replicate a research project in a different setting or with a different population
- Consider how various subpopulations might behave differently in the same situation
- Apply an existing perspective or theory to a new situation
- Explore unexpected or contradictory findings in previous studies
- Challenge research findings that seem to contradict what you personally know or believe to be true (Neuman, 2011)

Reading the literature has other advantages as well. It gives you a theoretical base on which to generate hypotheses and build a rationale for your study. It offers potential research designs and methods of measurement. And it can help you interpret your results and relate them to previous research findings in your field.

As you read about other people's research related to your topic, *take time to consider how you can improve your own work because of it.* Ask yourself: What have I learned that I would (or would not) want to incorporate into my own research? Perhaps it is a certain way of writing, a specific method of data collection, or a particular approach to data analysis. You should constantly question and reflect on what you read.

We also urge you to *keep a running record of helpful journal articles and other sources.* Include enough information that you will be able to track each source down again—perhaps including the author's name, the title and year of the journal or book, key words and phrases that capture the focus of the work, and (if applicable) the appropriate library call number or Internet address. You may think you will always be able to recall where you found a helpful source and what you learned from it. However, our own experiences tell us that you probably *will* forget a good deal of what you read unless you keep a handwritten or electronic record of it.

3. ***Seek the advice of experts.***   Another simple yet highly effective strategy for identifying a research problem is to ask an expert: What needs to be done? What burning questions are still out there? What previous research findings seemingly don't make sense? Your professors will almost certainly be able to answer each of these questions, as will other scholars you might contact through e-mail or meet on campus and elsewhere.

Some beginning researchers—including many students—are reluctant to approach well-known scholars for fear that these scholars don't have the time or patience to talk with novices. Quite the opposite is true: Most experienced researchers are happy to talk with people who are just starting out. In fact, they may feel flattered that you are familiar with their work and would like to extend or apply it in some way.

4. *Attend professional conferences.* Many researchers have great success finding new research projects at national or regional conferences in their discipline. By scanning the conference program and attending sessions of interest, they can learn "what's hot and what's not" in their field. Furthermore, conferences are a place where novice researchers can make contacts with more experienced individuals in their field—where they can ask questions, share ideas, and exchange e-mail addresses that enable follow-up communication.

5. *Choose a topic that intrigues and motivates you.* As you read the professional literature, attend conferences, and talk with experts, you will uncover a number of potential research problems. At some point you need to pick just *one* of them, and your selection should be based on what you personally want to learn more about. Remember, the project you are about to undertake will take you many months, quite possibly a couple of years or even longer. So it should be something you believe is worth your time and effort—even better, one you are truly passionate about. Peter Leavenworth, at the time a doctoral student in history, explained the importance of choosing an interesting dissertation topic this way: "You're going to be married to it for a while, so you might as well enjoy it."

6. *Choose a topic that others will find interesting and worthy of attention.* Ideally, your work should not end simply with a thesis, dissertation, or other unpublished research report. If your research adds an important piece to what the human race knows and understands about the world, then you will, we hope, want to share your findings with a larger audience. In other words, you will want to present what you have done at a regional or national conference, publish an article in a professional journal, or both (we talk more about doing such things in Chapter 13). Conference coordinators and journal editors are often quite selective about the research reports they accept for presentation or publication, and they are most likely to choose those reports that will have broad appeal.

Future employers may also make judgments about you, at least in part, based on the topic you have chosen for a thesis or dissertation. Your résumé or curriculum vitae will be more apt to attract their attention if, in your research, you are pursuing an issue of broad scientific or social concern—especially one that is currently a hot topic in your field.

7. *Be realistic about what you can accomplish.* Although it is important to address a problem that legitimately needs addressing, it is equally important that the problem be a *manageable* one. For example, how much time will it take you to collect the necessary data? Will you need to travel great distances to get the data? Will you need expensive equipment? Will the project require knowledge and skills far beyond those you currently have? Asking and then answering such questions can help you keep your project within reasonable, accomplishable bounds.

GUIDELINES Stating the Research Problem

Remember, the heart of any research project is the problem. At every step in the process, successful researchers ask themselves: What am I doing? For what purpose am I doing it? Such questions can help you focus your efforts toward achieving your ultimate purpose for gathering data: to resolve the problem.

Researchers get off to a strong start when they begin with an unmistakably clear statement of the problem. Thus, after identifying a research problem, you must articulate it in such a way that *it is carefully phrased and represents the single goal of the total research effort.* Following are several general guidelines to help you do exactly that.

1. *State the problem clearly and completely.*   When communicating your research problem to others—for instance, when you present it in your research proposal—you should state it so clearly that anyone else can understand the issue(s) or question(s) you want to investigate. However, you can state your problem clearly only when you also state it completely. At a minimum, you should describe it in one or more *grammatically complete sentences*. As examples of what *not* to do, following are some meaningless half-statements—verbal fragments that only hint at the problem. Ask yourself whether you understand exactly what each student researcher plans to do.

From a student in sociology:

Welfare on children's attitudes.

From a student in music:

Palestrina and the motet.

From a student in economics:

Busing of schoolchildren.

From a student in social work:

Retirement plans of adults.

All four statements lack clarity. It is imperative to think in terms of specific, researchable goals expressed in complete sentences. We take the preceding fragments and develop each of them into one or more complete sentences that describe a researchable problem.

Welfare on children's attitudes becomes:

What effect does welfare assistance to parents have on the attitudes of their children toward work?

Palestrina and the motet becomes:

This study will analyze the motets of Giovanni Pierluigi da Palestrina (1525?–1594) written between 1575 and 1580 to discover their distinctive contrapuntal characteristics and will contrast them with the motets of his contemporary William Byrd (1542?–1623) written between 1592 and 1597. During the periods studied, each composer was between 50 and 55 years of age.

Busing of schoolchildren becomes:

What factors must be evaluated and what are the relative weights of those several factors in constructing a formula for estimating the cost of busing children in a midwestern metropolitan school system?

Retirement plans of adults becomes:

How do retirement plans for adults compare with the actual realization, in retirement, of those plans in terms of self-satisfaction and self-adjustment? What does an analysis of the difference between anticipation and realization reveal for a more intelligent approach to planning?

Notice that, in the full statement of each of these problems, the areas studied are carefully limited so that the study is of manageable size. The author of the Palestrina-Byrd study carefully limited the motets that would be studied to those written when each composer was between 50 and 55 years of age. A glance at the listing of Palestrina's works in *Grove's Dictionary of Music and Musicians* demonstrates how impractical it would be for a student to undertake a study of all the Palestrina motets. He wrote 392 of them!

2. *Think through the feasibility of the project that the problem implies.*   Novice researchers sometimes identify a research problem without thinking about its implications. Consider the following research proposal submitted by John:

This study proposes to study the science programs in the secondary schools in the United States for the purpose of . . . .

Let's think about that. The United States has somewhere around 40,000 public and private secondary schools. These schools, north to south, extend from Alaska to Florida; east to west, from Maine to Hawaii. How does John intend to contact each of these schools? By personal visit? At best, he might be able to visit two or three schools per day, so if he worked 365 days a year—in which case many school officials would have to agree to meet with him on a weekend or holiday—he would need more than 40 years to collect his data. And even if John had exceptional longevity—not to mention exceptional persistence—the financial outlay for his project would be exorbitant.

"But," John explains, "I plan to gather the data by sending a questionnaire." Fine! Each letter, with an enclosed questionnaire and a return postage-paid envelope, might cost two dollars to mail. At best, he could expect a 50% return rate on the first mailing, so one or more follow-up mailings would be required for nonreturnees. And we would need to figure in the cost of envelopes, stationery, printing, and data analysis.

A faster and less expensive option, of course, would be to conduct the survey by e-mail. In that case, John would need to track down the name and chief administrator of every one of those 40,000 schools. How long might it take him to do that? And how many of his e-mail messages might end up in a chief administrator's spam filter and thus never be read?

Obviously, John didn't intend to survey every secondary school in the United States, yet that is what he wrote that he would do.

3. *Say precisely what you mean.* When you state your research problem, you should say exactly what you mean. You cannot assume that others will be able to read your mind. People will always take your words at their face value: You mean what you say—that's it. In the academic community, a basic rule prevails: *Absolute honesty and integrity are assumed in every statement a scholar makes.*

Look again at John's problem statement. We could assume that John means to fulfill precisely what he has stated (although we would doubt it, given the time and expense involved). Had he intended to survey only *some* schools, he should have said so plainly:

> This study proposes to survey the science programs *in selected secondary schools throughout the United States* for the purpose of . . . .

Or perhaps he could have limited his study to a specific geographical area or to schools serving certain kinds of students. Such an approach would give the problem constraints that the original statement lacked and would communicate to others what John intended to do—what he realistically *could* commit to doing. Furthermore, it would have preserved his reputation as a researcher of integrity and precision.

Ultimately, an imprecisely stated research problem can lead others to have reservations about the quality of the overall research project. If a researcher cannot be meticulous and precise in stating the nature of the problem, others might question whether the researcher is likely to be any more meticulous and precise in gathering and interpreting data. Such uncertainty and misgivings are serious indeed, for they reflect on the basic integrity of the whole research effort.

We have discussed some common difficulties in the statement of the problem, including statements that are unclear or incomplete and statements that suggest impractical or impossible projects. Another difficulty is this one: A researcher *talks about the problem* but never actually *states what the problem is.* Using the excuse that the problem needs an introduction or needs to be seen against a background, the researcher launches into a generalized discussion, continually obscuring the problem, never clearly articulating it. Take, for example, the following paragraph that appeared under the heading "Statement of the Problem":

> The upsurge of interest in reading and learning disabilities found among both children and adults has focused the attention of educators, psychologists, and linguists on the language syndrome. In order to understand how language is learned, it is necessary to understand what language is. Language acquisition is a normal developmental aspect of every individual, but it has not been studied in sufficient depth. To provide us with the necessary background information to understand the anomaly of language deficiency implies a knowledge of the

> developmental process of language as these relate to the individual from infancy to maturity. Grammar, also an aspect of language learning, is acquired through pragmatic language usage. Phonology, syntax, and semantics are all intimately involved in the study of any language disability.

Can you find a statement of problem here? Several problems are suggested, but none is articulated with sufficient clarity that we might put a finger on it and say, "There, that is the problem."

Earlier in this chapter we have suggested that you look at examples of dissertations that students have completed at your university and elsewhere. Look at the abstracts for a few of those dissertations and notice with what directness the problems are set forth. The problem should be stated in the first sentence or two: "The purpose of this study was to . . . ." No mistaking it, no background buildup necessary—just a straightforward plunge into the task at hand. All research problems should be stated with the same clarity.

4. *State the problem in a way that reflects an open mind about its solution.*   In our own research methods classes, we have occasionally seen research proposals in which the authors state that they intend to *prove* that such-and-such a fact is true. For example, a student once proposed the following research project:

> In this study, I will prove that obese adults experience greater psychological distress than adults with a healthy body mass index.

This is not a research question; it is a presumed—and quite presumptuous!—*answer* to a research question. If this student already knew the answer to her question, why was she proposing to study it? Furthermore, as noted in Chapter 1, it is quite difficult to prove something definitively, beyond a shadow of a doubt. We might obtain data consistent with what we believe to be true, but in the world of research we can rarely say with 100% certainty that it *is* true.

Good researchers try to keep open minds about what they might find. Perhaps they will find the result they hope to find, perhaps not. Any hypothesis should be stated as exactly that—a *hypothesis*—rather than as a foregone conclusion. As you will see later in the chapter, hypotheses play important roles in many research proposals. However, they should not be part of the problem statement.

Let's rewrite the preceding research problem, this time omitting any expectation of results that the research effort might yield:

> In this study, I will investigate the possible relationship between body mass index and psychological stress, as well as two more specific psychological factors (depression and anxiety) that might underlie such a relationship.

Such a statement clearly communicates that the researcher is open-minded about what she may or may not find.

5. *Edit your work.*   You can avoid the difficulties we have been discussing by carefully editing your words. *Editing* is sharpening a thought to a gemlike point and eliminating useless verbiage. Choose your words precisely, ideally selecting simple words, concrete nouns, and active, expressive verbs.

The sentences in the preceding paragraph began as a mishmash of foggy thought and jumbled verbiage. The original version of the paragraph contained 71 words. These were edited down to 41 words, yielding a reduction of about 40% and a great improvement in clarity and readability. Figure 2.1 shows the original version and how it was edited. The three lines under the *c* in *choose* mean that the first letter should be capitalized. We present some of the common editing marks when we discuss editing in more detail in Chapter 5.

Notice the directness of the edited copy. We eliminated unnecessarily wordy phrases— "relating to the statement of the problem," "a process whereby the writer attempts to bring what is said straight to the point"—replacing the verbosity with seven words: "sharpening

FIGURE 2.1 ■ Editing
to Clarify Your Writing:
An Example

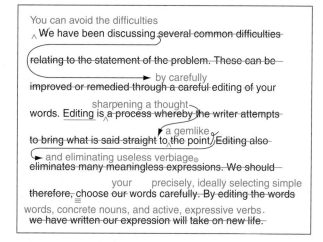

a thought to a gemlike point." As we edited, we also pinned down what good word choice might involve.

Editing almost invariably improves your thinking and your prose. Many students think that any words that approximate a thought are adequate to convey it to others. This is not so. Approximation is never precision.

The following checklist can help you formulate a research problem that is clear, precise, and accurate.

✓ CHECKLIST

Evaluating the Research Problem

_____   1. Write a clear statement of a problem for research.

_____

_____

_____

_____

_____

_____   2. Review your written statement and ask yourself the following questions:
   • Is the problem stated in one or more complete, grammatical sentences?
   • Is it clear how the area of study will be limited or focused?
   • Is it clear that you have an open mind about results that the research effort might yield?

_____   3. On the basis of your answers to the questions in Item 2, edit your written statement.

_____

_____

_____

_____

_____

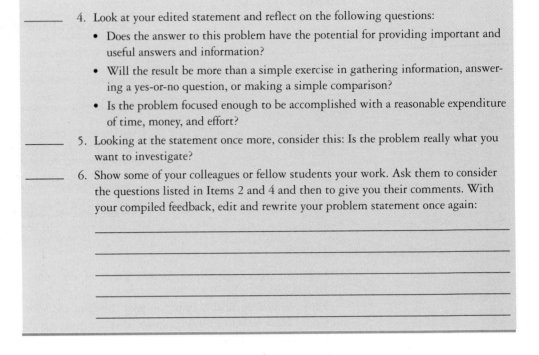

_____ 4. Look at your edited statement and reflect on the following questions:
- Does the answer to this problem have the potential for providing important and useful answers and information?
- Will the result be more than a simple exercise in gathering information, answering a yes-or-no question, or making a simple comparison?
- Is the problem focused enough to be accomplished with a reasonable expenditure of time, money, and effort?

_____ 5. Looking at the statement once more, consider this: Is the problem really what you want to investigate?

_____ 6. Show some of your colleagues or fellow students your work. Ask them to consider the questions listed in Items 2 and 4 and then to give you their comments. With your compiled feedback, edit and rewrite your problem statement once again:

_____

_____

_____

_____

_____

DIVIDING THE RESEARCH PROBLEM INTO SUBPROBLEMS

Most research problems are too large or complex to be solved without subdividing them. A good strategy, then, is to divide and conquer. Almost any problem can be broken down into smaller units, or subproblems—sometimes in the form of specific questions—that are easier to address and resolve. Furthermore, by viewing the main problem through its subproblems, a researcher can often get a better idea of how to approach the entire research endeavor.

Subproblems Versus Pseudo-Subproblems

The researcher must distinguish subproblems that are integral parts of the main problem from things that look like problems but are really nothing more than procedural issues. The latter, which we might call *pseudo-subproblems,* involve decisions a researcher must make before being able to resolve the research problem and its subproblems. Consider the following as examples:

- What is the best way to choose a sample from the population to be studied?
- How large should the sample be?
- What instruments or methods should be used to gather the data?
- What statistical procedures should be used to analyze the data?

For each pseudo-subproblem, you must decide whether (a) a little common sense and some creative thinking might help in solving it, or (b) you lack the knowledge to address the difficulty. In the latter case, you have several options:

1. Turn to the index of this text to see whether your pseudo-subproblem regarding sample selection, instrumentation, statistical analysis, or some other issue is discussed.
2. Peruse the "For Further Reading" lists at the end of each chapter in this book to see whether they include sources that might help you, and consult general research methods books in your discipline.
3. Search your university library's catalog and online databases to find potentially helpful books and journal articles. If your library doesn't own what you need, you can typically obtain it through interlibrary loan.

4. Seek the suggestions and advice of more experienced researchers in your field. Recall a point previously made in Chapter 1: One of the most effective strategies for using the human mind is *collaborating with other minds.*

Characteristics of Subproblems

Following are four key characteristics of subproblems.

1. *Each subproblem should be a completely researchable unit.* A subproblem should constitute a logical subarea of the larger research undertaking. Each subproblem might be researched as a separate subproject within the larger research goal. The solutions to the subproblems, taken together, can then be combined to resolve the main problem.

It is essential that each subproblem be stated clearly and succinctly. Often a subproblem is stated in the form of a question. A question tends to focus the researcher's attention more directly on the research target of the subproblem than does a declarative statement. As we have seen, a questioning, open-minded attitude is the mark of a true researcher.

2. *Each subproblem must be clearly tied to the interpretation of the data.* Just as is true for the main problem, each subproblem should involve interpretation as well as collection of data. This fact may be expressed as a part of each subproblem statement, or it may be reflected in a separate but related subproblem.

3. *The subproblems must add up to the totality of the problem.* After you have stated the subproblems, check them against the statement of the main problem to make sure that (a) they do not extend beyond the main problem and (b) they address all significant aspects of the main problem.

4. *Subproblems should be small in number.* If the main problem is carefully stated and properly limited to a feasible research effort, the researcher will find that it usually contains two to six subproblems. Sometimes a researcher will come up with as many as 10, 15, or 20 subproblems. When this happens, a careful review of the problem and its attendant subproblems is in order. If you find yourself in this situation, you should study the individual subproblems to see whether (a) some are actually procedural issues (pseudo-subproblems), (b) some might reasonably be combined into larger subproblems, or (c) the main problem is more complex than you originally believed. If the last of these is true, you may want to reconsider whether the solution to the overall research problem is realistically achievable given the time and resources you have.

Identifying Subproblems

To identify subproblems, you must begin with the problem itself. Write down the main problem, and then carefully scrutinize it to detect more specific problems that should be isolated for in-depth study. The old axiom that the *sum of the parts equals the whole* applies here. All of the subproblems must add up to the total problem.

You can use either paper and pencil or brainstorming software to help you identify your subproblems. We briefly describe each of these strategies.

Taking a Paper-and-Pencil Approach

Using this approach, you write the problem on paper and then box off the subproblem areas. More specifically, you might follow these steps:

1. Copy the problem on a clean sheet of paper, leaving considerable space between the lines.
2. Critically read the problem to identify specific topics that require in-depth treatment in order for the problem to be resolved. Draw a box around each topic.

3. Make sure that the words within each box include a word that indicates the need for data interpretation (e.g., *analyze, discover, compare*). Underline this word.
4. Arrange the entire problem—which now has its subproblems in boxes—in a graphic that shows the structure of the whole research design.

We use a problem in musicology to illustrate this technique. More specifically, we revisit the problem of the motets of Palestrina presented earlier in the chapter:

> This study will analyze the motets of Giovanni Pierluigi da Palestrina (1525?–1594) written between 1575 and 1580 to discover their distinctive contrapuntal characteristics and will contrast them with the motets of his contemporary William Byrd (1542?–1623) written between 1592 and 1597. During the periods studied, each composer was between 50 and 55 years of age.

Let's first delete the factual matter, such as lifespan dates and the fact that the two men were contemporaries. These facts merely help in giving a rationale for certain elements within the problem. Modified to reflect its essential parts, the motet problem becomes the following:

> The purpose of this study will be *to analyze* the motets of Palestrina written between 1575 and 1580 to discover their distinctive contrapuntal characteristics, *to analyze* the same characteristics in the motets of William Byrd written between 1592 and 1597, and to determine what *a comparison of these two analyses* may reveal.

Notice that we have broken up the "will contrast them with" phrase in the original statement into two distinct tasks, *analyzing* Byrd's motets in the same manner that Palestrina's motets have been analyzed, and *comparing* the two analyses. The three italicized phrases in the revised problem statement reflect three subproblems, each of which involves interpretation of data that is necessary for resolving the main research problem.

Let's now arrange the problem so that we can see precisely what the overall research design will be. Figure 2.2 is a graphic depiction of the problem. We have divided the problem into three subproblems. The first and second of these have the same structural configuration: The analytical aspect of the subproblem is stated in one box and the purpose of the analysis is stated in the box right below it. Addressing the third subproblem involves comparing the analyses conducted for the two preceding subproblems to determine what similarities and differences may exist. The last of the three subproblems—the comparison step—should ultimately resolve the main research problem.

FIGURE 2.2 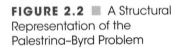 A Structural Representation of the Palestrina–Byrd Problem

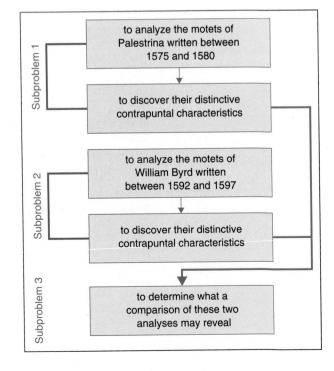

Subproblem 1
to analyze the motets of Palestrina written between 1575 and 1580

to discover their distinctive contrapuntal characteristics

Subproblem 2
to analyze the motets of William Byrd written between 1592 and 1597

to discover their distinctive contrapuntal characteristics

Subproblem 3
to determine what a comparison of these two analyses may reveal

Using Brainstorming (Mind Mapping) Software

USING TECHNOLOGY

Some computer software programs can facilitate the process of breaking problems into subproblems; you might see these referred to as either *brainstorming* or *mind mapping* software. Examples of commercially available programs are BrainStorm, Inspiration, MindJet, and XMind; a free online alternative is Coggle (coggle.it). Such programs allow you to brainstorm research ideas and construct graphic networks of interrelated concepts, terms, and principles. For example, in Inspiration, you put the main problem, idea, or concept inside a box or oval in the middle of your computer screen. As you brainstorm other, related ideas, you put those on the screen as well, and you draw (and perhaps label) arrows to represent how various ideas are interconnected. You can break each concept or problem into subparts and, if helpful, break down each subpart even further. The process is fast and flexible, and you can save and print your final diagram (Figure 3.1 in Chapter 3 is an example). Some brainstorming software programs also allow you to convert your diagram into an outline that lists major topics and various levels of subtopics.

EVERY PROBLEM NEEDS FURTHER DELINEATION

Up to this point, we have been discussing only the problem and its subparts. The statement of the problem establishes the goal for the research effort. The subproblems suggest ways of approaching that goal in a manageable, systematic way. But a goal alone is not enough. To comprehend fully the meaning of the problem, we need other information as well. Both the researcher and those reading the research proposal should ultimately have a clear understanding of every detail of the process.

At the beginning of any research endeavor, the researcher should minimize possible misunderstandings by

- Stating any *a priori* hypotheses
- Identifying specific variables under investigation (especially important in quantitative research)
- Defining terms
- Stating underlying assumptions
- Identifying delimitations and limitations

Such things comprise *the setting of the problem.* We look at each of them in more detail in the following sections. We also include a section titled "Importance of the Study," as a special section on this topic frequently appears in dissertations and other lengthy research reports.

Stating Hypotheses

As noted in Chapter 1, hypotheses are intelligent, reasonable guesses about how the research problem might be resolved. Our focus here is on *a priori* hypotheses—those that a researcher poses in advance, usually in conjunction with the research problem and its subproblems.[1] Often a one-to-one correspondence exists between the subproblems and their corresponding hypotheses, in which case there are as many hypotheses as there are subproblems.

Hypotheses can guide the researcher toward choosing particular types of research designs, collecting particular kinds of data, and analyzing those data in particular ways. The data may, in turn, support or not support each hypothesis. Notice how we just said that the data may *support* or *not support* each hypothesis; we intentionally did *not* say that the data would "prove" a hypothesis. Ultimately, hypotheses are nothing more than *tentative propositions set forth to assist in guiding the investigation of a problem or to provide possible explanations for observations made.*

A researcher who deliberately sets out to prove a hypothesis does not have the objective, impartial open-mindedness so important for good research. The researcher might bias the procedure by looking only for data that would support the hypothesis (recall the discussion of

---

[1]*A priori* has Latin origins, meaning "from before."

confirmation bias in Figure 1.3 of Chapter 1). Difficult as it may be at times, we must let the chips fall where they may. Hypotheses have nothing to do with proof. Rather, their acceptance or rejection depends on what the data—and the data alone—ultimately reveal.

A priori hypotheses are essential to most experimental research (see Chapter 7), and they are sometimes posed in other kinds of quantitative research as well. In contrast, many researchers who conduct strictly qualitative studies intentionally *do not* speculate in advance about what they will find, in large part as a way of keeping open minds about where their investigations will take them and what patterns they will find in their data.

Distinguishing Between Research Hypotheses and Null Hypotheses in Quantitative Research

The preceding discussion has been about *research* hypotheses—those educated guesses that researchers hope their data might support. But because researchers can never really prove a hypothesis, they often set out to cast doubt on—and therefore to *reject*—an opposite hypothesis. For example, imagine that a team of social workers believes that one type of after-school program for teenagers (Program A) is more effective in reducing high school dropout rates than is another program (Program B). The team's research hypothesis is:

> Teenagers enrolled in Program A will graduate from high school at a higher rate than teenagers enrolled in Program B.

Because the social workers cannot actually prove this hypothesis, they instead try to discredit an opposite hypothesis:

> There will be no difference in the high school graduation rates of teenagers enrolled in Program A and those enrolled in Program B.

If, in their research, the social workers find that there *is* a substantial difference in graduation rates between the two programs—and in particular, if the graduation rate is higher for students in Program A—they can reject the no-difference hypothesis and thus have, by default, supported their research hypothesis.

When we hypothesize that there will be *no* differences between groups, *no* consistent relationships between variables, or, more generally, *no* patterns in the data, we are forming a null hypothesis. Most null hypotheses are *not* appropriate as *a priori* hypotheses. Instead, they are used primarily during statistical analyses; we support a research hypothesis by showing, statistically, that its opposite—the null hypothesis—probably is *not* true. Accordingly, we examine null hypotheses again in our discussion of statistics in Chapter 8.

Identifying the Variables Under Investigation

We have occasionally used the term *variable* in earlier discussions in this chapter and in Chapter 1, but we haven't yet explained what we've meant by the term. We do so now: A variable is any quality or characteristic in a research investigation that has two or more possible values. For example, variables in studies of how well seeds germinate might include amounts of sun and water, kinds of soil and fertilizer, presence or absence of various parasites and microorganisms, genetic makeup of the seeds, speed of germination, and hardiness of the resulting plants. Variables in studies of how effectively children learn in classrooms might include instructional methods used; teachers' educational backgrounds, emotional warmth, and beliefs about classroom discipline; and children's existing abilities and personality characteristics, prior learning experiences, reading skills, study strategies, and achievement test scores.

Explicit identification of variables at the beginning of a study is most common in quantitative research, especially in experimental studies (see Chapter 7) and certain kinds of descriptive studies (see Chapter 6). In contrast, many qualitative researchers prefer to let important variables "emerge" as data are collected (see the discussion of grounded theory studies in Chapter 9).

Whenever a research project involves an investigation of a possible cause-and-effect relationship—as is typically true in experimental studies—at least two variables must be specified up front. A variable that the researcher studies as a possible cause of something else— in many cases, this is one that the researcher directly manipulates—is called an independent variable. A variable that is potentially caused or influenced by the independent variable—that "something else" just mentioned—is called a dependent variable, because its status *depends* to some degree on the status of the independent variable. In research in the social sciences and education, the dependent variable is often some form of human behavior. In medical research, it might be people's physical health or well-being. In agricultural research, it might be quality or quantity of a particular crop. In general, a cause-and-effect relationship can be depicted like this:

Independent variable → Dependent variable

To illustrate the two kinds of variables, let's take an everyday situation. One hot summer morning you purchase two identical cartons of chocolate ice cream at the supermarket. When you get home, you put one carton in your refrigerator freezer but absentmindedly leave the other one on the kitchen counter. You then leave the house for a few hours. When you return home, you discover that the ice cream on the counter has turned into a soupy mess. The ice cream in the freezer is still in the same condition it was when you purchased it. Two things vary in this situation. One, the temperature at which the ice cream is stored, is the independent variable. The other, consistency of the ice cream, depends on the temperature and is therefore the dependent variable.

Now let's consider an example in medical research. Imagine that you want to compare the relative effectiveness of two different drugs that are used to treat high blood pressure. You take a sample of 60 men who have high blood pressure and randomly assign each man to one of two groups: The men in one group take one drug, and the men in the other group take the other drug. Later, you compare the blood pressure measurements for the men in the two groups. In this situation, you are manipulating the particular drug that each man takes; the drug, then, is the independent variable. Blood pressure is the dependent variable: It is presumably influenced by the drug taken and so its measured value depends to some extent on the drug.

A research question or *a priori* hypothesis may occasionally specify other variables as well. For example, a mediating variable (also known as an *intervening variable*) might help explain *why* a certain independent variable has the effect that it does on a dependent variable. In particular, the independent variable influences the mediating variable, which in turn influences the dependent variable. Thus, the independent variable's influence on the dependent variable is an *indirect one,* as follows:

Independent variable → Mediating variable → Dependent variable

For example, consider the common finding that people who are confident in their ability to perform a particular new task do, on average, actually perform it better than less-confident people, even if the two groups of people had the same ability levels prior to performing the task. Looking at the situation from a simple independent-and-dependent-variables perspective, the situation would be depicted this way:

Confidence level	→	Performance quality
(independent variable)		(dependent variable)

But *why* does this relationship exist? One likely mediating variable is that highly confident people exert more effort in performing the new task than do people with less confidence (e.g., Bandura, 1997; Schunk & Pajares, 2005). The mediating variable, then, is *amount of effort,* as follows:

Confidence level	→	Amount of effort	→	Performance quality
(independent variable)		(mediating variable)		(dependent variable)

Still another variable of potential interest is a moderating variable—a variable that, while not intervening between the independent and dependent variables, influences the nature and strength of their cause-and-effect relationship. For example, consider the fact that, on average, children from very-low-income homes are more likely to have difficulties in adolescence and adulthood; for instance, compared to their financially more advantaged peers, they are less likely to complete high school and more likely to get in trouble with the law. Yet some very poor youngsters are resilient to their circumstances: They do quite well in life, sometimes going on to become physicians, lawyers, college professors, or other successful professionals. One factor that apparently increases the odds of resilience—in other words, it *reduces* the cause-and-effect relationship between childhood poverty and later problems—is a warm, supportive mother (Kim-Cohen, Moffitt, Caspi, & Taylor, 2004). Maternal warmth is a moderating variable: It affects the *nature of the relationship* between family income level and adult problems, like this:

Maternal warmth
(moderating variable)
↓

Childhood income level   →   Problems later in life
(independent variable)   (dependent variable)

The distinction between mediating and moderating variables is an important but often confusing one; even some experienced researchers get them confused (Holmbeck, 1997). A helpful way to keep them straight is to remember that an independent variable may potentially influence a mediating variable but does *not,* in and of itself, influence a moderating variable. For example, in the earlier *mediating variable* example, a high confidence level might increase the amount of effort exerted, but in the *moderating variable* example, we would certainly not suggest that having a low income increases (i.e., causes) a mother's warmth toward her children. Rather, moderating variables provide potential *contexts or conditions* that alter—that is, they *moderate*—an independent variable's effects. When researchers refer to *risk factors* or *protective factors* in their research reports, they are talking about moderating variables—variables that affect the likelihood that certain cause-and-effect relationships will come into play.

Identifying independent and dependent variables is often quite helpful in choosing both (a) an appropriate research design and (b) an appropriate statistical analysis. However, an important caution is in order here. In particular, *identifying independent and dependent variables does **not** guarantee that the research data will support the existence of a cause-and-effect relationship.* We return to this point in the discussion of correlational research in Chapter 6.

At various points in the book we present exercises to help you apply concepts and ideas we have presented. In the first of these exercises, which follows, you can gain practice in distinguishing among independent, dependent, mediating, and moderating variables.

CONCEPTUAL ANALYSIS EXERCISE Identifying Independent, Dependent, Mediating, and Moderating Variables

Following are eight proposed research problems. Each one of them implies one or more independent variables and one or more dependent variables. Some of them also imply one or more mediating or moderating variables. Identify the independent and dependent variables—and, if applicable, any mediating and/or moderating variables—in each problem. We warn you that some of these scenarios may challenge you, as the writer's hypotheses may lie well below the surface of the words. We encourage you, then, to try to put yourself in each researcher's mind and guess what the person is probably thinking about a possible cause-and-effect relationship in the phenomenon under investigation. The answers appear after the "For Further Reading" list at the end of the chapter.

1. In this study, I will examine the possible effects of regular physical exercise on the health and longevity of laboratory rats.
2. In this study, I will investigate the extent to which placing recycling bins in convenient locations in classroom buildings affects college students' recycling behaviors.
3. In this study, I will examine the relationship between amount of cell phone use while driving and the frequency of car accidents.

4. I propose to study the degree to which test anxiety may influence test performance by increasing the frequency of distracting thoughts.
5. This investigation will examine the extent to which a supportive student–teacher relationship reduces the negative emotional impact of peer bullying on a child's emotional well-being.
6. I will investigate the degree to which male and female adolescents choose gender-stereotypical careers in three different countries: Canada, Lebanon, and Japan.
7. This study will investigate the extent to which a particular tumor-suppressing gene reduces the risk of getting melanoma [a potentially deadly form of skin cancer] after a history of frequent exposure to sunlight.
8. In this study, I will investigate the possible relationship between body mass index and psychological stress, as well as two more specific psychological factors (depression and anxiety) that might underlie such a relationship. (You previously saw this problem statement in the guidelines for "Stating the Research Problem" earlier in the chapter.)

Defining Terms

What, precisely, do the terms in the problem and the subproblems mean? For example, if we say that the purpose of the research is to analyze the contrapuntal characteristics of motets, what are we talking about? What are *contrapuntal characteristics?* Or if we say that a study will investigate the relationship between people's self-confidence levels and the quality of their performance on a task, we need to pin down what we mean by both *self-confidence* and *performance quality.* Without knowing explicitly what specific terms mean—or, more specifically, what the *researcher* means by them—we cannot evaluate the research or determine whether the researcher has carried out what was proposed in the problem statement.

Sometimes novice researchers rely on dictionary definitions, which are rarely either adequate or helpful. Instead, each term should be defined *as it will be used in the researcher's project.* In defining a term, the researcher makes the term mean whatever he or she wishes it to mean within the context of the problem and its subproblems. Other individuals who read the researcher's research proposal or report must know how the researcher defines the term. Those individuals won't necessarily agree with such a definition, but as long as they know what the researcher means when using the term, they can understand the research and appraise it appropriately.

The researcher must be careful to avoid *circular definitions,* in which the terms to be defined are used in the definitions themselves. For example, if a researcher were to define *self-confidence* as "degree of confidence one has in one's own abilities," readers would still be in the dark about what *confidence* actually means within the context of that particular study.

Especially when talking about phenomena that have no cut-and-dried, easy-to-pinpoint manifestation in the physical world, it is often helpful to include an operational definition. That is, the researcher defines a characteristic or variable in terms of how it will be identified or measured in the research study. For instance, a researcher might, for purposes of his or her study, define *self-confidence* as a high score on a self-report questionnaire that has items such as "I can usually achieve what I set out to do" and "I think of myself as a smart person." Likewise, a researcher might define *intelligence* as a score on a certain intelligence test or define *popularity* as the number of peers who specifically identify an individual as being a desirable social partner. As another example, let's return to the first scenario in the earlier Conceptual Analysis Exercise: examining the possible effects of regular physical exercise on the health and longevity of laboratory rats. Longevity is easily defined and measured: It's simply the length of a rat's lifespan in days or some other unit of time. Somewhere in the research proposal, however, the researcher will need to be more specific about how he or she will define and measure physical exercise and health, thereby providing operational definitions for these terms. For example, physical exercise might involve putting a treadmill in some rats' cages but not in others. Health might be measured in any number of ways—for instance, through measurement of hypertension or analyses of blood or hair samples.

Stating Assumptions

We have previously discussed assumptions in Chapter 1. Assumptions are so basic that, without them, the research problem itself could not exist. For example, suppose we are attempting to determine, by means of a pretest and a posttest, whether one method of classroom instruction is superior to another. A basic assumption in such a situation is that the pretest and posttest measure knowledge of the subject matter in question.[2] We must also assume that the teacher(s) in the study can teach effectively and that the students are capable of learning the subject matter. Without these assumptions, our research project would be meaningless.

In research, we try to leave nothing to chance in order to prevent any misunderstandings. All assumptions that have a material bearing on the problem should be openly and unreservedly set forth. If others know the assumptions a researcher is making, they are better prepared to evaluate the conclusions that result from such assumptions.

To discover your own assumptions, ask yourself: What am I taking for granted with respect to the problem? Ideally, your answer should bring your assumptions into clear view.

Identifying Delimitations and Limitations

The statement of the research problem describes what the researcher intends to do. But it is also important to know what the researcher does *not* intend to do. What the researcher is not going to do is stated in the *delimitations.*

Research problems typically emerge out of larger contexts and larger problem areas. The researcher can easily be beguiled and drawn off course by addressing questions and obtaining data that lie beyond the boundaries of the problem under investigation. For example, in the Palestrina-Byrd problem, it's possible that, because the two men were contemporaries, Byrd may have met Palestrina or at least come in contact with some of his motets. Such contact may have been a determinative influence on Byrd's compositions. But given how the problem has been stated, the researcher does not need to be concerned with *influences* on the motets of the two composers. He or she should be primarily interested in the *characteristics* of the motets, including their musical style, musical individualism, and contrapuntal likenesses and differences. Study the contrapuntal characteristics—that is what a researcher of this problem will do. What the researcher does *not* need to do is to worry about collecting data extraneous to this goal, no matter how enticing or interesting such an exploratory safari might be (see Figure 2.3).

FIGURE 2.3 ▨ Delimitation of a Problem

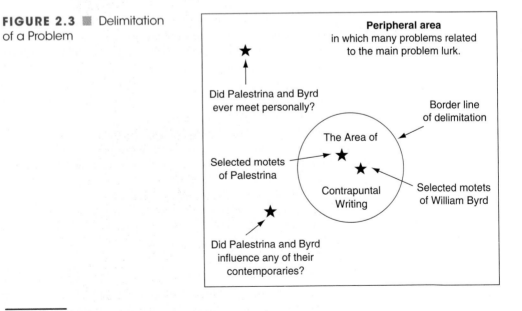

---

[2]Alternatively, we might make no such assumption; instead, we might set out to determine the *validity* of the tests as measures in this situation. We discuss the nature of validity of measurement in Chapter 4.

Good researchers also acknowledge that their research projects have certain weaknesses, or *limitations,* that might cast shadows of doubt on results and conclusions. No research project can be perfect, and an honest researcher will not pretend that it is. For example, when studying a certain aspect or quality of human behavior, a researcher might consider such questions as these:

▪ Will my sample consist only of people of a certain age range, geographic location, or cultural background? If so, how generalizable are my results likely to be to other populations?

▪ In what environment will I be conducting the study—in a laboratory, in a classroom, in a real-world setting, on the Internet, or elsewhere? How might this environmental context affect the results I obtain?

▪ How will I be measuring the variables in my study? How accurate are my measures likely to be?

▪ What personal biases might I be bringing to the study? Are they likely to influence the data I collect or my interpretations of the data?

▪ What "shortcuts" will I be taking in order to make my study logistically feasible? Might these shortcuts weaken the strength of any conclusions I might draw?

Weaknesses related to these and other issues must be clearly stated in a discussion of limitations, either in an introductory section or in a final "Discussion" or "Conclusions" section. Often researchers mention them in both places.

Importance of the Study

In most dissertations and other research reports, researchers set forth their reasons for undertaking the study. Such a discussion may be especially important in a research proposal. Some studies seem to go far beyond any relationship to the practical world. Of such research efforts readers might silently ask, "Of what *use* is it? What *practical value* does the study have? Will it make an appreciable difference in the health of the planet or in the well-being of one or more species living on it?" Such questions need to be answered.

WRITING THE FIRST CHAPTER OR SECTION OF A RESEARCH PROPOSAL

In any research proposal or research report, the first order of business is to present the general research problem, typically within its larger context. For example, as a doctoral student at the University of Maryland, Baltimore County, Christy Leung conducted a mixed-methods study concerning the experiences of Chinese women who had immigrated to the United States. She began the first chapter of her dissertation this way:

> America has long been recognized as a nation of immigrants . . . many immigrants believe that having freedom and equal opportunity for success and prosperity is possible. Immigrants come to the U.S. with a belief that through hard work, motivation, and persistence, they will be able to earn a better living and provide a better life for their children (Clark, 2003). Many groups, including the Chinese, have chosen to leave their home country because of this belief. The Chinese people have a long history of migration to and settlement in the U.S. to pursue the American dream. Chinese immigrants were once predominantly men who migrated as contract labor workers (e.g., Yung, Chang, & Lai, 2006). However, a series of political incidents and subsequent legislations led to a different wave of Chinese immigration to the U.S. after World War II (Yung et al., 2006; Zhoa, 2002). Changes in the pattern of international migration are important for understanding the adaptation and well-being of immigrants (Massey, Arange, Hugo, Kouaouci, Pellegrino, & Taylor, 1993). (Leung, 2012, p. 1)

In the three paragraphs that followed, Leung expanded on the diverse characteristics and motives of Chinese immigrants and described some of the unique challenges that women were apt to face in moving to the United States. At that point, Leung had provided sufficient information for readers to understand her research problem:

> [T]he overall goal of this research project was to examine Chinese immigrant mothers' reasons for migration, experiences of migrating to the U.S., . . . acculturation strategies, adjustment, and parenting. . . . (Leung, 2012, p. 3)

After stating the main research problem, a research proposal should identify more specific subproblems to be addressed, along with any *a priori* hypotheses related to these subproblems. Somewhere in the introductory section or chapter, key terms should be defined, basic assumptions should be elucidated, and delimitations and limitations should be put forth. A discussion of the importance of the study might have its own section or, alternatively, might be integrated into early paragraphs that introduce the research problem.

In a dissertation or other lengthy research report, such topics often comprise the first chapter or section. The document then generally continues with an in-depth discussion of investigations that others have done, usually titled "Review of the Related Literature" or something of that nature. We discuss this review in the next chapter.

PRACTICAL APPLICATION Writing the First Section of a Proposal

In a checklist earlier in this chapter, you stated your main research problem. In doing so, you took the first step in creating a research proposal. Now you can add the subproblems and identify the setting of the problem by doing the following exercise.

1. *State the subproblems.*   On a blank sheet of paper or new computer document, write the research problem statement you developed earlier. Now inspect your problem carefully and do these things:
   a. Within the problem, box off or highlight those areas that need in-depth treatment in order for the problem to be fully explored. Consecutively number these areas.
   b. Underline the words that indicate your intention to interpret the data (e.g., *analyze, compare*).
   c. Below the problem, which has been thus treated, write the several subproblems of your study in complete sentences. Make sure each subproblem includes a word that reflects data interpretation.

2. *State any a priori hypotheses.*   Are you expecting to find certain kinds of results related to one or more of your subproblems? If so, write your research hypotheses, along with a brief rationale for each one. Your rationales should be either theoretically or logically defensible. The sections on deductive logic, inductive reasoning, and theory building in Chapter 1 can help you complete this step.

3. *Identify and define key variables.*   Specify the particular characteristics, conditions, and/or behaviors that are either stated or implied in your problem and subproblems. Give a short but precise explanation of what each variable means *in your particular study*—for instance, how you intend to measure it or in some other way determine its values.

4. *Write your assumptions.*   Reread the section "Stating Assumptions." Now write a list of the specific assumptions you will be making as you design and carry out your research project—perhaps assumptions related to the people you will be studying, the relevance (or nonrelevance) of the environmental context in which you will be conducting your study, and your measurement techniques.

5. *Write the delimitations.*   Review the earlier discussion of delimitations. Now write several topics and questions related to your research problem that your research project will *not* address.

6. ***Write the limitations.*** Identify potential weaknesses of your study related to your proposed sample, data-collection environment, measurement techniques, and personal biases, as well as any "shortcut" strategies that may affect the quality of your results and credibility of your conclusions.

7. ***Describe the importance of the study.*** In a short paragraph or two, explain why your study is important. Eventually you may want to move this discussion to an earlier point in your proposal where you introduce your topic and provide an overall context for it. For now, however, keeping it in a separate section with its own label can help you remember that *talking* about your study's importance is important in its own right.

8. ***Type your proposal.*** Ideally, use word processing software so that you will easily be able to make future edits (there will be many!). Set margins at least an inch wide, and double-space the entire document; double-spacing makes proofreading easier and allows room for handwritten edits.

Now that you have written the first sections of a proposal, reflect on your proposed project using the following checklist.

✓ CHECKLIST

Evaluating Your Proposed Research Project

_____ 1. Have you read enough literature relevant to your topic to know that your research project is worth your time and effort?

- Will the project advance the frontiers of knowledge in an important way?

_____

_____

- Have you asked an expert in your field to advise you on the value of your research effort?

_____

_____

_____ 2. Have you looked at your research problem from all angles to minimize unwanted surprises?

- What is good about your potential project?

_____

_____

- What are the potential pitfalls of attempting this research effort?

_____

_____

_____ 3. What research procedure will you follow?

- Do you have a tentative plan to review the literature?

_____

_____

- Do you have a tentative plan for data collection?

_____

_____

- Do you have a tentative plan for data analysis?

_____

_____

- Do you have a tentative plan to interpret the data you collect?

    ———

    ———

———— 4. What research tools are available for you to use? Make a list and check their availability. Determine how you will use them.

    ———

    ———

    ———

    ———

———— 5. Ask two or three peers to read your proposal. Do they understand what you are proposing to do? What questions do they have? What concerns do they express?

- I have discussed this plan with ———————————————————————————

   ————————————————————, and ————————————————————.

- They have the following questions and concerns:

    ———

    ———

    ———

PRACTICAL APPLICATION Reappraising a Proposed Research Problem

In this chapter we have given you many suggestions for identifying an appropriate problem or question for your research. Because the problem is the center and driving force of any research project, we have devoted considerable space to its discussion. We can't overemphasize this fact: If the problem is not correctly selected and stated, you may put considerable time, energy, and resources into an endeavor that is much less than what it could be.

GUIDELINES   Fine-Tuning Your Research Problem

Earlier in the chapter, we presented guidelines for identifying and stating an appropriate research problem. Here we offer a few general suggestions for fine-tuning the problem you have identified.

1. *Conduct a thorough literature review.*   You have presumably already looked at some of the literature related to your research problem. A next critical step is to make sure you know enough about your topic that you can ask important questions and then make solid decisions about how you might answer them through your research endeavor. You may find that you need to revise your research plan significantly once you have delved more deeply into the literature related to your topic.

2. *Try to see the problem from all sides.*   What is good about this potential project? What is not? Try to take an objective, critical view of what you are proposing to do. Such a perspective can help minimize unwanted surprises.

3. *Think through the process.*   Once you have brought your research problem into clear focus, imagine walking through the whole research procedure, from literature review through data collection, data analysis, and interpretation. You can gain valuable insights as you mentally

walk through the project. Pay close attention to specific bottlenecks and pitfalls that might cause problems later on.

4. ***Discuss your problem with others.*** Beginning researchers frequently need to revise their problem statement in order to clarify it and make it more manageable. One good way to do this is to show it to other people. If they don't understand what you intend to do, further explanation and clarity are needed. One can learn a great deal from trying to explain something to someone else.

As you continue to refine your research problem, also continue to ask other people for their feedback. Ask people questions about your problem, and ask them to ask *you* questions about it. Do not be overly discouraged by a few individuals who may get some sense of satisfaction from impeding the progress of others. Many great discoveries have been made by people who were repeatedly told that they could not do what they set out to do.

5. ***Remember that your project will take time—lots of time.*** All too often, we authors have had students tell us that they anticipate completing a major research project, such as a thesis or dissertation, in a semester or less. In the vast majority of cases, such a belief is unrealistic. Consider all the steps involved in research: formulating a research problem, conducting the necessary literature search, collecting and interpreting the data, describing what you have done in writing, and improving on your research report through multiple drafts. If you think you can accomplish all of these things within 2 or 3 months, you're almost certainly setting yourself up for failure and disappointment. We would much rather you think of any research project—and especially your first project—as something that is a valuable learning experience in its own right. As such, it's worth however much of your time and effort it takes to do the job well.

6. ***Remember that the first drafts of whatever you write will almost certainly not be your last ones.*** Good researchers continually revise their thinking and, as a result, their writing. Furthermore, as mentioned in Chapter 1, writing about one's project often helps to clarify and enhance one's thinking. So get used to writing . . . and rewriting . . . and rewriting once again.

Nevertheless, by putting your problem statement on paper early in your research project, you have begun to focus your research efforts.

✔ Check your understanding in the Pearson etext

 Practice Thinking Like a Researcher

Practice Thinking Like a Researcher Activity 2.1: Stating the Research Problem
Practice Thinking Like a Researcher Activity 2.2: Identifying Research Subproblems
Practice Thinking Like a Researcher Activity 2.3: Selecting Variables to Study

FOR FURTHER READING

Booth, W. C., Colomb, G. G., & Williams, J. M. (2008). *The craft of research* (3rd ed.). Chicago: University of Chicago Press.

Cooper, H. (2006). Research questions and research designs. In P. A. Alexander & P. H. Winne (Eds.), *Handbook of educational psychology* (2nd ed., pp. 849–877). Mahwah, NJ: Erlbaum.

Gay, L. R., Mills, G. E., & Airasian, P. (2012). *Educational research: Competencies for analysis and application* (10th ed.). Upper Saddle River, NJ: Pearson Education. [See Chapter 2.]

Hayes, A. F. (2013). *Introduction to mediation, moderation, and conditional process analysis.* New York: Guilford Press.

Hesse-Biber, S. N. (2010). *Mixed methods research: Merging theory with practice.* New York: Guilford Press. [See Chapter 2.]

Holmbeck, G. N. (1997). Toward terminological, conceptual, and statistical clarity in the study of mediators and moderators: Examples from the child-clinical and pediatric psychology literatures. *Journal of Consulting and Clinical Psychology, 65,* 599–610.

McBurney, D. H. (1995). The problem method of teaching research methods. *Teaching of Psychology, 22*(1), 36–38.

McMillan, J. H., & Schumacher, S. (2010). *Research in education: Evidence-based inquiry* (7th ed.). Upper Saddle River, NJ: Pearson. [See Chapter 3.]

Medawar, P. B. (1979). *Advice to a young scientist.* New York: Harper & Row.

Neuman, W. L. (2011). *Social research methods: Qualitative and quantitative approaches* (7th ed.). Upper Saddle River, NJ: Pearson.

Plano Clark, V. L., & Badiee, M. (2010). Research questions in mixed methods research. In A. Tashakkori & C. Teddlie (Eds.), *Mixed methods in social & behavioral research* (2nd ed., pp. 275–304). Thousand Oaks, CA: Sage.

Roberts, C. M. (2010). *The dissertation journey: A practical and comprehensive guide to planning, writing, and defending your dissertation* (2nd ed.). Thousand Oaks, CA: Corwin.

Schram, T. H. (2006). *Conceptualizing and proposing qualitative research* (2nd ed.). Upper Saddle River, NJ: Pearson/Merrill/Prentice Hall. [See Chapter 5.]

Wimmer, R. D., & Dominick, J. R. (2005). *Mass media research: An introduction* (10th ed.). Boston: Wadsworth/Cengage.

ANSWERS TO THE CONCEPTUAL ANALYSIS EXERCISE "Identifying Independent, Dependent, Mediating, and Moderating Variables":

1. The phrase "effects of . . . on" tells us the direction of a hypothesized cause-and-effect relationship. Amount of physical exercise is the independent variable. Health and longevity are two dependent variables.

2. Placement of recycling bins is the independent variable; for example, the researcher might vary the number of recycling bins available and/or their proximity to classrooms and high-student-traffic areas. Recycling behavior is the dependent variable; for example, the researcher might count the number of recyclable objects (aluminum cans, sheets of paper, etc.) found in recycling bins each day or week.

3. The problem statement uses the term *relationship* without necessarily implying that this is a cause-and-effect relationship; for instance, the statement does not include a term such as *influence* or *affect*. However, we can reasonably guess that the researcher is hypothesizing that cell phone usage *increases the risk of* an accident, in which case amount of cell phone use is the independent variable and accident rate is the dependent variable. (To some degree, car accidents lead to cell phone use as well—someone in an accident is likely to call a family member or 9-1-1—but that cause-and-effect relationship hardly seems worthy of a research study.)

4. Don't let the sequence of variables mentioned in the problem statement lead you astray here. Test anxiety is the independent variable; test performance is the dependent variable. The third variable mentioned—distracting thoughts—is hypothesized to be the mediating variable: Level of anxiety (independent variable) affects the degree to which one has distracting thoughts (mediating variable), which in turn affects test performance (dependent variable).

5. The word *impact* implies a possible causal connection between bullying (independent variable) and emotional well-being (dependent variable). The nature of a student's relationship with his or her teacher can influence the impact of bullying; thus, the student–teacher relationship is a moderating variable.

6. The problem statement includes no words to suggest the direction of a relationship. Certainly, however, career choices *can't* affect one's gender, so any possible causal relationship must go in the other direction: from gender (independent variable) to career choice (dependent variable). The comparative aspect of the problem statement suggests that gender might have more of an influence on career choice in some countries (presumably those that adhere to traditional ideas about occupations appropriate for men and women) than in others. Country of residence, then, would be a moderating variable affecting the strength of the gender–career choice relationship.

7. The cause-and-effect relationship between frequent exposure to sunlight (independent variable) and melanoma (dependent variable) is well established in the medical literature. The presence or absence of a particular gene is hypothesized to be a moderating variable: The chances of sunlight leading to melanoma may be reduced—that is, the cause-and-effect relationship may be considerably weaker or possibly nonexistent—if a person has the tumor-suppressing gene.

8. Once again the problem statement talks only about a *relationship*, without using verbs such as *cause, affect,* or *influence* to imply causation. However, the mention of two psychological factors that *underlie* the relationship suggests that the researcher is assuming that either body mass index affects psychological stress or vice versa. Although the problem statement does not clarify which of these two variables is the independent variable and which is the dependent variable, two other variables—levels of depression and anxiety—are apparently hypothesized to be *mediating variables*. Perhaps a higher body mass index (independent variable) increases depression and anxiety (mediating variables) that, in turn, increase psychological stress (dependent variable). Or perhaps, instead, greater psychological stress (independent variable) increases depression and anxiety (mediating variables) that, in turn, lead to more food consumption and/or less physical exercise (two more, unstated and apparently unmeasured mediating variables), which in turn increase body mass index (dependent variable).

3

Review of the Related Literature

Many who have conducted research before you have laid foundational elements—not only previous research findings but also insightful concepts and theories—on which you might productively build. As groundbreaking physicist and mathematician Isaac Newton wrote in 1675, "If I have seen further it is by standing on the shoulders of giants."

Learning Outcomes

3.1 Describe several purposes that a literature review can serve during the planning of a research project.

3.2 Explain how you might effectively use five general resources to locate related literature: (a) the library catalog, (b) online databases, (c) reference

librarians, (d) Internet search engines, and (e) other researchers' reference lists.

3.3 Describe concrete strategies you can use to evaluate, organize, and synthesize literature related to a research problem.

As noted in Chapter 2, reading the literature related to your topic of interest can help you formulate a specific research problem. It can also help you tie your problem—and, later, your findings as well—to a larger body of research and theoretical understandings about your topic. In this chapter we discuss the importance of the literature review and give you suggestions for reviewing the related literature thoroughly but efficiently.

UNDERSTANDING THE ROLE OF THE LITERATURE REVIEW

Research proposals and research reports typically have a section—in the case of a thesis or dissertation, often an entire chapter—that describes theoretical perspectives and previous research findings related to the problem at hand. Its function is to review—to "look again" at (*re* + *view*)—what others have done in areas that are similar, though not necessarily identical to, one's own topic of investigation.

As a researcher, you should ultimately know the literature related to your topic *very, very well.* An extensive literature review has many benefits:

1. It can help you ascertain whether other researchers have already addressed and answered your research problem or at least some of its subproblems.
2. It can offer new ideas, perspectives, and approaches that may not have occurred to you.
3. It can inform you about other individuals who conduct work in this area—individuals whom you may wish to contact for advice or feedback.
4. It can alert you to controversial issues and gaps in understanding that have not yet been resolved—issues and gaps you might address in your own work.
5. It can show you how others have handled methodological and design issues in studies similar to your own.

6. It can reveal sources of data you may not have known existed.
7. It can introduce you to measurement tools that other researchers have developed and effectively used.
8. It can help you interpret and make sense of your findings and, ultimately, help you tie your results to the work of those who have preceded you.
9. It can bolster your confidence that your topic is one worth studying, because you will find that others have invested considerable time, effort, and resources in studying it.

Simply put, the more you know about investigations and perspectives related to your topic, the more effectively you can address your own research problem.

In most instances, researchers begin their review of the literature early in the game, and they draw on existing theories and previous research studies to help them pin down their research problem. Extensive literature reviews *up front* are especially common in quantitative research, where they can help researchers formulate specific *a priori* hypotheses in conjunction with their problem or its subproblems. In some forms of qualitative research, however, researchers worry that too much knowledge about current perspectives and previous findings might unduly bias their own data collection and interpretation; hence, they postpone a thorough literature review until relatively late in the research process (e.g., see the discussion of grounded theory research in Chapter 9).

STRATEGIES FOR LOCATING RELATED LITERATURE

You might find literature related to your topic in a number of places—for instance, in books, journals, newspapers, government publications, conference presentations, and Internet websites. Obviously you can't simply wander aimlessly through the library stacks or Internet with the hope that you will eventually stumble on items that may help you; you must focus your search from the very beginning.

A good way to start is to identify one or more keywords—words or short phrases summarizing your research topic—that can point you toward potentially useful resources. A prime source of such keywords is your statement of your research problem. For example, imagine that you want to investigate possible reasons why some children bully other children at school. Obvious keywords for this topic are *peer relationships, bullying,* and *aggression.* These are very general concepts, but they should get you started. They will lead you to thousands of potential resources, however, and so you will soon want to identify more specific keywords. As you begin to look at books, journal articles, websites, and other resources related to your topic and initial set of keywords, you should come across words and phrases that more closely capture what you want to study—for the bullying problem, these might include such terms as *social goals, social cognition,* and *cyberbullying*—and may also help you focus your research problem a bit more.

Armed with your keywords—which you will undoubtedly continue to revise—you can proceed in several directions. In the following sections, we describe five good starting points: the library catalog, online databases, reference librarians, the Internet, and other researchers' citations and reference lists.

Using the Library Catalog

The library catalog has come a long way from the tool it was in the mid-20th century. If you were a student in, say, 1960, when you entered the library you would go straight to the card catalog—a set of free-standing dressers-of-sorts with many small drawers containing 3-by-5 index cards. The catalog would have three cards for every book in the library—one card each for a book's title, author, and general topic. You would rifle through the cards in search of books relevant to your topic and then write down the call numbers of books you wanted to track down in the library's numerous shelves of books (i.e., the "stacks"). If you were conducting an extensive literature review, the process might involve going through drawer after drawer in the card catalog, writing down a lengthy list of books and call numbers, and then heading to the stacks to determine whether or not each book you wanted was currently available. The whole process could be incredibly tedious and time-consuming.

In today's college library, a researcher's plan of attack is entirely different. Although you may occasionally find a small public library that still uses a physical card catalog, college and university libraries rely almost exclusively on electronic catalogs of their collections. In place of those rows upon rows of index-card drawers are computer terminals at which users can quickly locate a library's holdings related to particular authors, titles, keywords, or call numbers. The database will tell you on what floor of the library—and, if relevant, in what building or on what branch campus—a particular book can be found. (Note that some widely used books are kept in the library's reserved books section rather than in the stacks; you must read these books in the library itself, as they cannot be checked out.) The database will also tell you the status of a book—whether it's currently available or, if not, when it is due to be returned. If you have any questions about how to use the library catalog and its many features, don't be afraid of "looking stupid"—ask a librarian to show you the basics.

A good college or university library will almost certainly have a number of books relevant to your research topic. Some books will be written entirely by one or two individuals. Others may be edited collections of chapters written by a variety of experts on the topic. And don't overlook general textbooks in your discipline. A good textbook can give you a broad overview of a topic, including important concepts, theoretical perspectives, a sampling of relevant research, and critical references.

The library's collection of academic journals, popular magazines, and newspapers—collectively known as periodicals—is another indispensable resource. The library catalog will tell you which periodicals the library owns, where each one is located, and the one or more forms (paper, electronic, microform) in which particular volumes and issues can be found. For instance, if the library has a periodical in paper form, you will find most volumes in the library stacks—usually in a section of the library devoted specifically to periodicals—but you are apt to find recently acquired, unbound issues (say, from the past year or two) on a separate set of shelves near the main desk for the periodicals section. Some university libraries organize and shelve their paper periodicals by call number; this approach enables you to find periodicals about any single topic close together, but you must know the call number(s) relevant to your discipline and topic. Other university libraries organize and shelve paper periodicals alphabetically by title; this approach enables you to find any particular periodical without having to consult the library catalog, but you will most likely go to many different shelves to retrieve all articles relevant to a particular literature review.

University libraries typically also have access to many periodicals in electronic form, which you can retrieve from a computer terminal (more about accessing electronic copies in the upcoming section on online databases). Finally, your library may have some periodicals (especially older ones) in *microform.* The microform area of a library is easy to spot, as it will have numerous file cabinets containing *microfilm, microfiche,* and the like, along with several large devices for viewing them. The devices may seem intimidating to a novice researcher, but they are quite easy to use once you have had a little practice. Don't be afraid to ask someone behind the periodicals desk to demonstrate how to use them.

One general rule of thumb is to use books and periodicals with recent copyright dates. The more recently a book or article has been written, the more likely it is to give you a sense of current perspectives in your field and alert you to recent research findings that may be pertinent to your research problem. You should ignore this rule, of course, if you are specifically interested in how perspectives about your topic have changed over the years.

A second rule of thumb is to focus on publications that are likely to have credibility with experts in the field. For example, credible books often come from publishing houses and university-affiliated publishers that specialize in scholarly works (e.g., Sage, Routledge, Oxford University Press). And as previously noted in Chapter 1, reputable journals are typically *juried,* in that notable scholars have carefully reviewed article manuscripts before they ever appear on the printed page; a quick look at the names and affiliations of a journal's editors and editorial board can give you a good sense of the rigor with which articles have been screened. We urge you *not* to be seduced by best-selling paperbacks on trendy topics, as their authors and contents have not necessarily been vetted by experts.

USING TECHNOLOGY

If you have access to the Internet from your home computer, then you already have access to countless online library catalogs around the world. An Internet search on Google, Bing, or Yahoo! can quickly give you links to many university and public library catalogs. Typically the Internet home page for your own institution will also have a quick link to the library and its catalog.

A Few Words About Call Numbers   The *call numbers* referred to earlier are the unique identification codes that books, journals, and similar items are given. A book's call number provides an "address" that enables you to find it in the library stacks. Books are coded and arranged on the library shelves in accordance with one of two principal classification systems, which divide areas of human knowledge in somewhat different ways:

- *The Dewey decimal (DD) classification system.*   Books are cataloged and shelved according to 10 basic areas of knowledge and subsequent subareas, each divided decimally. The Dewey decimal system is the principal classification system used in many public libraries.
- *The Library of Congress (LC) classification system.*   Books are assigned to particular areas of knowledge that are given special alphabetical categories. This system is widely used in college and university libraries.

Table 3.1 provides a rough overview of how the two systems generally classify many traditional academic subject areas. For each subject area listed in the table, the entries in the DD column to its left and the LC column to its right provide either starting points or general ranges for the Dewey decimal and Library of Congress designations, respectively. You can find descriptions of more specific categories and subcategories on many Internet websites.

TABLE 3.1 ■ A General Conversion Chart: Dewey Decimal Classification System (DD) Versus the Library of Congress Classification System (LC) for Various Subject Areas

DD	Subject	LC	DD	Subject	LC
630	Agriculture	S	070	Journalism	PN
301	Anthropology	GN	400	Language	P
930	Archaeology	CC	340	Law	K
700	Art	N	020	Library and Information Sciences	Z
520	Astronomy	QB	800	Literature	P
920	Biography	CT	510	Mathematics	QA
570	Biology	QH	610	Medicine and Public Health	QS–QZ, W
580	Botany	QK	355	Military Science	U
650	Business	HF	780	Music	M
540	Chemistry	QD	100	Philosophy	B
004–006	Computer Science	QA	530	Physics	QC
550	Earth Sciences	QE	320	Political Science	J
330, 380	Economics and Commerce	HB–HJ	150	Psychology	BF
370	Education	L	200	Religion	B
620	Engineering	T	500	Science (General)	Q
910	Geography	G	301	Sociology	HM
350	Government	JF, JK, JS	790	Sports and Recreation	GV
930–995	History	D, E, F	600	Technology	T
640	Hospitality	TX	590	Zoology	QL

Be aware, however, that neither the Dewey decimal system nor the Library of Congress system is as simple and cut-and-dried as Table 3.1 might suggest, in part because virtually any academic discipline includes many topics and draws from many research areas and—often—from other disciplines. Furthermore, we authors have found that books in our own areas of expertise are not always classified exactly as we ourselves might have classified them.

Browsing the Library's Holdings   Although keywords and knowledge of specific book titles and authors can get you off to a good start in locating helpful volumes in your library, they will give you *only* a start, because you probably won't be able to think of every potentially useful keyword, and you certainly won't be aware of every book and author relevant to your topic.

We therefore suggest that you also browse the library, either physically by walking among the stacks or electronically by "browsing" the entries in the library's online catalog. In many cases, when one goes to a library shelf to get a particular book or journal, the most useful information is found not in the material that was originally targeted, but rather in one or more volumes nearby.

Remember, too, that most academic disciplines are becoming increasingly interdisciplinary in both their problems and their methodologies. For example, to identify the needs and shopping patterns of different populations, marketing researchers often draw on sociologists' and geographers' concepts and data collection techniques, and psychologists can learn a great deal about human thought processes by using the positron emission tomography (PET) and magnetic resonance imaging (MRI) technologies of neurophysiologists. Thus, you are apt to find helpful sources under more than one range of call numbers. Good researchers are flexible and creative in their searches for relevant literature.

USING TECHNOLOGY

Using Online Databases

Although the library catalog will tell you which periodicals your library owns and in what form it owns them, it won't tell you the specific articles that each volume of a journal contains. Virtually all college and university libraries provide access to many online databases that enable searches of thousands of journals and such other sources as books, chapters in edited books, dissertations, government documents, technical reports, and newspapers. Table 3.2 lists examples.

A typical database allows you to limit your search in a variety of ways—perhaps by keywords, title, author, year, source (e.g., journal title), language, or any combination of these. Many databases focus on particular disciplines and subject areas. As an example, let's consider PsycINFO, a database that includes information not only about sources in psychology but also about psychology-related sources in such disciplines as physiology, sociology, anthropology, education, medicine, and business. As this edition of *Practical Research* goes to press, PsycINFO works as follows:

1. When you enter the database, you can conduct either a "basic search" (the default mode) or an "advanced search." If you click on "advanced search," you can type one to three words or phrases in boxes at the top of the screen. In pull-down menus to the right of the boxes, you can indicate whether each word or phrase you have typed is an author, title, keyword, word or phrase in the abstract, or some other entity.

2. In pull-down menus to the left of the second and any subsequent boxes at the top of the screen, you can tell the computer to

   a. Identify only those items that include *all* of the words/phrases you have entered (for this, you select the "and" option)
   b. Identify items that include *any* of the words/phrases you have entered (for this, you select the "or" option)
   c. Exclude items that have one of the words/phrases you have entered (for this, you select the "not" option)

3. Options in the lower portion of the computer screen allow you to limit your search results still further, perhaps by specifying a particular journal, range of publication dates, population, age-group, or language.

TABLE 3.2 ▪ Examples of Online Databases

Database	Subject Area(s) Covered
Academic Search Premier	Education, humanities, multicultural issues, sciences, social sciences
America: History and Life	History of the United States and Canada
AnthroSource	Anthropology
Applied Science and Technology Source	Applied sciences and technology (e.g., computing, engineering, resource management, telecommunications, transportation)
Art Source	Broad range of art topics (e.g., advertising, architecture, art history, folk art, graphic arts, video)
Biological Abstracts	Biology, medicine
Business Source Premier	Business, economics
EconLit	Economics
ERIC (Educational Resources Information Center)	Education and education-related topics
Historical Abstracts	World history (excluding the United States and Canada; for these, use America: History and Life)
IngentaConnect	All disciplines
JSTOR	Business, fine arts, humanities, sciences, social sciences
Linguistics and Language Behavior Abstracts (LLBA)	Language
MathSciNet	Mathematics (pure and applied), statistics
Medline	Dentistry, health care, medicine, veterinary medicine
National Criminal Justice Reference Service Abstracts	Courts, crime, justice, law enforcement, victimization
PAIS (Public Affairs Information Service) International	Public and social policy, social sciences
ProQuest Dissertations and Theses: Full Text	All disciplines
PsycINFO	Psychology and psychological aspects of other disciplines (e.g., physiology, sociology, anthropology, education, medicine, business)
Sociological Abstracts	Sociology and related topics in the social and behavioral sciences
SPORTDiscus	Physical education, physical fitness, recreation, coaching, sports medicine
Web of Science	Humanities, sciences, social sciences
WorldCat	All disciplines

4. Once you have limited your search to some degree (at a minimum by completing Step 1), you click on the "Search" button near the top of your computer screen.

5. The next screen will either (a) give you one or more references or (b) tell you that it has come up empty-handed ("No results were found"). If references appear, you can click on their titles to view abstracts and, in some cases, see and download the entire articles or other texts. If your search has been unsuccessful, you probably need to eliminate one or more of the limitations you imposed on your original search—you should also check for spelling errors in what you have typed—and click on the "Search" button once again.

6. Each time you identify a potentially useful source, you can use one or more tools to keep track of it, perhaps adding it to an electronic folder, printing it, or e-mailing it to yourself. You might also import the source to a bibliographic database software program on your computer; we will examine such software later in the chapter.

As is true for some of the articles in PsycINFO, many databases provide entire documents. For example, ProQuest Historical Newspapers: *The New York Times* allows you to search—and then also read—news articles, editorials, letters to the editor, birth announcements, obituaries, advertisements, and virtually any other entry in any issue of the *Times* dating back to its first issue in 1851. Another good general resource is JSTOR (pronounced "jay-stor"), which contains electronic copies of articles from many journals in the sciences, social sciences, arts, humanities, business, and law.

One easy way to access a university library's online databases is through computer terminals located throughout the library building. Often a library's Internet home page will provide a link to its online databases, and users may be able to access them on their home computers as well as at the library. However, because a library pays large annual fees for its online databases, it typically restricts off-site use of them to current students and employees. Hence, students who want to use a database at home may need to enter a preassigned user name and password before gaining access to it. A reference librarian at your own library can give you the details.

Researchers not currently connected to a university have other possible ways to access online databases. Many professional associations give current members access to electronic copies of articles published in the associations' journals. Some online databases are available without charge on the Internet. An example is Google Scholar (scholar.google.com), through which you can search the general topics and contents of books, journal articles, and other scholarly works in a wide range of disciplines. Some of the websites it identifies provide complete articles and other documents you can download and print (e.g., look for sites labeled "pdf"), whereas others provide abstracts and links to companies that charge a service fee for the complete documents. Another, more specialized database—one especially helpful for researchers interested in medicine and related topics—is PubMed, developed and updated by the National Library of Medicine (nlm.nih.gov). And for documents produced by various federal agencies in the United States, you can use the Federal Digital System, or FDsys, developed and maintained by the U.S. Government Printing Office (gpo.gov/fdsys). Also, check out Google Books (books.google.com), which provides excerpts from—and in some cases the entire texts of—out-of-print books.

One especially helpful database during a literature search is the Web of Science, which can tell you which publications cite *other* publications. For example, imagine that you are particularly intrigued by a 1999 article in the journal *Nature Neuroscience* indicating that the human brain is not fully mature until its owner reaches adulthood in the 20-something age range (Sowell, Thompson, Holmes, Jernigan, & Toga, 1999). Given the rapid-pace advances in neuroscience in recent years, this article is an "old" one, and so you want to find more up-to-date articles on the same topic. In the Web of Science database, the "Cited Reference Search" option allows you to search the reference lists of all other articles in its database and find more recently published articles that cite the article by Sowell and her colleagues. If you were to use the Web of Science for this specific purpose (as we did), you would find that the Sowell and colleagues' article has been cited by hundreds of other researchers and so obviously has been an influential one in neuroscience.

Another invaluable database is WorldCat, which combines the library catalogs of thousands of academic libraries, large public libraries, and other specialized collections throughout the world. Through this database, you can identify libraries that have particular books, periodicals, visual materials, sound recordings, and other items that might be rare and hard to come by.

Our list of databases and their features is hardly exhaustive. Databases become more sophisticated with each passing year. Please don't hesitate to consult with a reference librarian about databases that might be especially suitable for your research purposes.

Consulting with Reference Librarians

When you visit the reference section of your library—and we urge you to do this very early in your literature search—you will almost certainly see one or more librarians sitting at the reference desk. These individuals are there for one reason only: to help you and others find needed information. They can show you reference materials you never dreamed existed. They can also demonstrate how to use the computer catalog, hard-bound reference resources, online databases, or any of the library's other resources.

Some new researchers are reluctant to approach a reference librarian for fear of looking foolish or stupid. Yet the reality is that library resources are changing so quickly that most of us can't possibly keep up with them all. Whatever you do, *don't* be afraid to ask librarians for assistance. Even as seasoned researchers, we authors sometimes seek the advice of these individuals; by doing so, we can often save ourselves a great deal of time and aggravation.

The best way to master the library as a research tool is to use it! Go in, explore, take stock of its resources; experiment with the various search options in its computer terminals; browse in the reference room; go into the stacks and browse some more. You may be surprised at what a magnificent research tool the library really is.

USING TECHNOLOGY

Surfing the Internet

We have already mentioned the Internet as a source of such free-access online databases as Google Scholar, PubMed, and Google Books. With each passing year, the Internet becomes an increasingly valuable source of information to researchers. As most of our readers already know, an Internet search begins with a search engine at a website such as Google, Bing, or Yahoo! These websites typically have a box in which you can type one or more keywords to start your search. Following are some general strategies to keep in mind when using search engines:

1. Use at least two keywords to limit your search. (For example, to locate research about children with autism, you might type the words *children* and *autism*.)

2. Type a plus sign (+) before any keyword you definitely want used in your search. (For example, to limit your search only to children who have autism, you should type "+children" and "+autism." Otherwise, you might get a listing of all resources involving children *or* autism, which would undoubtedly be a long list indeed.)

3. If you want to look for a phrase rather than a single word, put quotation marks around the phrase. (For example, if you are looking for the home page of the Autism Society, you should type "Autism Society" within quotation marks. This way, your search will be restricted to items specifically about that particular organization.)

Surfing the Internet will lead you to many different types of websites. For instance, it may lead you to government websites that can provide helpful documents and information, including those for the U.S. Census Bureau (census.gov), Department of Education (ed.gov), Department of Labor (dol.gov), National Aeronautics and Space Administration (nasa.gov), and U.S. Geological Survey (usgs.gov). Most professional associations have websites as well, and these sites often provide a wealth of information about their areas of expertise.

One site to which an Internet search will often lead you is Wikipedia (wikipedia.org), an online encyclopedia that virtually anyone can add to and edit. Wikipedia contains millions of entries on a diverse range of topics, with people adding new ones every day. In our experience, Wikipedia provides good general overviews of many topics and can help a novice researcher identify key concepts and issues related to a topic. Keep in mind, however, that *its contents are not juried:* There is no oversight of any entry's accuracy by experts in the subject matter at hand. Accordingly, although you might use ideas you find in Wikipedia to guide your subsequent searches, as a general rule *you should not—we repeat, **not**—use Wikipedia as an authoritative source about your topic.*

An Internet search may also lead you to research articles and opinion papers that individual researchers have made available on the Internet, and you can typically print such documents or download them to your own computer. We caution you to keep in mind that such articles and papers vary widely in quality. Although most academic publications have a review process that enhances the quality of the research articles they include, many unpublished research reports posted on the Internet have not yet been reviewed or judged by professional colleagues. Obviously you will want to read *any* research report with a somewhat critical eye, but you should be especially careful when you find research reports on the Internet that you cannot verify as the work of credible scholars.

In your searches of the Internet, you will probably have to wade through many listings that aren't terribly helpful. On the plus side, however, if you have access to the Internet from a home computer, you can browse anytime day or night—weekends, holidays, even 3:00 a.m. if you like. Libraries are sometimes closed, but the Internet is always open.

Whenever you find a useful resource on the Internet, you should make a note of where or how you found it. One common practice is to record the address (Uniform Resource Locator, or URL) at which you found the resource and the date on which you did so. Alternatively, many on-line documents posted since the year 2000 have a Digital Object Identifier, or DOI—a unique, permanent number that enables others to find a document again even if its precise location on the Internet has changed in the meantime. DOIs are especially helpful when research reports and other scholarly works are available only in electronic form (for more information, go to doi.org).

Using Citations and Reference Lists of Those Who Have Gone Before You

No library or computer search—no matter how extensive—is foolproof. Ultimately any search depends on the particular keywords you use and the particular databases you include in your search. One additional—in our minds, *essential*—resource is the literature reviews of researchers whose own writings you have consulted. Such reviews, especially if they have been published recently, can give you valuable guidance about seminal research studies and cutting-edge ideas related to your research topic. As a rule of thumb, we suggest that you track down *any references you see cited by three or more other researchers.* Such references are clearly influencing current work in your field and should not be overlooked.

The preceding paragraph brings us to another important point: Don't depend on what other authors say about a particular reference. Too often we have seen two or more authors misrepresent the work of a particular researcher in the same, particular way; apparently, they are reading one another's descriptions of that researcher's work rather than reading the researcher's own words! Whenever possible, *go to the original source and read it yourself.*

Considering all of the resources we have described in this chapter, you might be thinking that you will be spending the next 10 years conducting your literature review! Don't worry. In the Practical Application sections that follow, we describe (a) how to plan an organized and efficient literature search, and (b) how to distinguish between research reports that are and are not worth taking seriously.

PRACTICAL APPLICATION   Planning a Literature Search

In Chapter 2 you learned how to select a research problem or question. You also learned that most problems, taken as a whole, are fairly complex and can be more easily solved when they are divided into two or more subproblems.

The main problem and subproblems provide a way to focus your attention as you read the literature. One concrete and effective approach, using either paper and pencil or brainstorming/mind mapping software, involves the following steps:

1. Write the problem in its entirety on the page or computer screen.

2. Write each subproblem in its entirety as well.

3. Identify the important words and phrases in each subproblem.

4. Translate these words and phrases into specific topics you must learn more about. These topics become your "agenda" as you read the literature.

5. Go to the library catalog, its online databases, and the Internet to seek out resources related to your agenda.

Let's take an example. For his dissertation research, doctoral student Arthur Benton wanted to develop a means of using an existing measurement instrument, the Strong Vocational Interest Blank (SVIB), to identify potential cartographers for the federal government. The SVIB assesses a person's interests in a wide variety of activities; the profile of interests that it generates is then compared with the interests of people in various occupations to identify career paths in which the person might find satisfaction and success. At the time the study was conducted, interest scales for 54 different occupational groups had been developed for the SVIB, but none had been developed for cartographers. The SVIB was published in two versions, the SVIB for Men and the SVIB for Women; to limit the scope of the project, Mr. Benton focused only on the SVIB for Men. In his dissertation proposal, he presented the following research problem:

> This researcher proposes to identify and evaluate the existing discrete interests among Federally employed male cartographers and to develop a scale for the revised Strong Vocational Interest Blank to aid recruitment of cartographers into Federal employment.

He then divided his problem into three subproblems:

> The first subproblem is to determine whether male cartographers employed by the Federal Government have a discrete pattern of interests different from those of men in general, as measured by the Strong Vocational Interest Blank for Men.

> The second subproblem is to construct a scoring key for the Strong Vocational Interest Blank to differentiate the interests of cartographers from those of men in general and also from the interests of other occupational groups.

> The third subproblem is to analyze and interpret the treated data so as to evaluate the discovered interests in terms of their discreteness in recruiting cartographers.

Figure 3.1 shows the literature-review agenda we created for the research problem and three subproblems using an early version of Inspiration mind mapping software. The four rectangles

FIGURE 3.1 Using Mind Mapping Software to Prepare for a Review of the Literature

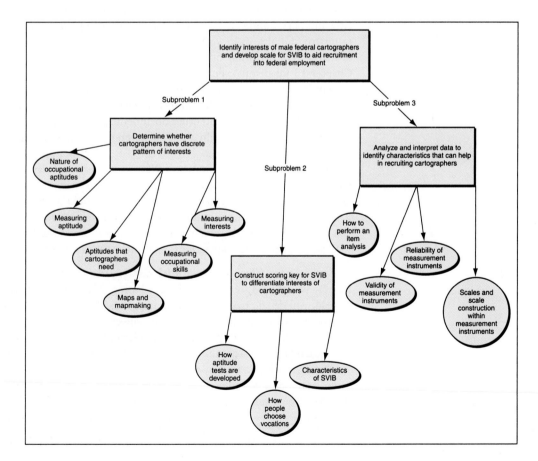

represent the research problem and its three subproblems. The ovals reflect the specific things we need to learn more about with respect to each subproblem.

The sequence of steps just described can help you keep your literature review within the realm of your research problem. It prevents you from wandering into other areas of the literature that, though potentially quite intriguing, may be of little or no use to you when the time comes to write your literature review.

Now that you have an idea of what to search for, let's consider how to make your search efforts efficient and productive.

GUIDELINES   Using Your Library Time Efficiently

Make no mistake about it: Conducting a thorough literature review takes a great deal of time. And almost certainly you will *not* be able to conduct your entire literature review from your home computer. So plan on going to the library—*not just once but several times,* especially as your analysis of the literature points you in potentially fruitful new directions. Following are suggestions for maximizing your efficiency at the library.

USING TECHNOLOGY

1. ***Before you go to the library, create a computer database for the resources you are going to gather.***   Earlier we spoke of the databases available through online searches. In fact, you can create your *own* database for the literature you read. One possibility is to use spreadsheet software to keep track of potentially useful literature sources (see Appendix A). Alternatively, you might use software specifically designed for creating bibliographic databases. Some are available commercially; examples are Biblioscape, EndNote, OneNote, and RefWorks. By searching the Internet, you can also find and download "freeware" (free software) that will serve your purpose; as this book goes to press, examples are BiblioExpress, ReadCube, and Zotero.

Bibliographic software programs typically have designated places, or *fields,* for all the information you would need in order to create a reference list—such as author, title, date, journal title and page numbers (for articles), and publishing company and location (for books). These programs can also *create your reference list for you!* Most programs allow you to use whatever format your institution or academic discipline requires (e.g., APA style or MLA style; see Chapter 13 for details). Furthermore, these programs have additional fields for call numbers, keywords, any notes you take while reading an item, and (often) any graphics you want to include. And some of them let you incorporate full texts of certain sources, especially journal articles, conference papers, and other documents in pdf form. If you decide to use a bibliographic software program, you might want to watch one or more of its online video tutorials to learn how to use its many features.

By putting the information you collect in an electronic database, you can later find anything you want in a matter of seconds. For example, perhaps you want to find books and articles written by a specific author. You can search the author field in the entire database; the program will identify every record for that author. In addition, you can rapidly sort the data by whatever field you choose. For example, if you want all of your sources listed by publication date, the program will, with appropriate instructions, rearrange them in chronological order.

2. ***Go to the library armed with data-gathering tools.***   If you have taken our advice in Step 1, you should, of course, bring a laptop with your database set up and ready to go. If, instead, you decide to go a low-tech, paper-and-pencil route, you should have some systematic way of recording the information you collect—ideally one that will also allow you to easily organize it. A paper-and-pencil approach involves taking note paper or index cards on which to write what you find—not only information relevant to your topic but also information about the sources in which you find it: titles, authors, journal titles (if applicable), publication dates, and so on. Some people going the paper-and-pencil route have found it helpful to print up a large number of note-taking forms similar to that shown in Figure 3.2.

3. ***Identify the materials you want to read (books, articles, etc.), and determine whether your library has them.***   You will probably identify many of the sources you need by consulting

FIGURE 3.2 ▪ Possible Format for a Paper-and-Pencil Note-Taking Form

Call No./Database _____

Author(s) _____ Date _____

Title of book or article _____

Journal title, volume/issue, pages _____

_____

Place of publication, publisher, date, edition (for books)

_____

Comments (use space below and reverse side)

the library catalog and perusing indexes and abstracts in online databases. As you make a list of your desired sources, keep the following suggestions in mind:

- *Keep track of the specific searches you conduct.* For example, make lists of which indexes and other databases you consult, as well as which keywords you use and in what order. Keeping such records ensures that you won't duplicate your efforts.
- *Let computers make your lists for you whenever possible.* For instance, if you are using one of your library's online databases, you will probably be able to print out the sources you identify or, if you prefer, e-mail your list (and in some cases actual journal articles) to yourself. And if you are using a bibliographic software program to organize your literature, you may be able to *import* all the bibliographic information for a particular source from a library database directly into your own database.
- *Check the library holdings for the books and journals you identify.* More specifically, make note of whether the library owns the sources you need and, if so, where they are located and whether they are currently on loan to another user. In the case of journals, you should also check to see whether they are in paper, online, or on microform (e.g., microfilm, microfiche). If the library does *not* have something you need, keep the reference; we will talk about alternative strategies for obtaining such materials shortly.

4. *Develop an organized plan of attack for finding the sources you have identified.* Arrange any paper and microform sources you need to obtain according to where they are located in the library. For instance, you can organize books by call number. You can organize journal articles first by paper versus microform, and then by the specific journals in which the articles appear. If your university has two or more separate libraries, you will also want to organize your sources by the specific buildings in which they are located.

5. *Track down your sources.* After you have organized your sources, you're ready to go find them and look them over. Keep a record of whether each item was (a) found and used, (b) found but determined not to be helpful, or (c) not found. As you peruse the stacks, don't forget to browse neighboring shelves.

6. *Record all basic information as you read each source.* "Make haste slowly" is a sound rule for any researcher. Be careful not to make careless, half-complete notes that—when you read them later—are either unintelligible or so lacking in essential information that they're practically useless. If you are using paper to record your findings, write legibly or print clearly. If you can't distinguish between undotted *i*'s and closed-up *e*'s, or between carelessly made *a*'s and *o*'s, you may eventually find yourself scurrying back to sources for such details.

In addition to recording any essential bibliographic information you haven't previously obtained, you will want to take sufficient notes about the content of the source to enable you to recreate its ideas when you are writing your literature review. As you do so, you may find it helpful to keep track of the pages on which you have found certain ideas; furthermore, page numbers are essential if you are quoting a source word for word. Also, put quotation marks around word-for-word transcriptions of phrases or sentences in a source. Later, the quotation marks can remind you that these are *someone else's words*—not yours—and must be identified as such in your literature review (more on this point in an upcoming discussion of plagiarism). In some cases, of course, a source will have so much information that you will simply want to make a photocopy of relevant pages[1] or, in the case of a book, check it out and take it home.

7. *Identify strategies for obtaining sources that are not immediately available.* We can almost guarantee that you won't find everything you need the first time around. Some books may be currently checked out to other users. Other books and a few journals may not be among the library's holdings. Following are several strategies to consider in such situations:

- *Put a hold on a checked-out book.* If you discover that a book has been checked out but is due to be returned shortly, your university catalog system will probably let you put a *hold* on the book so that you are the next one in line to check it out when it comes in. If your system doesn't provide this option, ask the librarian at the circulation desk to put a hold on the book for you. The library will contact you (typically by e-mail) as soon as the book is returned and save it for you for a few days at the circulation desk.
- *Recall the book.* Many university libraries allow professors to check out books for an entire semester or academic year, but the professors must return them earlier if someone else wants to use them. If you discover that a book you need is checked out for a long period of time—maybe for several months or longer—you can ask for the book to be *recalled* so that you can have access to it. Some university catalog systems let you recall a book yourself; for example, if you see a "request" button on the catalog page for the book, clicking on it will probably initiate a recall notice to the person who currently has it.
- *Submit a request for the source through interlibrary loan.* Almost all libraries have cooperative arrangements to exchange resources with other libraries. In all likelihood, you will be able to order a book or journal article through such interlibrary loan using your library's catalog system. A "low-tech" alternative is to make the request through your library's interlibrary loan office. Typically you can get books and journal articles from other libraries at little or no charge except, perhaps, for photocopying.
- *Check Google Books for older, out-of-print books.* Some books available on Google Books are no longer protected by copyright and are typically available free of charge. Those still under copyright are available only to the extent that the copyright holders have given permission; in such cases, you may be able to view excerpts from the book but may need to pay a small fee to see the entire book.
- *Order books from a bookstore.* Most bookstores will order any book that is currently in print and obtain it for you within a week or two. You can also order both new and used books through such online booksellers as Amazon (amazon.com) and Barnes & Noble (barnesandnoble.com).
- *Use an online document delivery service.* Some of the online databases listed in Table 3.2 (e.g., Academic Search Premier, JSTOR, PsycINFO) provide electronic copies of articles from selected journals. Others (e.g., ERIC) provide electronic copies of conference papers and other nonpublished works. If you find one or more doctoral dissertations that pertain directly to your research problem, you can order complete copies through ProQuest Dissertations and Theses: Full Text (proquest.com). Some of these services may be available to you free of charge through your university library; others may charge you a fee.

---

[1] In the United States, federal copyright law allows one copy for personal use.

As you conduct your literature review, you will undoubtedly need to repeat this cycle of steps several times. With each go-around, however, you will become more and more of an expert about the topic you are pursuing. You will also become increasingly knowledgeable about the library and its resources.

PRACTICAL APPLICATION Evaluating the Research of Others

An important skill for any researcher is the ability to review the work of others and evaluate the quality of their methods, results, and conclusions. *Never take other people's conclusions at face value; determine for yourself whether their conclusions are justified based on the data presented.* Critically examining what others have done has three distinct benefits:

■ It can help you determine which ideas, research findings, and conclusions you should take seriously and which you can reasonably discredit or ignore.
■ It can help you reconcile inconsistent findings obtained in previous research studies.
■ It can give you some ideas about how you might improve your own research efforts.

As you proceed through the rest of this book and learn more about research methodology, you will become increasingly knowledgeable about the kinds of conclusions that are and are not warranted from various methodologies and types of data. At this point, you may be able to judge the work of other researchers only in a fairly superficial fashion. Even so, there's no better time than the present to begin examining other researchers' work with a critical eye. We suggest that you begin to sharpen your evaluation skills by locating several research articles relevant to your interests. As you read and study the articles, consider the questions in the following checklist.

✔ CHECKLIST

Evaluating a Research Article

_____ 1. In what journal or other source did you find the article? Was it reviewed by experts in the field before it was published? That is, was the article in a *juried* (refereed) publication?

_____

_____

_____ 2. Does the article have a stated research question or problem? That is, can you determine the focus of the author's work?

_____

_____

_____ 3. Does the article describe the collection of new data, or does it describe and synthesize previous studies in which data were collected?

_____

_____

_____ 4. Is the article logically organized and easy to follow? What could have been done to improve its organization and readability?

_____

_____

_____   5. Does the article contain a section that describes and integrates previous studies on this topic? In what ways is this previous work relevant to the research problem?

_____

_____

_____   6. If the author explained procedures that were followed in the study, are these procedures clear enough that you could repeat the work and get similar results? What additional information might be helpful or essential for you to replicate the study?

_____

_____

_____   7. If data were collected, can you describe how they were collected and how they were analyzed? Do you agree with what was done? If you had been the researcher, what additional things might you have done?

_____

_____

_____

_____   8. Do you agree with the author's interpretations and conclusions? Why or why not?

_____

_____

_____   9. Finally, think about the entire article. What is, for you, most important? What do you find most interesting? What do you think are the strengths and weaknesses of this article? Will you remember this article in the future? Why or why not?

_____

_____

_____

KNOWING WHEN TO QUIT

Certainly you shouldn't read only one or two articles and think that you're done. Get used to looking for and reading new research reports; for a researcher, this is a lifelong endeavor. There are always, *always* new things to learn about a topic.

At some point, however, you must be practical and bring your preliminary literature review to a close. How will you know when that time has arrived? The best advice we can give you is this: *Look for repetitive patterns in the materials you are finding and reading.* As you read more and more sources, eventually familiar arguments, methodologies, and findings will start to appear. Perhaps you will see the same key people and studies cited over and over. You will get a feeling of *déjà vu*—"I've seen this (or something very similar to it) before." When you are no longer encountering new viewpoints, you can be reasonably sure that you are familiar with the critical parts of the literature.

Notice our use of the adjective *preliminary* to modify "literature review" in the second paragraph of this section. As you begin to write your review of the literature, you may find certain gaps in your knowledge that need filling. And later on, after you've collected your data, you may find intriguing results within them that additional explorations of related literature might help you sensibly interpret. Thus, you should plan on spending some additional time in your university library or its online equivalent as your project proceeds.

ORGANIZING AND SYNTHESIZING THE LITERATURE INTO A COHESIVE REVIEW

Too many literature reviews do nothing more than report what other people have done and said. Such reviews, which are typically written by novice researchers, go something like this:

In 1998, Jones found that such-and-such. . . . Also, Smith (2004) discovered that such-and-such. . . . Black (2012) proposed that so-on-and-so-forth. . . .

We learn nothing new from such a review; we would be better off reading the original books, articles, and other sources for ourselves.

In a good literature review, the researcher doesn't merely report the related literature. He or she also *evaluates, organizes, and synthesizes what others have done.* A checklist earlier in the chapter gave you a taste of what the *evaluation* component involves. But in addition to evaluating what you read, you must also *organize* the ideas you encounter during your review. In many cases, the subproblems within your main problem can provide a general organizational scheme you can use. Looking at how other authors have organized literature reviews related to your topic can be helpful as well.

Finally, and perhaps most importantly, you must *synthesize* what you have learned from your review. In other words, you must pull together the diverse perspectives and research results you have read into a cohesive whole. Here are some examples of what you might do:

- Identify common themes that run throughout the literature.
- Show how approaches to the topic have changed over time.
- Compare and contrast varying theoretical perspectives on the topic.
- Describe general trends in research findings.
- Identify discrepant or contradictory findings, and suggest possible explanations for such discrepancies.

When you write a literature review that does such things, you have contributed something new to the knowledge in the field even *before* you have conducted your own study. In fact, a literature review that makes such a contribution is often publishable in its own right. (We talk more about writing for publication in Chapter 13.)

PRACTICAL APPLICATION Writing the Literature Review

Soon after you have read, evaluated, organized, and synthesized the literature relevant to your research problem, you should begin writing the section or chapter that describes the literature you have examined. We offer several guidelines to help you in the process.

GUIDELINES Writing a Clear and Cohesive Literature Review

As university professors, we authors have written many literature reviews ourselves. We have also read countless master's theses and dissertations written by novice researchers. From such experiences, we have developed the following general guidelines for writing a solid review of the related literature.

1. *Get the proper psychological orientation.* Be clear in your thinking. Know precisely what you are trying to do. The review of the related literature section is a discussion of the research studies and other scholarly writings that bear directly on your own research effort.

You might think of your written review of related literature as a description for one or more of your peers about what other people have written in relation to what you plan to do. Viewing the literature section in this way can help both you and your readers see your own effort within the context of the efforts of researchers who have preceded you.

2. ***Develop a plan for the overall organizational structure of your review.***   Writing a good review of the related literature requires advance planning. Before beginning to write the review of the related literature, create an outline of the topics you intend to address and the points you intend to make. A careful consideration of your problem and subproblems should suggest relevant areas for discussion and the order in which they should be addressed.

Begin your discussion of the related literature from a comprehensive perspective, like an inverted pyramid—broad end first. Then, as you proceed, you can deal with more specific ideas and studies and focus in more and more on your own particular problem.

Throughout your discussion of the related literature, your organizational scheme should be crystal clear to both you and your readers. For example, start off with an *advance organizer*—an overview of the topics you will discuss and the sequence in which you will discuss them (see Chapter 1). And use headings and subheadings throughout your literature review to alert readers to the particular topics that each section addresses.

Early in the review, you will probably want to consider the classic works—those groundbreaking studies that have paved the way for much of the research about the topic. Such studies give an overall historical perspective and provide a context for your own efforts.

3. ***Continually emphasize relatedness to your research problem.***   Keep your readers constantly aware of how the literature you are discussing has relevance to your own project. Point out precisely what the relationship is. Remember that you are writing a review of the *related* literature.

Literature reviews should never be a chain of isolated summaries of other people's research and writing; when written in this manner, no attempt is made to demonstrate the relatedness of the literature to the problem being researched. If you can't identify a relationship, you would do well to consider whether you should include the source at all.

4. ***Provide transitional phrases, sentences, or paragraphs that help your readers follow your train of thought.***   If one idea, paragraph, or section leads logically to the next, say so! Furthermore, give readers some sort of signal when you change the course of your discussion in the middle of a section. For example, in a doctoral dissertation examining the various thinking processes that students might use when listening to a lecture, Nancy Thrailkill finished a discussion of the effects of visual imagery (mental "pictures" of objects or events) and was making the transition to a more theoretical discussion of imagery. She made the transition easy to follow with this sentence:

> Although researchers have conducted numerous studies on the use and value of imagery in learning, they seem to have a difficult time agreeing on why and how it works. (Thrailkill, 1996, p. 10)

The first clause in this transitional sentence recaps the discussion that immediately preceded it, whereas the second clause introduces the new (albeit related) topic.

5. ***Know the difference between describing the literature and plagiarizing it.***   Our own experiences tell us—and research confirms our observations—that many novice researchers don't fully understand the various forms that plagiarism might take (Cizek, 2003; McGue, 2000). In particular, plagiarism involves either (a) presenting another person's work as being one's own or (b) insufficiently acknowledging and identifying the sources from which one has drawn while writing. Reproducing another person's work word-for-word without crediting that person constitutes plagiarism, of course. But so, too, is making small, insignificant changes in someone else's words a form of plagiarism. For example, early in Chapter 2 we say:

> Some research projects can enhance our general knowledge about our physical, biological, psychological, or social world or shed light on historical, cultural, or aesthetic phenomena. . . . Such projects, which can advance theoretical conceptualizations about a particular topic, are known as **basic research**.

You would be plagiarizing our work if you said something like this without giving your source proper credit:

> Basic research can enhance our general knowledge about our physical, biological, psychological, or social world or shed light on historical, cultural, or aesthetic phenomena. Such research can advance theoretical conceptualizations about a topic.

All you would have done here is to replace "Some research projects" with "Basic research" at the beginning of your first sentence and make a few minor adjustments to the second sentence.

6. ***Always give credit where credit is due.***   Note the second part of our earlier definition of plagiarism: *insufficiently acknowledging and identifying the sources from which one has drawn while writing.* In writing the literature review, you must always, *always* credit those people whose ideas you are using or whose research results you are reporting. Such is true regardless of whether you are making use of printed materials, Internet resources, conference presentations, or informal conversations with others in your field. Omitting this crucial step leads your readers to infer that certain ideas are your own rather than those of someone else. Recall that all-important rule we previously presented in Chapter 2: *Absolute honesty and integrity are assumed in every statement a scholar makes.*

Citing other sources also means citing them *correctly.* Making major errors in citations—even if you do so unintentionally—constitutes plagiarism. For example, you must take care not to cite "Smith and Jones (2005)" when the correct citation is "Greene and Black (2007)." Sloppiness in your record keeping is no excuse. Although you haven't meant to, you are plagiarizing from Greene and Black's work.

The specific way in which you give credit to scholars whose ideas you are presenting—for instance, whether you use footnotes or, as we do, citations in parentheses within the body of the text—must depend on the particular style manual you're using, which, in turn, depends on your particular discipline. We provide more details about various style manuals in Chapter 13 (e.g., see Table 13.1).

7. ***Minimize your use of direct quotations from other people's work.***   Sometimes you may decide that someone else's prose captures an idea so well or so vividly that you want to present it word for word. Occasionally, too, certain excerpts provide examples of a point you are trying to make about the literature in general; such is the case when we authors present excerpts from students' dissertations and master's theses in this book. You can legitimately use other people's words if you present them within quotation marks (for a phrase or sentence) or in an indented passage (for a longer quotation). For example, we used the indentation strategy earlier when we presented Thrailkill's transitional sentence in Guideline 4. Notice that we immediately cited the source of the sentence. Consistent with our use of APA style in this book, we gave the author's last name, the date of her dissertation, and the page number on which we found the sentence. That information would be sufficient for any of our readers to find the exact source in our reference list (located near the end of the book) and, after obtaining a copy of Thrailkill's dissertation, finding the actual sentence on page 10.

All too often, however, we have seen literature reviews that appear to be little more than a sequence of quoted excerpts from various published sources. We strongly recommend that you *use quotations only when you have a very good reason*—for example, when the specific words that an author uses are as important as the ideas that the author presents. Consistently using other people's words, even when you give those people appropriate credit, can convey the impression that you aren't willing to take the time to write a clear, cohesive literature review on your own.

Current law allows what is known as *fair use* of a quotation, but some publishers have their own rules of thumb about how much material you can quote without their permission. When in doubt, check with the publisher or other copyright holder.[2]

As important as what others say about their research, and perhaps even more important, is what *you* say about their research. Your emphasis should always be on how a particular idea or research finding relates to your own problem—something only *you* can discuss.

8. ***Summarize what you have said.***   Perhaps the most important question any researcher can ask—and should continue to ask throughout the research process—is, "What does it all mean?" In a thesis or dissertation, every discussion of related literature should end with a brief

---

[2]Many publishers now use their websites to post their guidelines about what and how much you can use without seeking their permission. If you do need their permission for what you want to use, you can often submit a permission request online.

summary section in which you gather up all that has been said and describe its importance in terms of the research problem. Under the simple heading "Summary," you can condense your review into a synopsis of how the existing literature on your topic contributes to an understanding of the specific problem you are trying to address.

9. ***Remember that your first draft will almost certainly not be your last draft.*** Here we are simply repeating a point made in Chapter 1—a point that applies to a literature review as well as to any other part of a research report. First drafts almost inevitably leave a lot to be desired, in part because (as also noted in Chapter 1) the human mind can handle only so much information at any single point in time.

Imperfections in a first draft are unavoidable. In fact, we urge you to write a first draft even before you have completely finished your literature review. Writing a first, incomplete draft can help you identify parts of the literature that are still unclear to you and places where you may need additional information or citations. One strategy we authors use as we write a literature review is to leave blanks for information we realize we still need, mark the blanks in bold red font or with Post-it notes, and then make a final visit to the library (either to the actual building or to its online resources) in order to fill them in.

Even when you have obtained all the information you need for a complete review, you will typically not be able to express your thoughts with total clarity the first time around. Write the review, print it out, and let it sit for a few days. Then reread it with a critical eye, looking for places where you have been ambiguous, incomplete, or self-contradictory.

10. ***Ask others for advice and feedback.*** In this book we frequently suggest that you seek feedback from other people, and your literature review is no exception. Talk with others about what you have found, ask others to read an early draft, and get ideas about additional avenues you should explore. Use e-mail to contact people who have an interest in this area of study (e.g., contact the authors of studies that have influenced your own work). Explain where you are working and what you are working on, send them a copy of what you have written, and ask for their feedback and suggestions. You will be amazed at how helpful and supportive people can be when you tell them you have read their work and would appreciate their opinion.

A SAMPLE LITERATURE REVIEW

At this point, it may be helpful to look at excerpts from what is, in our view, a well-written review of the related literature for a doctoral dissertation proposal. The author of the review, Kay Corbett, wanted to identify possible relationships between cognitive development and motor development (i.e., between the development of children's thinking abilities and that of their movement patterns), especially between ages 4 and 8. Thus, the literature review focuses on both the cognitive and motor development of young children.

Two qualities of the proposal are particularly worth noting. First, the author did not present the studies she had read in a piecemeal, one-at-a-time fashion; instead, she continually synthesized the literature into a cohesive whole. Second, the author's organizational scheme is obvious throughout; she used an advance organizer, numerous headings and subheadings, and transitional paragraphs to help readers follow her as she moved from one topic to the next.

Excerpts from the proposal itself appear on the left-hand side and our commentary appears on the right. The ellipses (. . .) indicate places where we have omitted portions of the text. In some cases, we have summarized the content of what we've omitted within brackets.

✔ Check Your Understanding in the Pearson etext

Practice Thinking Like a Researcher

Practice Thinking Like a Researcher Activity 3.1: Beginning a Literature Review
Practice Thinking Like a Researcher Activity 3.2: Citing and Paraphrasing Previous Research

REVIEW OF LITERATURE

The literature review will include three areas: (a) empirical studies relating motor and cognitive development, (b) motor development, and (c) the neo-Piagetian theories of development as they relate to both motor and cognitive development. The present review is limited to investigations of children within the 4- to 8-year-old age range. Studies targeting children with special needs are excluded.	*The author begins with an advance organizer that outlines the upcoming chapter and describes the scope of the literature review.*
[The remainder of the chapter is divided into three main sections: "Motor and Cognitive Development," "The Development of Gross Motor Skills," and "The Neo-Piagetian Theories of Development." We pick up the chapter midway through the section on "The Development of Gross Motor Skills."]	*Notice how the three sections correspond roughly to the "a," "b," and "c" that the author describes in the first paragraph.*

The Development of Gross Motor Skills

. . . [T]he early childhood period is when many fundamental motor patterns are most efficiently learned. During this age period, children must have daily practice and participation in movement education programs to develop the fundamental movement skills to a mature pattern (Gallahue, 1993, 1995b, 1996; Halverson & Roberton, 1984; Haubenstricker & Seefeldt, 1986; Haywood, 1993; Miller, 1978, cited in Gallahue, 1989; Williams, 1983). If opportunity for this practice is not provided, children may move into adolescence with immature motor patterns that will hinder their ability to enter games or sports activities (Gallahue, 1995a; Haubenstricker & Seefeldt, 1986). Mature patterns can be acquired later in the developmental life span, but it requires much more time and practice to relearn the patterns.	*Notice how the author integrates and summarizes the results of several studies—an approach that is quite appropriate when researchers have all come to a similar conclusion. Several of the studies are (in 1997, the year the proposal is written) quite recent, communicating the (probably accurate) impression that the author is presenting an up-to-date perspective on the topic. A citation such as "Miller, 1978, cited in Gallahue, 1989" should be used only when the original source (in this case, Miller, 1978) is difficult to obtain.*
. . . The fundamental patterns for the 4- to 8-year-old age range include four categories of movements: (a) locomotor movements, (b) stability movements, (c) manipulative movements, and (d) axial movements (Gallahue, 1995b).	*Notice how this sentence alerts the reader to the organizational structure that follows.*
The locomotor movements acquired and/or refined during this period of childhood are running, jumping, hopping, galloping and sliding, leaping, skipping, and climbing (Gallahue, 1995b). These movements "involve a change in location of the body relative to a fixed point on the surface" (Gallahue, 1989, p. 46).	*To indicate that she is using Gallahue's definition of locomotor movements, the author uses quotation marks and, within the citation, lists the page on which she found the definition.*
Stability movements refer to the "ability to maintain one's balance in relationship to the force of gravity even though the nature of the force's application may be altered or parts of the body may be placed in unusual positions" (Gallahue, 1989, p. 494). Stability movements include weight transfer skills (Haywood, 1993). Weight transfer skills include inverted supports, in which the body assumes an upside-down position for a number of seconds before the movement is discontinued. "Stabilization of the center of gravity and maintenance of the line of gravity within the base of support apply to the inverted posture as well as to the erect standing posture" (Gallahue, 1989, p. 275). Other stability movements are dodging, one-foot balancing, beam walking, and rolling.	*The author quotes Gallahue several times. As a general rule, you should limit your quotations to situations in which an author's presentation of ideas or information is exceptionally vivid, precise, or in some other way highly effective. Otherwise, just paraphrase what your sources have said, giving them appropriate credit, of course, for their ideas.*

The manipulative movements involve giving force to objects and receiving force from them (Gallahue, 1989). Movements practiced during childhood are overhand throwing, catching, kicking, striking, dribbling, ball rolling, trapping (feet or body used to absorb the force of the ball instead of the hands and arms), and volleying.

The axial movements are "movements of the trunk or limbs that orient the body while it remains in a stationary position" (Gallahue, 1989, p. 271). Bending, stretching, twisting, turning, swinging, swaying, reaching, and lifting are all axial movements. They are used in combination with other movements to execute more complex movement skills.

Researchers investigating the development of fundamental movement skills focus on qualitative changes as children's developing movement patterns become more smooth and efficient. The following section will review studies investigating the development of fundamental movement patterns in children 4 to 8 years of age.

This paragraph helps the reader follow the author's train of thought as she makes the transition from one topic to another, related one.

Development of Locomotor Skills

The locomotor skills, from earliest acquisition until mature patterns are established, develop through qualitatively different stages (e.g., Gallahue, 1995b; Haywood, 1993; Haubenstricker & Seefeldt, 1986). The studies reviewed investigated qualitative changes that occur as fundamental locomotor patterns are developed.

Walking. The mature walking pattern is achieved between the fourth and seventh years (Eckert, 1987; Guttridge, 1939; Wickstrom, 1983; Williams, 1983). At this level, there are a reflexive arm swing and a narrow base of support (feet are placed no further apart than the width of the shoulders), the gate is relaxed, the legs lift minimally, and there is definite heel-toe contact (Gallahue, 1989). Although the mature pattern is achieved during the early childhood period, walking is not targeted in movement education programs as a skill needing concentrated focus (Gallahue, 1989, 1996; Werder & Bruininks, 1988).

Here the headings "Walking," "Running," "Jumping," and so on, under the more general "Development of Locomotor Skills" heading, communicate quite clearly how the section is organized.

Notice how, in this paragraph, the author synthesizes what previous researchers have found. She intentionally does not describe studies one by one because they all point to the same conclusion. The result is a smooth-flowing, easy-to-read, summary of work that has been done related to the topic.

Running. Many investigators have studied the running pattern. Roberton and Halverson (1984) document the development of running by rating arm action separately from leg action but base the documentation on earlier work (Wickstrom, 1983; Seefeldt et al., 1972, cited in Gallahue, 1989). Gallahue (1995b) proposes a whole-body sequence of development based on the same earlier work. Running patterns develop from flat-footed, uneven patterns with arms swinging outward to smoother patterns with step length increased and a narrower base of support. The mature pattern includes a reflexive arm swing, narrow base of support, relaxed gait, minimal vertical lift, and a definite heel to toe contact. Several University of Wisconsin studies of children between 1.5 and 10 years of age have documented the qualitative changes in the running pattern (Haywood, 1993).

In the second and third sentences of the "Running" paragraph, the verbs docu-ment, base, and proposes should be documented, based, and proposed (past tense). In general, use past tense (e.g., pro-posed or has proposed) to describe what has been done in the past. Use present tense to represent general ideas that are not re-stricted to a single time period. For instance, present tense is appropriately used in the paragraph's fourth sentence ("Running patterns develop from . . .").

Jumping. Early developmentalists defined age norms for children's jumping achievements (Wickstrom, 1983). The children step down from a higher surface from one foot to the other before jumping off the floor with both feet. Then they learn to jump from progressively greater heights onto both feet. Later, they can jump forward, and over objects (Haywood, 1993).

Developmental sequences in both the horizontal and vertical jumps are based on research on the standing long jump (Clark & Phillips, 1985; Hellebrandt et al., 1961; Seefeldt et al., 1972, cited in Gallahue, 1989; Wickstrom, 1983; Roberton, 1984; Roberton &

Halverson, 1984). The one-footed takeoff is one salient characteristic of the earliest jump pattern and persists in some children well into their elementary school years (Roberton, 1984). The jumping motor patterns develop during the ages from two to seven years (Haubenstricker & Seefeldt, 1986). Some elements of the jumping pattern remain stable across ages and type of jump; specifically, 3-, 5-, 7-, and 9-year olds and adults all use the same pattern of leg coordination. All people do not obtain a mature pattern in childhood. In fact many immature patterns are found in adults (Haywood, 1993). . . .

[The author devotes additional sections to "Hopping," "Galloping and Sliding," "Skipping," and "Leaping and Climbing." She then proceeds to the development of other categories of motor skills and, eventually, to a discussion of the third major topic of the chapter—neo-Piagetian theories.]

Note: Excerpt is from a research proposal submitted by Katherine E. Corbett to the University of Northern Colorado, Greeley, in partial fulfillment of the requirement for the degree of Doctor of Philosophy. Reprinted with permission.

In this paragraph the author clarifies the types of studies (i.e., research on the standing long jump) on which certain conclusions have been drawn. By doing so, she helps the reader put the conclusions in perspective and, perhaps, judge the quality of those conclusions.

Throughout the chapter, various levels of headings continue to be important guideposts that reflect this overall organizational scheme.

FOR FURTHER READING

Boote, D. N., & Beile, P. (2005). Scholars before researchers: On the centrality of the dissertation literature review in research preparation. *Educational Researcher, 34*(6), 3–15.

Chan, L. M. (1999). *A guide to the Library of Congress classification* (5th ed.). Englewood, CO: Libraries Unlimited.

Fink, A. (2010). *Conducting research literature reviews: From the Internet to paper* (4th ed.). Thousand Oaks, CA: Sage.

Galvan, J. L. (2012). *Writing literature reviews: A guide for students of the social and behavioral sciences* (5th ed.). Los Angeles: Pyrczak.

Hardy, J., & Dittman, H. (2007). *Learn Library of Congress classification* (2nd North American ed.). Friendswood, TX: Total Recall Publications.

Jesson, J. K. (2011). *Doing your literature review: Traditional and systematic techniques.* London: Sage.

Machi, L. A., & McEvoy, B. T. (2012). *The literature review: Six steps to success.* Thousand Oaks, CA: Corwin.

Reed, J. G., & Baxter, P. M. (2003). *Library use: A handbook for psychology* (3rd ed.). Washington, DC: American Psychological Association.

Stebbins, L. F. (2005). *Student guide to research in the digital age: How to locate and evaluate information sources.* Westport, CT: Libraries Unlimited.

Taylor, A. G. (2006). *Introduction to cataloging and classification* (10th ed.). Westport, CT: Libraries Unlimited.

Chapter 4

Planning your Research Project

Before constructing a home, a builder acquires or develops a detailed set of plans—how to frame the walls and roof, where to put doors and windows of various sizes, where to put pipes and electrical wiring, what kinds of materials to use, and the like. These plans enable the builder to erect a strong, well-designed structure. Researchers should pay similar attention to detail in planning a research project.

Learning Outcomes

4.1 Distinguish between primary data and secondary data, and describe a variety of forms that data for a research project might take.

4.2 Compare quantitative versus qualitative research methodologies in terms of their typical purposes, processes, data collection strategies, data analyses, and nature of the final reports.

4.3 Explain the difference between the internal validity and external validity of a research study. Also explain how you might use different strategies to determine the validity of a quantitative study versus that of a qualitative study.

4.4 Differentiate between substantial and insubstantial phenomena, as well

as among nominal, ordinal, interval, and ratio scales.

4.5 Describe several different types of validity and reliability related to specific measurement techniques. Also, describe various strategies you might use to either determine or enhance the validity and/or reliability of a measurement technique.

4.6 Discuss ethical issues related to protection from harm, voluntary and informed participation, right to privacy, and honesty with professional colleagues. Also, explain the roles of internal review boards and professional codes of ethics in minimizing potential ethical problems in a research study.

When we talk about a general strategy for solving a research problem, we are talking about a research design. The research design provides the overall structure for the procedures the researcher follows, the data the researcher collects, and the data analyses the researcher conducts. Simply put, research design is *planning.*

Nothing helps a research effort be successful so much as carefully planning the overall design. More time and expense are wasted by going off half-prepared—with only a vague set of ideas and procedures—than in any other way. You will be much more efficient and effective as a researcher if you identify your resources, your procedures, and the forms your data will take—always with the central goal of solving your research problem in mind—at the very beginning of your project.

PLANNING A GENERAL APPROACH

In planning a research design, a researcher in quest of new knowledge and understandings cannot be shackled by discipline-specific methodological restraints. The course of a research project will frequently lead the researcher into new and unfamiliar territories that have historically been associated with other content areas. The sociologist trying to resolve a problem in sociology may come face to face with problems that are psychological or economic. The educational researcher exploring the causes of a learning disability may need to consider the domains of neurophysiology, psychopathology, endocrinology, and family counseling. On the way to finding a solution for a problem in criminology, the student in criminal justice may venture into the realms of abnormal psychology and behavioral genetics. Any good researcher must be *eclectic,* willing to draw on whatever sources seem to offer productive methods or data for resolving the research problem.

Instead of limiting their thinking to departmentalized knowledge, researchers might better think of problems as arising out of broad generic areas within whose boundaries all research falls: people, things, records, thoughts and ideas, and dynamics and energy. Let's briefly consider some research problems that may fall within each of these areas.

- *People.* In this category are research problems relating to children, senior citizens, families, communities, cultural groups, ancestors, employees, mental and physiological processes, learning, motivation, social and educational problems, crime, rehabilitation, medical treatments, nutrition, language, and religion.
- *Things.* In this category are research problems relating to animal and vegetable life, viruses and bacteria, inanimate objects (rocks, soil, buildings, machines), matter (molecules, atoms, subatomic matter), stars, and galaxies.
- *Records.* In this category are research problems relating to newspapers, personal journals, letters, Internet websites, registers, speeches, minutes, legal documents, mission statements, census reports, archeological remains, sketches, paintings, and music.
- *Thoughts and ideas.* In this category are research problems relating to concepts, theories, perceptions, opinions, beliefs, reactions, issues, semantics, poetry, and political cartoons.
- *Dynamics and energy.* In this category are research problems relating to human interactions, metabolism, chemical reactions, radiation, radio and microwave transmissions, quantum mechanics, thermodynamics, hydrodynamics, hydrologic cycles, atomic and nuclear energy, wave mechanics, atmospheric and oceanic energy systems, solar energy, and black holes.

We do not intend the preceding lists to be mutually exclusive or all-inclusive. We merely present them to give you an idea of the many research possibilities that each category suggests.

Research Planning Versus Research Methodology

Do not confuse overall research planning with research methodology. Whereas the general approach to *planning* a research study may be similar across disciplines, the techniques one uses to collect and analyze data—that is, the *methodology*—may be specific to a particular academic discipline. Such is the case because data vary so widely in nature. You cannot deal with a blood cell in the same way that you deal with a historical document, and the problem of finding the sources of Coleridge's "Kubla Khan" is entirely different from the problem of finding the sources of radio signals from extragalactic space. You cannot study chromosomes with a questionnaire, and you cannot study attitudes with a microscope.

In planning a research design, therefore, it is extremely important for the researcher not only to choose a viable research problem but also to consider the kinds of data that an investigation of the problem will require, as well as reasonable means of collecting and interpreting those data. Many beginning researchers become so entranced with the glamour of the problem that they fail to consider practical issues related to data availability, collection, and interpretation.

Comparing the brain wave patterns of children who are gifted versus those of average ability may be an engaging project for research, but consider the following issues:

- Will you be able to find a sufficient number of children who are willing to participate in the study and whose parents will grant permission for their children to participate?
- Do you have an electroencephalograph at your disposal?
- If so, do you have the technical skills to use it?
- Are you sufficiently knowledgeable to interpret the electroencephalographic data you obtain?
- If so, do you know how you would interpret the data and organize your findings so that you could draw conclusions from them?

Unless the answer to all of these questions is *yes,* it is probably better that you abandon this project in favor of one for which you have the appropriate knowledge, skills, and resources. Your research should be *practical* research, built on precise and realistic *planning* and executed within the framework of a clearly conceived and feasible *design.*

THE NATURE AND ROLE OF DATA IN RESEARCH

Research is a viable approach to a problem only when data can be collected to support it. The term *data* is plural (singular is *datum)* and comes from the past participle of the Latin verb *dare,* which means "to give." Data are those pieces of information that any particular situation *gives* to an observer.

Researchers must always remember that data are not absolute reality or truth—if, in fact, any single "realities" and "truths" can ever be determined. (Recall the discussions of *postpositivism* and *constructivism* in Chapter 1.) Rather, data are merely *manifestations* of various physical, social, or psychological phenomena that we want to make better sense of. For example, we often see what other people do—the statements they make, the behaviors they exhibit, the things they create, and the effects of their actions on others. But the actual people "inside"—those individuals we will never know!

Data Are Transient and Ever Changing

Data are rarely permanent, unchanging entities. Instead, they are transient—they may have validity for only a split second. Consider, for example, a sociologist who plans to conduct a survey in order to learn about people's attitudes and opinions in a certain city. The sociologist's research assistants begin by administering the survey in a particular city block. By the time they move to the next block, the data they have collected are already out of date. Some people in the previous block who voiced a particular opinion may have seen a television program or heard a discussion that changed their opinion. Some people may have moved away, and others may have moved in; some may have died, and others may have been born. Tomorrow, next week, next year—what we thought we had "discovered" may have changed completely.

Thus is the transient nature of data. We catch merely a fleeting glance of what seems to be true at one point in time but is not necessarily true the next. Even the most carefully collected data may have an elusive quality about them; at a later point in time they may have no counterpart in reality whatsoever. Data are volatile: They evaporate quickly.

Primary Data Versus Secondary Data

For now, let's take a *positivist* perspective and assume that out there—somewhere—is a certain Absolute Truth waiting to be discovered. A researcher's only perceptions of this Truth are various layers of truth-revealing facts. In the layer closest to the Truth are primary data; these are often the most valid, the most illuminating, the most truth-manifesting. Farther away is a layer consisting of secondary data, which are derived not from the Truth itself, but from the primary data.

Imagine, for a moment, that you live in a dungeon, where you can never see the sun—the Truth. Instead, you see a beam of sunlight on the dungeon floor. This light might give you an idea of what the sun is like. The direct beam of sunlight is *primary data.* Although the shaft is not the sun itself, it has come directly from the sun.[1]

But now imagine that, rather than seeing a direct beam of light, you see a diffused pattern of shimmering light on the floor. The sunlight (primary data) has fallen onto a shiny surface and then been reflected—distorted by imperfections of the shiny surface—onto the floor. The pattern is in some ways similar but in other ways dissimilar to the original shaft of light. This pattern of reflected light is *secondary data.*

As another example, consider the following incident: You see a car veer off the highway and into a ditch. You have witnessed the entire event. Afterward, the driver says he had no idea that an accident might occur until the car went out of control. Neither you nor the driver will ever be able to determine the Truth underlying the accident. Did the driver have a momentary seizure of which he was unaware? Did the car have an imperfection that the damage from the accident obscured? Were other factors involved that neither of you noticed? The answers lie beyond an impenetrable barrier. The true cause of the accident may never be known, but the things you witnessed, incomplete as they may be, are primary data that emanated directly from the accident itself.

Now along comes a newspaper reporter who interviews both you and the driver and then writes an account of the accident for the local paper. When your sister reads the account the next morning, she gets, as it were, the reflected-sunlight-on-the-floor version of the event. The newspaper article provides secondary data. The data are inevitably distorted—perhaps only a little, perhaps quite a bit—by the channels of communication through which they must pass to her. The reporter's writing skills, your sister's reading skills, and the inability of language to reproduce every nuance of detail that a firsthand observation can provide—all of these factors distort what others actually observed.

Figure 4.1 represents what we have been saying about data and their relation to any possible Truth that might exist. Lying farthest away from the researcher—and, hence, least accessible—is The Realm of Absolute Truth. It can be approached by the researcher only by passing through two intermediate areas that we have labeled The Realm of the Data. Notice that a barrier exists between The Realm of Absolute Truth and The Region of the Primary Data. Small bits of information leak through the barrier and manifest themselves as data. Notice, too, the foggy barrier between The Realm of the Data and The Realm of the Inquisitive Mind of the Researcher. This barrier is comprised of many things, including the limitations of the human senses, the weaknesses of instrumentation, the inability of language to communicate people's thoughts precisely, and the inability of two human beings to witness the same event and report it in exactly the same way.

Researchers must never forget the overall idea underlying Figure 4.1. Keeping it in mind can prevent them from making exaggerated claims or drawing unwarranted conclusions. No researcher can ever glimpse Absolute Truth—if such a thing exists at all—and researchers can perceive data that reflect that Truth only through imperfect senses and imprecise channels of communication. Such awareness helps researchers be cautious in the interpretation and reporting of research findings—for instance, by using such words and phrases as *perhaps, it seems, one might conclude, it would appear to be the case,* and *the data are consistent with the hypothesis that. . . .*

Planning for Data Collection

Basic to any research project are several fundamental questions about the data. To avoid serious trouble later on, the researcher must answer them specifically and concretely. Clear answers can help bring any research planning and design into focus.

1. *What data are needed?*   This question may seem like a ridiculously simple one, but in fact a specific, definitive answer to it is fundamental to any research effort. To resolve the

---

[1]For readers interested in philosophy, our dungeon analogy is based loosely on Plato's Analogy of the Cave, which he used in Book VII of *The Republic.*

FIGURE 4.1 ▪ The
Relation Between Data
and Truth

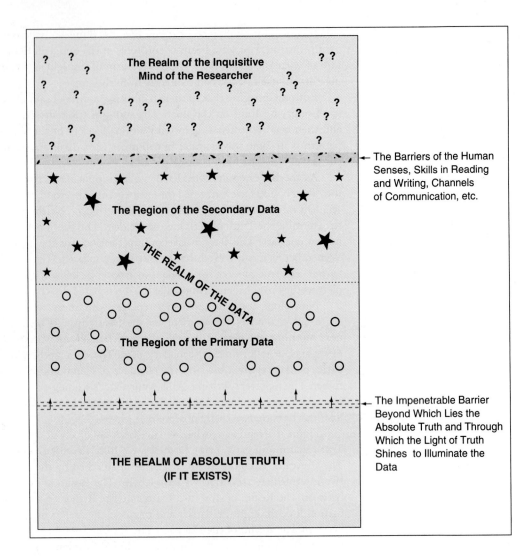

FIGURE 4.1 ▪ The Relation Between Data and Truth

problem, what data are mandatory? What is their nature? Are they historical documents? Interview excerpts? Questionnaire responses? Observations? Measurements made before and after an experimental intervention? Specifically, what data do you need, and what are their characteristics?

2. *Where are the data located?*   Those of us who have taught courses in research methodology are constantly awed by the fascinating problems that students identify for research projects. But then we ask a basic question: "Where will you get the data to resolve the problem?" Some students either look bewildered and remain speechless or else mutter something such as, "Well, they must be available *somewhere.*" Not *somewhere,* but *precisely where?* If you are planning a study of documents, where are the documents you need? At exactly which library and in what collection will you find them? What society or what organization has the files you must examine? Where are these organizations located? Specify geographically—by town, street address, and postal code! Suppose a nurse or a nutritionist is doing a research study about Walter Olin Atwater, whose work has been instrumental in establishing the science of human nutrition in the United States. Where are the data on Atwater located? The researcher can go no further until that basic question is answered.

3. *How will the data be obtained?*   To know where the data are located is not enough; you need to know how you might acquire them. With privacy laws, confidentiality agreements, and so on, obtaining the information you need might not be as easy as you think. You may indeed know what data you need and where you can find them, but an equally important question is,

How will you get them? Careful attention to this question marks the difference between a viable research project and a pipe dream.

4. *What limits will be placed on the nature of acceptable data?* Not all gathered data will necessarily be acceptable for use in a research project. Sometimes certain criteria must be adopted, certain limits established, and certain standards set up that all data must meet in order to be admitted for study. The restrictions identified are sometimes called the **criteria for the admissibility of data.**

For example, imagine that an agronomist wants to determine the effect of ultraviolet light on growing plants. *Ultraviolet* is a vague term: It encompasses a range of light waves that vary considerably in nanometers. The agronomist must narrow the parameters of the data so that they will fall within certain specified limits. Within what nanometer range will ultraviolet emission be acceptable? At what intensity? For what length of time? At what distance from the growing plants? What precisely does the researcher mean by the phrase "effect of ultraviolet light on growing plants"? All plants? A specific genus? A particular species?

Now imagine a sociologist who plans to conduct a survey to determine people's attitudes and beliefs about a controversial issue in a particular area of the country. The sociologist constructs a 10-item survey that will be administered and collected at various shopping malls, county fairs, and other public places over a 4-week period. Some people will respond to all 10 items, but others may respond to only a subset of the items. Should the sociologist include data from surveys that are only partially completed, with some items left unanswered? And what about responses such as "I don't want to waste my time on such stupid questions!"—responses indicating that a person was not interested in cooperating?

The agronomist and the sociologist should be specific about such things—ideally, in sufficient detail that another researcher might reasonably replicate their studies.

5. *How will the data be interpreted?* This is perhaps the most important question of all. The four former hurdles have been overcome. You have the data in hand. But you must also spell out precisely what you intend to do with them to solve the research problem or one of its subproblems.

Now go back and look carefully at how you have worded your research problem. Will you be able to get data that might adequately provide a solution to the problem? And if so, might they reasonably lend themselves to interpretations that shed light on the problem? If the answer to either of these questions is *no,* you must rethink the nature of your problem. If, instead, both answers are *yes,* a next important step is to consider an appropriate methodology.

LINKING DATA AND RESEARCH METHODOLOGY

Data and methodology are inextricably intertwined. For this reason, the methodology chosen for a particular research problem must always take into account the nature of the data that will be collected in the resolution of the problem.

An example may help clarify this point. Imagine that a man from a remote village decides to travel to the big city. While he is there, he takes his first ride on a commercial airliner. No one else in his village has ever ridden in an airplane, so after he returns home, his friends ask him about his trip. One friend asks, "How fast did you move?" "How far did you go?" and "How high did you fly?" A second one asks, "How did you feel when you were moving so fast?" "What was it like being above the clouds?" and "What did the city look like from so high?" Both friends are asking questions that can help them learn more about the experience of flying in an airplane, but because they ask different kinds of questions, they obtain different kinds of information. Although neither of them gets the "wrong" story, neither does each one get the whole story.

In research, too, different questions yield different kinds of information. Different research problems lead to different research designs and methods, which in turn result in the collection of different types of data and different interpretations of those data.

Furthermore, many kinds of data may be suitable only for a particular methodology. To some extent, *the desired data dictate the research method.* As an example, consider historical data, those pieces of information gleaned from written records of past events. You can't extract much meaning from historical documents by conducting a laboratory experiment. An experiment is simply not suited to the nature of the data.

Over the years, numerous research methodologies have emerged to accommodate the many different forms that data are likely to take. Accordingly, we must take a broad view of the approaches the term *research methodology* encompasses. Above all, we must not limit ourselves to the belief that only a true experiment constitutes "research." Such an attitude prohibits us from agreeing that we can better understand Coleridge's poetry by reading the scholarly research of John Livingston Lowes (1927, 1955) or from appreciating Western civilization more because of the historiography of Arnold Toynbee (1939–1961).

No single highway leads us exclusively toward a better understanding of the unknown. Many highways can take us in that direction. They may traverse different terrain, but they all converge on the same destination: the enhancement of human knowledge and understandings.

Comparing Quantitative and Qualitative Methodologies

On the surface, quantitative and qualitative approaches involve similar processes—for instance, they both entail identifying a research problem, reviewing related literature, and collecting and analyzing data. But by definition, they are suitable for different types of data: Quantitative studies involve numerical data, whereas qualitative studies primarily make use of nonnumerical data (e.g., verbal information, visual displays). And to some degree, quantitative and qualitative research designs are appropriate for answering different kinds of questions.

Let's consider how the two approaches might look in practice. Suppose two researchers are interested in investigating the "effectiveness of the case-based method for teaching business management practices." The first researcher asks the question, "How effective is case-based instruction in comparison with lecture-based instruction?" She finds five instructors who are teaching case-based business management classes; she finds five others who are teaching the same content using lectures. At the end of the semester, the researcher administers an achievement test to students in all 10 classes. Using statistical analyses, she compares the scores of students in case-based and lecture-based courses to determine whether the achievement of one group is significantly higher than that of the other group. When reporting her findings, she summarizes the results of her statistical analyses. This researcher has conducted a *quantitative* study.

The second researcher is also interested in the effectiveness of the case method but asks the question, "What factors make case-based instruction more effective or less effective?" To answer this question, he sits in on a case-based business management course for an entire semester. He spends an extensive amount of time talking with the instructor and some of the students in an effort to learn the participants' perspectives on case-based instruction. He carefully scrutinizes his data for patterns and themes in the responses. He then writes an in-depth description and interpretation of what he has observed in the classroom setting. This researcher has conducted a *qualitative* study.

Table 4.1 presents typical differences between quantitative and qualitative approaches. We briefly discuss these differences in the next few paragraphs—not to persuade you that one approach is better than the other, but to help you make a more informed decision about which approach might be better for your own research question.

Purpose   Quantitative researchers tend to seek explanations and predictions that will generalize to other persons and places. The intent is to identify relationships among two or more variables and then, based on the results, to confirm or modify existing theories or practices.

Qualitative researchers tend to seek better understandings of complex situations. Their work is sometimes (although not always) exploratory in nature, and they may use their observations to build theory from the ground up.

TABLE 4.1 ▨ Typical Characteristics of Quantitative Versus Qualitative Approaches

Question	Quantitative	Qualitative
What is the purpose of the research?	• To explain and predict • To confirm and validate • To test theory	• To describe and explain • To explore and interpret • To build theory
What is the nature of the research process?	• Focused • Known variables • Established guidelines • Preplanned methods • Somewhat context-free • Detached view	• Holistic • Unknown variables • Flexible guidelines • Emergent methods • Context-bound • Personal view
What are the data like, and how are they collected?	• Numerical data • Representative, large sample • Standardized instruments	• Textual and/or image-based data • Informative, small sample • Loosely structured or nonstandardized observations and interviews
How are data analyzed to determine their meaning?	• Statistical analysis • Stress on objectivity • Primarily deductive reasoning	• Search for themes and categories • Acknowledgment that analysis is subjective and potentially biased • Primarily inductive reasoning
How are the findings communicated?	• Numbers • Statistics, aggregated data • Formal voice, scientific style	• Words • Narratives, individual quotes • Personal voice, literary style (in some disciplines)

Process Because quantitative studies have historically been the mainstream approach to research, carefully structured guidelines exist for conducting them. Concepts, variables, hypotheses, and methods of measurement tend to be defined before the study begins and to remain the same throughout. Quantitative researchers choose methods that allow them to objectively measure the variable(s) of interest. They also try to remain detached from the phenomena and participants in order to minimize the chances of collecting biased data.

A qualitative study is often more holistic and *emergent,* with the specific focus, design, measurement tools (e.g., observations, interviews), and interpretations developing and possibly changing along the way. Researchers try to enter the situation with open minds, prepared to immerse themselves in its complexity and to personally interact with participants. Categories (variables) emerge from the data, leading to information, patterns, and/or theories that help explain the phenomenon under study.

Data Collection Quantitative researchers typically identify only a few variables to study and then collect data specifically related to those variables. Methods of measuring each variable are identified, developed, and standardized, with considerable attention given to the validity and reliability of the measurement instruments (more about such qualities later in the chapter). Data are often collected from a large sample that is presumed to represent a particular population so that generalizations can be made about the population.

Qualitative researchers operate under the assumption that reality is not easily divided into discrete, measurable variables. Some qualitative researchers describe themselves as *being* the research instrument because the bulk of their data collection is dependent on their personal involvement in the setting. Rather than sample a large number of participants with the intent of making generalizations, qualitative researchers tend to select a few participants who might best shed light on the phenomenon under investigation. Both verbal data (interview responses, documents, field notes) and nonverbal data (drawings, photographs, videotapes, artifacts) may be collected.

Data Analysis All research requires logical reasoning. Quantitative researchers tend to rely more heavily on deductive reasoning, beginning with certain premises (e.g., hypotheses, theories)

and then drawing logical conclusions from them. They also try to maintain objectivity in their data analysis, conducting predetermined statistical procedures and using relatively objective criteria to evaluate the outcomes of those procedures.

In contrast, qualitative researchers make considerable use of inductive reasoning: They make many specific observations and then draw inferences about larger and more general phenomena. Furthermore, their data analysis is more subjective in nature: They scrutinize the body of data in search of patterns—subjectively identified—that the data reflect.

It is important to note, however, that quantitative research is not exclusively deductive, nor is qualitative research exclusively inductive. Researchers of all methodological persuasions typically use both types of reasoning in a continual, cyclical fashion. Quantitative researchers might formulate a preliminary theory through inductive reasoning (e.g., by observing a few situations), engage in the theory-building process described in Chapter 1, and then try to support their theory by drawing and testing the conclusions that follow logically from it. Similarly, after qualitative researchers have identified a theme in their data using an inductive process, they typically move into a more deductive mode to verify or modify it with additional data.

Reporting Findings   Quantitative researchers typically reduce their data to summarizing statistics (e.g., means, medians, correlation coefficients). In most cases, *average* performances are of greater interest than the performances of specific individuals (you will see exceptions in the single-subject designs described in Chapter 7). Results are typically presented in a report that uses a formal, scientific style with impersonal language.

Qualitative researchers often construct interpretive narratives from their data and try to capture the complexity of a particular phenomenon. Especially in certain disciplines (e.g., anthropology), qualitative researchers may use a more personal, literary style than quantitative researchers do, and they often include the participants' own language and perspectives. Although all researchers must be able to write clearly, effective qualitative researchers must be especially skillful writers.

Combining Quantitative and Qualitative Designs

Given that quantitative and qualitative methodologies are useful in answering somewhat different kinds of questions and solving somewhat different kinds of research problems, we can gain better understandings of our physical, social, and psychological worlds when we have both methodologies at our disposal. Fortunately, the two approaches aren't necessarily mutually exclusive; many researchers successfully combine them in a *mixed-methods design*. For example, it isn't unusual for researchers to *count* (and therefore quantify) certain kinds of data in what is, for all intents and purposes, a qualitative investigation. Nor is it unusual for quantitative researchers to report participants' perceptions of or emotional reactions to various experimental treatments. Especially in studies of human behavior, mixed-methods designs with both quantitative and qualitative elements often provide a more complete picture of a particular phenomenon than either approach could do alone. We explore mixed-methods designs in more detail in Chapter 12.

PRACTICAL APPLICATION Choosing a General Research Approach

Although we believe that research studies are sometimes enhanced by combining both quantitative and qualitative methods, we also realize that many novice researchers may not have the time, resources, or expertise to effectively combine approaches for their initial forays into research. Furthermore, good research doesn't necessarily have to involve a complex, multifaceted design. For example, in an article reviewing classic studies in his own discipline, psychologist Christopher Peterson had this to say in his abstract:

> Psychology would be improved if researchers stopped using complicated designs, procedures, and statistical analyses for the sole reason that they are able to do so. . . . [S]ome of the classic studies in psychology [are] breathtakingly simple. . . . More generally, questions should dictate research methods and statistical analyses, not vice versa. (Peterson, 2009, p. 7)

As you choose your own general approach to addressing your research problem—whether to use a quantitative approach, a qualitative approach, or a combination of the two—you should base your decision on the research problem you want to address and the skills you have as a researcher, *not* on what tasks you want to avoid. For example, disliking mathematics and wanting to avoid conducting statistical analyses are not good reasons for choosing a qualitative study over a quantitative one. The guidelines we offer here can help you make a reasonable decision.

GUIDELINES Deciding Whether to Use a Quantitative or Qualitative Approach

Qualitative studies have become increasingly popular in recent years, even in some disciplines that have historically placed heavy emphasis on quantitative approaches. Yet we have met many students who have naively assumed that qualitative studies are easier or in some other way more "comfortable" than quantitative designs. Be forewarned: Qualitative studies require as much effort and rigor as quantitative studies, and data collection alone often stretches over the course of many months. In the following paragraphs, we offer important considerations for novice researchers who might be inclined to "go qualitative."

1. *Consider your own comfort with the assumptions of the qualitative tradition.*   If you believe that no single reality underlies your research problem but that, instead, different individuals may have constructed different, possibly equally valid realities relevant to your problem, then qualitative research might be more appropriate.

2. *Consider the audience for your study.*   If your intended audience (e.g., a dissertation committee, a specific journal editor, or colleagues in your field) is not accustomed to or supportive of qualitative research, it makes little sense to spend the time and effort needed to do a good qualitative study (e.g., see S. M. Miller, Nelson, & Moore, 1998).

3. *Consider the nature of your research question.*   Qualitative designs can be quite helpful for addressing exploratory or interpretive research questions. But they may be of little use in testing specific hypotheses about cause-and-effect relationships.

4. *Consider the extensiveness of the related literature.*   If the literature base is weak, underdeveloped, or altogether missing, a qualitative design can give you the freedom and flexibility you need to explore a specific phenomenon and identify important variables affecting it.

5. *Consider the depth of what you wish to discover.*   If you want to examine a phenomenon in depth with a relatively small number of participants, a qualitative approach is ideal. But if you are skimming the surface of a phenomenon and wish to do so using a large number of participants, a quantitative study will be more efficient.

6. *Consider the amount of time you have available for conducting the study.*   Qualitative studies typically involve an extensive amount of time both on and off the research site. If your time is limited, you may not be able to complete a qualitative study satisfactorily.

7. *Consider the extent to which you are willing to interact with the people in your study.*   Qualitative researchers who are working with human beings must be able to establish rapport and trust with their participants and interact with them on a fairly personal level. Furthermore, gaining initial entry into one or more research sites (e.g., social meeting places, people's homes) may take considerable advance planning and numerous preliminary contacts.

8. *Consider the extent to which you feel comfortable working without much structure.*   Qualitative researchers tend to work with fewer specific, predetermined procedures than quantitative researchers do; their work can be exploratory in many respects. Thus, they must think creatively about how best to address various aspects of a research problem, and they need a high tolerance for ambiguity.

9. *Consider your ability to organize and draw inferences from a large body of information.*   Qualitative research often involves the collection of a great many field notes, interview responses, and the like, that aren't clearly organized at the beginning of the process. Working

with extensive amounts of data and reasoning inductively about them require considerable self-discipline and organizational ability. In comparison, conducting a few statistical analyses—even for those who have little affection for mathematics—is a much easier task.

10. *Consider your writing skills.* Qualitative researchers must have excellent writing skills. Communicating findings is the final step in all research projects; the success of your research will ultimately be judged by how well you accomplish this final component of the research process.

Once you have decided whether to take a quantitative or qualitative approach, you need to pin down your research method more precisely. Table 4.2 lists some common research methodologies and the types of problems for which each is appropriate. In later chapters of the book, we look more closely at most of these methodologies.

TABLE 4.2 ■ Common Research Methodologies

Methodology	General Characteristics and Purposes
Action research	A type of applied research that focuses on finding a solution to a local problem in a local setting. For example, a teacher might investigate whether a new spelling program she has adopted leads to improvement in her students' achievement scores. (For example, see Efron & Ravid, 2013; Mertler, 2012; Mills, 2014.)
Case study	A type of qualitative research in which in-depth data are gathered relative to a single individual, program, or event for the purpose of learning more about an unknown or poorly understood situation. (See Chapter 9.)
Content analysis	A detailed and systematic examination of the contents of a particular body of material (e.g., television shows, magazine advertisements, Internet websites, works of art) for the purpose of identifying patterns, themes, or biases within that material. (See Chapter 9.)
Correlational research	A statistical investigation of the relationship between two or more variables. Correlational research looks at surface relationships but does not necessarily probe for causal reasons underlying them. For example, a researcher might investigate the relationships among high school seniors' achievement test scores and their grade point averages a year later when they are first-year college students. (See Chapter 6.)
Design-based research	A multistep, iterative study in which certain instructional strategies or technologies are implemented, evaluated, and modified to determine possible factors influencing learning or performance. (For example, see T. Anderson & Shattuck, 2012; Brown, 1992; Cobb, Confrey, diSessa, Lehrer, & Schauble, 2003.)
Developmental research	An observational-descriptive type of research that either compares people in different age groups (a *cross-sectional study*) or follows a particular group over a lengthy period of time (a *longitudinal study*). Such studies are particularly appropriate for looking at developmental trends. (See Chapter 6.)
Ethnography	A type of qualitative inquiry that involves an in-depth study of an intact cultural group in a natural setting. (See Chapter 9.)
Experimental research	A study in which participants are randomly assigned to groups that undergo various researcher-imposed treatments or interventions, followed by observations or measurements to assess the effects of the treatments. (See Chapter 7.)
Ex post facto research	An approach in which one looks at conditions that have already occurred and then collects data to investigate a possible relationship between these conditions and subsequent characteristics or behaviors. (See Chapter 7.)
Grounded theory research	A type of qualitative research aimed at deriving theory through the use of multiple stages of data collection and interpretation. (See Chapter 9.)
Historical research	An effort to reconstruct or interpret historical events through the gathering and interpretation of relevant historical documents and/or oral histories. (See Chapter 10.)
Observation study	A type of quantitative research in which a particular aspect of behavior is observed systematically and with as much objectivity as possible. (See Chapter 6.)
Phenomenological research	A qualitative method that attempts to understand participants' perspectives and views of physical or social realities. (See Chapter 9.)
Quasi-experimental research	A method similar to experimental research but without random assignment to groups. (See Chapter 7.)
Survey research	A study designed to determine the incidence, frequency, and distribution of certain characteristics in a population; especially common in business, sociology, and government research. (See Chapter 6.)

CONSIDERING THE VALIDITY OF YOUR METHOD

No matter what research methodology you choose, you must think about the general *validity* of your approach for your purpose—the likelihood that it will yield accurate, meaningful, and credible results that can potentially help you address your research problem. Your research effort will be worth your time and effort only to the extent that it allows you to draw meaningful and defensible conclusions from your data.

Researchers use a variety of strategies to support the validity of their findings. Different strategies are appropriate in different situations, depending on the nature of the data and the specific methodologies used. In the following sections, we examine two concepts—internal validity and external validity—that originated in discussions of quantitative research (Campbell & Stanley, 1963). However, some qualitative researchers have questioned the relevance of these two concepts to qualitative designs; thus, in a subsequent section, we present validation strategies that qualitative researchers often use.

Internal Validity

The **internal validity** of a research study is the extent to which its design and the data it yields allow the researcher to draw accurate conclusions about cause-and-effect and other relationships within the data. To illustrate, we present three situations in which the internal validity of a study is suspect:

1. A marketing researcher wants to study how humor in television commercials affects sales in the United States and Canada. To do so, the researcher studies the effectiveness of two commercials that have been developed for a new soft drink called Zowie. One commercial, in which a well-known but humorless television actor describes how Zowie has a zingy and refreshing taste, airs during the months of March, April, and May. The other commercial, a humorous scenario in which several teenagers spray one another with Zowie on a hot summer day, airs during the months of June, July, and August. The researcher finds that in June through August, Zowie sales are almost double what they were in the preceding 3 months. "Humor boosts sales," the researcher concludes.

2. An industrial psychologist wants to study the effects of soft classical music on the productivity of a group of typists in a typing pool. At the beginning of the month, the psychologist meets with the typists to explain the rationale for the study, gets their consent to play the music during the working day, and then begins to have music piped into the office where the typists work. At the end of the month, the typists' supervisor reports a 30% increase in the number of documents completed by the typing pool that month. "Classical music increases productivity," the psychologist concludes.

3. An educational researcher wants to study the effectiveness of a new method of teaching reading to first graders. The researcher asks all 30 of the first-grade teachers in a particular school district whether they would like to receive training in the new method and then use it during the coming school year. Fourteen teachers volunteer to learn and use the new method; 16 teachers say that they would prefer to use their current approach. At the end of the school year, students who have been instructed with the new method have, on average, significantly higher scores on a reading achievement test than students who have received more traditional reading instruction. "The new method is definitely better than the old one," the researcher concludes.

Did you detect anything wrong with the conclusions these researchers drew? If not, go back and read the three descriptions again. *None of the conclusions is warranted from the study conducted.*

In the first research study, the two commercials differed from each other in several ways (e.g., the presence of teenagers, the amount of action) in addition to humor. And we shouldn't overlook the fact that the humorous commercial aired during the summer months. People are more likely to drink soft drinks (including Zowie) when they're hot.

In the second study, the typists *knew* they were participating in a research study; they also knew the nature of the researcher's hypothesis. Sometimes the participants in a research study change their behavior simply because they know they are in a research study and are getting extra attention as a result. This effect, known as the **Hawthorne effect**,[2] is an example of **reactivity**, a more general phenomenon in which people change their behavior when they're aware that they are being observed. But other explanations for the second study's results are possible as well. Perhaps the typists typed more because they liked the researcher and wanted to help him support his hypothesis. Perhaps the music energized the typists for a few weeks simply because it created a change in their environment—a phenomenon known as the **novelty effect**. (In such a situation, reverting back to *no* music after a month or two might *also* lead to an increase in productivity.) Furthermore, the researcher didn't consider the number of people who were working before and after the music started. Perhaps productivity increased simply because two people in the typing pool had just returned from vacation!

In the third study, notice that the researcher looked for *volunteers* to use the new method for teaching reading. Were the volunteer teachers different in some way from the nonvolunteers? Were they better educated or more motivated? Did they teach with more enthusiasm and energy because they *expected* the new method to be more effective? Or did the volunteer teachers happen to teach in areas of the school district where children had had a better head start in reading skills before beginning school? Perhaps the children in the volunteers' classrooms performed better on the achievement test not because the instructional method was more effective, but because, as a group, they had been read to more frequently by their parents or gone to more academically oriented preschools.

To ensure the internal validity of a research study, researchers take precautions to *eliminate other possible explanations for the results observed.* Following are several strategies researchers sometimes use to increase the probability that *their explanations are the most likely ones* for the observations they have made:

- ▪ *A controlled laboratory study.*   An experiment is conducted in a laboratory setting so that environmental conditions can be carefully regulated.
- ▪ *A double-blind experiment.*   In a **double-blind experiment**, two or more different interventions are presented, with neither the participants in the study nor the people administering the interventions (e.g., teachers, research assistants) knowing which intervention various participants are receiving. Such lack of knowledge ("blindness") decreases the likelihood that people's expectations for outcomes might influence the *actual* outcomes.
- ▪ *Unobtrusive measures.*   In an **unobtrusive measure**, people are observed in such a way that they don't know their actions are being recorded. We offer two real-life examples to illustrate. In one case, a university library measured student and faculty use of different parts of the library by looking at wear-and-tear patterns on the carpet. In another situation, researchers for the U.S. National Park Service looked at hikers' frequency of using different hiking trails by installing electronic counters in hard-to-notice locations beside the trails (R. K. Ormrod & Trahan, 1982). (Note that ethical issues sometimes arise when we observe people without their permission; we discuss ethics later in this chapter.)
- ▪ *Triangulation.*   In **triangulation**, multiple sources of data are collected with the hope that they will all converge to support a particular hypothesis or theory. This approach is especially common in qualitative research; for instance, a researcher might engage in many informal observations in the field *and* conduct in-depth interviews, then look for common themes that appear in the data gleaned from both methods. Triangulation is also common in mixed-methods designs, in which both quantitative and qualitative data are collected to address a single research question.

---

[2]The effect owes its name to the Hawthorne Works, an industrial complex in Illinois where the effect was first observed.

Internal validity is especially of concern in experimental designs, where the specific intent is to identify cause-and-effect relationships; accordingly, we revisit this issue in Chapter 7. But to some degree, internal validity is important in *any* research study. Researchers and those who read their research reports must have confidence that the conclusions drawn are warranted from the data collected.

External Validity

The **external validity** of a research study is the extent to which its results apply to situations beyond the study itself—in other words, the extent to which the conclusions drawn can be *generalized* to other contexts. Following are three commonly used strategies that enhance the external validity of a research project:

- *A real-life setting.* Earlier we mentioned that researchers sometimes use laboratory experiments to help them control the environmental conditions in which a study takes place. Laboratory studies have a downside, however: They provide an artificial setting that might be quite different from real-life circumstances. Research that is conducted in the outside world, although it may not have the tight controls of a laboratory project, may be more valid in the sense that it yields results with broader applicability to other real-world contexts.[3]

- *A representative sample.* Whenever researchers seek to learn more about a particular category of objects or creatures—whether they are studying rocks, salamanders, or human beings—they often study a *sample* from that category and then draw conclusions about the category as a whole. (Here is a classic example of inductive reasoning.) For example, to study the properties of granite, researchers might take pieces of granite from anywhere in the world and assume that their findings based on those pieces might be generalizable to the same kinds of granite found in other locations. The same might hold true for salamanders if researchers limit their conclusions to the particular species of salamander they have studied.

  Human beings are another matter. The human race is incredibly diverse in terms of culture, childrearing practices, educational opportunities, personality characteristics, and so on. To the extent that researchers restrict their research to people with a particular set of characteristics, they may not be able to generalize their findings to people with a very different set of characteristics. Ideally, then, researchers want participants in a research study to be a *representative sample* of the population about which they wish to draw conclusions. In Chapter 6 we consider a number of strategies for obtaining representative samples.

- *Replication in a different context.* Imagine that one researcher draws a conclusion from a particular study in a specific context, and another researcher who conducts a similar study in a very different context reaches the same conclusion, and perhaps additional researchers also conduct similar studies in dissimilar contexts and, again, draw the same conclusion. Taken together, these studies provide evidence that the conclusion has validity and applicability across diverse situations.

You have previously encountered the distinction between *basic research* and *applied research* in Chapter 2. Well-designed basic research—research conducted under tightly controlled (and possibly artificial) conditions—ensures internal validity; that is, it allows the researcher to rule

---

[3]The artificial nature of laboratory research has been a concern in psychology for many years. In most cases, however, studies conducted in a laboratory and those conducted in real-world settings lead to the same conclusions about human nature, especially when lab-based studies reveal large differences among treatment groups (e.g., see C. A. Anderson, Lindsay, & Bushman, 1999; G. Mitchell, 2012).

out other possible explanations for the results obtained. Applied research—research conducted in more naturalistic but invariably more complex environments—is more useful for external validity; that is, it increases the chances that a study's findings are generalizable to other real-life situations and problems. Keep in mind, however, that the basic-versus-applied distinction is really a continuum rather than a dichotomy: Research studies can have varying degrees of artificiality versus real-world authenticity.

Validity in Qualitative Research

Qualitative researchers don't necessarily use the term *validity* in describing their research; they may instead use such words as *quality, credibility, trustworthiness, confirmability,* and *interpretive rigor* (Creswell, 2013; Lincoln & Guba, 1985; O'Cathain, 2010; Teddlie & Tashakkori, 2010). Nevertheless, they do take certain precautions to substantiate their methods, findings, and conclusions. As noted earlier, they often use *triangulation*—comparing multiple data sources in search of common themes—to give credence to their findings. Following are several additional strategies they employ:

- *Extensive time in the field.*   A researcher may spend several months, perhaps even a year or more, studying a particular phenomenon, forming tentative hypotheses, and continually looking for evidence that either supports or disconfirms those hypotheses.
- *Analysis of outliers and contradictory instances.*   A researcher actively looks for examples that are inconsistent with existing hypotheses, then continually revises his or her explanation or theory until all examples have been accounted for.
- *Thick description.*   A researcher who uses **thick description** describes a situation in sufficiently rich, "thick" detail that readers can draw their own conclusions from the data presented.
- *Acknowledgment of personal biases.*   Rather than claim to be an objective, impartial observer, a researcher describes personal beliefs and attitudes that may potentially be slanting observations and interpretations.
- *Respondent validation.*   In **respondent validation**, a researcher takes conclusions back to the participants in the study and asks quite simply, Do you agree with my conclusions? Do they make sense based on your own experiences?
- *Feedback from others.*   A researcher seeks the opinion of colleagues in the field to determine whether they agree or disagree that the researcher has made appropriate interpretations and drawn valid conclusions from the data.

Regardless of the kind of study you decide to conduct, you must address the validity of your study at the very beginning of your project—that is, *at the planning stage.* If you put off validity issues until later in the game, you may end up conducting a study that has little apparent credibility and worth, either in terms of minimizing alternative explanations for the results obtained (internal validity) or in terms of being generalizable to the world "out there" (external validity). As a result, you are almost certainly wasting your time and effort on what is, for all intents and purposes, a trivial enterprise.

IDENTIFYING MEASUREMENT STRATEGIES

Especially if you are planning a quantitative research project, you must also determine how you will *measure* the variables you intend to study. In some cases you will be able to use one or more existing instruments—perhaps an oscilloscope to measure patterns of sound, a published personality test to measure a person's tendency to be either shy or outgoing, or a rating scale that a previous researcher has developed to assess parents' childrearing practices. In other situations you may have to develop your *own* measurement instruments—perhaps a survey to assess people's opinions about welfare reform, a paper-and-pencil test to measure what students have learned from a particular instructional unit, or a checklist to evaluate the quality of a new product.

Appropriate measurement procedures provide a solid basis on which any good quantitative study rests. Just as a building with a questionable foundation is unlikely to be safe for habitation, so, too, will a research effort employing faulty measurement tools provide little of value in solving the problem under investigation.

We should note here that *some* measurement is almost inevitable in qualitative research as well. At a minimum, qualitative researchers are apt to *count* things—perhaps the members of certain groups or the frequencies of certain events. And during data analyses, many of them *code* their observations to reflect various categories into which different observations fall. Because their measurement strategies are often specific to certain qualitative designs and may continue to be refined over the course of a study (recall our earlier point that qualitative designs are often *emergent* in nature), we postpone discussion of such strategies until Chapter 11.

Defining Measurement

What exactly *is* measurement? Typically we think of measurement in terms of such objects as rulers, scales, gauges, and thermometers. In research, **measurement** takes on a somewhat different meaning:

> Measurement is limiting the data of any phenomenon—substantial or insubstantial—so that those data may be interpreted and, ultimately, compared to a particular qualitative or quantitative standard.

Let's zoom in on various parts of this definition. The first five words are *measurement is limiting the data.* When we measure something, we constrain the data in some way; we erect a barrier beyond which those data cannot go. What is a foot, a mile, a pound? Each is a unit of measure governed by a numerical constraint: 12 inches constrain a foot; 5,280 feet, a mile; and 16 ounces, a pound.

Now let's look at the next six words: *of any phenomenon—substantial or insubstantial.* In some cases, observable physical entities are measured. These are **substantial phenomena**; that is, the things being measured have physical substance, an obvious basis in the physical world. An astronomer measures patterns and luminosity of light in the night sky; a neurologist measures intensity and location of activity in the brain; a chemist measures the mass of a compound both before and after transforming it in some way. All of these are attempts to measure substantial phenomena. Some devices designed to measure substantial phenomena, such as high-powered telescopes and MRI machines, are highly specialized and used only in particular disciplines. Others, such as balance scales and tape measures, are applicable to many fields of inquiry.

We can also measure those things—if "things" they be—that are **insubstantial phenomena**, that exist only as concepts, ideas, opinions, feelings, or other intangible entities. For example, we might attempt to measure the economic "health" of business, the degree to which students have "learned," or the extent to which people "value" physical exercise. We seek to measure these intangibles, not with tape measures or scales, but with the Dow Jones Index, achievement tests, questionnaires, or interviews.[4]

We continue with the next seven words of our definition of measurement: *so that those data may be interpreted.* We cannot emphasize this point enough: Research involves not only the collection but also the interpretation of data—the transformation of data into new discoveries, revelations, and enlightenments.

---

[4]You may sometimes see the substantial–insubstantial distinction referred to as *manifest variables* (which can be directly observed and measured) versus *latent variables* (which lie below the surface and can be measured only indirectly through their effects on another, observable entity; e.g., see Bartholomew, 2004).

Now we finish our definition: *and, ultimately, compared to a particular qualitative or quantitative standard.* A researcher must have a goalpost, a true north, a point of orientation. In research, we call these standards *norms, averages, conformity to expected statistical distributions, goodness of fit, accuracy of description,* and the like.

Measurement is ultimately a comparison: a thing or concept measured against a point of limitation. We compare the length of an object with the scale of a ruler or a measuring tape. We "measure" an ideology against the meaning of it as articulated by its originator. For example, the essence of a philosophy arises from the writings and teachings of its founder: Platonism from Plato, Marxism from Karl Marx, and romanticism, perhaps, from Jean-Jacques Rousseau. The essence of a religious belief lies in its sacred writings, in the precepts of its great teachers, and in its creed. The meaning of freedom is articulated in many political documents—for instance, in the Declaration of Independence and the Constitution of the United States. Against these original sources, it is possible to measure the thoughts and ideas of others and to approximate their similarity to or deviance from those sources.

As you can see, then, our definition of measurement implies much more than an everyday understanding of measurement might suggest. Measurement provides an important tool with which data may be inspected, analyzed, and interpreted so that the researcher may probe the meaning that lies below their surface.

Measuring Insubstantial Phenomena: An Example

Measuring insubstantial phenomena—those phenomena that have no obvious, concrete basis in the physical world—can sometimes involve considerable creativity. For example, imagine that we want to examine—and also to *measure*—the interpersonal dynamics within a small group of people. Let's take a group of nine people who work together in the human resources department of a large corporation. They attend a recognition dinner at an exclusive hotel and enter the hotel in the following order: Terri, Sara, Greg, Tim, Gretchen, Matt, Peter, Jeff, and Joe. They greet one another and have time for a brief conversation before dinner. Most of them position themselves in conversation groups, as shown in Figure 4.2.

To the perceptive observer, the interpersonal dynamics within the group soon become apparent. Who greets whom with enthusiasm or with indifference? Who joins in conversation with whom? Who seems to be a relative outsider? However, *to merely observe the behavior of individuals in a particular situation is not to measure it.*

One possible approach to measuring the group's interpersonal dynamics is to give each group member a slip of paper on which to write three sets of names, one set each for (a) one or more individuals in the group whom the person likes most, (b) one or more individuals whom the person likes least, and (c) one or more individuals for whom the person has no strong feeling one way or the other. When using this method, we should poll each person in the group individually and guarantee that every response will be kept confidential.

We can then draw a chart, or sociogram, of these interpersonal reactions, perhaps in the manner depicted in Figure 4.3. We might also assign "weights" that place the data into

FIGURE 4.2 ▦
Conversation Groups in a Hypothetical Human Resources Department

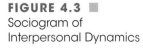

FIGURE 4.3 ■
Sociogram of
Interpersonal Dynamics

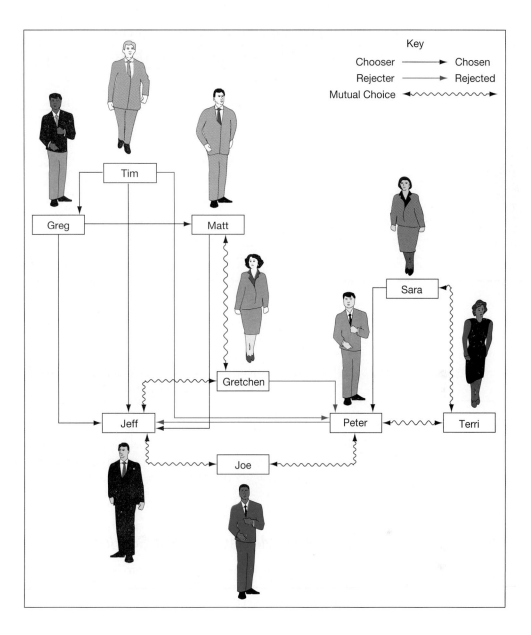

three numerical categories: +1 for a positive choice, 0 for indifference, and −1 for a negative reaction. Categorizing the data in this way, we can then construct a sociometric matrix. To create a matrix, we arrange the names of each person twice: vertically down the left side of a grid and horizontally across the top of the grid. The result is shown in Table 4.3. The dashes in the grid reflect the fact that the people can choose other individuals but cannot choose *themselves*.

Certain relationships begin to emerge. As we represent group dynamics in multiple forms, clusters of facts suggest the following conclusions:

■ Jeff seems to be the informal or popular leader (sometimes called the "star") of the group. He received five choices and only one rejection (see the "Jeff" column in Table 4.3). The sociogram also reveals Jeff's popularity with his colleagues.

■ Probably some factions and interpersonal tensions exist within the group. Notice that Peter, Sara, and Terri form a subclique, or "island," that is separated from the larger clique that Jeff leads. The apparent liaison between these two groups is Joe, who has mutual choices with both Jeff and Peter.

TABLE 4.3 ▮ Data from Figure 4.3 Presented as a Sociometric Matrix

				How Each Person Was Rated by the Others					
		Gretchen	Joe	Greg	Sara	Peter	Jeff	Tim	Matt	Terri
How Each Person Rated the Others	Gretchen	—	0	0	0	−1	+1	0	+1	0
	Joe	0	—	0	0	+1	+1	0	0	0
	Greg	0	0	—	0	0	+1	0	+1	0
	Sara	0	0	0	—	+1	0	0	0	+1
	Peter	0	+1	0	0	—	−1	0	0	+1
	Jeff	+1	+1	0	0	0	—	0	0	0
	Tim	0	0	+1	0	−1	+1	—	0	0
	Matt	+1	0	0	0	0	+1	0	—	0
	Terri	0	0	0	+1	+1	0	0	0	—
	Totals	2	2	1	1	1	4	0	2	2

▮ Friendship pairs may lend cohesion to the group. Notice the mutual choices: Matt and Gretchen, Gretchen and Jeff, Jeff and Joe, Joe and Peter, Peter and Terri, Terri and Sara. The sociogram clearly reveals these alliances.

▮ Tim is apparently the isolate of the group. He received no choices; he is neither liked nor disliked. In such a position, he is probably the least influential member of the group.

With this example we have illustrated what it means to interpret data by measuring an insubstantial phenomenon and analyzing the resulting data. Notice that we didn't just observe the behaviors of nine individuals at a social event; we also looked below the surface to identify possible hidden social forces at play. Our example is a simple one, to be sure. Measurement of interpersonal dynamics and social networks can certainly take more complex forms, including some that are especially helpful in studying social forces within large, extended groups (e.g., Chatterjee & Srivastava, 1982; Freeman, 2004; Wasserman & Faust, 1994).

Types of Measurement Scales

Virtually any form of measurement falls into one of four categories, or scales: nominal, ordinal, interval, and ratio (Stevens, 1946). The scale of measurement will ultimately dictate the statistical procedures (if any) that can be used in processing the data.

Nominal Scales

The word *nominal* comes from the Latin *nomen,* meaning "name." Hence we might "measure" data to some degree simply by assigning a name to each data point. Recall that the definition of measurement presented earlier includes the phrase *limiting the data.* That is what a nominal scale does—it limits the data—and just about all that it does. Assign a specific name to anything, and you have restricted that thing to the meaning of its name. For example, we can measure a group of children by dividing it into two groups: girls and boys. Each subgroup is thereby measured—restricted—by virtue of gender as belonging to a particular category.

Things can be measured nominally in an infinite number of ways. We can further measure girls and boys according to where each of them lives. Imagine that the town in which the children live is divided into two sections by Main Street, which runs from east to west. Those children who live north of Main Street are "the Northerners"; those who live south of it are "the Southerners." In one period of U.S. history, people measured the population of the entire nation in just such a manner.

Nominal measurement is quite simplistic, but it does divide data into discrete categories that can be compared with one another. Let's take an example. Imagine that we have six children: Zahra, Paul, Kathy, Binh, Ginger, and Nicky. They can be divided into six units of one child each. They can also form two groups: Zahra, Kathy, and Ginger (the girls) in one group and Paul, Binh, and Nicky (the boys) in the other. Perhaps all six children are students in a class that meets in Room 12 at Thompson's Corner School. By assigning a room number, we have provided the class with a name, even though that "name" is a number. In this case, the number has no quantitative meaning: Room 12 isn't necessarily bigger or better than Room 11, nor is it inferior to Room 13.

Only a few statistical procedures are appropriate for analyzing nominal data. We can use the *mode* as an indicator of the most frequently occurring category within our data set; for example, we might determine that there are more boys than girls in Room 12 at Thompson's Corner School. We can find the *percentage* of people in various subgroups within the total group; for example, we could calculate the percentage of boys in each classroom. We can use a *chi-square test* to compare the relative frequencies of people in various categories; for example, we might discover that more boys than girls live north of Main Street but that more girls than boys live south of Main Street. (We discuss these statistics, as well as the statistics listed in the following discussions of the other three scales, in Chapter 8.)

Ordinal Scales

With an **ordinal scale**, we can think in terms of the symbols > (greater than) and < (less than). We can compare various pieces of data in terms of one being greater or higher than another. In essence, this scale allows us to *rank-order* data—hence its name *ordinal*.

As an example, we can roughly measure level of education on an ordinal scale by classifying people as being unschooled or having completed an elementary, high school, college, or graduate education. Likewise, we can roughly measure members of the workforce by grades of proficiency: unskilled, semiskilled, or skilled.

An ordinal scale expands the range of statistical techniques we can apply to our data. In addition to the statistics we can use with nominal data, we can also determine the *median*, or halfway point, in a set of data. We can use a *percentile rank* to identify the relative position of any item or individual in a group. We can determine the extent of the relationship between two characteristics by means of Spearman's *rank order correlation*.

Interval Scales

An **interval scale** is characterized by two features: (a) it has equal units of measurement, and (b) its zero point has been established arbitrarily. The Fahrenheit (F) and Celsius (C) scales for measuring temperature are examples of interval scales: The intervals between any two successive numbers of degrees reflect equal changes in temperature, but the zero point doesn't indicate a total absence of heat. For instance, when Gabriel Fahrenheit was developing his Fahrenheit scale, he made his zero point the lowest temperature obtainable with a mixture of salt and ice, and his 100 degrees was what he determined to be human beings' average body temperature. These were purely arbitrary decisions. They placed the freezing point of water at 32° and the boiling point at 212° above zero.

Interval scales of measurement allow statistical analyses that aren't possible with nominal or ordinal data. Because an interval scale reflects equal distances among adjacent points, any statistics that are calculated using addition or subtraction—for instance, *means, standard deviations,* and *Pearson product moment correlations*—can now be used.

Many people who conduct surveys use rating scales to measure certain insubstantial characteristics, and they often assume that the results such scales yield are interval data. But are they *really* interval data? In some cases they might be, but in other situations they might not. Let's look at an example. Many universities ask students to use rating scales to evaluate the teaching effectiveness of various professors. Following is an example of an item from one university's teaching evaluation form:

Place an X on the scale below at the point
where you would rate the availability of your
professor for conferences.

| ....!.........!.........!.........!.........!.........!.........!.........!.........!.........!

| 0 | 10 | 20 | 30 | 40 | 50 | 60 | 70 | 80 | 90 | 100 |

Never
available   Seldom   Available by   Generally   Always
                   available   appointment only   available   available

Notice that the scale includes points ranging from 0 to 100. At five points along the scale are descriptive labels that can help students determine how they should rate their professor's availability. The numbers themselves reflect equal intervals, but the specific ratings that students assign may not. For instance, is the difference between "never available" and "seldom available" equivalent to the difference between "available by appointment only" and "generally available"? Not necessarily: Some students may think of the word *seldom* as being almost as bad as the word *never,* or they might think of "generally available" as being quite a bit better than "available by appointment only." If this is true, then the rating scale is really yielding ordinal rather than interval data.

Ratio Scales

Two commonly used measurement instruments—a thermometer and a yardstick—might help you understand the difference between the interval and ratio scales. If we have a thermometer that measures temperature on the Fahrenheit scale, we can*not* say that 80°F is twice as warm as 40°F. Why? Because this scale doesn't originate from a point of absolute zero; a substance may have some degree of heat even though its measured temperature falls *below* zero. With a yardstick, however, the beginning of linear measurement is absolutely the beginning. If we measure a desk from the left edge to the right edge, that's it. There's no more desk in either direction beyond those limits. A measurement of "zero" means there is no desk at all, and a "minus" desk width isn't even possible.

More generally, a **ratio scale** has two characteristics: (a) equal measurement units (similar to an interval scale) and (b) *an absolute zero point,* such that 0 on the scale reflects a total absence of the entity being measured.

Let's consider once again the "availability" scale presented earlier for measuring professor effectiveness. This scale could never be considered a ratio scale. Why? Because there is only one condition in which the professor would be absolutely unavailable—if the professor were dead!—in which case we wouldn't be asking students to evaluate this individual.

What distinguishes the ratio scale from the other three scales is that *the ratio scale can express values in terms of multiples and fractional parts,* and the ratios are *true* ratios. A yardstick can do that: A yard is a *multiple* (by 36) of a 1-inch distance; an inch is one-twelfth (a *fractional part*) of a foot. The ratios are 36:1 and 1:12, respectively.

Ratio scales outside the physical sciences are relatively rare. And whenever we cannot measure a phenomenon in terms of a ratio scale, we must refrain from making comparisons such as "this thing is three times as great as that" or "we have only half as much of one thing as another." Only ratio scales allow us to make comparisons that involve multiplication or division.

We can summarize our description of the four scales this way:

If you can say that
- One object is different from another, you have a *nominal scale;*
- One object is bigger or better or more of anything than another, you have an *ordinal scale;*
- One object is so many units (degrees, inches) more than another, you have an *interval scale;*
- One object is so many times as big or bright or tall or heavy as another, you have a *ratio scale.*
  (Senders, 1958, p. 51)

TABLE 4.4 ■ A Summary of Measurement Scales, Their Characteristics, and Their Statistical Implications

	Measurement Scale	Characteristics of the Scale	Statistical Possibilities of the Scale
Non-Interval Scales	Nominal scale	A scale that "measures" only in terms of names or designations of discrete units or categories	Enables one to determine the mode, percentage values, or chi-square
	Ordinal scale	A scale that measures in terms of such values as "more" or "less," "larger" or "smaller," but without specifying the size of the intervals	Enables one also to determine the median, percentile rank, and rank correlation
Interval Scales	Interval scale	A scale that measures in terms of equal intervals or degrees of difference, but with an arbitrarily established zero point that does not represent "nothing" of something	Enables one also to determine the mean, standard deviation, and product moment correlation; allows one to conduct most inferential statistical analyses
	Ratio scale	A scale that measures in terms of equal intervals and an absolute zero point	Enables one also to determine the geometric mean and make proportional comparisons; allows one to conduct virtually any inferential statistical analysis

Table 4.4 provides a quick reference for the various types of scales, their distinguishing characteristics, and the statistical analysis possibilities for each scale. When we consider the statistical interpretation of data in later chapters (especially in Chapter 8), you may want to refer to this table to determine whether the type of measurement instrument you have used will support the statistical operation you are contemplating.

CONCEPTUAL ANALYSIS EXERCISE Identifying Scales of Measurement

USING TECHNOLOGY

Each of the following scenarios involves measuring one or more variables. Decide whether the various measurements reflect nominal, ordinal, interval, or ratio scales, and justify your choices. Be careful, as the answers are not always as obvious as they might initially appear. The answers are provided after the "For Further Reading" list at the end of the chapter.

1. An environmental scientist collects water samples from streams and rivers near large industrial plants and saves exactly 1 liter of water from each sample. Then, back at the lab, the researcher determines the amounts of certain health-jeopardizing bacteria in each sample. What measurement scale does the measurement of bacteria content reflect?

2. A tourism researcher is studying the relationship between (a) a country's average annual temperature and (b) the amount of tourist dollars that the country brings in every year. What scales underlie the two variables in this study?

3. A political science researcher in the United States wants to determine whether people's political party membership is correlated with the frequency with which they have voted in local elections in the past 5 years. The researcher can easily obtain information about people's party membership and voting records from town clerks in several communities. To simplify data collection, the researcher uses the following coding scheme for party membership: 1 = Registered as Democrat, 2 = Registered as Republican, 3 = Registered as member of another party, 0 = No declared party affiliation. What measurement scale(s) underlie (a) political party membership and (b) voting frequency?

4. A marketing researcher in the United States wants to determine whether a certain product is more widely used in some parts of the country than others. The researcher

separates the country into 10 regions based on zip code; zip codes below 10000 are northeastern states, zip codes of 90000 and above are western states, and so on. What measurement scale does the researcher's coding scheme for the regions represent?

5. An economist is studying the home-buying behaviors of people of different income levels. The researcher puts people into four categories: Group A includes those earning up to $20,000 per year, Group B includes those earning between $20,001 and $50,000 per year, Group C includes those earning between $50,001 and $100,000 per year, and Group D includes those earning more than $100,000 per year. In this study, what kind of scale is income level?

6. A geographer is studying traffic patterns on four different types of roads that vary in quality: superhighways (i.e., roads accessible only by relatively infrequent on–off ramps), highways (i.e., roads that allow relatively high speeds for long distances but may have an occasional traffic light), secondary roads (i.e., well-paved two-lane roads), and tertiary roads (narrow, infrequently traveled roads; some may consist only of gravel). The type of road in this study reflects which type of measurement scale?

7. A psychologist is developing an instrument designed to measure college students' test anxiety. The instrument includes 25 statements—for example, "My heart starts to pound when I see the word *test* on a course syllabus" and "My palms get sweaty while I'm taking a multiple-choice test." Students must rate each of these statements on a 5-point scale, as follows:

   0   This is never true for me.
   1   This is rarely true for me.
   2   This is sometimes true for me.
   3   This is often true for me.
   4   This is always true for me.

Students who answer "never" to each of the 25 questions get the lowest possible score of 0 on the instrument. Students who answer "always" to each of the 25 questions get the highest possible score of 100 on the instrument. Thus, scores on the instrument range from 0 to 100. What kind of scale do the scores represent?

Validity and Reliability in Measurement

Earlier in the chapter we discussed the importance of determining that your chosen method will have validity for your purpose—that it will yield meaningful, credible results. When used to describe a measurement tool, however, the term *validity* has a somewhat different meaning. Regardless of the type of scale a measurement instrument involves, the instrument must have both validity and another, related characteristic—*reliability*—for its intended purpose. The validity and reliability of measurement instruments influence the extent to which a researcher can legitimately learn something about the phenomenon under investigation, the probability that the researcher will obtain statistical significance in any data analysis, and the extent to which the researcher can draw meaningful conclusions from the data.

Validity of Measurement Instruments

The validity of a measurement instrument is the extent to which the instrument measures what it is intended to measure. Certainly no one would question the premise that a yardstick is a valid means of measuring length. Nor would most people doubt that a thermometer measures temperature; for instance, in a mercury thermometer, the level to which the mercury rises is a function of how much it expands, which is a function of the degree to which it is hot or cold.

But to what extent does an intelligence test actually measure a person's intelligence? How accurately do people's annual incomes reflect their social class? And how well does a sociogram capture the interpersonal dynamics in a group of nine people? Especially when we are measuring *insubstantial* phenomena—phenomena without a direct basis in the physical world—our measurement instruments may be somewhat suspect in terms of validity.

Let's return to the rating-scale item presented earlier to assess a professor's availability to students and consider its validity as such a measure. Some of the labels are quite fuzzy and hard to pin down. The professor is "always available." What does *always* mean? Twenty-four hours a day? Could you call the professor at 3:00 a.m. any day of the week or, instead, only whenever the professor is on campus? If the latter is the case, could you call your professor out of a faculty meeting or out of a conference with the college president? We might have similar problems in interpreting "generally available," "seldom available," and "never available." On careful inspection, what seems at first glance to be a scale that anyone could understand has limitations *as a measurement instrument* for research purposes.

A paper-and-pencil test may be intended to measure a certain characteristic, and it may be *called* a measure of that characteristic, but these facts don't necessarily mean that the test actually measures what its creator says it does. For example, consider a paper-and-pencil test of personality traits in which, with a series of check marks, a person indicates his or her most representative characteristics or behaviors in given situations. The person's responses on the test are presumed to reveal relatively stable personality traits. But *does* such a test, in fact, measure the person's personality traits, or does it measure something else altogether? The answer depends, at least in part, on the extent to which the person is or *can* be truthful in responding. If the person responds in terms of characteristics and behaviors that he or she believes to be socially desirable, the test results may reveal not the person's actual personality, but rather an idealized portrait of how he or she would like to be perceived by others.

The validity of a measurement instrument can take several different forms, each of which is important in different situations:

- Face validity is the extent to which, on the surface, an instrument *looks like* it is measuring a particular characteristic. Face validity is often useful for ensuring the cooperation of people who are participating in a research study. But because it relies entirely on subjective judgment, it is not, in and of itself, a terribly dependable indicator that an instrument is truly measuring what the researcher wants to measure.

- Content validity is the extent to which a measurement instrument is a representative sample of the content area (domain) being measured. Content validity is often a consideration when a researcher wants to assess people's *achievement* in some area—for instance, the knowledge students have acquired during classroom instruction or the new skills employees have acquired in a training program. A measurement instrument has high content validity if its items or questions reflect the various parts of the content domain in appropriate proportions and if it requires the particular behaviors and skills that are central to that domain.

- Criterion validity is the extent to which the results of an assessment instrument correlate with another, presumably related measure (the latter measure is, in this case, the *criterion*). For example, a personality test designed to assess a person's shyness or outgoingness has criterion validity if its scores correlate with other measures of a person's general sociability. An instrument designed to measure a salesperson's effectiveness on the job should correlate with the number of sales the individual actually makes during the course of a business week.

- Construct validity is the extent to which an instrument measures a characteristic that cannot be directly observed but is assumed to exist based on patterns in people's behavior (such a characteristic is a *construct*). Motivation, creativity, racial prejudice, happiness—all of these are constructs, in that none of them can be *directly* observed and measured. When researchers ask questions, present tasks, or observe behaviors as a way of assessing an underlying construct, they should obtain some kind of evidence that their approach does, in fact, measure the construct in question.

Sometimes there is universal agreement that a particular instrument provides a valid instrument for measuring a particular characteristic; such is the case for yardsticks, thermometers, barometers, and oscilloscopes. But whenever we do *not* have such widespread agreement, we must provide evidence that an instrument we are using has validity for our purpose.

It is critical to note that the validity of any measurement instrument can vary considerably depending on the purpose for which it is being used. In other words, *the validity of an instrument is specific to the situation.* For example, a tape measure wrapped horizontally around a person's head is a valid measure of the person's head circumference but *not* a valid measure of the person's intelligence. Likewise, a widely used intelligence test might provide a reasonable estimate of children's general cognitive development but is *not* suitable for determining how well the children can perform in, say, a geometry class or interpersonal conflict.

Determining the Validity of a Measurement Instrument   An in-depth discussion of how to determine validity is beyond the scope of this book; measurement textbooks such as those listed in this chapter's "For Further Reading" section provide more detailed information. But here we offer three examples of what researchers sometimes do to demonstrate that their measurement instruments have validity for their purposes:

- *Table of specifications.*   To construct a measurement instrument that provides a representative sample of a particular content domain—in other words, to establish content validity—a researcher often constructs a two-dimensional grid, or **table of specifications**, that lists the specific topics and behaviors that reflect achievement in the domain. In each cell of the grid, the researcher indicates the relative importance of each topic–behavior combination. He or she then develops a series of tasks or test items that reflects the various topics and behaviors in appropriate proportions.
- *Multitrait–multimethod approach.*   In a **multitrait–multimethod approach**, two or more different characteristics are each measured using two or more different approaches (Campbell & Fiske, 1959; Campbell & Russo, 2001). The different measures of the same characteristic should be highly correlated. The same ways of measuring different characteristics should *not* be highly correlated. For example, in a classroom situation, the constructs *academic motivation* and *social motivation* might each be measured by both self-report questionnaires and teacher observation checklists. Statistical analyses should reveal that the two measures of academic motivation are highly correlated and that the two measures of social motivation are also highly correlated. Results from the two self-report questionnaires—because they are intended to assess different and presumably unrelated characteristics—should *not* be highly correlated, nor should results from the two teacher checklists.
- *Judgment by a panel of experts.*   Several experts in a particular area are asked to scrutinize an instrument and give an informed opinion about its validity for measuring the characteristic in question.

Although none of the approaches just described guarantees the validity of a measurement instrument, each one increases the likelihood of such validity.

Reliability of Measurement Instruments

Imagine that you are concerned about your growing waistline and decide to go on a diet. Every day you put a tape measure around your waist and pull the two ends together snugly to get a measurement. But just how tight is "snug"? Quite possibly, the level of snugness might be different from one day to the next. In fact, you might even measure your waist with different degrees of snugness from one *minute* to the next. To the extent that you aren't measuring your waist in a consistent fashion—even though you always use the same tape measure—you have a problem with reliability.

More generally, **reliability** is the consistency with which a measurement instrument yields a certain, consistent result when the entity being measured hasn't changed. As we have just seen in our waist-measuring situation, instruments that measure physical phenomena aren't necessarily completely reliable. As another example, think of a measuring cup that a baker might use while making a cake. When measuring a half-cup of flour, the baker won't always measure *exactly* the same amount of flour each time.

Instruments designed to measure social and psychological characteristics (insubstantial phenomena) tend to be even less reliable than those designed to measure physical (substantial) phenomena. For example, a student using the rating-scale item presented earlier for measuring professor availability might easily rate the professor as "70" one day and "90" the next, not because the professor's availability has changed overnight but because the student's interpretations of the phrases "generally available" and "always available" *have* changed. Similarly, if we asked the nine people portrayed in Figure 4.2 (Gretchen, Joe, Greg, etc.) to indicate the people they liked best and least among their colleagues, they wouldn't necessarily always give us the same answers they had given us previously, even if the interpersonal dynamics within the group have remained constant.

Determining the Reliability of a Measurement Instrument

Like validity, reliability takes different forms in different situations. But in the case of reliability, its particular form is essentially equivalent to the procedure used to determine it. Following are four forms of reliability that are frequently of interest in research studies:

- Interrater reliability is the extent to which two or more individuals evaluating the same product or performance give identical judgments.
- Test–retest reliability is the extent to which a single instrument yields the same results for the same people on two different occasions.
- Equivalent forms reliability is the extent to which two different versions of the same instrument (e.g., "Form A" and "Form B" of a scholastic aptitude test) yield similar results.
- Internal consistency reliability is the extent to which all of the items within a single instrument yield similar results.

For each of these forms, determining reliability involves two steps:

1. Getting two measures for each individual in a reasonably large group of individuals—in particular by doing one of the following:
   a. Having two different raters evaluate the same performance for each individual (interrater reliability)
   b. Administering the same instrument to the individuals at two different points in time—perhaps a day, a week, or a month apart (test–retest reliability)
   c. Giving each individual two parallel versions of the same instrument (equivalent forms reliability)
   d. Administering only one instrument but calculating two subscores for the instrument—for instance, calculating one score for odd-numbered items and another score for even-numbered items (internal consistency reliability)
2. Calculating a correlation coefficient that expresses the degree to which the two measures are similar (see Chapter 8 for a discussion of correlation coefficients)

You can find more in-depth discussions about determining reliability in almost any general measurement textbook.

Enhancing the Reliability and Validity of a Measurement Instrument

Both validity and reliability reflect the degree to which we may have *error* in our measurements. In many instances—and especially when we are measuring insubstantial phenomena—a measurement instrument may allow us to measure a characteristic only indirectly and so may be subject to a variety of biasing factors (e.g., people's responses on a rating scale might be influenced by their interpretations, prejudices, memory lapses, etc.). In such cases, we have error due to the imperfect *validity* of the measurement instrument. Yet typically—even when we are measuring substantial phenomena—we may get slightly different measures from one time to the next simply because our measurement tool is imprecise (e.g., the waist or head size we measure may depend on how snugly we pull the tape measure). In such cases, we have error due to the imperfect *reliability* of the measure. Generally speaking, validity errors reflect biases in the instrument itself and are relatively constant sources of error. In contrast, reliability errors reflect *use* of the instrument and are apt to vary unpredictably from one occasion to the next.

We can measure something accurately only when we can also measure it consistently. Hence, by increasing the reliability of a measurement instrument, we might also increase its validity. A researcher can enhance the reliability of a measurement instrument in several ways. First, the instrument should always be administered in a consistent fashion. In other words, there should be standardization in use of the instrument from one situation or individual to the next. Second, to the extent that subjective judgments are required, specific *criteria* should be established that dictate the kinds of judgments the researcher makes. And third, any research assistants who are using the instrument should be *well trained* so that they obtain similar results for any single individual or phenomenon being measured.

Yet even if we enhance the reliability of our measurements, we don't necessarily increase their accuracy. In other words, *reliability is a necessary but insufficient condition for validity*. For example, we could use a tape measure to measure a person's head circumference and claim that the result is a good reflection of intelligence. In this situation, we might have reasonable reliability—we are apt to get similar measures of an individual's head circumference on different occasions—but absolutely no validity. As noted earlier, head size is *not* a good indication of intelligence level.

Creative researchers use a variety of strategies to enhance the validity of their measurement instruments. One important strategy is to consult the literature in search of measurement techniques that other researchers have effectively used. Another is to show a first draft of an instrument to experienced colleagues and ask for their feedback and suggestions. Still another strategy is to conduct one or more *pilot studies* specifically to try out a particular instrument, carefully scrutinizing it for obvious or possible weaknesses and then modifying it in minor or major ways.

We cannot overemphasize the importance of determining and maximizing the validity and reliability of your measurement instruments. Without reasonably valid and reliable measures of the characteristics and phenomena under investigation, you cannot possibly obtain informative and useful data for addressing and solving your research problem.

As you plan your research project, you should clearly identify the nature of the measurement instruments you will use and carefully examine them with respect to their potential validity and reliability. Furthermore, in your research proposal and final research report, you should describe any instrument in explicit, concrete terms. For example, if you are using a particular piece of equipment to measure a certain physical characteristic or phenomenon, you should describe the equipment's specific nature (e.g., its manufacturer, model number, and level of precision). And if you are assessing some aspect of human thought or behavior, you should describe the questions asked or tasks administered, the overall length of the instrument (e.g., number of items, time required for administration), and the method of scoring responses.

CONCEPTUAL ANALYSIS EXERCISE Identifying Problems with Validity and Reliability in Measurement

USING TECHNOLOGY

In each of the scenarios in this exercise, a researcher encounters a measurement problem. Some of the scenarios reflect a problem with the validity of a measure. Others reflect a problem with a measure's reliability—a problem that indirectly also affects the measure's validity. For each scenario, choose the most obvious problem from among the following alternatives:

- Face validity
- Content validity
- Criterion validity
- Construct validity

- Interrater reliability
- Test–retest reliability
- Equivalent forms reliability
- Internal consistency reliability

The answers appear after the "For Further Reading" list at the end of this chapter.

1. After using two different methods for teaching basic tennis skills to non-tennis-playing adults, a researcher assesses the effectiveness of the two methods by administering a true–false test regarding the rules of the game (e.g., faults and double-faults, scoring procedures).

2. A researcher writes 120 multiple-choice questions to assess middle school students' general knowledge of basic world geography (e.g., what the equator is, where Africa is located). To minimize the likelihood that students will cheat on the test by copying one another's answers, the researcher divides the questions into three different sets to create three 40-item tests. In collecting data, the researcher distributes the three tests randomly to students in any single classroom. After administering the tests to students at many different middle schools, the researcher computes the students' test scores and discovers that students who answered one particular set of 40 questions scored an average of 3 points higher than students who answered either of the other two 40-question sets.

3. In order to determine what kinds of situations provoke aggression in gorillas, two researchers observe mountain gorillas in the Virunga Mountains of northwestern Rwanda. As they watch a particular gorilla family and take notes about family members' behaviors, the researchers often disagree about whether certain behaviors constitute "aggression" or, instead, reflect more benevolent "assertiveness."

4. A researcher uses a blood test to determine people's overall energy level after drinking or not drinking a can of a high-caffeine cola drink. Unfortunately, when two research assistants independently rate people's behaviors for energy level for a 4-hour period after drinking the cola, their results don't seem to have any correlation with the blood-test results.

5. In a 2-week period during the semester, a researcher gains entry into several college classrooms in order to administer a short survey regarding college students' beliefs about climate change. The survey consists of 20 statements about climate change (e.g., "Devastating floods in recent years are partly the result of the Earth's gradually rising overall temperature"), to which students must respond "Strongly disagree," "Disagree," "Agree," or "Strongly agree." Many of the students voluntarily put their names on their surveys. Thanks to the names on many survey forms, the researcher discovers that a few students were in two of the classes surveyed and thus completed the survey twice. Curiously, however, these students sometimes gave different responses to particular statements on the two different occasions, and hence their overall scores were also different.

6. In order to get a sense of how harmonious most long-term marriages are, a researcher administers a questionnaire to married couples who have been married for at least 20 years. The questionnaire consists of 60 statements to which both spouses must individually respond either "This describes my marriage" or "This doesn't describe my marriage." All 60 statements describe a possible characteristic of an unharmonious marriage (e.g., "We fight all the time," "We rarely agree about how to spend our money"), and the researcher has sequenced them in a random order on the questionnaire. Even so, the researcher discovers that respondents more frequently agree with the first 30 items than with the last 30 items. If one were to look only at responses to the first 30 items, then one would think that married couples fight a lot. But if one were to look only at responses to the last 30 items, one would conclude that most long-term couples live in relative peace and harmony. (*Note:* We recommend that questionnaires *not* be slanted in a one-way direction, as this one is; see the "Constructing a Questionnaire" guidelines in Chapter 6).

7. A researcher develops and uses a questionnaire intended to measure the extent to which college students display tolerance toward a particular religious group. However, several experts in the researcher's field of study suggest that the questionnaire measures not how tolerant students actually *are,* but what students would like to *believe* about their tolerance for people of a particular religion.

8. Students in an introductory college psychology course must satisfy their "research methods" requirement in one of several ways; one option is to participate in a research study called "Intelligence and Motor Skill Learning." When students choosing this option report to the laboratory, one of their tasks is to respond as quickly as possible to a series of simple computer-generated questions. Afterward, the researcher debriefs the students about the nature of the study and tells them that the reaction-time measure was designed to be a simple measure of intelligence. Some of the students object, saying, "That's not a measure of intelligence! Intelligence isn't how quickly you can do something, it's how *well* you can do it."

ETHICAL ISSUES IN RESEARCH

In certain disciplines—the social sciences, education, medicine, and similar areas of study—the use of human beings in research is, of course, quite common. And in biology the subjects of investigation are often nonhuman animals. Whenever human beings or other creatures with the potential to think, feel, and experience physical or psychological distress are the focus of investigation, researchers must look closely—during the *planning* stage—at the ethical implications of what they are proposing to do.

Most ethical issues in research fall into one of four categories: protection from harm, voluntary and informed participation, right to privacy, and honesty with professional colleagues. In the following sections we raise issues related to each of these categories. We then describe the internal review boards and professional codes of ethics that provide guidance for researchers.

Protection from Harm

Researchers should not expose research participants—whether they be human beings or nonhuman animals—to unnecessary physical or psychological harm. When a study involves human beings, the general rule of thumb is that the risk involved in participating in a study should not be appreciably greater than the normal risks of day-to-day living. Participants should not risk losing life or limb, nor should they be subjected to unusual stress, embarrassment, or loss of self-esteem.

In thinking about this issue, researchers must be particularly sensitive to and thoughtful about potential harm they might cause participants from especially vulnerable populations (Sieber, 2000). For example, some participants may have allergies or health conditions that place them at greater-than-average risk in certain environments or with certain foods or medications. Participants of a particular gender, cultural background, or sexual orientation might feel embarrassed or otherwise uncomfortable when asked to answer some kinds of questions or to engage in some kinds of activities. Special care must be taken with participants who cannot easily advocate for their own needs and desires—such as children, elderly individuals, and people with significant physical or mental disabilities.

Especially when working with human participants, a researcher should ideally also think about potential *benefits* that participation in a study might offer. At a minimum, the researcher should treat all participants in a courteous and respectful manner. A researcher can also consider how people might gain something useful from participating in a study—perhaps unique insights about a topic of personal interest or perhaps simply a sense of satisfaction about contributing in a small way to advancements in society's collective knowledge about the world. In some cases a researcher can offer an incentive for participating (e.g., money or course credit), provided that it isn't so excessive that it's essentially a form of disguised coercion (Scott-Jones, 2000).[5]

---

[5]Two qualifications should be noted here. When working with children, enticing incentives should be offered *only after* parents have already given permission for their participation. And when offering course credit to college students, alternative ways to earn the same credit must be provided as well—for instance, reading and writing a review of a research article (Scott-Jones, 2000).

In cases where the nature of a study involves creating a small amount of psychological discomfort, participants should know this ahead of time, and any necessary debriefing or counseling should follow immediately after their participation. A debriefing can simultaneously accomplish several things (Sales & Folkman, 2000):

- It can help alleviate any uncomfortable reactions—either anticipated or unanticipated—to certain questions, tasks, or activities.
- It can alert the researcher to necessary follow-up interventions for any participants experiencing extreme reactions.
- It provides an opportunity for the researcher to correct any misinformation participants might have gotten during the study.
- It provides a time during which participants can learn more about the nature and goals of the study, about how its results may fit in with what is already known about a topic, and about the nature of research more generally.

Voluntary and Informed Participation

When research involves public documents or records that human beings have previously created—such as birth certificates, newspaper articles, and Internet websites—such documents and records are generally considered to be fair game for research investigation. But when people are specifically recruited for participation in a research study, they should be told the nature of the study to be conducted and given the choice of either participating or not participating. Furthermore, they should be told that, if they agree to participate, they have the right to withdraw from the study at any time. And under no circumstances should people feel pressure to participate from employers or other more powerful individuals. *Any participation in a study should be strictly voluntary.*

In general, research with human beings requires **informed consent**. That is, participants—or legal guardians in the case of children and certain other populations—must know the nature of the study and grant written permission. One common practice—and one that is *required* for certain kinds of studies at most research institutions—is to present an **informed consent form** that describes the nature of the research project, as well as the nature of one's participation in it. Such a form should contain the following information:

- A brief description of the nature and goal(s) of the study, written in language that its readers can readily understand
- A description of what participation will involve in terms of activities and duration
- A statement indicating that participation is voluntary and can be terminated at any time without penalty
- A description of any potential risk and/or discomfort that participants might encounter
- A description of potential benefits of the study, including those for participants, science, and/or human society as a whole
- A guarantee that all responses will remain confidential and anonymous
- The researcher's name, plus information about how the researcher can be contacted
- An individual or office that participants can contact if they have questions or concerns about the study
- An offer to provide detailed information about the study (e.g., a summary of findings) upon its completion
- A place for the participant to sign and date the letter, indicating agreement to participate (when children are asked to participate, their parents must read and sign the letter)

An example of such a form, used by Rose McCallin in a research project for her doctoral dissertation, is presented in Figure 4.4. The form was used to recruit college students who were enrolled in a class in a teacher preparation program. It is missing one important ingredient: an offer to provide information about the study after its completion. Instead, McCallin appeared in class a few weeks after she had collected data to give a summary of the study and its implications for teachers.

Understanding How Students Organize Knowledge

You are being asked to participate in a study investigating ways in which students organize their knowledge.

We are interested in determining how students organize their knowledge in memory and use that knowledge. It is hoped that the results of this study can be useful in helping teachers understand why students perform differently from one another in the classroom.

As a future teacher, you will most likely have to use your knowledge in a variety of situations. However, relatively little is known about relationships among factors involved in knowledge application. Your participation may help to clarify some of these relationships so that we can better identify why students perform differently. And, although you may not directly benefit from this research, results from the study may be useful for future students, both those you teach and those who, like yourself, plan to be teachers.

If you agree to participate, you will complete two activities. In addition, we need to use your anonymous grade point average (GPA) as a control variable in order to account for initial differences among students. To ensure anonymity, we will submit only your social security number to the UNC Registrar, who will use this number to locate your GPA. The Registrar will black out the first three digits of your social security number before giving us this information, and the remaining 6-digit number will be used only to keep track of your performance on the other activities. You will not be putting your name on anything except this form. And, there will be no attempt to link your name with the last 6 digits of your social security number because individual performance is not of interest in this study. Only group results will be reported.

In the first activity, you will be asked to complete a 15-minute Self-Rating Checklist. This checklist consists of statements about knowledge application that you will judge to be true or false according to how each statement applies to you. In the second activity (which will be administered 2 days later), you will be given a list of concepts and asked to organize them on a sheet of paper, connect concepts you believe to be related, and describe the type of relationship between each connected pair of concepts. This activity should take about 30 minutes.

Although all studies have some degree of risk, the potential in this investigation is quite minimal. All activities are similar to normal classroom procedures, and all performance is anonymous. You will not incur any costs as a result of your participation in this study.

Your participation is voluntary. If at any time during this study you wish to withdraw your participation, you are free to do so without prejudice.

If you have any questions prior to your participation or at any time during the study, please do not hesitate to contact us.

AUTHORIZATION: I have read the above and understand the nature of this study. I understand that by agreeing to participate in this study I have not waived any legal or human right and that I may contact the researchers at the University of Northern Colorado (Dr. Jeanne Ormrod or Rose McCallin, 303-555-2807) at any time. I agree to participate in this study. I understand that I may refuse to participate or I may withdraw from the study at any time without prejudice. I also grant permission to the researchers to obtain my anonymous grade point average from the UNC Registrar for use as a control variable in the study. In addition, I understand that if I have any concerns about my treatment during the study, I can contact the Chair of the Internal Review Board at the University of Northern Colorado (303-555-2392) at any time.

Participant's signature: _____   Date: _____

Researcher's signature: _____   Date: _____

FIGURE 4.4 ■ Example of an Informed Consent Form

Source: Adapted from *Knowledge Application Orientation, Cognitive Structure, and Achievement* (pp. 109–110), by R. C. McCallin, 1988, unpublished doctoral dissertation, University of Northern Colorado, Greeley. Adapted with permission.

A dilemma sometimes arises as to *how informed* potential participants should be. If people are given too much information—for instance, if they are told the specific research hypothesis being tested—they may behave differently than they would under more normal circumstances (recall the earlier description of a study involving classical music and typists' productivity). A reasonable compromise is to give potential participants a general idea of what the study is about (e.g., "This study is investigating the effects of a physical exercise program on people's overall mental health") and to describe what specific activities their participation will involve—in other words, to give them sufficient information to make a reasonable, informed judgment about whether they want to participate.

On rare occasions (e.g., in some studies of social behavior), telling participants the true nature of a study might lead them to behave in ways that would defeat the purpose of the study. In general, deception of any kind is frowned on and should be used only when the study cannot meaningfully be conducted without it. Even then, the degree of deception should be as minimal as possible, and participants should be told the true nature of the research as soon as their involvement is over. (An internal review board, to be described shortly, can give you guidance regarding this matter.)

Earlier in the chapter we mentioned the use of unobtrusive measures as a strategy for measuring behavior. Strictly speaking, unobtrusive measures violate the principle of informed consent. But if people's behaviors are merely being recorded in some way during their normal daily activities—if people are not being asked to do something they ordinarily would not do—and if they are not being scrutinized in any way that might be potentially invasive or embarrassing, then unobtrusive measures are quite appropriate. Recall our two earlier examples: examining the frequency with which people used different parts of the library and the frequency with which people hiked along certain trails in a national park. Both of these examples involved behaviors within the scope of participants' normal activities.

Right to Privacy

Any research study involving human beings must respect participants' right to privacy. Under no circumstances should a research report, either oral or written, be presented in such a way that other people become aware of how a particular participant has responded or behaved—unless, of course, the participant has specifically granted permission *in writing* for this to happen.

In general, a researcher must keep the nature and quality of individual participants' performance strictly confidential. For instance, the researcher might give each participant a unique, arbitrary code number and then label any written documents with that number rather than with the person's name. And if a particular person's behavior is described in depth in the research report, he or she should be given a pseudonym—and other trivial, irrelevant details that might give away the person's identity should be changed—to ensure anonymity.

In this age of the Internet, researchers must also take precautions that computer hackers cannot access participants' individual data. Our advice here is simple: Don't post raw data or easily decodable data about individual participants online in any form. If you use the Internet to share your data with co-researchers living elsewhere, use e-mail and well-encoded attachments to transmit your data set; send your coding scheme in a separate e-mail message at another time.

Occasionally employers or other powerful individuals in a research setting might put considerable pressure on a researcher to reveal participants' individual responses. The researcher must not give in to such pressure. Knowledge about participants' individual performances should be revealed *only* to any co-researchers who have a significant role in the research investigation unless participants have specifically granted permission *in writing* that it be shared with certain other individuals. There is one important exception to this rule: Researchers are legally obligated to report to the proper authorities any information that suggests present or imminent danger to someone (e.g., child abuse, a planned terrorist act).

Honesty with Professional Colleagues

Researchers must report their findings in a complete and honest fashion, without misrepresenting what they have done or intentionally misleading others about the nature of their findings. And under no circumstances should a researcher fabricate data to support a particular conclusion, no matter how seemingly "noble" that conclusion might be. Such an action constitutes scientific fraud, plain and simple.

Within this context, we ask you to recall our discussion in Chapter 3 about giving appropriate credit where credit is due. Any use of another person's ideas or words demands full acknowledgment; otherwise, it constitutes plagiarism and—to be blunt—makes you a thief. Full acknowledgment of all material belonging to another person is mandatory. To appropriate the thoughts, ideas, or words of another without acknowledgment—even if you paraphrase the borrowed ideas in your own language—is dishonest, unethical, and highly circumspect. Honest researchers don't hesitate to acknowledge their indebtedness to others.

Internal Review Boards

Historically, some researchers had few (if any) scruples about the harm they inflicted on certain people or animals. Among the most notorious were German doctors who conducted horrific experiments on concentration camp prisoners during World War II—experiments that sometimes resulted in death or permanent disabilities. Other researchers, too, exposed people or animals to conditions that created significant physical or psychological harm, with virtually no oversight by more ethical colleagues. Fortunately, safeguards are now in place in many countries to keep inappropriate experimentation in check.

In the United States, in Canada, and among members of the European Union, any college, university, or research institution must have an internal review board (IRB)[6] that scrutinizes all proposals for conducting human research under the auspices of the institution. This board, which is made up of scholars and researchers across a broad range of disciplines, checks proposed research studies to be sure that the procedures are not unduly harmful to participants, that appropriate procedures will be followed to obtain participants' informed consent, and that participants' privacy and anonymity are ensured.

It is important to note that the research is reviewed at the proposal stage. *A proposal must be submitted to and approved by the IRB before a single datum is collected.* Depending on the extent to which the study intrudes in some way on people's lives and imposes risk to participants, the board's chairperson may (a) quickly declare it *exempt from review,* (b) give it an *expedited review,* or (c) bring it before the board for a *full review.* In any case, the researcher cannot begin the study until either the board has given its seal of approval or the researcher has made modifications that the board requests.

The criteria and procedures of an IRB vary slightly from one institution to another. For examples of institutional policies and procedures, you might want to visit the websites of Tufts University (tnemcirb.tufts.edu), the University of Northern Colorado (unco.edu/osp/ethics), or the University of Texas (utexas.edu/research/rsc). You can find other helpful sites on the Internet by using a search engine (e.g., Google, Bing, or Yahoo!) and such keywords as *IRB, human participants,* and *human subjects.*

Universities and other research institutions have review boards for animal research as well. Any research that may potentially cause suffering, distress, or death to animals must be described and adequately justified to an institutional animal care and use committee (IACUC). Furthermore, the researcher must minimize or prevent such suffering and death to the extent that it's possible to do so. For examples of research institutions' IACUC policies and procedures, we refer you to the University of Maryland (umresearch.umd.edu/IACUC) and the University of Arizona (uac.arizona.edu).

Many novice researchers view IRB and IACUC reviews as a bothersome hurdle to jump in their efforts to carry out a successful research project. We authors can assure you that members of these boards want to encourage and support research—*not* impede it—and typically work hard to make their proposal reviews as quick and painless as possible. Also, they can give helpful advice to ensure that your study does not needlessly jeopardize the welfare of participants in your study.

Professional Codes of Ethics

Many disciplines have their own codes of ethical standards governing research that involves human subjects and, when applicable, research involving animal subjects as well. One good source of discipline-specific ethical codes is the Internet. Following are examples of organizational websites with ethical codes related to research in their disciplines:

American Anthropological Association (aaanet.org)

American Association for Public Opinion Research (aapor.org)

---

[6]Some institutions use a different label (e.g., *Institutional Review Board, Committee for Protection of Human Subjects*).

American Educational Research Association (aera.net)
American Psychological Association (apa.org)
American Sociological Association (asanet.org)
Society for Conservation Biology (conbio.org)

PRACTICAL APPLICATION Planning an Ethical Research Study

Ethical practices in research begin *at the planning* stage. The following checklist can help you scrutinize your own project for its potential ethical implications.

✔ CHECKLIST

Determining Whether Your Proposed Study Is Ethically Defensible

_____ 1. Might your study present any physical risks or hazards to participants? If so, list them here.

_____

_____

_____ 2. Might your study incur any psychological harm to all or some participants (e.g., offensive stimulus materials, threats to self-esteem)? If so, identify the specific forms of harm that might result.

_____

_____

_____ 3. Will participants incur any significant financial costs (e.g., transportation costs, mailing expenses)? If so, how might you minimize or eliminate those costs?

_____

_____

_____ 4. What benefits might your study have for (a) participants, (b) your discipline, and (c) society at large?

_____

_____

_____ 5. Do you need to seek informed consent from participants? Why or why not?

_____

_____

_____ 6. If you need to seek informed consent, how might you explain the nature and goals of your study to potential participants in a way that they can understand? Write a potential explanation here.

_____

_____

_____

_____ 7. What specific steps will you take to ensure participants' privacy? List them here.

_____

_____

_____ 8. If applicable, what format might a post-participation debriefing take? What information should you include in your debriefing?

_____

_____

CRITICALLY SCRUTINIZING YOUR OVERALL PLAN

At this point, you have presumably (a) attended to the nature and availability of the data you need; (b) decided whether a quantitative, qualitative, or mixed-methods methodology is best suited to address your research problem; (c) possibly identified valid, reliable ways of measuring certain variables; and (d) examined the ethical implications of what you intend to do. But ultimately, you must step back a bit and look at the overall forest—the big picture—rather than at the specific, nitty-gritty trees. And you must definitely be realistic and practical regarding what you can reasonably accomplish. Remember the title of this book: ***Practical*** *Research*.

PRACTICAL APPLICATION Judging the Feasibility of a Research Project

Many beginning researchers avoid looking closely at the practical aspects of a research endeavor. Envisioning an exotic investigation or a solve-the-problems-of-the-world study sometimes keeps a researcher from making an impartial judgment about practicality. Completing the following checklist can help you wisely plan and accurately evaluate the research you have in mind. After you have finished, review your responses. Then answer this question: Can you reasonably accomplish this study? If your answer is *no,* determine which parts of the project are not terribly practical, and identify things you might do to make it more realistically accomplishable.

✓ CHECKLIST

Determining Whether a Proposed Research Project Is Realistic and Practical

THE PROBLEM

_____ 1. With what area(s) will the problem deal?

_____ People

_____ Things

_____ Records

_____ Thoughts and ideas

_____ Dynamics and energy

_____ 2. Are data that relate directly to the problem available for each of the categories you've just checked? _____ Yes _____ No

_____ 3. What academic discipline is primarily concerned with the problem?

_____

_____ 4. What other academic disciplines are possibly also related to the problem?

_____

_____ 5. What special qualifications do you have as a researcher for this problem?

_____ Interest in the problem

_____ Experience in the problem area

_____ Education and/or training

_____ Other (specify): _____

THE DATA

_____ 6. How available are the data to you?

_____ Readily available

_____ Available with permission

_____ Available with great difficulty or rarely available

_____ Unavailable

_____ 7. How often are you personally in contact with the source of the data?

_____ Once a day   _____ Once a week   _____ Never

_____ Once a month   _____ Once a year

_____ 8. Will the data arise directly out of a situation you create?

_____ Yes   _____ No

If your answer is no, where or how will you obtain the data?

_____

_____

_____

_____ 9. How do you plan to gather the data?

_____ Observation _____ Questionnaire _____ Test _____ Rating scale

_____ Photocopying of records _____ Interview and audio recording

_____ Specialized machine/device _____ Computer technology

_____ Other (explain): _____

_____

_____ 10. Is special equipment or are special conditions necessary for gathering or processing the data?

_____ Yes   _____ No

If your answer is yes, specify: _____

_____

_____ 11. If you will need special equipment, do you have access to such equipment and the skill to use it?

_____ Yes   _____ No

If your answer is no, how do you intend to overcome this difficulty?

_____

_____

_____ 12. What is the estimated cost in time and money to gather the data?

_____

_____ 13. What evidence do you have that the data you gather will be valid and reliable indicators of the phenomena you wish to study?

_____

_____

OVERALL ASSESSMENT

_____   14.   As you review your responses to this checklist, might any of the factors you've just considered, or perhaps any other factors, hinder a successful completion of your research project?

_____ Yes   _____ No

If your answer is yes, list those factors. _____

_____

_____

When You Can't Anticipate Everything in Advance: The Value of a Pilot Study

Did you have trouble answering some of the questions in the checklist? For instance, did you have difficulty estimating how much time it would take you to gather your data? Did you realize that you might need to develop your own questionnaire, test, or other measurement instrument but then wonder how valid and reliable the instrument might be for your purpose?

Up to this point, we have been talking about planning a research project as something that occurs all in one fell swoop. In reality, a researcher may sometimes need to do a brief exploratory investigation, or pilot study, to try out particular procedures, measurement instruments, or methods of analysis. *A brief pilot study is an excellent way to determine the feasibility of your study.* Furthermore, although it may take some time initially, it may ultimately save you time by letting you know—after only a small investment on your part—which approaches will and will not be effective in helping you solve your overall research problem.

PRACTICAL APPLICATION Developing a Plan of Attack

Once you have determined that your research project is feasible, you can move ahead. Yet especially for a novice researcher, all the things that need to be done—writing and submitting the proposal, getting IRB or IACUC approval, arranging for access to one or more research sites, setting up any experimental interventions you have planned, collecting data, analyzing and interpreting it, and writing the final research report (almost always in multiple drafts)—may, in combination, seem like a gigantic undertaking. We authors recall, with considerable disappointment and sadness, the many promising doctoral students we have known who took all required courses, passed their comprehensive exams with flying colors, and then never earned their doctoral degrees because they couldn't persevere through the process of completing a dissertation. Such a waste! we thought then . . . and continue to think now.

You must accept the fact that *your project will take time—lots of time.* All too often, we have had students tell us that they anticipate completing a major research project (e.g., a thesis or dissertation) in a semester or less. In the vast majority of cases, such a belief is unrealistic. Consider the many steps listed in the preceding paragraph. If you think you can accomplish all these things within 2 or 3 months, you are almost certainly setting yourself up for failure and disappointment. We would much rather you think of any research project—and especially your first project—as something that is a valuable learning experience in its own right. As such, it is worth however much of your time and effort it takes to do the job well.

The most effective strategy we can suggest here is to *develop a research and writing schedule and try to stick to it.* Figure 4.5 provides a workable format for your schedule. In the left-hand column, list all the specific tasks you need to accomplish for your research project (writing the proposal, getting approval from the IRB and any other relevant faculty committees, conducting

Task to Complete	Estimated Amount of Time Needed	Target Date for Completion	Task Completed (indicate with a ✔)

FIGURE 4.5 ■ Establishing a Schedule for Your Project

any needed pilot studies, etc.) in the order in which you need to accomplish them. In the second column, estimate the number of weeks or months it will take you to complete each task, always giving yourself a little more time than you think you will need. In the third column, establish appropriate target dates for accomplishing each task, taking into account any holidays, vacations, business trips, and other breaks in your schedule that you anticipate. Also include a little bit of slack time for unanticipated illnesses or family emergencies. Use the right-hand column to check off each step as you complete it.

USING TECHNOLOGY

Using Project Management Software and Electronic Planners

Project management software is available both commercially (e.g., FastTrack Schedule, Manymoon, Milestones, ToDoList) and in freeware available for download from the Internet (e.g., go to ganttproject.biz or freedcamp.com). You can use such software to organize and coordinate the various aspects of a research project. For example, it will let you outline the different phases of the project, the dates by which those phases need to be completed, the ways in which they are interconnected, and the person who is responsible for completing each task. This information can be displayed in graphic form with due dates and milestones highlighted.

Project management software is especially helpful when a research project has many separate parts that all need to be carefully organized and coordinated. For example, suppose a large research effort is being conducted in a local school district. The effort requires a team of observers and interviewers to go into various schools and observe teachers in class, interview students during study halls, and discuss administrative issues with school principals. Coordinating the efforts of the many observers, teachers, students, and administrators is a complex task that can be easily laid out and scheduled by project management software.

You might consider electronically organizing your schedule even if you don't expect your research project to be as multifaceted as the one just described. For example, you might use the *calendar* application that comes with your laptop or smartphone, or you might download day-planning freeware from the Internet (e.g., My Daily Planner and Free Day Planner are two possibilities). With such applications you can insert electronic reminders that you need to do certain things on such-and-such a date, and you can easily revise your long-term schedule if unforeseen circumstances occur.

Keeping an Optimistic and Task-Oriented Outlook

In our own experiences, we authors have found that a schedule goes a long way in helping us complete a seemingly humongous task. In fact, this is exactly the approach we took when we wrote various editions of this book. Make no mistake about it: Writing a book such as this one can be even more overwhelming than conducting a research project!

A schedule in which you break your project into small, easily doable steps accomplishes several things for you simultaneously. First, it gives you the confidence that you *can* complete your project if you simply focus on one piece at a time. Second, it helps you persevere by giving you a series of target dates that you strive to meet. And last (but certainly not least!), checking off each task as you complete it provides a regular reminder that you are making progress toward your final goal of solving the research problem.

✔ Check Your Understanding in the Pearson etext

Practice Thinking Like a Researcher

Practice Thinking Like a Researcher Activity 4.1: Selecting a Method that Suits Your Purpose
Practice Thinking Like a Researcher Activity 4.2: Ensuring Validity
Practice Thinking Like a Researcher Activity 4.3: Identifying Potential Risks in Research Plans

FOR FURTHER READING

Planning Your Research Design

Bordens, K. S., & Abbott, B. B. (2010). *Research design and methods: A process approach* (8th ed.). New York: McGraw-Hill.

Butler, D. L. (2006). Frames of inquiry in educational psychology: Beyond the quantitative-qualitative divide. In P. A. Alexander & P. H. Winne (Eds.), *Handbook of educational psychology* (2nd ed., pp. 903–927). Mahwah, NJ: Erlbaum.

Creswell, J. W. (2014). *Research design: Qualitative, quantitative, and mixed methods approaches* (4th ed.). Thousand Oaks, CA: Sage.

Ercikan, K., & Roth, W.-M. (2006). What good is polarizing research into qualitative and quantitative? *Educational Researcher, 35*(5), 14–23.

Ethridge, D. (2004). *Research methodology in applied economics: Organizing, planning, and conducting economic research* (2nd ed.). New York: Wiley.

Firestone, W. A. (1987). Meaning in method: The rhetoric of quantitative and qualitative research. *Educational Researcher, 16*(7), 16–21.

Hedrick, T. E., Bickman, L., & Rog, D. J. (1993). *Applied research design: A practical guide.* Thousand Oaks, CA: Sage.

Jacob, H. (1984). *Using published data: Errors and remedies.* Thousand Oaks, CA: Sage.

Johnson, R. B., & Onwuegbuzie, A. J. (2004). Mixed methods research: A research paradigm whose time has come. *Educational Researcher, 33*(7), 14–26.

Kerlinger, F. N., & Lee, H. B. (1999). *Foundations of behavioral research* (4th ed.). New York: Harcourt.

Malhotra, N. K. (2010). *Marketing research: An applied orientation* (6th ed.). Upper Saddle River, NJ: Prentice Hall.

Maxfield, M. G., & Babbie, E. R. (2011). *Research methods for criminal justice and criminology* (6th ed.). Belmont, CA: Wadsworth/Cengage Learning.

Miles, M. B., Huberman, A. M., & Saldaña, J. (2014). *Qualitative data analysis: A methods sourcebook* (3rd ed.). Los Angeles: Sage.

Neuman, W. L. (2011). *Social research methods: Qualitative and quantitative approaches* (7th ed.). Upper Saddle River, NJ: Pearson.

O'Cathain, A. (2010). Assessing the quality of mixed methods research: Toward a comprehensive framework. In A. Tashakkori & C. Teddlie (Eds.), *Mixed methods in social & behavioral research* (2nd ed., pp. 531–555). Thousand Oaks, CA: Sage.

Singleton, R. A., Jr., & Straits, B. C. (2009). *Approaches to social research* (5th ed.). New York: Oxford University Press.

Tashakkori, A., & Teddlie, C. (Eds.) (2010). *SAGE handbook of mixed methods in social and behavioral research* (2nd ed.). Thousand Oaks, CA: Sage.

Vogt, W. P., Gardner, D. C., & Haeffele, L. M. (2012). *When to use what research design.* New York: Guilford Press.

Wood, M. J., & Ross-Kerr, J. C. (2011). *Basic steps in planning nursing research: From question to proposal* (7th ed.). Sudbury, MA: Jones & Bartlett.

Measurement

Aft, L. (2000). *Work measurement and methods improvement.* New York: Wiley.

Campbell, D. T., & Russo, M. J. (2001). *Social measurement.* Thousand Oaks, CA: Sage.

Earickson, R., & Harlin, J. (1994). *Geographic measurement and quantitative analysis.* Upper Saddle River, NJ: Prentice Hall.

Fried, H. O., Knox Lovell, C. A., & Schmidt, S. S. (Eds.) (2008). *The measurement of productive efficiency and productivity growth.* New York: Oxford University Press.

Miller, D. C., & Salkind, N. J. (2002). *Handbook of research design and social measurement* (6th ed.). Thousand Oaks, CA: Sage.

Thorndike, R. M., & Thorndike-Christ, T. (2010). *Measurement and evaluation in psychology and education* (8th ed.). Upper Saddle River, NJ: Merrill/Pearson Education.

Ethics

American Educational Research Association. (1992). Ethical standards of the American Educational Research Association. *Educational Researcher, 21*(7), 23–36.

American Psychological Association. (2002). Ethical principles of psychologists and code of conduct. *American Psychologist, 57,* 1060–1073.

Bankowski, Z., & Levine, R. J. (Eds.) (1993). *Ethics and research on human subjects: International guidelines.* Albany, NY: World Health Organization.

Cheney, D. (Ed.). (1993). *Ethical issues in research.* Frederick, MD: University Publishing Group.

Christians, C. G. (2000). Ethics and politics in qualitative research. In N. K. Denzin & Y. S. Lincoln (Eds.), *Handbook of qualitative research* (2nd ed., pp. 133–155). Thousand Oaks, CA: Sage.

Eiserman, W. C., & Behl, D. (1992). Research participation: Benefits and considerations for the special educator. *Teaching Exceptional Children, 24,* 12–15.

Elliott, D., & Stern, J. E. (Eds.) (1997). *Research ethics: A reader.* Hanover, NH: University Press of New England.

Erwin, E., Gendin, S., & Kleiman, L. (Eds.). (1994). *Ethical issues in scientific research: An anthology.* New York: Garland.

Hemmings, A. (2009). Ethnographic research with adolescent students: Situated fieldwork ethics and ethical principles governing human research. *Journal of Empirical Research on Human Research Ethics, 4*(4), 27–38.

Israel, M., & Hay, I. (2006). *Research ethics for social scientists.* Thousand Oaks, CA: Sage.

King, N. M. P., & Churchill, L. R. (2000). Ethical principles guiding research on child and adolescent subjects. *Journal of Interpersonal Violence (Special Issue: The Ethical, Legal, and Methodological Implications of Directly Asking Children About Abuse), 15,* 710–724.

Loue, S., & Case, S. L. (2000). *Textbook of research ethics: Theory and practice.* New York: Plenum Press.

Macrina, F. L. (2005). *Scientific integrity: Text and cases in responsible conduct of research* (3rd ed.). Washington, DC: American Society for Microbiology.

Mertens, D. M., & Ginsberg, P. (Eds.) (2008). *The handbook of social research ethics.* Thousand Oaks, CA: Sage.

Neuman, W. L. (2011). *Social research methods: Qualitative and quantitative approaches* (7th ed.). Upper Saddle River, NJ: Pearson. [Provides an excellent discussion of ethical issues.]

Panter, A. T., & Sterba, S. K. (Eds.) (2012). *Handbook of ethics in quantitative methodology.* New York: Routledge.

Pimple, K. D. (2008). *Research ethics.* Aldershot, England: Ashgate.

Pimple, K. D., Orlans, F. B., & Gluck, J. P. (1997). *Ethical issues in the use of animals in research.* Mahwah, NJ: Erlbaum.

Rhodes, C. S., & Weiss, K. J. (Eds.) (2013). *Ethical issues in literacy research.* New York: Routledge.

Roberts, L. W. (2006). Ethical principles and practices for research involving human participants with mental illness. *Psychiatric Services, 57,* 552–557.

Sales, B. D., & Folkman, S. (Eds.) (2000). *Ethics in research with human participants.* Washington, DC: American Psychological Association.

Sieber, J. E., & Tolich, M. B. (2013). *Planning ethically responsible research* (2nd ed.). Thousand Oaks, CA: Sage.

Yan, E. G., & Munir, K. M. (2004). Regulatory and ethical principles in research involving children and individuals with developmental disabilities. *Ethics & Behavior, 14*(1), 31–49.

ANSWERS TO THE CONCEPTUAL ANALYSIS EXERCISE "Identifying Scales of Measurement":

1. This is a *ratio* scale, with an absolute zero point (i.e., no bacteria at all).

2. A country's average temperature is an *interval* scale, because an average temperature of 0—regardless of whether the temperature is reported in Fahrenheit or Celsius—still means *some* heat. (In the Kelvin scale, a temperature of 0 means no heat at all, but people typically don't use this scale in reporting climatic temperature.) Amount of tourist dollars is, of course, a *ratio* scale.

3. The party membership coding scheme is a *nominal* scale, because the numbers assigned indicate only category membership, not quantity or order. For example, a Republican (who is coded "2") does not have "twice as much" party membership as a Democrat (who is coded "1"). Meanwhile, voting frequency—how many times each person has voted in the past 5 years—is a *ratio* scale, with equal units of measurement (every trip to the polls is counted once) and an absolute zero point (a score of 0 means that a person has not voted at all in the past 5 years).

4. The zip code strategy for creating regions is a *nominal* scale, reflecting only category membership. Regions with higher zip codes don't necessarily have "more" of anything, nor are they necessarily "better" in some respect.

5. Don't be misled by the absolute zero point here (an income of $0 means no money at all). The ranges of income are different in each group: Group A has a $20,000 range, Group B has a $30,000 range, Group C has a $50,000 range, and Group D—well, who knows how much the richest person in the study makes each year? Because of the unequal measurement units, this is an *ordinal* scale.

6. This is an *ordinal* scale that reflects varying levels of quality. There is no indication that the four categories each reflect the same range of quality, and a true zero point (no road at all) is not represented by the categorization scheme.

7. This is a tricky one. Despite the 0, this is *not* a ratio scale because virtually all students have at least a tiny amount of anxiety about tests, even if they respond "never" to all 25 questions. But the scale does involve an *amount* of something, so this must be either an ordinal or interval scale. Many psychologists would argue that the scores reflect an *interval* scale and would treat it as such in their statistical analyses. We authors don't necessarily agree, for two reasons. First, some of the statements on the instruments might reflect higher levels of test anxiety than others, so a "4" response to one item isn't necessarily the equivalent of a "4" response to another. Second, the 5-point rating scale embedded within the instrument ("never" to "always") doesn't necessarily reflect equal intervals of frequency; for instance, perhaps a student thinks of "sometimes" as being a broad range of frequencies of test-anxiety occurrence but thinks of "often" as being a more limited range. Thus, we argue that, in reality, the scores on the test anxiety instrument reflect an *ordinal* scale.

ANSWERS TO THE CONCEPTUAL ANALYSIS EXERCISE "Identifying Problems with Validity and Reliability in Measurement":

1. The test lacks *content validity:* It does not reflect the content domain that the instruction has covered—actual tennis *skills.*

2. This is a problem of *equivalent forms reliability:* The different versions of the same instrument yield different results.

3. The issue here is *interrater reliability:* The researchers are evaluating the same behaviors differently.

4. The problem in this case is *criterion validity:* Two measures of energy level—blood-test results and observer ratings—yield very different results.

5. This is a problem of *test–retest reliability:* The students responded differently within a very short time interval (2 weeks at most), even though their general opinions about climate change probably changed very little, if at all, during that interval.

6. The questionnaire lacks *internal consistency reliability:* Different items in the instrument yield different results, even though all items are intended to measure a single characteristic: matrimonial harmony.

7. In this case the instrument's *construct validity* is suspect: Religious tolerance is a hypothesized internal characteristic that can be inferred and measured only indirectly through observable patterns in people's behaviors. Here the behaviors being observed are simply responses to a questionnaire.

8. *Face validity* is at stake here: Although many psychologists contend that intelligence involves reaction time to some degree—and thus the reaction-time task might be a valid measure—on the surface the task doesn't *appear* to be a good measure. Although face validity is not "true" validity, a lack of it can sometimes negatively impact participants' cooperation in a research project.

Chapter 5

Writing the Research Proposal

Research is never a solo flight, an individual excursion. In today's world, researchers must communicate objectives, plans, and methods for others to read, discuss, and react to. The formal mechanism that initiates such a dialogue is the research proposal. As a point of departure, it must be a precise document from the first word to the last.

Learning Outcomes

5.1 Describe three general characteristics of a good research proposal, and identify strategies for organizing and writing the first draft of a proposal.

5.2 Identify strategies for effectively revising and strengthening your first draft of a proposal.

5.3 Describe common weaknesses in research proposals.

Research is never a solitary activity. It involves many people and requires access to and use of resources far beyond one's own. For that reason, it must be carefully planned, described, inspected, and, in nearly every instance, approved by others. The graduate student conducting research for a thesis or dissertation must get the approval of an advisor and, in the case of a dissertation, a doctoral committee. A researcher seeking grant funding must get approval from the university or the organization for which he or she works, and the project must be deemed worthy of funding by the grant-awarding agency. Any researcher who plans to work with human subjects must get the approval of an internal review board, and one who plans to work with animals must get approval from an institutional animal care and use committee (see Chapter 4). Such approvals are usually secured through the submission of a document known as a *research proposal*. The proposal lays out the problem for research, describes exactly how the research will be conducted, and outlines in precise detail the resources the researcher will use to achieve the desired results.

A proposal is as essential to successful research as a building contractor's plans are to the construction of a new home. No one would start building a house by digging a hole for the foundation. Before one turns a shovelful of earth, many questions must be addressed, many decisions made. Will the house be two stories, a split-level, or a one-story ranch? How will the building be placed on the lot? Where will the doors be located? How will the roof be pitched and shingled? What kind of heating system will be installed? Each of these questions is important, and each should be addressed *before* a single pound of dirt is excavated, a single nail driven.

Even after all these decisions have been made, does the digging begin? Not at all! Further planning is necessary. The contractor needs a floor plan of the entire structure, floor by floor, showing to the inch exactly where each room, door, window, and closet will be located. The contractor also needs a series of elevations of the proposed structure, showing each wall to scale as it will appear when completed. Finally, the contractor requires a set of specifications for the building, indicating exactly what lumber will be used, how far apart certain beams will be placed, what kinds of doors and windows will be put in what locations, and all other details. Nothing is left to chance.

So is it now time to stake off the building's location and start digging for the foundation? Not so fast! Before the construction crew can do anything, they need *permission*. The contractor must get a building permit. Most communities have building codes that govern the kinds of buildings that can be constructed—including codes regarding plumbing, wiring, and distance from the street. A permit provides a means of ensuring that new buildings meet these codes. The point is this: *Permission is essential to the plan.*

Like the contractor who presents detailed plans for a building, the researcher develops a written proposal for a research project. In this proposal, the problem and its attendant subproblems are clearly stated, hypotheses or questions are articulated, all necessary terms are defined, delimitations and limitations are carefully spelled out, and the reason for conducting the study—why it is important—is explained. The researcher then specifies every anticipated detail of acquiring, organizing, analyzing, and interpreting the data. The researcher sets forth the resources at hand for carrying out the research: his or her qualifications (and those of any assistants), the availability of the data, the means by which the data will be obtained, any needed equipment and facilities, and any other aspects of the total research process that merit explanation. Nothing is overlooked. All questions that may arise in the minds of those who review the proposal are anticipated and answered. Any unresolved matter is a weakness in the proposal and can jeopardize its approval.

Sometimes novice researchers think that a proposal is merely a necessary formality and thus don't give it the serious consideration it deserves. They try to describe their project in a few hastily written pages. Such an approach often fails. Those sponsoring a project, whether a graduate committee or a funding agency, realize that a researcher invests considerable time, effort, and (sometimes) money when doing research. Accordingly, no one should rush into a project without a clearly conceived goal and a thorough, objective evaluation of all aspects of the research endeavor.

No matter whether you are seeking financial support for a project from a funding agency or seeking approval for a thesis or dissertation from a faculty committee, a clear, well-written proposal is essential. Nothing else can substitute for an explicit setting forth of both problem and procedure.

CHARACTERISTICS OF A PROPOSAL

Good research requires that those who undertake it be able to think clearly, without confusion. The proposal will demonstrate—for better or for worse—whether the author has this ability. When readers receive a proposal that is unfocused, poorly organized, and lacking in critical details, they are apt to get the impression that the mind producing such a document is incapable of thinking precisely, logically, systematically, and thoroughly about the job that needs to be done. More often than not, the perceived qualifications of a researcher rest squarely on the quality of the proposal submitted.

Therefore, as you embark on the task of writing a research proposal, you should understand exactly what characteristics a proposal should have.

A Proposal Is a Straightforward Document

A proposal should not be cluttered with extraneous and irrelevant material. Whatever does not contribute directly to the delineation of the problem and its solution must be omitted. Anything else is a distraction. Remember the building contractor's drawings: clean, clear, and economical. They contain all the information that's necessary, not one detail more.

Right off the bat, a proposal should open with a straightforward statement of the problem to be researched. It needs no explanatory props—no introduction, prologue, or discussion about why the researcher became interested in the problem or feels a burning desire to research it. Nor does it need explanations of why the researcher decided *not* to study certain other topics. Those who will review your proposal are not interested in such autobiographical excursions. Indeed, they may suggest to readers that you cannot separate essentials from irrelevancies; thus, they will neither enhance your stature as a researcher nor recommend you as one who can think in a clear and focused manner.

Imagine a proposal that begins with these words: "Five decades ago, the social and economic status of minority groups in the United States was. . . ." A reader's reaction might easily be: "Who cares, at this moment, what the social and economic status of minorities was 50 years ago? That's history. What does the researcher *propose* to do *in the near future?*"

If your first sentence irritates readers, you are immediately put at a disadvantage, and you have possibly sacrificed their interest. More significantly, readers may infer that you can't distinguish between history and future planning, and thus they may wonder about your ability as a researcher to think clearly and critically.

Keep in mind the meaning of *proposal.* The word suggests looking forward, to what the researcher *plans to do in the future.* A writer who intends to compare the past and present social and economic conditions of minority groups might begin, "This study *will* analyze the social and economic status of certain minority groups today in comparison with their similar status five decades ago for the purpose of. . . ." This is a no-nonsense beginning, and it indicates that the writer knows what a proposal should be.

A Proposal Is Not a Literary Production

A contractor's drawings of to-be-built homes are not works of art. Similarly, a proposal is not a creative production that strives to engage readers with complex characters, vivid imagery, and a spellbinding plot. The purpose of both is simply to communicate clearly. Just as a contractor's drawings present a plan for construction with economy of line and precision of measurement, a proposal describes a future research project with an economy of words and precision of expression.

The language must be clear, sharp, and exact. The proposal provides a chance to show how clearly and completely the researcher can state a research problem, delineate the collection of relevant data, and explain how those data will be interpreted and brought to bear on the problem.

A Proposal Is Clearly Organized

Proposals are written in conventional prose style, and thoughts are expressed in simple paragraph form. In professional writing, headings and subheadings are the single most commonly used strategy to express the writer's overall organizational scheme. Examine your textbooks—as well as current articles in popular magazines—and you will discover how frequently headings are used to indicate the organizational structure of what has been written. You should communicate the outline of your thoughts to your own readers in the same explicit fashion.

If you are currently working on a master's thesis or doctoral dissertation, your faculty advisor and committee may have a particular organizational scheme they want you to follow, possibly including certain chapter titles and within-chapter headings. Alternatively, if you are writing a grant proposal for a public or private funding agency, it is likely that the agency mandates that a proposal be divided into specific, labeled sections (e.g., "Research Objective," "Relevant Literature," "Proposed Method," "Implications for Professional Practice").

ORGANIZING AND WRITING A RESEARCH PROPOSAL

Proposals follow a simple, logical train of thought. Although there are conceivably many ways to arrange the various topics within a proposal, most proposals use similar formats, especially in quantitative studies. The following is an example of a format you might use in a proposal for a quantitative research study:

I. The problem and its setting
   A. Statement of the problem and subproblems
   B. Hypotheses
   C. Definitions of terms
   D. Assumptions
   E. Delimitations and limitations
   F. Importance of the study

  II. Review of the related literature
 III. Data and the treatment of the data
    A. The data needed and the means for obtaining the data
    B. The research methodology
    C. The specific treatment of the data for each subproblem
       1. Subproblem 1 *(The subproblem presented in Part I above is restated here.)*
          a. The data needed to address the subproblem
          b. The treatment of the data
       2. Subproblem 2 *(The same format for Subproblem 1 is followed here.)*
       3. *Additional subproblems are discussed in the same manner.*
 IV. Qualifications of the researcher and any assistants
  V. Outline of the proposed study (steps to be taken, timeline, etc.)
 VI. References
VII. Appendixes

Proposals for qualitative studies sometimes use a slightly different format. The following format is an example of an outline you might use for a qualitative proposal:

  I. Introduction
    A. Purpose of the study
    B. General background for the study
    C. Guiding questions
    D. Delimitations and limitations
    E. Significance of the study
 II. Methodology
    A. Theoretical framework
    B. Type of design and its underlying assumptions
    C. Role of the researcher (including qualifications and assumptions)
    D. Selection and description of the site and participants
    E. Data collection strategies
    F. Data analysis strategies
    G. Methods of achieving validity
III. Findings
    A. Relationship to literature
    B. Relationship to theory
    C. Relationship to practice
 IV. Management plan, timeline, feasibility
  V. References
 VI. Appendixes

One rule governs the writing of proposals and final documents: *The arrangement of the material should be presented in such a manner that it forms for readers a clear, progressive presentation.* It keeps items together that belong together—for example, the problem and its resultant subproblems, as well as the subproblems and their corresponding hypotheses.

Formatting Headings and Subheadings

You must use different formats to indicate the different levels of headings you use. For example, if you have five different levels of headings, the American Psychological Association's *Publication Manual* (2010) specifies the following formats:

- *Level 1 headings*—the most important ones—are in **Boldface Uppercase and Lowercase Letters** and are **centered** on the page. These are headings of the largest organizational units; for instance, they may be the titles of the various chapters in a proposal or research report. They correspond with Roman numerals I, II, III, and so on, in an outline.
- *Level 2 headings* are in **Boldface Uppercase and Lowercase Letters** that begin at the **left side** of the page—in other words, they are *flush left*. They correspond with the capital letters A, B, C, and so on, in an outline.

■ *Level 3 headings* are in **Boldface first-letter-only-uppercase, ending with a period.** They are **indented** to the same degree that a paragraph is indented, and the first paragraph in the section follows on the same line. (Such headings are sometimes known as *run-in headings.*) They correspond with the numbers 1, 2, 3, and so on, in an outline.

■ *Level 4 headings* are in ***Italicized boldface first-letter-only-uppercase, ending with a period.*** They are placed, ***indented,*** at the beginning of the first paragraph in the section. They correspond with the lowercase letters a, b, c, and so on, in an outline.

■ *Level 5 headings* are in *Italicized nonboldface first-letter-only-uppercase, ending with a period.* They are placed, *indented,* at the beginning of the first paragraph in the section. They correspond with the numbers (1), (2), (3), and so on, that you sometimes see in an outline.

If you were to use this format, your various headings would look like this on the page:

First Level Heading

The first paragraph of this section begins here. . . .

Second Level Heading

The first paragraph of this section begins here. . . .

> **Third level heading.** The first paragraph of this section begins here. . . .

> ***Fourth level heading.*** The first paragraph of this section begins here. . . .

> *Fifth level heading.* The first paragraph of this section begins here. . . .

To help the headings stand out on the page, you may want to have an extra space (that is, an empty line) immediately preceding each one.

The format we suggest here is not the only one you might use. When choosing appropriate formats for your headings, you should check with any style manuals in your discipline and, if you are a student, with any graduate school requirements.

Above all, you should be *consistent* in how you format your headings. We have seen too many proposals, theses, and dissertations in which headings of equal importance sometimes appear in ALL CAPITALS and at other times in Capitals and Lowercase, or perhaps they appear both

Centered

and

Flush Left.

Such inconsistency points to a careless, sloppy writer and, a proposal reviewer might think, perhaps an equally careless and sloppy researcher.

PRACTICAL APPLICATION Writing Your Proposal

Challenging as writing a proposal can be, especially for the beginning researcher, it isn't rocket science. Here we offer two sets of guidelines, one each for writing a first draft and for revising your proposal.

GUIDELINES Writing the First Draft

The following suggestions are based both on our own experiences as proposal writers and as faculty members who have advised numerous master's and doctoral students.

1. *Use word processing software.* Whether you begin writing your proposal on a word processor or on paper should depend on which medium allows you to think and write most easily. For example, if you have had considerable experience using a keyboard and can type as fast as you write, you will undoubtedly want to use a word processor from the get-go. In contrast, if you use the more tedious hunt-and-peck approach and have considerable trouble finding such letters as *Q, X,* and *Z,* you might want to start off with paper and pencil. At some point, however, you should put your first draft on a word processor to facilitate those inevitable revisions (there will be many!).

Early in the game, take the time to learn any special features of your word processing software that you will need for typing your proposal or your final research report. For example, learn how to insert tables, graphs, footnotes, and other specially formatted features. If you will be including words with accent marks or using punctuation marks different from those in English (e.g., *déjà, señor, Günter, ¿*), find out how to type them. If you will need to use certain symbols (e.g., α, Σ, π) or mathematical formulas, learn how to include them in your document.

2. *Adhere to any guidelines required by the institution, organization, or funding agency to which you are submitting the proposal.* If the group to which you are submitting the proposal requires that you (a) use certain headings, (b) follow a particular style manual, or (c) include certain information, do it! Blatant disregard for such guidelines is, for many proposal reviewers, a red flag that the researcher may not have his or her act together sufficiently to conduct the proposed research.

As their names imply, most style manuals also prescribe a certain writing style—for instance, whether to describe the researcher in first person ("I will conduct interviews . . .") or third person ("The researcher will conduct interviews . . .") and whether to use active voice ("The researcher will instruct participants to . . .") or passive voice ("Participants will be instructed to . . .") in describing procedures. Various academic disciplines have different style preferences, and you should not stray too far from the style typically used in your own field.

3. *When writing the first draft, focus more on organization and logical thought sequences than on exact wording, grammatical correctness, spelling, and nitty-gritty formatting details.* In Chapter 1 we mentioned that human beings can think about only a limited number of things at one time. All of the processes that skillful writing involves—such as organizing thoughts, following a logical sequence, expressing ideas clearly and succinctly, using acceptable grammar and punctuation, and spelling words correctly—may far exceed that capacity. In other words, you may very well *not* be able to do it all at once!

In the first draft, then, you should focus your attention on the big picture—that is, on presenting your ideas in a logical, organized, and coherent fashion. At this point, don't worry about picky details. If you can't immediately think of the right word to use somewhere, leave a blank where it should go and move on. If you can't remember how a word is spelled, spell it in whatever way you can for the time being and then perhaps indicate your uncertainty by adding a question mark in parentheses. If you're not sure about where commas should go, either insert them or don't, and then check a style manual later on.

As you write, you may even discover that you're missing an important piece of information, perhaps something that you need to track down online or at the library. Never mind; let it go for now. Leave a blank and make a note of what you need. Chances are that you will need several such bits of information. You can track them all down later, *after* you have finished your first draft.

4. *Present the research problem at the very beginning.* As we stated earlier in the chapter, *always* lead off with your research problem. The problem is at the very center of—and so drives—the entire project.

5. *Provide a context for your research problem.* A good proposal places the research problem within a specific context that helps readers understand why the problem to be investigated *is* a problem in need of solution. For example, perhaps the problem reflects an alarming state of affairs in our physical or social environment—say, an increase in sightings of frogs with birth defects or a high incidence of eating disorders in adolescent girls. Perhaps the problem involves inadequacies in an existing theory or conflicting findings in previous research. Perhaps the problem is a need to evaluate the effectiveness (or lack thereof) of a particular intervention—say, a new medical procedure or instructional method. Whatever form the context for the problem

takes, it should be documented with appropriate citations of relevant research, theory, and other literature.

If you are writing a three-chapter proposal for a master's thesis or doctoral dissertation, you should include literature and citations that are key and central to your research problem near the beginning of the very first chapter. A more in-depth review of related literature should be presented later, perhaps in the second chapter.

6. *Convince readers of the importance of your project.*   You must convince your readers that your planned research is not a trivial, meaningless undertaking—that, on the contrary, it can potentially make a substantial contribution to the body of human knowledge and may even, in some small way, help make the world a better place. Although you won't want to get emotional in your presentation, you nevertheless want to generate interest in what you are doing: You want your readers to *want to know* what your project's outcome will be.

As shown in the proposal outlines presented earlier in the chapter, researchers sometimes include a section specifically called "Importance of the Study," "Significance of the Study," or something of that ilk. In other cases researchers simply make a study's importance crystal clear within the introductory discussion of the overall context for the problem.

7. *Assume that your readers know nothing whatsoever about your proposed project.* Novice researchers often leave out critical pieces of information, assuming, somehow, that their readers are already aware of these things. (We have found this to be especially true for students who are writing a proposal for a faculty committee that already has some knowledge about the planned research.) Such omissions may lead to many misunderstandings along the way, and these misunderstandings can get you in trouble later on.

Your proposal is the mechanism through which you describe, in a permanent written form, what you intend to do from beginning to end. In this respect, it is very much like a contract to which you and your reviewers will ultimately agree. Accordingly, leave nothing unsaid, no question unanswered.

8. *Communicate that you have an open mind about the outcomes of your study.* Researchers often embark on research studies with the hope that they will uncover evidence in support of their hypotheses. But some novice researchers go too far and assert that they *will* find such evidence. Such statements as "I will show that" or "I will prove that" imply that the results of the study are already known. If the results can be predicted with 100% accuracy ahead of time, then what is the point of conducting the research? Truly objective, open-minded researchers place no bets in advance; they keep all options on the table. For instance, they might say "The purpose of this study is to determine *whether* . . ." or "The proposed research project is designed to investigate the *possible* effects of. . . ."

9. *Describe your proposed methodology with as much detail and precision as possible.* The extent to which you can describe your methodology will depend to some degree on whether you are using a quantitative or qualitative approach. If you are using a quantitative approach, you will need to specify your sample, measurement instruments, and procedures in the utmost detail. If you are using a qualitative approach, you will probably be making some sampling and procedural decisions as the study proceeds. Nevertheless, at the proposal stage you should outline your sources of data and procedures as specifically as possible. Remember, the more information your reviewers have about your proposed project, the better position they will be in to determine its worth and potential contributions.

10. *If you intend to use data that already exist, describe where the data are located and how you plan to obtain them.*   In some studies, and especially in historical research, a researcher may need certain kinds of records. In such a situation, the researcher should know their exact location. Many novice researchers begin research projects by assuming that records are available but learn too late that either no records exist or the needed records are in an inaccessible location or under such heavy restriction that they aren't available. Answer the question "Where are the data located?" in no uncertain terms, and determine that you have access to them.

Suppose that the necessary data are letters written by an important historical figure and that they are in the possession of the person's family. You may know where the letters are located, but do you know how you will get them for your research purposes? Perhaps, in a case like this—or in any situation in which records are under other people's control—you might provide the names and addresses of the individuals who possess the data. You might also state that these custodians of the data have consented to your using the data for research purposes. Such details should be clearly stated in the proposal so that your sponsor, your academic committee, individuals at a funding agency, or whoever else is reading your proposal can feel confident that you will have ready access to the data you need.

11. ***Describe how you will use the data to address your research problem.*** Even though you have not yet collected your data, you will nevertheless need to describe how you intend to organize, analyze, and interpret them so that you can solve your research problem. Do not assume that others will know what you intend to do. Spelling out the treatment and interpretation of the data is a tedious, time-consuming process. But the alternative—presenting only a broad sweep, describing only a general approach—almost invariably courts disaster. Interpretation of the data is the step that gives meaning to the entire enterprise and makes it a genuine research endeavor, and it must therefore be planned and specified well in advance.

To see how some novice researchers fail to answer this most important question—How will the data be interpreted?—let's consider Figure 5.1, which shows an excerpt from an economics doctoral student's proposal for a dissertation about labor relations. The student's main research

FIGURE 5.1 ■ Where Is the Interpretation of the Data? An Excerpt from a Student's Proposal

Restatement of Subproblem 1. The first subproblem is to determine through an analysis of employee responses the attitudes of employees toward certain aspects of management policy for salary increases and merit pay.

The Data Needed

The data needed to resolve this subproblem are those employee responses to questions concerning salary increases and merit pay.

Where the Data Are Located

The data are located in the employee responses to Questions 3, 7, and 13 of the questionnaire, "Survey of Employee Attitudes Toward Management."

How the Data Will Be Secured

The data will be secured by accurately tabulating all of the responses of employees to the above questions on the questionnaire.

How the Data Will Be Interpreted

From the responses of the questions, a table will be constructed similar to the following structural model. It will indicate the employee attitudes, their frequency, and the percentages of these attitudes of the total attitude response to each question.

Attitude	Frequency	Percentage
Totals		

A graph will then be constructed to show which attitudes received the greatest number of reactions and which had the least number of reactions. The median and the mean will also be found for the total group as a basis for comparison.

problem is to "analyze the attitudes of professional employees toward certain aspects of management policy and to evaluate the relationship between these attitudes and the responsibility of management to articulate such policy for its employees." The student has organized his discussion of the data in terms of specific subproblems, describing both data collection and data interpretation with respect to each subproblem. In the excerpt, we see how the student says he will resolve the following subproblem:

> What does an analysis of the attitudes of employees toward management policy for salary increases and merit pay reveal?

First read the student's restatement of the subproblem, his description of the data needed to resolve the problem, and his discussion of how he intends to secure those data; information about all of these issues appears under appropriate headings in Figure 5.1. Now, with such information in mind, read the section "How the Data Will Be Interpreted." What does the researcher really intend to do? Is he really going to *interpret* the data, to derive meaning from them? Is he going to "determine" anything *through an analysis of employee responses?*

Unfortunately, the student isn't talking about interpreting the data. He is merely planning to *tabulate* and *graph* the data. He will rearrange them and present them in another form. The data remain almost as raw as they were originally in employees' responses to the questionnaire. The researcher also tells us that he will find two points of central tendency ("averages") for the data: the median and the mean. The median and mean of *what?* The frequencies? The percentages? Both? And *why* will he calculate the median and mean? What do these statistics tell us about "attitudes of employees toward certain aspects of management policy"? These are critical questions that should be answered *in the proposal.* In the student's proposal as it presently exists, there's no discussion of how the data relate to *attitudes of employees,* even though an understanding of these attitudes is central to resolving the subproblem.

What might the student do to interpret his data? After tabulating the data in the manner he describes, he might collapse the responses into two categories—or perhaps into a continuum of categories—that reflect either support of or opposition to management policies. Then he could carefully review each category to identify the characteristics of each. Were people who supported management lukewarm in their support? What keywords did they use in their responses? What did the overall category responses indicate about the employees' attitudes?

Despite its obvious weakness, the excerpt in Figure 5.1 does illustrate one effective strategy for discussing the analysis and interpretation of the data. In particular, it can be quite helpful to *address each subproblem separately.* For each subproblem, you might:

a. Restate the subproblem.
b. Clearly identify the data that relate to the subproblem.
c. Explain fully and unequivocally how you intend to analyze and interpret the data to resolve the subproblem.

More generally, *the plan for the treatment of the data should be so specific and unequivocal that any other qualified person could carry out your research project solely by following your proposal.* Every contingency should be anticipated; every methodological problem should be resolved. The degree to which you delineate how the data will be interpreted will play a significant role in the success or failure of your research project. The method of data interpretation is the key to research success, and it should be described with utmost care and precision.

12. *Use appendixes to present informed consent letters, specific measurement instruments, and other detailed materials.*   Although you need to describe your procedures precisely and completely, too much detail all in one place can interfere with the overall flow of your writing. Appendixes provide an easy way to present any necessary details that aren't central to the points you are trying to make. Simply refer to each appendix as it is relevant to your discussion, perhaps like this: "To recruit participants, the nature of the study will be described, and volunteers will be asked to read and sign an informed consent letter (see Appendix D)." If you have more than one appendix, assign them letters that reflect the order in which you refer to them in the text: The first appendix you mention should be labeled "Appendix A," the second should be labeled "Appendix B," and so on.

GUIDELINES   Revising Your Proposal

Your first draft will almost certainly *not* be your final proposal. We remind you of a point first made in Chapter 1: *Anticipate that you will almost certainly have to write multiple drafts.* Here we offer suggestions for polishing your proposal into its final form.

1. *Set the proposal aside for a few days.*   After writing your first draft, put it aside for a while so that, later, you can approach it with a fresh eye. If you reread it too soon, you will read it with what you *thought you had said* still fresh in your mind and so you won't necessarily read what you *actually wrote.*

2. *Read a paper copy—rather than electronic version—of your first draft.*   As we have previously mentioned in Chapter 1, paper copies often reveal problems with a text that somehow escape our attention on the computer screen. We aren't sure why this is, but we have repeatedly found it to be so.

Your proposal should, at this point at least, be double-spaced rather than single-spaced and have wide margins, leaving lots of room for writing corrections and comments. You should expect that *you will write all over your first draft.* Figure 5.2 presents many commonly used editing marks for small-scale changes. For more significant changes (e.g., adding and moving text), you may want to use arrows, indicate pages where sentences or paragraphs should be moved to or from, and have blank sheets of paper or your computer nearby for major rewrites.

3. *Carefully scrutinize what you have written, looking for disorganized thoughts, illogical thinking, and inconsistencies in terminology.*   Look for places where you move unpredictably from one topic to another, go off on unnecessary tangents, or draw unwarranted conclusions. Also, look at each paragraph under each one of your headings: All paragraphs under a particular heading should deal specifically with the topic that the heading identifies.

In addition, strive for consistency in your terminology. Novice researchers sometimes bounce from one label to another when talking about a single characteristic or variable, and the inconsistency can be confusing for readers. For instance, imagine that an educational researcher is

FIGURE 5.2 ■
Commonly Used Editing
Marks

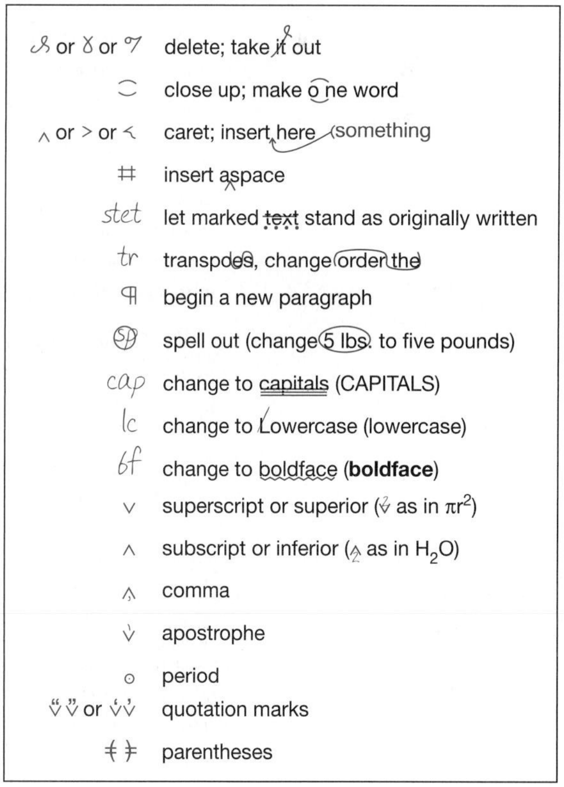

investigating an aspect of human motivation—in particular, the kinds of goals that students set for themselves as they study academic material. One such goal is the desire to truly learn and understand the topic of study—a goal that some motivation theorists call a *learning goal* and others call a *mastery goal.* In writing a research proposal, then, the researcher decides to appease both groups of theorists, using one term in some places and the other term in other places. Readers of the proposal are apt to be perplexed, perhaps thinking, "What's the difference between these two?" when there *isn't* a noteworthy difference between them. Better to choose one term or the other and stick to it.

Consistency is important, too, when referring to the different groups of participants you might have in a study. For instance, imagine a medical researcher who wants to study the effects of a new pain reliever for alleviating the symptoms of chronic arthritis. The researcher plans for some arthritis sufferers to take the pain reliever and for others to take a sugar pill that, on the surface, looks identical to the pain reliever.[1] The researcher might call the first group *Group 1,* the *Treatment Group,* or the *Experimental Group,* and might call the second group *Group 2,* the *Placebo Group,* or the *Control Group.* The researcher should decide which terms to use and be consistent in using them. Unpredictably moving back and forth among the different labels might lead a befuddled reader to conclude that the proposed research project will have six groups instead of two!

4. ***Look for places where you are not as clear as you might be.***   Ambiguous phrases and sentences—those with several possible meanings and those with no obvious meaning at all—significantly weaken the power of a research proposal. As an example, consider this excerpt from a literature review written by a master's student:

> It appears to be the case that not only is note taking superior for recall immediately after a lecture, but that the entire memory storage and recall process is further strengthened as time goes on when one takes notes on a lecture. And, of course, this is generally how American college students are tested.

What did the student mean by the phrase "the entire memory storage and recall process is further strengthened"? And to what does the word *this* refer in the second sentence? Even though one of us authors is an educational psychologist who knows a great deal about both human memory processes and American testing procedures, neither of us has any idea what this student was trying to communicate.

5. ***Keep your sentences simple and straightforward.***   As a general rule, try to keep your sentences short. Vary the length, of course, but break up those long, contorted sentences into shorter, more succinct ones. Be alert to how and where you use adjectives, adverbs, and other modifiers. Misplaced phrases and clauses can wreak havoc with the thoughts you want to communicate. As a simple, nonacademic example, consider this example of misplaced modification in a classified ad: "Piano for sale by a woman with beautifully carved mahogany legs that has arthritis and cannot play anymore." Move the prepositional phrase and add a comma, and the ad makes more sense: "FOR SALE: A piano with beautifully carved mahogany legs, by a woman who has arthritis and cannot play anymore."

6. ***Choose your words carefully.***   A thesaurus—perhaps a book, the "thesaurus" feature in your word processing software, or an online thesaurus (e.g., merriam-webster.com)—can help you find the exact word you need. Never use a long word where a short one will do. In a straightforward discussion, use one- or two-syllable words rather than longer ones. Use professional jargon only when you need it to relate your ideas to existing theories and literature in the discipline.

---

[1]In such a study, the researcher must not deceive the sugar pill recipients that they are getting a pain reliever. Such a deception would be a violation of basic ethical standards for research (see Chapter 4, especially the section "Voluntary and Informed Participation"). Instead, all participants in the study should be informed of the nature of the study: a comparison of the effects of a new pain reliever with those of a placebo. They do not need to be informed about which kind of pill they are taking, as such information might affect their subjective *perceptions* of pain and thereby distort the results of the study.

7. *Check carefully for errors in grammar, punctuation, spelling, and formatting.* Now is the time to attend to grammar, punctuation, spelling, correct and consistent heading formats, and other minor details. Ultimately you want your proposal to be, if not perfect, then as close to perfect as any human being can reasonably make it. Careless errors and other signs of sloppiness may suggest to your reviewers that the way you conduct your research project may be equally careless and sloppy.

Your word processing software can certainly be helpful in this respect. For instance, *use the grammar checker.* Grammar checkers can search for word expressions, clichés, multiple negation, too many prepositional phrases, and other common problems. Some word processors even have a built-in function to measure the reading level of your writing; such information might be helpful in ensuring that you are writing at the appropriate level for your audience.

In addition, *use the spell checker, but don't rely on it exclusively.* As pointed out in Chapter 1, a spell checker typically does nothing more than check each word to see if it is a "match" with a word in the English language or in some other list you specify. It won't tell you whether you have used the *right* words in every case. So even if you take advantage of the spell checker, always, *always* follow up by reading your document, word for word, to be sure that every word is correctly spelled. If you're a poor speller, then ask someone else—a good speller, obviously—to proofread the entire document for errors.

You or your proofreader should be alert not only for spelling errors but also for the use of *homonyms*—sound-alike words that are spelled differently and have different meanings—in place of words you actually intended to use. Following are commonly misused homonyms that we authors have often seen in research proposals and research reports:

it's **versus** *its*
it's is a contraction for "it is"
its is the possessive form of the pronoun *it*

there **versus** *their* **versus** *they're*
there is typically used either as (a) an adjective or adverb referring to a location or (b) an indefinite pronoun that begins a sentence (e.g., "There is no reason to . . .")
their is the possessive form of the pronoun *they*
they're is a contraction for "they are"

affect **versus** *effect*
affect as a *verb* means to have an influence on (e.g., "motivation affects learning")
affect as a *noun* is a synonym for emotion (e.g., "sadness and guilt are both forms of unpleasant
   affect")
effect as a *verb* means to bring something about (e.g., "to effect change")
effect as a *noun* means the causal result of an event (e.g., "rainfall has an effect on crop
   production")

The difference between *affect* and *effect* can be especially troublesome, in large part because *affect* as a verb and *effect* as a noun both involve an influence of some sort. But using the incorrect word instead of its more appropriate homonym, especially when done frequently throughout the proposal, communicates to readers that you have not taken the proposal-writing task seriously.

Speaking of *it's* versus *its,* we urge you to watch your use of apostrophes to indicate possessive nouns. In general, an apostrophe comes before the *s* in a singular noun (e.g., "a *person's* income level") but after the *s* in a plural noun (e.g., "companies' marketing strategies"). However, when a plural noun has no *s* unless it is possessive, the apostrophe comes before the *s* (e.g., "children's behaviors," "people's attitudes"). And when a singular noun ends in *s* even when it is *not* a possessive, you should add an apostrophe and an *s* (in that order) to indicate possession (e.g., "in Dr. Strauss's research").

8. *Make sure that items in bulleted lists are parallel in structure.* In writing a research proposal, a sequence of bullets or numbered items is often an effective way to present such things

as the definitions of key terms and the major assumptions underlying a research project. All of the items in the sequence should have the same general grammatical structure—at a minimum by all being short phrases *or* by all being complete sentences. Mixing complete and incomplete sentences within a single list is frowned upon. For example, in his dissertation proposal regarding cartographers and the Strong Vocational Interest Blank, previously mentioned in Chapter 3, Arthur Benton defined two of his terms as follows:

> *Cartographer.* A cartographer is a professional employee who engages in the production of maps, including construction of projections, design, drafting (or scribing), and preparation through the negative stage for the reproduction of maps, charts, and related graphic materials.
>
> *Discrete interests.* Discrete interests are those empirically derived qualities or traits common to an occupational population that serve to make them distinct from the general population or universe.

Notice how both definitions use complete sentences to describe the meanings of terms. Alternatively, the author might have used *in*complete sentences, perhaps like the following:

> *Cartographer.* A professional employee who engages in the production of maps, including construction of projections, design, drafting (or scribing), and preparation through the negative stage for the reproduction of maps, charts, and related graphic materials.
>
> *Discrete interests.* Those empirically derived qualities or traits common to an occupational population that serve to make them distinct from the general population or universe.

Careful attention to parallelism in form is yet another sign of a careful, meticulous researcher.

9. *Make sure there is a one-to-one correspondence between the citations in the text and the references in the reference list.*   Every source you cite in the text or in footnotes should be included in more complete form in the proposal's reference list—no matter whether the source is a book, journal article, conference presentation, Internet website, or some other entity to which you are giving credit. Furthermore, every item in the reference list should be cited at least once in the text. The formats for citations and reference lists should be consistent with the style manual typically used in your particular academic discipline. The four most commonly used styles are listed in Table 13.1 in Chapter 13.

10. *Consider the feasibility of your project once again.*   Now that you have laid everything out in the proposal, check one more time to be sure you have the time, resources, and energy to do everything you say you are going to do.

11. *Print out your second draft, and read your proposal carefully once again.*   Look critically at each thought as it stands on paper. Do the words say exactly what you want them to say? Read carefully phrase by phrase. See whether one word will carry the burden of two or more. Throw out superfluous words.

12. *Seek the feedback of others, and take it seriously when writing subsequent drafts.* We cannot stress this point enough. No matter how hard you try, you cannot be as objective as you would like to be when you read your own writing. Ask people to read and critique what you have written. Don't ask friends or relatives who are likely to give you a rubber stamp of approval. Instead, ask people who will read your work thoroughly, give you critical feedback, and make constructive suggestions. If you are writing a dissertation proposal, your doctoral committee will almost certainly request some revisions to what you have planned and written. If you are writing a master's thesis, your advisor and any advisory committee members will probably make requests and recommendations.

One final comment: *Get used to writing!* Researchers write continuously—sometimes to communicate with others, at other times to facilitate their own thinking. Paper or a word processor can be effective for personal brainstorming sessions. Take time to sit back and use a pencil or keyboard to help you clarify your thoughts and ideas.

PRACTICAL APPLICATION Strengthening Your Proposal

Not all research proposals get approved. Rejections are common for proposals requesting funding from a private or government agency. But some proposals to conduct nonfunded research get turned down as well, usually for one or more good reasons. In Figure 5.3 we list shortcomings that experienced proposal reviewers have often observed. Proposals submitted by students for academic research projects (e.g., for theses and dissertations) tend to have a number of these shortcomings.

FIGURE 5.3
Common Weaknesses
in Research Proposals

Weaknesses Related to the *Research Problem:*

- The description of the project is so nebulous and unfocused that the purpose of the research is unclear.
- The problem as presented is not empirically testable.
- The problem is not framed within an appropriate theoretical or conceptual context.
- The problem is unimportant or unlikely to yield new information.
- The hypothesis is ill-defined, doubtful, or unsound; it is based on insufficient evidence or illogical reasoning.
- The problem is more complex than the investigator realizes.
- The problem is of interest only to a particular, localized group, or in some other way has limited relevance to the field as a whole.
- The project is unrelated to the funding agency's purposes and reasons for sponsoring new research.

Weaknesses Related to the *Research Design and Methodology:*

- The description of the design and/or method is so vague and unfocused as to prevent adequate evaluation of its worth.
- The proposed methodology violates basic ethical standards.
- The data the investigator wishes to use are either difficult to obtain or inappropriate for the research problem.
- The proposed methods, measurement instruments, or procedures are inappropriate for the research problem (e.g., proposed measurement instruments may have poor reliability and validity).
- Appropriate controls are either lacking or inadequate.
- The equipment to be used is outdated or inappropriate.
- The statistical analysis has not received adequate consideration, is too simplistic, or is unlikely to yield accurate and clear-cut results.
- Potential limitations of the project, even if unavoidable, are not adequately addressed.

Weaknesses Related to the *Investigator:*

- The investigator does not have sufficient training or experience for the proposed research.
- The investigator appears to be unfamiliar with important literature relevant to the research problem.
- The investigator has insufficient time to devote to the project.

Weaknesses Related to *Resources:*

- The institutional setting is inadequate or unsuitable for the proposed research.
- Proposed use of equipment, support staff, or other resources is unrealistic.

Weaknesses Related to the *Quality of Writing:*

- The proposal does not stay focused on the research problem; it rambles unpredictably.
- The proposal inadequately or incorrectly cites related literature.
- The proposal does not adhere to the appropriate style manual.
- The proposal has grammatical and/or spelling errors.

Sources: Based on Allen, 1960; Cuca & McLoughlin, 1987; Dahlberg, Wittink, & Gallo, 2010; Davitz & Davitz, 1996; Wong, n.d.

Once you have written what you believe to be your final proposal, you should scrutinize it one more time, preferably after you have set it aside for a few more days. *Take a critical approach, looking for what's wrong rather than what's right.* The following checklist can provide guidance about what to look for.

✔ CHECKLIST

Evaluating an Early Draft of a Research Proposal

Check each item—or have a friend or colleague in your discipline check it—to be sure that your proposal exhibits *none* of the following characteristics:

FOR ANY RESEARCH PROPOSAL

_____ 1. The statement of the problem is vague, or it is so obscured by discussions of other topics that it is impossible to find.

_____ 2. The methodology is incompletely described; an explanation of exactly how the research will be conducted is not specifically delineated.

_____ 3. The proposed treatment of each subproblem is general and cursory; it does not convey clearly how the data will be used and interpreted to resolve the subproblem or the overall research problem.

_____ 4. The proposal lacks sharpness. It is not logically organized. Without clear divisions that set forth the areas of the research project, it rambles. Readers have difficulty isolating the discussion of the problem, the subproblems, the related studies, the methodology, the interpretation of the data, and other important parts of the proposal.

_____ 5. The proposal is phrased in terms that are too general, ambiguous, or imprecise to be useful for evaluation. Such phrases as "tests will be given" and "measurements will be taken" are largely meaningless.

_____ 6. The format of the proposal deviates from the guidelines set forth by the approval group or funding agency.

_____ 7. Some cited sources do not appear in the reference list; alternatively, they are incompletely or incorrectly cited.

FOR A PROPOSAL TO A FUNDING AGENCY

_____ 8. The problem does not address the research area outlined by the funding agency.

_____ 9. The proposal is too ambitious for the grant money available.

_____ 10. Items included in the budget are disallowed by the terms of the grant.

_____ 11. A clear and explicit budget statement outlining program expenditures is lacking, or the summary of estimated costs is ambiguous and indefinite.

_____ 12. The section of the proposal explaining the study's importance is not set forth clearly enough for the funding agency to see a relationship of the study to the purpose for which the grant is awarded.

FINAL THOUGHTS ABOUT PROPOSAL WRITING

When drawing up a contract, an attorney meticulously includes all of the rights and obligations of the parties included in the contract. The proposal writer should prepare a proposal with the same precision. In a sense, a proposal is, under certain circumstances, a form of contract, or what we might call a *quasi* contract.

Are you submitting a proposal for a grant to underwrite a research project? If so, you (as the party of the first part) are proposing to undertake a research project in exchange for a monetary consideration from the agency providing the grant (the party of the second part). Regarded from a legal standpoint, your proposal, on acceptance by the granting agency, is a formal contractual relationship.

Now let's look at the situation from an academic standpoint. Certainly there are differences between a proposal presented to a funding agency and a proposal presented by a student to an academic advisor. Yet in another way the two kinds of proposals are very similar: In both cases, the basic elements of the research problem, the methodology, the data, and any other factors critical to conducting the inquiry must be clearly set forth and mutually agreed on before the actual research activity can begin.

Any thesis or dissertation project must begin with a proposal, and any project involving human subjects must get IRB approval before it ever gets off the ground. But even when a proposal isn't mandatory, it's always *advisable*, regardless of the magnitude of the project or its academic sophistication. From a student's perspective, a proposal has two distinct advantages:

1. It helps the student organize the research activity.
2. It communicates to the student's advisor what the student intends to do, thereby enabling the advisor to provide counsel and guidance in areas that may pose exceptional difficulty.

Most faculty advisors will want to review a thesis or dissertation proposal periodically as it is being developed. Such a process of ongoing guidance from an experienced professional and researcher is to be welcomed, not avoided. It is perhaps the single best way you can learn the tricks of the research trade.

A proposal for any research endeavor merits words that are carefully chosen, a style that is clear and concise, an attention to the most minute procedural detail, and for each procedure, a rationale that is logically and clearly stated. All of this is a tall order, but the result reveals the scholarship of the proposal author as perhaps no other academic assignment can ever do.

To no small degree *your proposal is you!* It defines your ability to think critically and to express your thoughts clearly. *It is the practical application of your research competence laid bare on a sheet of paper.*

✔ Check Your Understanding in the Pearson etext

Practice Thinking Like a Researcher

Practice Thinking Like a Researcher Activity 5.1: Organizing a Research Proposal
Practice Thinking Like a Researcher Activity 5.2: Planning for Data Interpretation
Practice Thinking Like a Researcher Activity 5.3: Revising a Proposal

A SAMPLE RESEARCH PROPOSAL

We conclude this chapter by presenting an example of an effective research proposal—in this case, a proposal for a doctoral dissertation at the University of Northern Colorado. The author, Rosenna Bakari, uses the very first paragraph of the proposal to present the research problem clearly and concisely:

> Attitudes that teachers bring into the classroom are a critical factor in the academic failure of African American students (Irvine, 1990). Preliminary research suggests that many in-service and prospective teachers do not hold positive attitudes toward teaching African American students (Irvine, 1990). As a result, many researchers see attitudes and values clarification of preservice teachers concerning race as a critical aspect of multicultural teacher education (Gay, 1994; Wiggins & Follo, 1999; Zeichner, 1996). However, there are no adequate instruments available to measure preservice teachers' attitudes about teaching African American students. Hence, the intent of this research is to develop and validate an instrument to measure preservice teachers' attitudes toward teaching African American students. (p. 1)

We now fast-forward to Bakari's methodology section. We present the proposal itself on the left and add our commentary on the right.

DISSERTATION **ANALYSIS** 2

Methodology

This study is intended to develop and validate a survey instrument that assesses preservice teachers' attitudes toward teaching African American students. The survey instrument was developed based on educational recommendations and research literature indicating that culture is an important consideration in educating African American students effectively. Two pilot studies were conducted as preliminary investigations. This chapter will summarize the pilot studies and discuss the methodology of the current study.

[The student describes the two pilot studies she conducted previously relative to her present study. We pick the proposal up later, as she describes her proposed sample, measurement instruments, data collection, and data analysis.]

Sample

Three sub-groups will be solicited for participation. The first group will represent institutions where preservice teachers have little exposure to African American issues in education. The majority of participants are expected to be White and have little exposure to African American populations.

In the second group, preservice teachers will be solicited from teacher education programs that have more program goals or objectives related to teaching African American students. For example, diversity courses may be a requirement for graduation. In addition, preservice teachers are likely to have greater exposure to African American student populations during student teaching, in their university courses, or in their living communities than group one. However, the majority of participants are still expected to be White.

The third group of preservice teachers will be solicited from historically Black colleges or universities (HBCUs). Although HBCUs may differ in many respects, their focus is a "commitment, dedication, and determination to enhance the quality of life for African Americans" (Duhon-Sells, Peoples, Moore, & Page, 1996, p. 795). The majority of participants from this group are expected to be African American.

A minimum of 100 students will be solicited from each group. Sample size is critical because it provides a basis for the estimation of sampling error (Hair, Anderson, Tatham, & Black, 1995). A sample size of at least 100 is recommended to conduct a confirmatory factor analysis because a sample less than 100 may not provide enough statistical power to reject the null hypothesis. A small sample could lead to acceptance of a model which is not necessarily a good fit, simply because there was not enough statistical power to reject the model. On the other hand, if the sample is too large, the model may be rejected due to sensitivity in detecting small differences, because the larger the sample, the more sensitive the test is to detecting differences (Hair, Anderson, Tatham, & Black, 1995). Hair, Anderson, Tatham, and Black (1995) recommend a sample size between 100 and 200.

Comments

The author begins by reminding the reader of the purpose of the proposed research. The repetition of the research problem at this point, though not essential, is helpful to the reader, who can then put the procedures that follow into proper perspective.

The first paragraph is an advance organizer *for the reader, who then can follow the author's subsequent train of thought more easily.*

Earlier in the proposal the author presented her rationale for giving the instrument to three different groups. She predicted that the three groups would, on average, respond differently to the instrument, thereby providing evidence for the validity *of the instrument.*

Although the author is expecting the three groups to have different proportions of students from different racial groups, she will nevertheless seek information in support of her prediction through a demographic information sheet that she describes later in her proposal.

Always spell out what an abbreviation stands for before using it. For instance, here the author refers to "historically Black colleges or universities" and identifies the abbreviation HBCU in parentheses. She can then use "HBCU" in future discussions and her readers will know to what she is referring.

Here the author provides a justification for her sample size. We discuss the issue of statistical power in Chapter 11; at that point, we also revisit the concept of a null hypothesis.

In order to achieve the minimum participant requirement for each group, involvement from more than one university may be necessary. For instance, four universities may represent group one while two universities may represent group two. This flexibility is important due to the variability in size of teacher education programs. Moreover, the reliance on instructors' willingness to contribute class time to this research may minimize the number of participants. All participants will be undergraduate or graduate preservice teachers and enrolled in a required course for a teacher preparation program. Graduate students must also be in pursuit of initial teacher certification. Students may be in any phase of their teacher preparation program. Preservice teachers who are not currently enrolled in any of the classes where the instrument will be distributed will not be selected for participation. Further, only students who are in attendance on the day the instrument is distributed will be selected for participation. For those students solicited to participate, participation will be voluntary and anonymous.

The author explains why she is drawing her sample from several universities. It appears that she is predicting, and then answering, the kinds of questions the reader might have about her method.

Instrumentation

Four instruments will be employed for data collection in this research. They include the demographic data sheet, Teaching African American Students Survey, Responding Desirably on Attitudes and Opinions measurement (RD-16), and General Attitudes toward Teaching Survey. The demographic data sheet and the Teaching African American Students Survey (TAASS) were both designed by the researcher for this particular study. The General Attitudes toward Teaching Survey is an adaptation from a published Teacher Efficacy Scale and the TAASS. The RD-16 is a published instrument designed to measure social desirability. A description of the four instruments follows.

The author gives enough information about her sample to enable any qualified reader to conduct the study she proposes. In addition, by describing the nature of her sample, she provides information about the population to which her study's results could reasonably be generalized.

Once again we see an advance organizer for the discussion that follows.

The author uses abbreviations (TAASS and RD-16) for two of her instruments. To be consistent, she should probably introduce them both in the second sentence of the paragraph, rather than leave TAASS for the third sentence as she does here.

[*Under four separate subheadings, the author then describes each instrument in detail, including the specific items that each one includes and any known information about validity and reliability.*]

Data Collection

Participants will be contacted in their classes, where the instructor has agreed to allow class time to conduct this research. Participants will be told that the objective of the research is to gather information about future teachers, particularly who they are (demographics) and what they believe about teaching. To avoid a social desirability response set, participants will not be informed about the specific focus of the study (developing and validating an instrument to measure preservice teachers' attitudes toward teaching African American students). A statement will be read aloud to the class that informs students of their right to refuse to participate without any negative consequences, as well as the possibility of being requested to participate in follow-up research (test–retest reliability for the TAASS).

The heading "Procedure" is more commonly used than "Data Collection" in human subjects research, but the latter is acceptable as well.

Here the author describes her procedures regarding informed consent.

Requests for names and student identification numbers will be prohibited as any part of the data collection. However, participants will be asked to create identifications for themselves that cannot be traced to them by others. Pseudo-identification is necessary for students to remain anonymous, yet allows the researcher to conduct a retest for reliability measures. Examples of anonymous identifications will be given, such as a favorite noun, verb, or adjective (chair, jump, lazy). Students will be duly cautioned

Here she describes the steps she will take to ensure participants' right to privacy.

about selecting identifications that can be traced to them, such as mothers' maiden names, any part of their social security numbers, or nicknames.

Individual surveys will not be seen by anyone other than the participant once they are completed. Students will be requested to place their completed surveys in a designated "return" envelope. The last student to return the surveys will be requested to seal the return envelope. Only when the last survey is placed in the return envelope, and the envelope is sealed, will the administrator be permitted to handle the materials.

Notice how the author uses future tense to describe her proposed methodology. Later, when she rewrites the methodology section for her final research report, she will, of course, change her description of procedures to past tense.

In classes where the researcher does not administer the instruments, research packets will be prepared for the person who does. Research packets will contain a disclosure statement to be read aloud to the participants. In addition to the disclosure sheet, the packets will include a demographic information sheet, the TAASS, and only one of the validity criteria instruments. Half of the participants will receive the RD-16 in their packet, and the other half will receive the General Attitudes Scale. The order of the instruments will also vary in the packets, with the exception of the demographic data sheet. The demographic data sheet will always appear last. Administrators will be instructed to avoid interpreting items on any of the three survey instruments. If students ask for interpretation of any items on the surveys, administrators will be instructed to respond, "Please use your best interpretation to answer all the items." However, clarifications may be made about the demographic information, if requested.

The author will vary the order in which participants respond to the instrument, presumably as a way of determining whether taking one instrument affects how a participant responds to the instruments that follow.

The author is taking steps to increase the reliability of the instrument by standardizing its administration.

Three weeks after the initial research data have been collected, classes will be selected (based on availability) for retest of the TAASS. Participants will be solicited in a minimum of three classes that participated in the initial research. Only the TAASS will be administered for the retest. Students will be required to use the pseudo-identification selected in the initial research.

The author will administer the TAASS to some participants twice so that she can determine its test–retest reliability.

Data Analysis

LISREL and SPSS statistical software will be used for all analyses. As Hair, Anderson, Tatham, and Black (1995) point out, there is no method of dealing with missing data that is free of disadvantages. Anytime missing data are imputed there is a risk of biasing the results (e.g., distributions or correlation). Even the option of using the complete case approach has disadvantages. When only completed data are used, there is a risk of reducing the sample size to an inappropriate number. Moreover, the results may no longer be generalizable to the intended population if the missing data are systematized rather than randomized (Hair, Anderson, Tatham, & Black, 1995). Before any approach will be decided as to how to handle missing data, the missing data will be reviewed for systematic avoidance of response.

Notice that the author describes her proposed methods of data analysis as well as her methods of data collection. By doing so, she helps the reader determine whether her analyses will be appropriate for her research questions.

Notice, too, that the author will consider the nature of the data before and during her data analyses.

A book by Hair, Anderson, Tatham, and Black (1995) is cited several times in the methodology section. To be consistent with APA style (which she adheres to in her proposal), the author should list all four authors only for the first citation; after that, she can shorten the citation to "Hair et al. (1995)."

[The author then describes the specific analyses she plans to conduct and how they relate to her research problem.]

Note: Excerpt is from a research proposal submitted by Rosenna Bakari to the University of Northern Colorado, Greeley, in partial fulfillment of the requirement for the degree of Doctor of Philosophy. Reprinted with permission.

FOR FURTHER READING

Bernstein, T. M. (1993). *The careful writer: A modern guide to English usage.* New York: Free Press.

Booth, W. C., Colomb, G. G., & Williams, J. M. (2008). *The craft of research* (3rd ed.). Chicago: University of Chicago Press.

Dahlberg, B., Wittink, M. N., & Gallo, J. J. (2010). Funding and publishing integrated studies: Writing effective mixed methods manuscripts and grant proposals. In A. Tashakkori & C. Teddlie (Eds.), *Mixed methods in social & behavioral research* (2nd ed., pp. 775–802). Thousand Oaks, CA: Sage.

Davitz, J. R., & Davitz, L. L. (1996). *Evaluating research proposals: A guide for the behavioral sciences.* Upper Saddle River, NJ: Pearson.

DeBakey, L. (1976). The persuasive proposal. *Journal of Technical Writing and Communication, 6*(1), 5–25.

Johnson-Sheehan, R. (2008). *Writing proposals* (2nd ed.). New York: Longman.

Krathwohl, D. R., & Smith, N. L. (2005). *How to prepare a dissertation proposal: Suggestions for students in education and the social and behavioral sciences.* Syracuse, NY: Syracuse University Press.

Locke, L. F., Spirduso, W. W., & Silverman, S. J. (2014). *Proposals that work: A guide for planning dissertations and grant proposals* (6th ed.). Thousand Oaks, CA: Sage.

Miner, L. E., & Miner, J. T. (2008). *Proposal planning and writing* (4th ed.). Westport, CT: Greenwood.

Ogden, T. E., & Goldberg, I. A. (Eds.). (2002). *Research proposals: A guide to success* (3rd ed.). San Diego, CA: Academic Press.

Roberts, C. M. (2010). *The dissertation journey: A practical and comprehensive guide to planning, writing, and defending your dissertation* (2nd ed.). Thousand Oaks, CA: Corwin.

Rudestam, K. E., & Newton, R. R. (2007). *Surviving your dissertation: A comprehensive guide to content and process* (3rd ed.). Thousand Oaks, CA: Sage.

Smith, M. C., & Carney, R. N. (1999). Strategies for writing successful AERA proposals. *Educational Researcher, 28*(1), 42–45, 58.

Chapter

6

Descriptive Research

Our physical and social worlds present overwhelming amounts of information. But if you study a well-chosen sample from one of those worlds—and draw reasonable inferences from your observations of this sample—you can learn a great deal.

Learning Outcomes

6.1 Describe general characteristics and purposes of (a) observation studies, (b) correlational research, (c) developmental designs, and (d) survey research. Also, describe effective strategies you might use in each of these four research methodologies.

6.2 Identify effective strategies for conducting a face-to-face, telephone, or video-conferencing interview.

6.3 Identify effective strategies for constructing and administering

a questionnaire and for analyzing people's responses to it.

6.4 Explain possible uses of checklists, rating scales, rubrics, computer software, and the Internet in data collection.

6.5 Determine an appropriate sample for a descriptive study.

6.6 Describe common sources of bias in descriptive research, as well as strategies for minimizing the influences of such biases.

In this chapter, we discuss types of quantitative study that fall under the broad heading *descriptive quantitative research.* This general category of research designs involves either identifying the characteristics of an observed phenomenon or exploring possible associations among two or more phenomena. In every case, descriptive research examines a situation *as it is.* It does not involve changing or modifying the situation under investigation, nor is it intended to determine cause-and-effect relationships.

DESCRIPTIVE RESEARCH DESIGNS

In the next few pages, we describe observation studies, correlational research, developmental designs, and survey research, all of which yield quantitative information that can be summarized through statistical analyses. We devote a significant portion of the chapter to survey research, because this approach is used quite frequently in such diverse disciplines as business, government, public health, sociology, and education.

Observation Studies

As you will discover in Chapter 9, many qualitative researchers rely heavily on personal observations—typically of people or another animal species (e.g., gorillas, chimpanzees)—as a source of data. In *quantitative* research, however, an observation study is quite different. For one thing, an observation study in quantitative research might be conducted with plants rather than animals, or it might involve nonliving objects (e.g., rock formations, soil samples) or dynamic physical phenomena (e.g., weather patterns, black holes).

Also, a quantitative observation study tends to have a limited, prespecified focus. When human beings are the topic of study, the focus is usually on a certain aspect of behavior. Furthermore, the behavior is quantified in some way. In some situations, each occurrence of the behavior is *counted* to determine its overall frequency. In other situations, the behavior is *rated* for accuracy, intensity, maturity, or some other dimension. But regardless of approach, the researcher strives to be *as objective as possible* in assessing the behavior being studied. To maintain such objectivity, he or she is likely to use strategies such as the following:

- Define the behavior being studied in such a precise, concrete manner that the behavior is easily recognized when it occurs.
- Divide the observation period into small segments and then record whether the behavior does or does not occur during each segment. (Each segment might be 30 seconds, 5 minutes, 15 minutes, or whatever other time span is suitable for the behavior being observed.)
- Use a rating scale to evaluate the behavior in terms of specific dimensions (more about rating scales later in the chapter).
- Have two or three people rate the same behavior independently, without knowledge of one another's ratings.
- Train the rater(s) to use specific criteria when counting or evaluating the behavior, and continue training until consistent ratings are obtained for any single occurrence of the behavior.

A study by Kontos (1999) provides an example of what a researcher might do in an observation study. Kontos's research question was this: What roles do preschool teachers adopt during children's free-play periods? (She asked the question within the context of theoretical issues that are irrelevant to our purposes here.) The study took place during free-play sessions in Head Start classrooms, where 40 preschool teachers wore cordless microphones that transmitted what they said (and also what people near them said) to a remote audiotape recorder. Each teacher was audiotaped for 15 minutes on each of two different days. Following data collection, the tapes were transcribed and broken into 1-minute segments. Each segment was coded in terms of the primary role the teacher assumed during that time, with five possible roles being identified: *interviewer* (talking with children about issues unrelated to a play activity), *stage manager* (helping children get ready to engage in a play activity), *play enhancer/playmate* (joining a play activity in some way), *safety/behavior monitor* (managing children's behavior), or *uninvolved* (not attending to the children's activities in any manner). Two research assistants were trained in using this coding scheme until they were consistent in their judgments at least 90% of the time, indicating a reasonably high *interrater reliability.* They then independently coded each of the 1-minute segments and discussed any segments on which they disagreed, eventually reaching consensus on all segments. (The researcher found, among other things, that teachers' behaviors were to some degree a function of the activities in which the children were engaging. Her conclusions, like her consideration of theoretical issues, go beyond the scope of this book.)

As should be clear from the preceding example, an observation study involves considerable advance planning, meticulous attention to detail, a great deal of time, and, often, the help of one or more research assistants. Furthermore, a pilot study is essential for ironing out any wrinkles in identifying and classifying the behavior(s) or other characteristic(s) under investigation. Embarking on a full-fledged study without first pilot testing the methodology can result in many hours of wasted time.

Ultimately, an observation study can yield data that portray some of the richness and complexity of human behavior. In certain situations, then, it provides a quantitative alternative to such qualitative approaches as ethnographies and grounded theory studies (see Chapter 9).

Correlational Research

A correlational study examines the extent to which differences in one characteristic or variable are associated with differences in one or more *other* characteristics or variables. A correlation exists if, when one variable increases, another variable either increases or decreases in a somewhat predictable fashion. Knowing the value of one variable, then, enables us to *predict* the value of the other variable with some degree of accuracy.

In correlational studies, researchers gather quantitative data about two or more characteristics for a particular group of people or other appropriate units of study. When human beings are the focus of investigation, the data might be test scores, ratings assigned by an expert observer, or frequencies of certain behaviors. Data in animal studies, too, might be frequencies of particular behaviors, but alternatively they could be fertility rates, metabolic processes, or measures of health and longevity. Data in studies of plants, inanimate objects, or dynamic physical phenomena might be measures of growth, chemical reactions, density, temperature, or virtually any other characteristic that human measurement instruments can assess with some objectivity. Whatever the nature of the data, at least two different characteristics are measured in order to determine whether and in what way these characteristics are interrelated.

Let's consider a simple example: As children grow older, most of them become better readers. In other words, there is a *correlation* between age and reading ability. Imagine that a researcher has a sample of 50 children, knows the children's ages, and obtains reading achievement scores for them that indicate an approximate "grade level" at which each child is reading. The researcher might plot the data on a scatter plot (also known as a *scattergram*) to allow a visual inspection of the relationship between age and reading ability. Figure 6.1 presents this hypothetical scatter plot. Chronological age is on the graph's vertical axis (the *ordinate*), and reading level is on the horizontal axis (the *abscissa*). Each dot represents a particular child; its placement on the scatter plot indicates both the child's age and his or her reading level.

If age and reading ability were two completely unrelated characteristics, the dots would be scattered all over the graph in a seemingly random manner. When the dots instead form a rough elliptical shape (as the dots in Figure 6.1 do) or perhaps a skinnier sausage shape, then we know that the two characteristics are correlated to some degree. The diagonal line running through the middle of the dots in Figure 6.1—sometimes called the *line of regression*—reflects a hypothetical perfect correlation between age and reading level; if all the dots fell on this line, a child's age would tell us *exactly* what the child's reading level is. In actuality, only four dots—the solid black ones—fall on the line. Some dots lie below the line, showing children whose reading level is, relatively speaking, advanced for their age; these children are designated by hollow black dots. Other dots lie above the line, indicating children who are lagging a bit in reading relative to their peers; these children are designated by colored dots.

As we examine the scatter plot, we can say several things about it. First, we can *describe* the homogeneity or heterogeneity of the two variables—the extent to which the children are similar to or different from one another with respect to age and reading level. For instance, if the

FIGURE 6.1 ▪ Example of a Scatter Plot: Correlation Between Age and Reading Level

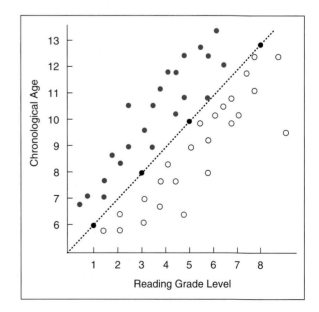

data were to include only children of ages 6 and 7, we would have greater homogeneity with respect to reading ability than would be the case for a sample of children ages 6 through 13. Second, we can *describe* the degree to which the two variables are intercorrelated, perhaps by computing a statistic known as a *correlation coefficient* (Chapter 8 provides details). But third—and most importantly—we can *interpret* these data and give them meaning. The data tell us not only that children become better readers as they grow older—that's a "no brainer"—but also that any predictions of children's future reading abilities based on age alone will be imprecise ones at best.

A Caution About Interpreting Correlational Results

When two variables are correlated, researchers sometimes conclude that one of the variables must in some way cause or influence the other. In some instances, such an influence may indeed exist; for example, chronological age—or at least the amount of experience that one's age reflects—almost certainly has a direct bearing on children's mental development, including their reading ability. But ultimately we can never infer a cause-and-effect relationship on the basis of correlation alone. Simply put, *correlation does not, in and of itself, indicate causation.*

Let's take a silly example. A joke that seems to have "gone viral" on the Internet is this one:

> I don't trust joggers. They're always the ones that find the dead bodies. I'm no detective . . . just sayin'.

The tongue-in-cheek implication here is that people who jog a lot are more likely to be murderers than people who don't jog very much and that perhaps jogging *causes* someone to become a murderer—a ridiculous conclusion! The faulty conclusion regarding a possible cause-and-effect relationship is crystal clear.

In other cases, however, it would be all too easy to draw an unwarranted cause-and-effect conclusion on the basis of correlation alone. For example, in a series of studies recently published in the journal *Psychological Science,* researchers reported several correlations between parenthood and psychological well-being: Adults who have children tend to be happier—and to find more meaning in life—than adults who don't have children (Nelson, Kushlev, English, Dunn, & Lyubomirsky, 2013). Does this mean that becoming a parent *causes* greater psychological well-being? Not necessarily. Possibly the reverse is true—that happier people are more likely to *want* to have children, and so they take steps to have them either biologically or through adoption. Or perhaps some other factor is at the root of the relationship—maybe financial stability, a strong social support network, a desire to have a positive impact on the next generation, or some other variable we haven't considered.

The data may not lie, but the causal conclusions we draw from the data may, at times, be highly suspect. Ideally, a good researcher isn't content to stop at a correlational relationship, because *beneath the correlation* may lie some potentially interesting dynamics. One way to explore these dynamics is through *structural equation modeling (SEM),* a statistical procedure we describe briefly in Table 8.5 in Chapter 8. Another approach—one that can yield more solid conclusions about cause-and-effect relationships—is to follow up a correlational study with one or more of the experimental studies described in Chapter 7 to test various hypotheses about what causes what.

Developmental Designs

Earlier we presented a hypothetical example of how children's ages might correlate with their reading levels. Oftentimes when researchers want to study how a particular characteristic changes as people grow older, they use one of two developmental designs, either a cross-sectional study or a longitudinal study.

In a **cross-sectional study**, people from several different age-groups are sampled and compared. For instance, a developmental psychologist might study the nature of friendships for children at ages 4, 8, 12, and 16. A gerontologist might investigate how retired people in their 70s, 80s, and 90s tend to spend their leisure time.

In a **longitudinal study**, a single group of people is followed over the course of several months or years, and data related to the characteristic(s) under investigation are collected at various times.[1] For example, a psycholinguist might examine how children's spoken language changes between 6 months and 5 years of age. Or an educational psychologist might get measures of academic achievement and social adjustment for a group of fourth graders and then, 10 years later, find out which students had completed high school (and what their high school GPAs were) and which ones had not. The educational psychologist might also compute correlations between the measures taken in the fourth grade and the students' high school GPAs; thus, the project would be a correlational study—in this case enabling predictions from Time 1 to Time 2—as well as a longitudinal one.

When longitudinal studies are also correlational studies, they enable researchers to identify potential mediating and moderating variables in correlational relationships. As previously explained in Chapter 2, *mediating variables*—also known as *intervening variables*—may help explain why a characteristic observed at Time 1 is correlated with a characteristic observed at Time 2. Mediating variables are typically measured at some point between Time 1 and Time 2—we might call it Time 1½. In contrast, *moderating variables* influence the nature and strength of a correlational relationship; these might be measured at either Time 1 or Time 1½. A statistical technique mentioned earlier—structural equation modeling (SEM)—can be especially helpful for identifying mediating and moderating variables in a longitudinal study (again we refer you to Table 8.5 in Chapter 8). Yet keep in mind that even with a complex statistical analysis such as SEM, *correlational studies cannot conclusively demonstrate cause-and-effect relationships.*

Obviously, cross-sectional studies are easier and more expedient to conduct than longitudinal studies, because the researcher can collect all the needed data at a single time. In contrast, a researcher who conducts a longitudinal study must collect data over a lengthy period and will almost invariably lose some participants along the way, perhaps because they move to unknown locations or perhaps because they no longer want to participate. An additional disadvantage of a longitudinal design is that when people respond repeatedly to the same measurement instrument, they are likely to improve simply because of their *practice* with the instrument, even if the characteristic being measured hasn't changed at all.

But cross-sectional designs have their disadvantages as well. For one thing, the different age groups sampled may have been raised under different environmental conditions. For example, imagine that we want to find out whether logical thinking ability improves or declines between the ages of 20 and 70. If we take a cross-sectional approach, we might get samples of 20-year-olds and 70-year-olds and then measure their ability to think logically about various scenarios, perhaps using a standardized multiple-choice test. Now imagine that, in this study, the 20-year-olds obtain higher scores on our logical thinking test than the 70-year-olds. Does this mean that logical thinking ability declines with age? Not necessarily. At least two other possible explanations readily come to mind. The quality of education has changed in many ways over the past few decades, and thus the younger people may have, on average, had a superior education to that of the older people. Also, the younger folks may very well have had more experience taking multiple-choice tests than the older folks have had. Such problems pose threats to the *internal validity* of this cross-sectional study: We can't eliminate other possible explanations for the results observed (recall the discussion of internal validity in Chapter 4).

A second disadvantage of a cross-sectional design is that we cannot compute correlations for potentially related variables that have been measured for different age groups. Consider, again, the educational psychologist who wants to use students' academic achievement and social adjustment in fourth grade to predict their tendency to complete their high school education. If the educational psychologist were to use a cross-sectional study, there would be different students in each age-group—and thus only one set of measures for each student—making predictions across time for any of the students impossible.

---

[1]Some longitudinal studies are conducted over a much shorter time period—perhaps a few minutes or a couple of hours. Such studies, often called *microgenetic studies*, can be useful in studying how children's thinking processes change as a result of short-term, targeted interventions (e.g., see Kuhn, 1995).

To address some of the weaknesses of longitudinal and cross-sectional designs, researchers occasionally combine both approaches in what is known as a **cohort-sequential study**. In particular, a researcher begins with two or more age-groups (this is the cross-sectional piece) and follows each age-group over a period of time (this is the longitudinal piece). As an example, let's return to the issue of how people's logical thinking ability changes over time. Imagine that instead of doing a simple cross-sectional study involving 20-year-olds and 70-year-olds, we begin with a group of 20-year-olds and a group of 65-year-olds. At the beginning of the study, we give both groups a multiple-choice test designed to assess logical reasoning; then, 5 years later, we give the test a second time. If both groups improve over the 5-year time span, we might wonder if practice in taking multiple-choice tests or practice in taking this *particular* test might partly account for the improvement. Alternatively, if the test scores increase for the younger (now 25-year-old) group but decrease for the older (now 70-year-old) group, we might reasonably conclude that logical thinking ability *does* decrease somewhat in the later decades of life.

Like a longitudinal study, a cohort-sequential study enables us to calculate correlations between measures taken at two different time periods and therefore to make predictions across time. For instance, we might determine whether people who score highest on the logical thinking test at Time 1 (when they are either 20 or 65 years old) are also those who score highest on the test at Time 2 (when they are either 25 or 70 years old). If we find such a correlation, we can reasonably conclude that logical thinking ability is a relatively stable characteristic—that certain people currently think and will continue to think in a more logical manner than others. We could also add other variables to the study—for instance, the amount of postsecondary education that participants have had and the frequency with which they engage in activities that require logical reasoning—and determine whether such variables mediate or moderate the long-term stability of logical reasoning ability.

Cross-sectional, longitudinal, and cohort-sequential designs are used in a variety of disciplines, but as you might guess, they are most commonly seen in developmental research (e.g., studies in child development or gerontology). Should you wish to conduct a developmental study, we urge you to browse in such journals as *Child Development* and *Developmental Psychology* for ideas about specific research strategies.

Survey Research

Some scholars use the term *survey research* to refer to almost *any* form of descriptive, quantitative research. We use a more restricted meaning here: Survey research involves acquiring information about one or more groups of people—perhaps about their characteristics, opinions, attitudes, or previous experiences—by asking them questions and tabulating their answers. The ultimate goal is to learn about a large population by surveying a sample of that population; thus, we might call this approach a *descriptive survey* or *normative survey*.

Reduced to its basic elements, a *survey* is quite simple in design: The researcher poses a series of questions to willing participants; summarizes their responses with percentages, frequency counts, or more sophisticated statistical indexes; and then draws inferences about a particular population from the responses of the sample. It is used with more or less sophistication in many areas of human activity—for instance, in a neighborhood petition in support of or against a proposed town ordinance or in a national telephone survey seeking to ascertain people's views about various candidates for political office. This is not to suggest, however, that because of their frequent use, surveys are any less demanding in their design requirements or any easier for the researcher to conduct than other types of research. Quite the contrary, a survey design makes critical demands on the researcher that, if not carefully addressed, can place the entire research effort in jeopardy.

Survey research captures a fleeting moment in time, much as a camera takes a single-frame photograph of an ongoing activity. By drawing conclusions from one transitory collection of data, we might generalize about the state of affairs for a longer time period. But we must keep in mind the wisdom of the Greek philosopher Heraclitus: There is nothing permanent but change.

Survey research typically employs a face-to-face interview, a telephone interview, or a written questionnaire. We discuss these techniques briefly here and then offer practical suggestions for conducting them in "Practical Application" sections later on. We describe a fourth approach—using the Internet—in a subsequent "Practical Application" that addresses strictly online methods of data collection.

Face-to-Face and Telephone Interviews

In survey research, interviews tend to be *standardized*—that is, everyone is asked the same set of questions (recall the discussion of *standardization* in Chapter 4). In a structured interview, the researcher asks certain questions and nothing more. In a semistructured interview, the researcher may follow the standard questions with one or more individually tailored questions to get clarification or probe a person's reasoning.

Face-to-face interviews have the distinct advantage of enabling a researcher to establish rapport with potential participants and therefore gain their cooperation. Thus, such interviews yield the highest response rates—the percentages of people agreeing to participate—in survey research. However, the time and expense involved may be prohibitive if the needed interviewees reside in a variety of states, provinces, or countries.

Telephone interviews are less time-consuming and often less expensive, and the researcher has potential access to virtually anyone on the planet who has a landline telephone or cell phone. Although the response rate is not as high as for a face-to-face interview—many people are apt to be busy, annoyed at being bothered, concerned about using costly cell phone minutes, or otherwise not interested in participating—it is considerably higher than for a mailed questionnaire. Unfortunately, the researcher conducting telephone interviews can't establish the same kind of rapport that is possible in a face-to-face situation, and the sample will be biased to the extent that people without phones are part of the population about whom the researcher wants to draw inferences.

Midway between a face-to-face interview and a telephone interview is an interview conducted using Skype (skype.com) or other video conferencing software. Such a strategy can be helpful when face-to-face contact is desired with participants in distant locations. However, participants must (a) feel comfortable using modern technologies, (b) have easy access to the needed equipment and software, and (c) be willing to schedule an interview in advance—three qualifications that can, like phone interviews, lead to bias in the sample chosen.

Whether they are conducted face-to-face, over the telephone, or via Skype or video conferencing software, personal interviews allow a researcher to clarify ambiguous answers and, when appropriate, seek follow-up information. Because such interviews take time, however, they may not be practical when large sample sizes are important.

Questionnaires

Paper-and-pencil questionnaires can be distributed to a large number of people, including those who live at far-away locations, potentially saving a researcher travel expenses and lengthy long-distance telephone calls. Also, participants can respond to questions with anonymity—and thus with some assurance that their responses won't come back to haunt them. Accordingly, some participants may be more truthful than they would be in a personal interview, especially when addressing sensitive or controversial issues.

Yet questionnaires have their drawbacks as well. For instance, when questions are distributed by mail or e-mail, the majority of people who receive questionnaires don't return them—in other words, there may be a low return rate—and the people who do return them aren't necessarily representative of the originally selected sample. Even when people are willing participants in a questionnaire study, their responses will reflect their reading and writing skills and, perhaps, their misinterpretation of one or more questions. Furthermore, a researcher must specify *in advance* all of the questions that will be asked—and thereby eliminates other questions that *could* be asked about the issue or phenomenon in question. As a result, the researcher gains only limited, and possibly distorted, information—introducing yet another possible source of bias affecting the data obtained.

If questionnaires are to yield useful data, they must be carefully planned, constructed, and distributed. In fact, *any* descriptive study requires careful planning, with close attention to each methodological detail. We now turn to the topic of planning.

PLANNING FOR DATA COLLECTION IN A DESCRIPTIVE STUDY

Naturally, a descriptive quantitative study involves measuring one or more variables in some way. With this point in mind, let's return to a distinction first made in Chapter 4: the distinction between substantial and insubstantial phenomena. When studying the nature of *substantial phenomena*—phenomena that have physical substance, an obvious basis in the physical world— a researcher can often use measurement instruments that are clearly valid for their purpose. Tape measures, balance scales, oscilloscopes, MRI machines—these instruments are indisputably valid for measuring length, weight, electrical waves, and internal body structures, respectively. Some widely accepted measurement techniques also exist for studying *insubstantial phenomena*— concepts, abilities, and other intangible entities that cannot be pinned down in terms of precise physical qualities. For example, an economist might use Gross Domestic Product statistics as measures of a nation's economic growth, and a psychologist might use the *Stanford-Binet Intelligence Scales* to measure children's general cognitive ability.

Yet many descriptive studies address complex variables—perhaps people's or animals' day-to-day behaviors, or perhaps people's opinions and attitudes about a particular topic—for which no ready-made measurement instruments exist. In such instances, researchers often collect data through systematic observations, interviews, or questionnaires. In the following sections, we explore a variety of strategies related to these data-collection techniques.

PRACTICAL APPLICATION Using Checklists, Rating Scales, and Rubrics

Three techniques that can facilitate quantification of complex phenomena are checklists, rating scales, and rubrics. A checklist is a list of behaviors or characteristics for which a researcher is looking. The researcher—or in many studies, each participant—simply indicates whether each item on the list is observed, present, or true or, in contrast, is *not* observed, present, or true.

A rating scale is more useful when a behavior, attitude, or other phenomenon of interest needs to be evaluated on a continuum of, say, "inadequate" to "excellent," "never" to "always," or "strongly disapprove" to "strongly approve." Rating scales were developed by Rensis Likert in the 1930s to assess people's attitudes; accordingly, they are sometimes called Likert scales.[2]

Checklists and rating scales can presumably be used in research related to a wide variety of phenomena, including those involving human beings, nonhuman animals, plants, or inanimate objects (e.g., works of art and literature, geomorphological formations). We illustrate the use of both techniques with a simple example involving human participants. In the late 1970s, park rangers at Rocky Mountain National Park in Colorado were concerned about the heavy summertime traffic traveling up a narrow mountain road to Bear Lake, a popular destination for park visitors. So in the summer of 1978, they provided buses that would shuttle visitors to Bear Lake and back again. This being a radical innovation at the time, the rangers wondered about people's reactions to the buses; if there were strong objections, other solutions to the traffic problem would have to be identified for the following summer.

Park officials asked a sociologist friend of ours to address their research question: How do park visitors feel about the new bus system? The sociologist decided that the best way to approach the problem was to conduct a survey. He and his research assistants waited at the parking lot to which buses returned after their trip to Bear Lake; they randomly selected people who exited the bus and administered the survey. With such a captive audience, the response rate was extremely high: 1,246 of the 1,268 people who were approached agreed to participate in the study, yielding a response rate of 98%.

---

[2]Although we have often heard *Likert* pronounced as "lie-kert," Likert pronounced his name "lick-ert."

FIGURE 6.2 ■ Excerpts from a Survey at Rocky Mountain National Park. Item 4 is a *Checklist.* Items 5 and 6 are *Rating Scales*

Source: From Trahan (1978, Appendix A).

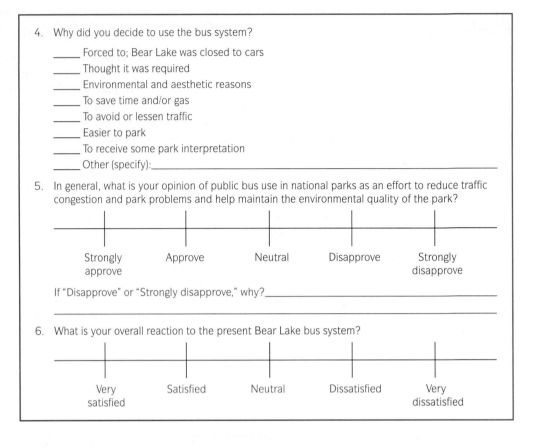

4. Why did you decide to use the bus system?

_____ Forced to; Bear Lake was closed to cars

_____ Thought it was required

_____ Environmental and aesthetic reasons

_____ To save time and/or gas

_____ To avoid or lessen traffic

_____ Easier to park

_____ To receive some park interpretation

_____ Other (specify):_____

5. In general, what is your opinion of public bus use in national parks as an effort to reduce traffic congestion and park problems and help maintain the environmental quality of the park?

Strongly approve   Approve   Neutral   Disapprove   Strongly disapprove

If "Disapprove" or "Strongly disapprove," why?_____

_____

6. What is your overall reaction to the present Bear Lake bus system?

Very satisfied   Satisfied   Neutral   Dissatisfied   Very dissatisfied

We present three of the interview questions in Figure 6.2. Based on people's responses, the sociologist concluded that people were solidly in favor of the bus system (Trahan, 1978). As a result, it continues to be in operation today, many years after the survey was conducted.

One of us authors was once a member of a dissertation committee for a doctoral student who developed a creative way of presenting a Likert scale to children (Shaklee, 1998). The student was investigating the effects of a particular approach to teaching elementary school science and wanted to determine whether students' beliefs about the nature of school learning—especially learning science—would change as a result of the approach. Both before and after the instructional intervention, she read a series of statements and asked students either to agree or to disagree with each one by pointing to one of four faces. The statements and the rating scale that students used to respond to them are presented in Figure 6.3.

Notice that in the rating scale items in the Rocky Mountain National Park survey, park visitors were given the option of responding "Neutral" to each question. In the elementary school study, however, the children always had to answer "Yes" or "No." Experts have mixed views about letting respondents remain neutral in interviews and questionnaires. If you use rating scales in your own research, you should consider the implications of letting respondents straddle the fence by including a "No opinion" or other neutral response, and design your scales accordingly.

Whenever you use checklists or rating scales, you simplify and more easily quantify people's behaviors or attitudes. Furthermore, when participants *themselves* complete these things, you can collect a great deal of data quickly and efficiently. In the process, however, you don't get information about *why* participants respond as they do—qualitative information that might ultimately help you make better sense of the results you obtain.

An additional problem with rating scales is that people don't necessarily agree about what various points along a scale mean; for instance, they may interpret such labels as "Excellent" or "Strongly disapprove" in idiosyncratic ways. Especially when researchers rather than participants are evaluating certain behaviors—or perhaps when they are evaluating certain *products* that participants have created—a more explicit alternative is a rubric. Typically a rubric includes two

FIGURE 6.3 ■ Asking Elementary School Children About Science and Learning

Source: From *Elementary Children's Epistemological Beliefs and Understandings of Science in the Context of Computer-Mediated Video Conferencing With Scientists* (pp. 132, 134) by J. M. Shaklee, 1998, unpublished doctoral dissertation, University of Northern Colorado, Greeley. Reprinted with permission.

Students responded to each statement by pointing to one of the faces below.

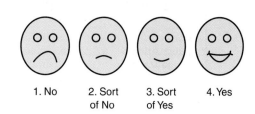

| 1. No | 2. Sort of No | 3. Sort of Yes | 4. Yes |

Students who were unfamiliar with Likert scales practiced the procedure using Items A and B; others began with Item 1.

A. Are cats green?
B. Is it a nice day?
1. The best thing about science is that most problems have one right answer.
2. If I can't understand something quickly, I keep trying.
3. When I don't understand a new idea, it is best to figure it out on my own.
4. I get confused when books have different information from what I already know.
5. An expert is someone who is born really smart.
6. If scientists try hard enough, they can find the truth to almost everything.
7. Students who do well learn quickly.
8. Getting ahead takes a lot of work.
9. The most important part about being a good student is memorizing the facts.
10. I can believe what I read.
11. Truth never changes.
12. Learning takes a long time.
13. Really smart students don't have to work hard to do well in school.
14. Kids who disagree with teachers are show-offs.
15. Scientists can get to the truth.
16. I try to use information from books and many other places.
17. It is annoying to listen to people who can't make up their minds.
18. Everyone needs to learn how to learn.
19. If I try too hard to understand a problem, I just get confused.
20. Sometimes I just have to accept answers from a teacher even if they don't make sense to me.

or more rating scales for assessing different aspects of participants' performance, with concrete descriptions of what performance looks like at different points along each scale. As an example, Figure 6.4 shows a possible six-scale rubric for evaluating various qualities in students' nonfiction writing samples. A researcher could quantify the ratings by attaching numbers to the labels. For example, a "Proficient" score might be 5, an "In Progress" score might be 3, and "Beginning to Develop" might be 1. Such numbers would give the researcher some flexibility in assigning scores (e.g., a 4 might be a bit less skilled than "Proficient" but really more than just "In Progress").

Keep in mind, however, that although rating scales and rubrics might yield numbers, a researcher can't necessarily add the results of different scales together. For one thing, rating scales sometimes yield *ordinal* data rather than *interval* data, precluding even such simple mathematical calculations as addition and subtraction (see the section "Types of Measurement Scales" in Chapter 4). Also, combining the results of different scales into a single score may make no logical sense. For example, imagine that a researcher uses the rubric in Figure 6.4 to evaluate students' writing skills and translates the "Proficient," "In Progress," and "Beginning to Develop" labels into scores of 5, 3, and 1, respectively. And now imagine that one student gets scores of 5 on the first three scales (all of which reflect writing mechanics) but scores of only 1 on the last three scales (all of which reflect organization and logical flow of ideas). Meanwhile, a second student

FIGURE 6.4 ▮ Possible Rubric for Evaluating Students' Nonfiction Writing

Source: Adapted from "Enhancing Learning Through Formative Assessments and Effective Feedback" (interactive learning module) by J.E. Ormrod, 2015, in *Essentials of Educational Psychology* (4th ed.). Copyright 2015, Pearson. Adapted by permission.

Characteristic	*Proficient*	*In Progress*	*Beginning to Develop*
Correct spelling	Writer correctly spells all words.	Writer correctly spells most words.	Writer incorrectly spells many words.
Correct punctuation & capitalization	Writer uses punctuation marks and uppercase letters where, and only where, appropriate.	Writer occasionally (a) omits punctuation marks, (b) inappropriately uses punctuation marks, or (c) inappropriately uses uppercase/lowercase letters.	Writer makes many punctuation and/or capitalization errors.
Complete sentences	Writer uses complete sentences throughout, except when using an incomplete sentence for a clear stylistic purpose. Writing includes no run-on sentences.	Writer uses a few incomplete sentences that have no obvious stylistic purpose, *or* writer occasionally includes a run-on sentence.	Writer includes many incomplete sentences and/or run-on sentences; writer uses periods rarely or indiscriminately.
Clear focus	Writer clearly states main idea; sentences are all related to this idea and present a coherent message.	Writer only implies main idea; most sentences are related to this idea; a few sentences are unnecessary digressions.	Writer rambles, without a clear main idea; *or* writer frequently and unpredictably goes off topic.
Logical train of thought	Writer carefully leads the reader through his/her own line of thinking about the topic.	Writer shows some logical progression of ideas but occasionally omits a key point essential to the flow of ideas.	Writer presents ideas in no logical sequence.
Convincing statements/ arguments	Writer effectively persuades the reader with evidence or sound reasoning.	Writer includes some evidence or reasoning to support ideas/opinions, but a reader could easily offer counterarguments.	Writer offers ideas/opinions with little or no justification.

gets scores of 1 on the three writing-mechanics scales and scores of 5 on the three organization-and-logical-flow scales. Both students would have total scores of 18, yet the quality of the students' writing samples would be quite different.

USING TECHNOLOGY

PRACTICAL APPLICATION Computerizing Observations

One good way of enhancing your efficiency in data collection is to record your observations on a laptop, computer tablet, or smartphone as you are making them. For example, when using a checklist, you might create a spreadsheet with a small number of columns—one for each item on the checklist—and a row for every entity you will observe. Then, as you conduct your observations, you can enter an "X" or other symbol into the appropriate cell whenever you see an item in the checklist. Alternatively, you might download free or inexpensive data-collection software for your smartphone or computer tablet; in smartphone lingo, this is called an application, or "app." Examples are OpenDataKit (opendatakit.org) and GIS Cloud Mobile Data Collection (giscloud.com).

For more complex observations, you might create a general *template* document in spreadsheet or word processing software and then electronically "save" a separate version of the document for each person, situation, or other entity you are observing. You can either print out these entity-specific documents for handwritten coding during your observations, or, if time and your keyboarding skills allow, you can fill in each document while on-site in the research setting.

For some types of observations, existing software programs can greatly enhance a researcher's accuracy and efficiency in collecting observational data. An example is CyberTracker (cybertracker.org), with which researchers can quickly record their observations and—using global positioning system (GPS) signals—the specific locations at which they make each observation. For instance, a biologist working in the field might use this software to record specific places at which various members of an endangered animal species or invasive plant species are observed. Furthermore, CyberTracker enables the researcher to custom-design either verbal or graphics-based checklists for specific characteristics of each observation; for instance, a checklist might include photographs of what different flower species look like or drawings of the different leaf shapes that a plant might have.

PRACTICAL APPLICATION Planning and Conducting Interviews in a Quantitative Study

In a quantitative study, interviews tend to be carefully planned in advance, and they are conducted in a similar, standardized way for all participants. Here we offer guidelines for conducting interviews in a quantitative study; some of them are also applicable to the qualitative interviews described in Chapter 9.

GUIDELINES Conducting Interviews in a Quantitative Study

Taking a few simple steps in planning and conducting interviews can greatly enhance the quality of the data obtained, as reflected in the following recommendations.

1. *Limit questions to those that will directly or indirectly help you answer your research question.* Whenever you ask people to participate in a research study, you are asking for their *time.* They are more likely to say *yes* to your request if you ask for only a short amount of their time—say, 5 or 10 minutes. If, instead, you want a half hour or longer from each potential participant, you're apt to end up with a sample comprised primarily of people who aren't terribly busy—a potential source of bias that can adversely affect the generalizability of your results.

2. *As you write the interview questions, consider how you can quantify the responses, and modify the questions accordingly.* Remember, you are conducting a *quantitative* study. Thus you will, to some extent, be coding people's responses as numbers and, quite possibly, conducting statistical analyses on those numbers. You will be able to assign numerical codes to responses more easily if you identify an appropriate coding scheme ahead of time.

3. *Restrict each question to a single idea.* Don't try to get too much information in any single question; in doing so, you may get multiple kinds of data—"mixed messages," so to speak—that are hard to interpret (Gall, Gall, & Borg, 2007).

4. *Consider asking a few questions that will elicit qualitative information.* You don't necessarily have to quantify *everything.* People's responses to a few open-ended questions may support or provide additional insights into the numerical data you obtain from more structured questions. By combining quantitative and qualitative data in this manner, you are essentially employing a *mixed-methods design.* Accordingly, we return to the topic of survey research in Chapter 12.

USING TECHNOLOGY

5. *Consider how you might use a computer to streamline the process.*   Some computer software programs allow you to record interviews directly onto a laptop computer and then transform these conversations into written text (e.g., see Dragon Naturally Speaking; nuance. com/dragon). Alternatively, if interviewees' responses are likely to be short, you might either (a) use a multiple-choice-format checklist to immediately categorize them or (b) directly type them into a spreadsheet or word processing program.

6. *Pilot-test the questions.*   Despite your best intentions, you may write questions that are ambiguous or misleading or that yield uninterpretable or otherwise useless responses. You can save yourself a great deal of time over the long run if you fine-tune your questions before you begin systematic data collection. You can easily find weak spots in your questions by asking a few volunteers to answer them in a pilot study.

7. *Courteously introduce yourself to potential participants and explain the general purpose of your study.*   You are more likely to gain potential participants' cooperation if you are friendly, courteous, and respectful and if you explain—up front—what you are hoping to learn in your research. The goal here is to motivate people to *want* to help you out by giving you a little bit of their time.

8. *Get written permission.*   Recall the discussion of *informed consent* in the section on ethical issues in Chapter 4. All participants in your study (or, in the case of children, their parents or legal guardians) should agree to participate in advance—and in writing.

9. *Save controversial questions for the latter part of the interview.*   If you will be touching on sensitive topics (e.g., opinions about gun control, attitudes toward people with diverse sexual orientations), put them near the end of the interview, after you have established rapport and gained a person's trust. You might also preface a sensitive topic with a brief statement suggesting that violating certain laws or social norms—although not desirable—is fairly commonplace (Creswell, 2012; Gall et al., 2007). For example, you might say something like this: "Many people admit that they have occasionally driven a car while under the influence of alcohol. Have you ever driven a car when you probably shouldn't have because you've had too much to drink?"

10. *Seek clarifying information when necessary.*   Be alert for responses that are vague or otherwise difficult to interpret. Simple, nonleading questions—for instance, "Can you tell me more about that?"—may yield the additional information you need (Gall et al., 2007, p. 254).

PRACTICAL APPLICATION Constructing and Administering a Questionnaire

Questionnaires seem so simple, yet in our experience they can be tricky to construct and administer. One false step can lead to uninterpretable data or an abysmally low return rate. We have numerous suggestions that can help you make your use of a questionnaire both fruitful and efficient. We have divided our suggestions into three categories: constructing a questionnaire, using technology to facilitate questionnaire administration and data analysis, and maximizing your return rate.

GUIDELINES   Constructing a Questionnaire

Following are 12 guidelines for developing a questionnaire that encourages people to be cooperative and yields responses you can use and interpret. We apologize for the length of the list, but, as we just said, questionnaire construction is a tricky business.

1. ***Keep it short.*** Your questionnaire should be as brief as possible and solicit only information that is essential to the research effort. You should evaluate each item by asking yourself two questions: "What do I intend to do with the information I'm requesting?" and "Is it absolutely essential to have this information to solve part of the research problem?"

2. ***Keep the respondent's task simple and concrete.*** Make the instrument as simple to read and respond to as possible. Remember, you are asking for people's *time,* a precious commodity for many people these days. People are more likely to respond to a questionnaire—and to do so quickly—if they perceive it to be quick and easy to complete (McCrea, Liberman, Trope, & Sherman, 2008).

Open-ended questions—those that ask people to respond with lengthy answers—are time-consuming and can be mentally exhausting for both the participants and the researcher. The usefulness of responses to open-ended items rests entirely on participants' skill to express their thoughts in writing. Those who write in the "Yes/no, and I'll tell you exactly why" style are few and far between. Some respondents may ramble, engaging in discussions that aren't focused or don't answer the questions. Furthermore, after answering 15 to 20 of these questions, your respondents will think you are demanding a book! Such a major compositional exercise is unfair to those from whom you are requesting a favor.

3. ***Provide straightforward, specific instructions.*** Communicate exactly how you want people to respond. For instance, don't assume that they are familiar with Likert scales. Some of them may never have seen such scales before.

4. ***Use simple, clear, unambiguous language.*** Write questions that communicate exactly what you want to know. Avoid terms that your respondents may not understand, such as obscure words or technical jargon. Also avoid words that have imprecise meanings, such as *several* and *usually.*

5. ***Give a rationale for any items whose purpose may be unclear.*** We cannot say this enough: You are asking people to do you a favor by responding to your questionnaire. Give them a reason to *want* to do the favor. Each question should have a purpose, and in one way or another, you should make its purpose clear.

6. ***Check for unwarranted assumptions implicit in your questions.*** Consider a very simple question: "How many cigarettes do you smoke each day?" It seems to be a clear and unambiguous question, especially if it is accompanied with certain choices so that all the respondent has to do is to check one of them:

How many cigarettes do you smoke each day? Check one of the following:
____ More than 25 ____ 25–16 ____ 15–11 ____ 10–6 ____ 5–1 ____ None

One underlying assumption here is that a person is likely to be a smoker rather than a non-smoker, which isn't necessarily the case. A second assumption is that a person smokes the same number of cigarettes each day, but for many smokers this assumption isn't viable; for instance, they may smoke when they're at home rather than at work, or vice versa. How are the people in this group supposed to answer the question?

Had the author of the question considered the assumptions on which the question was predicated, he or she might first have asked questions such as these:

Do you smoke cigarettes?
____ Yes
____ No (If you mark "no," skip the next two questions.)

Are your daily smoking habits reasonably consistent; that is, do you smoke about the same number of cigarettes each day?
____ Yes
____ No (If you mark "no," skip the next question.)

7. ***Word your questions in ways that don't give clues about preferred or more desirable responses.*** Take another question: "What strategies have you used to try to quit smoking?"

By implying that the respondent has, in fact, tried to quit, it may lead the respondent to describe strategies that have never been seriously tried at all.

8. ***Determine in advance how you will code the responses.***   As you write your questions—perhaps even *before* you write them—develop a plan for recoding participants' responses into numerical data you can statistically analyze. Data processing procedures may also dictate the form a questionnaire should take. If, for example, people's response sheets will be fed into a computer scanner, the questionnaire must be structured differently than if the responses will be tabulated using paper and pencil (we'll say more about computer scanning in the subsequent set of guidelines).

9. ***Check for consistency.***   When a questionnaire asks questions about a potentially controversial topic, some respondents might give answers that are socially acceptable rather than accurate in order to present a favorable impression. To allow for this possibility, you may want to ask the same question two or more times—using different words each time—at various points in your questionnaire. For example, consider the following two items, appearing in a questionnaire as Items 2 and 30. (Their distance from each other increases the likelihood that a person will answer the second without recalling how he or she answered the first.) Notice how one individual has answered them:

> 2. Check one of the following choices:
>   _X_ In my thinking, I am a liberal.
>   _____ In my thinking, I am a conservative.

> 30. Check one of the following choices:
>   _____ I find new ideas stimulating and attractive, and I would
>   find it challenging to be among the first to try them.
>   _X_ I subscribe to the position of Alexander Pope:
>   "Be not the first by whom the new is tried,
>   nor yet the last to lay the old aside."

The two responses are inconsistent. In the first, the respondent claims to be a liberal thinker but later, when given liberal and conservative positions in other forms, indicates a position generally thought to be more conservative than liberal. Such an inconsistency might lead you to question whether the respondent really *is* a liberal thinker or only wants to be seen as one.

When developing a questionnaire, researchers sometimes include several items designed to assess essentially the same characteristic. This approach is especially common in studies that involve personality characteristics, motivation, attitudes, and other complex psychological traits. For example, one of us authors once worked with two colleagues to explore factors that might influence the teaching effectiveness of college education majors who were completing their teaching internship year (Middleton, Ormrod, & Abrams, 2007). The research team speculated that one factor potentially affecting teaching effectiveness was willingness to try new teaching techniques and in other ways take reasonable risks in the classroom. The team developed eight items to assess risk taking. Following are four examples, which were interspersed among items designed to assess other characteristics:

		Not at All True		Somewhat True		Very True
11.	I would prefer to teach in a way that is familiar to me rather than trying a teaching strategy that I would have to learn how to do.	1	2	3	4	5
16.	I like trying new approaches to teaching, even if I occasionally find they don't work very well.	1	2	3	4	5
39.	I would choose to teach something I knew I could do, rather than a topic I haven't taught before.	1	2	3	4	5
51.	I sometimes change my plan in the middle of a lesson if I see an opportunity to practice teaching skills I haven't yet mastered.	1	2	3	4	5

Notice how a response of "Very True" to Items 16 and 51 would be indicative of a *high* risk taker, whereas a response of "Very True" to Items 11 and 39 would be indicative of a *low* risk taker. Such counterbalancing of items—some reflecting a high level of a characteristic and others reflecting a low level of the characteristic—can help address some people's general tendency to agree or disagree with a great many statements, including contradictory ones (Nicholls, Orr, Okubo, & Loftus, 2006).

When several items assess the same characteristic—*and* when the responses can reasonably be presumed to reflect an interval (rather than ordinal) measurement scale—responses to those items might be combined into a single score. But a researcher who uses a counterbalancing approach cannot simply add up a participant's numerical responses for a particular characteristic. For example, for the four risk-taking items just presented, a researcher who wants high risk takers to have higher scores than low risk takers might give 5 points each for "Very True" responses to the high-risk-taking items (16 and 51) and 5 points each for "Not at All True" responses to the low-risk-taking items (11 and 39). In general, the values of the low-risk-taking items would, during scoring, be opposite to what they are on the questionnaire, with 1s being worth 5 points each, 2s being worth 4 points, 3s being worth 3, 4s being worth 2, and 5s being worth 1. In Appendix A, we describe how to recode participants' responses in precisely this way.

Especially when multiple items are created to assess a single characteristic, a good researcher mathematically determines the degree to which, overall, participants' responses to those items are consistent—for instance, the extent to which each person's responses to all "risk-taking" items yield similar results. Essentially, the researcher is determining the *internal consistency reliability* of the set of items. Most statistical software packages can easily compute internal consistency reliability coefficients for you.[3]

Ideally, preliminary data on internal consistency reliability is collected in advance of full-fledged data collection. This point leads us to our next suggestion: Conduct at least one pilot test.

10. *Conduct one or more pilot tests to determine the validity of your questionnaire.* Even experienced researchers conduct test runs of newly designed questionnaires to make sure that questions are clear and will effectively solicit the desired information. At a minimum, you should give your questionnaire to several friends or colleagues to see whether they have difficulty understanding any items. Have them actually fill out the questionnaire. Better still, ask your pilot test participants what thoughts run through their minds as they read a question:

> Please read this question out loud. . . . What is this question trying to find out from you? . . . Which answer would you choose as the right answer for you? . . . Can you explain to me why you chose that answer? (Karabenick et al., 2007, p. 143)

Through such strategies you can see the kinds of responses you are likely to get and make sure that, in your actual study, the responses you obtain will be of sufficient quality to help you answer your research question.

If your research project will include participants of both genders and various cultural backgrounds, be sure to include a diverse sample in your pilot test(s) as well. Gender and culture *do* play a role in people's responses to certain types of questionnaire items. For instance, some researchers have found a tendency for males to play up their strengths and overrate their abilities, whereas females are apt to ruminate on their weaknesses and *under*rate their abilities (Chipman, 2005; Lundeberg & Mohan, 2009). And people from East Asian cultures are more likely to downplay their abilities than people from Western cultures (Heine, 2007). Keep such differences in mind when asking people to rate themselves on their strengths and weaknesses, and experiment with different wordings that might minimize the effects of gender and culture on participants' responses.

Conducting a pilot study for a questionnaire—and especially asking participants what they are thinking as they read and respond to particular items—is one step toward determining whether a questionnaire has validity for its purpose—in other words, whether it truly measures

---

[3]Two common reliability coefficients, known by the researchers who originated them, are the Kuder-Richardson Formula 20 (for either–or responses such as *yes* vs. *no* or *true* vs. *false*) and Cronbach's alpha coefficient (for multinumber rating scales such as the 5-point scale for the risk-taking items).

TABLE 6.1 ■ Guide for the Construction of a Questionnaire

Write the question in the space below.	Why are you asking the question? How does it relate to the research problem?

what it is intended to measure. Some academic disciplines (e.g., psychology and related fields) insist that a researcher use more formal and objective strategies to determine a questionnaire's validity, especially when the questionnaire is intended to measure complex psychological traits (e.g., personality, motivation, attitudes). We refer you to the section "Determining the Validity of a Measurement Instrument" in Chapter 4 for a refresher on three potentially relevant strategies: creating a table of specifications, taking a multitrait–multimethod approach, and consulting with a panel of experts.

11. *Scrutinize the almost-final product one more time to make sure it addresses your needs.*   Item by item, a questionnaire should be quality tested again and again for precision, objectivity, relevance, and probability of favorable reception and return. Have you concentrated on the recipient of the questionnaire, putting yourself in the place of someone who is being asked to invest time on your behalf? If you received such a questionnaire from a stranger, would *you* agree to complete it? These questions are important and should be answered impartially.

Above all, you should make sure that *every question is essential for you to address the research problem.* Table 6.1 can help you examine your items with this criterion in mind. Using either paper and pencil or appropriate software (e.g., a spreadsheet or the *table* feature in a word processing program), insert each item in the left-hand column and then, in the right-hand column, explain why you need to include it. If you can't explain how an item relates to your research problem, throw it out!

12. *Make the questionnaire attractive and professional looking.*   Your final instrument should have clean lines, crystal-clear printing (and certainly no typos!), and perhaps two or more colors. It should ultimately communicate that its author is a careful, well-organized professional who takes his or her work seriously and has high regard for the research participants.

USING TECHNOLOGY

GUIDELINES Using Technology to Facilitate Questionnaire Administration and Data Analysis

Throughout most of the 20th century, questionnaire-based surveys were almost exclusively paper-and-pencil in nature. But with continuing technological advances and people's increasing computer literacy in recent years, many survey researchers are now turning to technology to share some of the burden of data collection and analysis. One possibility is to use a dedicated website both to recruit participants and to gather their responses to survey questions; we address this strategy in a Practical Application feature a bit later in the chapter. Following are several additional suggestions for using technology to make the use of a questionnaire more efficient and cost-effective.

1. *When participants are in the same location that you are, have them respond to the questionnaire directly on a laptop or tablet.*   Electronic questionnaires can be highly effective if participants feel comfortable with computer technology. When participants enter their responses directly into a computer, you obviously save a great deal of time. Furthermore, when appropriately programmed to do so, a computer can record how *quickly* people respond—information that may in some situations be relevant to your research question.

2. *When participants are at diverse locations, use e-mail to request participation and obtain participants' responses.*   If the people you want to survey have easily obtainable e-mail addresses and are regularly online, an e-mail request to participate can be quite appropriate. Furthermore, you can send the survey either within the body of your e-mail message or as an attachment. Participants can respond in a return e-mail message or electronically fill out and return your attachment.

3. *If you use paper mail delivery rather than e-mail, use a word processing program to personalize your correspondence.*   Inquiry letters, thank-you letters, and other correspondence can be personalized by using the *merge* function of most word processing programs. This function allows you to combine the information in your database with the documents you wish to send out. For example, when printing the final version of your cover letter, you can include the person's name immediately after the greeting (e.g., "Dear Carlos" or "Dear Mr. Asay")—a simple touch that is likely to yield a higher return rate than letters addressed to "Potential Respondent" or "To whom it may concern." The computer inserts the names for you; you need only tell it where to find the names in your database.

4. *Use a scanner to facilitate data tabulation.*   When you need a large sample to address your research problem adequately, you should consider in advance how you will tabulate the responses after the questionnaires are returned to you. One widely used strategy is to have a computer scan preformatted answer sheets and automatically sort and organize the results. To use this strategy, your questions must each involve a small set of possible answers; for instance, they might be multiple-choice, have yes-or-no answers, or involve 5-point rating scales. You will want participants to respond using a pencil or dark-colored ink. Enclosing a small number 2 pencil with the questionnaire you send is common courtesy. Furthermore, anything you can do to make the participants' task easier—even something as simple as providing the writing implement—will increase your response rate.

5. *Use a computer database to keep track of who has responded and who has not.*   An electronic spreadsheet or other database software program provides an easy way of keeping track of people's names and addresses, along with information regarding (a) which individuals have and have not yet received your request for participation, (b) which ones have and have not responded to your request, and (c) which ones need a first or second reminder letter or e-mail message. Also, many spreadsheet programs include templates for printing mailing labels.

GUIDELINES   Maximizing Your Return Rate for a Questionnaire

As university professors, we authors have sometimes been asked to distribute questionnaires in our classes that relate, perhaps, to some aspect of the university's student services or to students' preferences for the university calendar. The end-of-semester teacher evaluation forms you often fill out are questionnaires as well. Even though participation in such surveys is voluntary, the response rate when one has such a captive audience is typically quite high, often 100%.

Mailing or e-mailing questionnaires to people one doesn't know is quite another matter. Potential respondents have little or nothing to gain by answering and returning the questionnaire, and thus many of them don't return it. As a result, the typical return rate for a mailed questionnaire is 50% or less, and that for an e-mailed questionnaire is even lower (Rogelberg & Luong, 1998; Sheehan, 2001).

We think of one doctoral student who conducted dissertation research in the area of reading. As part of her study, she sent a questionnaire to reading teachers to inquire about their beliefs and attitudes regarding a certain kind of children's literature. Initially, the student sent out 103 questionnaires; 14 teachers completed and returned them (a return rate of 13%). In a second attempt, she sent out 72 questionnaires to a different group of teachers; 12 responded (a return rate of 15%). In one final effort, she sought volunteers on the Internet by using two lists of teachers' e-mail addresses; 57 teachers indicated that they were willing to fill out her questionnaire, and 20 of them actually did so (a return rate of 35%).

Was the student frustrated? Absolutely! Yet she had made a couple of mistakes that undoubtedly thwarted her efforts from the beginning. First, the questionnaire had 36 questions, 18 of which were open-ended ones requiring lengthy written responses. A quick glance would tell any discerning teacher that the questionnaire would take an entire evening to complete. Second, the questionnaires were sent out in the middle of the school year, when teachers were probably already quite busy planning lessons, grading papers, and writing reports. Even teachers who truly wanted to help this struggling doctoral student (who was a former teacher herself) may simply not have found the time to do it. Fortunately for the student, the questionnaire was only one small part of her study, and she was able to complete her dissertation successfully with the limited (and almost certainly nonrepresentative) sample of responses she received.

Should you decide that a mailed or e-mailed questionnaire is the most suitable approach for answering your research question, the following guidelines can help you increase your return rate.

1. *Consider the timing.*   The student just described mailed her questionnaires in the winter and early spring because she wanted to graduate at the end of the summer. The timing of her mailing was convenient for her, but it was *not* convenient for the people to whom she sent the questionnaire. Her response rate—and her study!—suffered as a result. Consider the characteristics of the sample you are surveying, and try to anticipate when respondents will be most likely to have time to answer a questionnaire. And as a general rule, stay away from peak holiday and vacation times, such as mid-December through early January.

2. *Make a good first impression.*   Put yourself in the place of a potential respondent. Imagine a stranger sending you the questionnaire you propose to send. What is your initial impression as you open the envelope or e-mail message? Is the questionnaire inordinately long and time-consuming? Is it cleanly and neatly written? Does it give an impression of uncluttered ease? Are the areas for response adequate and clearly indicated? Is the tone courteous, and are the requests reasonable?

3. *Motivate potential respondents.*   Give people a reason to *want* to respond. Occasionally, researchers may actually have the resources to pay people for their time or offer other concrete inducements. But more often than not, you will have to rely on the power of persuasion to gain cooperation. Probably the best mechanism for doing so is the cover letter or e-mail message that accompanies your questionnaire.

One potentially effective strategy is to send a letter soliciting people's cooperation *before* actually sending them the questionnaire. For example, Figure 6.5 shows an example of a letter that a researcher might use to gain people's cooperation in responding to a questionnaire about the quality of a particular academic program. Several aspects of the letter are important to note:

- The letter begins with the name of the sponsoring institution. Ideally, a cover letter is written on the institution's official letterhead stationery. (Alternatively, an e-mail request for participation might include an eye-catching banner with the institution's name and logo.)
- Rather than saying "Dear Sir or Madam," the letter is personalized for the recipient.
- The letter describes the potential value of the study, both for the individual and for alumni in general, hence giving the potential responder a reason to *want* to respond.

FIGURE 6.5 ■ A Letter of Inquiry

A B C University
Address

Date

Dear [person's name],

Your alma mater is appealing to you for help. We are not asking for funds, merely for a few minutes of your time.

We know you are proud of your accomplishments at A B C University, and your degree has almost certainly helped you advance your professional aspirations. You can help us maintain—and ideally also improve—your program's reputation by giving us your honest opinion of its strengths and weaknesses while you were here. We have a questionnaire that, with your permission, we would like to send you. It should take at most only 15 minutes of your time.

Our program is growing, and with your help it can increase not only in size but also in excellence and national prominence. We are confident that you can help us make it the best that it can possibly be.

Enclosed with this letter is a return postcard on which you can indicate your willingness to respond to our questionnaire. Thank you in advance for your kind assistance. And please don't hesitate to contact me at ___[telephone number]___ or ___[e-mail address]___ if you have any questions or concerns.

Respectfully yours,

Your Signature

Your Name

- The letter assures the individual that his or her cooperation will not place any unreasonable burden—in particular, that the questionnaire will take a maximum of 15 minutes to complete.
- By filling out and sending a simple enclosed postcard (for example, see Figure 6.6)—a quick and easy first step—the researcher gains the individual's commitment to completing a lengthier, more complex task in the near future. The postcard should be addressed and stamped for easy return.
- The letter includes two means of communicating with the researcher in case the individual has any reservations about participating in the study.
- The overall tone of the letter is, from beginning to end, courteous and respectful.

Compare the letter in Figure 6.5 with the brief note in Figure 6.7 that was sent to one of us authors and that, unfortunately, is all too typical of students' first attempts at drafting a cover letter. A focus only on the researcher's needs in letters of this sort may be another reason for the poor return of questionnaires in some research projects.

FIGURE 6.6 ■ Questionnaire Response Card

Dear [your name]:

☐ Please send the questionnaire; I will be happy to cooperate.

☐ I am sorry, but I do not wish to answer the questionnaire.

Comments:

Date: _____   _____

Name

X Y Z UNIVERSITY
Campus Station

Dear Sir:

I am a graduate student at X Y Z University, and the enclosed questionnaire is sent to you in the hope that you will assist me in obtaining information for my master's thesis.

I should appreciate your early reply since I am attempting to get my degree this June.

Yours truly,

John Doe

John Doe

The cover letter is extremely important. It should be carefully and thoughtfully composed and should stress the concerns of the recipient rather than any selfish interests of the sender. Some students forget this and, in doing so, unintentionally reveal their own self-centeredness.

4. *If mailing your questionnaire, include a self-addressed envelope with return postage.*   To impose on a person's time and spirit of cooperation and then to expect that person also to supply the envelope and pay the postage is unreasonable.

5. *Offer the results of your study.*   In return for the investment of time and the courtesy of replying to your questions, offer to send your respondent a summary of your study's results. At either the beginning or end of your instrument, you might provide a box to check to indicate the desire for a summary, together with a place for name and either mailing or e-mailing address. If anonymity is important, a mailed questionnaire might include a separate postcard on which the respondent can request the summary; this postcard should, of course, have a place for the respondent's name and address, along with the suggestion that the card be mailed separately from the questionnaire. For e-mailed questionnaires, a respondent can simply hit the "reply" button twice, once to return the completed questionnaire and a second time (perhaps a few hours later) to request the study's results.

6. *Be gently persistent.*   Many experts suggest that when people don't initially respond to a questionnaire, you can increase your response rate by sending two follow-up reminders, perhaps sending each one out a week or two after the previous mailing (e.g., Neuman, 2011; Rogelberg & Luong, 1998). But if the questionnaire is meant to be anonymous, how do you know who has returned it and who has not?

To address this problem, many researchers put a different code number on each copy they send out and keep a list of which number they have sent to each person in their sample. When a questionnaire is returned, they remove the number and person's name from the list. When it is time to send a follow-up letter, they send it only to the people who are still on the list. Researchers should use the list of names and code numbers *only* for this purpose. At no point should they use it to determine who responded in what way to each question—a practice that violates the right to privacy discussed in Chapter 4.

Let's return to the solicitation letter and postcard in Figures 6.5 and 6.6. We have modeled them after a letter and postcard that an American University faculty member successfully used to get alumni feedback about the university's nursing program. After receiving a card that indicated willingness to cooperate, the faculty member immediately mailed the questionnaire. She kept a log of questionnaires mailed, the names and addresses of people to whom they were mailed, and the date of mailing. If she didn't receive a reply within 3 weeks' time, she sent a reminder letter. The reminder was written in the same tone as the initial letter. An example of such a reminder letter appears in Figure 6.8.

The faculty member's follow-up letter brought results. She was being firm and persuasive, but with considerable skill and tact. Courtesy, understanding, and respect for others pay large dividends in a situation in which a researcher needs others' cooperation, especially in questionnaire studies.

FIGURE 6.8 ■ A Follow-Up Letter

A B C University
Address

Date

Dear [person's name],

We are all very busy these days, and sometimes we have trouble staying on top of our many commitments. Despite our best intentions, we may sometimes overlook something we have said we would do.

Three weeks ago I sent you a questionnaire asking for your input regarding your program at A B C University. To date I have not yet received your completed questionnaire. Perhaps you have simply mislaid it, or perhaps it has been lost in the mail—any one of several reasons might account for its delay in reaching me.

In any event, I am enclosing another copy of the questionnaire, along with another self-addressed, stamped envelope. I am hoping you can find 15 minutes somewhere in your busy schedule to complete and return the questionnaire. I would really appreciate your personal insights and suggestions regarding your experiences in our program.

Thank you once again for your assistance and generosity in helping us enhance our program. And remember that if you have any questions, you can easily reach me at [telephone number] or [e-mail address].

Respectfully yours,

Your Signature

Your Name

USING TECHNOLOGY

PRACTICAL APPLICATION Using the Internet to Collect Data for a Descriptive Study

In recent years, some researchers have collected descriptive data directly on the Internet. For instance, they may put a questionnaire on a website and ask people who visit the site to respond. One site providing links to a wide variety of online research projects is "Psychological Research on the Net," maintained by John Krantz, Professor of Psychology at Hanover College (psych.hanover.edu). As this edition of the book goes to press, the site is hosting research projects on such diverse topics as eating habits, music preferences, religious beliefs, friendships, and parental disciplinary strategies. Dr. Krantz checks to be sure that each project has been approved by the appropriate internal review board and incorporates informed consent procedures. There is no fee for using the site.

Commercial websites for data collection are available as well. Two popular ones are SurveyMonkey (surveymonkey.com) and Zoomerang (zoomerang.com), each of which charges a modest monthly fee. These websites provide templates that make questionnaire design easy and enable a researcher to present a variety of item types (e.g., multiple-choice items, rating scales). They also include features for communicating with a preselected sample of participants (e.g., through e-mail invitations), as well as features through which the researcher can tabulate, statistically analyze, and download the results.

Conducting a survey online has several advantages (Kraut et al., 2004). When the desired sample size is quite large, an online questionnaire is far more cost-effective than a mailed questionnaire. Often a questionnaire can be adapted based on a participant's previous responses; for instance, if a person responds *no* to the question "Do you smoke cigarettes?" the questionnaire software will subsequently skip questions related to smoking habits. Furthermore, some evidence indicates that online surveys yield data comparable to those obtained through face-to-face contact (Gosling, Vazire, Srivastava, & John, 2004).

If you choose to collect data on the Internet, keep in mind that your ethical standards must be just as rigorous as they would be if you were collecting data through face-to-face contacts or the postal service. Participants must be informed about and agree to the general nature of a study, perhaps by means of a website page that serves as an informed consent letter and a virtual "click to accept" button with which participants can indicate consent (Kraut et al., 2004). Also, participants' responses must remain as confidential as they would in any study. The *protection from harm* ethical standard can be especially troublesome in an online study, as it may be virtually impossible to determine that a participant has found a task or question extremely stressful or upsetting and needs some sort of follow-up intervention. Your research advisor and university's internal review board can help you work through ethical issues and develop appropriate precautions for any study that might potentially cause even minor harm or distress to participants.

Sampling, too, must be a source of concern in an online study. SurveyMonkey and Zoomerang enable a researcher to zero in on a predetermined sample of participants—for example, by uploading a list of e-mail addresses to which the participation request will be sent. Other online research projects, such as those on the "Psychological Research on the Net" website mentioned earlier, are open to anyone who wants to participate. But in virtually any online study, the people who participate won't be representative either of a particular group of people or of the overall population of human beings (Gosling et al., 2004; McGraw, Tew, & Williams, 2000). After all, participants will be limited to people who (a) are comfortable with computers, (b) spend a fair amount of time on the Internet, (c) enjoy partaking in research studies, and (d) have been sufficiently enticed by your research topic to do what you ask of them. In cases where a questionnaire can be completed by anyone who has access to the Internet, many responders are apt to be college students who are earning course credit for their participation. In short, *your sample will be biased to some degree.*

Sampling is a concern for any researcher, but it is especially so for the researcher who wants to draw inferences about a large population. In the following section, we look at strategies for selecting an appropriate sample.

CHOOSING A SAMPLE IN A DESCRIPTIVE STUDY

Any researcher who conducts a descriptive study wants to determine *the nature of how things are.* Especially when conducting survey research, the researcher may want to describe one or more characteristics of a fairly large population—perhaps the television viewing habits of 10-year-olds, the teaching philosophies of elementary school teachers, or the attitudes that visitors to Rocky Mountain National Park have about a shuttle bus system. Whether the population is 10-year-olds, elementary school teachers, or national park visitors, we are talking about *very large* groups of people; for example, more than 3 million people visit Rocky Mountain National Park every year.

In such situations, researchers typically do not study the entire population of interest. Instead, they select a subset, or sample, of the population. But they can use the results obtained from their sample to make generalizations about the entire population only if *the sample is truly representative of the population.* Here we are talking about a research study's *external validity,* a concept introduced in Chapter 4.

When stating their research problems, many novice researchers forget that they will be studying a sample rather than a population. They announce, for example, that their goal is

> to survey the legal philosophies of the attorneys of the United States and to analyze the relationship of these several philosophical positions with respect to the recent decisions of the Supreme Court of the United States.

If the researcher means what he or she has said, he or she proposes to survey "the attorneys"—all of them! The American Bar Association consists of approximately 400,000 attorneys distributed over more than 3.5 million square miles. Surveying all of them would be a gargantuan undertaking.

A researcher who intends to survey only a subset of a population should say so, perhaps by using such qualifying words as *selected, representative, typical, certain,* or *a random sample of.* For example, the researcher who wants to study the philosophical perspectives of American Bar Association members might begin the problem statement by saying, "The purpose of this research is to survey the legal philosophies of a random sample of attorneys. . . ." Careful researchers say precisely what they mean.

The specific sampling procedure used depends on the purpose of the sampling and a careful consideration of the parameters of the population. But in general, *the sample should be so carefully chosen that, through it, the researcher is able to see characteristics of the total population in the same proportions and relationships that they would be seen if the researcher were, in fact, to examine the total population.*

When you look through the wrong end of a set of binoculars, you see the world in miniature. If the lenses aren't precision-made and accurately ground, you get a distorted view of what you're looking at. In the same way, a sample should, ideally, be a population microcosm. If the sampling procedure isn't carefully planned, any conclusions the researcher draws from the data are likely to be distorted. We discuss this and other possible sources of bias later in the chapter.

Sampling Designs

Different sampling designs may be more or less appropriate in different situations and for different research questions. Here we consider eight approaches to sampling, which fall into two major categories: probability sampling and nonprobability sampling.

Probability Sampling

In probability sampling, the sample is chosen from the overall population by *random selection*— that is, it is selected in such a way that each member of the population has an equal chance of being chosen. When such a *random sample* is selected, the researcher can assume that the characteristics of the sample approximate the characteristics of the total population.

An analogy might help. Suppose we have a beaker containing 100 ml of water. Another beaker holds 10 ml of a concentrated acid. We combine the water and acid in proportions of 10:1. After thoroughly mixing the water and acid, we should be able to extract 1 ml from any part of the solution and find that the sample contains 10 parts water for every 1 part acid. In the same way, if we have a population with considerable variability in ethnic background, education level, social standing, wealth, and other factors, and if we have a perfectly selected random sample—a situation usually more theoretical than logistically feasible—we will find in the sample the same characteristics that exist in the larger population, and we will find them in roughly the same proportions.

There are many possible methods of choosing a random sample. For example, we could assign each person in the population a unique number and then use an arbitrary method of picking certain numbers, perhaps by using a roulette wheel (if the entire population consists of 36 or fewer members) or drawing numbers out of a hat. Many computer spreadsheet programs and Internet websites also provide means of picking random numbers (e.g., search for "random number generator").

A popular paper-and-pencil method of selecting a random sample is to use a table of random numbers, which you can easily find on the Internet and in many statistics textbooks. Figure 6.9 presents an excerpt from such a table. Typically a table of random numbers includes blocks of digits that can be identified by specific row and column numbers. For instance, the excerpt in Figure 6.9 shows 25 blocks, each of which includes 50 digits arranged in pairs. Each 50-digit block can be identified by both a row number (shown at the very left) and a column number (shown at the very top). To ensure a truly random sample, the researcher identifies a starting point in the table *randomly*.

How might we identify a starting entry number? Pull a dollar bill from your wallet. The one we have just pulled as we write this book has the serial number L45391827A. We choose the first 2 digits of the serial number, which makes the entry number 45. But which is the row

FIGURE 6.9 ■
Choosing the Starting
Point in a Random
Numbers Table

	1	2	3	④	5
	38 01 08 18 62	82 52 01 82 29	02 56 28 19 24	88 42 9‑2 63 07	23 99 90 93 57
	51 10 40 21 24	04 69 90 71 43	04 78 84 81 84	41 31 8‑2 31 79	40 79 15 65 18
1	92 12 24 41 22	72 73 42 19 31	84 53 15 16 78	98 77 8‑6 76 75	66 51 70 90 93
	94 72 67 55 42	52 52 26 41 89	32 38 14 58 97	71 94 9‑3 90 49	66 42 05 69 12
	77 75 72 87 20	86 70 64 02 44	89 24 08 35 53	32 96 0‑0 84 78	48 68 39 83 83
	92 44 11 50 85	05 70 08 70 64	91 81 58 48 16	61 87 4‑8 52 08	60 42 80 59 20
	60 04 91 78 89	71 40 77 32 66	11 30 10 01 21	49 12 8‑8 73 47	68 54 94 32 12
2	28 39 28 16 75	92 57 77 21 95	56 93 73 19 17	94 62 1‑8 76 31	00 85 74 86 15
	88 49 94 80 45	16 20 72 31 64	74 04 31 00 86	97 79 3‑3 98 04	55 26 34 15 70
	71 23 62 84 00	35 01 41 52 70	05 91 02 35 24	53 74 6‑0 11 41	36 34 18 08 46
	96 96 31 54 02	00 91 92 76 35	15 68 62 95 24	32 12 7‑3 38 93	77 48 20 37 37
	42 24 86 51 17	60 92 31 00 55	68 99 02 84 40	43 90 6‑7 66 07	93 58 14 66 19
3	48 04 03 20 10	64 51 11 11 69	31 07 84 90 36	84 56 5‑0 31 14	58 67 15 93 17
	24 82 46 95 57	73 54 42 99 51	33 72 12 89 86	63 44 3‑4 78 78	62 23 04 30 78
	81 67 50 87 94	68 85 73 36 83	04 80 31 52 66	70 04 3‑2 61 56	87 67 45 06 85
	13 45 91 94 98	03 88 43 86 42	98 65 79 38 10	91 12 8‑1 98 30	31 10 49 95 83
	72 24 96 81 87	52 68 73 61 17	51 94 47 58 01	13 88 4‑0 38 70	51 11 02 00 63
4	55 05 71 44 11	66 04 57 07 14	92 20 82 92 33	30 08 9‑6 22 15	50 11 40 49 63
	92 36 97 30 14	88 41 90 80 35	07 75 80 26 05	94 14 3‑1 80 07	55 41 14 57 90
	89 92 58 84 08	73 41 65 61 95	43 97 81 33 05	74 67 2‑2 23 00	86 26 66 99 63
	26 80 83 98 13	77 10 83 11 03	00 44 16 60 42	30 88 02 35 74	26 31 51 32 71
	10 71 47 27 12	75 45 51 26 23	19 59 86 21 70	98 76 96 40 12	97 70 77 57 74
⑤	44 94 81 62 78	00 77 55 27 14	52 71 25 82 30 →	52 02 54 04 07	51 23 05 30 59
	33 85 26 45 29	22 81 84 43 83	11 60 71 38 45	93 07 22 30 42	99 30 52 21 40
	45 50 56 50 40	26 05 25 93 64	78 17 59 58 83	80 47 43 71 41	03 06 18 79 54

and which is the column? We flip a coin. If it comes down heads, the first digit will designate the row; otherwise, the digit will designate the column. The coin comes down tails. This means that we will begin in the fourth column and the fifth row. The block where the two intersect is the block where we begin within the table, as shown in Figure 6.9.

We don't have to use a dollar bill to determine the entry point, of course. We could use any source of numbers, such as a telephone directory, a license plate, a friend's social security number, or the stock quotations page in a newspaper. Not all of these suggested sources reflect strictly random numbers; instead, some numbers may appear more frequently than others. Nevertheless, using such a source ensures that the entry point into the table is chosen *arbitrarily,* eliminating any chance that the researcher might either intentionally or unintentionally tilt the sample selection in one direction or another.

Having determined the starting block, we must now consider the size of the proposed sample. If it is to be fewer than 100 individuals, we will need only 2-digit numbers. If it is to be more than 99 but fewer than 1,000, we will need 3 digits to accommodate the sample size.

At this point, let's go back to the total population to consider the group from which the sample is to be drawn. It will be necessary to designate individuals in some manner. A reasonable approach is to arrange the members of the population in a logical order—for instance, alphabetically by surname—and assign each member a serial number for identification purposes.

We are now ready for the random selection. We start with the upper left-hand digits in the designated starting block and work downward through the 2-digit column in the rest of the table. If we need additional numbers, we proceed to the top of the next column, work our way down, and so on, until we have selected the sample we need. For purposes of illustration, we will assume that the total population consists of 90 individuals from which we will select a sample of 40.

We will need random numbers of 2 digits each. Beginning in the upper left-hand corner of the designated block and remembering that only 90 individuals are in the total population, we see that the first number in the leftmost column is 30, so we choose individual number 30 in the population. The next number (98) doesn't apply because only 90 people are in the population. Our next choice is 52, we ignore 93, and then we choose 80. Proceeding to the next block down, we choose 23 and 12, ignore 92, choose 3 and 33. We continue down the column and proceed to any additional columns we need, ignoring the numbers 91–99, 00, and any numbers we've already selected, until we get a sample of 40.

We have probably said enough about the use of a random numbers table. We turn now to specific probability sampling techniques.

Simple Random Sampling
Simple random sampling is exactly the process just described: Every member of the population has an equal chance of being selected. Such an approach is easy when the population is small and all of its members are known. For example, one of us authors once used it in a study to evaluate the quality of certain teacher training institutes one summer (Cole & Ormrod, 1995). Fewer than 300 people had attended the institutes, and we knew who and where they all were. But for very large populations—for instance, all 10-year-olds or all lawyers—simple random sampling is neither practical nor, in many cases, possible.

Stratified Random Sampling
Think of Grades 4, 5, and 6 in a public school. This is a *stratified population*. It has three different layers (*strata)* of distinctly different types of individuals. In stratified random sampling, the researcher samples equally from each of the layers in the overall population.

If we were to sample a population of fourth-, fifth-, and sixth-grade children in a particular school, we would assume that the three strata are roughly equal in size (i.e., there are similar numbers of children at each grade level), and thus we would take equal samples from each of the three grades. Our sampling method would look like that in Figure 6.10.

Stratified random sampling has the advantage of guaranteeing equal representation of each of the identified strata. It is most appropriate when the strata are roughly equal in size in the overall population.

FIGURE 6.10
Stratified Random
Sampling Design

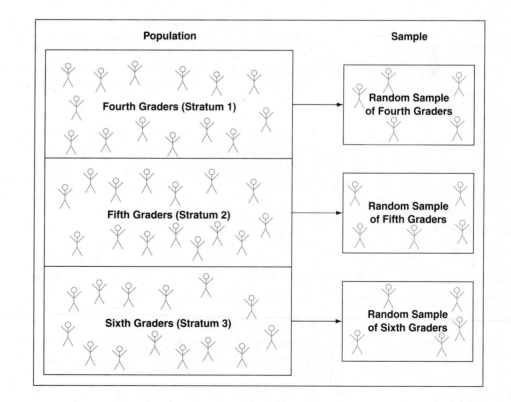

FIGURE 6.11 ■
Proportional Stratified
Sampling Design

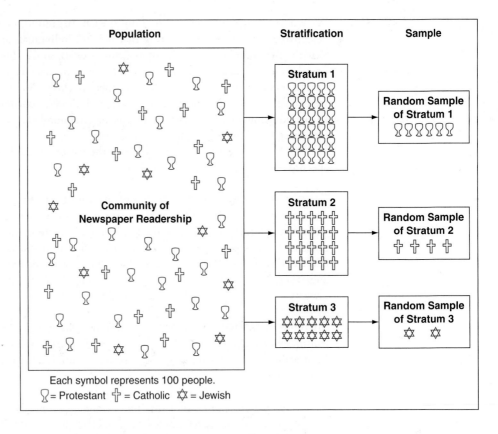

Proportional Stratified Sampling

Proportional Stratified Sampling   Proportional stratified sampling is appropriate when various strata are *different* in size. For example, imagine a small town that has 1,000 Jewish residents, 2,000 Catholics, and 3,000 Protestants. A local newspaper publishes a section dealing with interfaith church news, religious events, and syndicated articles of interest to the religious community in general. The editor decides to conduct a survey in order to obtain certain information and opinions from the paper's readers.

In this situation, the editor chooses his sample in accordance with the proportions of each religious group in the paper's readership. For every Jewish person, there should be two Catholics and three Protestants. In this situation, the people are not obviously segregated into the different strata, so the first step is to identify the members of each stratum and then select a random sample from each one. Figure 6.11 represents this type of sampling.

Cluster Sampling   Sometimes the population of interest is spread over a large area, such that it isn't feasible to make a list of every population member. Instead, we might obtain a map of the area showing political boundaries or other subdivisions. We can then subdivide the area into smaller units, or *clusters*—perhaps precincts, school boundary areas, or counties. In cluster sampling, clusters should be as similar to one another as possible, with each cluster containing an equally heterogeneous mix of individuals.

A subset of the clusters is randomly selected, and the members of these clusters comprise our sample. For example, imagine that we want to learn the opinions of Jewish, Catholic, and Protestant residents in a fairly large community. We might divide the community into 12 areas, or clusters. We randomly select clusters 1, 4, 9, and 10, and their members become our sample. This sampling design is depicted in Figure 6.12.

Systematic Sampling   Systematic sampling involves choosing individuals—or perhaps clusters—according to a predetermined sequence, with the sequence being determined by chance. For instance, we might create a randomly scrambled list of units that lie within the population of interest and then select every 10th unit on the list.

Let's return to the 12 clusters shown in Figure 6.12. Half of the cell numbers are odd, and the other half are even. Using a systematic sampling approach, we choose, by *predetermined*

FIGURE 6.12 ■
Cluster Sampling Design

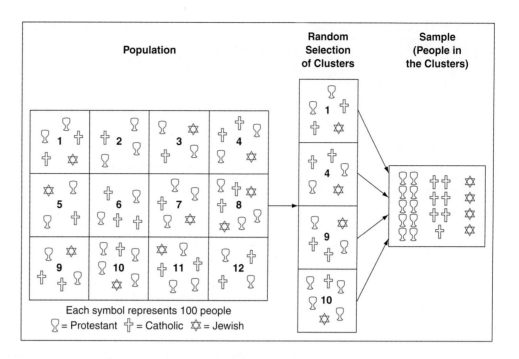

sequence, the clusters for sampling. Let's toss a coin. Heads dictates that we begin with the first odd-numbered cluster; tails dictates that we begin with the first even-numbered cluster. The coin comes down tails, which means that we start with the first even-numbered digit, which is 2, and select the systematically sequential clusters 4, 6, 8, 10, 12. Figure 6.13 illustrates this process.

FIGURE 6.13 ■
Systematic Sampling
Design

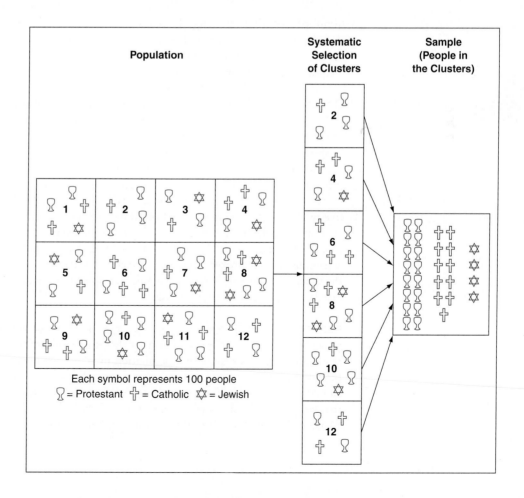

TABLE 6.2 ■ Population Characteristics and Probability Sampling Techniques Appropriate for Each Population Type

Population Characteristic	Example of Population Type	Appropriate Sampling Technique(s)
1. Population is generally a homogeneous group of individual units.	A particular variety of flower seeds, which a researcher wants to test for germination potential.	• Simple random sampling • Systematic sampling of individual units (when large populations of human beings are involved)
2. Population contains definite strata that are approximately equal in size.	A school with six grade levels: kindergarten, first, second, third, fourth, and fifth.	• Stratified random sampling
3. Population contains definite strata that appear in different proportions within the population.	A community in which residents are Catholic (25%), Protestant (45%), Jewish (15%), Muslim (5%), or nonaffiliated (10%).	• Proportional stratified sampling
4. Population consists of discrete clusters with similar characteristics. The units within each cluster are as heterogeneous as units in the overall population.	Travelers in the nation's 20 leading air terminals. (It is assumed that all air terminals are similar in atmosphere, purpose, design, etc. The passengers who use them differ widely in such characteristics as age, gender, national origin, socioeconomic status, and belief system, with such variability being similar from one airport to the next.)	• Cluster sampling • Systematic sampling (of clusters)

Each of the sampling designs just described is uniquely suited to a particular kind of population; thus, you should consider the nature of your population when selecting your sampling technique. Table 6.2 identifies the various kinds of populations for which different probability sampling techniques might be appropriate.

Nonprobability Sampling

In nonprobability sampling, the researcher has no way of predicting or guaranteeing that each element of the population will be represented in the sample. Furthermore, some members of the population have little or no chance of being sampled. Following are three common forms of nonprobability sampling.

Convenience Sampling   Convenience sampling—also known as *accidental sampling*—makes no pretense of identifying a representative subset of a population. It takes people or other units that are readily available—for instance, those arriving on the scene by mere happenstance.

Convenience sampling may be quite appropriate for some research problems. For example, suppose you own a small restaurant and want to sample the opinions of your patrons on the quality of food and service at your restaurant. You open for breakfast at 6 a.m., and on five consecutive weekdays you question a total of 40 of your early-morning arrivals. The opinions you get are from 36 men and 4 women. It is a heavily lopsided poll in favor of men, perhaps because the people who arrive at 6 a.m. are likely to be in certain occupations that are predominantly male (e.g., construction workers and truck drivers). The data from this convenience sample give you the thoughts of robust, hardy men about your breakfast menu—that's all. Yet such information may be all you need for your purpose.

Quota Sampling   Quota sampling is a variation of convenience sampling. It selects respondents in the same proportions that they are found in the general population, but not in a random fashion. Let's consider a population in which the number of African Americans equals the number of European Americans. Quota sampling would choose, say, 20 African Americans and 20 European Americans, but without any attempt to select these individuals randomly from the overall population. Suppose, for example, that you are a reporter for a television station. At noon, you position yourself with a microphone and television camera beside Main Street in the center of a particular city. As people pass, you interview them. The fact that people in the two categories may come in clusters of two, three, or four is no problem. All you need are the opinions of 20 people from each category. This type of sampling regulates only the size of each category within the sample; in every other respect, the selection of the sample is nonrandom and, in most cases, convenient.

Purposive Sampling   In purposive sampling, people or other units are chosen, as the name implies, for a particular *purpose.* For instance, we might choose people who we have decided are "typical" of a group or those who represent diverse perspectives on an issue.

Pollsters who forecast elections frequently use purposive sampling: They may choose a combination of voting districts that, in past elections, has been quite helpful in predicting the final outcomes.

Purposive sampling may be very appropriate for certain research problems. However, researchers should always provide a rationale explaining why they selected their particular sample of participants.

Sampling in Surveys of Very Large Populations

Nowhere is sampling more critical than in surveys of large populations. Sometimes a researcher reports that $x\%$ of people believe such-and-such, that $y\%$ do so-and-so, or that $z\%$ are in favor of a particular political candidate. *Such percentages are meaningless unless the sample is representative of the population about which inferences are to be drawn.*

But now imagine that a researcher wants to conduct a survey of the country's *entire adult population.* How can the researcher possibly hope to get a random, representative sample of such a large group of people? The Survey Research Center of the University of Michigan's Institute for Social Research has successfully used a *multistage sampling of areas,* described in its now-classic *Interviewer's Manual* (1976):

1. *Primary area selection.*   The country is divided into small "primary areas," each consisting of a specific county, a small group of counties, or a large metropolitan area. A predetermined number of these areas are randomly selected.

2. *Sample location selection.*   Each of the selected primary areas is divided into smaller sections ("sample locations"), such as specific towns. A small number of these locations is randomly selected.

3. *Chunk selection.*   The sample locations are divided into even smaller "chunks" that have identifiable boundaries such as roads, streams, or the edges of a city block. Most chunks have 16 to 50 dwellings, although the number may be larger in large cities. Once again, a random sample is selected.

4. *Segment selection.*   Chunks are subdivided into areas containing a relatively small number of dwellings, and some of these "segments" are, again, chosen randomly.

5. *Housing unit selection.*   Approximately four dwellings are selected (randomly, of course) from each segment, and the residents of those dwellings are asked to participate in the survey. If a doorbell is unanswered, the researcher returns at a later date and tries again.

As you may have deduced, the approach just described is a multistage version of cluster sampling (see Figure 6.14). At each stage of the game, units are selected randomly. "Randomly" does *not* mean haphazardly or capriciously. Instead, a mathematical procedure is employed to ensure that selection is entirely random and the result of blind chance. This process should yield a sample that is, in all important respects, representative of the country's population.

FIGURE 6.14 ▦
Multistage Sampling

Source: From the *Interviewer's Manual* (Rev. ed., p. 36) by the Survey Research Center, Institute for Social Research, 1976, Ann Arbor: University of Michigan. Reprinted with permission.

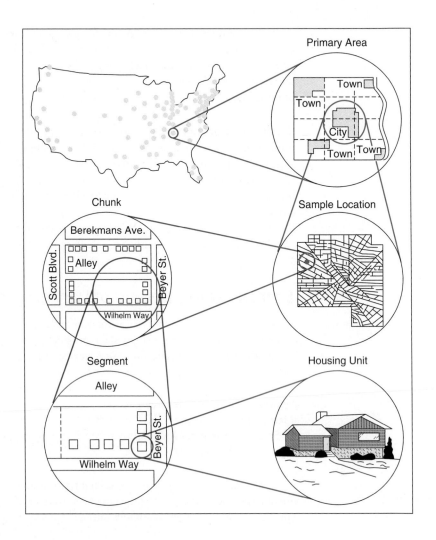

PRACTICAL APPLICATION Identifying a Sufficient Sample Size

A basic rule in sampling is: *The larger the sample, the better.* But such a generalized rule isn't very helpful to a researcher who must make a practical decision about a specific research situation. Gay, Mills, and Airasian (2012, p. 139) have offered the following guidelines for selecting a sample size, which we'll refer to by the symbol *N:*

▦ For smaller populations, say, $N = 100$ or fewer, there is little point in sampling; survey the entire population.

▦ If the population size is around 500 (give or take 100), 50% should be sampled.

▦ If the population size is around 1,500, 20% should be sampled.

▦ Beyond a certain point (about $N = 5,000$), the population size is almost irrelevant and a sample size of 400 will be adequate.

Generally speaking, then, the larger the population, the smaller the percentage—but not the smaller the number!—one needs to get a representative sample.

To some extent, the size of an adequate sample depends on how homogeneous or heterogeneous the population is—how alike or different its members are with respect to the characteristics of research interest. If the population is markedly heterogeneous, a larger sample is necessary than if the population is fairly homogeneous. Important, too, is the degree of precision with which the researcher wants to draw conclusions or make predictions about the population under study.

Statisticians have developed formulas for determining the desired sample size for a given population. Such formulas are beyond the scope of this book, but you can find them in many introductory statistics books and on many Internet websites (e.g., search "calculating sample size").

PRACTICAL APPLICATION Analyzing the Population in a Descriptive Study

Select a particular population and conduct an analysis of its structure and characteristics. Analyze the population you have chosen by completing the following checklist.

✔ CHECKLIST

Analyzing Characteristics of the Population Being Studied

_____ 1. On the following line, identify the particular population you have chosen:

_____

_____ 2. Now answer the following questions with respect to the *structure of the population:*

	YES	NO
a. Is the population a relatively homogeneous group of individuals or other units?	_____	_____
b. Could the population be considered to consist generally of equal "layers," each of which is fairly homogeneous in composition?	_____	_____
c. Could the population be considered to be composed of separate homogeneous layers differing in size and number of units comprising them?	_____	_____
d. Could the population be envisioned as isolated islands or clusters of individual units, with the clusters being similar to one another in composition?	_____	_____

_____ 3. Through what means would you extract a representative sample from the total population? Describe your procedure on the following lines:

_____

_____

_____

_____ 4. Refer to Table 6.2. Is your sampling procedure appropriate for the characteristics of the population? _____ Yes _____ No

_____ 5. Have you guaranteed that your sample will be chosen by chance and yet will be representative of the population? _____ Yes _____ No

_____ 6. If the preceding answer is yes, explain how this will be done.

_____

_____

_____ 7. Indicate what means will be employed to obtain the information you need from the sample.

_____

_____

_____ 8. What are the weaknesses inherent in this method of obtaining the data?

_____

_____

_____

COMMON SOURCES OF BIAS IN DESCRIPTIVE STUDIES

In this and preceding chapters, we have occasionally mentioned that a particular research strategy might in some way *bias* the results. In general, **bias** in a research study is any influence, condition, or set of conditions that singly or in combination distort the data obtained or conclusions drawn. Bias can creep into a research project in a variety of subtle ways. For example, when conducting an interview, a researcher's tone of voice in asking questions might predispose a participant to respond in one way rather than in another, or the researcher's personality might influence a participant's willingness to reveal embarrassing facts.

Most sources of bias in descriptive research fall into one of four categories, each of which we examine now.

Sampling Bias

A key source of bias in many descriptive studies is **sampling bias**—any factor that yields a nonrepresentative sample of the population being studied. For example, imagine that a researcher wants to conduct a survey of a certain city's population and decides to use the city telephone book as a source for selecting a random sample. She opens to a page at random, closes her eyes, puts her pencil down on the page, and selects the name that comes closest to the pencil point. "You can't get more random than this," she thinks. But the demon of bias is there. Her possible selections are limited to people who are listed in the phone book. People with very low income levels won't be adequately represented because some of them can't afford telephone service. Nor will wealthy individuals be proportionally represented because many of them have unlisted numbers. And, of course, people who use only cell phones—people who, on average, are fairly young—aren't included in the phone book. Hence, the sample will consist of disproportionately large percentages of people at middle-income levels and in older age-groups (e.g., Keeter, Dimock, Christian, & Kennedy, 2008). Likewise, as noted in earlier sections of the chapter, studies involving online interviews or Internet-based questionnaires are apt to be biased—this time in favor of computer-literate individuals with easy access to the Internet.

Studies involving mailed questionnaires frequently fall victim to bias as well, often without the researcher's awareness. For example, suppose that a questionnaire is sent to 100 citizens, asking, "Have you ever been audited by the Internal Revenue Service (IRS) to justify your income tax return?" Of the 70 questionnaires returned, 35 are from people who say that they have been audited, whereas 35 are from people who respond that they have never been audited. The researcher might therefore conclude that 50% of American citizens are likely to be audited by the IRS at one time or another.

The researcher's generalization isn't necessarily accurate. We need to consider how the nonrespondents—30% of the original sample—might be different from those who responded to the questionnaire. Many people consider an IRS audit to be a reflection of their integrity. Perhaps for this reason, some individuals in the researcher's sample may not have wanted to admit that they had been audited and so tossed the questionnaire into the wastebasket. If previously audited people were less likely to return the questionnaire than nonaudited people, the sample was biased, and thus the results didn't accurately represent the facts. Perhaps, instead of a 50-50 split, an estimate of 60% (people audited) versus 40% (people not audited) is more accurate. The data the researcher has obtained don't enable the researcher to make such an estimate, however.

The examples just presented illustrate two different ways in which bias can creep into the research sample. In the cases of telephone and Internet-based data collection, *sample selection* itself was biased because not everyone in the population had an equal chance of being selected. For instance, people not listed in the phone book had *zero* chance of being selected. Here we see the primary disadvantage of nonprobability sampling, and especially of convenience sampling: People who happen to be readily available for a research project—those who are in the right place at the right time—are almost certainly *not* a random sample of the overall population.

In the example concerning IRS audits, *response rate*—and, in particular, potential differences between respondents and nonrespondents—was the source of bias. In that situation, the researcher's return rate of 70% was quite high. More often, the return rate in a questionnaire study is 50% or less, and the more nonrespondents there are, the greater the likelihood of bias. Likewise, in telephone surveys, a researcher won't necessarily reach certain people even with 10 or more attempts, and those who *are* eventually reached won't all agree to an interview (Witt & Best, 2008).

Nonrespondents to *mailed questionnaires* might be different from respondents in one or more ways (Rogelberg & Luong, 1998). They may have illnesses, disabilities, or language barriers that prevent them from responding. And on average, they have lower educational levels. In contrast, people who are hard to reach *by telephone* are apt to be young working adults who are *more* educated than the average individual (Witt & Best, 2008).

Even when potential participants' ages, health, educational levels, language skills, and computer literacy are similar, they can differ widely in their *motivation* to participate in a study: Some might have other priorities, and some might worry that a researcher has sinister intentions. Participants in longitudinal studies may eventually grow weary of being "bothered" time after time. Also, a nonrandom subset of them might die before the study is completed!

Look once again at the five steps in the University of Michigan's Survey Research Center procedure for obtaining a sample in a national survey. Notice the last sentence in the fifth step: "If a doorbell is unanswered, the researcher returns at a later date and tries again." The researcher does *not* substitute one housing unit for another; doing so would introduce bias into the sampling design. The center's *Interviewer's Manual* describes such bias well:

> The house on the muddy back road, the apartment at the top of a long flight of stairs, the house with the growling dog outside must each have an opportunity to be included in the sample. People who live on back roads can be very different from people who live on well paved streets, and people who stay at home are not the same as those who tend to be away from home. If you make substitutions, such important groups as young men, people with small families, employed women, farmers who regularly trade in town, and so on, may not have proportionate representation in the sample. (Survey Research Center, 1976, p. 37)

Instrumentation Bias

By instrumentation bias, we mean the ways in which particular measurement instruments slant the obtained results in one direction or another. For instance, in our earlier discussion of questionnaires, we mentioned that a researcher must choose certain questions—and by default must omit *other* questions. The same is true of structured interviews: By virtue of the questions asked, participants are encouraged to reflect on and talk about some topics rather than other ones. The outcome is that some variables are included in a study, and other potentially important variables are overlooked.

As an example, imagine that an educational researcher is interested in discovering the kinds of goals that students hope to accomplish when they're at school. Many motivation researchers have speculated that students might be concerned about either (a) truly mastering classroom subject matter, on the one hand, or (b) getting good grades by any expedient means, on the other. Accordingly, they have designed and administered rating-scale questionnaires with such items as "I work hard to understand new ideas" (reflecting a desire to master a topic) and "I occasionally copy someone else's homework if I don't have time to do it myself" (reflecting a desire to get good grades). But in one study (Dowson & McInerney, 2001), researchers instead asked middle students what things were most important for them to accomplish at school. Many participants focused not on a desire to do well academically but instead on *social* goals, such as being with and helping classmates and avoiding behaviors that might adversely affect their popularity.

Response Bias

Whenever we gather data through interviews or questionnaires, we are relying on *self-report* data: People are telling us what they believe to be true or, perhaps, what they think we want to hear. To the extent that people describe their thoughts, beliefs, and experiences inaccurately, response bias is at work. For example, people's descriptions of their attitudes, opinions, and motives are often constructed on the spot—sometimes they haven't really thought about a certain issue until a researcher poses a question about it—and thus may be colored by recent events, the current context, or flawed self-perceptions (McCaslin, Vega, Anderson, Calderon, & Labistre, 2011; Schwarz, 1999). Furthermore, some participants may intentionally or unintentionally misrepresent the facts in order to give a favorable impression—a source of bias known as a *social desirability effect* (e.g., Uziel, 2010). For example, if we were to ask parents the question, "Have you ever abused your children?" the percentage of parents who told us *yes* would be close to zero, and so we would almost certainly underestimate the prevalence of child abuse in our society. And when we ask people about *past* events, behaviors, and perspectives, interviewees must rely on their memories, and human memory is rarely as accurate as a video recorder might be. People are apt to recall what *might* or *should* have happened (based on their attitudes or beliefs) rather than what actually *did* happen (e.g., Schwarz, 1999; Wheelan, 2013).

Researcher Bias

Finally, we must not overlook the potential effects of a researcher's expectations, values, and general belief systems, which can predispose the researcher to study certain variables and not other variables, as well as to draw certain conclusions and not other conclusions. For example, recall the discussion of philosophical assumptions in Chapter 1: Researchers with a *positivist* outlook are more likely to look for cause-and-effect relationships—sometimes even from correlational studies that don't warrant conclusions about cause and effect!—than postpositivists or constructivists.

Ultimately, we must remember that *no human being can be completely objective.* Assigning numbers to observations helps a researcher quantify data but it does not necessarily make the researcher any more objective in collecting or interpreting those data.

PRACTICAL APPLICATION Acknowledging the Probable Presence of Bias in Descriptive Research

When conducting research, it's almost impossible to avoid biases of one sort or another—biases that can potentially influence the data and thus also influence the conclusions drawn. Good researchers demonstrate their integrity by admitting, without reservation, that certain biases may well have influenced their findings. For example, in survey research, you should *always* report the percentages of people who have and have not consented to participate, such as those who have agreed and refused to be interviewed or those who have and have not returned questionnaires. Furthermore, you should be candid about possible sources of bias that result from differences between participants and nonparticipants. Here we offer guidelines for identifying possible sampling biases in questionnaire research. We then provide a checklist that can help you pin down various biases that can potentially contaminate descriptive studies of all sorts.

GUIDELINES Identifying Possible Sampling Bias in Questionnaire Research

Rogelberg and Luong (1998) have suggested several strategies for identifying possible bias in questionnaire research. Following are three especially useful ones.

1. *Carefully scrutinize the questionnaire for items that might be influenced by factors that frequently distinguish respondents from nonrespondents.* For example, ask yourself questions such as these:

- Might some people be more interested in this topic than others? If so, would their interest level affect their responses?
- How much might people's language and literacy skills influence their ability and willingness to respond?
- Are people with high education levels likely to respond differently to certain questions than people with less education? (Remember, responders tend, on average, to be more highly educated than nonresponders.)
- Might younger people respond differently than older ones do?
- Might people with full-time jobs respond differently than people who are retired and unemployed? (Fully employed individuals may have little or no free time to complete questionnaires, especially if they have young children.)
- Might healthy people respond differently than those who are disabled or chronically ill? (Healthy people are more likely to have the time and energy to respond.)

2. *Compare the responses on questionnaires that were returned quickly with responses on those that were returned later, perhaps after a second reminder letter or after the deadline you imposed.* The late ones may, to some extent, reflect the kinds of responses that nonrespondents would have given. Significant differences between the early and late questionnaires probably indicate bias in your results.

3. *Randomly select a small number of nonrespondents and try to contact them by mail or telephone.* Present an abridged version of your survey, and, if some people reply, compare their answers to those in your original set of respondents.

One of us authors once used a variation on the third strategy in the study of summer training institutes mentioned earlier in the chapter (Cole & Ormrod, 1995). A research assistant had sent questionnaires to all attendees at one summer's institutes so that the institutes' leaders could improve the training sessions the following year, and she had gotten a return rate of 50%. She placed telephone calls to small random samples of both respondents and nonrespondents and asked a few of the questions that had been on the questionnaire. She obtained similar responses from both groups, leading the research team to conclude that the responses to the questionnaire were probably fairly representative of the entire population of institute participants.

✔ **CHECKLIST**

Identifying Potential Sources of Bias in a Descriptive Study

_____ 1. Do you have certain expectations about the results you will obtain and/or the conclusions you are likely to draw? If so, what are they?

_____

_____

_____ 2. Do you have any preconceived notions about cause-and-effect relationships within the phenomenon you are studying? If so, what precautions might you take to ensure that you do *not* infer causal relationships from cross-variable correlations you might find?

_____

_____

_____ 3. How do you plan to identify a sample for your study? What characteristics of that sample might limit your ability to generalize your findings to a larger population?

_____

_____

_____ 4. On what specific qualities and characteristics will you be focusing? What potentially relevant qualities and characteristics will you *not* be looking at? To what degree might omitted variables be as important or more important in helping to understand the phenomenon you are studying?

_____

_____

_____ 5. Might participants' responses be poor indicators of certain characteristics, attitudes, or opinions? For example:

- Might they say or do things in order to create a favorable impression?
  _____ Yes _____ No
- Might you be asking them questions about topics they haven't really thought about before?
  _____ Yes _____ No
- Will some questions require them to rely on their memories of past events?
  _____ Yes _____ No

If any of your answers are *yes,* how might such sources of bias influence your findings?

_____

_____

INTERPRETING DATA IN DESCRIPTIVE RESEARCH

In our discussion of descriptive research methods in this chapter, we have focused largely on strategies for acquiring data. But at this juncture, we remind you of two basic principles of research:

1. The purpose of research is to seek the answer to a problem in light of data that relate to the problem.
2. Although collecting data for study and organizing it for inspection require care and precision, extracting meaning from the data—the interpretation of the data—is all-important.

A descriptive study is often a very "busy" research method: The researcher must decide on a population; choose a technique for sampling it; develop a valid means of collecting the desired information; minimize the potential for bias in the study; and then actually collect, record, organize, and analyze all the necessary data. The activities connected with descriptive research can be complex, time-consuming, and occasionally distracting. Therein lies an element of danger. With all this action going on, it wouldn't be surprising if the researcher lost sight of the problem and subproblems. But the problem and its subproblems are precisely the reason for the entire endeavor.

Activity for activity's sake is seductive. Amassing great quantities of data can provide a sense of well-being, and a researcher might lose sight of the ultimate demands that the problem itself makes on those data. Presenting the data in displays and summaries—graphs, charts, tables—does nothing more than demonstrate the researcher's acquisitive skills and consummate ability to present the same data in various ways.

All research activity is subordinate to the research problem itself. Sooner or later, the entire effort must result in an interpretation of the data and a setting forth of conclusions, drawn from the data, to resolve the problem under investigation. Descriptive research ultimately aims to solve problems through the *interpretation* of the data that have been gathered.

SOME FINAL SUGGESTIONS

As we approach the end of the chapter, it is important to reflect on several issues related to descriptive research. Consider each of the following questions within the context of the research project you have in mind:

- Why is a description of this population and/or phenomenon valuable?
- What specific data will I need to solve my research problem and its subproblems?
- What procedures should I follow to obtain the necessary information? How can I best implement those procedures?
- How do I get a sample that will be reflective of the entire population about which I am concerned?
- How can I collect my data in a way that minimizes misrepresentations and misunderstandings?
- How can I control for possible bias in the collection and description of the data?
- What do I do with the data once I have collected them? How do I organize and prepare them for analysis?
- Above all, in what ways might I reasonably interpret the data? What conclusions might I reach from my investigation?

✔ Check Your Understanding in the Pearson etext

 ### Practice Thinking Like a Researcher

Practice Thinking Like a Researcher Activity 6.1: Selecting a Design
Practice Thinking Like a Researcher Activity 6.2: Developing Measurement Instruments
Practice Thinking Like a Researcher Activity 6.3: Selecting a Sampling Technique

A SAMPLE DISSERTATION

We conclude the chapter by illustrating how questionnaires might be used in a correlational study to address the topic of violence in intimate relationships (e.g., husband and wife, boyfriend and girlfriend) in American society. The excerpts we present are from Luis Ramirez's doctoral dissertation in sociology completed at the University of New Hampshire (Ramirez, 2001).

Ramirez hypothesized that violence between intimate partners—in particular, assault by one partner on the other—is, in part, a function of ethnicity, acculturation (e.g., adoption of mainstream American behaviors and values), criminal history, and social integration (e.g., feelings of connectedness with family and friends). He further hypothesized that as a result of such factors, differences in intimate partner violence might be observed in Mexican Americans and non-Mexican Americans.

Ramirez begins Chapter 1 by discussing the prevalence of violence (especially assault) in intimate relationships. We pick up Chapter 1 at the point where he identifies his research questions and hypotheses. We then move into Chapter 2, where he describes his methodology. As has been true for earlier proposal and dissertation samples, the research report appears on the left-hand side, and our commentary appears on the right.

Comments

RESEARCH QUESTIONS

[T]he following questions will be addressed: What role does acculturation into American society have on intimate partner violence for Mexican Americans? What are the effects of a person's criminal history on intimate partner violence? What are the extent of criminal history and its relation to intimate partner violence, and is criminal history restricted to one type of crime or is it a more general tendency (violent versus property crimes)? Are crimes that are committed early in life more indicative of a pattern of crime as compared to crimes that begin later in life? Do people who assault their partners possess weak social bonds with the society they live in? Finally, this study will ask the question, "Are there differences between criminal history and bond to society for Mexican Americans and Non-Mexican Whites, and how do these factors affect intimate partner violence?"

If relations are found between these characteristics, it suggests that social agencies that deal with intimate partner violence need to adjust their policies and intervention procedures to better meet the characteristics of their clients. The focus of primary prevention could be put on the social bonding process, the criminal history of the individual, or the acculturation process in order to help solve future problems. Furthermore, a comparative study of intimate partner assault among ethnic groups could provide further clarification to a body of literature and research that has produced mixed results.

[The author briefly reviews theoretical frameworks related to ethnicity and acculturation, criminal history, and control theory, which he then uses as a basis for his hypotheses.]

HYPOTHESES

The theoretical frameworks reviewed led to the following hypotheses:

Ethnicity and Acculturation

1. The rate of intimate partner violence is lower for Mexican Americans than Non-Mexicans.

2. The higher the acculturation into American Society, the higher the probability of assaulting a partner for Mexican Americans.

Criminal History

3. Criminal history is more prevalent for Mexican Americans than for Non-Mexicans.

4. The more crimes committed in the past, the higher the probability of physically assaulting a partner.

5. Criminal history is more associated with an increased risk of intimate partner violence for Mexican Americans than Non-Mexicans.

6. Early onset crime is more associated with an increased risk of intimate partner violence than criminal behavior beginning later in life.

7. Previous violent crime is more associated with an increased risk of intimate partner violence than property crime.

To understand factors underlying violence in intimate partner relationships—his main research problem—the author identifies a number of subproblems, which he expresses here as research questions.

Here the author addresses the importance of the study, both pragmatic (results have potential implications for social policy and practice) and theoretical (results may shed light on inconsistencies in previous research studies).

The hypotheses are organized by the theoretical frameworks from which they have been derived, helping the reader connect them to rationales the author has previously provided.

Notice how the hypotheses are single-spaced. Single-spaced hypotheses often appear in theses and dissertations, but check the guidelines at your own institution to see whether such formatting is desired.

Social Integration

8. Mexican Americans are more socially integrated than Non-Mexican Whites.

9. The more socially integrated an individual is, the lower the probability of physically assaulting a partner.

10. Social integration is more associated with a decreased risk of intimate partner violence for Mexican Americans than Non-Mexicans.

A more detailed review of the literature will be presented in . . . following chapters. Literature for all hypotheses will be reviewed in their respective chapters.

Figure 1.1 is a diagrammed representation of what I believe is the causal process that could affect intimate partner violence. It includes demographic and control variables, the main independent variables (acculturation, criminal history, social integration), and intimate partner violence. These variables will be described in detail in the next chapter.

FIGURE 1.1 Model of Intimate Partner Violence

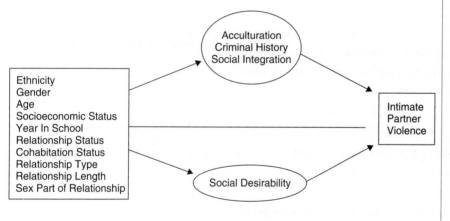

CHAPTER 2
Methods

Sample

The issues discussed in the previous chapter will be investigated using data from a sample of college students who have been or are currently in a dating or married relationship. A sample of college students is appropriate for this study for the following reasons: (1) The National Crime Victimization Survey found that the rates of non-lethal intimate partner violence was greatest for the 20 to 24 year age group, followed by the 16 to 19 age group, and then the 25 to 34 age group (Renison & Welchans, 2000). The majority of college students fall into the high-risk age categories. Sugarman and Hotaling (1989) identified eleven studies that provided rates for physical assault of dating partners and concluded the rates of assaulting a partner range from 20% to 59%. (2) College students make up about a third of the 18 to 22 year old population. College students are a sizable population in reference to the general population (about 15 million). (3) College students are in a formative period of their lives in relation to the habits that they develop with an intimate partner. These habits could surface in other intimate relations (O'Leary, Malone, & Tyree, 1994; Pan, Neidig, & O'Leary, 1994).

An in-depth review of the literature is postponed until Chapters 3 through 5, where the author also relates his own results to previous research findings. Although this is an unusual organizational structure, it works well in this situation, allowing the reader to connect results relative to each hypothesis to the appropriate body of literature.

Note the transition to the next chapter, which immediately follows.

Figure 1.1 effectively condenses and summarizes the researcher's hypotheses. Also, it graphically demonstrates that four variables —acculturation, criminal history, social integration, and social desirability— are hypothesized to be mediating variables in the relationship between demographics and violence.

Some style manuals suggest that an author include at least a small amount of text between two headings of different levels. For example, before beginning the "Sample" section, the author might provide an advance organizer, describing the topics he will discuss in the chapter and in what order.

It is important to mention that a sample of college students is not a representative sample of the general population in the United States. This group generally has lower levels of criminal behavior, substance abuse, and marriage rates. Additionally, college students may be more socially integrated into society and are engaged in education as a tool for upward mobility. In short, this is a segment of society that plays by the rules.

Data Collection

Six hundred and fifty questionnaires were passed out to students at The University of Texas at El Paso and Texas Tech University during the fall 1999, spring 2000, and summer 2000 semesters. Students who were enrolled in Sociology, Anthropology, and History classes [were] the respondents.

Respondents filled out the questionnaire (Appendix A) in a classroom setting. Each respondent received a booklet consisting of: (1) a cover sheet explaining the purpose of the study, the participant's rights, and the name of a contact person and telephone number for those who might have questions after the test session was over; (2) the demographic questions; (3) the instruments described in this section. The purpose, task demands, and rights were explained orally as well as in printed form at the beginning of each session. Respondents were told that the questionnaire would include questions concerning attitudes, beliefs, and experiences they may have had. They were guaranteed anonymity and confidentiality of their responses and they were told that the session would take an hour or slightly more. In actuality, the range of time that it took students to finish was between 30 minutes to 1 hour. All students were asked to sign a written consent form before completing their questionnaires. Students were also given instructions on how to properly fill out three scantron sheets before they were left to fill out the questionnaire at their own pace.

A debriefing form was given to each participant, as [he or she] turned in [his or her] questionnaire. It explained the study in more detail and provided names and telephone numbers of local mental health services and community resources, such as services for battered women. Students that voluntarily participated in the study were offered extra credit points by their professors.

The initial sample consisted of 650 respondents, of which 576 chose to complete the questionnaire. Of these, 33 questionnaires were omitted because they were illegible or partially completed. Finally, of the 543 remaining questionnaires, 348 were selected for this study because they met the criteria of having no missing data for any specific question, were either Mexican American/Mexican National or Non-Mexican White, and had been in a heterosexual romantic relationship for a month or longer during the previous 12 months.

The author clearly realizes that his sample (college students) is not representative of the entire U.S. population. He presents a good case that the sample is quite appropriate for his research questions. At the same time, he acknowledges that his sample has some shortcomings.

The author, whose home town is El Paso, has numerous acquaintances at both institutions and so can easily gain access to these students. He must, of course, seek approval from the internal review boards at the two institutions, as well as at the institution where he is completing his doctorate.

The author has combined his informed consent forms and questionnaires into a single booklet that he can easily distribute. Doing so is quite common in descriptive research, especially with adult samples, and increases the efficiency of data collection.

The author is using computer technology (scantron sheets) in his data collection. Given the nature of his sample (college students) and his sample size (576), this approach is reasonable.

Given the sensitive nature of some questionnaire items, the debriefing that follows data collection appropriately includes information about community resources for individuals who have been victims of partner violence.

Here the author describes his criteria for including completed questionnaires in his data set. In essence, he is addressing the issue of admissibility of the data (see Chapter 4).

Note: Excerpt is from *The Relation of Acculturation, Criminal History, and Social Integration of Mexican American and Non-Mexican Students to Assaults on Intimate Partners* (pp. 3–4, 14–20) by I. L. Ramirez, 2001, unpublished doctoral dissertation, University of New Hampshire, Durham. Reprinted with permission.

FOR FURTHER READING

Alreck, P. L., & Settle, R. B. (2003). *The survey research handbook* (3rd ed.). New York: McGraw-Hill.

Berdie, D. R., Anderson, J. F., & Niebuhr, M. A. (1986). *Questionnaires: Design and use* (2nd ed.). Metuchen, NJ: Scarecrow Press.

Bourque, L. B., & Fielder, E. P. (Eds.). (2002a). *How to conduct self-administered and mail surveys* (2nd ed.). Thousand Oaks, CA: Sage.

Bourque, L. B., & Fielder, E. P. (2002b). *How to conduct telephone surveys* (2nd ed.). Thousand Oaks, CA: Sage.

Daniel, J. (2011). *Sampling essentials: Practical guidelines for making sampling choices.* Thousand Oaks, CA: Sage.

Delandshere, G., & Petrosky, A. R. (1998). Assessment of complex performances: Limitations of key measurement assumptions. *Educational Researcher, 27,* 14–24.

Fink, A. (2009). *How to conduct surveys: A step-by-step guide* (5th ed.). Thousand Oaks, CA: Sage.

Fowler, F. J., Jr. (2014). *Survey research methods* (5th ed.). Thousand Oaks, CA: Sage.

Friedman, H. H., & Amoo, T. (1999). Rating the rating scales. *Journal of Marketing Management, 9*(3), 114–123.

Gosling, S. D., Vazire, S., Srivastava, S., & John, O. P. (2004). Should we trust Web-based studies? A comparative analysis of six preconceptions about Internet questionnaires. *American Psychologist, 59,* 93–104.

Gubrium, J. F., Holstein, J. A., Marvasti, A. B., & McKinney, K. D. (Eds.). (2012). *The SAGE handbook of interview research: The complexity of the craft* (2nd ed.). Thousand Oaks, CA: Sage.

Gwartney, P. A. (2007). *The telephone interviewer's handbook: How to conduct standardized conversations.* San Francisco, CA: Jossey-Bass.

Henry, G. T. (1990). *Practical sampling.* Thousand Oaks, CA: Sage.

Kraut, R., Olson, J., Banaji, M., Bruckman, A., Cohen, J., & Couper, M. (2004). Psychological research online: Report of Board of Scientific Affairs' Advisory Group on the Conduct of Research on the Internet. *American Psychologist, 59,* 105–117.

Laursen, B., Little, T. D., & Card, N. A. (Eds.). (2013). *Handbook of developmental research methods.* New York: Guilford Press.

Litwin, M. S. (1995). *How to measure survey reliability and validity.* Thousand Oaks, CA: Sage.

Magnusson, D., Bergman, L. R., Rudinger, G., & Torestad, B. (Eds.). (2010). *Problems and methods in longitudinal research: Stability and change.* New York: Cambridge University Press.

Marsden, P. V., & Wright, J. D. (Eds.). (2010). *Handbook of survey research* (2nd ed.). Bingley, United Kingdom: Emerald Group.

Menard, S. (Ed.). (2007). *Handbook of longitudinal research: Design, measurement, and analysis.* Burlington, MA: Academic Press.

Neuman, W. L. (2011). *Social research methods: Qualitative and quantitative approaches* (7th ed.). Boston: Allyn & Bacon. (See Chapter 10, "Survey Research.")

Oppenheim, A. N. (1992). *Questionnaire design, interviewing, and attitude measurement.* New York: St. Martin's Press.

Pianta, R. C., & Hamre, B. K. (2009). Conceptualization, measurement, and improvement of classroom processes: Standardized observation can leverage capacity. *Educational Researcher, 38,* 109–119.

Rogelberg, S. G., & Luong, A. (1998). Nonresponse to mailed surveys: A review and guide. *Current Directions in Psychological Science, 7,* 60–65.

Schuman, H., & Presser, S. (1996). *Questions and answers in attitude surveys: Experiments on question form, wording, and context.* Thousand Oaks, CA: Sage.

Schwarz, P. N., & Sudman, S. (1996). *Answering questions: Methodology for determining cognitive and communicative processes in survey research.* San Francisco: Jossey-Bass.

Sue, V. M., & Ritter, L. A. (2012). *Conducting online surveys* (2nd ed.). Thousand Oaks, CA: Sage.

Valliant, R., Dever, J. A., & Kreuter, F. (2013). *Practical tools for designing and weighting survey samples.* New York: Springer.

7

Experimental, Quasi-Experimental, and Ex Post Facto Designs

Progress is relative: We measure it by noting the amount of change between what was and what is. And we attempt to account for the change by identifying the dynamics that have caused it. Ideally, we must manipulate one possible causal factor while controlling all other possible causal factors; only in this way can we determine whether the manipulated factor has a direct influence on the phenomenon we are studying. To the extent that many potentially causal factors all vary at once in an entangled, confounded manner, we learn little or nothing about what causes what.

Learning Outcomes

7.1 Identify examples of independent and dependent variables, and describe several strategies for controlling for confounding variables in experimental studies.

7.2 Recognize examples of pre-experimental, experimental,

quasi-experimental, ex post facto, and factorial designs, as well as of meta-analyses.

7.3 Describe potential biases in these designs and how they might affect a study's internal or external validity.

In the descriptive designs described in the preceding chapter, we make no systematic attempt to determine the underlying causes of the phenomena being studied. But sometimes we *do* want to know what leads to what; in other words, we want to identify *cause-and-effect relationships.*

A researcher can most convincingly identify cause-and-effect relationships by using an experimental design. In such a design, the researcher considers many possible factors that might cause or influence a particular condition or phenomenon. The researcher then attempts to control for all influential factors *except* those whose possible effects are the focus of investigation.

An example can help clarify the point. Imagine that we have two groups of people. We take steps to make sure that, on average, the two groups are so similar that we can, for all intents and purposes, call them equivalent. We give members of both groups a pretest to measure a particular characteristic in which we are interested—for instance, this might be blood pressure, academic achievement, or purchasing habits. Then we expose only one of the groups to a treatment or intervention of some sort—perhaps a new pharmaceutical drug, an instructional method, or an advertising campaign—that we think may have an effect on the characteristic we are studying. Afterward, we give members of both groups a posttest to measure the characteristic once again. If the characteristic changes for the group that received the intervention but does *not* change for the other group, and if everything about the two groups has been the same *except for the intervention,* we can reasonably conclude that the treatment or intervention brought about the change we observed. Because we have systematically *manipulated* the situation, we have used an experimental design.

Some of the research designs we describe in this chapter are true experimental designs; as such, they allow us to identify cause-and-effect relationships. Other designs in this chapter eliminate some—but not all—alternative explanations of an observed change. Yet all of the designs in the chapter have one thing in common: clearly identifiable independent and dependent variables.

We have previously introduced you to independent and dependent variables in Chapter 2, but because these concepts guide so much of our discussion in this chapter, a brief refresher might be in order. An independent variable is one that the researcher studies as having a possible effect on one or more other variables. In many of the designs described in this chapter, the researcher directly manipulates and controls at least one independent variable. In contrast, a dependent variable is a variable that is potentially influenced by an independent variable; that is, its value *depends* to some degree on the value of the independent variable. In other words, the hypothesized relationship is this:

Independent variable → Dependent variable

As an example, let's look at a dissertation in educational psychology written by Nancy Thrailkill (1996), who wanted to study the effects of three different kinds of lecture material on people's ability to remember information contained in the lecture. Working with undergraduate students, she presented different parts of a lecture on an obscure American Civil War battle in one of three ways: (a) she described certain historical figures and events in such a manner that they were easy to imagine and visualize (*imagery* condition), (b) she included attention-grabbing phrases in the lecture (*attention* condition), or (c) she did neither of these things (*control* condition). In the following examples from Thrailkill's dissertation, the underscored phrases illustrate the modifications made for each of the three conditions; other variations in wording made the three lectures equivalent in length:

> *Imagery:* Lincoln also created the Army of Virginia, incorporating several forces which had been under different commanders. Lincoln set <u>the dimpled, baby-faced young blond</u> Major General John Pope in charge of this new combined force. Being put under his command was objectionable to some of the former commanders. . . .

> *Attention:* Lincoln also created the Army of Virginia, incorporating several forces which had been under different commanders. <u>LISTEN TO ME NOW.</u> Lincoln set the less experienced Major General John Pope in charge of this new combined force. Being put under the command of Pope was objectionable to some of the former commanders. . . .

> *Control:* Lincoln also created the Army of Virginia, incorporating several forces which had been under different commanders. Lincoln set the less experienced <u>junior officer</u> Major General John Pope in charge of this new combined force. Being put under the command of Pope was objectionable to some of the former commanders. (Thrailkill, 1996, p. 62, some underscoring added)

After presenting different parts of the lecture under the three different conditions, Thrailkill measured the students' recall for the lecture in two ways. She first gave students blank sheets of paper and asked them to write down as much of the lecture as they could remember (a *free recall* task). When they had completed that task, she gave them a multiple-choice test that assessed their memory for specific facts within the lecture. In this study, the independent variable was the nature of the lecture material: easily visualized, attention-getting, or neutral. There were two dependent variables, both of which reflected students' ability to recall facts within the lecture: students' performance on the free recall task and their scores on the multiple-choice test. Thrailkill's hypothesis was confirmed: The students' ability to recall lecture content *depended,* to some extent, on the way in which the content was presented.

THE IMPORTANCE OF CONTROL

A particular concern in any experimental study is its internal validity, the extent to which its design and the data it yields allow the researcher to draw legitimate conclusions about cause-and-effect and other relationships (see Chapter 4). In experimental designs, internal validity is essential. Without it, a researcher cannot draw firm conclusions about cause and effect—and that is, after all, the whole point of conducting an experimental study.

As an example, suppose we have just learned about a new method of teaching science in elementary school. We want to conduct an experiment to investigate the method's effect on students' science achievement test scores. We find two fifth-grade teachers who are willing to participate in the study. One teacher agrees to use the new method in the coming school year; in fact, she's quite eager to try it. The other teacher wants to continue using the same approach he has always used. Both teachers agree that at the end of the school year we can give their students a science achievement test.

Are the two classes the same in every respect *except for the experimental intervention?* If the students taught with the new method obtain higher achievement test scores at the end of the year, will we know that the method was the *cause* of the higher scores? The answer to both questions is a resounding *no!* The teachers are different: One is female and the other male, and they almost certainly have different personalities, educational backgrounds, and teaching styles. In addition, the two groups of students may be different; perhaps the students instructed by the new method are, on average, more intelligent or motivated than the other, or perhaps they live in a more affluent school district. Other, more subtle differences may be at work as well, including the interpersonal dynamics in the two classes, and the light, temperature, and noise levels within each classroom. Any of these factors—and perhaps others we haven't thought of—might be reasons for any group differences in achievement test scores we obtain.

Whenever we compare two or more groups that are or might be different in ways *in addition to* the particular treatment or intervention we are studying, we have confounding variables in our study. The presence of such variables makes it extremely difficult to draw conclusions about cause-and-effect relationships, because we can't pin down exactly *what* is the cause of any pattern in the data observed after the intervention. In other words, confounding variables threaten a study's internal validity. In a now-classic book chapter, Campbell and Stanley (1963) identified several potential threats to the internal validity of an experimental study; we describe them in Figure 7.1.

Controlling for Confounding Variables

To maximize internal validity when a researcher wants to identify cause-and-effect relationships, the researcher needs to control confounding variables in order to rule them out as explanations for any effects observed. Researchers use a variety of strategies to control for confounding variables. Following are several common ones.

1. ***Keep some things constant.***   When a factor is the *same* for everyone, it cannot possibly account for any differences observed. Oftentimes researchers ensure that different treatments are imposed in the same or very similar environments. They may also seek research participants who share a certain characteristic, such as age, gender, grade level, or socioeconomic status. Keep in mind, however, that restricting the nature of one's sample may lower the *external validity,* or generalizability, of any findings obtained (see the discussion of this concept in Chapter 4).

2. ***Include a control group.***   In Chapter 4 we described a study in which an industrial psychologist begins playing classical music as employees in a typing pool go about their daily task of typing documents. At the end of the month, the psychologist finds that the typists' productivity is 30% higher than it was during the preceding month. The increase in productivity may or may not be due to the classical music. There are too many possible confounding variables—personnel changes, nature of the documents being typed, numbers of people out sick or on vacation during the 2-month period, even just the knowledge that an experiment is being conducted—that may also account for the typing pool's increased productivity.

To better control for such extraneous variables, researchers frequently include a control group, a group that receives either no intervention or a "neutral" intervention that should have little or no effect on the dependent variable. The researchers then compare the performance of this group to an experimental group—also known as a treatment group—that participates in an intervention.

FIGURE 7.1 ■
Potential Threats to the
Internal Validity in an
Experimental Study

When a researcher studies the possible effects of an intervention on some other (dependent) variable, a number of confounding variables can come into play that threaten the study's internal validity and thereby also jeopardize any cause-and-effect conclusions the researcher might hope to draw. Campbell and Stanley (1963) have identified the following potential threats to internal validity, which can be present either singly or in combination:

1. *History:* An uncontrolled outside event occurring between two measurements of the dependent variable brings about a change in the dependent variable. For example, a noteworthy event in the local community might change participants' knowledge, abilities, or emotional states in ways that affect the second measurement of the dependent variable.
2. *Maturation:* A change in participants' characteristics or abilities might simply be the result of the passage of time. For example, children might make normal developmental gains in eye-hand coordination or intellectual ability.
3. *Testing:* Taking a test at one time influences participants' performance during a subsequent administration of the test, perhaps simply as a result of practice in taking the test. For example, people who take a multiple-choice test at one time may gain general test-taking skills that enhance their performance on a subsequent multiple-choice test.
4. *Instrumentation:* A change occurs in how a measurement instrument is used from one time to the next. For example, a researcher might have one research assistant rate participants' performance on the first occasion but have a different research assistant judge their performance on the subsequent occasion. Any observed change might be the result of the two assistants' differing standards for rating the performance. (This threat to internal validity reflects a problem with *interrater reliability;* see Chapter 4.)
5. *Statistical regression:* In a common phenomenon known as statistical regression, people who score extremely high or low on a measure at one time are likely to score in a less extreme manner on the same measure at a later time; that is, extreme scorers tend to "drift" toward more average performance during a subsequent measure. For example, a researcher might assign people to one of two groups—"high-anxiety" or "low-anxiety"—based on their extremely high or low scores on a self-report questionnaire designed to measure general anxiety level. Especially if the initially extreme scores were the result of people's temporary circumstances—circumstances that might make them feel either exceptionally anxious or, instead, quite "mellow" on the first testing—the supposedly high-anxiety people would become less anxious and the supposedly low-anxiety people would become more anxious regardless of any experimental interventions the two groups might undergo.
6. *Selection:* A bias exists in how members of different groups in a study are chosen. For example, when recruiting college students for a study, a researcher might put all students enrolled in an 8:00 a.m. class in one treatment group and all students enrolled in a 2:00 p.m. class in another treatment group. Students taking the early-morning class might be different in some significant way from those taking the afternoon class (e.g., the sleeping habits of the two groups might be different).
7. *Attrition:** Members of different groups drop out of the study at proportionally different rates. For example, one group in a study might lose 25% of its members before the final measurement, whereas another group might lose only 5% of its members. Thus, even if the two groups were equivalent with regard to important characteristics at the beginning of the study, they might be different in some significant way later in the study simply as a result of the differential dropout rate.

Campbell and Stanley listed an eighth threat to internal validity as well: an *interaction* among two of the threats listed above. For example, if students in an 8:00 a.m. class are assigned to one treatment group and students in a 2:00 p.m. class are assigned to a different treatment group, and if students in the 8:00 a.m. group drop out of the study in greater numbers than students in the 2:00 p.m. group, any final differences observed in the dependent variable might be the result of the fact that early risers are, for some reason, more likely to drop out than students who like to sleep in a bit. In this situation, it becomes virtually impossible to disentangle possible effects of an experimental intervention from effects of (a) the selection bias, (b) the differing dropout rates, and (c) the interaction of these two confounding variables.

**Note:* Campbell and Stanley use the term *experimental mortality* for this threat to internal validity, but the term *attrition* is more commonly seen in contemporary research literature.

As you should recall from Chapter 4, people sometimes show improved performance simply because they know they're participating in a research study—a phenomenon known as *reactivity* and, more specifically, the *Hawthorne effect.* To take this fact into account, a researcher sometimes gives the people in a control group a placebo that might, on the surface, *appear* to be influential but in reality should *not* be influential. For instance, a researcher studying the effects of a new arthritis medication might give some participants a particular dosage of the medicine and give others a similar-looking sugar pill. Or a researcher investigating a new approach to treating test anxiety might use the new treatment with some individuals but give other individuals general relaxation training that, although possibly beneficial in other ways, won't necessarily address their test anxiety.

We must emphasize—and we emphasize it quite strongly—that any researcher who incorporates placebos in a study must consider *three ethical issues* related to the use of placebos. First is the principle of informed consent: Participants in the study must be told that the study includes a placebo treatment as well as an experimental treatment and that they won't know which treatment they have received until the study has ended. Second, if participants in the study have actively sought help for a medical, psychological, or other significant problem, those who initially receive the placebo treatment should, at the conclusion of the study, be given the opportunity to receive more effective treatment. (This is assuming, of course, that the treatment *is* more effective than the placebo.) Third, and most important, when studying a treatment related to life-threatening situations (e.g., a new drug for terminal cancer, a new psychotherapeutic technique for suicidal teenagers), the researcher must seriously weigh (a) the benefits of the new knowledge that can be gained by a control group receiving no treatment—or perhaps, instead, a less-intensive version of the experimental intervention—against (b) the lives that might be saved by including all participants in the treatment group.

Our last point raises an issue we cannot possibly resolve for you here. Should you find yourself having to make a decision about the best research design to use in a life-and-death situation, you should consult with your professional colleagues, the internal review board at your institution, and your own conscience.

3. ***Randomly assign people to groups.***   In Chapter 6 we spoke at length about the value of selecting people at random to participate in a descriptive research study; such random selection enhances the probability that any results obtained for the sample also apply to the population from which the sample has been drawn. In experimental studies, researchers use random selection for a different purpose: to assign participants within their sample to various groups.

In any research study involving human beings or other living things, members of the sample are apt to be different from one another in many ways that are relevant to the variables under investigation. For example, earlier in this chapter we described a situation in which a researcher wants to compare two methods of teaching elementary school science. The students in the study will almost certainly differ from one another in intelligence, motivation, educational opportunities at home, and other factors that will affect their performance on the achievement test given at the end of the school year. It would be virtually impossible to control for such variables by having all students in the study have the *same* intelligence, the *same* motivation, the *same* kinds of outside opportunities, and so on.

As an alternative to keeping some characteristics the same for everyone, a researcher can, instead, randomly assign participants to groups. When people have been selected for one group or another on a random basis, the researcher can reasonably assume that, *on average, the groups are quite similar* and that *any differences between them are due entirely to chance.* In fact, many inferential statistical tests—especially those that allow a researcher to make comparisons among two or more groups—are based on the assumption that group membership is randomly determined and that any pretreatment differences between the groups result from chance alone.

4. ***Use one or more pretests to assess equivalence before the treatment(s).***   Sometimes random assignment to two different groups simply isn't possible; for instance, researchers may have to study groups that already exist (e.g., students in classrooms, participants in different medical treatment programs). An alternative in this situation is to assess other variables that might influence the dependent variable and determine whether the groups are similar with respect to

those variables. If the groups *are* similar, the probability that such variables could account for any future group differences is reduced considerably.

Another strategy is to identify matched pairs: pairs of people—one in each of two groups being compared—who are identical or very similar with respect to characteristics that might possibly have an effect on the dependent variable. For instance, a researcher comparing the achievement test scores of students in two different instructional programs might identify pairs of students of the same age and gender who have similar IQ scores. A researcher comparing two different treatments for a particular illness might match patients according to age, gender, and duration and intensity of the illness. In either case, the researcher does not study the data collected for *all* people in the two groups, only the people who are part of "matched sets" that he or she has identified. A researcher who uses this approach should, in the final research report, explain in what way(s) the participants in the study have been matched, for example, by saying, "Pairs were matched on the basis of age, gender, and previous grade point average."

One problem with assessing before-treatment equivalence with pretests is that the researcher rules out *only the variables that he or she has actually assessed and determined to be equivalent across groups.* The design does not rule out other influential factors that the researcher hasn't assessed and perhaps not even considered.

5. *Expose participants to all experimental treatments.*   Still another strategy for controlling for individual differences is to *use participants as their own controls*—that is, to have every participant in the study undergo all experimental and control treatments and then assess the effects of each treatment independently. Any independent variable that is systematically varied for every participant is known as a within-subjects variable, and an approach that includes a within-subjects variable is known as a within-subjects design. You may also see the term repeated-measures design used in reference to this approach.

As an example, let's return to Thrailkill's (1996) dissertation involving three different lecture methods and their possible effects on recall for lecture content. Thrailkill's sample consisted of volunteer students who were enrolled in three sections of an undergraduate class in educational psychology, and she planned to give the lecture just three times, once to each class. The lecture was about a little-known American Civil War battle that participants were unlikely to have learned about in school; thus, participants' prior knowledge about the battle was a constant—they all had *zero* prior knowledge—rather than a confounding variable. The researcher divided the lecture into three parts of approximately equal length and wrote three versions of each part, one version each for the imagery, attention, and control conditions. She combined the three versions of the three lecture parts such that each class received the different treatments in a different sequence, as follows:

	PART OF LECTURE		
	First Part	*Middle Part*	*Last Part*
Group 1	Attention	Imagery	Control
Group 2	Control	Attention	Imagery
Group 3	Imagery	Control	Attention

In this manner, all participants in her study were exposed to the two treatments and the control condition, and each condition occurred in all possible places (first, second, and third) in the sequence.

In the study just described, the researcher used a within-subjects variable (type of intervention: imagery vs. attention vs. control) to compensate for the fact that participants had not been randomly assigned to the three class sections in her sample. Sometimes researchers use a similar strategy with just a single group, and in some cases with just a single individual. You will learn some strategies for showing causation in single-group and single-individual studies later in the chapter, when we explore *quasi-experimental designs.*

6. *Statistically control for confounding variables.* Sometimes researchers can control for known confounding variables, at least in part, through statistical techniques. Such techniques as *partial correlation, analysis of covariance* (ANCOVA), and *structural equation modeling* (SEM) are suitable for this purpose. We briefly describe each of these in Chapter 8. Should you choose to use one of them in your own research, we urge you to consult one or more statistics books for guidance about their use and appropriateness for various research situations.

Keep in mind, however, that statistically controlling confounding variables is no substitute for controlling for them in one's research design if at all possible. *A carefully controlled experimental design is the only approach that allows you to draw firm conclusions about cause and effect.*

OVERVIEW OF EXPERIMENTAL, QUASI-EXPERIMENTAL, AND EX POST FACTO DESIGNS

In true experimental research, the researcher manipulates the independent variable and examines its effects on another, dependent variable. A variety of research designs have emerged that differ in the extent to which the researcher manipulates the independent variable and controls for confounding variables—in other words, the designs differ in the degree to which they have *internal validity.* In the upcoming sections, we present a number of possible designs, which we have divided into five general categories: *pre-experimental designs, true experimental designs, quasi-experimental designs, ex post facto designs,* and *factorial designs.* Altogether we describe 16 different designs that illustrate various ways—some more effective than others—of attempting to identify cause-and-effect relationships. Some of our discussion is based on designs identified by Campbell and Stanley (1963).[1]

We illustrate the designs using tables that have this general format:

Group	Time →		
Group 1			
Group 2			

Each group in a design is shown in a separate row, and the things that happen to the group over time are shown in separate cells within the row. The cells have one of four notations:

Tx: Indicates that a *treatment* (reflecting the independent variable) is presented.

Obs: Indicates that an *observation* (reflecting the dependent variable) is made.

—: Indicates that nothing occurs during a particular time period.

Exp: Indicates a previous *experience* (an independent variable) that some participants have had and others have not; the experience has *not* been one that the researcher could control.

The nature of these tables will become more apparent as we proceed.

As you read about the 16 designs, keep in mind that they are hardly an exhaustive list; researchers can modify or combine them in various ways. For example, although we will be limiting ourselves to studies with only one or two groups (perhaps one treatment group and one control group), it's entirely possible to have two or more treatment groups (each of which is exposed to a different variation of the independent variable) and, in some cases, two control groups (perhaps one getting a placebo and another getting no intervention at all). More generally, the designs we describe here should simply provide starting points that get you thinking about how you might best tackle your own research problem.

---

[1]In particular, Designs 1 to 6 and Designs 8 to 11 are based on those that Campbell and Stanley described. However, when describing Design 11, we use the contemporary term *reversal time-series design* rather than Campbell and Stanley's original term *equivalent time-samples design.*

PRE-EXPERIMENTAL DESIGNS

In pre-experimental designs, it isn't possible to show cause-and-effect relationships, because either (a) the independent "variable" doesn't vary or (b) experimental and control groups are not comprised of equivalent or randomly selected individuals. Such designs are helpful only for forming tentative hypotheses that should be followed up with more controlled studies.

Design 1: One-Shot Experimental Case Study

The one-shot experimental case study is probably the most primitive type of experiment that might conceivably be termed "research." An experimental treatment (Tx) is introduced, and then a measurement (Obs)—a posttest of some sort—is administered to determine the effects of the treatment. This design is shown in the following table:

Group	Time →	
Group 1	Tx	Obs

The design has low internal validity because it's impossible to determine whether participants' performance on the posttest is the result of the experimental treatment per se. Many other variables may have influenced participants' performance, such as physiological maturation or experiences elsewhere in the participants' general environment. Perhaps the characteristic or behavior observed after the treatment existed *before* the treatment as well. The reality is that with a single measurement or observation, we have no way of knowing whether the situation has changed or not, let alone whether it has changed as a result of the intervention.

One-shot experimental case studies may be at the root of many common misconceptions. For example, imagine that we see a child sitting on the ground on a damp, rainy day. The next day the child has a sore throat and a cold. We conclude that sitting on the damp earth caused the child to catch cold. Thus, the design of our "research" thinking is something like this:

Exposure to cold, damp ground (Tx) → Child has a cold (Obs)

Such "research" may also "support" such superstitious folk beliefs as these: If you walk under a ladder, you will have bad luck; Friday the 13th is a day of catastrophes; a horseshoe above the front door brings good fortune to one's home. Someone observed an event, then observed a subsequent event, and linked the two together as cause and effect.

Be careful not to confuse the one-shot experimental case study method with the qualitative case study design described in Chapter 9. Case study research involves extensive engagement in a research setting—a far cry from basing conclusions on a single observation.

Although the one-shot experimental case study is simple to carry out, its results are, for all intents and purposes, meaningless. At the very least, researchers should use the design described next.

Design 2: One-Group Pretest–Posttest Design

In a one-group pretest–posttest design, a single group (a) undergoes a pre-experimental observation or evaluation, then (b) is administered the experimental treatment, and finally (c) is observed or evaluated again after the treatment. This design can be represented as follows:

Group	Time →		
Group 1	Obs	Tx	Obs

Suppose an elementary school teacher wants to know if simultaneously reading a story and listening to it on audiotape will improve the reading skills of students in his class. He gives his students a standardized reading test, then has them simultaneously read and listen to simple stories every day for 8 weeks, and then administers an alternate form of the same standardized reading test. If the students' test scores improve over the 8-week period, the teacher might conclude—perhaps accurately, but perhaps not—that the simultaneous-reading-and-listening intervention was the cause of the improvement.

Now suppose an agronomist crossbreeds two strains of corn. She finds that the resulting hybrid strain is more disease-resistant and has a better yield than either of the two parent types. She concludes that the crossbreeding process has made the difference. Once again we have an Obs–Tx–Obs design: The agronomist measures the disease level of the parent strains (Obs), then develops a hybrid of the two strains (Tx), and then measures the disease level of the next generation (Obs).

In a one-group pretest–posttest design, we at least know that a change has taken place. However, we haven't ruled out other possible explanations for the change. In the case of the elementary school teacher's study, improvement in reading scores may have been due to other activities within the classroom curriculum, to more practice taking the reading test, or simply to the fact that the students were 8 weeks older. In the case of the agronomist's experiment, changes in rainfall, temperature, or soil conditions may have been the primary reason for the healthier corn crop.

Design 3: Static Group Comparison

The static group comparison involves both an experimental group and a control group. Its design takes the following form:

Group	Time →	
Group 1	Tx	Obs
Group 2	—	Obs

An experimental group is exposed to a particular experimental treatment; the control group is not. After the treatment, both groups are observed and their performance compared. In this design, however, no attempt is made to obtain equivalent groups or even to examine the groups to determine whether they are similar before the treatment. Thus, we have no way of knowing if the treatment actually causes any observed differences between the groups.

Designs 1, 2, and 3 leave much to be desired in terms of drawing conclusions about what causes what. The experimental designs we describe next are far superior in this respect.

TRUE EXPERIMENTAL DESIGNS

In contrast with the three very simple designs just described, experimental designs offer a greater degree of control and, as a result, greater internal validity. The first three of the four designs we discuss in this section share one thing in common: People or other units of study are *randomly assigned to groups.* Such random assignment guarantees that any differences between the groups are probably quite small and, in any case, are due entirely to chance. The last design in this section involves a different strategy: presenting all treatments and any control conditions to a single group.

Design 4: Pretest–Posttest Control-Group Design

In a pretest–posttest control-group design, people or other units of study (e.g., members of a particular plant or animal species) are randomly assigned to either an experimental group or a control group. The experimental group is observed, subjected to the experimental treatment, and observed again. The control group is isolated from any influences of the experimental treatment; it is simply observed both at the beginning and at the end of the experiment. The basic format for the pretest–posttest control-group design is as follows:

	Group	Time →		
Random Assignment	Group 1	Obs	Tx	Obs
	Group 2	Obs	—	Obs

Such a design, simple as it is, solves two major problems associated with pre-experimental designs. We can (a) determine whether a change takes place after the treatment, and, if so, we can (b) eliminate most other possible explanations (in the form of confounding variables) as to why the change has taken place. Thus, we have a reasonable basis on which to draw a conclusion about a cause-and-effect relationship.

Design 5: Solomon Four-Group Design

One potential problem in the preceding design is that the process of observing or assessing people before administering the experimental treatment may, in and of itself, influence how people respond to the treatment. For instance, perhaps the pretest increases people's motivation: It makes them want to benefit from the treatment they receive. Such an effect is another instance of the *reactivity* effect described in Chapter 4.

To address the question *What effect does pretesting have?*, Solomon (1949) proposed an extension of the pretest–posttest control-group design that involves four groups, as depicted in the following table:

	Group	Time →		
	Group 1	Obs	Tx	Obs
Random Assignment	Group 2	Obs	—	Obs
	Group 3	—	Tx	Obs
	Group 4	—	—	Obs

The addition of two groups who are not pretested provides a particular advantage. If the researcher finds that in the final observation, Groups 3 and 4 differ in much the same way that Groups 1 and 2 do, then the researcher can more easily generalize his or her findings to situations in which no pretest has been given. In other words, the Solomon four-group design enhances the *external validity* of the study.

Compared to Design 4, this design obviously involves a larger sample and demands more of the researcher's time and energy. Its principal value is in eliminating pretest influence; when such elimination is desirable, the design is ideal.

Design 6: Posttest-Only Control-Group Design

Some life situations defy pretesting. You can't pretest the forces in a thunderstorm or a hurricane, nor can you pretest growing crops. Additionally, sometimes you may be unable to locate a suitable pretest, or, as just noted, the very act of pretesting can influence the results of the experimental manipulation. In such circumstances, the posttest-only control-group design offers a possible solution. The design may be thought of as the last two groups of the Solomon four-group design. The paradigm for the posttest-only approach is as follows:

	Group	Time →	
Random Assignment	Group 1	Tx	Obs
	Group 2	—	Obs

Random assignment to groups is critical in the posttest-only design. Without it, the researcher has nothing more than a static group comparison (Design 3), from which, for reasons previously noted, the researcher has a difficult time drawing inferences about cause and effect.

Design 7: Within-Subjects Design

Earlier we introduced you to the nature of a within-subjects design—also known as a repeated-measures design—in which all participants receive all treatments (including any control conditions) in a research study. Note that we have switched from the term *participant* to the term *subject* here. The latter term has a broader meaning than *participants* in that it can be used to refer to a wide variety of populations—perhaps human beings, dogs, or laboratory rats.

In a good within-subjects design, the various treatments are administered very close together in time, in some cases simultaneously. If we use the subscripts a and b to designate the different treatments and treatment-specific measures, then in its simplest form a within-subjects design is as follows:

Group	Time →	
Group 1	Tx_a	Obs_a
	Tx_b	Obs_b

As an example, imagine that a researcher wants to study the effects of illustrations in an instructional software program that teaches 20 science concepts to sixth graders. The software defines and describes all 20 concepts with similar precision and depth. In addition, the software illustrates 10 of those concepts (chosen randomly) with pictures or diagrams. After students have completed the software curriculum, they take a quiz that assesses their understanding of the 20 concepts, and the researcher computes separate quiz scores for the illustrated and nonillustrated concepts. If the students perform better on quiz items for illustrated concepts than on items for nonillustrated ones, the researcher can reasonably conclude that, yes, illustrations help students learn science more effectively. In other words, the researcher has identified a cause-and-effect relationship: Illustrations improve science learning.

For a within-subjects design to work, the various forms of treatment must be such that their effects are fairly localized and unlikely to "spread" beyond specifically targeted behaviors. Such is the case in the study just described: The illustrations help students learn the particular concepts that have been illustrated but don't help students learn science more generally. In contrast, it would not make sense to use a within-subjects design to study the effects of two different psychotherapeutic techniques to reduce adolescents' criminal behaviors: If the same group of adolescents receives both treatments and then shows a significant reduction in juvenile offenses, we might suspect that either treatment could have had a fairly broad impact; we wouldn't know whether one of the treatments was more effective than the other.

Ideally, too, the two different treatments should be administered repeatedly, one after another, in a balanced but somewhat random order. For example, in the instructional software that presents both illustrated and nonillustrated science concepts, we might begin with an illustrated concept, then have two nonillustrated ones, then another illustrated one, another nonillustrated one, two illustrated ones, and so on, with the presentation of the two conditions being evenly balanced throughout the program.

With the last point in mind, let's return once again to Thrailkill's dissertation involving a lecture about the American Civil War. Each group received each of the three treatments: the imagery, attention, and control conditions. The logistics of the study were such that it was difficult to intermingle the three treatments throughout the lecture; instead, Thrailkill administered first one treatment (e.g., attention), then another (e.g., imagery), and finally the third (e.g., control). Had she limited her study to a single group, she could not have ruled out an alternative explanation— *when* in the lecture the information appeared (whether it appeared near the beginning, in the middle, or at the end)—for the results she obtained. By using three different groups, each of which had any particular condition in a different part of the lecture, she was able to eliminate that alternative explanation. Strictly speaking, however, because she could neither randomize assignment to groups nor randomly distribute different treatment conditions throughout the lecture, her study is probably better characterized as a quasi-experimental study than a true experimental study. We look more closely at quasi-experimental designs now.

QUASI-EXPERIMENTAL DESIGNS

In the preceding discussion of true experimental designs, we have emphasized the importance of *randomness,* either in the selection of group members in a multiple-groups study or in the presentation of different treatments in a single-group study. Sometimes, however, randomness is either impossible or impractical. In such situations, researchers often use quasi-experimental designs. When they conduct quasi-experimental studies, they don't control for all confounding variables and so can't completely rule out some alternative explanations for the results they obtain. They must take whatever variables and explanations they haven't controlled for into consideration when they interpret their data.

Design 8: Nonrandomized Control-Group Pretest–Posttest Design

The nonrandomized control-group pretest–posttest design can perhaps best be described as a compromise between the static group comparison (Design 3) and the pretest–posttest control-group design (Design 4). Like Design 3, it involves two groups to which participants haven't been randomly assigned. But it incorporates the pretreatment observations of Design 4. In sum, the nonrandomized control-group pretest–posttest design can be depicted as follows:

Group	Time →		
Group 1	Obs	Tx	Obs
Group 2	Obs	—	Obs

Without random assignment, there's no guarantee that the two groups are similar in every respect prior to the experimental treatment or intervention—no guarantee that any differences between them are due entirely to chance. However, an initial observation (e.g., a pretest) can confirm that the two groups are at least similar in terms of the dependent variable under investigation. If, after one group has received the experimental treatment, we then find group differences with respect to the dependent variable, we might reasonably conclude that the post-treatment differences are probably the result of that treatment.

Identifying matched pairs in the two groups is one way of strengthening the pretest–posttest control-group design. For instance, if we are studying the effect of a particular preschool program on children's IQ scores, we might find pairs of children—each pair including one child who is enrolled in the preschool program and one who is not—who are the same age and gender and have similar IQ scores before the program begins. Although we cannot rule out all other possible explanations in this situation (e.g., it may be that the parents who enroll their children in the preschool program are, in general, more concerned about their children's cognitive development), we can at least rule out *some* alternative explanations.

Design 9: Simple Time-Series Design

In its simplest form, a time-series design consists of making a series of observations (i.e., measuring the dependent variable on several occasions), introducing an intervention or other new dynamic into the system, and then making additional observations. If a substantial change is observed in the second series of observations in comparison to the first series, we might reasonably conclude that the cause of the change was the factor introduced into the system. This design thus looks something like the following:

Group	Time →								
Group 1	Obs	Obs	Obs	Obs	Tx	Obs	Obs	Obs	Obs

In such studies, the sequence of observations made prior to the treatment is typically referred to as baseline data.

Such a design has been widely used in the physical and biological sciences. Sir Alexander Fleming's discovery that *Penicillium notatum* (a mold) could inhibit staphylococci (a type of bacteria) is an example of this type of design. Fleming had been observing the growth of staphylococci on a culture plate. Then, unexpectedly, a culture plate containing well-developed colonies of staphylococci was contaminated with the spores of *Penicillium notatum.* Fleming observed that the bacteria near the mold seemed to disappear. He intentionally repeated the situation: After periodically observing the bacteria, he introduced the mold. Each time he used this procedure, his subsequent observations were the same: no staph germs near the mold.

The major weakness of this design is the possibility that some other, unrecognized event in the laboratory or outside world may occur at approximately the same time that the experimental treatment does, reflecting the *history* factor described in Figure 7.1. If this other event is actually the cause of the change, any conclusion that the treatment has brought about the change will obviously be incorrect.

Design 10: Control-Group Time-Series Design

In a variation of the time-series design, two groups are observed over a period of time, but one group (a control) doesn't receive the experimental treatment. The general design takes the following form:

Group	Time →								
Group 1	Obs	Obs	Obs	Obs	Tx	Obs	Obs	Obs	Obs
Group 2	Obs	Obs	Obs	Obs	—	Obs	Obs	Obs	Obs

This design has greater internal validity than the simple time-series design (Design 9). If an outside event is the cause of any changes we observe, then presumably the performance of *both* groups will be altered after the experimental treatment takes place. If, instead, the experimental treatment is the factor that affects performance, we should see a change only for Group 1.

Design 11: Reversal Time-Series Design

The reversal time-series design uses a within-subjects approach as a way of minimizing—though not entirely eliminating—the probability that outside effects might bring about any changes observed. The intervening experimental treatment is sometimes present, sometimes absent, and we measure the dependent variable at regular intervals. Thus, we have the following design:

Group	Time →							
Group 1	Tx	Obs	—	Obs	Tx	Obs	—	Obs

To illustrate, suppose we are interested in whether audiovisual materials help a single class of students learn astronomy. On some days we might include audiovisual materials in a lesson, and on other days we might omit them. We can then measure how effectively the students learn under both conditions. If the audiovisual materials do, in fact, promote student learning, we should see consistently better student performance on those days.

Design 12: Alternating-Treatments Design

A variation on the reversal time-series design involves including two or more different forms of experimental treatment in the design. Referring to the two different forms of treatment with the notations Tx_a and Tx_b, we can depict this design in the following manner:

Group	Time →											
Group 1	Tx_a	Obs	—	Obs	Tx_b	Obs	—	Obs	Tx_a	Obs	—	Obs	Tx_b	Obs

If such a sequence were pursued over a long enough time span, we would hope to see different effects for the two different treatments.

Design 13: Multiple-Baseline Design

Designs 11 and 12 are based on the assumption that the effects of any single treatment are temporary and limited to the immediate circumstances. Thus, these designs won't work if a treatment is likely to have long-lasting and perhaps fairly general effects. Furthermore, if an experimental treatment is apt to be quite beneficial for all participants, then ethical considerations may discourage us from including an untreated control group. In such instances, a multiple-baseline design provides a good alternative. This design requires at least two groups. Prior to the treatment, baseline data are collected for all groups, and then the treatment itself is introduced at a different time for each group. In its simplest form, a multiple-baseline design might be configured as follows:

Group	Time →					
Group 1	*Baseline* →		*Treatment* →			
	—	Obs	Tx	Obs	Tx	Obs
Group 2	*Baseline* →				*Treatment* →	
	—	Obs	—	Obs	Tx	Obs

A study by Heck, Collins, and Peterson (2001) provides an example of this approach. The researchers wanted to determine if instruction in playground safety would decrease elementary school children's risky behaviors on the playground. The treatment in this case involved a 5-day intervention in which a woman visited children's classrooms to talk about potentially risky behaviors on slides and climbing equipment, as well as about the unpleasant consequences that might result from such behaviors. The woman visited four different grade levels over a 3-week period; a random selection process resulted in her visiting first-grade classes one week, second-grade classes the following week, and kindergarten and third-grade classes (which went to recess at the same time) the week after that. Meanwhile, two independent observers simultaneously

FIGURE 7.2 ◼

Instances of Risky Behavior on Slides and Climbers by Grade Level; Third Graders and Kindergartners Shared a Single Recess

Reprinted from "Decreasing Children's Risk Taking on the Playground" by A. Heck, J. Collins, and L. Peterson, 2001, *Journal of Applied Behavior Analysis, 34,* p. 351. Reprinted with permission of the Society for the Experimental Analysis of Behavior, Inc.

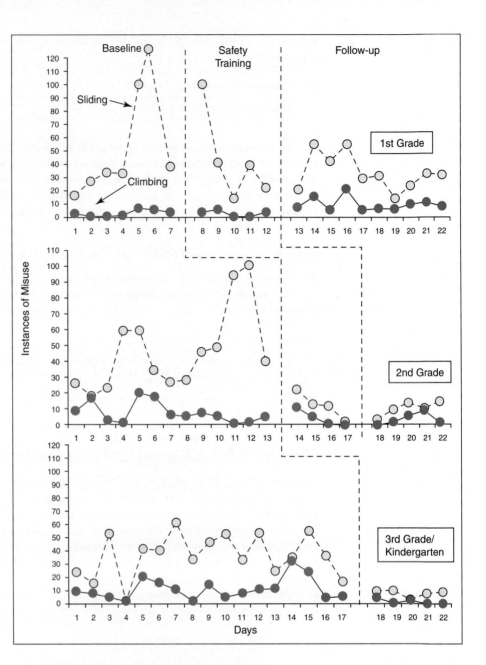

counted the number of risky behaviors on the playground before, during, and (for two of the four grade levels) after the interventions. The data they collected are depicted in Figure 7.2; numbers of risky behaviors on the slide are shown with the lighter dots, whereas those on the climbing equipment are shown with the darker dots. As you can see, once safety training began, the children in the second-grade and third-grade/kindergarten groups showed noticeable declines in risky behaviors on the slide and, to a lesser extent, on the climbing equipment (where risky behavior was relatively infrequent to begin with). Because the behavior changes occurred at different times for these two groups, and in particular because the changes for each group occurred at about the time that the group began its safety training, the researchers reasonably concluded that the training itself (rather than some other factor) was probably the reason for the changes. The first graders, who received the training first, showed little or no benefit from it, especially for the climbing equipment. Perhaps the trainer was still perfecting her training procedures that first week; however, we have no way of knowing for sure why the training appeared to be relatively ineffective for the first group.

Using Designs 11, 12, and 13 in Single-Subject Studies

Reversal, alternating-treatments, and multiple-baseline designs can be used not only with groups but also with single individuals, in what are collectively known as single-subject designs. A study by Deaver, Miltenberger, and Stricker (2001) illustrates how a researcher might use two of these—reversal and multiple-baseline—simultaneously. A 2-year-old girl named Tina had been referred for treatment because she often twirled her hair with her fingers so vigorously that she pulled out some of her hair. On one occasion she wrapped her hair around a finger so tightly that the finger began to turn blue and the hair had to be removed with scissors. Tina engaged in such behavior primarily when she was alone (e.g., at naptime); hence, there was no parent or other adult present to discourage it. The researchers identified a simple treatment—putting thin cotton mittens on Tina's hands—and wanted to document its effect. They videotaped Tina's behaviors when she was lying down for a nap in either of two settings, her bedroom at home or her daycare center, and two observers independently counted the number of hair twirling incidents as they watched the videotapes. Initially, the observers collected baseline data. Then, during separate time periods for the bedroom and daycare settings, they gave Tina the mittens to wear during naptime. After reversing back to baseline in both settings, they had Tina wear the mittens once again. The percentages of time that Tina twirled her hair in the two settings over the course of the study are presented in Figure 7.3.

In both the bedroom and daycare settings, the researchers alternated between baseline and treatment; this is the *reversal* aspect of the study. Furthermore, they initiated and then later

FIGURE 7.3 ◾

Percentage of Session Time in Which Hair Twirling Was Observed Both in the Bedroom and at Daycare

Reprinted from "Functional Analysis and Treatment of Hair Twirling in a Young Child" by C. M. Deaver, R. G. Miltenberger, & J. M. Stricker, 2001, *Journal of Applied Behavior Analysis, 34,* p. 537. Reprinted with permission of the Society for the Experimental Analysis of Behavior, Inc.

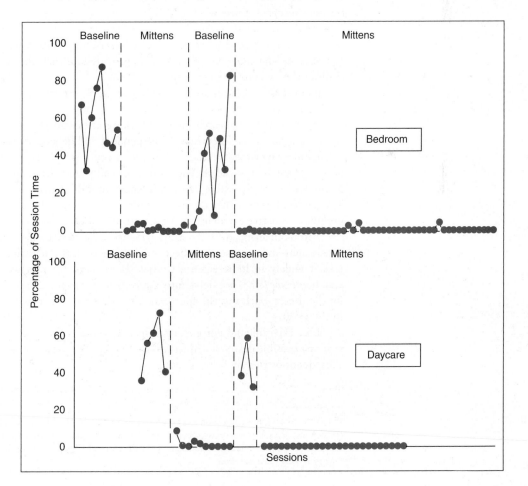

reinstituted the treatment at different times in the two settings; this is the *multiple-baseline* aspect of the study. Figure 7.3 consistently shows dramatic differences in hair twirling during baseline versus mittens conditions, leading us to conclude that the mittens, rather than some other factor, were almost certainly the reason for the disappearance of hair twirling.

EX POST FACTO DESIGNS

In many situations, it is unethical or impossible to manipulate certain variables in order to investigate their potential influence on other variables. For example, a researcher cannot intentionally infect people with a potentially lethal new virus, withhold instruction, ask parents to abuse their children, or modify a person's personality to compare the effects of these factors on the dependent variables in one's research problem.

Ex post facto designs[2] (the term *ex post facto* literally means "after the fact") provide an alternative means by which a researcher can investigate the extent to which specific independent variables—perhaps involving a virus, lack of schooling, a history of family violence, or a personality trait—may possibly affect the dependent variable(s) of interest. In an ex post facto study, a researcher identifies *events that have already occurred or conditions that are already present* and then collects data to investigate a possible relationship between these factors and subsequent characteristics or behaviors. In particular, after observing that differing circumstances have prevailed for two or more different groups—such circumstances comprise the independent variable—the researcher tries to determine whether the groups differ on some other, dependent variable. For example, a researcher might identify two groups of adults with different immunization records—those who, as children, were vaccinated against measles and those who were not—and then calculate the percentage of reported cases of measles in each group. Similarly, a researcher might identify two groups of 10-year-olds—those who had extensive musical training in preschool and those whose preschools provided no such training—and compare the musical skills of the two groups of children.

Ex post facto designs are often confused with correlational or experimental designs because they share certain characteristics with each of these other design types. Like correlational research, ex post facto research involves looking at existing circumstances. But like experimental research, it has clearly identifiable independent and dependent variables.

Unlike experimental studies, however, ex post facto designs involve no direct manipulation of the independent variable: The presumed "cause" has already occurred. To the extent that such manipulation isn't possible, the researcher cannot draw firm conclusions about cause and effect. The problem here is that the experimenter can't control for confounding variables that might provide alternative explanations for any group differences observed.

Although an ex post facto study lacks the control element—and thus doesn't enable definite conclusions about cause and effect—it is nevertheless a legitimate research method. Medicine uses it widely in its research activities. Physicians discover an illness and then initiate their search *after the fact*. They delve into antecedent events and conditions to discover a possible cause for the illness. Such was the approach of medical researchers when the AIDS virus came to light in the 1980s.

Like experimental designs, ex post facto designs can take a variety of forms. Here we present one possible design for illustrative purposes. We present a second ex post facto design in the subsequent section on factorial designs.

---

[2]Ex post facto designs are also known as *causal-comparative* designs. However, as B. Johnson (2001) has pointed out, the latter term may mislead novice researchers to believe that such designs show cause and effect as clearly and definitively as true experimental designs. In reality, such designs never eliminate all other possible explanations for an observed effect; thus, they can't truly show cause and effect.

Design 14: Simple Ex Post Facto Design

Design 14 is similar to the static group comparison (Design 3) described in the previous section on pre-experimental designs. The important difference is one of timing: In this case, the "treatment" in question occurred long before the study began; hence, we call it an *experience* rather than a treatment because the researcher hasn't been responsible for imposing it. A simple ex post facto design can be depicted as follows, where Exp refers to a prior experience that one group has had and another has not:

Group	Time →	
	Prior event(s)	*Investigation period*
Group 1	Exp	Obs
Group 2	—	Obs

An obvious variation on this design is one in which Group 2 has an experience as well, albeit a different experience from that of Group 1.

Such designs are common in studying the possible effects of previously occurring environmental variables such as television viewing habits, child abuse, and malnutrition. They are also used in studying the potential influences of pre-existing characteristics—perhaps those that are inherited or congenital—such as gender, mental illness, and physical disability. (In the latter instances, we might want to replace the term *experience* with a term such as *characteristic*.) The most we can conclude from these studies is that certain behaviors or other variables tend to be *associated* with certain pre-existing conditions; we can never determine that those other variables were actually caused by those conditions.

FACTORIAL DESIGNS

Thus far we have been describing designs in which only one independent variable is studied. Yet in many situations, a researcher examines the effects of two or more independent variables in a single study; this approach is known as a factorial design.

Design 15: Two-Factor Experimental Design

In its simplest form—one involving two independent variables, which we will call *Variable 1* and *Variable 2*—such a design might look like the following:

	Group	Time →		
		Treatments related to the two variables may occur simultaneously or sequentially		
		Treatment related to Variable 1	*Treatment related to Variable 2*	
Random Assignment	Group 1	Tx$_1$	Tx$_2$	Obs
	Group 2	Tx$_1$	—	Obs
	Group 3	—	Tx$_2$	Obs
	Group 4	—	—	Obs

We can determine the effects of the first independent variable by comparing the performance of Groups 1 and 2 with that of Groups 3 and 4. We can determine the effects of the second independent variable by comparing Groups 1 and 3 with Groups 2 and 4. If you think you've seen this design before, in a way you have. This is simply a more generalized form of the Solomon four-group design (Design 5), but we are no longer limiting ourselves to having the presence or absence of a pretest be one of our independent variables.

Such a design allows us to examine not only the possible effects of two independent variables but also the possible *interaction* of the variables as they influence the dependent variable. For example, imagine that, after presenting both treatments, we find that Groups 2, 3, and 4 show similar performance but that Group 1 outperforms the other three. Such a result might indicate that neither independent variable produces a particular effect on its own—that *both* variables are necessary to bring about the effect.

Design 16: Combined Experimental and Ex Post Facto Design

In the factorial design just presented, participants are randomly assigned to groups in a true experimental study. But it is also possible to combine elements of experimental research and ex post facto research into a single factorial design. In its simplest form, such a design looks like the following:

Group	Time →				
	Prior event(s)	*Investigation period →*			
Group 1	Exp$_a$	Random Assignment	Group 1a	Tx$_a$	Obs
			Group 1b	Tx$_b$	Obs
Group 2	Exp$_b$	Random Assignment	Group 2a	Tx$_a$	Obs
			Group 2b	Tx$_b$	Obs

In this case, the researcher initially divides the sample into two groups based on the participants' previous experiences or pre-existing conditions; this is the *ex post facto* part of the study. Then the researcher randomly assigns members of each group to one of two treatment groups (or perhaps a treatment group and a control group); this is the *experimental* part of the study. The result is four groups that represent all four possible combinations of the previous experience/pre-existing characteristic and the treatment variable. Such a design enables the researcher to study how an experimental manipulation might influence a particular dependent variable *and* how a previous experience or pre-existing characteristic might interact with that manipulation.

In a variation of such a design, the experimental manipulation might be a within-subjects variable rather than a between-groups variable. As an example, one of us authors once joined forces with two colleagues and a graduate student to test the hypothesis that people with different educational backgrounds interpret and remember maps differently and, more specifically, that only people with a background in geography apply general principles of geography when they interpret maps (J. E. Ormrod, Ormrod, Wagner, & McCallin, 1988). We constructed two maps to test our hypothesis. One map was arranged in accordance with patterns of a typical city; for instance, a downtown business district was located at a point where it could be easily reached from different directions (this is typical), and factories, a lumberyard, and low-income housing were situated near railroad tracks (also typical). The second map was less "logical" in the sense that it violated basic geographic principles; for instance, a river originated in the plains and ran *up* into a mountain range, and various transportation networks didn't interconnect in ways that they normally do. The two different maps reflected one of our independent variables: logic (or lack thereof) of the spatial arrangement of features within a map.

Three groups of college professors—geographers, sociologists, and educational psychologists—provided the basis for our second independent variable: academic background. We asked each professor to study each of the two maps aloud for three 2-minute intervals (we tape-recorded what they said during the study sessions) and then, after each interval, to draw as much of the map as he or she could remember.

Thus, if we call the two maps Tx_a (logical map) and Tx_b (illogical map), our design looks like the following:

Group	Time →							
Geographers	Tx_a	Obs	Obs	Obs	Tx_b	Obs	Obs	Obs
Sociologists	Tx_a	Obs	Obs	Obs	Tx_b	Obs	Obs	Obs
Educational psychologists	Tx_a	Obs	Obs	Obs	Tx_b	Obs	Obs	Obs

In this situation, one independent variable—the logic or illogic of the map presented—was a variable we directly manipulated, and we presented it to all participants in a *within-subjects* (repeated-measures) manner. The second independent variable, academic background, was a preexisting condition and therefore something we could *not* control; this was the ex post facto part of the design.

The upshot of the study was that there was an *interaction* between the two independent variables, map logic and academic background. In particular, the geographers remembered more of the logical map than they did of the illogical map; in contrast, the sociologists and educational psychologists remembered each map with equal accuracy. We interpreted this result to indicate that only the geographers were applying geographic principles to study the maps and that they could use such principles effectively only with the geographically logical one. We supported our conclusion with a qualitative element in our study; that is, we used a *mixed-methods design*. In particular, we conducted content analyses of the professors' study sessions. Indeed, the content analyses revealed that the geographers had applied many geographic principles to the logical map but had trouble applying them to the illogical one. Meanwhile, the sociologists and educational psychologists studied both maps in a haphazard manner, with few attempts to make sense of what they saw on the maps.

Table 7.1 provides a summary of the pre-experimental, experimental, quasi-experimental, ex post facto, and factorial designs described in the preceding sections. Keep in mind that, as stated earlier, this is not an exhaustive list of experimental and ex post facto designs. You can combine and expand on these designs in a number of ways—and perhaps incorporate elements of qualitative or descriptive-quantitative designs (e.g., content analysis or longitudinal data collection) as well—to more effectively address your own research question.

TABLE 7.1 ■ Summary of Experimental and Ex Post Facto Designs

Name of the Design	Goal of the Research	Graphic Depiction	Comments on the Design
Pre-Experimental Designs			

Pre-Experimental Designs

Name of the Design	Goal of the Research	Graphic Depiction	Comments on the Design
1. One-shot experimental case study	To show that one event (a treatment) precedes another event (the observation)	Group — Time → : Group 1 | Tx | Obs	Shows a before-and-after sequence but cannot substantiate that it reflects a cause-and-effect relationship.
2. One group pretest–posttest design	To show that change occurs after a treatment	Group — Time → : Group 1 | Obs | Tx | Obs	Provides a measure of change but yields no conclusive results about the cause of the change.
3. Static group comparison	To show that a group receiving a treatment behaves differently than a group receiving no treatment	Group — Time → : Group 1 | Tx | Obs ; Group 2 | — | Obs	Fails to determine pretreatment equivalence of groups.

True Experimental Designs

Name of the Design	Goal of the Research	Graphic Depiction	Comments on the Design
4. Pretest–posttest control-group design	To show that change occurs following, but only following, a particular treatment	Random Assignment — Group — Time → : Group 1 | Obs | Tx | Obs ; Group 2 | Obs | — | Obs	Controls for many potential threats to internal validity.
5. Solomon four-group design	To investigate the possible effect of pretesting	Random Assignment — Group — Time → : Group 1 | Obs | Tx | Obs ; Group 2 | Obs | — | Obs ; Group 3 | — | Tx | Obs ; Group 4 | — | — | Obs	Enables the researcher to determine how pretesting might affect the final outcome observed.
6. Posttest-only control-group design	To determine the effects of a treatment when pretesting cannot or should not occur	Random Assignment — Group — Time → : Group 1 | Tx | Obs ; Group 2 | — | Obs	Uses the last two groups in the Solomon four-group design; random assignment to groups is critical for maximizing group equivalence.
7. Within-subjects design	To compare the relative effects of different treatments for the same participants	Group — Time → : Group 1 | Tx_a | Obs_a / Tx_b | Obs_b	Useful only when effects of each treatment are temporary and localized.

Quasi-Experimental Designs

Name of the Design	Goal of the Research	Graphic Depiction	Comments on the Design
8. Nonrandomized control-group pretest–posttest design	To show that two groups are equivalent with respect to the dependent variable prior to the treatment, thus eliminating initial group differences as an explanation for posttreatment differences	Group — Time → : Group 1 | Obs | Tx | Obs ; Group 2 | Obs | — | Obs	Differs from experimental designs because test and control groups are not totally equivalent; equivalence on the pretest ensures equivalence only for variables that have specifically been measured.

TABLE 7.1 ■ Summary of Experimental and Ex Post Facto Designs *(continued)*

Name of the Design	Goal of the Research	Graphic Depiction	Comments on the Design
		Quasi-Experimental Designs *(continued)*	
9. Simple time-series experiment	To show that, for a single group, change occurs during a lengthy period only after the treatment has been administered	Group Time → Group 1 | Obs | Obs | Tx | Obs | Obs	Provides a stronger alternative to Design 2; external validity can be increased by repeating the experiment in different places under different conditions.
10. Control-group time-series design	To bolster the internal validity of the preceding design with the addition of a control group	Group Time → Group 1 | Obs | Obs | Tx | Obs | Obs Group 2 | Obs | Obs | — | Obs | Obs	Involves conducting parallel series of observations for experimental and control groups.
11. Reversal time-series design	To show, in a single group or individual, that a treatment consistently leads to a particular effect	Group Time → Group 1 | Tx | Obs | — | Obs | Tx | Obs	Is an on-again, off-again design in which the experimental treatment is sometimes present, sometimes absent.
12. Alternating-treatments design	To show, in a single group or individual, that different treatments have different effects	Group Time → Group 1 | Tx_a | Obs | — | Obs | Tx_b | Obs	Involves sequentially administering different treatments at different times and comparing their effects against the possible consequences of nontreatment.
13. Multiple-baseline design	To show the effect of a treatment by initiating it at different times for different groups or individuals, or perhaps in different settings for a single individual	Group Time → Group 1 | — | Obs | Tx | Obs | Tx | Obs Group 2 | — | Obs | — | Obs | Tx | Obs	Involves tracking two or more groups or individuals over time, or tracking a single individual in two or more settings, for a lengthy period of time, as well as initiating the treatment at different times for different groups, individuals, or settings.
		Ex Post Facto Designs	
14. Simple ex post facto design	To show the possible effects of an experience that occurred, or a condition that was present, prior to the investigation	Group Time → Group 1 | Exp | Obs Group 2 | — | Obs	May show a difference between groups but does not conclusively demonstrate that the difference is due to the prior experience/condition in question.
		Factorial Designs	
15. Two-factor experimental design	To study the effects of two experimenter-manipulated variables and their possible interaction	Group Time → Random Assignment: Group 1 | Tx_1 | Tx_2 | Obs Group 2 | Tx_1 | — | Obs Group 3 | — | Tx_2 | Obs Group 4 | — | — | Obs	Requires a larger sample size than two-group studies; random assignment to treatments is essential.
16. Combined experimental and ex post facto design	To study the possible effects of an experimenter-manipulated variable, a previously existing condition, and the interaction between the two	Group Time → Group 1 | Exp_a | Random Assignment: Group 1a | Tx_a | Obs / Group 1b | Tx_b | Obs Group 2 | Exp_b | Random Assignment: Group 2a | Tx_a | Obs / Group 2b | Tx_b | Obs	Requires a larger sample size than two-group studies; random assignment to the experimenter-manipulated variable is essential.

CONCEPTUAL ANALYSIS EXERCISE Identifying
Quantitative Research Designs

As a way of reviewing the designs described in this chapter, we offer a brief pop quiz. Following are short summaries of five research studies. The studies don't necessarily fit exactly into one of the design categories presented, but each one is definitely *experimental, quasi-experimental,* or *ex post facto* in nature. Identify the type of research that each study reflects. The answers appear after the "For Further Reading" section at the end of the chapter.

1. Two researchers want to see if a particular training program is effective in teaching horses to enter a horse trailer without misbehaving in the process—that is, without rearing, trying to turn around, or in some other way resisting entry into the trailer. Five horses (Red, Penny, Shadow, Sammy, and Fancy) go through the training, with each horse beginning training on a different day. For each horse, an observer counts the number of misbehaviors every day prior to and during training, with data being collected for a time span of at least 45 days (Ferguson & Rosales-Ruiz, 2001).

2. Two researchers wonder whether an eyewitness's memory of an event is affected by questions that he or she is asked subsequent to the event. To find out, the researchers show adults a film that depicts a car accident. Each adult is then asked one of five questions (randomly selected) about the accident:
   - About how fast were the cars going when they *contacted* each other?
   - About how fast were the cars going when they *hit* each other?
   - About how fast were the cars going when they *bumped into* each other?
   - About how fast were the cars going when they *collided into* each other?
   - About how fast were the cars going when they *smashed into* each other?

   The researchers compute the average speed given in response to each of the five questions to determine whether the questions have influenced participants' "memory" for the accident (Loftus & Palmer, 1974).

3. A researcher studies the effects of two different kinds of note-taking training (one of which is a placebo) on the kinds of notes that college students take. Her sample consists of students enrolled in two sections of an undergraduate course in educational psychology; with the flip of a coin, she randomly determines which section will be the treatment group and which will be the control group. She analyzes the content of students' class notes both before and after the training, making the prediction that the two groups' notes will be similar before the training but qualitatively different after the training (Jackson, 1996).

4. At the request of the National Park Service, two researchers at Rocky Mountain National Park investigate the degree to which signs along hiking trails might influence hikers' behaviors. Park Service officials are concerned that the heavy traffic on one particular hiking trail, the trail to Emerald Lake, may be having a negative impact on the local environment; they would like to divert some traffic to a lesser-used trail to Lake Haiyaha, which begins at the same place as the Emerald Lake trail. One day in early summer, the researchers hide battery-operated, optic counters at key locations along the two trails to record the number of hikers. The study has four phases: (1) at the spot where the two trails originate, only signs indicating the destinations of the two trails are present; (2) a "positively worded" sign is added that describes the attractive features of the Lake Haiyaha trail and encourages hikers to use it; (3) the positively worded sign is replaced by a "negatively worded" sign that describes the crowdedness of the Emerald Lake trail and discourages its use; and (4) both the positively worded and negatively worded signs are posted. The researchers compare the frequency of hikers during each of the four phases (R. K. Ormrod & Trahan, 1982).

5. A team of researchers has a sample of elementary school boys, some of whom have been identified as having attention-deficit hyperactivity disorder (ADHD) and some of whom have not. One of the researchers asks each boy to interpret several social situations that are depicted in a series of black-and-white drawings (e.g., one sequence

of drawings shows a sequence of events at a Halloween party). Some of the situations involve antisocial behavior (e.g., aggression), and other situations involve prosocial behavior (e.g., sharing). The researchers compare the interpretations that boys with ADHD make with the interpretations that boys without ADHD make with respect to both kinds of situations (Milch-Reich, Campbell, Pelham, Connelly, & Geva, 1999).

PRACTICAL APPLICATION Determining Possible Cause-and-Effect Relationships

The research designs described in this chapter vary considerably in the degree to which they control for potential confounding variables—variables that threaten a study's internal validity—and thus they also vary in terms of the degree to which they enable a researcher to draw firm conclusions about cause-and-effect relationships. The following checklist can help you evaluate a research design with respect to its internal validity.

✓ CHECKLIST

Looking for Confounding Variables

If you are planning a study in which you hope to find one or more cause-and-effect relationships—or if, instead, you are evaluating another person's research proposal or report—scrutinize the study with the following questions in mind:

_____ 1. What are the independent and dependent variables in the study:
Independent variable(s):

_____

Dependent variable(s):

_____

_____ 2. Is every independent variable actively manipulated by the researcher?
_____ Yes _____ No

_____ 3. If the researcher is manipulating one or more independent variables, what precautions is the researcher taking to ensure that the manipulation is minimizing or eliminating the potential effects of confounding variables? For example, is the researcher:

• Keeping certain other variables constant? If so, which ones?

_____

_____

• Including a control group or at least two treatment groups?

_____

• Randomizing assignment to groups?

_____

• Using a within-subjects (repeated-measures) design?

_____

• Using other appropriate strategies? If so, which ones?

_____

_____

_____ 4. If the researcher is *not* manipulating one or more independent variables, what precautions is the researcher taking to control for confounding variables? For example, is the researcher:

- Using one or more pretests to assess before-treatment group equivalence? If so, what variables are being pretested?

  _____

  _____

- Identifying matched pairs? If so, on the basis of what variables?

  _____

  _____

- Statistically controlling for confounding variables? If so, which ones?

  _____

_____ 5. If the researcher is conducting a single-group or single-subject study, is the researcher:

- Conducting a series of observations both before and after the intervention (a time-series design)? _____

- Alternating either between two or more treatments or between treatment and nontreatment, with a new observation being made after each treatment or non-treatment (a reversal design)? _____

- Beginning an intervention at different times for different individuals or different contexts (a multiple-baseline design)? _____

_____ 6. What other variables in the study (either identified or not identified by the researcher) might potentially affect the dependent variable? _____

  _____

  _____

_____ 7. To what extent might each of the following factors threaten the study's internal validity? If any of these factors pose a potential threat, how is the researcher minimizing or eliminating its influence? (Refer to Figure 7.1.)

History:

_____

Maturation:

_____

Testing:

_____

Instrumentation:

_____

Statistical regression:

_____

Selection:

_____

Attrition:

_____

_____ 8. With your answers to the preceding questions in mind, explain whether the study's results justifiably demonstrate a cause-and-effect relationship:

_____

_____

_____

_____

META-ANALYSES

Remember, we can conclude that a cause-and-effect relationship exists between an independent variable and a dependent variable only if we have directly manipulated the independent variable and have controlled for confounding variables that might offer alternative explanations for any changes in the dependent variable. Even when we have taken such precautions, however, there is the possibility that our alleged "cause" doesn't really produce the effect we think it does—that the situation we have just observed is a one-time-in-a-million fluke.

In Chapter 4 we introduced the idea of *replication:* We gain greater confidence in our research findings when a study is repeated over and over again—perhaps with a different population, in a different setting, or with slight variations on the treatment implementation.

Once researchers have conducted many such replications, another researcher may come along and conduct a meta-analysis—that is, an analysis of the analyses. In particular, the researcher combines the results of many experimental and/or ex post facto studies to determine whether they lead to consistent conclusions. A meta-analysis is primarily a statistical technique, and thus we describe this procedure in greater depth in Chapter 8.

CONDUCTING EXPERIMENTS ON THE INTERNET

USING TECHNOLOGY

In Chapter 6 we mentioned that some researchers now conduct research studies on the Internet. Although most of these studies can best be categorized as descriptive studies, we occasionally see experimental studies as well. For instance, one of us authors once visited the website "Psychological Research on the Net," which provides links to numerous sites that host online research projects.[3] To learn more about this growing approach to data collection, she became a participant in several online studies that were active at the time. Although most of the studies involved completing questionnaires and so appeared to be correlational or survey studies, one of them was clearly an experimental study. In particular, this author was asked to (a) read and study a story that was illustrated by several photographs; (b) read three additional stories, one of which was quite similar to the initial story; and (c) answer a series of questions about details in the stories. In a subsequent debriefing on the website, she learned that she had been randomly assigned to the experimental group in the second part of the study; other participants were assigned to a control group, in which all three stories were quite different from the initial story. The researcher was investigating the possible effects that a similar story in Part b might have on recall for the story in Part a.

Internet-based experimental studies don't necessarily have to be one-shot affairs. For example, in one online study (Cepeda, Vul, Rohrer, Wixted, & Pashler, 2008), researchers enticed people into participating in a three-session experiment with the promise that for every session they completed, their name would be entered into an end-of-study lottery that would award cash prizes. A total of 1,354 people completed all three sessions; they ranged in age from 18 to 72 and lived in various countries around the world. In Session 1 of the experiment, participants studied a list of 32 obscure trivia facts, such as the answer to "What European nation consumes the most spicy Mexican food?" (p. 1097), and they continued to study each fact until they could correctly recall it.[4] After this first session, participants were divided into different treatment groups that varied in terms of the timing for Sessions 2 and 3, and they were sent e-mail messages when it was time to complete these subsequent sessions. In Session 2 (which might be as little as 3 minutes or as much as 105 days after Session 1), participants studied the trivia facts again, this time studying each one twice. Then, in Session 3 (which was 7, 35, 70, or 350 days after Session 2), participants were asked to remember as many of the facts as they could. The findings of the study are important for any conscientious student to note: Especially when the final test session was considerably delayed

---

[3]As noted in Chapter 6, this website is maintained by John Krantz, Professor of Psychology at Hanover College (psych .hanover.edu).

[4]In case you're curious, Norwegians are especially partial to spicy Mexican food, at least in comparison with other Europeans.

(e.g., by 2½ months or almost a year), people who spread out their studying more (i.e., those with a longer delay between Sessions 1 and 2) remembered more facts. (If you've noticed a possible problem with *attrition* in the study, give yourself a pat on the back! We'll address this problem shortly.)

In some instances, an Internet-based research study might be quite suitable for your research question. Keep in mind, however, that ethical practices ensuring protection from harm, informed consent, and right to privacy are as important in online experimental research as they are in any face-to-face studies. The suggestions for ethical practices presented in Chapter 6 for online questionnaires are equally applicable to online experiments (see the Practical Application "Using the Internet to Collect Data for a Descriptive Study" in Chapter 6).

Remember, too, that the sample you get in an online study will hardly be representative of the overall population; for instance, it is likely to consist largely of college-educated, computer-literate people who enjoy participating in research studies. An additional problem is that you cannot observe your participants to determine whether they are accurately reporting demographic information (their age, gender, etc.) and whether they are truly following the instructions you present. Accordingly, unless you are interested in a topic such as very-long-term memory (as Cepeda and his colleagues were in their 2008 study) and can carefully control the conditions under which people are participating, we suggest that you use an Internet-based study primarily to formulate tentative hypotheses or to pilot test experimental materials you plan to use in a more controlled and observable situation.

TESTING YOUR HYPOTHESES, AND BEYOND

Experimental and ex post facto studies typically begin with specific research hypotheses, and subsequent statistical analyses should, of course, be conducted to test these hypotheses. Such analyses often take the form of a *t* test, analysis of variance, or analysis of covariance. We briefly describe these procedures in Chapter 8.

Yet one's analyses need not be restricted *only* to the testing of initially stated hypotheses. Oftentimes a study may yield additional results—results that are unexpected yet intriguing— that merit analysis. There is no reason why the researcher can't examine these findings as well, perhaps statistically, perhaps not.

PRACTICAL APPLICATION Acknowledging the Probable Presence of Bias in Experimental Research

Despite the tight controls in many experiments—and in some cases *because* of such controls—one or more forms of bias can wiggle their ways into the data or into interpretations of the data. Some of these biasing factors, such as group selection procedures, statistical regression, and differing attrition rates, can adversely affect the *internal validity* of a study (look once again at Figure 7.1). For example, as you were reading about the memory-for-trivia experiment in the earlier discussion of Internet-based experiments, you might have wondered if the dropout (attrition) rate was higher for participants with longer between-session delays, and indeed it was (Cepeda et al., 2008). Were participants who had poor memories more likely to drop out over the long run than participants who had good memories? If so, by Session 3, the people who remained in spread-out-studying treatment groups might simply have had better memories *in general* than people who remained in close-together-studying treatment groups. To determine the extent to which the differing attrition rates for various treatment groups might jeopardize the study's internal validity, the researchers collected basic demographic data at the beginning of Session 1. In their data analyses, the researchers found no significant differences in any demographic variables or in Session 1 performance between participants who completed all three sessions and those who did not—thus lending support to their premise that the members of the various treatment groups were similar in all ways *except* for the differing study intervals.

Other biasing factors can negatively impact the *external validity* of an experimental study. For example, when conducting their online study of studying and memory, Cepeda and his colleagues not only had a biased sample—computer-literate individuals who volunteered to participate—but they also had participants study *trivial facts* in an *atypical learning situation.* Would their conclusions apply to more important learning tasks in everyday learning contexts? Their results alone can't answer this question.

Furthermore, a researcher's expectations and hypotheses are likely to bias a study from the get-go: By focusing only on certain variables and by measuring those variables in predetermined ways, no researcher can discover the "whole truth" about the phenomenon under investigation— if there *is* a general, underlying truth. Try as we might, we human beings cannot be completely objective and unbiased in our well-intended efforts to make better sense of our physical, social, and psychological worlds. But we can—and *must*—be honest about our biases so that others can realistically evaluate the merits of our work.

✓ CHECKLIST

Identifying Potential Sources of Bias and Potential Threats to External Validity in an Experimental, Quasi-Experimental, or Ex Post Facto Study

The previous checklist, "Looking for Confounding Variables," can help you identify biasing factors that can adversely affect the internal validity of a study. Following are additional questions to keep in mind when looking for possible biases in an experimental, quasi-experimental, or ex post facto study, as well as for factors that might adversely affect a study's external validity.

_____ 1. What one or more hypotheses about cause-and-effect relationships has the researcher formed about the phenomenon being studied? What potentially important variables might these hypotheses be leading the researcher to ignore?

_____

_____

_____

_____ 2. How is the sample being selected for the study? Is this sample likely to be representative of the population about which generalizations are being made? Why or why not?

_____

_____

_____ 3. If the study involves human beings, what are participants being asked to do? To what degree are these tasks similar to real-world activities?

_____

_____

_____ 4. In what setting is the study being conducted? To what degree is it similar to the settings of everyday life?

_____

_____

_____ 5. With your answers to Questions 2, 3, and 4 in mind, describe the extent to which the results of the study should be generalizable to diverse individuals, tasks, and settings.

_____

_____

_____

✔ **Check Your Understanding in the Pearson etext**

Practice Thinking Like a Researcher

Practice Thinking Like a Researcher Activity 7.1: Selecting and Controlling Variables
Practice Thinking Like a Researcher Activity 7.2: Planning for an Experimental Design
Practice Thinking Like a Researcher Activity 7.3: Planning for a Quasi-Experimental Design

A SAMPLE DISSERTATION

To illustrate how an experimental study might appear in its written form, we present excerpts from Virginia Kinnick's doctoral dissertation conducted at the University of Colorado (Kinnick, 1989). The researcher, a faculty member in the School of Nursing at another university, had considerable experience teaching nursing students the knowledge and skills they would need when working with women who were in the process of delivering a baby, and her interest lay in learning more about teaching such knowledge and skills effectively.

During a woman's labor prior to the delivery of her baby, a fetal monitor is often used to assess the baby's heart rate, and the maternity nurse must frequently check the monitor for signs that the baby might be experiencing exceptional and potentially harmful stress. Kinnick wanted to determine whether a particular method of teaching concepts (one described by Tennyson and Cocchiarella) might be more effective for teaching fetal monitoring skills than the method traditionally used in nursing education programs. In Kinnick's dissertation, the problem statement is as follows:

> This study is designed to determine if use of an instructional design model for concept attainment in teaching the critical concepts related to fetal monitoring will make a significant difference in preparation of nursing students in this skill, compared to the traditional teaching method which exists in most schools. (Kinnick, 1989, p. 8)

The research design was not one of the designs we have specifically described in this chapter. Instead, it involved administering three different instructional methods to three treatment groups (with participants assigned randomly to groups) and then observing the effects of the treatments at two different times: once immediately after instruction and then later after students had completed the clinical rotation portion of their nursing program. Thus, the design of the study was the following:

	Group	Time →		
Random Assignment	Group 1	Tx_1	Obs	Obs
	Group 2	Tx_2	Obs	Obs
	Group 3	Tx_3	Obs	Obs

In the following pages, we present excerpts from the methodology chapter of the researcher's dissertation. Our comments and observations appear on the right-hand side.

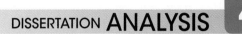

DISSERTATION **ANALYSIS** 4

METHODOLOGY

[After an introductory paragraph outlining the chapter's contents, the author describes the sample used in the study: students enrolled in maternity nursing courses at two universities. Then, as she begins a discussion of her procedure, she explains that the experimental treatments were based on the Tennyson-Cocchiarella concept-teaching model (1986) and presents the key elements of the model. We pick up the methodology chapter at the point where the author describes the specific treatments used for each of the three treatment groups.]

Description of the Treatment Groups

[The author first explains that, for each of the three groups, treatment consisted of instruction in the basic concepts of fetal monitoring, plus additional instructional strategies, or "teaching variables," that differed for the groups.] . . . Starting with a basic class and adding new teaching variables to each treatment group, however, did require additional time. The length of time required for teaching the three treatment groups varied between 1 and 2 hours. These timeframes were established based on the results of the survey of baccalaureate nursing schools, in which 36% of the schools responding had less than 1 hour to teach fetal monitoring theory, and 52% had 1 to 2 hours (Kinnick, 1989).

The teaching variables for the first treatment group included labels and definitions plus presentation of best examples. According to Merrill and Tennyson, these variables usually include additional information needed to aid in the clarification and understanding of the concepts (Merrill & Tennyson, 1977, p. 100). Therefore, the design of this didactic presentation began with a very basic overview of physiology at the uterofetoplacental unit. Electronic fetal monitoring patterns are a reflection of uterofetoplacental physiology. Understanding the normal physiology and changes in the physiology that cause inadequate fetal oxygenation help the learner to identify the various patterns, and whether patterns are normal or abnormal. Understanding the physiology is also the basis to identifying appropriate nursing intervention which promotes normal physiology (reduction or even elimination of fetal distress) when abnormal patterns occur.

When the classes were taught, the majority of students did not have any theory about the process of labor and delivery. In addition, they had not seen a fetal monitor. Methods of monitoring the fetus and a brief description and discussion of external versus internal monitoring, therefore, needed to be discussed. In addition, it was necessary to show the students a print-out of a fetal monitor as well as explain what the graphs meant. Before the basic concepts related to interpretation of the fetal heart could be taught, the student also needed to recognize critical characteristics of a contraction pattern as seen on a monitor strip. Contraction patterns can be a cause of physiological changes at the uterofetoplacental site. After these areas had been covered, the concept label, definitions, and best examples were presented. . . .

Comments

The author points out a possible confounding variable in her study: The three forms of instruction took varying amounts of time.

The survey to which the author refers was administered during a pilot study that she conducted prior to conducting the dissertation itself. She published the pilot study as a research article, which she cites here.

In this and subsequent paragraphs the author describes the treatment used for each treatment group; in a later "Procedure" section, she describes the general procedure she used to conduct the study. More often, a researcher will include a description of how each group was treated within the procedure section itself. Either approach is acceptable, however, as long as the writer makes the organization of the methodology section clear (e.g., through headings and subheadings).

This description of what most students knew (and did not know) before instruction gives the reader greater confidence that the results observed after instruction (i.e., students' test performance) were probably due to the instructional treatments, rather than to any earlier learning experiences that the students may have had.

This 1-hour presentation included labels, definitions, best examples, and clarifying information. In the experience of this researcher, this presentation reflects closely the method for teaching fetal monitoring used in most schools of nursing, especially when the allocated time for teaching this content is limited. This treatment group is referred to as Group 1 throughout the study.

The second treatment group began with the same presentation used with the first treatment group, plus the addition of expository presentations for each major concept. An expository presentation was added after the labels, definition, and best examples of each set of coordinate concepts had been completed. For example, following the definition and display of the best examples of baseline fetal heart rate and its coordinate concepts, an expository presentation was done of the coordinate concepts. When that was completed, the concept of baseline variability was introduced and the same order of teaching variables was used. The addition of the expository presentations added approximately half an hour, so that this treatment group was scheduled for one and one-half hours. This group (labels, definitions, best examples, and expository presentation) is referred to as Group 2.

The design in Group 2 was chosen based on the results of Dunn's research (1984) on concept learning with college age students.... *[The author briefly describes Dunn's findings and their relevance for the instruction presented to Group 2.]*

The treatment design for the third group used the same teaching variables as in Group 2, plus the addition of an interrogatory presentation to follow each expository presentation. This involved the addition of ... transparencies specifically developed for the interrogatory presentation. When a fetal monitor pattern was shown on the screen, students were requested to compare it with their handout of definitions (list of critical characteristics) and best examples, and to identify the concept shown on the fetal monitoring pattern. This treatment design incorporated all of the teaching variables of the Tennyson-Cocchiarella concept-teaching model.

Development of the Instruments

[In this section, the author describes the tests she used to assess what participants knew about fetal monitoring following instruction, as well as a short questionnaire she used to determine the extent to which each participant knew something about fetal monitoring before instruction.]

Procedure

Prior to implementing this research, approval for the project was obtained from the Human Research Committee at the University of Colorado and the Internal Review Board for Research at the University of Northern Colorado (Appendix E). The researcher then met with all students in each maternity nursing course during their first class to explain the research and ask their consent to participate. Consent forms were provided for each student (Appendix E). Once this process was completed, the research design was implemented.

Each maternity nursing course had three groups participating in the research. Students in each of the courses were randomly assigned to one of these three groups. One group received the instructional method described in the Tennyson-Cocchiarella

Notice that the author's notion of what is "traditional" instruction is based on her own experiences, and she says so here.

After describing Group 1, the author proceeds to descriptions of Group 2 and then Group 3 in a logical and systematic fashion. The use of three subheadings (something along the lines of Treatment for Group 1 *or* Group 1 Instruction*) might have been helpful, however.*

By "expository presentation," the author means giving a short explanation or lecture about important ideas and concepts.

A rationale for a particular experimental treatment strengthens any research report. A brief rationale can easily be incorporated into the description of procedures; a longer one should probably be presented earlier in the research report.

By "interrogatory presentation," the author means asking questions to assess students' understanding of, and ability to apply, what they have learned.

Because the author conducted the study at two universities, she followed the necessary human research review procedures at both institutions.

As noted earlier in Chapter 7, random assignment is one effective way of ruling out the possible effects of confounding variables.

model of concept attainment. A second group received the same instructional method with the exception of the interrogatory presentation. The third group had a didactic presentation using only labels, definitions, best examples, and clarifying information. In other words, both the expository and interrogatory presentations were eliminated from the presentation for the third group. In both schools, the researcher taught all three methods. A script (or lecture) was developed for the researcher to use in all the treatment groups so that the content was the same in each group (Appendix F). The students were tested in a class session within 2 to 3 days following the class (treatment). After the completion of the clinical experience of all groups in each university, a parallel form of the classification test was again administered. The sequence can be summarized as follows:

Class instruction → Posttest → Clinical
Rotation → Delayed Test Upon Completion
of Clinical Rotation

In addition, each student was requested to keep a record of the number of contacts each of them had with fetal monitoring tracings, the context, and type of pattern (Appendix G). For example, the student may have been assigned to a labor patient who had a normal pattern. The contact, however, could have been in clinical conference where actual monitor strips of patients were discussed, or also in a prenatal clinic where a nonstress test was done on a patient. The purpose of keeping these records [was] to identify the number of interrogatory examples the students encountered clinically and the range of examples. This information [could] be compared with the posttest results.

Ideally, none of the students were to have had any contact in the clinical setting before the instruction and first test were done. However, it was impossible to schedule all three treatments before students in each maternity nursing course were assigned to the clinical setting since they began their clinical experiences the second week of classes. A few students in this situation were assigned to patients with fetal monitors attached. Since they did not have any theory on fetal monitoring, they were not responsible for interpretation of fetal monitor patterns. However, staff nurses and/or clinical instructors may have demonstrated how to attach and detach the equipment and talked about tracings seen by students on their individual patients.

Statistical Analysis

[The author continues with a discussion of the statistical analyses she used to compare the performance of the three groups.]

Note: Excerpt is from *Learning Fetal Monitoring Under Three Conditions of Concept Teaching* (pp. 58–69) by V. Kinnick, 1989, unpublished doctoral dissertation, University of Colorado, Boulder. Reprinted with permission.

The first group mentioned here ("one group") is actually Group 3, and the last ("the third group") is actually Group 1; this reversal might cause confusion for the reader.

The use of a "script" here would help the researcher teach the content similarly for all three treatment groups (except, of course, for the things she intentionally wanted to do differently for the three groups). Thus, it should help minimize any influences the researcher's hypotheses might have on her delivery of different instructional methods.

This graphic display of the procedure used is a helpful summary for the reader.

The author presumably asked students to keep such records as a way of helping her interpret any unexpected results related to the delayed (postclinical rotation) test. Keep in mind, however, that such self-reporting techniques, dependent as they are on participants' diligence and memories, will not always yield totally accurate information.

Here the author points out a potential weakness in her study: Some students had additional exposure to fetal monitoring outside of the instruction she had given them in their respective treatment groups. The exposure was apparently minimal, however, and so probably did not jeopardize the quality of her study. Such honesty is essential in any research report.

FOR FURTHER READING

Antony, J. (2003). *Design of experiments for engineers and scientists.* Oxford, England: Butterworth-Heineman/Elsevier.

Barlow, D. H., Nock, M. K., & Hersen, M. (2009). *Single case experimental designs: Strategies for studying behavior change* (3rd ed.). Upper Saddle River, NJ: Pearson.

Bausell, R. B. (1994). *Conducting meaningful experiments: Forty steps to becoming a scientist.* Thousand Oaks, CA: Sage.

Canavos, G. C., & Koutrouvelis, I. A. (2009). *An introduction to the design and analysis of experiments.* Upper Saddle River, NJ: Pearson.

Dugard, P., File, P., & Todman, J. (2012). *Single-case and small-n experimental designs: A practical guide to randomization tests* (2nd ed.). New York: Routledge.

Friedman, D., & Sunder, S. (1994). *Experimental methods: A primer for economists.* New York: Cambridge University Press.

Glass, D. J. (2007). *Experimental design for biologists.* Cold Spring Harbor, NY: Cold Spring Harbor Laboratory Press.

Glass, G. V. (1988). Quasi experiments: The case of interrupted time series. In R. M. Jaeger (Ed.), *Complementary methods for research in education* (pp. 445–464). Washington, DC: American Educational Research Association.

Kirk, R. E. (2013). *Experimental design: Procedures for the behavioral sciences* (4th ed.). Thousand Oaks, CA: Sage.

Montgomery, D. C. (2012). *Design and analysis of experiments* (8th ed.). New York: Wiley.

Morgan, D. L., & Morgan, R. K. (2001). Single participant research design: Bringing science to managed care. *American Psychologist, 56,* 119–127.

O'Neill, R. E., McDonnell, J. J., Billingsley, F., & Jenson, W. (2011). *Single case research designs in educational and community settings.* Upper Saddle River, NJ: Pearson.

Phillips, D. C. (1981). Toward an evaluation of the experiment in educational contexts. *Educational Researcher, 10*(6), 13–20.

Pukelsheim, F. (2006). *Optimal design of experiments (Classics in applied mathematics).* New York: Wiley.

Ruxton, G., & Colegrave, N. (2010). *Experimental design for the life sciences* (3rd ed.). Oxford, England: Oxford University Press.

Schneider, B., Carnoy, M., Kilpatrick, J., Schmidt, W. H., & Shavelson, R. J. (2007). *Estimating causal effects using experimental and observational designs.* Washington, DC: American Educational Research Association.

Shadish, W. R., Cook, T. D., & Campbell, D. T. (2001). *Experimental and quasi-experimental designs for generalized causal inference.* Boston: Houghton Mifflin.

Solso, R. S., & MacLin, K. (2008). *Experimental psychology: A case approach* (8th ed.). Upper Saddle River, NJ: Pearson.

ANSWERS TO THE CONCEPTUAL ANALYSIS EXERCISE "Identifying Quantitative Research Designs":

1. This is a *quasi-experimental* study. In particular, it involves a *multiple-baseline* design: Each of the horses begins training on a different day. In the section of the chapter "Using Designs 11, 12, and 13 in Single-Subject Studies," a multiple-baseline study is described in which a single 2-year-old girl successively received a particular treatment (having mittens) in two different contexts. In this example, however, we see the approach being used with five different horses, each of which receives the treatment only once.

2. This is an *experimental* study in which the researchers randomly assign participants to one of five groups, each of which is asked a different question.

3. Don't let the random selection of treatment and control groups fool you. This is a *quasi-experimental* study because participants are not randomly assigned as *individuals* to the treatment and control groups. More specifically, the study is a *nonrandomized control-group pretest–posttest* design (Design 8).

4. This, too, is a *quasi-experimental* study. It is a *time-series* design in which the effects of no intervention (Phase 1) are compared to the effects of two different interventions (the two new signs) imposed either singly or in combination. Of the designs described in this chapter, it is probably most similar to Design 12. Note, however, that no phase of the study is repeated; this omission is a decided weakness in the design.

5. This is a *combined experimental and ex post facto factorial* design with two independent variables, one of which is a *within-subjects* variable. One independent variable is the presence or absence of attention-deficit hyperactivity disorder, which the researchers do not (and *cannot*) manipulate; this is the ex post facto component of the design. The other independent variable is the content of the drawings (aggression vs. prosocial behavior); this is the experimental, within-subjects component of the design.

Chapter 8

Analyzing Quantitative Data

Numbers are meaningless unless we can find the patterns that lie beneath them. With statistics, we can summarize large numerical data sets, make predictions about future trends, and determine whether various experimental treatments have led to significantly different outcomes. Thus, statistical procedures are among the most powerful tools in the researcher's toolbox.

Learning Outcomes

8.1 Describe several strategies for organizing a data set in order to reveal possible patterns within the data.

8.2 Describe several ways in which the nature of the data partly determines the kinds of statistics that can be used in data analysis.

8.3 Distinguish between descriptive statistics and inferential statistics, and describe various purposes that each

of these two categories of statistics can serve, including (a) estimating central tendency, variability, and correlation; (b) estimating population parameters; (c) testing hypotheses; and (d) conducting a meta-analysis.

8.4 Describe several ways in which you might use the results of statistical analyses to help you interpret a data set.

In quantitative research, we try to make better sense of the world through measurement and numbers. Sometimes the numbers represent aspects of the observable, physical world, such as the weights of concrete objects, the growth rates of invasive species, or the number of people engaging in particular activities. We may also use numbers to represent nonphysical phenomena, such as how much students learn in the classroom, what beliefs people have about controversial topics, or how much influence various news media are perceived to have. We can then summarize and interpret the numbers by using statistics.

In general, we can think of statistics as a group of computational procedures that enable us to find patterns and meaning in numerical data. Statistics help us answer a critical question: *What do the data mean?* In other words, what message do they communicate?

EXPLORING AND ORGANIZING A DATA SET

Before using any statistical procedure—before making a single computation—look closely at your data and consider potentially productive ways of organizing them. Using an open mind and your imagination, look for patterns in the numbers. Nothing takes the place of looking carefully, inquiringly, critically—perhaps even naively—at the data.

We take a simple example—although admittedly a very artificial one—to illustrate the point. Following are the scores on a reading achievement test for 11 children, arranged alphabetically:

Adam	76	Mary	92
Alice	80	Ralph	64
Bill	72	Robert	60
Chuck	68	Ruth	96
Kathy	84	Tom	56
Margaret	88		

What do you see? Perhaps you've noticed that the highest score was earned by a girl and the lowest score was earned by a boy. Hmm, might gender be an important dynamic in the data set? Let's arrange the scores horizontally across the page, attach gender designations to each one, and see what happens:

76   80   72   68   84   88   92   64   60   96   56

♂   ♀   ♂   ♂   ♀   ♀   ♀   ♂   ♂   ♀   ♂

Look! Now we can discern a symmetrical pattern that wasn't previously apparent. No matter whether we start from the left or from the right, we have *one* boy, then *one* girl, then *two* boys, *three* girls, *two* boys, *one* girl, and *one* boy.

Now let's arrange the data differently, separating girls from boys:

Girls		*Boys*	
Alice	80	Adam	76
Kathy	84	Bill	72
Margaret	88	Chuck	68
Mary	92	Ralph	64
Ruth	96	Robert	60
		Tom	56

Represented graphically in Figure 8.1, the trends are clear: The girls' scores increase as we proceed through the alphabet, and the boys' scores decrease. Furthermore, the scores are equidistant from one another: Each score is 4 points either above or below the preceding one.

FIGURE 8.1 ▥
A Visual Representation of the Reading Achievement Test Scores

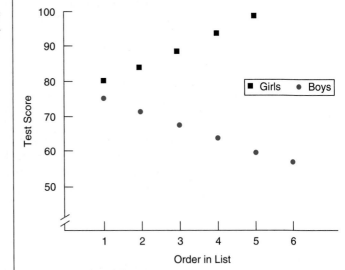

Whatever we have observed may have no relevance whatsoever for our project, but because it represents *dynamics within the data,* it's important that we see it. In the preceding example, we would be hard pressed to find much meaning in diverging trends for girls versus boys that appear simply through an alphabetical arrangement of first names. Yet for the researcher working in an area of science, observations of a similar kind can reveal important new insights. Take the case of a paleontologist and an astronomer who examined growth marks on the spiral-shaped shells of a particular marine mollusk, the chambered nautilus (Kahn & Pompea, 1978). They noticed that each chamber in a shell had an average of 30 growth lines and deduced that (a) the growth lines had appeared at the rate of 1 per day and (b) one chamber had been laid down every lunar month, specifically every 29.53 days. They also concluded that, if their interpretation of the data was correct, it might be possible to determine from fossil shells the length of the ancient lunar months. Because the distance of the moon from Earth can be calculated from the length of the lunar month, the scientists examined nautilus fossils—some of them 420 million years old—and noticed a gradual decrease in the number of growth lines in each chamber as the fossils came from further and further back in prehistoric time. This finding indicated that the moon was once closer to Earth and revolved around it more rapidly than it does now—an observation consistent with contemporary scientific theory.

In the examples just presented, we find a fundamental principle about data exploration: *How the researcher prepares the data for inspection or interpretation will affect the meaning that those data reveal. Therefore, every researcher should be able to provide a clear, logical rationale for the procedure used to arrange and organize the data.* We had no rationale whatsoever for arranging the data according to the children's first names. Had we used their last names—which would have been equally illogical—we would still have seen that the girls had higher scores than the boys, but we wouldn't necessarily have seen the diverging trends depicted in Figure 8.1.

In research questions regarding the physical world, the method for organizing data is apt to be fairly straightforward. Data often come to the scientist prepackaged and prearranged. The sequence of growth rings on a nautilus shell is already there, obvious and nondebatable. But in other disciplines—for instance, in the social sciences, humanities, and education—a researcher may need to give considerable thought to the issue of how best to organize the data.

Organizing Data to Make Them Easier to Think About and Interpret

As previously mentioned in Chapter 1, the human mind can think about only so much information at one time. A data set of, say, 5,000 tidbits of information is well beyond a human being's mental capacity to consider all at once. In fact, unless a researcher has obtained *very* few pieces of data (perhaps only seven or eight numbers), he or she will want to organize them in one or more ways to make them easier to inspect and think about.

In the preceding example of 11 children and their reading achievement test scores, we experimented with various organizational schemes in an effort to find patterns in the data. Let's take another everyday example. Joe is in high school. In February he gets the following quiz grades: 92, 69, 91, 70, 90, 89, 72, 87, 73, 86, 85, 75, 84, 76, 83, 83, 77, 81, 78, 79. Here Joe's grades are listed in a *simple linear sequence*—the order in which Joe earned them. These are the raw numerical facts—the data—obtained directly from the situation. Listed in chronological order, they don't seem to say very much, except that Joe's performance has been inconsistent.

Let's put Joe's grades in a *two-dimensional table* organized by weeks and days, as shown in Figure 8.2. The table reveals some patterns in Joe's grades. If we compare the five columns, we notice that the grades on Mondays, Wednesdays, and Fridays are considerably higher than those on Tuesdays and Thursdays. And if we look at successive numbers in each column, we see that the grades get progressively worse on Mondays, Wednesdays, and Fridays, but progressively better on Tuesdays and Thursdays.

Now let's represent Joe's grades as a *line graph,* shown in Figure 8.3. In this graph, we see phenomena that weren't readily apparent in the two-dimensional table. It's hard to miss the considerable variability in grades during the first and second weeks, followed by a gradual leveling-out process in the latter part of the month. A profile of this sort should

FIGURE 8.2 ▨
The Reading
Achievement Test
Scores in Table Form

Grade Record for February					
	Monday	**Tuesday**	**Wednesday**	**Thursday**	**Friday**
First week	92	69	91	70	90
Second week	89	72	87	73	86
Third week	85	75	84	76	83
Fourth week	83	77	81	78	79

FIGURE 8.3 ▨
Line Graph of Joe's
Daily Grades

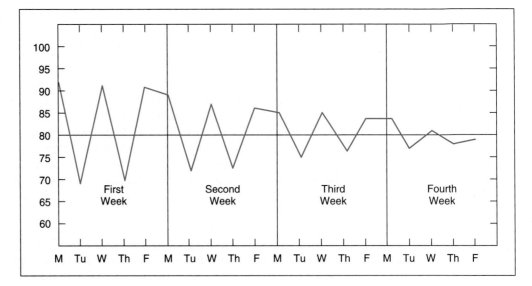

prompt the alert researcher to explore the data further in an attempt to explain the pattern the graph reveals.

Graphing data is often quite useful for revealing patterns in a data set. For example, let's return to a study first described in a Practical Application exercise near the end of Chapter 7:

> Two researchers want to see if a particular training program is effective in teaching horses to enter a horse trailer without misbehaving in the process—that is, without rearing, trying to turn around, or in some other way resisting entry into the trailer. Five horses (Red, Penny, Shadow, Sammy, and Fancy) go through the training, with each horse beginning training on a different day. For each horse, an observer counts the number of misbehaviors every day prior to and during training, with data being collected for a time span of at least 45 days (Ferguson & Rosales-Ruiz, 2001).

In Chapter 7 we were concerned only with the design of this study, concluding that it was a quasi-experimental (and more specifically, a multiple-baseline) study. But now let's look at the results of the study. When the researchers plotted the numbers of five different misbehaviors for each horse before and during training, they constructed the graph presented in Figure 8.4. Was the training effective? Absolutely yes! Once training began, Penny had one really bad day plus another day in which she turned a couple of times, and Shadow and Fancy each tossed their heads during one of their loading sessions. Aside from these four occasions, the horses behaved perfectly throughout the lengthy training period, despite the fact that all five had been quite ornery prior to training. These data have what we might call a *hit-you-between-the-eyes* quality: We don't need a fancy statistical analysis to tell us that the training was effective.

Time-series studies often yield data that show clear hit-you-between-the-eyes patterns; for another example, return to Figure 7.3 in Chapter 7. But generally speaking, simply organizing the data in various ways will not, in and of itself, reveal everything the data have to offer. Instead, a quantitative researcher will need to perform statistical analyses to fully discover the patterns and meanings the data hold. Before we turn to the nature of statistics, however, let's briefly look at how a researcher can use computer software to assist with the data organization process.

FIGURE 8.4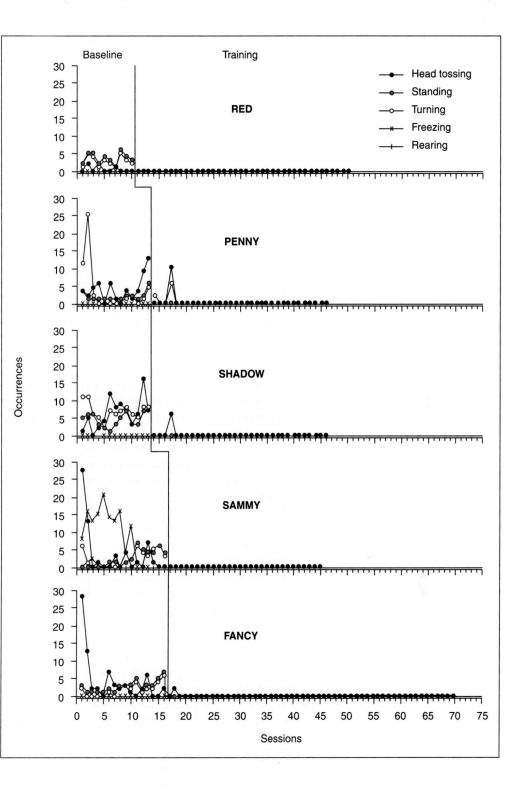
Undesirable Trailer-Loading Behaviors for Five Horses Before and After Training

Source: Reprinted from "Loading the Problem Loader: The Effects of Target Training and Shaping on Trailer-Loading Behavior of Horses" by D. L. Ferguson & J. Rosalez-Ruiz, 2001, *Journal of Applied Behavior Analysis, 34,* p. 419. Reprinted with permission of the Society for the Experimental Analysis of Behavior, Inc.

Using Computer Spreadsheets to Organize and Analyze Data

USING TECHNOLOGY

The process of organizing large amounts of data was once a tedious, time-consuming task. Fortunately, computers have made the process much simpler and more efficient. One important tool is an electronic spreadsheet, a software program that enables a researcher to enter and then manipulate data in a two-dimensional table. Undoubtedly, the best known spreadsheet software is Microsoft's Excel, but other software packages are available as well, including "freeware" you can download without charge from the Internet (e.g., LibreOffice, Sphygmic Software Spreadsheet, Simple Spreadsheet, Spread32).

The beauty of an electronic spreadsheet is that once you enter data into it, the software can quickly and easily help you organize the data and perform simple calculations. For example, you can add several test scores together to create a new column that you might call "Total of Test Scores," or you might divide the numbers in one column by the numbers in another column to get proportions that are potentially meaningful in the context of your study. If you change a data point—for example, perhaps you discover that you miskeyed a test score and so must correct it—all of the relevant calculations are automatically updated. The software typically also lets you copy *(import)* data from databases, word processing documents, or other spreadsheets into a new spreadsheet.

Spreadsheets would be useful to researchers even if they were capable only of listing data and adding up different columns and rows. But in fact, they allow the researcher to do many other things as well:

- *Sorting.*   Once the data have been organized into rows and columns, it's possible to reorganize them in any way you wish. For example, suppose you have math test scores for a large number of children of various ages. You originally entered the scores in the order in which you obtained them. But now you decide that you want to consider them on the basis of the children's ages. In a matter of seconds, an electronic spreadsheet can sort the scores by age and list them from youngest to oldest child, or vice versa.

- *Recoding.*   A spreadsheet typically allows you to make a new column that reflects a transformation of data in an existing column. For instance, imagine that you have reading scores for children ages 7 to 15. Perhaps you want to compare the scores for children in three different age groups: Group 1 will consist of children who are 7- to 9-years old, Group 2 will include 10- to 12-year-olds, and Group 3 will include 13- to 15-year-olds. You can tell the computer to form a new column called "Group" and to give each child a group number (1, 2, or 3) depending on the child's age.

- *Formulas.*   Current spreadsheet programs have the capability to calculate many complex mathematical and statistical formulas. Once the data are organized into rows and columns, you can specify formulas that describe and analyze one or more groups of data. For example, you can enter the formula for computing the average, or mean, of a set of numbers, and the spreadsheet will perform the necessary calculations. Many commonly used formulas are often preprogrammed, so you merely select the statistic or function you need (e.g., you might select "AVERAGE") and highlight the data you wish to include in the calculation. The software does the rest.

- *Graphing.*   Most spreadsheet programs have graphing capabilities. After you highlight the appropriate parts of the data, the program will automatically produce a graph from those data. Generally, the type of graph produced is selected from several options (e.g., line graphs, bar graphs, pie charts). Users can select how the axes are labeled, how the legend is created, and how data points are depicted.

- *"What Ifs."*   Thanks to the speed and ease with which an electronic spreadsheet can manipulate and perform calculations on large bodies of data, you can engage in numerous trial-and-error explorations. For example, if you're examining data for a sample of 5,000 people and decide that an additional comparison between certain subgroups might prove interesting, the spreadsheet can complete the comparison in a matter of seconds. This capability allows you to continually ask *what if . . . ?*—for instance, What if the data were analyzed on the basis of gender, rather than on the basis of age? or What if results from administering only one level of a specific medication were analyzed instead of grouping all levels together?

In the discussion of Microsoft Excel in Appendix A, you can learn how to use some of the many features that an electronic spreadsheet offers.

We have said enough about organizing a data set. We now turn to one of the most important tools in a researcher's toolbox—statistical analysis.

CHOOSING APPROPRIATE STATISTICS

In a single chapter we cannot thoroughly describe the many statistical procedures that researchers might use. Here we must limit ourselves to a description of basic statistical concepts and principles and a brief overview of some of the most commonly used procedures. We authors are assuming that you have taken, or will take, at least one course in statistics—better still, take two, three, or even more!—to get a firm foundation in this essential research tool.

Earlier we looked at Joe's test scores in three ways: a simple linear sequence, a two-dimensional table, and a line graph. All of these depicted Joe's day-to-day performance. Now, instead, let's begin to summarize what we're seeing in the test scores. We can, for example, use a statistic known as a *mean*—in everyday terms, an *average*—to take out the jagged irregularities of Joe's daily performance. In Figure 8.5, we represent Joe's average scores for the 4 weeks of February with four broken lines. When we do this, we get an entirely new view of Joe's achievement. Whereas Figure 8.3 showed only an erratic zigzagging between daily extremes, with the zigzags becoming less extreme as the weeks went by, the dotted lines in Figure 8.5 show that, week by week, very little change occurred in Joe's average test performance.

Yet it may be that we also want to summarize how much Joe's grades *vary* each week. The means presented in Figure 8.5 tell us nothing about how consistent or inconsistent Joe's grades are in any given week. We would need a different statistic—perhaps a *range* or a *standard deviation*—to summarize the variability we see each week. (We will describe the nature of such measures of variability shortly.)

Thus far we have discovered an important point: *Looking at data in only one way yields an incomplete view of those data and their underlying patterns and meanings.* For this reason, we have many statistical techniques, each of which is suitable for a different purpose and can answer a different question for a particular set of data.

In the next few pages, we consider two general functions that statistics can serve. We also discuss the various ways in which the nature of the data may limit the particular statistical procedures that can be used.

Functions of Statistics

Statistics have two major functions. Some statistics describe what the data look like—where their center or midpoint is, how broadly they are spread, how closely two or more variables within the data are intercorrelated, and the like. Such statistics are, appropriately, called descriptive statistics.

FIGURE 8.5
Line Graph of Joe's
Weekly Average Grades

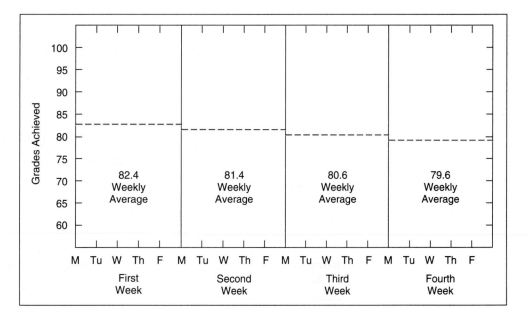

Other statistics, known as inferential statistics, serve a different purpose: They allow us to draw *inferences* about large populations by collecting data on relatively small samples. For example, imagine that you are an immigration officer. Although you have never been to Egypt, you have met numerous Egyptians as they disembark from incoming planes and ships. Perhaps you have even become well acquainted with a small number of Egyptians. From this small sample of the Egyptian population, you might infer what Egyptian people in general are like. (Your inferences may or may not be accurate because your sample, which consists entirely of visitors and immigrants to your own country, isn't necessarily representative of the entire population of Egypt. However, that is a sampling problem, not a statistical one.)

More generally, inferential statistics involve using one or more small samples and then *estimating* the characteristics of the population from which each sample has been drawn. For instance, we might estimate a population mean from the mean we obtain for a sample. Or we might determine whether two or more groups of people are actually different, given the differences we observe between samples taken from each of those groups. Inferential statistics provide a way of helping us make reasonable guesses about a large, unknown population by examining a small sample that *is* known. In the process, they also allow us to test hypotheses regarding what might be true for that large population.

Statistics as Estimates of Population Parameters

Especially when we use statistics to draw inferences about a population from which a research sample has been drawn, we are using them as *estimates of population parameters.* A parameter is a characteristic or quality of a population that, in *concept,* is a constant; however, its *value* is variable.

As an illustration, let's consider a circle. One of the parameters of a circle is its radius. In concept, the radius is a constant: It is the same for every circle—the distance from the center of the circle to the perimeter. In value, it varies, depending on the size of the circle. Large circles have long radii; small circles, short radii. The value—that is, the length of the radius in linear units (centimeters, feet, etc.)—is variable. Thinking of a parameter in this way, we see that each circle has several parameters: The diameter is always twice the radius *(r),* the circumference is always $2\pi r$, and the area is always πr^2. These concepts are constants, even though their particular values vary from one circle to the next.

Within the context of quantitative data analysis, a parameter is a particular characteristic (e.g., a mean or standard deviation) of the entire population—which is sometimes called a *universe*—about which we want to draw conclusions. In most cases, we can study only a small sample of a population. Any calculation we perform for the sample rather than the population (the sample mean, the sample standard deviation, etc.) is a statistic. Statisticians distinguish between population parameters and sample statistics by using different symbols for each. Table 8.1 presents a few commonly used symbols in statistical notation.

TABLE 8.1 ■
Conventional Statistical Notation for Population Parameters and Sample Statistics

The Characteristic in Question	The Symbol Used to Designate the Characteristic	
	Population Parameter	Sample Statistic
The mean	μ	M or $\overline{X}$
The standard deviation	σ	s or SD
Proportion or probability	P	p
Number or total	N	n

Note: The symbol μ is the lowercase form of the Greek letter *mu.* The symbol σ is the lowercase form of the Greek letter *sigma.*

Considering the Nature of the Data

As you begin to think about statistical procedures that might be most appropriate for your research problem, keep in mind that different statistics are suitable for different kinds of data. In particular, you should consider whether your data

- Have been collected for a single group or, instead, for two or more groups
- Involve continuous or discrete variables
- Represent nominal, ordinal, interval, or ratio scales
- Reflect a normal or non-normal distribution

After we look at each of these distinctions, we will relate them to another distinction—that between parametric and nonparametric statistics.

Single-Group Versus Multi-Group Data

In some cases, a research project yields data about a single group of people, objects, or events. In other cases, it may yield parallel sets of data about two or more groups. Analyzing characteristics of a single group will often require different statistical techniques than those for making comparisons among two or more groups.

Continuous Versus Discrete Variables

In Chapter 2 we defined a *variable* as a quality or characteristic in a research investigation that has two or more possible values. Simply put, a variable *varies*. However, it may vary in different ways. A **continuous variable** reflects an infinite number of possible values falling along a particular continuum. An example is chronological age. The participants in a research study can be an infinite number of possible ages. Some might be 2 years old, others might be 92, and we might have virtually any age (including fractions of years) in between. Even if the study is limited to a small age range—say, 2- to 4-year-old children—we might have children who are exactly 2 years old, children who are 2 years and 1 month old, children who are 2 years and 2 months old, and so on. We could, in theory, be even more precise, perhaps specifying participants' ages in days, hours, minutes, seconds, or even fractions of a second.

In contrast, a **discrete variable** has a finite and small number of possible values. An example is a student's high school grade level. At a 4-year high school, a student can be in only one of four grades: 9th, 10th, 11th, or 12th. At most high schools, it isn't possible to be in anything else. One cannot be somewhere between two grade levels, such as in the "9.25th grade."

Nominal, Ordinal, Interval, and Ratio Data

In Chapter 4 we described four different scales of measurement; these scales, in turn, dictate how we can statistically analyze the numbers we obtain relative to one another. To refresh your memory, we briefly describe each of the scales again.

- *Nominal data* are those for which numbers are used only to identify different categories of people, objects, or other entities; they do not reflect a particular quantity or degree of something. For instance, a researcher might code all males in a data set as 1 and all females as 2. The researcher might also code political affiliation with numbers, perhaps using 1 for Republicans, 2 for Democrats, 3 for "Other affiliation," and 4 for "No affiliation." In neither case do the numbers indicate that participants have more or less of something; girls don't have more "gender" than boys, and Democrats don't have more "political affiliation" than Republicans.
- *Ordinal data* are those for which the assigned numbers reflect an order or sequence. They tell us the degree to which people, objects, or other entities have a certain quality or characteristic (a variable) of interest. They do not, however, tell us anything about how

great the differences are between the people, objects, or other entities. For example, in a group of graduating high school seniors, each student might have a class rank that reflects his or her relative academic standing in the group: A class rank of 1 indicates the highest grade point average (GPA), a rank of 2 indicates the second highest GPA, and so on. These numbers tell us which students surpassed others in terms of GPA, but it doesn't tell us precisely how similar or different the GPAs of any two students in the sequence are.

▓ *Interval data* reflect equal units of measurement. As is true for ordinal data, the numbers reflect differences in degree or amount. But in addition, differences between the numbers tell us *how much difference* exists in the characteristic being measured. As an example, scores on intelligence tests (IQ scores) are, because of the way in which they are derived, assumed to reflect an interval scale. Thus, if we take four IQ scores at equal intervals—for instance, 85, 95, 105, and 115—we can assume that the 10-point difference between each pair reflects equivalent differences in intelligence between the people who have obtained those scores. The one limitation of interval data is that a value of zero (0) does *not* necessarily reflect a complete lack of the characteristic being measured. For example, it is sometimes possible to get an IQ score of 0, but such a score doesn't mean that a person has no intelligence whatsoever.

▓ *Ratio data* are similar to interval data, in that they reflect equal intervals between values for the characteristic being measured. However, they also have a true zero point: A value of 0 tells us that there's a complete absence of the characteristic. An example is income level: People with an annual income of $30,000 make $10,000 more than people with an annual income of $20,000, and people with an annual income of $40,000 make $10,000 more than people with an annual income of $30,000. Furthermore, people who make $0 a year have *no* income.

Normal and Non-Normal Distributions

Many theorists have proposed that characteristics of living populations (e.g., populations of maple trees, platypuses, human beings, or a certain subgroup of human beings) often reflect a particular pattern, one that looks like this:

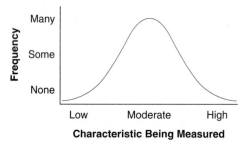

This pattern, commonly called the normal distribution or normal curve—you may also see the term *bell curve*—has several distinguishing characteristics:

▓ *It is horizontally symmetrical.*   One side is the mirror image of the other.
▓ *Its highest point is at its midpoint.*   More people (or whatever other entities are the focus of investigation) are located in the exact middle than at any other point along the curve. In statistical terms, three widely used measures of central tendency—the mode, the median, and the mean (all to be described shortly)—are equivalent.
▓ *Predictable percentages of the population lie within any given portion of the curve.*   If we divide the curve according to its standard deviation (also to be described shortly), we know that certain percentages of the population lie within each portion. In particular, approximately 34.1% of the population lies between the mean and one standard deviation below the mean, and another 34.1% lies between the mean and one standard

FIGURE 8.6 ▣
Percentages Within Each
Portion of the Normal
Distribution

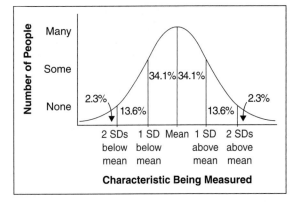

deviation above the mean. Approximately 13.6% of the population lies between one and two standard deviations below the mean, with another 13.6% lying between one and two standard deviations above the mean. The remaining 4.6% lies two or more standard deviations away from the mean, with 2.3% at each end of the distribution. This pattern is shown in Figure 8.6. The proportions of the population lying within any particular section of the normal distribution can be found in most introductory statistics books. You can also find them online by using the keywords "normal distribution table" in a search engine such as Google, Bing, or Yahoo!

To better understand the normal distribution, take any fortuitous happening and analyze its distribution pattern. For example, let's take corn production in Iowa—the state that produces more corn than any other U.S. state. If we could survey the per-acre yield of every farmer in Iowa—the total population, or universe, of the cornfields and corn farmers in Iowa—we would probably find that a few farmers had an unusually small corn crop per acre for no discernible reason except that "that's the way it happened." A few other farmers, for an equally unknown reason, may have had especially bountiful yields from their fields. However, most farmers would have had middle-of-the-road yields—some a little bit more than average, others a little bit less than average. The normal curve might describe Iowa's corn production. No one planned it this way; it's simply how nature behaves.

Watch an approaching thunderstorm. An occasional flash of lightning heralds the coming of the storm. Soon the flashes occur more frequently. At the height of the storm, the number of flashes per minute reach a peak. Gradually, with the passing of the storm, the number of flashes subsides. The normal curve is at work once again.

We could think of thousands of situations, only to find that nature often behaves in a way consistent with the normal distribution. The curve is a constant; it's always bell-shaped. In any one situation, the *values* within it vary. The mean is not always the same number, and the overall shape may be more broadly spread or more compressed, depending on the situation.

Sometimes, however, a variable doesn't fall in a normal distribution. For instance, its distribution might be lopsided, or skewed; the "skew" is the part of the distribution that stretches out a bit to one side. If the peak lies to the left of the midpoint, the distribution is **positively skewed**; if the peak lies to the right of the midpoint, the distribution is **negatively skewed**. Or perhaps a distribution is unusually pointy or flat, such that the percentages within each portion of the distribution are notably different from those depicted in Figure 8.6. Here we are talking about kurtosis, with an unusually peaked, or pointy, distribution, being a **leptokurtic distribution**, and an unusually flat one being a **platykurtic distribution** (see Figure 8.7).

Of course, some data sets don't resemble a normal distribution, not even a lopsided, pointy, or overly flattened variation of one. In general, ordinal data, by virtue of how they are created, *never* fall in a normal distribution. For instance, a data set might look more like a stairway that progresses upward in regular intervals. Or, take a graduating high school class. If each student is given a class rank according to academic grade point average, Luis might rank first, Janene might rank second, Marietta third, and so on. We don't see a normal distribution in this situation because we have only one student at each academic rank. If we construct a graph that depicts

FIGURE 8.7 ▨
Common Departures
from the Normal
Distribution

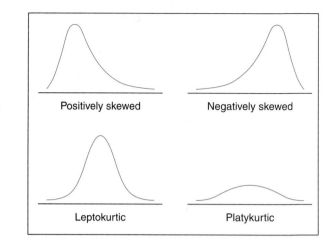

the frequencies of the class ranks, we see a low, flat distribution rather than one that rises upward and peaks in the middle.

Percentile ranks also form a flat distribution rather than a bell-shaped curve. Percentile ranks—sometimes simply called percentiles—are often used to report performance on scholastic aptitude and achievement tests. To calculate them, a researcher first determines the raw score—the number of test items correctly answered or number of points accumulated—that each person in the sample earns on a test or other research instrument. Each person's percentile rank is then calculated as follows:

$$\text{Percentile rank} = \frac{\text{Number of other people scoring } \textit{lower} \text{ than the person}}{\text{Total number of people in the sample}}$$

By the very nature of how they are calculated, percentile ranks spread people evenly over the number of possible ranks one might get; for instance, there will be roughly the same number of people earning percentile ranks of 5, 35, 65, and 95. Furthermore, although percentile ranks tell us how people have performed relative to one another, they don't tell us *how much* they differ from one another in the characteristic being assessed. In essence, percentile ranks are *ordinal data* and must be treated as such.

Choosing Between Parametric and Nonparametric Statistics

Your choice of statistical procedures must depend to some degree on the nature of your data and the extent to which they reflect a normal distribution. Some statistics, known as parametric statistics, are based on certain assumptions about the nature of the population in question. Two of the most common assumptions are these:

▨ The data reflect an interval or ratio scale.
▨ The data fall in a normal distribution (e.g., the distribution has a central high point, and it is not seriously skewed, leptokurtic, or platykurtic).

When either of these assumptions is violated, the results one obtains from parametric statistics can be flawed.

Other statistics, called nonparametric statistics, are not based on such assumptions. For instance, some nonparametric statistics are appropriate for data that are ordinal rather than interval in nature. Others may be useful when a population is highly skewed in one direction or the other.

You may be thinking, "Why not use nonparametric statistics all the time to avoid having to make (and possibly violate) any assumptions about the data?" The reason is simple: Our most complex and powerful inferential statistics are based on parametric statistics. Nonparametric statistics are, by and large, appropriate only for relatively simple analyses.

On an optimistic note, we should point out that some statistical procedures are robust with respect to certain assumptions. That is, they yield generally valid results even when an assumption isn't met. For instance, a particular procedure might be as valid with a leptokurtic or platykurtic distribution as it is with a normal distribution; it might even be valid with ordinal rather than interval data. When using any statistical technique, you should consult with a statistics textbook to determine what assumptions are essential for that technique and what assumptions might reasonably be disregarded. Some statistical software packages routinely provide information about whether a particular data set meets or violates certain assumptions and make appropriate adjustments for non-normal distributions.

DESCRIPTIVE STATISTICS

As their name implies, descriptive statistics *describe* a body of data. Here we discuss how to determine three things a researcher might want to know about a data set: points of central tendency, amount of variability, and the extent to which two or more variables are associated with one another.

Measures of Central Tendency

A *point of central tendency* is a point around which the data revolve, a middle number around which the data regarding a particular variable seem to hover. In statistical language, we use the term *measures of central tendency* to refer to techniques for finding such a point. Three commonly used measures of central tendency are the mode, the median, and the mean, each of which has its own characteristics and applications.

The mode is the single number or score that occurs most frequently. For instance, in this data set

3 4 6 7 7 9 9 9 9 10 11 11 13 13 13 15 15 21 26

the mode is 9, because 9 occurs more frequently (four times) than any other number. Similarly, if we look at the previous list of Joe's grades for February (see Figure 8.2), we see that only one grade (83) appears more than once; thus, 83 is the mode. As a measure of central tendency, the mode is of limited value, in part because it doesn't always appear near the middle of the distribution and in part because it isn't very stable from sample to sample. However, the mode is the *only* appropriate measure of central tendency for nominal data.

The median is the numerical center of a set of data; to facilitate our discussion, we will call each piece of data in the set a "score." The median is the number in the very middle of the scores, with exactly as many scores above it as below it. Recall that Joe's record has 20 grades for February. Thus, 10 grades are above the median, and 10 are below it. The median is midway in the series between the 10th and 11th scores, or in this case midway between the scores of 81 and 83—that is, 82 (see Figure 8.8).

You might think of the mean as the fulcrum point for a set of data: It represents the single point at which the two sides of a distribution "balance." Mathematically, the mean is the *arithmetic average*[1] of the scores within the data set. To find it, we calculate the sum of all the scores (adding each score every time it occurs) and then divide by the total number of scores. If we use the symbol X to refer to each score in the data set and the symbol N to refer to the total number of scores, we calculate the mean as follows:

$$M = \frac{X_1 + X_2 + X_3 + \ldots + X_N}{N}$$

---

[1] As noted in Chapter 1, when the word *arithmetic* is used as an adjective, it is pronounced with emphasis on the third syllable ("ar-ith-MET-ic").

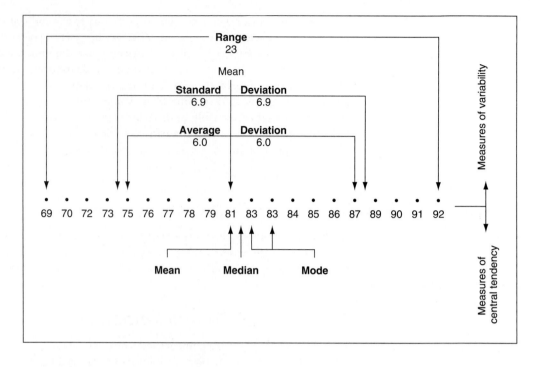

Statisticians frequently use the symbol Σ (uppercase form of the Greek letter *sigma*) to designate adding all of the numbers related to a particular variable; thus, we can rewrite the formula for a mean as follows:

$$M = \frac{\Sigma X}{N}$$

Using the formula, we find that the mean for Joe's grades is 81, as shown in Figure 8.8. (The variation in Joe's grades, depicted in the figure as *measures of variability,* is discussed shortly.)

The mean is the measure of central tendency most commonly used in statistical analyses and research reports. However, it is appropriate only for interval or ratio data, because it makes mathematical sense to compute an average only when the numbers reflect equal intervals along a particular scale.

The median is more appropriate for dealing with ordinal data. The median is also used frequently when a researcher is dealing with a data set that is highly skewed in one direction or the other. As an example, consider this set of scores:

3   4   5   5   6   9   15   17   125

The mean for these scores is 21, a number that doesn't give us a very good idea of the point near which most of the scores are located. The median, which in this case is 6, is a better reflection of central tendency because it isn't affected by the single extreme score of 125. Similarly, medians are often used to reflect central tendency in family income levels, home values, and other such financial variables; most family incomes and home values are clustered at the lower end of the scale, with only a very few extending into the million-dollar range.

Curves Determine Means

The mean as we have just described it—sometimes known as the *arithmetic* mean[2]—is most appropriate when we have a normal distribution, or at least a distribution that is somewhat symmetrical. But not all phenomena fit a bell-shaped pattern. Growth is one: It often follows an ogive curve that eventually flattens into a plateau, as shown in Figure 8.9.

---

[2]Again, the emphasis in *arithmetic* is on the third syllable ("ar-ith-MET-ic").

FIGURE 8.9 ▩
Typical Growth Curve

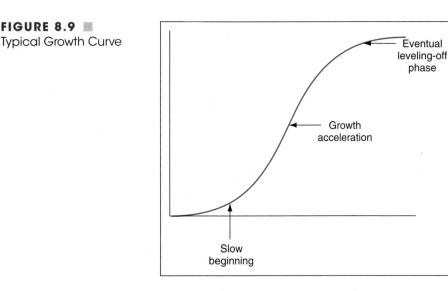

Growth is a function of geometric progression. As an example, let's consider the work of Thomas Robert Malthus, an English clergyman and economist who theorized about the potential for a population explosion and resulting worldwide famine. In *An Essay on the Principle of Population* (1826/1963), Malthus contended that, when unchecked, a population increases at an exponential rate, in which each successive value depends, multiplicatively, on the preceding value; for example, in the series 2, 4, 8, 16, 32, 64, 128 . . ., each number is twice the preceding number. But Malthus also predicted that the size of the human population would eventually flatten out because there's an upper limit to what Mother Earth can produce in the way of food to sustain the population. Thus, many growth curves resemble a stretched-out *S,* as the curve in Figure 8.9 does.

If we are recording the growth of beanstalks in an agronomy laboratory, we don't find the average growth by assuming a normal distribution and calculating the arithmetic mean. The statistical technique doesn't fit the data. Instead, we use the geometric mean, which is computed by *multiplying* all of the scores together and then finding the Nth root of the product. In other words, the geometric mean, which we can symbolize as Mg, is calculated as follows:

$$M_g = \sqrt[N]{(X_1)(X_2)(X_3) \ldots (X_N)}$$

For growth phenomena, we use the geometric mean because that is the way things grow and the way cells divide—geometrically.

Demographers, biologists, physicists, ecologists, and economists all encounter growth phenomena in one form or another. They all witness the same typical aspects of change: a slow beginning (a few settlers in an uninhabited region; a few bacteria on a culture); then, after a period of time, rapid expansion (the boom period of city growth; the rapid multiplication of microorganisms); and finally—sometimes but not always—a leveling-off period (the land becomes scarce and the city sprawl is contained by geographical and economic factors; the bacteria have populated the entire culture). Following are examples of situations in which the application of the geometric mean is appropriate:

- ▩ Population growth
- ▩ Biological growth
- ▩ Increments of money at compound interest
- ▩ Decay or simple decelerative situations

In every situation, one basic principle applies: The configuration of the data dictates the measure of central tendency most appropriate for that particular situation. If the data fall in a distribution that approximates a normal curve (as most data do), they call for one measure of central tendency. If they have an ogive-curve nature (characteristic of a growth situation), they

Measure of Central Tendency	How It Is Determined (N = number of scores)	Data for Which It Is Appropriate
Mode	The most frequently occurring score is identified.	• Data on nominal, ordinal, interval, and ratio scales • Multimodal distributions (two or more modes may be identified when a distribution has multiple peaks)
Median	The scores are arranged in order from smallest to largest, and the middle score (when N is an odd number) or the midpoint between the two middle scores (when N is an even number) is identified.	• Data on ordinal, interval, and ratio scales • Data that are highly skewed
Arithmetic mean	All the scores are added together, and their sum is divided by the total number (N) of scores.	• Data on interval and ratio scales • Data that fall in a normal distribution
Geometric mean	All the scores are multiplied together, and the Nth root of their product is computed.	• Data on ratio scales • Data that approximate an ogive curve (e.g., growth data)

demand another measure. A *polymodal distribution*—one with several peaks—might call for still a third approach; for instance, the researcher might describe it in terms of its two or more modes. Only after careful and informed consideration of the characteristics of the data can the researcher select the most appropriate statistic.

Thus, we must emphasize an essential rule for researchers who use statistics in their data analysis: *The nature of the data—the facts of life—governs the statistical technique, not the other way around.* Just as the physician must know what drugs are available for specific diseases and disorders, so the researcher must know what statistical techniques are suited to specific research demands. Table 8.2 presents a summary of the measures of central tendency and their uses, together with the various types of data for which each measure is appropriate.

Measures of Central Tendency as Predictors

Sometimes a researcher uses a measure of central tendency as a rough estimate of the most likely outcome—essentially trying to answer the question *What is the best prediction?* As an example, suppose you are walking down the street. Suddenly you come to a crowd of people forming in a normal-curve-like manner. Where, based on your best prediction, will you find the cause for the crowd forming? The answer is simple. Where the crowd is deepest, where the greatest number of people are, you will probably find the cause for the gathering. It might be an accident, a street fight, or a person giving away free candy bars. But whatever the occasion, your best guess about the cause of the gathering lies at the point where the human mass is at its peak.

Similarly, we can often make reasonable predictions about a population based on our knowledge of central tendency. When we speak of "the average citizen," "the average student," and "the average wage earner," we are referring to those citizens, students, and wage earners who are huddled around the point of central tendency. In the broad spectrum of possibilities, we are betting on the average as being the best single guess about the nature of the total population.

Measures of Variability: Dispersion and Deviation

Up to this point, we have been discussing the question *What is the best guess?* Now we turn to the opposite question: *What are the worst odds?* This, too, is important to know. The more the data cluster around the point of central tendency, the greater the probability of making a correct guess

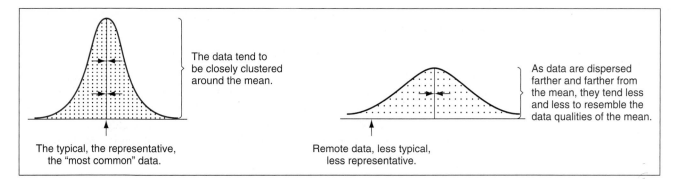

The data tend to be closely clustered around the mean.

The typical, the representative, the "most common" data.

As data are dispersed farther and farther from the mean, they tend less and less to resemble the data qualities of the mean.

Remote data, less typical, less representative.

FIGURE 8.10 ▓ Distributions That Differ in Variability

about where any particular data point lies. As illustrated in Figure 8.10, data are more similar if they cluster about the mean. Scatter them, and they lose some of their uniformity; they become more diverse, more heterogeneous. As specific data points recede farther from the mean, they lose more and more of the quality that makes them "average."

Consider, for example, the case of Stephen Jay Gould, a renowned evolutionary biologist who in 1982 learned that he had abdominal mesothelioma, an especially lethal form of cancer. His prognosis was grim: Medical literature at the time reported a median life expectancy of 8 months following the diagnosis. Two years later, Gould—still very much alive—wrote a classic essay, "The Median Isn't the Message" (1985), which you can easily find and read on the Internet. In fact, Gould lived for 20 years after his diagnosis, eventually succumbing to a very different form of cancer. Clearly the median was *not* a good predictor in his case.[3]

To derive meaning from data, then, it's important to determine not only their central tendency but also their spread. And it often helps to pin down their spread in terms of one or more statistics.

How Great Is the Spread?

The simplest measure of variability is the **range**, which indicates the spread of the data from lowest to highest value:

$$\text{Range} = \text{Highest score} - \text{Lowest score}$$

For instance, the range for Joe's test scores is $92 - 69$, or 23 (see Figure 8.8).

Although the range is easy to compute, it has limited usefulness as a measure of variability and can even be misleading if the extreme upper or lower limits are atypical of the other values in the series. Let's take an example. Following are the numbers of children in each of 10 families: 1, 3, 3, 3, 4, 4, 5, 5, 6, 15. We might say that the families range from one with a single child to a family of 15 children (a range of $15 - 1$, or 14). But this figure is misleading: It suggests that the sample shows a great deal of variability in family size. We give a more realistic estimate of variability in this sample if we say something such as "Eighty percent of the families have from 3 to 6 children."

Other measures of variability use less extreme values as starting points. One such measure is the **interquartile range**. If we divide the distribution into four equal parts, Quartile 1 lies at a point where 25% of the members of the group are below it. Quartile 2 divides the group into two equal parts and is identical to the median. Quartile 3 lies at a point where 75% of the values are below it.[4]

---

[3]Here you can see an example of a positively skewed distribution. At most, people could die only 8 months earlier than the 8-month median time period—that is, at the very moment of diagnosis—but people might survive much, much longer than the 8-month median, as Gould did.

[4]If, instead of dividing the data into four equal parts, we divide them into 10 equal parts, each part is called a *decile;* if into 100 equal parts, each part is called a *percentile.*

The interquartile range is equal to Quartile 3 (the 75th percentile point) minus Quartile 1 (the 25th percentile point), as follows:

$$\text{Interquartile range} = \text{Quartile 3} - \text{Quartile 1}$$

Thus, the interquartile range gives us the range for the middle 50% of the cases in the distribution. Because quartiles are associated with the median, any researcher using the median as a measure of central tendency should also consider the quartile deviation as a possible statistical measure for variability. When working with either ordinal data or highly skewed data, some researchers report what is called a five-number summary, which consists of the lowest and highest numbers (depicting the range) plus Quartile 1, the median (which is also Quartile 2), and Quartile 3.

Now, instead, let's use the mean as a starting point. Imagine that we determine how far away from the mean each score is in the distribution. That is, we calculate the *difference* between each score and the mean (we call this difference the *deviation*). If we were to add all of these differences (ignoring the plus and minus signs) and then divide the sum by the *number* of scores (which reflects the number of score–mean differences as well), we get the *average* of the differences between any score and the mean. This number is sometimes called the *average deviation (AD)*. The equation for the average deviation is:

$$AD = \frac{\sum |X - M|}{N}$$

Here $|X - M| = X - M$ without regard for plus and minus signs; in other words, it is the *absolute value* of the difference between each score and the mean.

The average deviation is easily understood and, for that reason, has some merit. It might be acceptable when no further statistical procedure is contemplated. It is a little-used value, however, and the measures of standard deviation and variance have largely replaced it in most research projects.

The standard deviation (σ or s, for population parameter and sample statistic, respectively) is the measure of variability most commonly used in statistical procedures. To understand the reason for using the standard deviation, we must think about what happens mathematically when we find the average deviation just described. Imagine that we were to compute the average deviation *without* using the absolute values of the differences. For any number lying to the left of the mean (and thus having a value smaller than the mean), the difference between the number and the mean ($X - M$) would be a negative number. In contrast, any number lying to the right of the mean would yield a positive $X - M$ value. When we added all the positive and negative deviations together, they would entirely counterbalance one another, essentially "canceling out" one another and yielding an overall sum of zero. To circumvent this problem, the average deviation uses absolute values, thereby allowing us to ignore the plus and minus signs. Yet this is a rather dubious procedure. It is neither sound mathematics nor sound statistics to ignore what we don't like. We can, however, change negatives to positives in a perfectly acceptable mathematical manner. In arithmetic, if we multiply a negative value by itself, it becomes positive. Thus, when we square all negative differences, they become positive.

To calculate a standard deviation, we follow a procedure similar to calculating an average deviation. However, rather than taking the absolute value of the score–mean differences, we *square* the differences. After we have added the squared differences together and then divided by the number of scores, we find the square root of the quotient. Thus, the formula for a standard deviation is as follows:

$$s = \sqrt{\frac{\sum (X - M)^2}{N}}$$

It is important to note that we square the differences first and *then* add them together. If we were to add them together first and then square their sum, we would get an entirely different—and incorrect!—result.

The average deviation and standard deviation are usually similar but not identical values. As an example, if we calculate these two statistics for Joe's grades, we get an average deviation of 6.0 and a standard deviation of 6.9 (see Figure 8.8).

Many statistical procedures use another measure of variability in addition to or instead of the standard deviation. This statistic is known as the variance, which is simply the standard deviation squared:

$$s^2 = \frac{\sum (X - M)^2}{N}$$

Four of the measures of variability just described are summarized in Table 8.3. The table omits the five-number summary, which isn't a single statistic, and the average deviation, which, as we've said, is mathematically suspect and rarely used.

Using the Mean and Standard Deviation to Calculate Standard Scores

Earlier we introduced the term *raw score,* the number of correct answers or points that a person gets on a test or other measurement instrument. Such scores typically need some context to make them meaningful. For instance, if we say that Mary has gotten a score of 35 on a test of extroversion (i.e., on a test assessing her tendency to be socially outgoing), you might ask, "What does that score *mean?*" Is it high? Low? Somewhere in the middle? Without a context, a score of 35 has no meaning. We have no idea how introverted or extroverted Mary is.

Sometimes researchers provide context by tying scores to a specific rating scale or rubric (see Chapter 6). On other occasions, they convert raw scores to norm-referenced scores—scores that reflect where each person is positioned in the distribution relative to a group of peers. This peer group, called a *norm group,* might be either the other participants in a research study or, instead, a nationwide group of individuals who have been given the same measurement instrument.

We have already seen one example of a norm-referenced score: A *percentile rank* is the percentage of people in the group that a particular individual has scored *better than.* For example, if Mary scores at the 95th percentile on a test of extroversion, then we know that she is quite

TABLE 8.3 ■ Using Measures of Variability for Different Types of Data

Measure of Variability	How It's Determined (N = number of scores)	Data for Which It's Appropriate
Range	The difference between the highest and lowest scores in the distribution	• Data on ordinal, interval, and ratio scales*
Interquartile range	The difference between the 25th and 75th percentiles	• Data on ordinal, interval, and ratio scales • Especially useful for highly skewed data
Standard deviation	$s = \sqrt{\dfrac{\sum(X - M)^2}{N}}$	• Data on interval and ratio scales • Most appropriate for normally distributed data
Variance	$s^2 = \dfrac{\sum(X - M)^2}{N}$	• Data on interval and ratio scales • Most appropriate for normally distributed data • Especially useful in inferential statistical procedures (e.g., analysis of variance)

*Measures of variability are usually inappropriate for nominal data. Instead, frequencies or percentages of each number are reported.

outgoing—more so than 95% of the people who have taken the test. But as noted earlier in the chapter, percentile ranks have a definite limitation: They are ordinal data rather than interval data, and thus we can't perform even such basic arithmetic operations as addition and subtraction on them. Accordingly, we will be very limited in the statistical procedures we can use with percentile ranks.

More useful in statistical analyses are standard scores. Simply put, a standard score tells us how far an individual's performance is from the mean with respect to standard deviation units. The simplest standard score is a z-score, which is calculated by using an individual's raw score (which we will symbolize as X), along with the mean and standard deviation for the entire group, as follows:

$$z = \frac{X - M}{s}$$

As an illustration, let's return to Mary's score of 35 on the extroversion test. If the mean of the scores on this test is 25, and if the standard deviation is 5, we would calculate Mary's z-score as follows:

$$z = \frac{35 - 25}{5} = \frac{10}{5} = 2$$

When we calculate z-scores for an entire group, we get a distribution that has a mean of 0 and a standard deviation of 1.

Because about half of the z-scores for any group of people will be a negative number—as just noted, the *mean* for the group is 0—researchers sometimes change z-scores into other standard-score scales that yield only positive numbers. To convert a z-score to another scale, we would simply multiply the z by the new scale's standard deviation (s_{new}) and then add the new scale's mean (M_{new}) to the product obtained, as follows:

$$\text{New standard score} = (z \times s_{new}) + M_{new}$$

Let's take an example. One common standard-score scale is the IQ scale, which uses a mean of 100 and a standard deviation of 15. (As you might guess, this scale is the one on which intelligence test scores are typically based.) If we were to convert Mary's extroversion score to the IQ scale, we would plug her z-score of 2, plus a standard deviation of 15 and a mean of 100, into the preceding formula, as follows:

$$\text{IQ score} = (2 \times 15) + 100 = 130$$

Thus, using the IQ scale, Mary's score on the extroversion test would be 130.

Another commonly used standard-score scale is the stanine. Stanines have a mean of 5 and a standard deviation of 2. Mary's stanine would be 9, as we can see from the following calculation:

$$\text{Stanine} = (2 \times 2) + 5 = 9$$

Stanines are *always* a whole number from 1 to 9. If our calculations gave us a number with a fraction or decimal, we would round it off to the nearest whole number. If some of our calculations resulted in numbers of 0 or less, or 10 or more, we would change those scores to 1 and 9, respectively.

Standard scores take a variety of forms, each with a prespecified mean and standard deviation; z-scores, IQs, and stanines are just three examples.[5] But in general, standard scores give us a context that helps us interpret the scores: If we know the mean and standard deviation on which the scores are based, then we also know where in the distribution any particular score lies. For instance, an IQ score of 70 is two standard deviations (30 points) below the mean of 100, and a stanine score of 6 is one half of a standard deviation (1 is half of 2) above the mean of 5.

Converting data to standard scores doesn't change the shape of the distribution; it merely changes the mean and standard deviation of that distribution. But imagine that, instead, we *do*

---

[5]A standard score gaining increasing popularity for reporting academic achievement test results is the *NCE score*, which has a mean of 50 and a standard deviation of 21.06. With this particular (and seemingly very odd) standard deviation, an NCE score of 1 is equivalent to a percentile score of 1 and, likewise, an NCE score of 99 is equivalent to a percentile score of 99.

want to change the nature of the distribution. Perhaps we want to change a skewed distribution into a more balanced, normally distributed one. Perhaps, in the process, we also want to change ordinal data into interval data. Several procedures exist for doing such things, but describing them would divert us from the basic nature and functions of statistics that we need to focus on here. You can find discussions of *normalizing* a data set in many basic statistics textbooks; another good resource is Harwell and Gatti (2001).

Keeping Measures of Central Tendency and Variability in Perspective

Statistics related to central tendency and variability help us summarize our data. But—so as not to lose sight of our ultimate goal in conducting research—we should remind ourselves that statistical manipulation of the data is *not,* in and of itself, research. Research goes one step further and demands *interpretation* of the data. In finding medians, means, interquartile ranges, or standard deviations, we have not interpreted the data, nor have we extracted any *meaning* from them. We have merely described the center and spread of the data. We have attempted only to see what the data look like. After learning their basic nature, we should then look for conditions that are forcing the data to behave as they do. For example, if we toss a pair of dice 100 times and one particular die yields a "5" in 80 of those tosses, we will have a distribution for that die much different from what we would expect. This may suggest to us that a reason lurks behind the particular results we have obtained. For example, perhaps we are playing with a loaded die!

Measures of Association: Correlation

The statistics described so far—measures of central tendency and variability—involve only a single variable. Oftentimes, however, we also want to know whether two or more variables are in some way associated with one another. For example, relationships exist between age and reading ability (as illustrated in Figure 6.1 in Chapter 6), between emotional state and physical health, and between the amount of rainfall and the price of vegetables in the marketplace. Consider, too, the relationships between temperature and pressure, between the intensity of light and the growth of plants, and between the administration of a certain medication and the resulting platelet agglutination in the blood. Relationships among variables are everywhere. One function of statistics is to capture the nature and strength of such relationships.

The statistical process by which we discover whether two or more variables are in some way associated with one another is called *correlation.* The resulting statistic, called a correlation coefficient, is a number between −1 and +1; most correlation coefficients are decimals (either positive or negative) somewhere between these two extremes. A correlation coefficient for two variables simultaneously tells us two different things about the relationship between those variables:

■ *Direction.* The direction of the relationship is indicated by the *sign* of the correlation coefficient—in other words, by whether the number is a positive or negative one. A positive number indicates a positive correlation: As one variable increases, the other variable also increases. For example, there is a positive correlation between self-esteem and school achievement: Students with higher self-esteem achieve at higher levels (e.g., Marsh, Gerlach, Trautwein, Lüdtke, & Brettschneider, 2007). In contrast, a negative number indicates an inverse relationship, or negative correlation: As one variable increases, the other variable *de*creases. For example, there is a negative correlation between the number of friends children have and the likelihood that they'll be victims of bullying: Children who have many friends are *less* likely to be bullied by their peers than are children who have few or no friends (e.g., Laursen, Bukowski, Aunola, & Nurmi, 2007).

■ *Strength.* The strength of the relationship is indicated by the *size* of the correlation coefficient. A correlation of +1 or −1 indicates a *perfect* correlation: If we know the degree to which one characteristic is present, we know exactly how much of the other characteristic exists. For example, if we know the length of a horseshoe crab in inches, we also know—or at least we can quickly calculate—exactly what its length is in centimeters. A number close to either +1 or −1 (e.g., +.89 or −.76) indicates a *strong* correlation: The two variables are closely related, such that knowing the level of one variable allows us to predict the level of the other variable with considerable accuracy. For example, we often find a strong relationship between two intelligence tests taken at the same time: People tend to get very similar scores on both tests, especially if the tests cover similar kinds of content (e.g., McGrew, Flanagan, Zeith, & Vanderwood, 1997). In contrast, a number close to 0 (e.g., +.15 or −.22) indicates a *weak* correlation: Knowing the level of one variable allows us to predict the level of the other variable, but we cannot predict with much accuracy. For example, there is a weak relationship between intellectual giftedness and emotional adjustment: Generally speaking, people with higher IQ scores show greater emotional maturity than people with lower scores (e.g., Shavinina & Ferrari, 2004), but many people are exceptions to this rule. Correlations in the middle range (for example, those in the .40s and .50s, positive or negative) indicate a *moderate* correlation.

The most widely used statistic for determining correlation is the Pearson product moment correlation, sometimes called the Pearson *r*. But there are numerous other correlation statistics as well. As is true for measures of both central tendency and variability, the nature of the data determines the technique that is most appropriate for calculating correlation. In Table 8.4, we

TABLE 8.4 ◼ Examples of Correlational Statistics

Statistic	Symbol	Data for Which It's Appropriate
Parametric Statistics		
Pearson product moment correlation	r	Both variables involve continuous data.
Coefficient of determination	R^2	This is the square of the Pearson product moment correlation; thus, both variables involve continuous data.
Point biserial correlation	r_{pb}	One variable is continuous; the other involves discrete, dichotomous, and perhaps nominal data (e.g., Democrats vs. Republicans, males vs. females).
Biserial correlation	r_b	Both variables are continuous, but one has been artificially divided into an either–or dichotomy (e.g., "above freezing" vs. "below freezing," "pass" vs. "fail").
Phi coefficient	Φ	Both variables are true dichotomies.
Triserial correlation	r_{tri}	One variable is continuous; the other is a trichotomy (e.g., "low," "medium," "high").
Partial correlation	$r_{12 \cdot 3}$	The relationship between two variables exists, in part, because of their relationships with a third variable, and the researcher wants to "factor out" the effects of this third variable (e.g., what is the relationship between motivation and student achievement when IQ is held constant statistically?).
Multiple correlation	$R_{12 \cdot 3}$	A single variable is correlated with two or more variables; here the researcher wants to compute the single variable's combined relationship with the others. This statistic is used in multiple regression.
Nonparametric Statistics		
Spearman rank order correlation (Spearman's rho)	ρ	Both variables involve rank-ordered data and so are ordinal in nature.
Kendall coefficient of concordance	W	Both variables involve rankings (e.g., rankings made by independent judges regarding a particular characteristic) and hence are ordinal data, and the researcher wants to determine the degree to which the rankings are similar.
Contingency coefficient	C	Both variables involve nominal data.
Kendall's tau correlation	τ	Both variables involve ordinal data; the statistic is especially useful for small sample sizes (e.g., $N < 10$).

present several parametric and nonparametric correlational techniques and the kinds of data for which they are appropriate.

One especially noteworthy statistic in Table 8.4 is the *coefficient of determination,* or R^2. This statistic, which is the square of the Pearson *r,* tells us *how much of the variance is accounted for* by the correlation. Although you will see this expression used frequently in research reports, researchers usually don't stop to explain what it means. By *variance,* we are specifically referring to a particular measure of variability mentioned earlier: the square of the standard deviation, or s^2. For example, if we find that, in our data set, the R^2 between Variable 1 and Variable 2 is .30, we know that 30% of the variability in Variable 1 is reflected in its relationship with Variable 2. This knowledge will allow us to control for—and essentially *reduce*—some of the variability in our data set through such statistical procedures as partial correlation and analysis of covariance (described in Table 8.4 and later in Table 8.5, respectively).

It is important to note, too, that the correlation statistics presented in Table 8.4 are all based on an important assumption: that the relationship between the two variables is a *linear* one—that is, as one variable continues to increase, the other continues to increase (for a positive correlation) or decrease (for a negative correlation). Not all relationships take a linear form, however. For example, consider the relationship between body mass index (a general measure of a person's body fat; often abbreviated as BMI) and anxiety. In one recent study (Scott, McGee, Wells, & Oakley Browne, 2008), researchers found that anxiety was highest in people who were either very underweight or very overweight; anxiety was lowest for people of relatively *average* weight. Such a relationship is known as a *U-shaped relationship* (see Figure 8.11). U-shaped and other nonlinear relationships can be detected through scatter plots and other graphic techniques, as well as through certain kinds of statistical analyses (e.g., see B. Thompson, 2008).

Always keep in mind that the nature of the data governs the correlational procedure that is appropriate for those data. Don't forget the cardinal rule: *Look at the data!* Determine their nature, scrutinize their characteristics, and then select the correlational technique suitable for the type of data with which you are working.

How Validity and Reliability Affect Correlation Coefficients

Beginning researchers should be aware that the extent to which one finds a statistical correlation between two characteristics depends, in part, on how well those characteristics have been measured. Even if there really *is* a correlation between two variables, a researcher won't necessarily find one if the measurement instruments being used have poor validity and reliability. For instance, we are less likely to find a correlation between age and reading level if the reading test we use is neither a valid (accurate) nor reliable (consistent) measure of reading achievement.

FIGURE 8.11
U-shaped Relationship Between Body Mass Index (BMI) and Anxiety

Source: Based on Scott et al., 2008.

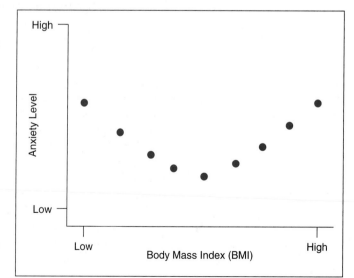

Over the years, we authors have had many students find disappointingly low correlation coefficients between two variables that they hypothesized would be highly correlated. By looking at the correlation coefficient alone, a researcher cannot determine the reason for a low correlation any more than he or she can determine the reason for a high one. Yet one thing is certain: *You will find substantial correlations between two characteristics only if you can measure both characteristics with a reasonable degree of validity and reliability.* We refer you back to the section "Validity and Reliability in Measurement" in Chapter 4, where you can find strategies for determining and enhancing both of these essential qualities of sound measurement.

A Reminder About Correlation

Whenever you find evidence of a correlation within your data, you must remember one important point: *Correlation does not necessarily indicate causation.* For example, if you find a positive correlation between self-esteem and classroom achievement, you can't necessarily conclude that students' self-esteem *influences* their achievement, nor can you assume the reverse—that achieving at high levels directly *enhances* students' self-esteem. The words *influence* and *enhance* both imply cause-and-effect—something that a correlation between two variables doesn't necessarily reflect. Only experimental studies, such as those described in Chapter 7, allow you to draw definitive conclusions about the extent to which one thing causes or influences another.

Finding a correlation in a data set is equivalent to discovering a signpost. That signpost points to the fact that two variables are associated, and it reveals the nature of the association (positive or negative, strong or weak). It should then lead you to wonder, "What is the underlying reason for the association?" But the statistic alone will not be able to answer this question.

INFERENTIAL STATISTICS

As mentioned earlier, inferential statistics allow us to draw inferences about large populations from relatively small samples. More specifically, inferential statistics have two main functions:

1. To estimate a population parameter from a random sample
2. To test statistically based hypotheses

In this text, we do not have the space to venture too far into these areas; statistics textbooks can give you more detailed information. However, the general concepts and principles we discuss in the following sections can help you appreciate just how useful inferential statistics can be.

Estimating Population Parameters

When we conduct research, more often than not we use a sample to learn about the larger population from which the sample has been drawn. Typically we compute various statistics for the sample we have studied. Inferential statistics can tell us how closely these sample statistics approximate parameters of the overall population. For instance, we often want to estimate population parameters related to central tendency (the mean, or μ), variability (the standard deviation, or σ), and proportion (P). These values in the population compare with the M or $\overline{X}$, the s, and the p of the sample (see Table 8.1).

A simple example can illustrate this idea of estimation. Jan is a production manager for a large corporation. The corporation manufactures a piece of equipment that requires a connecting-rod pin, which the corporation also manufactures. The pin fits snugly into a particular joint in the equipment, permitting a metal arm to swivel within a given arc. The pin's diameter is critical: If the diameter is too small, the arm will wobble while turning; if it's too large, the arm will stick and refuse to budge. Jan has received complaints from customers that some of the pins are faulty. She decides to estimate, on the basis of a random sample of the connecting-rod pins, how many units of the equipment may have to be recalled in order to replace their faulty pins. From this sample, Jan wants to know three facts about the thousands of equipment units that have been manufactured and sold:

1. What is the average diameter of the pins?
2. How widely do the pins vary in diameter?
3. What proportion of the pins are acceptable in the equipment units already sold?

The problem is to determine population parameters on the basis of sample statistics. From the sample, Jan can estimate the mean and variability of the pin diameters and the proportion of acceptable pins within the population universe. These are the values represented by the symbols μ, σ, and P.

Statistical estimates of population parameters are based on the assumption that *the sample is randomly chosen and representative of the total population.* Only when we have a random, representative sample can we make reasonable guesses about how closely our statistics estimate population parameters. To the extent that a sample is nonrandom and therefore nonrepresentative—to the extent that its selection has been *biased* in some way—our statistics may be poor reflections of the population from which it has been drawn.

An Example: Estimating a Population Mean

Imagine that we want to estimate the average (mean) height of 10-year-old boys in the state of Iowa. Measuring the heights of the entire population would be incredibly time-consuming, so we decide to measure the heights of a random and presumably representative sample of, let's say, 200 boys.

Random samples from populations—please note the word *random* here—display roughly the same characteristics as the populations from which they were selected. Thus, we should expect the mean height for our sample to be approximately the same as the mean for the overall population. It will not be *exactly* the same, however. In fact, if we were to collect data on the heights of a second random sample of 200 boys, we would be likely to compute a slightly different mean than we had obtained for the first sample.

Different samples—even when each one has been randomly selected from the same population—will almost certainly yield slightly different estimates of the overall population. The difference between the population mean and a sample mean constitutes an *error* in our estimation. Because we don't know what the exact population mean is, we also don't know how much error is in our estimate. We *do* know three things, however:

1. The means we might obtain from an infinite number of random samples form a normal distribution.
2. The *mean of this distribution of sample means* is equal to the mean of the population from which the samples have been drawn (μ). In other words, the population mean equals the average, or mean, of all the sample means.
3. The standard deviation of this distribution of sample means is directly related to the standard deviation of the variable that has been measured—the variable for which we've calculated all the means—for the overall population.[6]

This situation is depicted in Figure 8.12.

The parameter mentioned in Number 3 of the preceding list—the standard deviation for the distribution of sample means—is called the standard error of the mean. This index tells us how much the particular mean we obtain is likely to vary from one sample to another *when all samples are the same size and are drawn randomly from the same population.* Statistically, when all of the samples are of a particular size *(n)*, the standard error of the mean for any variable being measured is related to the standard deviation *for the variable itself* in the following way:

$$\sigma_M = \frac{\sigma}{\sqrt{n}}$$

---

[6]Taken together, these assumptions form the core of what statisticians refer to as the *central limit theorm.*

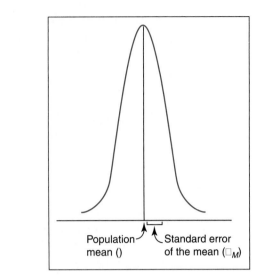

FIGURE 8.12
Distribution of
Sample Means

Here we are faced at once with a problem. The formula just presented involves using the population standard deviation (σ), but the purpose of using the sample was to *avoid* having to measure the entire population. Fortunately, statisticians have devised a way to estimate the standard error of the mean from the standard deviation of a *sample* drawn from the population. This formula is

$$\text{Estimated } \sigma_M = \frac{s}{\sqrt{n-1}}$$

Notice how, in both formulas, the standard error of the mean (σ_M) is directly related to the standard deviation of the characteristic being measured (σ or s): More variability in the population leads to a larger standard error of the mean—that is, to greater variability in the sample means we might obtain. In addition, the standard error is *inversely* related to n, the size of the sample. As the sample size increases, the standard error of the mean decreases. Thus, a larger sample size will give us a sample mean that more closely approximates the population mean. This principle holds true for estimates of other population parameters as well. In general, *larger samples yield more accurate estimates of population parameters.*

Point Versus Interval Estimates

When using sample statistics to estimate population parameters, we can make two types of estimates: point estimates and interval estimates.

A point estimate is a single statistic that is used as a reasonable estimate of the corresponding population parameter; for instance, we might use a sample mean as a close approximation to the population mean. Although point estimates have the seeming benefit of being precise, in fact this precision is illusory. A point estimate typically does *not* correspond exactly with its equivalent in the population. Let's return to our previous example of the connecting-rod pins. Perhaps the company has produced 500,000 pins, and Jan has selected a sample of 100 of them. When she measures the diameters of these pins, she finds that the mean diameter is 0.712 centimeter, and the standard deviation is 0.020 centimeter. She guesses that the mean and standard deviation of the diameters of *all* of the pins are also 0.712 and 0.020, respectively. Her estimates will probably be close—and they're certainly better than nothing—but they won't necessarily be dead-on.

A more accurate approach—although still not 100% dependable—is to identify interval estimates of parameters. In particular, we specify a range within which a population parameter probably lies, and we state the probability that it actually lies there. Such an interval is often called a confidence interval because it attaches a certain level of probability to the estimate—a certain level of *confidence* that the estimated range includes the population parameter.

As an example, Jan might say that she is 95% certain that the mean of the 500,000 connecting-rod pin diameters her company has produced is somewhere between 0.708 and 0.716.

What Jan has done is to determine that the standard error of the mean is 0.002 (see the previously presented formula for estimated σ_M). Jan knows that sample means fall in a normal distribution (look once again at Figure 8.12). She also knows that normal distributions have predictable proportions within each section of the curve (look once again at Figure 8.6). In particular, Jan knows that about 68% (34.1% + 34.1%) of the sample means lie within one standard error of the population mean, and that about 95% (13.6% + 34.1% + 34.1% + 13.6%) lie within two standard errors of the population mean. What she has done, then, is to go two standard errors (2 × 0.002, or 0.004) to either side of her sample mean (0.712) to arrive at her 95% confidence interval of 0.708 to 0.716.

We have said enough about estimation for you to appreciate its importance. For more information and guidance, we urge you to consult one or more statistics textbooks, such as those listed in the "For Further Reading" section at the end of the chapter.

Testing Hypotheses

The second major function of inferential statistics is to test hypotheses. At the outset, we should clarify our terminology. The term *hypothesis* can confuse you unless you understand that it has two different meanings in research literature. The first meaning relates to a *research hypothesis;* the second relates to a *statistical hypothesis.*

Most of the discussions of hypotheses in earlier chapters have involved the first meaning of the word *hypothesis.* In forming a research hypothesis, a researcher speculates about how the research problem or one of its subproblems might be resolved. A research hypothesis is a reasonable conjecture, an educated guess, a theoretically or empirically based prediction. Its purpose is a practical one: It provides a logical framework that guides a researcher while designing a research study and collecting data.

When we encounter the phrase "testing a hypothesis," however, the matter is entirely different. Here the word *hypothesis* refers to a statistical hypothesis, usually a *null* hypothesis. A **null hypothesis** (often symbolized as H_0) postulates that any result observed is the result of chance alone. For instance, if we were to compare the means of two groups, our null hypothesis would be that both groups are parts of the same population and that any differences between them—including any difference we see between their means—are strictly the result of the fact that *any* two samples from the population will yield slightly different estimates of a population parameter.

Now let's say that we look at the *probability* that our result is due to chance alone. If, for example, we find that a difference between two group means would, if due entirely to chance, occur *only one time in a thousand,* we could reasonably conclude that the difference is *not* due to chance—that, instead, something in the situation we are studying (perhaps an experimental treatment we have imposed) is systematically leading to a difference in the groups' means. This process of comparing observed data with the results we would expect from chance alone is called *testing the null hypothesis.*

At what point do researchers decide that a result has *not* occurred by chance alone? One commonly used cutoff is a 1-in-20 probability: Any result that would occur by chance only 5% of the time—that is, a result that would occur, on average, only one time in every 20 times—probably is *not* due to chance but instead to another, systematic factor that is influencing the data. Other researchers use a more rigorous 1-in-100 criterion: The observed result would occur by chance only one time in 100. The probability that researchers use as their cutoff point, whether .05, .01, or some other figure, is the **significance level,** or **alpha** (α). A result that, based on this criterion, we deem *not* to be due to chance is called a **statistically significant** result. When we decide that a result is due to something other than chance, we *reject the null hypothesis.*

In the "Results" section of a research report, you will often see the researcher's alpha level implied in parentheses. For example, imagine that a researcher reports that "a *t*-test revealed significantly different means for the two treatment groups ($p < .01$)." The "$p < .01$" here means that the difference in means for the two groups would occur by chance less than one time in 100 *if* the two groups had been drawn from the same population. Sometimes, instead, a researcher will state the actual probability with which a result might occur by chance alone. For example, a researcher might report that "a *t*-test revealed significantly different means for the two treatment groups ($p = .003$)." The "$p = .003$" here means that a difference this large would occur only three times in 1,000 for two groups that come from the same population. In this situation, then, chances are good that the two groups come from *different* populations—a roundabout way of saying that the two treatments differentially affected the outcome.

When we reject the null hypothesis, we must look to an alternative hypothesis—which might be the *research hypothesis*—as being more probable. For example, if our null hypothesis is that two groups are the same and we then obtain data that lead us to reject this hypothesis, we indirectly support the opposite hypothesis: The two groups are *different*.

In brief, we permit a certain narrow margin of variation within our data, which we deem to be natural and the result of pure chance. Any variation within this statistically permissible range isn't considered to be important enough to claim our attention. Whatever exceeds these limits, however, is considered to be the result of some determinative factor other than chance, and so the influence is considered to be an important one. The term *significant,* in the statistical sense in which we have been using it, is close to its etymological meaning—namely, "giving a signal" that certain dynamics are operating within the data and merit attention.

Making Errors in Hypothesis Testing

It is possible, of course, that we make a mistake when we decide that a particular result is not the result of chance alone. In fact, *any* result might conceivably be due to chance; our sample, although selected randomly, may be a fluke that displays atypical characteristics simply through the luck of the draw. If we erroneously conclude that a result was not due to chance when in fact it *was* due to chance—if we incorrectly reject the null hypothesis—we are making a Type I error (also called an *alpha error*).

Yet in another situation, we might conclude that a result is due to chance when in fact it is *not*. In such a circumstance, we have failed to reject a null hypothesis that is actually false—something known as a Type II error (also called a *beta error*). For example, imagine that we are testing the relative effects of a new medication versus the effects of a placebo in lowering blood cholesterol. Perhaps we find that people who have been taking the new medication have, on average, a lower cholesterol level than people taking the placebo, but the difference is a small one. We might find that such a difference could occur 25 times out of 100 due to chance alone, and so we *retain the null hypothesis.* If, in actuality, the medication does reduce cholesterol more than a placebo does, we have made a Type II error.

Statistical hypothesis testing is all a matter of probabilities, and there is always the chance that we could make either a Type I or Type II error. We can decrease the odds of making a Type I error by lowering our level of significance, say, from .05 to .01, or perhaps to an even lower level. In the process of doing so, however, we increase the likelihood that we will make a Type II error—that we will fail to reject a null hypothesis that is, in fact, incorrect. To decrease the probability of a Type II error, we would have to increase our significance level (α), which, because it increases the odds of rejecting the null hypothesis, also increases the probability of a Type I error. Obviously, then, there is a trade-off between Type I and Type II errors: Whenever you decrease the risk of making one, you increase the risk of making the other.

To illustrate this trade-off, we return to our study of the potentially cholesterol-reducing medication. There are four possibilities:

1. We correctly conclude that the medication reduces cholesterol.
2. We correctly conclude that it does *not* reduce cholesterol.
3. We mistakenly conclude that it is effective when it *isn't.*
4. We mistakenly conclude that it isn't effective when it *is.*

These four possibilities are illustrated in Figure 8.13. The three vertical lines illustrate three hypothetical significance levels we might choose. Imagine that the dashed middle line, Line A, represents a significance level of, say, .05. In this particular situation (such will not always be the case), we have a slightly greater chance of making a Type I error (represented by the upper shaded area) than of making a Type II error (represented by the lower shaded area). But the significance

FIGURE 8.13
The Trade-off Between
Type I and Type II Errors

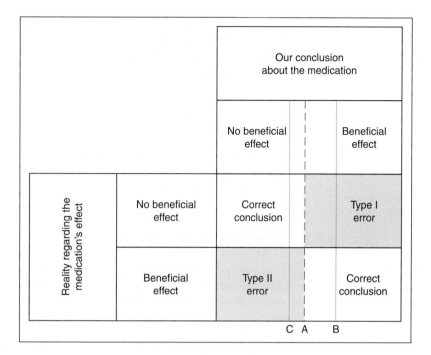

level we choose is an arbitrary one. We could reduce our chance of a Type I error by decreasing our significance level to, say, .03. Line B to the right of Line A in the figure represents such a change; notice how it would create a smaller box (lower probability) for a Type I error but create a larger box (greater probability) for a Type II error. Alternatively, if we raise the significance level to, say, .06 (as might be represented by Line C, to the left of Line A in the figure), we decrease the probability of a Type II error but increase the probability of a Type I error.

For a novice researcher, it can be extremely frustrating to get insignificant results—those that, from a statistical standpoint, could have been due to chance alone. Following are three suggestions for decreasing the likelihood of making a Type II error and thereby increasing the likelihood of correctly rejecting an incorrect null hypothesis. In other words, these are suggestions for increasing the power of a statistical test:

- *Use as large a sample size as is reasonably possible.* The larger the sample, the less the statistics you compute will diverge from actual population parameters.[7]
- *Maximize the validity and reliability of your measures.* Measures of variables in a research study rarely have perfect (100%) validity and reliability, but some measures are more valid and reliable than others. Research projects that use measures with high validity and reliability are more likely to yield statistically significant results. (Again we refer you to the section "Validity and Reliability in Measurement" in Chapter 4.)
- *Use parametric rather than nonparametric statistics whenever possible.* As a general rule, nonparametric statistical procedures are less powerful than parametric techniques. By "less powerful," we mean that nonparametric statistics typically require larger samples to yield results that enable the researcher to reject the null hypothesis. When characteristics of the data meet the assumptions for parametric statistics, then, we urge you to use these statistics. (Look once again at the section "Choosing Between Parametric and Nonparametric Statistics" earlier in this chapter.)

It is important—in fact, critical—to keep in mind that *whenever we test more than one statistical hypothesis, we increase the probability of making at least one Type I error.* Let's say that, for a particular research project, we have set the significance level at .05, such that we will reject the

---

[7]Formulas exist for computing the power of statistical procedures for varying sample sizes. For example, see Lipsey (1990) or Murphy, Myors, and Wolach (2009).

null hypothesis whenever we obtain results that would be due to chance alone only 1 time in 20. And now let's say that as we analyze our data, we perform 20 different statistical tests, always setting α at .05. In this situation, although we won't necessarily make a Type I error, the odds are fairly high that we will.[8]

Another Look at Statistical Hypotheses Versus Research Hypotheses

Novice researchers sometimes become so wrapped up in their statistical analyses that they lose track of their overall research problem or hypothesis. In fact, testing a null hypothesis involves nothing more than a statistical comparison of two distributions of data—one hypothetical (a theoretical ideal) and one real (the distribution of data collected from a research sample). A researcher simply uses one or more statistical procedures to determine whether calculated values sufficiently diverge from the statistical ideal to reject the null hypothesis.

Testing a statistical hypothesis does not, in and of itself, contribute much to the fulfillment of the basic aim of research: a systematic quest for undiscovered knowledge. Certainly statistical analyses are invaluable tools that enable us to find patterns in the data and thus help us detect possible dynamics working within the data. But we must never stop with statistical procedures that yield one or more numerical values. We must also *interpret* those values and give them meaning. The latter process includes the former, but the two should never be confused.

It is often the case that the statistical hypothesis is the opposite of the research hypothesis. For example, we might, as our research hypothesis, propose that two groups are different from one another. As we begin our statistical analysis, we set out to test the statistical hypothesis that the two groups are the same. *By disconfirming the null hypothesis, we indirectly find support for our research hypothesis.* This is, to be sure, a backdoor approach to finding evidence for a research hypothesis, yet it is the approach that a researcher typically takes. The reasons for this approach are too complex to be dealt with in a text such as this one. Suffice it to say that it is mathematically much easier to test a hypothesis that an equivalence exists than to test a hypothesis that a difference exists.

Examples of Statistical Techniques for Testing Hypotheses

Table 8.5 lists many commonly used parametric and nonparametric statistical techniques for testing hypotheses. We hope it will help you make decisions about the techniques that are most appropriate for your own research situation. As you can see in the table, however, nonparametric techniques exist only for relatively simple statistical analyses, such as comparing measures of central tendency or testing the statistical significance of correlations. When your research problem calls for a sophisticated analysis (e.g., multiple regression or structural equation modeling), parametric statistical procedures—with certain underlying assumptions about the nature of your data—are your only viable option.

We urge you to consult one or more statistics texts to learn as much as you can about whatever statistical procedures you use. Better still, enroll in one or more statistics courses! You can successfully solve your research problem only if you apply statistical procedures appropriately and conduct defensible analyses of your data.

Meta-Analysis

Occasionally researchers use inferential statistics not to analyze and draw conclusions from data they have collected but instead to analyze and draw conclusions about *other researchers' statistical analyses.* Such analysis of analyses is known as meta-analysis. A meta-analysis is

---

[8]When testing 20 hypotheses at a .05 significance level, the probability of making at least one Type I error is .642—in other words, chances are better than 50–50 that at least one Type I error is being made. In general, the probability of making a Type I error when conducting multiple statistical tests is $1 - (1 - \alpha)^n$, where α (alpha) is the significance level and n is the number of tests conducted.

TABLE 8.5 Examples of Inferential Statistical Procedures and Their Purposes

Statistical Procedure	Purpose
Parametric Statistics	
Student's *t*-test	To determine whether a statistically significant difference exists between two means. A *t*-test takes slightly different forms depending on whether the two means come from separate, independent groups (an *independent-samples t*-test) or, instead, from a single group or two interrelated groups (a *dependent-samples t*-test).
Analysis of variance (ANOVA)	To examine differences among three or more means by comparing the variances (s^2) both within and across groups. As is true for *t*-tests, ANOVAs take slightly different forms for separate, independent groups and for a single group; in the latter case, a *repeated-measures* ANOVA is called for. If an ANOVA yields a significant result (i.e., a significant value for *F*), the researcher should follow up by comparing various pairs of means using a *post hoc comparison of means.*
Analysis of covariance (ANCOVA)	To look for differences among means while controlling for the effects of a variable that is correlated with the dependent variable (the former variable is called a *covariate*). This technique can be statistically more powerful than ANOVA (i.e., it decreases the probability of a Type II error).
t-test for a correlation coefficient	To determine whether a Pearson product moment correlation coefficient (*r*) is larger than would be expected from chance alone.
Regression	To examine how accurately one or more variables enables(s) predictions to be made regarding the values of another (dependent) variable. A *simple linear regression* generates an equation in which a single independent variable yields predictions for the dependent variable. A *multiple linear regression* yields an equation in which two or more independent variables are used to predict the dependent variable. The researcher must keep in mind, however, that an independent variable's accuracy in predicting a correlated dependent variable does *not* necessarily indicate a cause-and-effect relationship.
Factor analysis	To examine the correlations among a number of variables and identify clusters of highly interrelated variables that reflect underlying themes, or *factors,* within the data.
Structural equation modeling (SEM)	To examine the correlations among a number of variables—often with different variables measured for a single group of people at different points in time—in order to identify possible causal relationships (*paths*) among the variables. SEM encompasses such techniques as *path analysis* and *confirmatory analysis* and is typically used to test a previously hypothesized model of how variables are causally interrelated. SEM enables a researcher to identify a *mediator* in a relationship: a third variable that may help explain why Variable A seemingly leads to Variable B (i.e., Variable A affects the mediating variable, which in turn affects Variable B). SEM also enables a researcher to identify a *moderator* of a relationship: a third variable that alters the nature of the relationship between Variables A and B (e.g., Variables A and B might be correlated when the moderating variable is high but not when it is low, or vice versa). (Mediating and moderating variables are discussed in more detail in Chapter 2.) When using SEM, the researcher must keep in mind that the data are *correlational* in nature; thus, any conclusions about cause-and-effect relationships are speculative at best.
Nonparametric Statistics	
Mann-Whitney *U*	To compare the medians of two groups when the data are ordinal rather than interval in nature. This procedure is the nonparametric counterpart of the independent samples *t*-test in parametric statistics.
Kruskal-Wallis test	To compare three or more group medians when the data are ordinal rather than interval in nature. This procedure is the nonparametric counterpart of ANOVA.
Wilcoxon signed-rank test	To compare the medians of two correlated variables when the data are ordinal rather than interval in nature. This procedure is a nonparametric equivalent of a dependent-samples *t*-test in parametric statistics.
Chi-square (X^2) goodness-of-fit test	To determine how closely observed frequencies or probabilities match expected frequencies or probabilities. A chi-square can be computed for nominal, ordinal, interval, or ratio data.
Odds ratio	To determine whether two dichotomous nominal variables (e.g., smokers vs. nonsmokers and presence vs. absence of heart disease) are significantly correlated. This is one nonparametric alternative to a *t*-test for Pearson's *r.*
Fisher's exact test	To determine whether two dichotomous variables (nominal or ordinal) are significantly correlated when the sample sizes are quite small (e.g., $n < 30$). This is another nonparametric alternative to a *t*-test for Pearson's *r.*

most useful when many studies have already been conducted on a particular topic or research problem and another researcher wants to pull all the results together into a neat and mathematically concise package.

The traditional approach to synthesizing previous studies related to a particular research question is simply to describe them all, pointing out which studies have yielded which conclusions, which studies have contradicted other studies, and what methodological differences might have accounted for inconsistencies in findings. In a meta-analysis, however, the researcher integrates the studies statistically rather than verbally. After pinning down the research problem, the researcher:

1. ***Conducts a fairly extensive search for relevant studies.*** The researcher doesn't choose arbitrarily among studies that have been reported about the research problem. Instead, the researcher uses some systematic and far-reaching approach (e.g., searching in several prespecified professional journals, using certain keywords in a search of online databases) to identify studies that have addressed the topic of interest.
2. ***Identifies appropriate studies to include in the meta-analysis.*** The researcher limits the chosen studies to those that involve a particular experimental treatment (in experimental studies), pre-existing condition (in ex post facto studies), or other variable that is the focus of the meta-analysis. He or she may further restrict the chosen studies to those that involve particular populations, settings, assessment instruments, or other factors that might impact a study's outcome.
3. ***Converts each study's results to a common statistical index.*** Previous researchers haven't necessarily used the same statistical procedures to analyze their data. For example, if each researcher has compared two or more groups that received two or more different experimental interventions, one investigator may have used a *t*-test, another may have conducted an analysis of variance, and a third may have conducted a multiple regression. The meta-analytic researcher's job is to find a common denominator here. Typically, when an experimental intervention has been studied, an **effect size (ES)** is calculated for each study; that is, the researcher determines how much of a difference each study's intervention makes (in terms of standard deviation units) relative to a control group or other comparison group. The effect sizes of all the studies are then used to compute an average effect size for that intervention.[9]

The statistical procedures used in meta-analyses vary widely, depending, in part, on the research designs of the included studies; for instance, correlational studies require different meta-analytic procedures than experimental studies. We must point out, too, that meta-analyses, although they make important contributions to the knowledge bases of many disciplines, are not for the mathematically fainthearted. If you are interested in conducting a meta-analysis, several of the resources listed in the "For Further Reading" section at the end of this chapter should prove helpful.

USING STATISTICAL SOFTWARE PACKAGES

USING TECHNOLOGY

Earlier in the chapter, we mentioned that general purpose spreadsheet programs can be used to describe and analyze sets of quantitative data. However, many spreadsheets are limited in their statistical analysis capabilities. As an alternative, you may want to consider using one of the several statistical software packages now widely available for use on

---

[9]Increasingly, researchers are including effect sizes in their reports of single research studies. Procedures for calculating effect sizes differ somewhat depending on the circumstances (e.g., see Cumming, 2014; Fidler & Cumming, 2013).

personal computers (e.g., SPSS, SAS, SYSTAT, Minitab, Statistica). Such packages have several advantages:

- *Range of available statistics.* Many of these programs include a wide variety of statistical procedures, and they can easily handle large data sets, multiple variables, and missing data points.
- *User-friendliness.* As statistical software programs become increasingly powerful, they also become more user-friendly. In most cases, the programs are logical and easy to follow, and results are presented in an easy-to-read table format. However, selections of the proper statistics and interpretations of the results are still left to the researcher.
- *Assumption testing.* A common feature of statistical software packages is to test for characteristics (e.g., skewness, kurtosis) that might violate the assumptions on which a parametric statistical procedure is based.
- *Graphics.* Many statistical programs allow the researcher to summarize and display data in tables, pie charts, bar graphs, or other graphics.

In Appendix B, we show you some of the basics of one statistical software program, SPSS, and use a small data set to illustrate some of the ways you might use it.

For frugal researchers—especially those whose research problems require small data sets and relatively simple statistical procedures (e.g., computing standard deviations, correlation coefficients, or chi-squares)—online statistics calculators provide another option. Two examples are easycalculation.com (easycalculation.com/statistics/statistics.php) and GraphPad Software's QuickCalcs (graphpad.com/quickcalcs). An Internet search for "online statistics calculator" can identify other helpful websites as well.

Yet we must caution you: *A computer cannot and should not do it all for you.* You may be able to perform sophisticated calculations related to dozens of statistical tests and present the results in a variety of ways, but if you don't understand how the results relate to your research problem, or if you can't otherwise make logical, theoretical, or pragmatic sense of what your analyses have revealed, then all your efforts have been for naught. Powerful statistical software programs make it all too easy to conduct studies so large and complex that the researcher loses sight of the initial research question. In the words of Krathwohl (1993), the researcher eventually behaves "like a worker in a laboratory handling radioactive material, . . . manipulating mechanical hands by remote control from a room outside a sealed data container. With no sense of the data, there is little basis for suspecting an absurd result, and we are at the mercy of the computer printout" (p. 608).

Ultimately *you* must be in control of your analyses; you must know what calculations are being performed and why. Only by having an intimate knowledge of the data can you derive true meaning from the statistics computed and use them to address your research problem.

INTERPRETING THE DATA

To the novice researcher, statistics can be like the voice of a bevy of Sirens. For those who have never studied or have forgotten the works of Homer, the *Odyssey* describes the perilous straits between Scylla and Charybdis. On these treacherous rocks resided a group of Sirens—svelte maidens who, with enticing songs, lured sailors in their direction and, by so doing, caused ships to drift and founder on the jagged shores.

For many beginning researchers, statistics hold a similar appeal. Subjecting data to elegant statistical routines may lure novice researchers into thinking they have made a substantial discovery, when in fact they have only calculated a few numbers. Behind every statistic lies a sizable body of data; the statistic may summarize these data in a particular way, but it cannot capture all the nuances of the data. The entire body of data collected—not any single statistic calculated—is what must ultimately be used to resolve the research problem. There is no substitute for the task the researcher ultimately faces: to discover the meaning of the data and its relevance to the research problem. Any statistical process you may use is merely a tool in pursuing this central quest.

At the beginning of the chapter, we presented a hypothetical data set for 11 school children and discovered that the five girls in the sample had higher reading achievement test scores than the six boys. Shortly thereafter, we presented actual data about growth marks on the shells of the chambered nautilus. Perhaps these examples piqued your curiosity. For instance, perhaps you wondered about questions such as these:

▨ Why were all of the girls' scores higher than those of the boys?
▨ Why were the intervals between each of the scores equidistant for both boys and girls?
▨ What caused the nautilus to record a growth mark each day of the lunar month?
▨ Is the relationship between the forming of the partitions and the lunar cycle singular to the nautilus, or are there other similar occurrences in nature?

Knowledge springs from questions like these. But we must be careful not to make snap judgments about the data we have collected. It's all too easy to draw hasty and unwarranted conclusions. Even the most thorough research effort can go astray at the point of drawing conclusions from the data.

For example, from our study of 11 children and their reading achievement scores, we might conclude that girls read better than boys. But if we do so, we aren't thinking carefully about the data. Reading is a complex and multifaceted skill. The data *do not* say that girls read better than boys. The data *do* say that, on a particular test given on a particular day to a particular group of 11 children, all girls' scores were higher than all boys' scores and that, for both boys and girls, the individual scores differed by intervals of 4. The apparent excellence of the girls over the boys was limited to test performance in those reading skills that were specifically measured by the test. Honesty and precision dictate that all conditions in the situation be considered and that we make generalizations only in strict accordance with the data. On the following day, the same test given to another 11 children might yield different results.

In general, interpreting the data means several things:

1. ***Relating the findings to the original research problem and to the specific research questions and hypotheses.***   Researchers must eventually come full circle to their starting point—why they conducted a research study in the first place and what they hoped to discover—and relate their results to their initial concerns and questions.

2. ***Relating the findings to pre-existing literature, concepts, theories, and research studies.***   To be useful, research findings must in some way be connected to the larger picture—to what people already know or believe about the topic in question. Perhaps the new findings confirm a current theoretical perspective, perhaps they cast doubt on common "knowledge," or perhaps they simply raise new questions that must be addressed before humankind can truly understand the phenomenon in question.

3. ***Determining whether the findings have practical significance as well as statistical significance.***   Statistical significance is one thing; practical significance—whether findings are actually useful—is something else altogether. For example, let's return to that new medication for lowering blood cholesterol level mentioned earlier in the chapter. Perhaps we randomly assign a large sample of individuals to one of two groups; one is given the medication, and the other is given a placebo. At the end of the study, we measure cholesterol levels for the two groups and then conduct a *t*-test to compare the group means. If our sample size is quite large, the standard error of the mean will be very small, and we might therefore find that even a minor difference in the cholesterol levels of the two groups is statistically significant. Is the difference *practically* significant as well? That is, do the benefits of the medication outweigh its costs and any unpleasant side effects? A calculation of *effect size*—how different the cholesterol levels are for the treatment and control groups relative to the standard deviation for one or both groups—can certainly help us as we struggle with this issue. But ultimately a statistical test cannot, in and of itself, answer the question. Only human minds—including those of the researcher, practitioners in the field of medicine, and individuals with unhealthy cholesterol levels—can answer it.

4. *Identifying limitations of the study.*   Finally, interpreting the data involves outlining the weaknesses of the study that yielded them. No research study can be perfect, and its imperfections inevitably cast at least a hint of doubt on its findings. Good researchers know—and also report—the weaknesses along with the strengths of their research.

PRACTICAL APPLICATION Analyzing and Interpreting Data in a Quantitative Study

You can gain a clearer understanding of various statistics and statistical procedures by reading about them in research reports and using them in actual practice. If your research project involves quantitative data, the following checklist can help you clarify which statistical analyses might be most appropriate for your situation.

✔ CHECKLIST

Choosing Statistical Procedures

CHARACTERISTICS OF THE DATA

_____ 1. Are the data _____ continuous or _____ discrete?

_____ 2. What scale do the data reflect? Are they _____ nominal, _____ ordinal, _____ interval, or _____ ratio?

_____ 3. _____ What do you want to do with the data?

_____ Calculate central tendency? If so, with which measure? _____

_____ Calculate variability? If so, with which measure? _____

_____ Calculate correlation? If so, with which measure? _____

_____ Estimate population parameters? If so, which ones? _____

_____ Test a null hypothesis? If so, at what confidence level? _____

_____ Other? (specify) _____

_____ 4. State your rationale for processing the data as you have just indicated you intend to do.

_____

_____

_____

INTERPRETATION OF THE DATA

_____ 5. After you have treated the data statistically to analyze their characteristics, what will you then have?

_____

_____

_____ 6. From a research standpoint, what will your interpretation of the data consist of? How will the statistical analyses help you solve any part of your research problem?

_____

_____

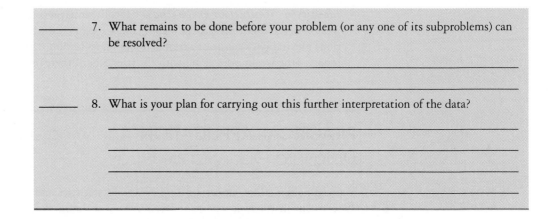

_____ 7. What remains to be done before your problem (or any one of its subproblems) can be resolved?

_____

_____

_____ 8. What is your plan for carrying out this further interpretation of the data?

_____

_____

_____

_____

✔ **Check Your Understanding in the Pearson etext**

Practice Thinking Like a Researcher

Practice Thinking Like a Researcher Activity 8.1: Organizing Data in Tables and Graphs
Practice Thinking Like a Researcher Activity 8.2: Finding and Estimating Central Tendency
Practice Thinking Like a Researcher Activity 8.3: Reducing Type I and Type II Errors

A SAMPLE DISSERTATION

To illustrate this final step in the research process—interpretation of the data—we present excerpts from Kimberly Mitchell's doctoral dissertation in psychology conducted at the University of Rhode Island (K. J. Mitchell, 1998). Mitchell was interested in identifying possible causal factors leading to eating disorders and substance abuse, and she hypothesized that family dynamics and child abuse might be among those factors. She drew on three theoretical perspectives that potentially had relevance to her research question: problem behavior theory, social cognitive theory, and the theory of cognitive adaptation. She administered several surveys to a large sample of undergraduate students and obtained a large body of correlational data about the students' childhoods, eating habits, drug use, and so on. She then used _structural equation modeling_ (described briefly in Table 8.5) as a means of revealing possible—we must emphasize the word _possible_—cause-and-effect relationships in her data set.

The excerpts refer to several psychological theories and concepts with which many of our readers may not be familiar. Nevertheless, as you read the excerpts, you should be able to see how the author frequently moves back and forth between her results and the broader theoretical framework. We pick up the dissertation at the point where Mitchell begins to summarize and interpret her results.

DISSERTATION ANALYSIS 5

DISCUSSION

<u>Summary of Results and Integration</u>

The purpose of this study was to integrate several theories that are beneficial for understanding health-risk behaviors. Problem Behavior Theory (Jessor, 1987), Social Cognitive Theory . . . (Bandura, 1977a), and the Theory of Cognitive Adaptation (Taylor, 1983) are similar in that they all pose a cognitive component within the individual that is crucial to overcome the potential negative consequences of life stressors. . . . This study supports these three theories, as well as previous research in the field. It extends the research by linking these theories into a single comprehensible framework for understanding the link between the childhood stressors of sexual abuse and negative family functioning and adult substance misuse of alcohol, illicit drugs, and eating.

A series of structural equation models revealed the powerful impact individuals' perceptions of their confidence and their interactions with their environment play on health-risk behavior. The first three models examined various ways childhood stressors (sexual abuse and family functioning) could predict current health-risk behaviors (alcohol use, illicit drug use, and binge eating). Examination of the first three models (Full, Direct, and Mediational) and chi-square difference tests revealed that the mediators (self-efficacy, life satisfaction, and coping) are extremely important in predicting health-risk behaviors. This [finding] supports Jessor's (1987) theory that problem behavior is the result of the interaction of the personality system, perceived environment, and the behavioral system. The personality system is measured by the cognitive mediator constructs; the perceived environment by the family functioning construct; and the behavioral system by the outcome constructs. . . . [T]he socialization an individual encounters throughout childhood through interactions with family members appears to influence both how the individual perceives the self and the environment around him/her. These factors seem to propel individuals to behave in ways that may or may not be risky for their health.

Furthermore, Jessor (1987) suggests that problem behaviors in which adolescents engage are interrelated and co-vary. Donovan and Jessor (1985) suggest that diverse problem behavior, such as alcohol abuse, risky sexual behavior, and drug use, constitute a single behavioral syndrome. The current study supports this notion. All of the structural models revealed a positive relationship between alcohol and drug use, as well as a positive relationship between drug use and binge eating. Although the relationship between alcohol use and binge eating was not found to be significant, they are indirectly related through drug use. Such relationships support the idea that these health-risk behaviors constitute a single behavioral syndrome. Future research with a longitudinal design is needed to see if there is a linear trend among these variables. . . .

[The author continues with a discussion of more specific aspects of her findings and their relevance to the three theoretical frameworks. We pick up her discussion again when she summarizes her conclusions.]

Comments

The author capitalizes the names of the three theories. More often, researchers use lowercase letters when referring to particular theoretical perspectives. Either approach is acceptable as long as the author is consistent.

Notice how the author begins with a "grand conclusion" of sorts, which she supports in subsequent paragraphs. She also explains how she has expanded on existing theories by integrating them to explain the phenomenon she has studied.

The "models" she refers to here are multivariable flowcharts that reflect how some variables may influence other variables, perhaps directly or perhaps indirectly through additional, mediator variables.

Self-efficacy refers to people's confidence in their ability to perform a task (e.g., resist the temptation to abuse alcohol) successfully. It is a central concept in Bandura's social cognitive theory, one of the three theoretical frameworks on which the author bases her study.

Notice how the author continually connects her findings with the theoretical frameworks she is using.

Here the author points out both what she has found and what she has not found.

Summary of Conclusions

There are several conclusions that can be drawn from this study. First, in support of Problem Behavior Theory (Jessor, 1987), health-risk behaviors may be part of a single behavioral syndrome. The consistent relationships found throughout the models between alcohol use and drug use, as well as [between] drug use and binge eating, reveal the presence of a higher order behavioral syndrome.

Second, there is a complex relationship between child sexual abuse and family functioning in terms of their ability to predict life satisfaction, coping, and self-efficacy. While child sexual abuse was found to significantly predict coping and life satisfaction, the inclusion of family functioning into the model made these paths disappear. The initial finding indicates a confounding of child sexual abuse and family functioning rather than sexual abuse itself. Furthermore, the constant relationship between child sexual abuse and family functioning shows that, although child sexual abuse does not directly predict the mediator constructs, it plays a role in the prediction indirectly.

Third, family functioning and cognitive mediators interact in specific and consistent ways to determine health-risk behaviors. Those students with high levels of family functioning are likely to have high life satisfaction, more effective coping strategies, and higher self-efficacy [related to] alcohol use, drug use, and eating. In turn, these cognitive factors interact to predict health-risk behavior.

[The author continues with additional conclusions, and then turns to the limitations of her study.]

Study Limitations

The present study offers several important findings to the literature. Yet there are some limitations to the study as well. First, the design was cross-sectional rather than longitudinal. Structural equation modeling is a multivariate technique that is well utilized with longitudinal data (Maruyama, 1998). By incorporating longitudinal data into the overall design, one can begin to establish causality in the results. The use of cross-sectional data with this sample does not allow the researcher to make causal statements about the findings. For example, the data cannot tell us whether self-efficacy for alcohol use comes before actual alcohol use or vice versa. Furthermore, the study asks the participant to answer a portion of the survey retrospectively, such as [is true for] the child sexual abuse and family functioning items. This brings up problems with how reliable the responses are due to the length of time that has passed between the incident(s) in question and the time of the study. . . .

A second limitation to this study is the nature of the sample itself. Although the sample size is excellent (n=469), there were disproportionate numbers of men and women (125 and 344, respectively). Furthermore, the sample was extremely homogeneous (87% White; 91% freshman or sophomore; 74% with family income over $35,000; and 73% Catholic or Protestant). This degree of similarity among participants limits the generalizability of the study results to other populations. Yet the results are still important because this is a population at high risk for alcohol use, drug use, and bulimia-related binge eating.

Another limitation to this study is the lack of response to the probing sexual abuse questions. Approximately one half of the 91 students who reported sexual abuse did

Although the author has previously presented each of her conclusions, she summarizes them all here. Such a summary is typical of lengthy research reports. It is quite helpful to readers, who might easily lose track of some important conclusions as they read earlier portions of a report.

The author makes the point that two of her independent (predictor) variables, child sexual abuse and family functioning, are highly interrelated. Their strong correlation is reflected in the models identified through her structural equation modeling procedures.

The author's use of the term cross-sectional *is somewhat different from our use of it in Chapter 8. She simply means that she collected all data from her sample at one time, rather than following the sample over a lengthy period and collecting data at two or more times. As the author states, a longitudinal design would have better enabled her to identify important factors that preceded—and so may have had a causal effect on—other factors.*

The author points out a problem with using surveys to learn about people's prior life experiences: Human memory is not always accurate. Her use of the word reliable *here refers to accuracy and dependability (i.e., validity) of the results, rather than to reliability as we have previously defined the term.*

The author explains ways in which her sample was not completely representative of the overall population of older adolescents and young adults but also makes a good case for the value of studying this sample.

not respond to the in-depth questions regarding the abuse experience(s) (e.g., degree of trust with perpetrator, frequency of abuse). This could be due to the nature of the survey itself or [to] the environment in which students filled out the survey. In terms of the nature of the survey, once students responded to the overall sexual abuse questions geared to determine whether they were abuse survivors or not, they were instructed to skip the next five questions if their responses to the previous seven questions were all "Never." It is possible that students who did not respond "Never" to the seven questions skipped the follow-up questions anyway in a desire to finish the survey quickly. The second possibility for the lack of response is the environment in which students took the survey. Students were asked to sign up for a designated one-hour time slot to participate in the study. It is highly likely that students signed up for the same time slots as their friends in class and subsequently sat next to each other while filling out the survey. Due to the close proximity and the sensitive nature of the questions, some sexual abuse survivors may not have wanted to fill out additional questions in fear that their friends might see. Better procedures in the future would be to have all students fill out all questions, whether they are abuse survivors or not, and/or to allow them to have more privacy while taking the survey....

A final limitation of the study is the use of self-report data only. Self-report data may be fraught with problems derived from memory restrictions and perception differences. A more comprehensive design would include actual physical ways to measure the outcome variables. For example, the researcher could have strengthened the design by taking blood or urine samples to examine drug use. The problem here is that [the latter] method requires a great deal of time and money to undertake.

[The researcher concludes the discussion by talking about potential implications of her findings for clinical practice and social policy.]

Note: Excerpt is from *Childhood Sexual Abuse and Family Functioning Linked With Eating and Substance Misuse: Mediated Structural Models* (pp. 92–94, 114–119) by K. J. Mitchell, 1998, unpublished doctoral dissertation, University of Rhode Island, Kingston. Reprinted with permission.

The author identifies gaps (missing data) in her survey data and suggests plausible explanations for them. At the end of the paragraph, she offers suggestions for how future research might minimize such gaps.

By perception differences, *the author is presumably referring to how different participants may have interpreted their prior experiences and/or items on the survey. An additional weakness of self-report data is that some participants may have intentionally misrepresented their prior experiences and/or current behaviors.*

In this chapter and the two preceding ones, we have focused on quantitative approaches to addressing research problems. In the next three chapters, we turn our attention to the very different methodologies and data analysis procedures that qualitative approaches might involve. Then, in Chapter 12, we explore how quantitative and qualitative approaches might be combined in *mixed-methods* research.

FOR FURTHER READING

Agresti, A., & Franklin, C. A. (2013). *Statistics: The art and science of learning from data* (3rd ed.). Upper Saddle River, NJ: Pearson.

Arthur, W., Jr., Bennett, W., Jr., & Huffcutt, A. I. (2001). *Conducting meta-analysis using SAS.* Mahwah, NJ: Erlbaum.

Azen, R., & Walker, C. M. (2011). *Categorical data analysis for the behavioral and social sciences.* New York: Routledge.

Borgatti, S. P., Everett, M. G., & Johnson, J. C. (2013). *Analyzing social networks.* London: Sage.

Cumming, G. (2011). *Understanding the new statistics: Effect sizes, confidence intervals, and meta-analysis.* New York: Routledge.

Coladarci, T., Cobb, C. D., Minium, E. W., & Clarke, R. C. (2011). *Fundamentals of statistical reasoning in education* (3rd ed.). New York: Wiley.

Coolidge, F. L. (2013). *Statistics: A gentle introduction* (3rd ed.). Thousand Oaks, CA: Sage.

Cooper, H. (2009). *Research synthesis and meta-analysis: A step-by-step approach* (4th ed.). Thousand Oaks, CA: Sage.

Cumming, G., & Finch, S. (2005). Inference by eye: Confidence intervals and how to read pictures of data. *American Psychologist, 60,* 170–180.

Fennessey, J. (1968). The general linear model: A new perspective on some familiar topics. *American Journal of Sociology, 74,* 1–27.

Fidler, F., & Cumming, G. (2013). Effect size estimation and confidence intervals. In J. A. Schinka & W. F. Velicer (Eds.), *Handbook of psychology: Vol. 2. Research methods in psychology* (2nd ed., pp. 142–163). Hoboken, NJ: Wiley.

Field, A. (2013). *Discovering statistics using IBM SPSS statistics* (4th ed.). Thousand Oaks, CA: Sage.

Fowler, F. J., Jr. (2008). *Survey research methods* (4th ed.). Thousand Oaks, CA: Sage. [See Chapter 10.]

Gonzalez, R. (2009). *Data analysis for experimental design.* New York: Guilford Press.

Gravetter, F. J., & Wallnau, L. B. (2011). *Essentials of statistics for the behavioral sciences* (7th ed.). Belmont, CA: Wadsworth/Cengage.

Grissom, R. J., & Kim, J. J. (2012). *Effect sizes for research: Univariate and multivariate applications* (2nd ed.). New York: Routledge.

Hayes, A. F. (2013). *Introduction to mediation, moderation, and conditional process analysis.* New York: Guilford Press.

Heiman, G. W. (2014). *Basic statistics for the behavioral sciences* (7th ed.). Boston: Cengage.

Hunter, J. E., & Schmidt, F. L. (2004). *Methods of meta-analysis: Correcting error and bias in research findings.* Thousand Oaks, CA: Sage.

Jose, P. E. (2013). *Doing statistical mediation and moderation.* New York: Guilford Press.

Kirk, R. E. (2008). *Statistics: An introduction* (5th ed.). Belmont, CA: Wadsworth/Cengage.

Kline, R. B. (2010). *Principles and practice of structural equation modeling* (3rd ed.). New York: Guilford Press.

Kranzler, J. H. (2011). *Statistics for the terrified* (5th ed.). Upper Saddle River, NJ: Pearson.

Kraska-Miller, M. (2013). *Nonparametric statistics for social and behavioral sciences.* New York: Routledge.

Lind, D. A., Marchal, W. G., & Wathen, S. A. (2013). *Basic statistics for business and economics* (8th ed.). New York: McGraw-Hill.

Montgomery, D. C. (2013). *Design and analysis of experiments* (8th ed.). New York: Wiley.

Phillemer, D. B. (1994). One- versus two-tailed hypothesis tests in contemporary educational research. *Educational Researcher, 20*(9), 13–17.

Phillips, J. L., Jr. (2000). *How to think about statistics* (6th ed.). New York: Henry Holt.

Prell, C. (2012). *Social network analysis: History, theory, and methodology.* London: Sage.

Rosner, B. (2011). *Fundamentals of biostatistics* (7th ed.). Monterey, CA: Brooks/Cole/Cengage.

Rowntree, D. (2004). *Statistics without tears: A primer for non-mathematicians.* Boston: Pearson.

Silver, N. (2012). *The signal and the noise: Why so many predictions fail— But some don't?* New York: Penguin.

Singer, J. D., & Willett, J. B. (2003). *Applied longitudinal data analysis: Modeling change and event occurrence.* Oxford, England: Oxford University Press.

Sweet, S. A., & Grace-Martin, K. (2012). *Data analysis with SPSS: A first course in applied statistics* (4th ed.). Upper Saddle River, NJ: Pearson.

Terrell, S. R. (2012). *Statistics translated: A step-by-step guide to analyzing and interpreting data.* New York: Guilford Press.

Thompson, B. (2008). *Foundations of behavioral statistics.* New York: Guilford Press.

Vogt, W. P., & Johnson, R. B. (2011). *Dictionary of statistics and methodology: A nontechnical guide for the social sciences* (4th ed.). Thousand Oaks, CA: Sage.

Wheelan, C. (2013). *Naked statistics: Stripping the dread from the data.* New York: Norton.

Wood, P. (2000). Meta-analysis. In G. M. Breakwell, S. Hammond, & C. Fife-Schaw (Eds.), *Research methods in psychology* (2nd ed., pp. 414–425). Thousand Oaks, CA: Sage.

Chapter
9

Qualitative Research Methods

To answer some research questions, we cannot skim across the surface. We must dig deep to get a complete understanding of the phenomenon we are studying. In qualitative research, we indeed dig deep: We collect various forms of data and examine them from various angles to construct a rich and meaningful picture of a complex, multifaceted situation.

Learning Outcomes

9.1 Identify several situations in which a qualitative methodology might be especially useful.

9.2 Describe general characteristics and purposes of (a) case studies, (b) ethnographies, (c) phenomenological studies, (d) grounded theory studies, and (e) content analyses. Also, describe effective strategies you might use in each of these five research methodologies.

9.3 Identify effective strategies for collecting data in a qualitative study. As you do so, explain how you can address issues related to (a) validity and reliability, (b) sampling, (c) making observations, and (d) conducting interviews.

9.4 Describe several general criteria that are often used in evaluating qualitative studies.

The term **qualitative research** encompasses a number of methodologies that are in some respects quite different from one another. Yet all qualitative approaches have two things in common. First, they typically focus on phenomena that are occurring or have previously occurred in natural settings—that is, in the "real world." And second, they involve capturing and studying the complexity of those phenomena. Qualitative researchers rarely try to simplify what they observe. Instead, they recognize that the issue they are studying has many dimensions and layers, and they try to portray it in its multifaceted form.

Qualitative research can be found in many academic disciplines, including anthropology, sociology, psychology, biology, history, political science, education, and medicine. In fact, it could be argued that inquiry in *any* discipline begins in a qualitative form (e.g., Lauer & Asher, 1988). When little information exists on a topic, when variables are unknown, when a relevant theory base is inadequate or missing, a qualitative study can help define what is important—that is, *what needs to be studied.* For example, the field of medicine makes extensive use of qualitative methods when unique or puzzling cases are first observed. Biologists' efforts to classify newly observed species, create taxonomies, and describe the social behaviors of primates and certain other animal species are largely qualitative efforts. Many analyses of historical data are almost entirely qualitative. And social scientists often look subjectively for patterns in the complex phenomena they observe, sometimes using qualitative methods exclusively and sometimes combining qualitative and quantitative methods into a *mixed-methods design* (details to follow in Chapter 12).

In this chapter we give you a general idea of what qualitative research is and what it strives to accomplish, with a particular focus on studies of human beings and their creations. Included in the chapter are descriptions of five kinds of qualitative studies: case studies, ethnographies, phenomenological studies, grounded theory studies, and content analyses. We describe a sixth kind, historical research, in Chapter 10.

As you proceed through the chapter, you will find several strategies—sampling, making observations, interviewing—that you previously encountered in the discussion of descriptive quantitative studies in Chapter 6. These are old news, you might think. On the contrary, such strategies can take on very different forms when we want them to yield qualitative data.

Qualitative research can be quite different from quantitative research in another important way as well. In discussions of quantitative designs and strategies in the preceding three chapters, we imply—intentionally—that data collection comes first, with data analysis to follow in a separate step. In qualitative research, however, the methodology often involves an *iterative process* in which the researcher moves back and forth between data collection and data analysis in what is sometimes called the constant comparative method. For example, the researcher might (a) collect some preliminary data in a natural setting; (b) inspect the data for possible patterns; (c) return to the setting to collect additional data that might substantiate, clarify, or contradict those patterns; and (d) conduct a more thorough, detailed analysis of the data—possibly repeating Steps c and d through additional iterations. Accordingly, if you are planning a qualitative study you should read both this chapter *and* the discussion of qualitative data analysis in Chapter 11 before beginning data collection.

RESEARCH PROBLEMS AND METHODOLOGY CHOICE IN QUALITATIVE RESEARCH

In Chapter 2 we emphasized the importance of pinning down the research problem with utmost precision. We sometimes find an exception in qualitative research. Some qualitative researchers often formulate only general research problems and ask only general questions about the phenomenon they are studying. For example, they might ask, "What is the nature of the culture of people living in Samoa?" or "What is it like to live with someone who has Alzheimer's disease?" Such research problems and questions don't remain so loosely defined, however. As a study proceeds, the qualitative researcher gains increasing understanding of the phenomenon under investigation and thus becomes increasingly able to ask more specific questions—and occasionally can begin to formulate and test specific hypotheses as well.

When qualitative researchers ask only open-ended research questions at the beginning of an investigation, they may have trouble identifying—at the outset—the exact methods they will use. Initially, they may select only a general approach suitable for their purpose, perhaps choosing a case study, ethnography, or content analysis. As they learn more about what they are studying and can therefore ask more specific questions, so, too, can they better specify what strategies they will use to answer those questions.

In some instances, then, the methodology of a qualitative study may continue to evolve over the course of the investigation. Despite this fact, we must emphasize that *qualitative research requires considerable preparation and planning.* Qualitative researchers must be well trained in observation techniques, interview strategies, and whatever other data collection methods are likely to be necessary to address their research problem. They must have a firm grasp of previous research related to the problem so that they know what to look for and can separate important information from unimportant details in what they observe (some grounded theory studies are exceptions, for reasons you will discover shortly). And they must be adept at wading through huge amounts of data and finding a meaningful order in what, to someone else, might appear to be chaos. For these reasons, a qualitative study can be a challenging task indeed. It is definitely *not* the approach to take if you're looking for quick results and easy answers.

Potential Advantages of a Qualitative Approach

Qualitative research studies typically serve one or more of the following purposes:

- *Exploration.* They can help you gain initial insights into what has previously been a little-studied topic or phenomenon.
- *Multifaceted description.* They can reveal the complex, possibly multilayered nature of certain situations, settings, processes, relationships, systems, or people.
- *Verification.* They allow you to test the validity of certain assumptions, claims, theories, or generalizations within real-world contexts.
- *Theory development.* They can enable you to develop new concepts or theoretical perspectives related to a phenomenon.
- *Problem identification.* They can help you uncover key problems, obstacles, or enigmas that exist within the phenomenon.
- *Evaluation.* They provide a means through which you can judge the effectiveness of particular policies, practices, or innovations.

As a general rule, however, qualitative studies do *not* allow you to identify cause-and-effect relationships—to answer questions such as *What caused what?* or *Why did such-and-such happen?* You will need quantitative research, especially experimental studies, to answer questions of this kind.

QUALITATIVE RESEARCH DESIGNS

In this section, we describe five commonly used qualitative research designs. We give you enough information to help you determine whether one of these approaches might be suitable for your research question, and we briefly describe the specific nature of each methodology. Later in the chapter, we discuss data collection strategies that are more broadly applicable to qualitative research. But our space is limited here. Should you choose to conduct a qualitative study, we urge you to take advantage of the resources listed in the "For Further Reading" section at the end of the chapter.

Remember, too, that of all the designs we describe in this book, qualitative research methods are the least prescriptive. There are no magic formulas, no cookbook recipes for conducting a qualitative study. This book, as well as any others you may read, can give you only general guidelines based on the experiences of those qualitative researchers who have gone before you. In a qualitative study, the specific methods you use will ultimately be constrained only by the limits of your imagination.

Case Study

In a case study—sometimes called *idiographic research*—a particular individual, program, or event is studied in depth for a defined period of time. For example, a medical researcher might study the nature, course, and treatment of a rare illness for a particular patient. An educator might study and analyze the instructional strategies that a master teacher uses to teach high school history. A political scientist might study the origins and development of a politician's campaign as he or she runs for public office. Case studies are common not only in medicine, education, and political science, but also in law, psychology, sociology, and anthropology.

Sometimes researchers focus on a single case, perhaps because its unique or exceptional qualities can promote understanding or inform practice for similar situations. At other times researchers study two or more cases—often cases that are either similar or different in certain key ways—to make comparisons, build theory, or propose generalizations; such an approach is called a *multiple* or *collective* case study.

In a typical case study, a researcher collects extensive data on the individual(s), program(s), or event(s) on which the investigation is focused. These data often include observations, interviews, documents (e.g., newspaper articles), past records (e.g., previous test scores), and audiovisual materials (e.g., photographs, videotapes, audiotapes). In many case studies, the researcher spends an extended period of time on site and regularly interacts with the person or people being studied. The researcher also records details about the context surrounding the case or cases of focus, including information about the physical environment and any historical, economic, and social factors that have bearing on the situation. By portraying such contexts, the researcher helps others who later read the research report to draw conclusions about the extent to which the study's findings might be generalizable to other situations.

A case study may be especially suitable for learning more about a little known or poorly understood situation. It can also be appropriate for investigating how an individual or program changes over time, perhaps as the result of certain conditions or interventions. In either circumstance, it tends to be most useful for generating or providing preliminary support for one or more hypotheses regarding the phenomenon being investigated. Its major limitation is that, especially when only a single case is involved, we cannot be sure that the findings are generalizable to other situations.

Ethnography

In a case study, a researcher looks in considerable depth at a particular person, program, or event. In contrast, in an ethnography, a researcher looks in depth at an *entire group*—more specifically, a group that shares a common culture. (The word *ethnography* comes from *ethnos,* Greek for "a nation or other close-knit group of people," and *graph,* "something written or recorded.") The ethnographic researcher studies a group in its natural setting for a lengthy time period, often several months or several years. The focus of investigation is on the everyday behaviors of the people in the group (e.g., interactions, language, rituals), with an intent to identify cultural norms, beliefs, social structures, and other patterns. Ideally, the ethnographic researcher identifies not only explicit cultural patterns—those readily acknowledged by group members or easily observable in objects or behaviors—but also *implicit* patterns—those beliefs and assumptions that have such a below-the-surface, taken-for-granted quality that even group members aren't always consciously aware of them.

Ethnographies were first used in cultural anthropology, but they are now seen in sociology, psychology, education, and marketing research as well. The conception of the type of "culture" that can be studied has also changed over time: Whereas ethnographies once focused on long-standing cultural groups (e.g., people living on the island of Samoa), more recently they have been used to study such "cultures" as those of adult work environments, elementary school classrooms, exclusive social cliques in adolescence, violence-prone adolescent groups, and Internet-based communities[1] (e.g., Bender, 2001; Kozinets, 2010; McGibbon, Peter, & Gallop, 2010; Mehan, 1979; Merten, 2011).

The group chosen for in-depth study should, of course, be appropriate for answering a researcher's general research problem or question. Ideally, it should also be one in which the researcher is a "stranger" and has no vested interest in the study's outcome. A group that the researcher knows well (perhaps one that involves close acquaintances) might be more accessible and convenient, but by being so close to the situation, the researcher may have trouble looking at it with sufficient detachment to gain a balanced perspective and portray an accurate picture of the processes observed (Creswell, 2013).

Site-based fieldwork is the *sine qua non*—the essence—of any ethnography. Prolonged engagement in a group's natural setting gives ethnographic researchers time to observe and record processes that would be almost impossible to learn about by using any other approach. Thus, an essential first step in an ethnographic study is to gain legitimate access to the site. Often researchers must go through a gatekeeper, a person who can smooth the way for their entrance into the situation. This individual might be a tribal chief in a community in a developing country, a principal or teacher in a school or classroom, or a program director at a homeless shelter. Then, after gaining entry into the site, researchers must establish rapport with and gain the trust

---

[1]See Kraut and colleagues (2004) for a good discussion of the research possibilities, potential pitfalls, and ethical issues related to studying people's postings on the Internet.

of the people being studied. At the same time, they must be open about why they are there. The principle of *informed consent* described in Chapter 4 is just as essential in an ethnography as it is in any other type of research.

Initially, researchers cast a broad net, intermingling with everyone and getting an overall sense of the social and cultural context. Gradually, they identify key informants who can provide information and insights relevant to their research question and can facilitate contacts with other helpful individuals.

In some ethnographic studies, researchers engage in participant observation, becoming immersed in the daily life of the people. In fact, over the course of the study, their role may gradually change from "outsider" to "insider." The advantage here is that they might gain insights about the group and its behaviors that could not be obtained in any other way. The disadvantage is that they may become so emotionally involved as to lose the ability to assess the situation accurately. In some situations, they may even "go native," joining the group and therefore becoming unable to complete the study (Creswell, 2013).

Throughout their fieldwork, ethnographic researchers are careful observers, interviewers, and listeners. Furthermore, they take extensive field notes (written either on site at the time or in private later in the day) in the forms of dialogues, diagrams, maps, and other written materials. Lengthy conversations and significant events can be recorded using audiotapes and videotapes. Researchers may also collect artifacts (e.g., tools, ritualistic implements, artistic creations) and records (e.g., accounting ledgers, personal journals, lesson plans) from the group. In order to test hypotheses about a group's unconsciously shared beliefs or assumptions, some ethnographic researchers occasionally conduct *breaching experiments*—that is, they intentionally behave in ways they suspect might violate an unspoken social rule—and observe people's reactions (Mehan & Wood, 1975).

We must caution you that conducting a good ethnography requires both considerable patience and considerable tolerance. One experienced ethnographer has described the process this way:

> It requires a great patience under any circumstances for me to "sit and visit." A rather inevitable consequence of being inquisitive without being a talker is that my conversational queries usually prompt others to do the talking. During fieldwork, I make a conscious effort to be sociable, thus providing opportunities for people to talk to me. . . . I never confront informants with contradictions, blatant disbelief, or shock, but I do not mind presenting myself as a bit dense, someone who does not catch on too quickly and has to have things explained. . . . (Wolcott, 1994, p. 348)

An ethnography is especially useful for gaining an understanding of the complexities of a particular sociocultural group. It allows considerable flexibility in the methods used to obtain information, which can be either an advantage (to an experienced researcher who knows what to look for) or a disadvantage (to a novice who may be overwhelmed and distracted by unimportant details). Hence, if you decide that an ethnography is the approach most suitable for your research problem, we urge you to get a solid grounding in cultural anthropology before you venture into the field (Creswell, 2013).

Phenomenological Study

In its broadest sense, the term *phenomenology* refers to a person's perception of the meaning of an event, as opposed to the event as it exists external to the person. A phenomenological study is a study that attempts to understand people's perceptions and perspectives relative to a particular situation. In other words, a phenomenological study tries to answer the question *What is it like to experience such-and-such?* For instance, a researcher might study the experiences of people caring for a chronically or terminally ill relative, living in an abusive relationship, or home-schooling a child.

In some cases, the researcher has had personal experience related to the phenomenon in question and wants to gain a better understanding of the experiences of others. By looking at multiple perspectives on the same situation, the researcher can then make some generalizations of *what something is like* from an insider's perspective.

Phenomenological researchers depend almost exclusively on lengthy interviews (perhaps 1 to 2 hours in length) with a small, carefully selected sample of participants. A typical sample size is from 5 to 25 individuals, all of whom have had direct experience with the phenomenon being studied.

The actual implementation of a phenomenological study is as much in the hands of the participants as in the hands of the researcher. The phenomenological interview is often a relatively unstructured one in which the researcher and participants work together to "arrive at the heart of the matter" (Tesch, 1994, p. 147). The researcher listens closely as participants describe their everyday experiences related to the phenomenon; the researcher must also be alert for subtle yet meaningful cues in participants' expressions, pauses, questions, and occasional sidetracks. A typical interview looks more like an informal conversation, with the participant doing most of the talking and the researcher doing most of the listening.

Throughout the data collection process, phenomenological researchers try to suspend any preconceived notions or personal experiences that may unduly influence what they "hear" participants saying. Such suspension—sometimes called *bracketing* or *epoché*—can be extremely difficult for researchers who have personally experienced the phenomenon under investigation. Yet it is essential if they are to gain an understanding of the typical experiences that people have had. The ultimate goal of a phenomenological study should be—not only for the researcher but also for readers of the final research report—to provide a sense that "I understand better what it is like for someone to experience that" (Polkinghorne, 1989, p. 46).

Grounded Theory Study

Of all the research designs described in this book, a grounded theory study is the one *least* likely to begin from a particular theoretical framework. On the contrary, the major purpose of a grounded theory approach is to *begin with the data and use them to develop a theory.* The term *grounded* refers to the idea that the theory that emerges from the study is derived from and rooted in data that have been collected in the field rather than taken from the research literature. Grounded theory studies are especially helpful when current theories about a phenomenon are either inadequate or nonexistent.[2]

Typically, a grounded theory study focuses on a *process* related to a particular topic—including people's actions and interactions—with the ultimate goal of developing a theory about the process. The approach has its roots in sociology (Glaser & Strauss, 1967) but is now also used in such fields as anthropology, geography, education, nursing, psychology, and social work. It has been used effectively for a wide range of topics—for instance, to study children's eating habits, college students' thoughts and feelings during classroom discussions, and workers' stress levels in public service agencies (Do & Schallert, 2004; Kime, 2008; Skagert, Dellve, Eklöf, Pousette, & Ahlborg, 2008).

As is true for the qualitative designs previously described, data collection in a grounded theory study is field-based, flexible, and likely to change over the course of the investigation. Interviews typically play a major role in data collection, but observations, documents, historical records, videotapes, and anything else of potential relevance to the research question might also be used. The only restriction is that the data collected *must* include the perspectives and voices of the people being studied (Charmaz, 2002, 2014; Corbin & Strauss, 2008).

More so than in any other qualitative methodology, data analysis in a grounded theory study begins almost immediately, at which point the researcher develops *categories* to classify the data. Subsequent data collection is aimed at *saturating* the categories—in essence, learning as much about them as possible—and at finding any disconfirming evidence that point to possible revisions in the categories identified or in interrelationships among them. The theory that ultimately evolves is one that includes numerous concepts and interrelationships among those concepts; in other words, it has *conceptual density* (Schram, 2006).

Virtually all experts agree that grounded theory researchers should have a firm grasp of general concepts and theoretical orientations in their discipline as a whole; hence, an in-depth literature review early in the process is essential. However, experts disagree about whether researchers should look closely at previous findings *directly related to the present research problem* before collecting

---

[2]Some researchers associate the term *grounded theory* with a particular method of data analysis—in particular, that of Corbin and Strauss (2008; Strauss & Corbin, 1990)—and suggest the term *emergent theory* as a broader, less prescriptive label for this approach (e.g., Jaccard & Jacoby, 2010).

and analyzing data. For example, Glaser (1978) has argued that too much advance knowledge of earlier research regarding a topic may limit a researcher's ability to be open-minded about how to analyze and interpret the data collected. In contrast, many others suggest that the advantages of conducting a relatively thorough literature review outweigh the disadvantages; in particular, previous works and writings about a topic can often help a researcher think more clearly and insightfully about the collected data (e.g., Hesse-Biber, 2010; Jaccard & Jacoby, 2010). Our own advice is to learn as much as you can about your research topic through a thorough review of the related literature but *to refrain from forming specific hypotheses about what you yourself might find.*

Content Analysis

A content analysis is a detailed and systematic examination of the contents of a particular body of material for the purpose of identifying patterns, themes, or biases. Content analyses are typically performed on *forms of human communication,* including books, newspapers, personal journals, legal documents, films, television, art, music, videotapes of human interactions, transcripts of conversations, and Internet blog and bulletin board entries.[3] For example, a researcher might use a content analysis to determine what religious symbols appear in works of art, how middle school science texts portray the nature of science, or what attitudes are reflected in the speeches or newspaper articles of a particular era in history. As you might infer from these examples, content analyses are found in a wide variety of disciplines, including the fine arts, education, history, psychology, journalism, and political science.

Of the five designs described in this chapter, a content analysis is apt to involve the greatest amount of planning at the front end of the project. The researcher typically defines a specific research problem or question at the very beginning (e.g., "Do contemporary children's books reflect traditional gender stereotypes?", "What religious symbols appeared in early Byzantine architecture, and with what frequency, during the years 527–867?"). Furthermore, the researcher takes measures to make the process as objective as possible. The following steps are typical:

1. The researcher identifies the specific body of material to be studied. If this body is relatively small, it is studied in its entirety. If it is quite large (e.g., if it consists of all newspaper articles written during a particular time period), a sample (perhaps a random sample) is selected.
2. The researcher defines the characteristics or qualities to be examined in precise, concrete terms. The researcher may identify specific examples of each characteristic as a way of defining it more clearly.
3. If the material to be analyzed involves complex or lengthy items (e.g., works of literature, transcriptions of conversations), the researcher breaks down each item into small, manageable segments that are analyzed separately.
4. The researcher scrutinizes the material for instances of each characteristic or quality defined in Step 2. When judgments are objective—for instance, when the study involves looking for the appearance of certain words in a text—only one judge, or *rater,* is necessary. When judgments are more subjective—for instance, when the study involves categorizing discrete sections of textbooks as conveying various messages about the nature of science—two or three raters are typically involved, and a composite of their judgments is used.

Content analyses are not necessarily stand-alone designs. For example, a systematic content analysis might be an integral part of the data analysis in a phenomenological study (e.g., see Wennick, Lundqvist, & Hallström, 2009). A content analysis might also be used to flesh out the complex, multidimensional aspects of a descriptive or experimental study, resulting in a *mixed-methods design* with both qualitative and quantitative elements.

Even when a content analysis *is* the sole research methodology, it's apt to have a quantitative component. In many instances, quantification may involve simply counting the frequencies

---

[3]Again, we refer you to Kraut and colleagues (2004) regarding ethical issues related to studying people's postings on the Internet.

with which various characteristics are observed in the body of data being examined. But alternatively, a researcher might conduct one or more statistical analyses on the numbers obtained—for instance, comparing the numbers obtained from two or more distinct subsets of the materials being analyzed (e.g., see Bergman, 2010).

Table 9.1 summarizes the nature of the five designs described in the preceding sections, including a brief description of general data analysis strategies. Keep in mind, however, that the five designs aren't necessarily as distinctly different as the table might indicate. Any particular study may include elements of two or more qualitative designs. Remember, much qualitative research is, by its very nature, somewhat flexible and may continue to evolve over the course of a project. To the extent that your research question leads you to believe that two or more designs are equally relevant to your purpose, think creatively about how you might combine them into a single study.

Such flexibility should *not,* however, lead you to believe that you can conduct a qualitative research project in a sloppy, poorly thought-through manner. On the contrary, the flexible nature of a qualitative study makes it just that much more challenging, especially for a novice researcher. *For anything you do in a qualitative study, you must have a definite rationale and a distinct purpose, and you must keep your overall goal—to answer your research question—clearly in sight at all times.*

TABLE 9.1 ▦ Distinguishing Characteristics of Different Qualitative Designs

Design	Purpose	Focus	Methods of Data Collection	Methods of Data Analysis
Case study	To understand one person or situation (or perhaps a very small number) in great depth	One case or a few cases within its/their natural setting	• Observations • Interviews • Appropriate written documents and/or audiovisual material	• Categorization and interpretation of data in terms of common themes • Synthesis into an overall portrait of the case(s)
Ethnography	To understand how behaviors reflect the culture of a group	A specific field site in which a group of people share a common culture	• Participant observation • Structured or unstructured interviews with "informants" • Artifact/document collection	• Identification of significant phenomena and underlying structures and beliefs • Organization of data into a logical whole (e.g., chronology, typical day)
Phenomenological study	To understand an experience from the participants' points of view	A particular phenomenon as it is typically lived and perceived by human beings	• In-depth, unstructured interviews • Purposeful sampling of 5–25 individuals	• Search for *meaningful concepts* that reflect various aspects of the experience • Integration of those concepts into a seemingly typical experience
Grounded theory study	To derive a theory from data collected in a natural setting	A process, including human actions and interactions and how they result from and influence one another	• Interviews • Any other relevant data sources	• Prescribed and systematic method of coding the data into categories and identifying interrelationships • Continual interweaving of data collection and data analysis • Construction of a theory from the categories and interrelationships
Content analysis	To identify the specific characteristics of a body of material	Any verbal, visual, or behavioral form of communication	• Identification and possible sampling of the specific material to be analyzed • Coding of the material in terms of predetermined and precisely defined characteristics	• Tabulation of the frequency of each characteristic • Descriptive or inferential statistical analyses as needed to answer the research question

CONCEPTUAL ANALYSIS EXERCISE Choosing a Qualitative Research Design

Following are brief summaries of five potential research projects. Identify the qualitative methodology that is probably most appropriate for each project. The answers appear after the "For Further Reading" section at the end of the chapter.

1. In an effort to learn the nature and appeal of long-standing men's social groups, a researcher plans to spend a 9-month period with a local chapter ("lodge") of the Benevolent and Protective Order of Elks. By observing and interacting with the Elks, he hopes to observe the chapter's meetings, rituals, and charitable activities and to discover the chapter's beliefs, values, goals, and interpersonal dynamics.

2. A researcher wants to determine to what degree and in what ways television commercials might portray men and women in traditionally gender-stereotypical ways (e.g., how often men versus women are shown cleaning house, how often men versus women are shown making important business decisions).

3. In order to learn how grassroots political parties emerge and develop over time, a researcher wants to study the origins and evolution of three recently established "Tea Party" groups, one in her own state and two in neighboring states.

4. A researcher is intrigued by Asperger syndrome, a cognitive disability in which people have average or above-average intelligence and language skills but poor social skills and little or no ability to interpret other people's nonverbal social cues (e.g., body language). The researcher wants to find out what it is like to be an adolescent with this syndrome—how a teenager is apt to feel about having few or no friends, being regularly excluded from classmates' social activities, and so on.

5. A researcher wants to determine how doctors, nurses, and other hospital staff members coordinate their actions when people with life-threatening traumatic injuries arrive at the emergency room. The researcher can find very little useful research on this topic in professional journals.

COLLECTING DATA IN QUALITATIVE RESEARCH

As you have seen, qualitative researchers often use multiple forms of data in any single study. They might use observations, interviews, objects, written documents, audiovisual materials, electronic entities (e.g., e-mail messages, Internet websites), and anything else that can help them answer their research question. Potential sources of data are limited only by a researcher's open-mindedness and creativity. For example, in a school setting, a researcher might consider where various students are seated in the lunch room, what announcements are posted on the walls, or what messages are communicated in graffiti (Eisner, 1998). In an ethnographic study of a cultural group, a researcher might ask one or more participants to keep a daily journal or to discuss the content and meaning of photographs and art objects (Creswell, 2013).

While collecting data, many qualitative researchers also begin jotting notes—sometimes called memos—about their initial interpretations of what they are seeing and hearing. Some of these "notes-to-self" might involve emerging themes in people's actions and statements. Others might make note of initial hunches and intuitions to pursue through further observations or interview questions. Still others might be preliminary theories about possible underlying dynamics within a social group.

Many qualitative studies are characterized by an emergent design, in which data collected early in the investigation influence the kinds of data the researcher subsequently gathers. The flexibility of qualitative methodologies is an advantage for experienced researchers but often a disadvantage for novices, who may not have sufficient background or training to determine how best to adjust data collection strategies midway through a study. Thus, many experts suggest that a novice researcher set forth a definite, fairly structured plan for data collection—a strategy that can minimize the degree to which the researcher wanders off into intriguing but ultimately unproductive diversions.

A predetermined, well-thought-out plan is also essential when submitting a qualitative research proposal to an internal review board (IRB). Most importantly, data collection methods must be consistent with the ethical principles presented in Chapter 4. The researcher must take precautions not to expose people (or animals) to unnecessary physical or psychological harm—as could happen, say, if the researcher were to inquire about highly personal and emotionally charged topics. The people being studied must know the nature of the study and be willing participants in it (this is *informed consent*), and any data collected should not be traceable back to particular individuals (thus maintaining participants' *right to privacy*). One common way of keeping personal data confidential is to assign various pseudonyms to different participants and to use those pseudonyms both during data collection and in the final research report.

PRACTICAL APPLICATION Addressing Validity and Reliability Issues in Qualitative Data Collection

As you should recall, Chapter 4 includes a section called "Validity and Reliability in Measurement." Qualitative researchers don't necessarily *measure* things—at least not in the numerical sense of the word. Nevertheless, they must be concerned about both the validity and the reliability of the data they collect. In particular, the data they collect must be both (a) reasonably *accurate* with regard to the characteristics and dynamics of the entities or situation being studied (this is *validity*) and (b) *consistent* in the patterns and dynamics they reflect (this is *reliability*).

A particular strength of qualitative methods is that a perceptive researcher might discern underlying patterns and dynamics in social interactions or cultural artifacts that a standardized, quantitative measurement instrument would never illuminate. In a sense, *the researcher is an instrument* in much the same way that an oscilloscope, questionnaire, or multiple-choice achievement test is an instrument. The potential downside of this instrument—the human mind—is that it can be biased by its preconceived theories and expectations, and such biases can adversely affect the quality of the data obtained.

Qualitative researchers use a variety of strategies to enhance the validity and reliability—and hence the credibility—of the data they collect. Following are five important strategies during the *data collection* phase of a qualitative study (we identify strategies related to *data analysis and interpretation* in Chapter 11):

- *Reflexivity.* Good qualitative researchers actively try to identify personal, social, political, or philosophical biases that are likely to affect their ability to collect and interpret data—this self-reflection is known as reflexivity—and take whatever steps they can to reduce such influences.
- *Triangulation.* Many qualitative researchers use a strategy called triangulation: They collect multiple forms of data related to the same research question, with the goal of finding consistencies or inconsistencies among the data. For example, imagine that a researcher wants to study the behaviors of an especially exclusive group of snobbish but so-called "popular" girls at a public high school. This researcher might not only interview both members and nonmembers of the group but also observe the girls in action in various locations in and around school—for instance, observing seating patterns in the cafeteria, group clusters in the hallways and school yard, and verbal interaction patterns during class sessions. The researcher might also scan school records regarding which students are members (and possibly officers or captains) of various extracurricular clubs and sports teams.
- *Clearly distinguishing between data and memos.* Right from the get-go, a qualitative researcher must keep interpretations separate from actual observations. For example, consider the ethnographic researcher who decides to take only handwritten notes in the field, perhaps as a way of blending in better with the social environment than would be possible with, say, a laptop or video camera. This researcher might draw a vertical line down the

middle of each page, recording observations, interview responses, and any helpful graphics (e.g., maps, diagrams) in the left column and jotting memos about these things in the right column. Only in this way can the researcher separate *fact* (what the researcher is actually seeing and hearing) from what could possibly be *fiction* (what the researcher currently thinks might be going on).

▪ *Seeking of exceptions and contradictory evidence.* By nature, human beings seem to be predisposed to look for and identify patterns and consistencies in their physical worlds (e.g., see Mandler, 2007; Rakison & Oakes, 2003). Furthermore, once they have zeroed in on their conclusions about these patterns and consistencies, they're often reluctant to revise their beliefs (recall the discussion of *confirmation bias* in Figure 1.3 in Chapter 1). A good qualitative researcher actively fights such mental predispositions, in part by continually asking the questions "Might I be wrong?" and "What disconfirming evidence can I find?" and then intentionally seeking out the answers.

▪ *Spending considerable time on site.* Many qualitative studies require extensive data collection in the field; such is true for virtually any ethnography and for many case studies, phenomenological studies, and grounded theory studies. Just a brief visit to the site under investigation—popping in and popping out, as it were—is unlikely to yield the quantity and quality of data (including potentially contradictory observations) essential for drawing accurate, multifaceted understandings of any complex phenomenon.

In planning for data collection, qualitative researchers must also identify one or more appropriate *samples* from which to acquire data. Furthermore, they are apt to rely heavily on *observations* and/or *interviews* as sources of data. We offer suggestions related to each of these three topics in the three Practical Application sections that follow. Some of our suggestions can, in one way or another, enhance the validity and reliability of the data obtained.

PRACTICAL APPLICATION Selecting an Appropriate Sample for a Qualitative Study

Qualitative researchers might draw their data from a variety of sources—not only from people but perhaps also from objects, text materials, and audiovisual and electronic records. The particular entities they select for analysis comprise their sample.

Only rarely—for instance, when a study involves a content analysis of a small number of items—can qualitative researchers look at *everything* that has potential relevance to a research problem. More typically, they must be choosy about the data they gather and analyze and, as a result, will get an incomplete picture of the phenomenon in question. One experienced qualitative researcher has described the situation this way:

> Whether observing, interviewing, experiencing, or pursuing some combination of strategies, you cannot be everywhere at once or take in every possible viewpoint at the same time. Instead . . . you develop certain perspectives by engaging in some activities or talking to certain people rather than others. . . . You build assertions toward the never-quite-attainable goal of "getting it right," approximating realities but not establishing absolutes.
>
> Your task, both derived from and constrained by your presence, is thus inherently interpretive and incomplete. The bottom line is that there is no bottom line: It is not necessary (or feasible) to reach some ultimate truth for your study to be credible and useful. (Schram, 2006, p. 134)

How you identify your sample must depend on the research question(s) you want to answer. If you want to draw inferences about an entire population or body of objects, you must choose a sample that can be presumed to *represent* that population or body. Ideally, this sample is chosen through a completely random selection process or through a process that incorporates appropriate proportions of each subgroup within the overall group of people or objects. For possible ways of choosing such a sample, return to the discussion of probability sampling in Chapter 6. (Remember, truly effective researchers often draw on methodologies from diverse research traditions.)

In other circumstances, however, you might need to be intentionally *non*random in your selection of data sources. In particular, your sampling would be selective, or *purposive:* You would choose those individuals or objects that will yield the most information about the topic under investigation. For example, grounded theory researchers tend to engage in theoretical sampling, choosing data sources that are most likely to help them develop a theory of the process in question. Later, they may employ discriminant sampling, returning to particular data sources that can help them substantiate the theory. (As you should recall from Chapter 6, some descriptive quantitative researchers also engage in purposive sampling.)

A novice qualitative researcher might ask *How large should my sample be? How much is enough?* There are no easy, cut-and-dried answers to these questions, but we offer several suggestions to guide decision making:

- Be sure that the sample includes not only seemingly "typical" but also seemingly "nontypical" examples.
- When a power hierarchy exists—as it does in the workplace and in many clubs and communities—sample participants from various levels in the hierarchy. For example, in the workplace, you might interview both bosses and employees; in a club or community, you might interview not only highly active, influential members but also less involved individuals (e.g., see Becker, 1970).
- Actively look for cases that can potentially discredit emerging hypotheses and theories.
- If appropriate for your research problem, sample from diverse contexts or situations.

Ideally, the sample should provide information not only about how things are *on average* but also about how much *variability* exists in the phenomenon under investigation.

In some instances, a research problem is best addressed by sampling from a large geographical area, perhaps one that includes diverse cultural groups. For example, in a dissertation project involving the experiences of White women who were raising biological children of mixed or other races,[4] doctoral student Jennifer Chandler (2014) wanted to interview mothers from diverse locations across the United States—locations that would differ in demographic makeup and possibly also in attitudes regarding multiracial families. To obtain such a sample, she created an "Invitation to Participate" letter that described the purpose of her study, the characteristics of desired participants, and the general nature of the interviews she would conduct. Many individuals across the country helped her distribute the invitation, including (a) personal friends and colleagues; (b) people she met at several professional conferences; (c) officers in parent-teacher organizations in numerous public school districts (e.g., Los Angeles, Houston, Denver, New York); and (d) people who had contributed to Internet blogs about topics related to interracial parenting. The resulting sample included 30 mothers from towns and cities in more than a dozen states across the country. It was certainly not a random sample, but it helped Chandler capture the diversity in experiences that mothers living in various geographical and cultural settings were likely to have had.

PRACTICAL APPLICATION Making Observations in a Qualitative Study

In the observation studies described in Chapter 6, observations typically have a limited, prespecified focus, and procedures are set in place in advance for quantifying the observations in some way, perhaps with a rating scale. In contrast, observations in a qualitative study are intentionally unstructured and free-flowing: The researcher shifts focus from one thing to another as new and

---

[4]More precisely, the sample included mothers who (a) *identified* themselves as being non-Hispanic White women and (b) *identified* their children as being of mixed or other races. Chandler's capitalization of "White" when referring to a racial group is consistent with APA style (2010).

potentially significant objects and events present themselves. The primary advantage of conducting observations in this manner is flexibility: The researcher can take advantage of unforeseen data sources as they surface. Observations are often recorded in great detail, perhaps with field notes or videotapes that capture the wide variety of ways in which people or other animal species act and interact. From these data, the researcher can construct a complex yet integrated picture of how certain humans or nonhumans spend their time.

Such an approach has its drawbacks, of course. A researcher (especially a novice researcher) won't always know what things are most important to look for, especially at the beginning, and so may waste considerable time observing and recording trivialities while overlooking entities that are more central to the research question. A second disadvantage is that *by his or her very presence,* the researcher may influence what people say and do or may change how significant events unfold (recall the discussion of *reactivity* in Chapter 4).

Recording events can be problematic as well. Written notes are often insufficient to capture the richness of what one is observing. Yet audiotapes and videotapes aren't always completely dependable either. Background noises may make tape-recorded conversations only partially audible. A video camera can capture only the events happening in a small, focused area. And the very presence of tape recorders and video cameras may make some participants uncomfortable.

If you decide to conduct observations as part of a qualitative study, we offer these recommendations:

1. Before you begin your study, experiment with various data recording strategies (field notes, audiotapes, videotapes), identify the particular methods that work best for you, and practice using them in diverse contexts.

2. When you first enter a research site, have someone introduce you to the people you hope to observe. This is the time to briefly describe your study and get potential participants' informed consent.

3. As you observe, remain relatively quiet and inconspicuous, yet be friendly to anyone who approaches you. You certainly don't want to discourage people from developing relationships with you and—perhaps later—taking you into their confidence.

Also remember a strategy alluded to earlier: *Clearly distinguish between your actual observations (data) and your interpretations (memos).* This strategy is important for two reasons. First, you need to be as objective as you can in the records you keep of what might otherwise be only subjective impressions. And second, your interpretations of what you have seen and heard may very well change over the course of the study.

PRACTICAL APPLICATION Planning and Conducting Interviews in a Qualitative Study

Interviews can often yield a rich body of qualitative information. A researcher might ask questions related to any of the following (Silverman, 1993):

- Facts (e.g., biographical information)
- People's beliefs and perspectives about the facts
- Feelings
- Motives
- Present and past behaviors
- Standards for behavior (i.e., what people think *should* be done in certain situations)
- Conscious reasons for actions or feelings (e.g., why people think that engaging in a particular behavior is desirable or undesirable)

Interviews in a qualitative study tend not to be as tightly prescribed and structured as the interviews conducted in a quantitative study. A second difference is the general "feel" of the interview: It tends to be informal and friendly in a qualitative study but more formal and emotionally neutral in a quantitative one. Participants in a qualitative interview may feel as if they're simply engaging in a friendly chat with the researcher, who is often someone they have come to know and trust. In contrast, participants in survey research are continually aware that, yes, this is an interview and that any temporary relationship they've formed with the researcher will end once the interview is complete.

In some cases, a qualitative researcher may want to interview several participants simultaneously in a focus group. To conduct a focus group, the researcher gathers several people (usually no more than 10 or 12) to discuss a particular issue for 1 to 2 hours. A moderator—someone who may or may not be the researcher—introduces the issues to be discussed, makes sure that no one dominates the discussion, and keeps people focused on the topic. Focus groups are especially useful when time is limited, group members feel comfortable sharing their thoughts and feelings with one another, and the group interaction might be more informative than individually conducted interviews (Creswell, 2013; Neuman, 2011).

GUIDELINES   Conducting a Productive Interview

Conducting an informative interview isn't as easy as it might seem. The following suggestions are based partly on our own experiences and partly on guidance offered by experts in qualitative research (Creswell, 2013; Eisner, 1998; Shank, 2006; Silverman, 1993).

1. ***Identify general interview questions and possible follow-up subquestions in advance.*** Some experienced qualitative researchers are quite skillful at conducting open-ended, unstructured interviews. As a result, they can gain intriguing information and perspectives they hadn't planned to ask for. However, a major disadvantage of an unstructured interview is that a researcher might ask different questions of different participants and thus may not be able to make cross-participant comparisons. Furthermore, the researcher must be alert to instances when a conversation is drifting in an unproductive direction and gently guide it back on course.

Novice researchers typically have greater success when they prepare their general interview questions in advance, along with possible follow-up questions that probe for details, and make sure that all questions are addressed at some point during the interview. Such planning increases the odds that a researcher can compare the responses of different participants in the event that certain comparisons are desired. Furthermore, IRB approval of a research project may in some instances require that questions be explicitly laid out in the initial research proposal.

Obviously, interview questions should be related to the research questions and overall research problem. As an example, in a qualitative study she conducted for her doctoral dissertation, Debby Zambo examined how children with reading disabilities believe their minds work when they read. She worked with and extensively studied 11 children in grades 5 through 9, interviewing them 10 to 15 times over the course of her investigation. Figure 9.1 presents an excerpt from her dissertation, in which she showed how her interview questions aligned with her research questions.

For any single interview, limit your list of questions to a small number, perhaps five to seven of them. (Although Debby Zambo had many more questions than this, she spread them throughout a dozen or so interviews with each child.) You will find that you won't necessarily need to ask every question explicitly, as the answers to some may emerge while a participant is responding to others.

Ideally, interview questions encourage people to talk about a topic *without* hinting that they should give a *particular* answer. In other words, avoid leading questions. Questions such as "What is going on now?" "What is it like to work here?" and "What's a typical day like?" can stimulate an informative conversation without suggesting that one kind of response is somehow more desirable than another (Shank, 2006).

2. ***Consider how participants' cultural backgrounds might influence their responses.*** In an effort to ascertain men's beliefs about ideal family size for a research project in what is now Bangladesh, Howard Schuman (1967) asked a seemingly simple question: "Suppose you had no

FIGURE 9.1 ■

Example of How a
Researcher Might Align
Interview Questions with
Research Questions

Source: From *Uncovering the
Conceptual Representations
of Students With Reading
Disabilities* (pp. 140–142) by
D. Zambo, 2003, unpublished
doctoral dissertation, Arizona
State University, Tempe. Re-
printed with permission.

Research Question	Interview Question
1. What do students with reading disabilities think about reading and themselves? a. What are their thoughts about reading?	What do they think reading is all about? What do they find easy/difficult to read? Who do they think good/poor readers are and what do good/poor readers do? How [does a person] become good/poor at reading?
b. What are their ideas about themselves and reading?	What are they reading? What do they think is easy/difficult to read? What goes on in their head when they read easy/difficult things? What is their activity level (calm/fidgety) when they read? What body parts do they use when they read? How do they think reading [has impacted or will] impact their lives in the past, present, and future?
2. What emotions are evoked when they read?	Do they get frustrated when they read? What other emotions may be involved when they read? Does believing they can get better at reading help them be a better reader? Does hoping they can get better at reading help them be a better reader? Does wishing they can get better at reading help them be a better reader?
3. What do children with reading difficulties know about the cognitive processes of reading? a. What do they know about attention?	What is attention? Do they recognize that they must focus their attention when they read? What do they focus on? Why do they focus on that? Do they have difficulty with attention? If so, what do they do? Is their attention easy or difficult to capture when they read? Can they sustain their attention enough when they read? What do they do to sustain their attention? How consistent is their attention? What do they do to make their attention consistent? Is their attention better on some days and when is it better? What do they do if their attention is better on some days? What distracts them when they read? Do ideas and memories pop into their heads and distract them when they read?
b. What do they know about their memory and reading?	What do they know about memory in general? What do they do to put things into their memory? What do they do to keep things in their memory? How do they remember what they read? How do they remember/understand what they have read?

(continued)

FIGURE 9.1 ■
Continued

Research Question	Interview Question
4. What do students with dyslexia know about the brain and reading?	Do they understand the brain is interconnected with external body parts? Analogy—Can they create an analogy for the brain? Metacognition—Thinking About Thinking—What do they wonder about their mind/brain? [What do they] think about their thinking? Can they differentiate mental entities (thoughts, dreams, and memories) from close imposters?
5. What do children with dyslexia know about their dyslexic mind?	How do their brains work when they read? Are their brains like or different [from] others' brains when they read? Do they listen/see/feel things in their brains when they read? How do they do this? Do they think their minds are active when they read? What happens in their minds when they read? What do they do to make this happen? Are they aware of what is in their minds as they read? Are their minds excited when they read? How do things get from a book to their brains?

children. How many would you like to have?" Most men responded, "As many as God wills." This response reflected a widespread cultural tradition at the time: to leave one's fate in the hands of God, or at least to *say* that one's fate is in God's hands. Wisely, Schuman revised the question: "Suppose you had no children. If God wished to give you as many children as you wished, how many would you wish for?" (p. 22). This revision yielded responses that were far more useful in addressing Schuman's research question.

As Schuman discovered, participants' cultural backgrounds can influence their interview responses in ways you haven't necessarily anticipated. For instance, if you are interviewing people from Asian cultures, you should be aware that they are less likely to brag about their individual accomplishments than Westerners are (Heine, 2007). A naive researcher might erroneously conclude that Asian individuals are less productive than Western individuals, when in reality Asian individuals are merely less *boastful* than their Western counterparts. On average, people from Asian cultures also tend to be more tentative in expressing their opinions than is true for Westerners—for example, they might begin a sentence by saying "I'm not sure, but perhaps . . ."—and they aren't as likely to reveal their emotions during conversations (Morelli & Rothbaum, 2007; Ward, Bochner, & Furnham, 2001).

Various cultural groups differ, too, in their general verbal interaction patterns—for instance, in how talkative and assertive they are and in how much physical distance *(personal space)* they prefer when conversing with another person (e.g., see Tyler et al., 2008; Ward et al., 2001). Given such diversity across cultural groups—and often among certain subgroups of a cultural group—we can give you only general, nonprescriptive advice here: Be sensitive to the fact that culture may play a significant role in how your participants interpret and respond to your questions, and experiment with multiple ways of asking for the kinds of information you ultimately want to obtain.

3. *Make sure your sample includes people who will give you the kinds of information you are seeking.*   You should, of course, choose people whom you expect to give you typical perceptions and perspectives. But as noted in the earlier discussion of sampling, you may also intentionally pick a few "extremists" or other exceptional individuals who might give you unique insights related to your research problem. When you do so, however, you should identify them as such in your notes.

4. *Find a suitable location.*   In theory, you can conduct an interview anywhere that people are willing to talk to you. But you will probably have a more successful interview if you find a quiet place where you and your interviewee are unlikely to be distracted or interrupted.

5. *Get written permission.* Explain the nature of the study and your plans for using the results. Ask the participant (or, in the case of a child, the participant's parent or legal guardian) to sign an informed consent form. Offer to provide an abstract or copy of the research report once you have completed the study.

6. *Establish and maintain rapport.* Begin the conversation with small talk that can break the ice. Be courteous and respectful at all times. Show genuine interest in what the person has to say. Ideally, you should try to motivate people to *want* to participate in your study. For example, in a dissertation research project with Chinese mothers who had immigrated to the United States, doctoral student Christy Leung and her research team began interviews by following this general script:

> As you know, we are doing this project because we really want to help Chinese families succeed in the U.S., and to have the children be happy and successful. So, we are trying to learn from the different experiences of the families, in order to find patterns of things that can help the transition, and also things that can be negative for the transition and ways to avoid those negative things. That is why we really appreciate your participation and sharing.
>
> After we started this project, we also found that there are aspects of the families' experiences that we were not able to understand in detail through some of the questionnaires that we are using. Many parents really wanted to talk about and share their experiences regarding how they and their children are doing in the U.S. We feel that these rich experiences (both positive and negative) can add so much to our understanding of the issues that Chinese families in the U.S. are facing. (Leung, 2012, p. 295)

Because interviews in qualitative studies tend to be rather informal, they might appear similar to casual conversation. There is one critical difference between a qualitative interview and normal dialogue, however: The researcher wants to gain information from the interviewee without also revealing his or her own perspectives. In other words, a critical element of most intimate conversations—disclosure of one's thoughts, beliefs, and feelings—is lopsided, with only one member of the pair doing the disclosing. To maintain rapport and general feelings of closeness and trust, therefore, you must show compassion and interest in other ways, perhaps through body language (smiling, maintaining eye contact, leaning forward) and such neutral encouragements as "Go on" and "What do you mean?" (Shank, 2006).

7. *Focus on the actual rather than on the abstract or hypothetical.* You are more likely to get revealing information if you ask what a person *does or would do in a specific situation*—that is, if you ask about actual behaviors. For example, if you are interviewing a teacher, ask questions about specific teaching strategies rather than about educational philosophy. Otherwise, you might get nothing more than what Eisner (1998) has described as "pious, canned proclamations that seem as though they had been snatched from a third-rate philosophy of education text" (p. 183).

8. *Don't put words in people's mouths.* Let people choose their own way of expressing their thoughts. A good interviewer is, above all, a good listener who lets people say what they want to say in the way they want to say it. Furthermore, a good interviewer recognizes that people may reveal inconsistencies in their recollections, attitudes, and logic: Their perceptions won't necessarily all fit together in a neat little package (Kvale & Brinkmann, 2009).

9. *Record responses verbatim.* Whether you use handwritten notes, shorthand, or a tape recorder, smartphone application, or laptop computer, capture everything the person says, especially if interview questions are fairly open-ended. If you suspect that an interviewee may have said something other than what he or she intended to communicate, read or play back the response and ask if it accurately reflects his or her thoughts.

10. *Keep your reactions to yourself.* Although you won't necessarily want to maintain a continual "poker face," you're more likely to get accurate information if you don't show surprise, agreement, or disapproval of what someone tells you.

11. *Remember that you are not necessarily getting the facts.* As confident and convincing as some of your participants may be, you should always treat their responses as *perceptions and opinions* rather than as facts.

12. *When conducting a focus group, take group dynamics into account.*   Whenever you gather two or more people into a single interview, these individuals will rarely act as true equals. Some participants are likely to dominate the conversation. Others may be reluctant to express their views, perhaps because they're shy or feel uncertain about the validity of their perspective. In most cases, you will get more representative data—and hence more *useful* data—if you make sure that everyone in the group has a chance to answer each question. Accordingly, you should keep your list of questions for a focus group quite short. And if you are recording the focus group session, ask participants to identify themselves by name at the beginning of the session; having them do so will help you identify different speakers when you transcribe the session later on.

An Example in International Relations

A student researcher wanted to interview certain United Nations personnel to get their opinions concerning issues related to his study. He planned to travel to New York City for a series of interviews and, to conserve both time and expense, wanted to schedule them as tightly as possible. His procedure was organized and logical.

Approximately 6 weeks before his trip, the student wrote the United Nations representatives with whom he wished to confer; he told them when he would be in New York and requested an interview that would last 30 minutes at most. He asked each prospective interviewee for an indication of several time slots when the interview might be scheduled. In his letter, he clearly explained what information he was seeking and why he was seeking it. His reasons were mature and meaningful and were phrased to pique the interest for those he wanted to interview. (*Not* among his reasons was the fact that he was writing a thesis! If you must reveal that you are collecting data for a thesis, use the word *study* instead of *thesis*. Aside from the student and the graduate advisor, theses hold very little glamour in the everyday world. "Studies" are much more acceptable.)

With the letter, the student enclosed a separate sheet containing the questions he intended to ask during the interview, arranged in the order he would ask them. He also suggested that if the interviewee had no objections, he would tape the interview in order to conserve time and lessen the distraction of handwritten notes. He provided a check box on a return postcard for the interviewee to indicate whether he or she had any objection to recording the interview.

After receiving potential interviewees' replies, he created a master chart of list appointments and, by letter, immediately confirmed each interviewee's appointment time and thanked the interviewee for his or her cooperation. When a time conflict arose, he sought to resolve it by suggesting alternative times that were still open.

Ten days before the scheduled interviews, the student mailed reminders along with another copy of the interview questions. He also enclosed his full interview schedule so that the interviewees might appreciate the time constraints under which he was working.

The student arrived promptly for each scheduled interview, introduced himself, asked whether the interviewee wanted a copy of the questions he had previously sent, and began with the first question. He tried to guide the interview, always keeping to his agenda of questions and seeking to preserve a relaxed, friendly, yet also professional atmosphere. He wrapped up each interview by thanking the interviewee for the courtesy of giving his or her time. In 3½ days, he interviewed 35 United Nations representatives and had more than four-fifths of his data on tape.

The student transcribed the substance of the interviews and, within 10 days of his visit, sent each interviewee a typed, double-spaced transcript accompanied by a thank-you letter for granting the interview. He asked each individual to read the transcript carefully and, if it was correct, to sign a statement that it was a correct record of the interview. If the person found it inexact or incorrect in any place, he or she could correct the script as desired. In the same mailing, the researcher included a request for permission to use any quotations from the interview in his final report, with the understanding that he would again send the interview content for the interviewee's approval. In his final thesis, the researcher acknowledged his interviewees and noted that they had inspected and approved all of their quoted statements. With the use of such strategies, the researcher and the readers of his report could all be confident that the participants' thoughts and opinions were accurately represented.

In summary, the researcher's use of the following steps led to a highly productive research effort:

1. Set up the interview well in advance.
2. Send the agenda of questions to ask the interviewee.
3. Ask for permission to tape the conference.
4. Confirm the date immediately in writing.
5. Send a reminder, together with another copy of the questions, 10 days before the interview.
6. Be prompt; follow the agenda; offer a copy of the questions in case the original copy has been mislaid.
7. After the interview, submit a transcript of the interview, and get from the interviewee either a written acknowledgment of its accuracy or a corrected copy.
8. After incorporating the material into a semifinal draft of the research report, send that section of the report to the interviewee for final approval and written permission to use the data in the report.

USING TECHNOLOGY

Using Technology to Facilitate Collection of Interview Data

With appropriate software, most laptops and many smartphones can serve as audio recorders. And, of course, videos recorded on a camcorder can be easily downloaded to a personal computer. Meanwhile, transcription software (e.g., HyperTRANSCRIBE) lets you mark key points in a videotaped or audiotaped interview, retrieve desired pieces of information quickly, and slow down what you have recorded so that you can transcribe it more easily. Other software programs (e.g., Dragon Naturally Speaking) will even do your transcribing for you.

In some cases, you can conduct qualitative interviews long-distance through various Internet mechanisms, including e-mail, Skype, or video conferencing. Focus groups might also be conducted online, perhaps through Internet-based chat rooms or bulletin boards (e.g., see Krueger & Casey, 2009, for suggestions). Keep in mind, however, that ethical standards don't fly out the window simply because you're conversing with people in cyberspace rather than in the same room. You must still seek participants' (or parents') informed consent, and you must protect participants' privacy. Furthermore, you must ensure that participants have appropriate characteristics and qualifications for your investigation—something that may be difficult to determine if you never see these individuals in the flesh.

CRITERIA FOR EVALUATING QUALITATIVE RESEARCH

How do readers, reviewers, and practitioners assess the worth of a qualitative proposal or research study? What characteristics are essential to a good study? What makes one study "excellent" and another study only "marginal"?

Experienced qualitative researchers have offered a variety of standards that might be used to evaluate a qualitative study (Altheide & Johnson, 1994; Creswell, 2013; Eisner, 1998; Gall, Gall, & Borg, 2007; Glaser, 1992; Howe & Eisenhardt, 1990). We have boiled down their suggestions to nine general criteria:

1. *Purposefulness.* The research question drives the methods used to collect and analyze data, rather than the other way around.

2. *Explicitness of assumptions and biases.*   The researcher identifies and communicates any assumptions, beliefs, values, and biases that may influence data collection and interpretation.

3. *Rigor.*   The researcher uses rigorous, precise, and thorough methods to collect, record, and analyze data. The researcher also takes steps to remain as objective as possible throughout the project.

4. *Open-mindedness.*   The researcher shows a willingness to modify hypotheses and interpretations when newly acquired data conflict with previously collected data.

5. *Completeness.*   The researcher depicts the object of study in all of its complexity. The researcher spends sufficient time in the field to understand all nuances of a phenomenon; describes the physical setting, behaviors, and perceptions of participants; and ultimately gives readers an in-depth, multifaceted picture of the phenomenon (i.e., *thick description*).

6. *Coherence.*   The data yield consistent findings, such that the researcher can present a portrait that "hangs together." Multiple data sources converge onto consistent conclusions *(triangulation),* and any contradictions within the data are reconciled.

7. *Persuasiveness.*   The researcher presents logical arguments, and the weight of the evidence suggests one interpretation to the exclusion of others.

8. *Consensus.*   Other individuals, including the participants in the study and other scholars in the discipline, agree with the researcher's interpretations and explanations.

9. *Usefulness.*   The project yields conclusions that promote better understanding of the phenomenon, enable more accurate predictions about future events, or lead to interventions that enhance the quality of life.

In this chapter we have addressed issues related to only some of these criteria—especially issues related to purposefulness, rigor, and open-mindedness. We address issues related to other criteria in discussions of data analysis in Chapter 11 and report writing in Chapter 13.

PRACTICAL APPLICATION Planning the Logistics of a Qualitative Study

As should be clear by now, a qualitative research project is not something to be entered into casually. One key consideration is that, regardless of the kinds of data involved, data collection in a qualitative study takes a great deal of time. The researcher should record any potentially useful data thoroughly, accurately, and systematically, using field notes, sketches, photographs, audio recordings, videos, or some combination of these. And as you will discover in Chapter 11, data organization and analysis must be equally meticulous and time-intensive.

If you think a qualitative approach might be suitable for your purposes, you may want to do a pilot study first to find out whether you feel comfortable with the ambiguity and relative lack of structure in the process. We urge you, too, to learn as much as you can about qualitative research strategies, perhaps by reading some of the sources listed in the "For Further Reading" section at the end of this chapter. Once you have determined that you have both the time and skills to conduct a qualitative study, you may find the following checklist helpful in your planning.

✓ CHECKLIST

Pinning Down the Methodology of a Qualitative Study

WHAT IS THE PURPOSE OF THE PROJECT?

_____   1. What is the current status of knowledge pertaining to the question?

_____

_____

_____

_____   2. Why is the study important?

_____

_____

_____

WHAT IS THE SPECIFIC FOCUS AND DESIGN OF THE PROJECT?

_____   3. Will the focus be on individuals, groups, cultures, experiences, processes, or content?

_____

_____   4. Will the design be a case study, ethnography, phenomenological study, grounded theory study, content analysis, a combination of two or more of these, or none of these?

_____

WHAT DATA ARE NEEDED?

_____   5. Will you need to gain access to one or more sites in the field? If so, how will you do it?

_____

_____

_____   6. How much time will you need?

_____

_____   7. What special resources are needed and available?

_____

_____

_____

_____   8. Are there any existing constraints on data collection?

_____

_____

HOW WILL THE DATA BE COLLECTED?

_____   9. How will the participants or materials be sampled?

_____

_____

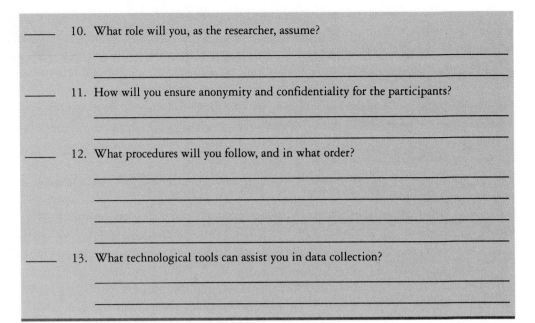

_____   10. What role will you, as the researcher, assume?

_____

_____

_____   11. How will you ensure anonymity and confidentiality for the participants?

_____

_____

_____   12. What procedures will you follow, and in what order?

_____

_____

_____

_____   13. What technological tools can assist you in data collection?

_____

_____

✔ **Check Your Understanding in the Pearson etext**

Practice Thinking Like a Researcher

Practice Thinking Like a Researcher Activity 9.1: Recognizing Qualitative Designs
Practice Thinking Like a Researcher Activity 9.2: Collecting Data for a Qualitative Study
Practice Thinking Like a Researcher Activity 9.3: Planning and Conducting Interviews

A SAMPLE DISSERTATION

As an example of a qualitative research study, we present excerpts from Robin Smith's doctoral dissertation conducted at Syracuse University (Smith, 1999). The study was a multiple case study that also incorporated elements of grounded theory research and content analysis.

The study focused on five high school students who had significant intellectual disabilities. In particular, it examined the nature of the students' involvement and participation in high school classrooms. It also looked at teachers' perceptions and interpretations of the students' disabilities and academic performance.

The dissertation's "Method" chapter begins with an overview of the research strategies used and a rationale for selecting the individuals to be studied. It then presents more specific information about each of the five students: Gerald, Trish, Nick, Tyrone, and Abe (all pseudonyms). We pick up the chapter at the point where it begins a discussion of data collection. As we have done in preceding chapters of this book, we present excerpts on the left and a running commentary on the right.

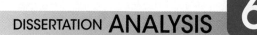

DISSERTATION ANALYSIS | 6

DATA COLLECTION PROCESSES

Data gained in the varied academic settings of the five students assisted in understanding the patterns of academic participation and the meanings and relationships of the five students regarding their academic participation in high school. I gathered data from the following sources:

Observations

Over three school semesters, I conducted observations of five high school students who were attending high school and enrolled in at least one academic subject in the general high school curriculum. These observations totaled 52 visits ranging in length ... the shortest was 15 minutes ... the longest, 6 hours.... *[The author continues with a detailed discussion of the kinds of observations made and the circumstances in which she made them.]*

Conversations and Interviews

I had conversations and interviews with adults involved and concerned with the students, such as general and special education teachers, assistants, and parents. I recorded and described these conversations in field notes and transcriptions....

The semi-structured interviews with the parents of each student included the following kinds of questions:

1. Tell me about the history of your child's schooling.
2. What are the child's strengths? That is, what is he or she good at?
3. Where does it get hard for the student?
4. How does he or she like high school? How can you tell?
5. What do you see your child learning?
6. What are your goals and dreams for your child?
7. What else should I know about your child to better understand what is happening for him or her in school?

I conducted similar interviews with the special education teachers, which included discussion of their educational goals for the student. I conducted one formal interview with each special education teacher, with further interviews as necessary to enhance my understanding of my data. These other interviews were often in the form of brief conversations during or in between class, interviews by appointment, and phone conversations.

I also conducted interviews with the general education teachers in the form of formal, informal, or brief conversations that fit into the teachers' schedules.... I also had some conversations with the general education teachers by staying a few minutes after class and asking them questions about what I had observed that day or how they thought the student was doing....

Comments

Here the author provides information about the amount of time she spent in the field. Her observations varied considerably in duration depending on the situation; we are more apt to see such flexibility in a qualitative study than in a quantitative one.

The interviews were presumably structured in this manner so that similar kinds of information would be obtained about each child.

The author used follow-up unstructured interviews to gather additional information as needed. This strategy is consistent with a grounded theory approach, in which the researcher moves back and forth between data collection and data analysis.

The author used audiotapes and transcriptions to capture the details of in-depth interviews; she also wrote notes about shorter, more informal conversations as soon after they took place as possible. The phrase "according to the comfort level of the

I taped and had transcribed in-depth interviews, and I embedded observer comments in the transcribed text as I reviewed it. I wrote down informal conversations as soon as possible, and when possible, wrote during the conversations according to the comfort level of the participants with note taking. I used a Hewlett Packard 200LX-palmtop computer, which enabled me to take legible and detailed notes and add more detail soon after an observation.

Official Records and Documents

Official records and documents were another source of information. At the very end of my study I went to the district office of special education, which kept the official records of all five of the students. I looked in each file to learn what I could about the students' grades and progress reports, along with the professional assessments and recommendations regarding the students' schooling. I took notes on my hand-held computer and read long quotes into my tape recorder for later reference and transcription. I took notes on students' work in class and from some student work I found in the files, and collected samples of their work where possible.

Finally, I relied heavily on very detailed field notes. At first I wrote everything I saw. As I narrowed my focus I consistently included the students' interactions with adults and peers, their reactions to what was going on, and what other students were doing at the same time. Describing interactions of the nonspeaking students was challenging; due to the crowded conditions of several of the general education classes and my being in a wheelchair, I was not always able to be close enough to the student to observe facial expressions. Fortunately, each student was accessible to me most of the time, especially when I was well into the study and a couple of sympathetic teachers invited the student to sit where I could be close by. Thus many of my observations were able to include whispered dialogue between the student and support person helping with an assignment.

CODING AND ANALYSIS

... As I collected and analyzed data from preliminary observations, I found issues to explore ... questions arose that created a need for further observing or interviewing. Using the constant comparative method of analysis (Glaser & Strauss, 1967), I collected data, looked for emerging themes and recurrent events, categorized them, and reevaluated my themes and categories. As I collected more data, I wrote analytic memos about my data, and reevaluated my previous theories as I compared old data with new (Bogdan & Biklen, 1992, pp. 72-75). The themes of academic engagement, generated by my pilot study, continued to expand in depth and breadth, and they generated more themes that guided the development of my study.

For example, Nick, one of the students I observed, sat with his assistant in the last row by the door, separated by another row of desks from the class; he seemed an observer in class lectures and discussions. When his assistant supported him to participate in hands-on activities, the assistant did the task for the student. The educators in the room said to me, "He doesn't understand much of what's going on," and they did not expect him to benefit from the actual curriculum content ("He's not getting much

participants with note taking" might have been better worded as "to the extent that participants felt comfortable with my note taking." However, the phrase reflects an appropriate sensitivity about taking notes only when it did not make a participant feel uneasy. And notice the author's use of a small computer to facilitate data collection!

Why did the author wait until the end to look at school records and documents? Later in this excerpt you will see her reason: She was worried that early knowledge of these records would bias her interpretations of what she observed in the classroom.

This narrowing of focus as the study proceeds is frequently found in qualitative research.

Notice how the author is looking for nonverbal as well as verbal information. Notice, too, how cooperative participants (in this case, some "sympathetic teachers") can facilitate data collection.

The author conducted an earlier pilot study—something we urge any beginning researcher to do, particularly when planning a qualitative study.

Notice the author's attention to Nick's physical distance from other students—a clear, nonverbal indicator that Nick is essentially a nonparticipant, an outsider, in this classroom.

out of it."). In contrast, Trish, a student with even less physical coordination and verbal expression, followed a full academic schedule, and many of her teachers considered her to be involved, interested, and learning. This led me to look for signs of expectations of the student and how people evaluated the students. Thus, early data codes such as "expectation," "perception," and "assessment" led to a chapter regarding expectations and another regarding types of assessments.

I used Q.S.R. Nudist (QSR-NUD*IST, 1995) to code my data. This program enabled me to identify text segments in various ways, including participants' names and roles, as well as assigned categories such as "engaged," "disengaged," and "academics," that resulted in 98 data codes. A few of these original codes survived my ongoing revisions and collapsing of categories to my final analysis. I printed categories out in groups and coded them again by hand, testing new coding categories by merging several categories and reexamining the data. For example, many of the text segments that I had labeled "expectation" evolved into "assessment." Once I had determined that assessment was an important category, I subdivided it into "formal," "informal," and "professional," each with its own set of categories which are explained in my data chapter, "Patterns of Assessment". . . . Further hand coding yielded the categories I finally used in the chapter on "participation". . . .

[The author continues the discussion of data coding and other issues and then turns to the subject of values.]

Exposing Researcher Values

During this research I have continuously inspected my expectations and values as a continuing reminder of the role that values have in inquiry. . . . Ongoing self-reflection in memos and discussions with mentors throughout the course of the study helped me identify and account for the interference of my assumptions in my study. . . . For example, sometimes I was tempted to express findings about expectations in cause and effect terms. . . .

I expose my values in my narrative as playing a significant role in my inquiry. In sharing my values in the introduction, and further here, I have attempted to take them into account as I share my data and analysis. For example, as a disability rights advocate, I have hoped that my research regarding students with disabilities would be a contribution toward achieving equality and full integration of people with disabilities. I remained aware of my bias against the self-contained setting, where four of the students in the study were based, in order to see what might actually benefit the students in that setting. I am aware that my bias is related to my advocacy stance against segregation and to the negative accounts of friends who have experienced segregated special education. I also had a prejudice against professional assessments along with the likelihood . . . that I might be influenced by the contents if I read them early in the study. To counter inappropriate influence of this prejudice, I read the assessments at the end of my study and took a class in how to administer psychoeducational assessments. . . .

As I listened to my informants, I was aware of my own assumption that students benefit from academic inclusion and that all students have the right to attain

The ability to contrast one situation with another is a key advantage of a multiple case study.

Here we see open coding, *the first step in data analysis in a grounded theory study (see Chapter 11).*

NUD*IST was an early, groundbreaking computer database program especially suited for data collection in qualitative research.

Here data analysis has moved on to axial coding, *where the author is refining her categories and their interconnections (see Chapter 11).*

In this section, the author reveals her biases and the strategies she used to counteract those biases. Regular conversations with her university advisor and others helped her identify assumptions she didn't initially realize she was making.

Here the author describes her bias in favor of inclusion, *where students with disabilities learn in general education classrooms alongside their nondisabled peers, rather than in* self-contained classrooms, *in which students with disabilities are segregated from nondisabled students.*

Here we discover why the author waited until the end of her study to look at school records.

knowledge . . . for my observations and interviews, I kept an open mind to the notion that special education settings do not preclude learning, may even enhance it, and that observing the special education academic experiences could also inform me about student engagement and how they [students] participated in the academic activities.

Here the author is looking for disconfirming evidence, one effective strategy for minimizing the influence of a researcher's biases on data interpretation.

LEAVING THE FIELD

The process of leaving the field was gradual. I was learning less and less from observations by the end of spring. Completing ceasing the first school year observation was precipitated by the beginning of the university summer session and my assignment to spend all day in a suburban school as a student teacher. I was assigned to Trish's summer school class the second summer session and took notes on that experience. I visited her twice in the fall but was excluded from her general education classes due to overcrowding. Also in the fall, I spent two days with Tyrone. . . . By then I had been analyzing data and felt the main thing lacking was the assessment of material from official records. Waiting until the following summer to look into the records proved wise, as I was able to find them a rich source of data. I actually eased my way out of the field (Bogdan & Biklen, 1992, pp. 104–105) rather than leaving, keeping contacts with many of my informants and calling to find out what is going on with a student or to clarify a question.

In grounded theory terminology, the author has probably saturated *her categories at this point: Any additional information is shedding little or no new light on the subject matter.*

Notice that the author didn't just disappear from the scene. Instead, she continued to maintain contact with her participants after her research was completed.

Note: Excerpt is from *Academic Engagement of High School Students With Significant Disabilities: A Competence-Oriented Interpretation* (pp. 18–30) by R. M. Smith, 1999, unpublished doctoral dissertation, Syracuse University, Syracuse, New York. Reprinted with permission.

FOR FURTHER READING

Agar, M. H. (1996). *The professional stranger: An informal introduction to ethnography* (2nd ed.). San Diego, CA: Academic Press.

Barlow, D. H., & Nock, M. K. (2009). Why can't we be more idiographic in our research? *Perspectives on Psychological Science, 4,* 19–21.

Birks, M., & Mills, J. (2011). *Grounded theory: A practical guide.* Thousand Oaks, CA: Sage.

Bloomberg, L. D., & Volpe, M. F. (Eds.) (2008). *Completing your qualitative dissertation: A roadmap from beginning to end.* Thousand Oaks, CA: Sage.

Brinkmann, S., & Kvale, S. (2014). *InterViews: Learning the craft of qualitative research interviewing* (3rd ed.). Thousand Oaks, CA: Sage.

Butler-Kisber, L. (2010). *Qualitative inquiry: Thematic, narrative and arts-informed perspectives.* London: Sage.

Chandler, S. (Ed.). (1992). Qualitative issues in educational research. *Theory Into Practice, 31,* 87–186.

Charmaz, K. (2014). *Constructing grounded theory: A practical guide through qualitative analysis* (2nd ed.). Thousand Oaks, CA: Sage.

Corbin, J., & Strauss, A. C. (2008). *Basics of qualitative research: Techniques and procedures for developing grounded theory* (3rd ed.). Thousand Oaks, CA: Sage.

Creswell, J. W. (2012). *Educational research: Planning, conducting, and evaluating quantitative and qualitative research* (4th ed.). Upper Saddle River, NJ: Pearson/Allyn & Bacon.

Creswell, J. W. (2013). *Qualitative inquiry and research design: Choosing among five approaches* (3rd ed.). Thousand Oaks, CA: Sage.

Creswell, J. W. (2014). *Research design: Qualitative, quantitative, and mixed methods approaches* (4th ed.). Los Angeles: Sage.

Denzin, N. K., & Lincoln, Y. S. (2013). *Strategies of qualitative inquiry* (4th ed.). Thousand Oaks, CA: Sage.

Eisner, E. W. (1998). *The enlightened eye: Qualitative inquiry and the enhancement of educational practice.* Upper Saddle River, NJ: Prentice Hall.

Fetterman, D. M. (2010). *Ethnography: Step by step* (3rd ed.). Thousand Oaks, CA: Sage.

Gast, D. L., & Ledford, J. R. (2014). *Single case research methodology: Applications in special education and behavioral sciences* (2nd ed.). New York: Routledge.

Gibson, B., & Hartman, J. (2014). *Rediscovering grounded theory.* London: Sage.

Glaser, B. (1992). *Basics of grounded theory analysis.* Mill Valley, CA: Sociology Press.

Graneheim, U. H., & Lundman, B. (2003). Qualitative content analysis in nursing research: Concepts, procedures and measures to achieve trustworthiness. *Nurse Education Today, 24*(2), 105–112.

Guest, G., Namey, E. E., & Mitchell, M. L. (2013). *Collecting qualitative data: A field manual for applied research.* Thousand Oaks, CA: Sage.

Hammersley, M. (2008). *Questioning qualitative inquiry: Critical essays.* Thousand Oaks, CA: Sage.

Hammersley, M., & Atkinson, P. (2007). *Ethnography: Principles in practice* (3rd ed.). New York: Routledge.

Hatch, A. J. (2006). *Early childhood qualitative research.* New York: Routledge.

Hays, D. G., & Singh, A. A. (2012). *Qualitative inquiry in clinical and educational settings.* New York: Guilford Press.

Heidegger, M. (2005). *Introduction to phenomenological research* (D. O. Dahlstrom, Trans.). Bloomington: Indiana University Press.

Hesse-Biber, S. N., & Leavy, P. (Eds.) (2011). *Handbook of emergent methods.* New York: Guilford Press.

Jaccard, J., & Jacoby, J. (2010). *Theory construction and model-building skills.* New York: Guilford Press. (See Chapter 10, "Grounded and Emergent Theory.")

James, N., & Busher, H. (2009). *Online interviewing.* London: Sage.

Johnson, R. B., & Onwuegbuzie, A. J. (2004). Mixed methods research: A research paradigm whose time has come. *Educational Researcher, 33*(7), 14–26.

Jorgensen, D. L. (2007). *Participant observation: A methodology for human studies.* Thousand Oaks, CA: Sage.

Josselson, R. (2013). *Interviewing for qualitative inquiry: A relational approach.* New York: Guilford Press.

Kamberelis, G., & Dimitriadis, G. (2013). *Focus groups: From structured interviews to collective conversations.* New York: Routledge.

King, N. (2010). *Interviews in qualitative research.* Thousand Oaks, CA: Sage.

Krueger, R. A., & Casey, M. A. (2009). *Focus groups: A practical guide for applied research* (4th ed.). Thousand Oaks, CA: Sage.

Latimer, J. (Ed.) (2003). *Advanced qualitative research for nursing.* New York: Wiley.

Lincoln, Y. S., & Guba, E. G. (1985). *Naturalistic inquiry.* Thousand Oaks, CA: Sage.

Locke, L. F. (1989). Qualitative research as a form of scientific inquiry in sport and physical education. *Research Quarterly for Exercise and Sport, 60,* 1–20.

Morgan, D. L. (1998). *The focus group guidebook.* Thousand Oaks, CA: Sage.

Moustakas, C. (1994). *Phenomenological research methods.* Thousand Oaks, CA: Sage.

Neuman, W. L. (2011). *Social research methods: Qualitative and quantitative approaches* (7th ed.). Boston: Allyn & Bacon. (See Chapter 13, "Field Research and Focus Group Research.")

Peshkin, A. (1988). Understanding complexity: A gift of qualitative research. *Anthropology and Education Quarterly, 19,* 416–424.

Richards, L., & Morse, J. M. (2013). *Read me first for a user's guide to qualitative methods* (3rd ed.). Thousand Oaks, CA.

Richardson, J. T. E. (1999). The concepts and methods of phenomenological research. *Review of Educational Research, 69,* 53–82.

Rubin, H. J., & Rubin, I. S. (2012). *Qualitative interviewing: The art of hearing data.* Thousand Oaks, CA: Sage.

Salmons, J. S. (2014). *Qualitative online interviews* (2nd ed.). Thousand Oaks, CA: Sage.

Sandelowski, M. (2000). Whatever happened to qualitative description? *Research in Nursing and Health, 23,* 334–340.

Savin-Baden, M., & Major, C. H. (2013). *Qualitative research: The essential guide to theory and practice.* New York: Routledge.

Schram, T. H. (2006). *Conceptualizing and proposing qualitative research* (2nd ed.). Upper Saddle River, NJ: Merrill/Prentice Hall.

Shank, G. D. (2006). *Qualitative research: A personal skills approach* (2nd ed.). Upper Saddle River, NJ: Merrill/Prentice Hall.

Smith, J. A., Flowers, P., & Larkin, M. (2009). *Interpretative phenomenological analysis: Theory, method and research.* London: Sage.

Smith, M. L. (1987). Publishing qualitative research. *American Educational Research Journal, 24,* 173–183.

Stake, R. E. (2006). *Multiple case study analysis.* New York: Guilford Press.

Stake, R. E. (2010). *Qualitative research: Studying how things work.* New York: Guilford Press.

Strauss, A., & Corbin, J. (1994). Grounded theory methodology: An overview. In N. Denzin & Y. Lincoln (Eds.), *Handbook of qualitative research* (pp. 273–285). Thousand Oaks, CA: Sage.

Tashakkori, A., & Teddlie, C. (Eds.) (2010). *Mixed methods in social & behavioral research.* Thousand Oaks, CA: Sage.

Yin, R. K. (2013). *Case study research: Design and methods* (5th ed.). Thousand Oaks, CA: Sage.

Yin, R. K. (2011). *Qualitative research from start to finish.* New York: Guilford Press.

ANSWERS TO THE CONCEPTUAL ANALYSIS EXERCISE "Choosing a Qualitative Research Design":

1. The researcher wants to learn about the general *culture* of an Elks group; hence, an *ethnography* is most appropriate.

2. A *content analysis* is called for here—in particular, a systematic sampling and analysis of television commercials that are broadcast within a specified time period.

3. By focusing on three specific examples of a grassroots political party, the researcher is presumably intending to conduct a *multiple case study.*

4. The focus here is on how adolescents *perceive* their situation, making a *phenomenological study* especially relevant to the research problem.

5. Because the research question involves a process—human interaction—and very little literature exists to shed light on the question, a *grounded theory* study is probably in order here.

Chapter

10

Historical Research

Looking at a string of seemingly random events, the historical researcher develops a rational explanation for their sequence, speculates about possible cause-and-effect relationships among them, and draws inferences about the effects of events on individuals and the society in which they lived.

Learning Outcomes

10.1 Recognize examples of primary sources and secondary sources in historical research.

10.2 Identify several good sources of data for historical research, and distinguish between external evidence and internal evidence in evaluating data gathered from these sources.

10.3 Describe several important strategies for writing a good historical research report.

In and of itself, history consists of nothing more than an ever-flowing stream of events and continuing changes in human life and its institutions, including its languages, customs, philosophies, religions, art, and architecture. Historical research tries to make sense of this maelstrom. It considers the currents and countercurrents of present and past events, with the hope of discerning patterns that tie them all together. At its core, historical research deals with the *meanings of events.*

Many people have the impression that historical research involves gathering significant facts about a major event—perhaps a war, an economic downturn, or the emergence of a new nation—and organizing these facts into a sequence, usually chronological. Such an enterprise may yield a historical narrative. It is not, however, true historical research. The heart of the historical method is, as with any other type of research, not the accumulation of the facts, but rather the *interpretation* of the facts. Interpretation of the data is central in all research. The task of the historical researcher is not merely to describe *what* events took place but to present a *factually supported rationale* to suggest *how* and *why* they may have happened.

Historical research is certainly not the domain of historians alone. On the contrary, it can be found in such disciplines as geography, anthropology, political science, economics, psychology, literature, and linguistics. For example, some social scientists engage in comparative-historical research, comparing historical events and processes across two or more societies or cultures, with the goal of identifying similarities, differences, and patterns that could conceivably reflect cause-and-effect relationships.

As you will see, historical research is largely a qualitative endeavor, although historical researchers often make use of quantitative data as well.

DATA SOURCES IN HISTORICAL RESEARCH

In Chapter 4 we distinguished between *primary data* and *secondary data,* with the former being closer to the reality, or Truth, that the researcher ultimately wants to uncover. In historical research, this distinction is often referred to in terms of *primary sources* versus *secondary sources.* Primary sources are those that appeared first in time—in particular, when or soon after the events in question occurred. These sources take such diverse forms as letters, diaries, newspaper articles, sermons, laws, census reports, immigration records, probate documents, deeds, photographs, paintings, films, buildings, and labor-saving tools. As an example, Matthew McKenzie, a doctoral student in history at the University of New Hampshire, studied the impact of the Boston Marine Society on political decision making and scientific advancements in colonial America and the early decades of the United States. McKenzie made extensive use of the society's minutes and other documents, as explained in the following excerpt from his dissertation:

> [A]s an organization of [sea] captains predicated upon fellowship and mutual aid and with a distinct role within the port [Boston Harbor], the Society went to great lengths to follow proper parliamentary procedures and to act only on decisions taken unanimously. As part of this process, the society maintained meeting minutes recording the society's (though not individuals') opinions, resolutions, and approved actions. Consequently, throughout its 250-year history, the society left committee reports, resolutions, and clear statements that reveal its collective will and motivations. These records allow historians to uncover not only what the organization did, but why. (McKenzie, 2003, pp. 2–3)

Another source of primary data, at least for events within the past few decades, can be found in interviews of people who participated in them. This approach is sometimes known as *narrative research* or *oral history*. A good example is Kevin Kearns's *Dublin Tenement Life* (1994), which pulls data from interviews with many residents of inner-city tenement buildings into a vivid description of inner-city Irish life in the early 1900s. To give you a taste of this approach, we present a brief excerpt from Kearns's description of teenage courting practices:

> [B]y age eighteen or thereabouts "marriage was their highest ambition," claims Peggy Pigott [a former tenement resident whom Kearns interviewed]. It was around this time that young women liked to go "clicking" in pairs. Clicking was an acceptable practice whereby respectable young women would stroll together along fashionable Dublin streets ostensibly window-viewing but in reality hoping to meet decent lads. When May Hanaphy [another interviewee] and one of her pals went clicking back in the 1920s, it was a perfectly proper way to meet a prospective husband:
>
> > Oh, clicking then was very popular. See, that's how flirting went on. That's how many a girl got her husband, going out at night time. Oh, you'd go out for that purpose at that time. We'd go clicking along mostly O'Connell Street or maybe down Henry Street, you know, slow walking . . . strolling, and two fellas come along and say 'there's two mots.' (Kearns, 1994, p. 46)

Interview data often give life to historical events. But just as is true in conducting any interview, the researcher must remember that participants' recollections aren't always accurate. Only when several people recall events similarly can a researcher have reasonable confidence in what the interviews reveal. More generally, the guidelines for "Conducting a Productive Interview" presented in Chapter 9 are as applicable to historical researchers as they are to other qualitative researchers.

Historical researchers don't necessarily limit themselves to words, images, and objects; they often use numbers as well. For instance, they might draw inferences about people's interests during a particular time period by looking at the numbers of books on various topics that were sold during that period (Marius, 1989). Or they might examine the frequencies with which the Puritans of colonial America named their children after figures in the Bible, chart trends in these frequencies over time, and then speculate about what the trends might mean for religious practices and beliefs (Marius, 1989). In his study of the Boston Marine Society, McKenzie (2003) used early tax rolls to determine the wealth of society members, and he used society records of new members to show the decline in the society's popularity and influence in the early 1800s (see Figures 10.1 and 10.2). In research for his master's thesis in history, Peter Leavenworth (1998) used early real estate deeds to find patterns in land sales in New England during the 1600s, with a focus on land sold by Native Americans to British colonists. At one point in his analysis, Leavenworth plotted the frequency of land sales for each month of the year (see Figure 10.3).

FIGURE 10.1 ■ Using Tax Rolls to Determine the Wealth of Boston Marine Society Members

Source: From *Vocational Science and the Politics of Independence: The Boston Marine Society, 1754–1812* (p. 25) by M. G. McKenzie, 2003, unpublished doctoral dissertation, University of New Hampshire, Durham. Reprinted with permission.

Wealth Bracket	No. in Bracket	Assessed Tax in 1771 (£ s)	Proportion of Population
Top 20%	8	£37 12s–£46 13s	11%
2nd	6	£28 6s–£37 12s	8%
3rd	19	£18 18s–£28 4s	26%
4th	19	£9 10s–£18 16s	26%
5th	20	0–£9 8s	28%
Total Population	72		100%

Source: Pruitt, *Massachusetts Tax Evaluation;* and Baker, *Boston Marine Society,* 318–361.

FIGURE 10.2 ■ Using New Membership Data to Reveal the Decline in the Boston Marine Society's Popularity and Influence During the Early 1800s

Source: From *Vocational Science and the Politics of Independence: The Boston Marine Society, 1754–1812* (p. 198) by M. G. McKenzie, 2003, unpublished doctoral dissertation, University of New Hampshire, Durham. Reprinted with permission.

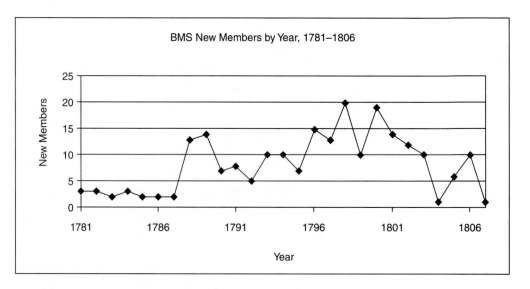

In the following excerpt from his thesis, Leavenworth finds considerable meaning in the month-to-month frequency data:

> One last use of the deed index is to chart times of the year when transactions were more prevalent. . . . [T]he dips in overall Indian deed activity shown in February and May are consistent throughout the century. The February dip was either hunting- or weather-related, while the May dearth may have been either a time of Indian removal to summer habitations, or the period of spring fishing runs, or both. Many early accounts, including missionary John Eliot's, mention large annual spring gatherings of many bands at traditional fishing locations on the Merrimack and Piscataqua Rivers. When distribution is separated by decade, large spikes in land sales increasingly cluster in the spring later in the century. This may point to a growing native need for sustenance from the English marketplace after the hardships of the winter months, especially as their increasing proximity to white society did not raise their standard of living. Both Indian and English land sale patterns, not surprisingly, display a marked decrease at harvest time. (Leavenworth, 1998, pp. 88–89)

In the examples just presented, the raw numerical values sufficed for the researchers' purposes. In other instances, however, historical researchers might perform statistical analyses on the numerical data they collect; in such instances, historical research is truly a blend of qualitative and quantitative methodologies. An excellent resource for beginning historical researchers is Haskins and Jeffrey's *Understanding Quantitative History* (1990), which suggests many potentially useful sources of quantitative information and describes a variety of ways to analyze quantitative historical data.

In contrast with primary sources, secondary sources are the works of historians who have interpreted and written about primary sources. These include history textbooks, as well

FIGURE 10.3 ■ Using Early Deeds to Track Patterns in Land Sales, Especially from Native Americans to British Colonists, in New England During the 1600s

Source: From *"The Best Title That Indians Can Claim: Native Agency and Consent in the Transferal of Penacook-Pawtucket Land in the Seventeenth Century"* (p. 88) by P. S. Leavenworth, 1998, unpublished master's thesis, University of New Hampshire, Durham. Reprinted with permission.

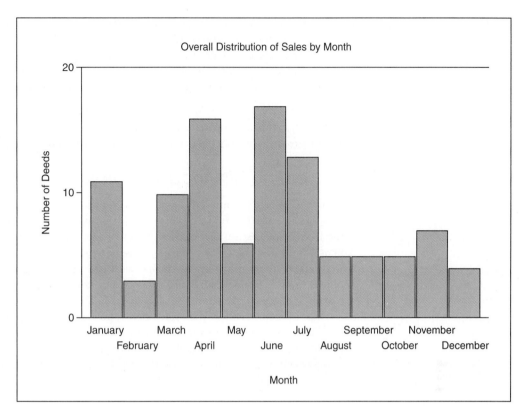

as more scholarly books and articles written about a particular event or time period. Secondary sources inevitably reflect the assumptions and biases of the people who wrote them. For example, 21st-century British historian Peter Heather has commented about the biases of fourth-century Roman historian Ammianus Marcellinus, who wrote comprehensive and widely used historical accounts of the Roman Empire:

> [W]hile claiming to be interested in the truth, Ammianus was not averse to deploying literary artistry in the service of what he considered to be true, and sometimes even evasion. The big cultural story unfolding around him in his own lifetime was the progressive Christianization of the Empire, but he deliberately minimized its appearance in his text, and may even have attempted to conceal a personal aversion to it in the guise of favoring religious toleration. (Heather, 2009, pp. 155–156)

Given that personal biases almost invariably infiltrate secondary sources, good historical researchers rely on primary sources whenever possible. Yet virtually *any* report of an event—even a report that historians would consider to be a primary source—is apt to be somewhat distorted in line with the writer's basic beliefs and assumptions. For example, a newspaper article describing a highly controversial event—perhaps an unprovoked attack that resulted in many human casualties—might very well be slanted in one direction or another, depending on the writer's political leanings.

As noted in Chapter 4, researchers can probably never determine the ultimate, objective Truth that lies beneath a body of data—if, in fact, a single Absolute Truth actually exists (recall the discussions of postpositivism and constructivism in Chapter 1). The historical researcher keeps this point in mind, as illustrated in the following excerpt from a geography dissertation that analyzed changes in Jamaican agricultural practices during the early 1800s:

> The sources of data are primarily printed documents published during the period of crisis, plus some surviving correspondence. Most important are island newspapers, the annual almanac, books, pamphlets, and government records. As with any historical data, [they] are incomplete in their coverage of contemporary events and may present a biased picture of the times.

> Some are also suspect as personal interpretations of interested parties participating in the events described. These problems are not insurmountable so long as we are aware of them and interpret source information in terms of its contemporary context. In fact, the opinions and biases reflected in much of the data [are themselves] an important component in our portrait of adaptive change. (R. K. Ormrod, 1974, pp. 217–218)

Notice how the author acknowledges the probable presence of bias in some of his sources, even those published during the time period he was studying. In fact, he uses that bias to his advantage: as a way of getting a better handle on the prevailing perspectives of the time.

USING TECHNOLOGY

Collecting Historical Records

Historical researchers often find it helpful to make copies of the primary sources (letters, minutes, deeds, etc.) they find in archival collections at libraries, museums, historical societies, and the like. Many institutions provide photocopies for a small fee. An alternative approach is to photocopy the sources using a *digital camera,* which requires less light than photocopying and so is less likely to inflict environmental wear and tear on fragile documents. Photographs from digital cameras can be loaded directly onto a personal computer, allowing for easy cutting-and-pasting into a research report.

As researchers collect their documents, however, they should keep track of where each one came from, perhaps in a form similar to the footnotes they might eventually use to describe the documents in a final research report. For paper photocopies, small Post-it notes attached at a corner and written comments on the flip side are obvious strategies. When a digital camera is used, an ongoing log of what each shot is and where and when it has been taken is essential.

USING TECHNOLOGY

Online Databases for Historical Events

Some historical documents and records can be found only in the archives of various libraries, museums, and historical societies around the world, and you may have to travel a great distance to see them. But many others have been painstakingly captured in electronic form and made available online. For example, many university libraries subscribe to such online databases as the following:

- *American History in Video.*   This resource has more than 5,000 newsreels, documentaries, and other videos capturing various events and trends in American history.
- *Ancestry Library.*   This resource is a genealogical database that includes such documents as census records; birth, marriage, and death certificates; and immigration and naturalization records.
- *Digitized Primary American History Resources.*   This resource provides links to many primary sources related to American history (e.g., historical documents, presidential papers, photographs).
- *Digitized World History Sources.*   This resource provides links to many primary sources related to world history (e.g., Magna Carta, Code of Hammurabi, Manifesto of the Communist Party).
- *Early American Newspapers.*   This resource is a digital archive of newspapers from all 50 states and the District of Columbia.
- *ProQuest Historical Newspapers: The New York Times.*   This resource includes every page of every issue of the *New York Times* since its first issue in 1851.
- *Historical Statistics of the United States.*   This resource is a compilation of statistical data on a wide range of topics (e.g., Native Americans, migration, slavery, health, crime).

In addition, government websites offer many historical documents online. One especially helpful site is that of the U.S. Library of Congress (loc.gov), which provides documents related to both American and world history and includes links to other helpful websites around the world.

Such resources open up many possibilities for researchers who might otherwise be restricted by location, disabilities, or other challenges. In addition, simple word processing functions (e.g., *copy* and *paste)* are invaluable time savers. As you locate relevant quotations, references, and so forth, that you want to keep for future reference, you can highlight and copy desired sections and then paste them into your own database. If you do such copying and pasting, however, you must take appropriate precautions to avoid copyright infringement. Furthermore, remember that you must *not* use the words and ideas of other people without proper citation.

PRACTICAL APPLICATION Handling Historical Data Systematically

In historical research, much of the data collected is recorded in terms of hundreds, perhaps thousands, of notes. In order to effectively *make sense* of those notes, however, a researcher must organize them in some logical, meaningful way. Historical data collection demands a systematic plan, not only for collecting data but also for retrieving and analyzing them. Therefore, before you begin a historical research project, you should have a specific plan for the acquisition, organization, storage, and retrieval of your data.

Computer technology facilitates data collection in several ways. For example, if you must travel to a particular library, museum, or other site that houses desired historical documents, use a laptop computer rather than paper and pencil to record your findings, and either type or dictate your notes directly into a laptop computer. Then, when you return home, enter your notes into a database or word processing file that will allow you to organize and search through your notes in various ways.

EVALUATING AND INTERPRETING HISTORICAL DATA

After researchers have located historical data relevant to a research problem, they must decide what is fact and what is fiction. In other words, they must determine the *validity* of their data.

In historical research, data require two types of evaluation. First, a researcher must judge whether a document or artifact is authentic. Second, if the item is indeed authentic, the researcher must decide what it means. In these two situations, the researcher is reviewing the data to determine their external evidence and internal evidence, respectively. You may also see these concepts referred to as *external criticism* and *internal criticism*.

External Evidence

External evidence is primarily concerned with the question *Is the article genuine?* Counterfeits and frauds are not uncommon, nor is their acceptance by the naive scholar and researcher unusual.

External evidence for the validity of a document is of paramount importance for the credibility of the research. Establishing authenticity of documents may in some cases involve carbon dating, handwriting analysis, identification of the types of ink and paper used, vocabulary usage and writing style, and other historical detective work. This aspect of historical methodology is a study in itself, and we cannot discuss it at length in a chapter as brief as this one.

Internal Evidence

Quite apart from the question of genuineness is the equally important question *What does it mean?* When considering a manuscript or a statement, the researcher asks such questions as, "What was the author trying to say?" "To what individuals or events do certain phrases refer?" "What interpretations can be extracted from the words?"

Let's take a well-known example. The date is November 19, 1863. Abraham Lincoln is speaking at the dedication of a national cemetery in Gettysburg, Pennsylvania. In his brief but famous address, the president said, "But, in a larger sense, we cannot dedicate—we cannot consecrate—we cannot hallow this ground. The brave men, living and dead, who struggled here, have consecrated it, far above our poor power to add or detract."

What did Lincoln mean by "the brave men, living and dead"? Did he mean only the brave men of the Union forces? (We must remember that he was dedicating a Union cemetery.) Did he mean the brave Confederate men as well? Or did he mean brave men, indiscriminately, with no thought of North or South but merely of courage and valor? To a researcher studying the life of Abraham Lincoln, it is important to determine what Lincoln specifically meant by his words or, alternatively, whether he was intentionally being ambiguous.

The matter of internal evidence applies not only to articles from the distant past but to more contemporary documents as well. What does the decision of a court mean? What do the words of the decision convey about the intent and will of the court? The question comes up frequently in legal interpretation. In such instances, the primary question is *What do the words mean?* This is the sole concern of internal evidence.

Considerable historical meaning can be found in graphic documents as well as strictly verbal ones. For example, in his dissertation about the Boston Marine Society, McKenzie analyzed nautical charts of the New England coastline created during the society's era. He noticed that one early mapmaker, DesBarres—whose nautical charts were typically rendered in painstaking detail—had a glaring omission in a map of the Bar Harbor area of Maine. McKenzie's dissertation interprets the omission in light of political concerns of the time:

> In at least one case, DesBarres consciously changed the shape of the coastline to suit imperial [British] needs, thus pitting local needs against imperial desires. In his chart of the coast of Maine from Frenchman Bay to Mosquito Harbor, DesBarres failed to indicate Northeast Harbor, the best harbor in the region, or anything that might resemble a harbor along the southern coast of Mount Desert island. . . . DesBarres' omission was almost certainly intentional, as the rest of the island's features, including its topography, coves, and hazardous rocks, were laid out in DesBarres' characteristic detail, and in more detail than the rest of land areas on the chart. DesBarres most likely left this strategically important harbor out of consideration for military reasons. In this case, imperial concerns outweighed the need for accurate local charts for free commerce. (McKenzie, 2003, p. 79)

When interpreting historical data, a researcher must inevitably impose certain assumptions on them. For instance, when looking at the laws that a democratic government created during a particular era, the researcher might assume that the laws reflected the *needs and beliefs of the majority of voting citizens* (Marius, 1989). Or, more generally, when tracking the course of events in a particular social or cultural group, a researcher might assume that the events reflected *economic or social progress* (Breisach, 1994). And for better or for worse, many historical researchers might be inclined to perceive practices that are consistent with their own culture's norms and values as being somehow "better" than other practices.

Good historical researchers identify, explicitly and concretely, the assumptions that have guided their interpretations of historical data. As an example, we look once again at the previously excerpted geography dissertation, this time focusing on the researcher's interpretation of events during a crisis in Jamaican sugar planting practices during the early 19th century:

> Our interpretation [of the data] will depend upon two primary assumptions: (1) an adaptation imperative existed which demanded that the island society respond to the events threatening its pattern of livelihood, and (2) most of the behaviors involved in the response, bounded by the constraints inherent in the functioning cultural ecosystem, were goal directed. These assumptions lead us to expect an orderly response to crisis rather than a random one and lead us to seek a behavior system which sought to relieve the stresses on the society. Although such a behavior system would function in a probabilistic manner rather than as a closely determined one, we should nevertheless be able to construct an orderly framework of interpretation around our data.
> (R. K. Ormrod, 1974, p. 227)

PSYCHOLOGICAL OR CONCEPTUAL HISTORICAL RESEARCH

Thus far, we have discussed conventional historical research—the study of significant events and the individuals who played important roles in them. But this chapter would not be complete without a brief discussion of another type of historical research—namely, that concerned with the origin, development, and influence of ideas and concepts. Ideas and concepts can influence the course of history just as surely as events and people do.

As an example, the idea of *democracy* was born in Greece; its development has run parallel to the events of the Greco-Roman world, the Middle Ages, and modern times. Over the years the idea evolved into such concepts as *representative government* and *political campaign.* The initial concept of democracy that began in ancient Athens is, perhaps, found in its purest form today in New England town meetings (e.g., those in Maine, Vermont, and Connecticut).

Consider other key ideas that have guided the course of civilization: capitalism, socialism, rationalism, individualism, communism, postmodernism. Each of them has a developmental history, which is just as "real" as the history of Europe, China, or your own hometown. Search any comprehensive paper-based or electronic encyclopedia for some of the principal ideas of civilization just listed, and you may well find some discussion of how these ideas have evolved over time.

Look, too, at Arnold Toynbee's monumental *A Study of History* (1939–1961). Here, you will find not the traditional approach to history—the description and interpretation of events—so much as the dynamic ideas that have powered the histories of nations and civilizations and that have been instrumental in bringing about cataclysmic changes in those histories.

SEARCHING FOR ROOTS

In Chapter 4 we mentioned the research of John Livingston Lowes, which is presented in *The Road to Xanadu* (1927, 1955). Lowes's book is remarkable because it is, in a sense, research in reverse. In it, Lowes searches for "the genesis of two of the most remarkable poems in English, 'The Rime of the Ancient Mariner' and 'Kubla Khan'" (Lowes, 1927, p. 3).

This type of research, which is the counterpart of a genealogical search of one's family origins, begins with such questions as *Where did it come from?* and *How did it all begin?* It is precisely the type of research that astronomers and astrophysicists conduct to try to account for the creation of the universe. But researchers don't have to conduct research projects on such a cosmic scale to engage in the same kind of detective work that reels backward instead of forward in search of answers to questions. The process of beginning with a phenomenon and going backward in time to identify possible—we repeat, *possible*—causal factors is sometimes called *ex post facto research,* but we caution you not to confuse ex post facto *historical* research with the ex post facto designs described in Chapter 7.

PRACTICAL APPLICATION Historical Research Writing

Descriptions of historical research projects are often quite different from those for other types of research, hence our inclusion of a brief discussion of historical research writing prior to the more general discussion of research reports in Chapter 13. In fact, written accounts of historical research vary widely, depending on the researchers and their idiosyncratic writing styles. Those historians whose works often appear on best-seller lists infuse their descriptions of history with colorfully depicted events and interesting personalities.

GUIDELINES Writing the Historical Research Report

Many of the suggestions we offer about writing in Chapter 1 and Chapter 5 apply to historical research as well as to any other type of research. In addition, Marius (1989) has offered several useful *rules for argument* that you should keep in mind when, in particular, you are writing about a historical research study.

1. ***State your own argument early in the game.*** Remember, you are not only presenting the data but also *interpreting* it. You should be up-front about your interpretation and not keep your readers guessing.

2. ***Provide examples to support any assertion you make.*** You make a more convincing case when you give examples of data that lend credence to your position.

3. ***Give the fairest possible treatment of any perspectives different from your own.*** You may very well be presenting an interpretation that differs from those of other scholars. Describe competing interpretations and provide evidence that supports them, as well as evidence that casts doubt on them.

4. ***Point out the weaknesses of your own argument.*** It is better to shoot holes in your own case than to have others do it for you. You portray yourself as a credible researcher when you appear to be objective—rather than blindly one-sided—in your analysis and interpretation of your data.

With regard to this fourth guideline, we should remind you that your research project, while answering your initial research question, may also yield new, unanswered questions. You can turn any inconsistent findings that you uncover into "unresolved issues" or "suggestions for future research."

✔ Check Your Understanding in the Pearson etext

Practice Thinking Like a Researcher

Practice Thinking Like a Researcher Activity 10.1: Selecting Sources for Historical Research
Practice Thinking Like a Researcher Activity 10.2: Using Online Databases

---

A SAMPLE DISSERTATION

We now return to Matthew McKenzie's dissertation on the Boston Marine Society, which McKenzie completed for his doctoral degree in history at the University of New Hampshire (McKenzie, 2003). We have previously shown brief snippets of the dissertation to illustrate certain aspects of historical research, but we now present a larger chunk with a running commentary. You will see that, overall, the dissertation has a different feel to it than the proposal and dissertation excerpts that appear in previous chapters. Unlike those earlier excerpts, this dissertation is written as a *narrative,* with historical events and interpretations seamlessly interwoven throughout the discussion. McKenzie spent an extra year overhauling major sections of his dissertation, and his efforts show clearly in the quality of his writing. Notice, too, how he used footnotes to identify his sources, reflecting the Chicago Manual style that historians typically use in their research reports (more about various styles in Chapter 13).

DISSERTATION ANALYSIS 7

Introduction

In the spring of 1755, Captain Hector McNeill was in command of a merchant vessel in a small flotilla convoying an army up the Bay of Fundy. The fleet had left Boston a few days before with the task of safely delivering 2,000 New England soldiers to fight against their French imperial rivals at Fort Beaussejour. As the fleet sailed along the current-swept, rocky shores, [Colonel] Robert Monckton worried about the fate of his army. Back in Boston, there had been almost no charts for him to consult, and even fewer descriptions of the currents and tides that made this region so dangerous. Moreover, his and his army's fate rested in the hands of a few Boston merchant skippers, like Captain McNeill, none of whom likely knew the latest and best techniques in navigation.

Despite his fears, however, and the dangerous shoals and hazardous headlands, the fleet proceeded safely. When Monckton approached McNeill about their progress, curious as to how a colonial trading skipper could successfully undertake such a hazardous job, McNeill showed him information which no British commander in North America or London knew existed. Trading along the coast, McNeill had collected five years of nautical observations, including (presumably) tides, currents, coastal descriptions, and manuscript drawings. From these observations, McNeill had drawn a chart covering the coast from Cape Cod to Cape St. Mary's including the Bay of Fundy. McNeill's chart impressed the British commander. And shortly after the Boston skipper safely delivered his regiments, Monckton dislodged the French from Beaussejour.[1]

McNeill was not alone in his interest in marine cartography in New England. In 1760, he joined a group of master mariners in Boston, called the Boston Marine Society (BMS), which had also been systematically collecting navigational observations since 1754. Both McNeill and the Marine Society understood that local navigational knowledge carried commercial, political, and imperial opportunities. Consequently, when the organization united senior captains for mutual aid, they also recognized that they stood in an important position between London imperial agents in North America and the coastline that interested them. Furthermore, they were actively collecting data as every member returned to Boston—a feature that they would try to barter for greater influence in Boston and within the [British] Empire.

Historians are fortunate in the Marine Society's meticulous record keeping and parliamentary procedure. Two key issues help modern researchers see the society's collective will and motivation. First, as membership was limited to captains alone, the society was self-conscious that they spoke as an elite body in Boston's maritime community. Second, as an organization of captains predicated upon fellowship and mutual aid and with a distinct role within the port, the society went to great lengths to follow proper parliamentary procedures and to act only on decisions taken unanimously. As part of this process, the society maintained meeting minutes recording the society's

Comments

In Chapter 6, we suggested that you always state your research problem at the very beginning of your research proposal. In a research report, however, researchers often begin with a few paragraphs of background information that provides a context for the research problem. A common strategy in historical writing is to begin with a story—a real-life drama of sorts—that draws readers in and motivates them to continue reading.

Here we get a glimpse of what will be one major thrust of the dissertation: describing and tracking the nature of early nautical charts, whose use and promotion were partly attributable to efforts of the Boston Marine Society.

Notice the use of footnotes to identify the sources for certain statements. The author is using the style required by the Journal of American History *(available online on the journal's website at journalofamericanhistory .org). Footnotes are also consistent with the* Chicago Manual of Style *(2010), which historians typically follow.*

Notice the smooth flow of the narrative from one event to another. In our experience, narrative writing is more challenging than traditional "scientific" report writing. However, when well executed (as is the case here), narrative reports are also more engaging than scientific reports tend to be.

Here we see the context in which the discussion of the society's minutes (excerpted earlier in the chapter) appeared.

---

[1]Hector McNeill to Lord Colville, January 17, 1763, Boston Marine Society Papers (Massachusetts Historical Society, Boston, Mass.).

(though not individuals') opinions, resolutions, and approved actions. Consequently, throughout its 250-year history, the society left committee reports, resolutions, and clear statements that reveal its collective will and motivations. These records allow historians to uncover not only what the organization did, but why.

This is not the first study of the Boston Marine Society. Earlier studies of the Marine Society have cataloged in some detail the work the Marine Society undertook during its long history. Nathaniel Spooner stitched together a rough narrative in his 1879 *Gleanings of the Boston Marine Society* (Boston, 1879, 1999). In 1982, William A. Baker's *A History of the Boston Marine Society* (Boston, 1982) integrated the Marine Society's history more closely with changes in Boston politics and economics and assembled systematic information on the society's more than 3,000 members. Both of these works greatly aided the project that follows. Yet neither delved into the society's influence upon the history of American science, [and] with the exception of Baker's study of the society during the American Revolution, neither Baker nor Spooner were interested in examining how the society operated as an active agent in Boston's historical development.

This study seeks to examine the society within the context of the history of American science. Academic centers and learned societies have been the focus for most considerations of American science because of their prominence in the nineteenth and twentieth centuries. The Marine Society's scientific interests indicate, however, that colonial groups could and did develop their own scientific agenda that they pursued through methods adapted from common vocational practices. In doing so, the Marine Society's navigational work draws important parallels to the history of colonial science in other areas during the late eighteenth century. In the simplest form, I argue that colonial Boston shipmasters were not dependent upon learned societies for their navigational research needs. Rather, they adapted their mutual aid society and developed methodologies to collect navigational observations, analyze them for reliability and accuracy, and in a few cases, publish their findings for the benefit of the community. Furthermore, given the close ties between seafaring, economic growth, and political influence in a mercantile economy, the Marine Society's work in navigational research granted them social and political influence in Boston. With this added influence—power would be too strong a term for it—the Marine Society tried to stabilize post-Revolutionary Boston politics and to legitimate their efforts to become one of the town's new elites. Ultimately, the Marine Society lost its political influence as changes in navigational research, shifts in Boston and national politics, and new market centers for scientific information combined to weaken the society's position in both the political and navigational research world.

The Marine Society gives us a glimpse of the rise and fall of what I call "vocational science." In many previous studies discussed below, science and research were considered as a purely intellectual—"academic"—exercise, centered in learned academies, universities, and laboratories. I argue, to the contrary, that those who used navigation to carry their vessels safely into port, and expanded navigational knowledge, pursued science just as much as those who approached navigation from theoretical understandings of geodesy, mathematical astronomy, and spherical trigonometry. Whether using complex mathematical models to develop an absolute understanding of coastal features, or using piloting techniques, rule of thumb guidelines, simple instruments, and best-as-possible guess-work, both vocational and academic

Here the author explains how his own research extends the boundaries of what is known and believed about the Boston Marine Society's role in American history.

Here the author also explains how his research represents a divergence from the traditional approach to the history of science: Rather than studying the effects of traditional academic groups (universities and academic organizations), he is studying the impact of a less academic, yet definitely influential, group.

The author makes his central hypothesis clear at this point: He believes that early shipmasters relied on one another rather than on traditional scientific investigations to get the information they needed to travel safely along the northern Atlantic coastline.

He posits a second hypothesis as well: The society's significant involvement in the local economy gave it considerable influence in early Boston.

The author introduces a new concept— vocational science—to describe the phenomenon he uncovers in his research.

The author contrasts his own viewpoint with more traditional views.

researchers formed part of a larger process by which the knowledge of New England's coast expanded.

The idea of vocational science also highlights an important mechanism by which specific groups used science to shore up their economic, social, and political positions within their local area. While most prior work on American science has shown how the pursuit of scientific knowledge translated into improved cultural and social reputation, most have seen these efforts as a neutral desire to expand humanity's understanding of the world. Yet in this case, engagement in scientific research carried immediate economic, political, and social benefits that were anything but neutral. As Joyce Chaplin has shown, colonial Carolina low-country planters sent botanical specimens to the Royal Society and the Royal Society of Arts in exchange for agricultural innovations. These innovations—seeds, water control mechanisms, and processing machinery—helped them secure political control over Carolina politics during the Early Republic and helped create the land-owning elite of the Ante-bellum south.[2] James McClellan argues that while French planters in Saint Domingue did not embrace science as openly as their Carolina counterparts, science did serve the mercantilist interests of the state, and helped perpetuate slavery in the French Caribbean.[3] Finally, John Lauritz Larson has shown that experimental engineering designs for locks, dams, and internal waterways promised America's post-Revolutionary elite a means to promote private improvement schemes with public funds and in the face of public opposition.[4] In all these situations, science—whether tied to European centers or not—worked to bolster a specific group's local political and economic positions. Not pursued solely for knowledge in its own right, science expanded knowledge of the natural world, yet at the same time advanced specific interests.

The author argues convincingly that, contrary to the popular perception of scientists as individuals who are more concerned about the general quest for knowledge than about their personal needs, these "vocational scientists" often had fairly self-serving motives at the root of their endeavors. He draws analogies to advancements in other locations and other times, where people may have been equally self-promoting. In doing so, he situates his research within a larger body of research literature that has preceded his own work.

Readers will find the terms "science," "navigational knowledge," and "research" used quite liberally and perhaps over-interchangeably in the pages that follow. This is intentional. The structured and distinct practices that we associate with science today had yet to develop in the second half of the eighteenth century. The lines between "amateur," "practitioner," and "interested gentleman" were blurry to say the least. As others have shown, to impose such categories on inquiries into the natural world and the inquirers themselves clouds more than clarifies. Only after science underwent dramatic changes in the early nineteenth century would science have such clear structures.[5]

Here the author anticipates and addresses a potential source of confusion for his readers. In particular, he provides a reasonable rationale for why he will use several terms interchangeably.

[The report continues with a discussion of earlier researchers' explanations of the interplay among science, politics, and social dynamics in colonial America and the early decades following the American Revolution.]

---

[2] Joyce Chaplin, *An Anxious Pursuit: Agricultural Innovation and Modernity in the Lower South, 1730–1815* (Chapel Hill, 1993), 131–142.

[3] James E. McClellan III, *Colonialism and Science: Saint Domingue in the Old Regime* (Baltimore, 1993), 9, 289–292.

[4] John Lauritz Larson, *Internal Improvement: National Public Works and the Promise of Popular Government in the Early United States* (Chapel Hill, 2001), 1–37.

[5] See McClellan, *Colonialism and Science,* 7; and Roy MacLeod, "On Visiting the Moving Metropolis: Reflections on the Architecture of Imperial Science," in *Scientific Aspects of European Expansion,* ed. William K. Storey (Hampshire, 1996), 24–27.

Note: Excerpt is from *Vocational Science and the Politics of Independence: The Boston Marine Society, 1754–1812* (pp. 1–6), by M. G. McKenzie, 2003, unpublished doctoral dissertation, University of New Hampshire, Durham. Reprinted with permission.

FOR FURTHER READING

Barzun, J., & Graff, H. (2003). *The modern researcher* (6th ed.). Belmont, CA: Wadsworth. (This text provides a comprehensive survey of historians' work.)

Breisach, E. (2008). *Historiography: Ancient, medieval, and modern* (3rd ed.). Chicago: University of Chicago Press.

Brundage, A. (2013). *Going to the sources: A guide to historical research and writing* (5th ed.). Chichester, West Sussex, United Kingdom: Wiley.

Clive, J. (1989). *Not by fact alone: Essays on the writing and reading of history.* New York: Knopf.

Creswell, J. W. (2012). *Educational research: Planning, conducting, and evaluating quantitative and qualitative research* (4th ed.). Upper Saddle River, NJ: Pearson. (See Chapter 15, "Narrative Research Designs.")

Daiute, D. (2013). *Narrative inquiry: A dynamic approach.* Thousand Oaks, CA: Sage.

Errante, A. (2000). But sometimes you're not part of the story: Oral histories and ways of remembering and telling. *Educational Researcher, 29*(2), 16–27.

Floud, R. (2006). *An introduction to quantitative methods for historians.* New York: Routledge.

Gray, W. (1991). *Historian's handbook: A key to the study and writing of history* (2nd ed.). Prospect Heights, IL: Waveland.

Haskins, L., & Jeffrey, K. (1990). *Understanding quantitative history.* New York: McGraw-Hill.

Hill, M. R. (1993). *Archival strategies and techniques.* Thousand Oaks, CA: Sage.

Janesick, V. J. (2010). *Oral history for the qualitative researcher.* New York: Guilford Press.

Knowles, A. K. (Ed.). (2008). *Placing history: How maps, spatial data, and GIS are changing historical scholarship.* Redlands, CA: ESRI Press.

Lewis, M. J., & Lloyd-Jones, R. (2009). *Using computers in history: A practical guide to data presentation, analysis, and the Internet* (2nd ed.). New York: Routledge.

Marius, R., & Page, M. E. (2012). *A short guide to writing about history* (8th ed.). New York: Longman.

Neuman, W. L. (2011). *Social research methods: Qualitative and quantitative approaches* (7th ed.). Boston: Allyn & Bacon. (See Chapter 14, "Historical-Comparative Research.")

Novick, P. (1988). *That noble dream: The "objectivity question" and the American historical profession.* Cambridge, England: Cambridge University Press.

Chapter

11

Analyzing Qualitative Data

In qualitative research, we closely examine the data to find the meanings that lie within them. In most qualitative methodologies data interpretation begins almost immediately, and initial interpretations are apt to drive subsequent data collection. As we engage in such an iterative data-collection-and-interpretation process, we must remember that, although the human mind is capable of amazing insights, it can be easily influenced by expectations and biases that prejudice our understandings.

Learning Outcomes

11.1 Describe general strategies you might effectively apply when organizing and analyzing qualitative data.

11.2 Explain how qualitative data analysis is typically an iterative, spiral-like process.

11.3 Explain what the term *researcher-as-instrument* means in qualitative research, and discuss its implications for data analysis.

In the quantitative designs described in Chapter 6 and Chapter 7, data collection, data analysis, and data interpretation are, in large part, three separate steps in a research project. In most qualitative designs, however, they are closely intertwined. Not only do data analysis and data interpretation often go hand in hand but they also begin early in data collection and may subsequently drive further data collection. For instance, data collected early in a qualitative study might suggest certain patterns or dynamics in the phenomenon being investigated, leading the researcher to seek additional information in an attempt to confirm, clarify, or disconfirm the hypothesized patterns or dynamics. As previously mentioned in Chapter 9, this process of continually, iteratively moving back and forth among data collection and data analysis/interpretation, with initial analyses and interpretations driving later data collection, is sometimes called the constant comparative method.

Strategies for analyzing qualitative data are less prescriptive than those for analyzing quantitative data. Also, they tend to rely heavily on *inductive* reasoning processes: The researcher observes a few specific situations or events and, from them, imposes specific meanings on them—often by *coding* them in some way—and then draws conclusions about a more general state of affairs. Such flexibility and open-endedness in data analysis strategies certainly have benefits—they can yield insights that might not come to light any other way—but they make it extremely difficult for a researcher to analyze data with total objectivity. Any qualitative researcher must continually acknowledge, both to self and to others, that personal attitudes and opinions are inevitably creeping into and biasing observations and interpretations.

No matter how you proceed, your data analysis in a qualitative study is apt to be a complex, time-consuming process. You must wade through a great deal of information, some of which will be useful and some of which will not. Furthermore, the data you obtain are apt to be multifaceted and may simultaneously reflect several distinct layers of meaning. This is not to say, however, that the process of analyzing qualitative data is dull and tedious. On the contrary, it can be stimulating, challenging, illuminating, and quite enjoyable—a very personally rewarding enterprise.

QUALITATIVE ANALYSIS STRATEGIES

Experienced qualitative researchers have offered many strategies for effectively analyzing and interpreting qualitative data, and the particular strategies employed must depend, in large part, on the nature of the research problem and the types of data for which the problem calls. In the upcoming pages we offer a few general considerations and suggestions—enough, we hope, to guide you as you plan a qualitative research project. For more explicit strategies, we urge you to consult one or more of the sources listed in the "For Further Reading" section at the end of the chapter.

General Strategies for Organizing and Analyzing Qualitative Data

Following are general strategies that might apply to virtually any qualitative study. They are meant—only very loosely—to be executed in the order we list them here. But please remember that many qualitative research studies involve an iterative process in which a researcher goes back and forth among data collection, analysis, and interpretation. You, too, should go back and forth among the strategies as needed.

   1. ***Convert the data into one or more forms that will be easy to organize and analyze.*** For example, transcribe audiotaped interviews. Put handwritten field notes into word processing documents or a spreadsheet. Electronically scan photocopied documents.

   2. ***Organize the data in a preliminary, superficial way that will enable you to locate them easily as you proceed.***   For example, in a case study, this initial organizational scheme might involve putting notes about various incidents and events in chronological order. In an ethnographic study, it might involve sorting electronic documents into desktop e-folders with such labels as *Field Observations, Interviews,* and *Artifacts.* In a content analysis, initial organization might involve separating the entities to be analyzed according to a variable central to the research problem—perhaps (in a study of historical trends) the chronological time periods in which different items were created or (in the field of child development) the ages of the children who created various writing samples, drawings, or other artifacts.
   You might think of Steps 1 and 2 as "getting your ducks in a row"—a commonly used idiom that essentially means gathering and arranging all needed materials before beginning an activity. With all the materials close at hand and in readily usable forms, you can more efficiently forge ahead and tackle the many mental challenges that your data analysis will ultimately involve.

   3. ***Identify preliminary categories that are likely to be helpful in coding the data.*** One of the biggest challenges in qualitative data analysis is to determine how best to organize it *meaningfully*—something the preceding ducks-in-a-row strategy doesn't fully accomplish. The first step in the meaning-making process is to identify a list of potentially helpful ways of categorizing and coding the data. For example, a researcher studying the course of a political campaign might think in terms of "campaign strategies," "fund-raising activities," "news media accounts," "setbacks," and the like.
   In some cases, a researcher begins with a *start list*—a predetermined list of categories or themes derived from the research problem and its subproblems or, instead, from a particular theoretical or conceptual framework. In other cases, the researcher peruses the collected data in search of general themes that seem to "pop out" as being important considerations in the

phenomenon under investigation. For example, a beginning list of codes might include codes related to some or all of the following:

- Specific topics
- Characteristics and attributes
- Actions
- Processes
- Emotions
- Beliefs
- Values
- Evaluations

Typically the researcher also identifies subcategories—*subcodes*—for some or all of the codes. For example, under a general code *Emotions,* a researcher might include such subcodes as *Joy, Anxiety,* and *Depression.* And sometimes researchers pull certain codes or subcodes directly from things that participants tell them (e.g., "I worry about my family" or "The popular kids are snobs"); such codes are called *in vivo* (i.e., "living") codes.

Lists of codes and subcodes are rarely meant to be mutually exclusive. In many studies, data might be simultaneously coded in two or more ways. Whatever approach you use to analyze your data—and we strongly recommend using one of the computer software programs we mention later in the chapter—your approach should readily accommodate multiple, possibly overlapping codings of your data.

4. ***Divide the data into meaningful units that will be individually coded.***   In some qualitative studies the meaningful units to be coded are clear-cut; for example, this might be true when the objects of study are paintings, television commercials, or specific movements in classical music. But especially in verbal materials, such as interview data or lengthy written works, the data need to be systematically broken into small segments—perhaps individual phrases or sentences—that will be coded separately.

5. ***Apply the initial coding scheme to a subset of the data.***   In a sense, this strategy involves pilot testing the list of codes to determine whether it will adequately capture the multidimensional meanings that the data hold. Such a pilot test is likely to reveal certain weaknesses in the list. For example, initial codes might:

- Be too vague to enable consistent, reliable categorization of the data
- Reflect overlapping ideas (and thus might be combined into a single code)
- Be too item-specific to be of use in making generalizations about the data
- Omit certain themes that appear to be important in the overall data set

This might also be a good time to identify parts of the data set that are, for all intents and purposes, irrelevant to the research problem and can be omitted from future analysis.

6. ***Construct a final list of codes and subcodes, and define each code and subcode as specifically and concretely as possible.***   The goal here is to create a list that ensures reasonable consistency—*reliability*—in coding the data. The list should be definitive enough that two different researchers would be highly likely to code any single item in the same way. One common strategy for enhancing coding reliability is to include specific examples (e.g., quotes from participant interviews) to illustrate each code and subcode. As an illustration, let's return once again to Christy Leung's dissertation study, a project briefly mentioned in Chapter 2 and subsequently revisited in Chapter 9. Leung's research questions centered around Chinese mothers, their experiences in immigrating to the United States, and their parenting practices. Her start list and final list of codes included many codes related to immigration and parenting. Figure 11.1 presents short excerpts from the two lists—in particular, codes related to the interviewee's negative and positive immigration experiences. Notice that the start list includes only general ideas to be coded, whereas the final list includes a

FIGURE 11.1 ■ Coding the Interviews of Chinese Immigrant Women: Excerpts from a Start List and a Final List of Codes and Subcodes

EXCERPTS FROM START LIST:

Number	Descriptive Label	Code
I-3	Negative Immigration Experiences	I-NIE
I-3(1)	Racial discrimination	I-NIE-RAC
I-3(2)	Language barriers	I-NIE-LAN
I-3(3)	Financial hardship	I-NIE-FIN
I-3(4)	Job limitations	I-NIE-EMP
I-3(5)	Lack of social support/networks	I-NIE-SSN
I-3(6)	Cultural shock	I-NIE-CUL
I-3	Positive Immigration Experiences	I-PIE
I-4(1)	Strong sense of family	I-PIE-FAM
I-4(2)	Perception of equal opportunities	I-PIE-EOP
I-4(3)	More educational opportunities or better quality education	I-PIE-EDU
I-4(4)	More employment opportunities or job advancement	I-PIE-EMP
I-4(5)	Higher standard of living or better living environment	I-PIE-LIV
I-4(6)	Cultural experiences	I-PIE-CUL

EXCERPTS FROM FINAL LIST:

Code	Full Name	Definitions	Direct Quote
		Negative Immigration Experiences	
NIE-DEL	Difficulties with Everyday Life	Mothers encountered difficulties with everyday lives, such as a lack of instrumental support from family or a lower standard of living in the U.S.	Our parents [who stayed in our home country] could not help us. We had to rely on ourselves for everything, [but] we could only do things within our own abilities. Of course, that was difficult.
NIE-LAN	Language or Cultural Barriers	Mothers had communication problems or job limitations due to language barriers or unfamiliarity with the cultural and social norms in the U.S.	[It] is mainly the language barrier. Because I cannot express myself very well, so it is very difficult to be recognized/valued at work, which is due to [my] limitations in language.
NIE-SSN	Small Networks or Disconnectedness	Mothers had a small social network in the U.S., or expressed a sense of disconnectedness from the mainstream society	The social network here [in the U.S.] is quite limited, whereas having a lot of friends, classmates and colleagues around in China makes us feel more like at home. Here, we also socialize with some Chinese and American friends, but the feeling is different. Sometimes, I feel lost and irritable.
NIE-RAC	Limitations or Discriminations	Mothers encountered various challenges such as job limitations, complicated immigration processes, or racial discrimination in the U.S.	[I] gave up [my job] after [I] came. In fact, [I] completely abandoned my previous work [and therefore,] the level of [my] work is declining.
		Positive Immigration Experiences	
PIE-GPE	General Positive Experiences	Mothers had positive social encounters, reunited with their spouses, or gained valuable life experiences after migrating to the U.S.	I learned many things after coming to the U.S.; [such experience] has widened my vision and changed my perspectives on many things. [I] realized that my thoughts were very narrow before. [I] just feel that many of my thoughts have changed now.
PIE-EDU	Education/Career Opportunities	Mothers had access to quality education, more employment opportunities, or better career development in the U.S.	In the U.S., the educational system gives you freedom to choose the subjects you like, whereas in Hong Kong, your major is actually based on the [academic] grades you received.

(Continued)

FIGURE 11.1 ⬛ *Continued*

PIE-EQU	Justice, Freedom, Equality	Mothers believed that social order and justice are better maintained and freedom and individual rights are guaranteed in the U.S.	The legal system is relatively sound; there is law in every aspect. Everyone obeys the legal system.
PIE-LIV	Better Living Environment	Mothers had a better living environment or a less stressful lifestyle after their migration to the U.S.	The U.S is quite good overall. Life here is relatively simple [and I] like the environment. It's very convenient to live here.
	Perceived Support at the Initial Stage of Migration and/or Throughout Their Transition		
HEP-INS	Instrumental Support	Tangible help with applications, employment, housing, financial difficulties, child care, transportation, or everyday needs.	[We received] a lot of help from our families. My parents helped us take care of our children and supported [us] financially.
HEP-INF	Informational Support	Information about universities or professional schools, or advice on everyday life and available resources in the U.S.	When I first came, she [a friend here in the U.S.] gave me a lot of advices on how to adapt to the life here, where to find a place to live, and on many things over everyday living.
HEP-ESS	Emotional or Spiritual Support	Emotional/psychological support, encouragement, and social contact, or spiritual support.	When I had difficulties, I had love and support [from friends from church]. Then I had the courage to overcome any difficulties. My friends and classmates also gave me psychological support. They encouraged and comforted me.
HEP-CUL	Culture or Language	Assistance in learning the American culture or improving their English language skills.	I went to the ESOL class offered in the county community college. They gave me a lot of help. They help new immigrants to learn English.

Source: From *The Immigration Experiences, Acculturation, and Parenting of Chinese Immigrant Mothers* (pp. 299, 303–305) by C. Y. Y. Leung, 2012, unpublished doctoral dissertation, University of Maryland, Baltimore County. Reprinted with permission.

definition and illustrative quote for each code. Notice, too, that the final list omits some codes in the start list (e.g., "Financial hardship"), substantially revises other codes, and includes new topics (e.g., "Instrumental support") that presumably emerged during Leung's early inspection of the data. Also, the category "Positive Immigration Experiences" in the final list includes a subcategory, "Perceived Support at the Initial Stage of Migration and/or Throughout Their Transition"; codes within this category are designated as "HEP" in the leftmost column.

7. ***Consider using two or more raters to code the data independently.*** When only a single researcher codes the data, it's all too easy for the researcher's expectations and biases to influence the codes assigned to each piece of data. To minimize such a contaminating influence, the researcher might, instead, have two or more people independently code the data. Here we are talking about interrater reliability: the extent to which two or more individuals provide identical judgments. When two individuals consistently rate the great majority of the data in similar ways, a researcher not only documents the reliability of the coding scheme but also enhances the credibility—the *validity*—of the results obtained.

When using two or more raters, qualitative researchers use strategies such as these to enhance interrater reliability of the final codes assigned:

- Include concrete definitions or significant characteristics of each code, along with specific examples from the data set (as illustrated in Figure 11.1).
- Provide training and practice in applying the codes to samples of data; continue until raters are consistently rating each data point.

- If necessary, revise the final list of codes or definitions to address ambiguities.
- After raters have independently coded the data, have them discuss and reach agreement about any inconsistently rated pieces of data.

8. ***Identify noteworthy patterns and relationships among the codes.***   For example, you might discern common themes that underlie many participants' experiences. If you look once again at Figure 11.1, you might notice that the codes "Racial discrimination" and "Job limitations" in Leung's start list became parts of a single larger category "Limitations or Discriminations" in her final list. Likewise, "More educational opportunities . . ." and "More employment opportunities . . ." became "Education/Career Opportunities."

Other patterns are apt to emerge as well. For instance, you might identify key sources of disagreement or conflict among participants, or you might detect inherent social hierarchies among members of a certain social group or community. You might also discover that certain events almost always precede other events, or that certain thoughts and feelings almost always precede certain actions. However, a qualitative researcher must always keep in mind that despite such *this-happens-and-then-that-happens* regularities, the researcher cannot conclude that the first event in the sequence definitely *causes* the second event. As we authors have stated before, *correlation does not necessarily indicate causation.* Although qualitative research can be especially useful in *describing* complex phenomena, only well-controlled experimental research can truly pin down causal, *this-variable-influences-that-variable* relationships.

Some patterns and relationships within the data might be readily apparent early in an analysis—and thus are reflected in a final list of codes—whereas others might come to light only after all the data have been coded. We must emphasize once again that in qualitative research, data analysis is often a back-and-forth, iterative process.

At this point we should introduce two terms frequently used in descriptions of qualitative data analysis. Initial passes through the data in an open-minded search for meanings and potential codes are often called *open coding.* Subsequent, more integrative analyses of the data and initial codings go by a variety of names, including *second-cycle coding, axial coding,* and *selective coding* (more on the last two of these in an upcoming discussion of grounded theory analysis).

9. ***Be alert for outliers, exceptions, and contradictions within the data set.***   A good qualitative researcher actively, consciously resists temptations to find commonalities that don't truly exist, make sweeping generalizations that aren't accurate, or jump to quick but unwarranted conclusions. Qualitative data are inevitably messy data that can't easily be wrapped up in one tight little package.

Such is the *nature of nature:* Diversity reigns supreme. And the more complex the phenomenon under investigation—and human beings are incredibly complex beings—the more diversity one is likely to see.

10. ***Interpret the data in light of your research problem.***   You must never forget the reason for conducting your study in the first place: to address a particular problem or question. Perhaps the data unequivocally provide one or more answers. Perhaps, instead, they only hint at certain answers and suggest that one or more follow-up investigations are in order. Only rarely do they offer nothing of value—an unfortunate outcome that is most common when a novice researcher naively embarks on a qualitative project with little or no advance planning and preparation.

The nature of your final interpretations—the *meanings* you ascribe to your data—can take a variety of forms. Following are common meaning-making strategies in qualitative research (Miles et al., 2014):

- Quantifying frequencies or probabilities of certain noteworthy characteristics or events
- Making comparisons or drawing contrasts within the data
- Connecting findings to one or more existing theories
- Developing a new, coherent theory to account for the findings
- Using metaphors to capture key phenomena or dynamics (e.g., describing the life of retirees as involving an "empty nest")

- Speculating about *possible* cause-and-effect relationships and *possible* mediating or moderating variables influencing those relationships (recall the discussion of mediating and moderating variables in Chapter 2)
- Creating graphics (e.g., tables, graphs, flowcharts) that summarize general patterns in the data

You should also look for convergence *(triangulation)* within your data: Many separate pieces of information should all point to the same conclusions.

Creswell's Data Analysis Spiral

We must repeat once again that qualitative data analysis is an iterative process, and thus a good qualitative researcher is apt to go back and forth a bit among the strategies just presented. Nevertheless, the researcher must gradually move forward, spending more time on the later strategies and leaving the earlier ones behind. Creswell (2013) has described a *data analysis spiral* that, in our view, offers a helpful perspective on how qualitative data analysis can reasonably proceed. Using Creswell's approach, you go through the data several times, taking the following steps:

1. Organize the data, perhaps using index cards, manila folders, or a computer database. You may also break down large bodies of text into smaller units, perhaps in the form of stories, sentences, or individual words.
2. Peruse the entire data set several times to get a sense of what it contains as a whole. In the process, you should jot down a few memos that suggest possible categories or interpretations. If your data are in paper form, you might write comments in the margins or use Post-it notes to capture your preliminary thoughts. If your data are in electronic form, you might use the *insert comment* feature available in many software programs, or you might add your initial impressions in a different font or color or, for a spreadsheet or database, in a separate column or field.
3. Identify general categories or themes, and perhaps subcategories or subthemes as well, and then classify each piece of data accordingly. At this point, you should be getting a general sense of patterns—a sense of *what the data mean.*
4. Integrate and summarize the data for readers. This step might include offering propositions or hypotheses that describe relationships among the categories. It might also involve packaging the data into an organizational scheme such as a table, figure, matrix, or hierarchical diagram.

We depict this spiral graphically in Figure 11.2.

An Example: Data Analysis in a Grounded Theory Study

In many types of research, and especially in experimental quantitative designs, a major goal is to test hypotheses related to one or more existing theories. But as you should recall from Chapter 9, the chief goal of a grounded theory study is to develop a *new* theory, one that arises from (i.e., is grounded in) the data themselves. In no other design, then, are data analysis strategies more central to the entire research effort.

Experts disagree about the best approach for analyzing data in a grounded theory study (e.g., see Charmaz, 2014; Corbin & Strauss, 2008; Glaser, 1992). One widely used approach is that proposed by Corbin and Strauss (2008; Strauss & Corbin, 1990), who have suggested the following steps:

1. ***Open coding.*** The data are divided into segments and then scrutinized for commonalities that reflect general categories or themes. After meaningful categories are identified, the data are further examined for *properties*—specific attributes or subcategories—that characterize each category. Properties are typically reflected in adjectives, adverbs, and adjectival and adverbial phrases in verbal material. For example, properties might be related to desirability

FIGURE 11.2 ■ The Data Analysis Spiral (based on Creswell, 2013)

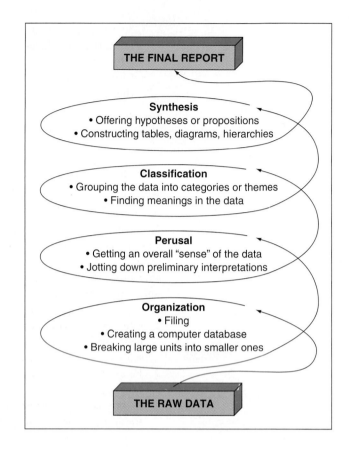

THE FINAL REPORT

Synthesis
• Offering hypotheses or propositions
• Constructing tables, diagrams, hierarchies

Classification
• Grouping the data into categories or themes
• Finding meanings in the data

Perusal
• Getting an overall "sense" of the data
• Jotting down preliminary interpretations

Organization
• Filing
• Creating a computer database
• Breaking large units into smaller ones

THE RAW DATA

(e.g., whether a certain object or event is to be sought or avoided), intensity (e.g., how angry someone feels), or duration (e.g., how long an event lasts). During this phase of analysis, data continue to be collected until it is clear that no new information is coming forward, no new categories are coming to light. At this point the categories are considered to be conceptually *saturated.*

2. *Axial coding.*   During the process of open coding, one or a few categories might emerge as being central to the phenomenon under investigation. In axial coding, one of these categories is chosen as a *core category,* and other categories are identified as possibly reflecting

   • The context in which the core category is embedded
   • Conditions that give rise to the core category
   • Strategies people use to manage or carry out the core category
   • Conditions that influence how the strategies are carried out
   • Consequences of those strategies

   In other words, the core category serves as an *axis* around which certain other categories appear to revolve in some way. Often the intercategory relationships are depicted as a diagram that encapsulates possible dynamics among various categories. If appropriate and helpful, the axial coding process is repeated using other codes as core categories.

3. *Selective coding and theory development.*   A single category is chosen as *the* core concept in the phenomenon, and a theory is developed based on this concept and its interrelationships with other categories. This theory—which might take the form of a verbal statement, visual model, or set of hypotheses—depicts the evolving nature of the phenomenon and describes how certain conditions lead to certain actions or interactions, how those actions or interactions lead to *other* actions, and so on, with the typical sequence of events being laid out. The result tends to be a general *story line* that describes "what happens" in the phenomenon being studied.

We have described these steps only in the most general terms. Corbin and Strauss's *Basics of Qualitative Research* (2008) offers more specific guidance and some helpful examples.

The steps just listed provide a structured and relatively systematic way of boiling down a huge body of data into a concise conceptual framework that describes and explains a particular phenomenon; as such, it has a semblance of rigor and objectivity that many researchers find appealing. Yet in some experts' eyes, these steps are *too* structured, to the point that they limit a researcher's flexibility and may predispose the researcher to identify categories prematurely (Charmaz, 2000; Glaser, 1992). Should you decide that a grounded theory study is the best way to tackle your research problem, we urge you to read experienced researchers' diverse approaches to data analysis techniques (e.g., see Charmaz, 2014; Corbin & Strauss, 2008; Garson, 2013; Martin & Gynnild, 2011).

An Example: Data Analysis in a Content Analysis Study

In one sense, virtually any qualitative study involves analyzing the contents of collected data. But in a content analysis study, determining the particular contents of verbal or nonverbal materials—typically human-created materials intended to communicate thoughts, ideas, and perceptions—is the *whole point* of conducting the study. For instance, a content analysis study might be aimed at identifying evolving techniques in ancient Greek sculptures, ideological biases in cable news channels, or popular topics on adolescents' Facebook pages.

Almost invariably, one crucial step in a content analysis is to tabulate the frequency of each characteristic found in the material being studied. Thus, virtually any content analysis is quantitative as well as qualitative. In some situations, appropriate statistical analyses are performed on the frequencies or percentages obtained to determine whether significant differences exist related to the research question. The researcher then uses the tabulations and statistical analyses to interpret the data as they reflect on the problem under investigation.

Sometimes the research problem is specific enough that the researcher can identify, in advance, certain characteristics that will be searched for and counted. For example, when archeologists want to determine which pre-Mayan cultural group lived at a newly discovered Peruvian archaeological site, they might look for specific characteristics in artifacts and architectural structures known to be used by various cultural groups in pre-Mayan times.

In other situations, however, the research problem is less precise, such that initial data analysis involves an open-minded perusal of the data for ideas about significant characteristics to consider. Such was the case for one of us authors, who with several graduate students once asked the question, "What general developmental trends characterize children's conceptions of geographical space, as reflected in the maps they create of their local environments?" (Forbes, Ormrod, Bernardi, Taylor, & Jackson, 1999). To answer the question, the team had children at various grade levels create maps of their local neighborhoods from memory. The two maps shown in Figure 11.3 can give you an idea of the kinds of maps the children created. The first (showing the route from home to school) was drawn by a 6-year-old boy; the second (showing a bird's-eye view of several streets and surrounding geographical features) was drawn by a 13-year-old girl.[1]

At the time the study was conducted, no systematic research had been conducted on the nature of children's maps; thus, the research team had to start from scratch in its determination of helpful coding categories for the maps. To get a sense of what this process might involve, look closely at the maps in Figure 11.3. What characteristics pop out at you as being of possible interest? Amount of detail? Area of geographical space depicted? Perspective (e.g., side view vs. bird's-eye view of features)? Consistent scale? (For instance, notice the disproportionately large stop sign, tree, and picket fence in the 6-year-old's map.) Labels? Signage? Actions? (For instance, in the first map, a child says "[T]hank you" to a school bus driver, and the second map mentions a dog that waddles.) Ultimately, the research team had to make decisions about which of these and other characteristics were most important to focus on—which ones were most significant from a developmental perspective—as they analyzed their data.

---

[1] At the time the study was conducted, neither the researchers nor the children's parents/legal guardians anticipated that any of the data might appear in a book such as this one. The two maps shown in Figure 11.3 have been created more recently, with the parents giving appropriate written permission to publish them in this book. We use them here only for illustrative purposes.

FIGURE 11.3 ■ What Qualitative Differences Are Evident in These Two Neighborhood Maps Drawn by a 6-Year-Old (Left) and 13-Year-Old (Right)?

FIGURE 11.3 ■ What Qualitative Differences Are Evident in These Two Neighborhood Maps Drawn by a 6-Year-Old (Left) and 13-Year-Old (Right)?

USING TECHNOLOGY

PRACTICAL APPLICATION Using Computer Databases to Facilitate Data Organization and Analysis

We authors are assuming that you will use computer software to record interviews and keep track of other collected data. By storing your data on a computer, you can easily retrieve any piece of information using one or more relevant keywords, and you can sort your data quickly and in multiple ways. As a precaution against some unforeseen catastrophe (e.g., a fire or flood), you should regularly back up your data either on an external storage device (e.g., flash drive) or in an electronic dropbox or other Internet-based storage mechanism. Regardless of the specific backup strategy you use, you should keep at least two copies of your data in different physical or electronic locations.

Most qualitative researchers also use computer software to organize and interpret a large body of data. For some studies, a simple spreadsheet program such as Excel may suffice (see Appendix A). Other software programs are especially suited for complex qualitative research studies (e.g., ATLAS.ti, Ethnograph, EthnoNotes, HyperQual, HyperRESEARCH, Kwalitan, MAXQDA, Nvivo, QDA Miner, Qualrus). Such programs provide a ready means of storing, segmenting, and organizing lengthy field notes, and they are designed to help you find patterns in your notes. Some of them also enable you to compare how different raters have coded the same material, thus providing a means of determining interrater reliability. Typically you can import (i.e., transfer) data from word processing files or electronic spreadsheets into the programs; some programs let you include graphic materials, photographs, audiotapes, and videotapes as well. Any one of these programs may take some time and practice to master, but keep in mind that the time you spend learning how to use it effectively is likely to *save* you time in the long run.

ACKNOWLEDGING THE ROLE OF RESEARCHER-AS-INSTRUMENT IN QUALITATIVE RESEARCH

Any research study requires the researcher to make important, informed decisions about how to proceed with data analysis. In quantitative designs, those decisions primarily involve selection of statistical procedures most appropriate for the research question and best suited to characteristics of the data. In quantitative data analysis, then, most important decisions occur up front, before data are collected. In contrast, qualitative research requires the researcher to make significant decisions and judgments throughout the data analysis process, not only about what strategies to use in general but also about which data are most likely to be noteworthy and how to evaluate and code specific pieces of data.

Because qualitative data analysis involves so much decision making—so many *judgments*—it can be especially vulnerable to a researcher's predispositions, expectations, biases, and values, reflecting the notion of *researcher-as-instrument* previously mentioned in Chapter 9.

True objectivity probably isn't possible in qualitative research (if, in fact, it's ever possible in *any* research project). Accordingly, good qualitative researchers take certain precautions to enhance the validity and credibility of their findings. Following are three widely recommended strategies.

1. *Strive for balance, fairness, and completeness in data analysis and interpretation.* As an alternative to maintaining complete objectivity—which, as just pointed out, is probably impossible, Wolcott (1994) has proposed that qualitative researchers should instead strive for *rigorous subjectivity*—in other words, they should take steps to ensure that their analyses and interpretations will ultimately be credible and defensible in the eyes of colleagues and other well-informed individuals. Such steps include the following:

- Triangulate multiple data sources.
- Intentionally look for outliers, exceptions, and contradictions both within the sample selected and within the data collected.
- Remember that participants won't necessarily give you the Ultimate Truth; rather, they may tell you what they (a) *believe* to be true, (b) *wish* were true, or (c) think you want to hear.
- Continue to collect data until you are no longer gaining new insights about the phenomenon of interest (recall the earlier discussion of *saturating* the categories).
- Have two or more individuals independently code the data.
- Seek feedback from both participants and professional colleagues about your findings and interpretations.

All of these strategies should look familiar, because in one context or another, we have mentioned them all in earlier chapters. We bring them up again here because, taken as a whole, they can greatly enhance the credibility and defensibility—and thus the likely validity—of a researcher's findings and conclusions.

2. *Carefully document your analysis procedures.* In a quantitative study, a researcher may need to describe only the specific statistical analyses performed and perhaps also the specific software programs used to perform them. In contrast, a qualitative researcher must document and defend every step along the way—for example, how an initial list of codes was identified, how and in what ways the list was modified for final coding, how raters were trained to code the data reliably, and how raters resolved discrepancies in their judgments about particular pieces of data. Ideally, data analysis procedures should be described in enough detail that another researcher could replicate them and obtain similar results.

3. *In your final report, be upfront about your personal biases.* Credible qualitative researchers don't claim that they have approached a project with complete objectivity. (If they did, the rest of us would never believe them!) Instead, they carefully look inward, reflecting on and then describing possible beliefs, expectations, and cultural values that might have

predisposed them to interpret their data in particular ways. With such knowledge, readers of the final report can better evaluate the credibility of a researcher's findings and interpretations. They are also more likely to perceive the researcher to be a person of honesty and integrity.

PRACTICAL APPLICATION Planning Data Analysis for a Qualitative Study

As you have probably realized by now, there is usually no single "right" way to analyze the data in a qualitative study. The researcher begins with a large body of information and must, through inductive reasoning, sort and categorize it and gradually boil it down to a small set of abstract, underlying themes. Even in content analysis—an approach that, on the surface, might seem quite straightforward and matter-of-fact—the researcher often determines the specific characteristics to be studied only after carefully scrutinizing the body of material in search of potentially meaningful characteristics to identify and count.

The following checklist can help you pin down specific strategies you might use as you consider how best to analyze qualitative data.

✔ CHECKLIST

Pinning Down the Data Analysis in a Qualitative Study

WHAT WILL BE THE NATURE OF YOUR DATA?

_____ 1. What form(s) will your data take?
   _____ Verbal materials
   _____ Concrete objects/artifacts
   _____ Video recordings
   _____ Audio recordings
   _____ Other (explain): _____

_____ 2. Will some or all of your data need to be broken down into smaller segments for coding? If so, what criteria might you use to identify appropriate segments?

   _____

   _____

HOW WILL YOU CODE YOUR DATA?

_____ 3. Do your research problem and/or its subproblems suggest particular categories you might use in coding? If so, what are they?

   _____

_____ 4. Do existing theories or previous research studies related to your problem offer possible categories? If so, what are they?

   _____

_____ 5. What steps will you take to create a final list of codes and subcodes?

   _____

   _____

   _____

_____ 6. Will you have two or more people code the data? If so, what steps will you take to ensure reasonable interrater reliability?
   _____ Concretely define each category and subcategory

_____ Provide examples of each category and subcategory

_____ Give explicit training and practice in applying the codes

_____ Establish a procedure for resolving inconsistent ratings (explain):

_____

_____ Other (explain): _____

_____

HOW WILL YOU ANALYZE AND INTERPRET THE CODED DATA?

_____　7.　What software program(s) might be helpful in analyzing the data?

_____

_____　8.　What strategies will you use to identify general trends within the data?

_____

_____

_____

_____　9.　What kinds of exceptions and inconsistencies might you find within the data?

_____

_____

_____ 10.　What personal or theoretical biases do you have relative to the outcomes
of your study? How can you minimize their influence on your analyses and
interpretations?

_____

_____

_____ 11.　Will it be helpful to analyze the coded data quantitatively as well as qualitatively?
If so, what computations might you perform?

_____ Frequency counts

_____ Percentages

_____ Measures of central tendency (modes, medians, means)

_____ Measures of variability (ranges, interquartile ranges, standard deviations)

_____ Correlation coefficients

_____ Other (explain): _____

_____ 12.　How will you document your data analysis procedures?

_____

_____

_____ 13.　What strategies will you use to ensure that you and others can have confidence in
your findings and interpretations?

_____ Triangulating multiple data sources

_____ Using two or more raters

_____ Saturating categories

_____ Using direct quotes from interview data to support your conclusions

_____ Getting feedback from participants

_____ Getting feedback from experts and professional colleagues (if yes, list these
individuals): _____

_____ Other (explain): _____

PRACTICAL APPLICATION Observing How Experienced Researchers Have Conducted Qualitative Research

In virtually any complex human endeavor—for example, in carpentry, figure skating, musical composition, and computer programming—novices gain new skills and increasing expertise through careful observation of what experienced individuals do. This principle certainly applies to research methodology: Beginning researchers gain considerable proficiency by observing what expert researchers do, in some cases by watching them in the field or in a lab and in other cases by reading their research reports. Especially in qualitative research—where possible data collection and analysis strategies are virtually endless—discovering how expert researchers have tackled research problems similar to your own can give you many useful ideas for planning a methodology and data analysis strategies. Thus, before you embark on a qualitative study, we urge you to read many, many qualitative research reports in search of ideas about how you might best carry out your own study.

As you read these reports, however, you must keep in mind that not all published research studies are good ones; some are apt to have methodological weaknesses that adversely affect the credibility of the results obtained and conclusions drawn. When you find one or more weaknesses in a particular study, think creatively about how the researcher might have strengthened the study—and, indirectly, also how you might strengthen your own study.

Drawing from our discussions in this chapter and in Chapter 9, as well as from guidelines offered by Good (1993) and Miles and colleagues (2014), we offer the following checklist to help you evaluate other researchers' qualitative studies and final research reports.

✔ CHECKLIST

Evaluating a Qualitative Study

METHODOLOGY   YES   NO

_____ 1. Is the context/setting of the study adequately described?   _____ _____

_____ 2. Are techniques for data collection appropriate for the research
            problem? Are they thoroughly and precisely described?   _____ _____

_____ 3. Are multiple data sources used?   _____ _____

_____ 4. Are sufficient data collected from a variety of participants
            over an appropriate length of time?   _____ _____

_____ 5. Are criteria for the selection of participants or materials pre-
            sented? Is the sample described in sufficient detail?   _____ _____

_____ 6. Are potential ethical concerns appropriately addressed?   _____ _____

_____ 7. Are the roles of the researcher and participants made clear?   _____ _____

_____ 8. Might the researcher's presence at the site influence what
            participants do or say?   _____ _____

_____ 9. Does the researcher identify any assumptions, beliefs, values,
            or biases that might influence data collection or analysis?   _____ _____

_____ 10. Does the researcher actively look for evidence that might
             disconfirm initial hypotheses?   _____ _____

FINDINGS AND INTERPRETATIONS

_____ 11. Are the data analysis techniques appropriate for the research
             question, methodology, and theoretical framework?   _____ _____

_____ 12. Are data analysis techniques explicitly described?   _____ _____

_____ 13. Do data analysis techniques allow for revision and reinterpre-
             tation as new data come to light?   _____ _____

_____ 14. Are various data sources triangulated? _____ _____

_____ 15. If used, are tables, figures, and other graphics easy to read and interpret? Do they enhance the reader's ability to understand the study? _____ _____

_____ 16. Are sufficient data reported to support the conclusions drawn? _____ _____

_____ 17. Are any irrelevant and unnecessary data reported? If so, what should be deleted? _____ _____

_____

_____

_____ 18. Are discrepant data discussed and reconciled? _____ _____

_____ 19. Have the setting and observations been sufficiently described to present a convincing case? _____ _____

_____ 20. Are participant "voices" used to support the assertions and present multiple perspectives? _____ _____

_____ 21. Is the report detailed enough that the findings can be compared to other studies in other contexts? _____ _____

_____ 22. Is the discussion congruent with the research question and rationale for the study? _____ _____

_____ 23. Are implications for theory and/or practice discussed? _____ _____

_____ 24. Have other scholars in the field reviewed the proposal or report? If so, do they agree that the approach, methodology, and conclusions are appropriate? _____ _____

_____ 25. Have participants in the project read the report? Do they agree with its findings? _____ _____

✔ **Check Your Understanding in the Pearson etext**

Practice Thinking Like a Researcher

Practice Thinking Like a Researcher Activity 11.1: Mapping the Initial Steps in Qualitative Data Analysis

Practice Thinking Like a Researcher Activity 11.2: Coding Qualitative Data

Practice Thinking Like a Researcher Activity 11.3: Minimizing the Impact of the Researcher-as-Instrument

A SAMPLE DISSERTATION

In Chapter 2, Chapter 9, and this chapter's Figure 11.1, we have previously looked at brief excerpts from Christy Leung's doctoral dissertation regarding Chinese mothers' reasons for immigrating to the United States, experiences prior to and after immigrating, and adjustment and parenting strategies. We now close the chapter by examining some of her qualitative data analysis strategies, which effectively illustrate several of the chapter's recommendations.

Leung conducted her study within the context of a large mixed-method research project for which her doctoral advisor, Dr. Charissa Cheah, was principal investigator. She collected and analyzed both quantitative and qualitative data related to several intertwined research questions. Many of the excerpts you will see in the following pages focus on Leung's efforts to learn about the women's "positive and negative experiences as well as their perceived support received at the initial stage of migration and/or throughout their time in the U.S." (Leung, 2012, p. 116).

DISSERTATION ANALYSIS

Comments

3.5.2 Preparation of qualitative data. Interviews were conducted with 50 mothers (27 boys and 23 girls) who migrated to the U.S. at the age of 13 years or above. . . . The 50 audio-taped interviews were transcribed and checked by multiple bilingual graduate and undergraduate students for accuracy. Prior to the content analyses, the transcripts of the interviews conducted in Chinese were translated into English and then reviewed by multiple bilingual graduate and undergraduate students. Students discussed any discrepancies in translations with each other until they agreed with the final version of the translation to ensure translation accuracy.

Leung used numbers in her headings to indicate her overall organizational scheme. Section 3.5.2 is a subsection of Section 3.5 ("Data Preparation") in Chapter 3 ("Methodology").

In order to provide a full description of the context of the qualitative content analysis, background information about the two coders and the auditor, the consensus process, and issues with potential biases are discussed below.

Many of the interviews were conducted in the participants' native Chinese. Notice the use of multiple raters to translate interview responses into English, thus ensuring that the data to be analyzed were accurate representations of what participants had said.

Coders and auditor. A team of two coders, which comprised a graduate assistant (the author of this dissertation project) and an undergraduate assistant, primarily developed the coding scheme and then coded the interview data. An auditor reviewed the coding process and analyses and provided feedback to the coders (Hill et al., 2005). . . . Regarding the first coder, the graduate assistant is a first-generation Chinese American who immigrated to the U.S. during her late adolescence. She is fluent in both spoken and written Chinese. She supervised all of the translation of research materials and the transcription and translation of interview transcripts. Prior to the coding of interview data for the present study, she was trained by the principal investigator of the larger project to independently code semi-structured interview data regarding: (a) the expressions of love and care as well as the long-term socialization goals of Chinese immigrant mothers, (b) the socialization of Aboriginal-Canadian and European-Canadian mothers, and (c) the social cognitive reasoning of Chinese-Malaysian adolescents.

The use of two coders and an auditor reflect the author's concern for reliability, especially interrater reliability. The descriptions of the coders in this paragraph and the following one should reasonably persuade readers that the two individuals had sufficient background to knowledgably code the data. Note that the first coder was the author herself.

Regarding the second coder, the undergraduate assistant is a second-generation Chinese American who grew up in an urban neighborhood with a large Chinese immigrant population in New York. She is fluent in spoken Chinese. She reviewed the English or English-translated version of all interview transcripts prior to the coding. She has knowledge of the literature of immigration, acculturation, and adaptation of Chinese immigrants. Under the mentorship of the principal investigator of the larger project and the first coder, she completed an independent research project on Chinese mothers' experiences in coming to the U.S. and expectations for their children's adaptation and success in the U.S. . . . Given their background and experiences, the two coders are familiar with Chinese immigrant communities. They can understand the narratives and experiences of Chinese immigrants as cultural insiders.

[In a subsequent paragraph, the author also describes the background and qualifications of Dr. Cheah, who served as auditor for the project.]

Consensus process. Using multiple coders is a preferable practice in qualitative research (Hill et al., 1997, 2005). The multiple perspectives and insights generated from the coders' discussions on coding disagreements help minimize their subjective bias and improve the quality of data analysis (Barbour, 2001). On the other hand, the process of developing a coding scheme and coding of interview transcripts involves consistent discussion and lengthy consensus between coders. Moreover, the nature of the consensus process requires that coders need to respect each other, value others' perspectives, have confidence to share their opinions, feel comfortable to negotiate disagreements, and welcome feedback from others (Brodsky et al., 2004; Hill et al., 1997, 2005).

Thus, both of the coders came to a mutual understanding that equal voice, willingness to share different opinions, and openness to negotiate intellectual conflicts were essential during the coding process. Despite the effort to develop a supportive relationship and facilitate open discussions among the coders, both of the coders recognized the existing power differentials between themselves due to the graduate/undergraduate student dynamics, mentor/mentee academic hierarchy, and differences in research knowledge and experiences. In order to avoid the potential dominant voice of one coder over the other coder, they consulted with the auditor throughout the consensus and coding process. . . .

Potential biases. Addressing potential biases at the initial stage of data analysis is also critical in qualitative research (Hill et al., 1997, 2005). Both of the coders believed that Chinese cultural values continue to play a significant and influential role in Chinese family socialization. Specifically, the two coders articulated their expectations that the Confucian ethic of filial piety would be reflected in the socialization goals and parenting practices of Chinese immigrants. To prevent biases from interfering with coding and data analysis, the two coders and the auditor acknowledged these expectations and came to a mutual understanding that the coders put aside their expectations throughout the process.

In addition, they reviewed and came to a consensus on some general coding guidelines, such as coding by themes, coding based on evidence in the transcripts, and multiple coding (Hill et al., 1997, 2005). In order to understand the context of the responses, coders [did] not utilize the line-by-line coding strategy because fragmenting sentences within a response might fail to capture the context of the response. Instead, coders coded responses by themes or ideas. Thus, one sentence might be coded more than once across different segments of a response. However, coders [had to] identify evidence in the transcripts to support their coding decisions. They might make short notes to indicate their interpretations of specific responses and to justify their coding decisions. Moreover, multiple codes [could] be assigned to one response as long as the response contained multiple themes.

[At this point the author begins Section 3.6, "Planned Analyses," and first addresses analyses of her quantitative data. We pick up the document again when she returns to her analyses of the qualitative data.]

3.6.2 Qualitative content analysis. *[In the first paragraph of this section, the author reminds readers of research questions that the qualitative data were collected to address.]*

Here the author accurately points out that using two coders can minimize the influence of any single coder's biases. It is possible, of course, that two coders would be influenced by the same assumptions, expectations, and/or values—a potential source of bias that any qualitative researcher should keep in mind.

Notice the author's concern that the two coders have equal say during the coding process. Regular involvement of the auditor helped to minimize the possibility that one coder's opinions would dominate over those of the other coder.

Here the author acknowledges that the coders might have had similar biases in how they coded the data. Making a conscious effort to put aside expectations can help reduce their biasing effect but would probably never eliminate it. (Look once again at Figure 1.3, "Common Pitfalls in Human Reasoning," in Chapter 1.)

Notice how the researcher/author (who was also the first coder) involved the second coder in the creation as well as the application of the coding scheme.

"Line-by-line coding" literally means separately coding each line of participants' written responses. As the coders appropriately concluded, such an approach to coding the data might lose some of the data's underlying meanings.

Notice that the coders kept track of their reasons for applying various codes to different parts of the data. Such notes-to-self might be useful in situations where the coders disagreed about how to code certain parts of an interview.

Based on Hill et al.'s (2005) consensual qualitative research method (CQR), a qualitative content analysis (Fereday & Muir-Cochrane, 2006) was conducted to systemically classify and describe the themes regarding the mothers' immigration experiences and parenting revealed from the audio-taped interview. Utilizing a mixed approach that integrates the deductive thematic analysis (Crabtree & Miller, 1999) with the inductive coding process (Boyatzis, 1998), some codes were derived theoretically to address the research questions at the initial phase, whereas other codes were generated to capture the new themes that emerged in the interviews (Fereday & Muir-Cochrane, 2006; Miles & Huberman, 1994). During the content analysis, a coding scheme was developed to create categories of themes, and a cross-analysis was conducted to identify similar and different themes across mothers with the four acculturation strategies.

Notice how some initial codes had a theoretical basis, whereas others emerged during initial inspections of the interview data. The author cites several well-regarded qualitative researchers, who have presumably recommended her methodological choices.

Open coding and development of a coding scheme. A start list of codes was created based on the theoretical concepts reviewed in the literature and the research questions stated in the present study (Miles & Huberman, 1994; see Appendix L). To develop a coherent and structured start list, each research question served as a higher-order code which was accompanied by a subset of corresponding codes that captured the themes in response to the specific research question. The start list was reviewed and discussed by the coders and then checked by the auditor to reach an agreement regarding the classification and definition of codes.

The cross-analysis involved comparing responses of four distinct groups of mothers whose quantitative data had revealed differing acculturation patterns (i.e., differing ways of adapting or not adapting to U.S. culture).

As you should recall, excerpts from both her start list and her final list appear earlier in the chapter (see Figure 11.1). Notice how the researcher uses her research questions as a basis for organizing the start list.

Based on the start list and the coding guidelines, open coding was conducted where the two coders independently analyzed and coded two interviews, chosen randomly by using the random numbers table. In coding the two interviews, each coder also identified new, distinct ideas and created conceptual codes based on similarities in the meaning of distinct ideas from the open-ended responses. Next, the team compared the codes, discussed any discrepancies, and consulted with the auditor to reach a consensus in order to generate new codes. They also discussed and revised the labeling and definition of the codes to better capture the meaning of each code. The coders repeated this process with an additional 22 interviews. They modified and refined the coding scheme and finalized the coding and classification guidelines in order to establish a common understanding of the coding scheme. The process of discussion, consultation, and consensus process involved coding two interviews at a time. They discussed any discrepancies in their coding and consulted with the auditor to resolve disagreement, to seek advice in interpretations of responses, or to clarify applications of the established codes. . . .

Using a random numbers table to choose a subset of the data here served as yet another means of minimizing potential effects of the researcher's biases on data analysis.

Notice the iterative process described here: The coders moved back and forth between revising the list of codes and applying it to additional data. This was undoubtedly a painstaking endeavor, but it helped to ensure that the final list of codes would capture the multiple nuances and meanings of the interview data.

Axial coding and cross-analysis. The remaining 26 interviews were coded based on the established coding scheme. At this point in the data analysis, the coding application and revision were conducted by the first coder, and then reviewed by the auditor. Based on a series of conjoint review and discussion sessions, they modified and refined the coding until any disagreements in coding were resolved by consensus (Hill et al., 2005). Given that the coding scheme was relatively comprehensive, no new codes were identified during the process of coding the additional 26 interviews. Next, axial coding was conducted where some of the codes representing similar or overlapping themes were combined and the definitions of those codes were revised to reduce the number of codes. Finally, a cross-analysis was conducted to compare themes across the mothers in this sample (see Appendix M for the final list of codes).

Here the author presents convincing evidence ("no new codes") that the list of codes developed from the first 24 interviews captured all noteworthy meanings within the interview data.

Based on the guidelines provided in Hill et al.'s (2005) CQR update, the percentages of the codes were categorized by using labels in order to determine how often the codes applied to the mothers in this sample. . . . In the present study, a code category was identified as *general* when it applied to *almost all or a majority of the cases* (80%–100%), *typical* when it applied to *most of the cases* (50%–77%), *sometimes* when it applied to *some of the cases* (20%–45%), or *rare* when it applied to a *small number of the cases* (1%–19%). . . .

Calculating percentages and defining what is meant by such terms as "typical" and "sometimes" are two simple yet effective ways through which the author enhances her ability to analyze and represent her data in an unbiased manner.

[After two additional sentences in the preceding paragraph, the author begins Chapter 4, which she straightforwardly calls "Results." We pick up the dissertation again when she turns to qualitative results related to the mothers' negative and positive immigration experiences. We present only small portions of the section in order to illustrate how a researcher might effectively communicate qualitative findings.]

<u>4.2.2 Qualitative results.</u> The second research aim in the qualitative portion was to explore Chinese immigrant mothers' (a) negative and positive immigration experiences, and (b) perceived support at the initial stage of migration and/or throughout their transition to the U.S. . . .

Once again, the author reminds the reader of her second research question relative to the qualitative data.

Negative immigration experiences. Regarding the negative experiences that the mothers in this sample had with their migration or since the being in the U.S., four themes emerged from the analyses . . .: (a) difficulties with everyday life, (b) language or cultural barriers, (c) small social networks or a sense of disconnectedness, and (d) limitations or discrimination (see Table 6). Different patterns of responses across the four acculturation groups were identified. . . .

The author uses many subheadings within the section to organize her findings, and in the first paragraph of this subsection, she provides an advance organizer for the upcoming discussion (recall the discussion of advance organizers in Chapter 1).

Many of these mothers, such as Ms. Gao, a marginalized mother who migrated at 30 years of age, discussed the problems they encountered communicating with individuals outside their own ethnic group due to language barriers: "When you are talking [with others] outside [the home], people sometimes do not understand what we mean by what we say." Thus, these mothers indicated that they often cannot express themselves well in English and experience a feeling of not being understood by the others. Moreover, several mothers mentioned that they had difficulties finding a job or suffered from a decline in their occupational status with a lower earning potential because of their poor English skills.

The term "marginalized" refers to one of the four acculturation groups the author had identified; the other three groups were labeled "assimilated," integrated," and "separated."

"Ms. Gao" and other names in the report are pseudonyms, thus maintaining confidentiality and protecting the participants' right to privacy.

In addition, mothers in all four acculturation groups had to face various challenges at work because they were not familiar with the cultural and social norms in the U.S. Specifically, some of these mothers had difficulties building professional relationships because they were not competent in socializing with their American colleagues. Other mothers believed that they missed professional opportunities because they had been socialized to be modest and reserved in their home country, whereas their American colleagues had been taught to be confident and assertive in the U.S. Mothers such as Ms. Hui, an assimilated mother who migrated at 25 years of age, also expressed that Chinese women might not present themselves with confidence effectively at work due to such cultural differences: "I can speak out only when I know something very well. However, I find out that it is not the case with others sometimes. Some people can speak out within one minute [even if] they only know a little bit."

Notice how the author effectively uses quotes from the interview data to illustrate her generalizations. Bracketed words in quoted responses reflect changes that the author or a translator had made in order to clarify what the women were talking about. In reporting interview data, this strategy is both appropriate and helpful, provided that it does not change the meanings of participants' statements.

Note: Excerpts are from *The Immigration Experiences, Acculturation, and Parenting of Chinese Immigrant Mothers* (pp. 109–113, 116–119, 146–149) by C. Y. Y. Leung, 2012, unpublished doctoral dissertation, University of Maryland, Baltimore County. Reprinted with permission.

FOR FURTHER READING

Altheide, D. L., & Schneider, C. J. (2013). *Qualitative media analysis* (2nd ed.). Thousand Oaks, CA: Sage.

Charmaz, K. (2014). *Constructing grounded theory* (2nd ed.). Thousand Oaks, CA: Sage.

Corbin, J., & Strauss, A. C. (2008). *Basics of qualitative research: Techniques and procedures for developing grounded theory* (3rd ed.). Thousand Oaks, CA: Sage.

Creswell, J. W. (2013). *Qualitative inquiry and research design: Choosing among five approaches* (3rd ed.). Thousand Oaks, CA: Sage.

Denzin, N. K., & Lincoln, Y. S. (2013). *Collecting and interpreting qualitative materials* (4th ed.). Thousand Oaks, CA: Sage.

Fereday, J., & Muir-Cochrane, E. (2006). Demonstrating rigor using thematic analysis: A hybrid approach of inductive and deductive coding and theme development. *International Journal of Qualitative Methods, 5*(1), 1–11.

Glaser, B. (1992). *Basics of grounded theory analysis.* Mill Valley, CA: Sociology Press.

Grbich, C. (2007). *Qualitative data analysis.* Thousand Oaks, CA: Sage.

Guest, G., MacQueen, K. M., & Namey, E. E. (2012). *Applied thematic analysis.* Thousand Oaks, CA: Sage.

Harding, J. (2013). *Qualitative data analysis from start to finish.* London: Sage.

Hill, C. E., Knox, S., Thompson, B. J., Williams, E. N., Hess, S. A., & Ladany, N. (2005). Consensual qualitative research: An update. *Journal of Counseling Psychology, 52,* 196–205.

Hill, C. E., Thompson, B. J., & Williams, E. N. (1997). A guide to conducting consensual qualitative research. *The Counseling Psychologist, 25,* 517–572.

Kuckartz, U. (2014). *Qualitative text analysis: A guide to methods, practice, and using software.* London: Sage.

Martin, V. B., & Gynnild, A. (Eds.). (2011). *Grounded theory: The philosophy, method, and work of Barney Glaser.* Boca Raton, FL: BrownWalker Press.

Merriam, S. B. (1995). What can you tell from an N of 1? Issues of validity and reliability in qualitative research. *PAACE Journal of Lifelong Learning, 4,* 51–60.

Miles, M. B., Huberman, A. M., & Saldaña, J. (2014). *Qualitative data analysis: A methods sourcebook* (3rd ed.). Los Angeles: Sage.

Saldaña, J. (2013). *The coding manual for qualitative researchers* (2nd ed.). London: Sage.

Tashakkori, A., & Teddlie, C. (Eds.) (2010). *Mixed methods in social & behavioral research.* Thousand Oaks, CA: Sage.

Wertz, F. J., Charmaz, K., McMullen, L. M., Josselson, R., Anderson, R., & McSpadden, E. (2011). *Five ways of doing qualitative analysis: Phenomenological psychology, grounded theory, discourse analysis, narrative research, and intuitive inquiry.* New York: Guilford Press.

Wolcott, H. F. (1994). *Transforming qualitative data: Description, analysis, and interpretation.* Thousand Oaks, CA: Sage.

Yin, R. K. (2011). *Qualitative research from start to finish.* New York: Guilford Press.

12

Mixed-Methods Designs

Many research problems have both quantitative and qualitative dimensions. To fully address them, then, the researcher must use both quantitative and qualitative techniques. Thus, quantitative and qualitative methodologies are not necessarily a case of either–or, but rather a case of more–or–less.

Learning Outcomes

12.1 Identify situations in which mixed-methods designs are especially useful.

12.2 Describe general characteristics and purposes of (a) convergent designs, (b) embedded designs, (c) exploratory designs, (d) explanatory designs, and (e) multiphase iterative designs.

12.3 Describe effective strategies for conducting mixed-methods research, especially those related to (a) identifying research questions

and hypotheses, (b) conducting a literature review, (c) choosing one or more samples, (d) maximizing the overall validity of a research project, and (e) addressing potential ethical concerns.

12.4 Identify appropriate and efficient approaches to analyzing data in a mixed-methods study.

12.5 Explain how you might conduct a systematic review of qualitative research studies regarding a particular topic.

Some research problems practically scream for both quantitative and qualitative data. These problems call for mixed-methods research. Such research involves not only collecting, analyzing, and interpreting both quantitative and qualitative data but also *integrating* conclusions from those data into a cohesive whole.

As you may have noticed, this chapter is a relatively short one. It is short not because mixed-methods studies are quick and easy—they definitely are *not* quick and easy—but because mixed-methods research draws largely on quantitative and qualitative research strategies addressed in previous chapters. For instance, in a typical mixed-methods investigation, the researcher must be well-versed in most or all of the following skill sets (Creswell & Plano Clark, 2011):

- Identifying focused and useful research questions
- Formulating and strategically testing hypotheses
- Choosing one or more samples that enable appropriate inferences about a larger population
- Controlling for confounding variables
- Creating and using measurement instruments that have validity and reliability for their purposes
- Conducting structured, semistructured, and open-ended interviews
- Analyzing qualitative data (identifying units suitable for coding, applying the codes, discerning general themes underlying the data, etc.)
- Calculating and drawing inferences from descriptive and inferential statistics
- Drawing and persuasively arguing for reasonable conclusions from qualitative data (through triangulation, negative case analysis, thick description, etc.)

Because a mixed-methods study requires both quantitative and qualitative research skills, it can be an especially challenging undertaking for a novice researcher. The trickiest part of mixed-methods research is in *combining* the two methodological traditions into a research endeavor in which all aspects substantially contribute to a single, greater whole. In other words, a good mixed-methods study is one that effectively and convincingly "hangs together."[1]

If you have the requisite skills and experience, however, we urge you to take on the challenge, because you might very well obtain a more complete, comprehensive answer to your research question than would be possible with only quantitative or only qualitative methodologies.

WHEN MIXED-METHODS DESIGNS ARE MOST USEFUL AND APPROPRIATE

In some disciplines, mixed-methods research is becoming increasingly fashionable, trendy, "hip"—so much so that many universities now offer specific courses on mixed-methods techniques. But fashion and trendiness are hardly legitimate reasons to conduct a mixed-methods study. Ultimately, decisions about research design must be driven by the research problem and its subproblems. Some problems and subproblems call for only quantitative data, some call for only qualitative data, and some are best addressed with *both* kinds of data.

On average, a mixed-methods research study requires more of a researcher's time and energy than a strictly qualitative or quantitative study. Why, then, would a researcher want to go to the trouble of collecting, analyzing, interpreting, and integrating both quantitative and qualitative data? Following are several good reasons (Bryman, 2006; Greene, Caracelli, & Graham, 1989):

- *Completeness.*   A researcher can fully address a research problem and its subproblems only by collecting, analyzing, and interpreting both quantitative and qualitative data.
- *Complementarity.*   Quantitative aspects of the study can compensate for weaknesses in qualitative research, and vice versa. For example, the results of unstructured interviews with only a small number of individuals (which might raise concerns about generalizability) can be replicated by administering a questionnaire to a larger, more representative sample.
- *Hypothesis generation and testing.*   Qualitative data often provide insights that help a researcher form hypotheses about cause-and-effect relationships—hypotheses that the researcher can subsequently test through controlled, quantitative research.
- *Development of appropriate research tools and strategies.*   One type of data can inform and guide subsequent collection of another type of data. For example, unstructured interviews (yielding qualitative data) can guide the construction of appropriate questions for a survey (which will yield quantitative data).
- *Resolution of puzzling findings.*   In a quantitative study, various results can sometimes seem inconsistent or contradictory; qualitative data may reveal underlying nuances and meanings that can help the researcher make sense of the numbers.
- *Triangulation.*   A researcher can make a more convincing case for particular conclusions if both quantitative and qualitative data lead to those conclusions.

COMMON MIXED-METHODS DESIGNS

In previous chapters we have touched on a few ways in which quantitative and qualitative methods might be combined into a single study. For example, in a large-scale survey, questionnaires might include both (a) rating scales or checklists that yield numerical data and (b) open-ended questions that yield verbal responses requiring qualitative analysis (see Chapter 6). Historical researchers often make use of both qualitative and quantitative data in a single research inquiry (see Chapter 10). And the effectiveness of people's study strategies might be measured both

---

[1]Teddlie and Tashakkori (2010) have suggested that a study that *doesn't* effectively integrate findings and conclusions from quantitative and qualitative data might better be called a *quasi-mixed* study.

quantitatively (e.g., by the number of facts they recall) and qualitatively (e.g., by the content of their think-aloud study sessions; see Chapter 7).

The ways in which a researcher might combine quantitative and qualitative methods are almost limitless, restricted only by the researcher's imagination and creativity, as well as by the nature of the research problem. To help you envision some of the possibilities, we describe five general types of mixed-methods designs, based on categories suggested by Creswell (2014).

Convergent Designs

In a convergent design, a researcher collects both quantitative and qualitative data in parallel, usually at the same time and with respect to the same general research problem. The researcher gives similar or equal weight to the two types of data and strives for triangulation, with the hope that analyses of both data sets lead to similar conclusions about the phenomenon under investigation.

Embedded Designs

An embedded design is similar to a convergent design, in that both quantitative and qualitative data are collected within the same general time frame. However, one general approach dominates—perhaps a qualitative approach, but more often a quantitative one—with the other approach serving in a secondary, supplementary role. For example, when planning a large-scale survey of people's attitudes or opinions about a controversial topic, a researcher might create a series of statements with which participants either "agree" or "disagree" at various points along a rating-scale continuum. Within this generally quantitative instrument, however, the researcher could embed several open-ended items in which participants explain their ratings. Such qualitative data could help the researcher make better sense of the numerical findings.

Exploratory Designs

An exploratory design typically encompasses two phases. In Phase 1, a researcher uses one or more qualitative methods to get a general sense of characteristics, phenomena, and/or issues related to the topic of study. The qualitative data—perhaps from observations, interviews, or both—provide a basis for a more systematic, quantitative study in Phase 2. For example, qualitative observations of a phenomenon in a real-world setting might help a researcher develop hypotheses to be systematically tested in an experimental study, or the results of a few unstructured interviews might help the researcher develop appropriate questions for a questionnaire administered to a much larger sample—and possibly also to determine important subgroup differences to keep in mind when identifying the Phase 2 sample.

Explanatory Designs

Like an exploratory design, an explanatory design is usually a two-phase process, but in this case the quantitative phase comes first. More specifically, Phase 1 involves collecting considerable quantitative data, perhaps in an experiment, ex post facto study, or survey. However, this first phase yields only numbers (e.g., percentages and/or averages). Collecting qualitative data in a Phase 2 follow-up—for instance, asking a subsample of Phase 1 participants to describe what they were thinking or feeling during an experimental intervention or to elaborate on their answers to survey questions—can help the researcher give greater substance and meaning to the numbers.

Multiphase Iterative Designs

A multiphase iterative design includes three or more phases, with early ones providing foundational data on which later phases can build. The design is *iterative* in that the researcher moves back and forth among quantitative and qualitative methods, with each new body of data informing the conceptualization and implementation of subsequent phases.

Multiphase iterative designs have become increasingly common in program evaluation research—that is, in determining the efficacy of certain intervention programs. For example, imagine that a team of researchers wants to evaluate the effectiveness of a program created to reduce drug abuse in teenagers who live in a particular city. The team might take steps such as the following, with Steps 3a and 3b being two complementary parts of a single data-collection step:

1. Collect baseline quantitative data regarding the current prevalence of illicit drug use in the city's teenage population.
2. Implement an intervention program based on current theories and previous research studies.
3a. Collect subsequent quantitative data regarding illicit drug use in teenagers who have participated in the intervention; compare the data to those for a control group of nonparticipants.
3b. Conduct qualitative interviews of both program staff members and program participants to discover their views about the strengths and weaknesses of the initial intervention.
4. Make modifications to the intervention program in an effort to improve its outcomes.
5. Collect follow-up quantitative and qualitative data (e.g., prevalence of drug use by program participants; staff members' and participants' opinions about the revised program).
6. If deemed necessary, repeat Steps 4 and 5 through additional iterations.

Another arena in which multiphase iterative designs are common is *design-based research* (also known as *design experiments*), in which researchers in educational technology and other learning sciences apply existing knowledge and theories about human learning processes to create effective instructional programs or curricula. As an example, imagine that a researcher wants to develop instructional software that can help middle school students learn how to *control for confounding variables* when conducting simple physics experiments—say, when determining what one or more variables (e.g., weight, length) influence the rate at which a pendulum swings back and forth. In developing a preliminary version of the software, the researcher draws on existing knowledge regarding educational strategies that have been empirically shown to enhance children's scientific reasoning skills. The researcher has a small sample of middle schoolers use the software to swing a virtual "pendulum" while controlling for such factors as weight, length, and height of initial drop. The researcher then quantitatively and/or qualitatively assesses the students' subsequent ability to control for confounding variables in other computer-based "experiments"—for instance, experiments in which students must determine (a) what environmental conditions influence how fast sunflowers grow and (b) what factors affect an automobile's fuel efficiency. After paying particular attention to parts of the software that seem to have worked well and to those that have not, the researcher modifies the program, has a second sample of students use it, tweaks the program again, and so on, until—ideally—a truly effective software program emerges.

Common Symbolic Notations for Mixed-Methods Designs

Mixed-methods researchers tend to use certain notational conventions to describe how the quantitative and qualitative aspects of a study contribute to its overall design. In general, they use uppercase "QUAN" or "QUAL" to indicate that quantitative and qualitative methods both play major roles; they use lowercase "quan" or "qual" to indicate that one of these methods plays only a minor, supplemental role (e.g., Creswell, 2010; Miles, Huberman, & Saldaña, 2014). For example, the notation "QUAN+QUAL" means that both quantitative and qualitative data contribute substantially and equally to a study or to one of its phases. The notation "QUAL(quan)" indicates that a study or phase is predominantly qualitative but has a minor quantitative element embedded within it. The notation "QUAL→QUAN→QUAL" might be used to summarize a three-phase study in which a researcher first (a) conducts qualitative interviews to identify various aspects and nuances of people's attitudes regarding a topic, then (b) uses the results to create and administer a quantitative survey to gather data from a much larger sample, and finally (c) interviews a subset of the survey participants to get in-depth qualitative information that can enhance the researcher's ability to interpret the survey responses.

When mixed-methods designs are lopsided in favor of one form of data over the other, they tend to lean in the quantitative direction (Hesse-Biber, 2010). Unless there's a compelling reason to do otherwise, we urge novice mixed-methods researchers to lean in the quantitative direction as well. A more quantitatively oriented approach can provide a reasonable structure to guide the overall research project—a structure that can keep a researcher on task and consistently focused on addressing the research problem. As one experienced mixed-methods researcher has put it, "Undertaking a qualitative approach to mixed methods is like taking a journey without always being in control of your destination" (Hesse-Biber, 2010, p. 211).

CONCEPTUAL ANALYSIS EXERCISE Identifying Mixed-Methods Research Designs

The following items describe four hypothetical mixed-methods research projects. For each one, identify the project's general design, choosing from one of these five options: convergent, embedded, exploratory, explanatory, and multiphase iterative. Also, depict the design using the symbolic notations "QUAN," "QUAL," "quan," and/or "qual." The answers are provided after the "For Further Reading" section at the end of the chapter.

1. A researcher conducts in-depth case studies of two average-intelligence middle school boys who have dyslexia; that is, these boys have reading abilities substantially lower than would be predicted from their IQ scores. In the case studies, the researcher especially focuses on (a) the challenges and frustrations the boys face in their daily academic work and (b) strategies they have developed to help them cope with these challenges and frustrations. The researcher then uses the case study data to develop checklist questions for interviews to be conducted with a sample of 45 middle school students with dyslexia.

2. A researcher recruits 500 adult volunteers to complete an online questionnaire regarding their beliefs about several politically charged topics (e.g., climate change, legalization of marijuana, capital punishment). The questionnaire includes 40 statements (e.g., "Over the past several decades, the Earth's atmosphere has gradually been getting warmer") to which participants respond "strongly agree," "agree," "disagree," or "strongly disagree." Also, each of the last four rating-scale items is immediately followed by an open-ended question that asks participants to explain why they rated the preceding statement as they did. Based on the rating-scale responses, the researcher identifies some participants as being politically "conservative" and others as being politically "liberal"; the researcher then statistically contrasts the political leanings of people in various age-groups and geographical regions. Also, the researcher and a second rater jointly code answers to the four open-ended questions as reflecting the use of either (a) empirical evidence or (b) ideological thinking; the researcher then looks for possible differences in how "conservatives" and "liberals" reason about certain issues.

3. At the request of the CEO of a large paper-products company, a researcher wants to determine why an 18-employee department within the company is especially dysfunctional. In a short paper-and-pencil questionnaire, the researcher asks each person in the department to identify (a) one to three individuals within the department whom the person likes best, (b) one to three individuals within the department whom the person especially *dis*likes, and (c) one to three individuals within the department for whom the person has no strong feelings. Based on the data collected, the researcher creates a sociogram similar to the one depicted in Figure 4.3 in Chapter 4; this sociogram enables the researcher to identify "leaders" and "isolates" within the group. The following week, the researcher interviews each department

member, asking him or her simply to "Describe what you like and dislike about _____," with the blank being filled by the names of the apparent leaders and isolates within the department.

4. Based on current theories and research evidence regarding effective study skills, a team of researchers creates a 6-month after-school program for low-achieving tenth graders. In a quasi-experimental study, the team compares the pre-program and post-program GPAs of program participants with those of control-group students who do not attend the program. Later, at the end of the school year, the team conducts unstructured interviews of program participants to discover which aspects of the program they did and did not find helpful for improving their study skills. Over the summer, the team revises the program's curriculum in line with Year 1 participants' interview responses and then, the following year, conducts the program again with the school's incoming tenth graders. Once again, pre-program and post-program GPAs are compared for program participants and nonparticipants.

PLANNING A MIXED-METHODS STUDY

Some mixed-methods designs are, in advance, planned in precise detail from start to finish. Others have a more *emergent* quality to them, with data collected early in the process revealing other kinds of data that might also be useful (recall the concept of *emergent design* in Chapter 9). For example, early data might yield difficult-to-interpret inconsistencies or suggest potentially fruitful new avenues of investigation; in either case, a subsequent phase of data collection might be in order.

But regardless of whether a mixed-methods study has a fixed or emergent design, it requires considerable advance planning. We have discussed planning in considerable depth in earlier chapters (especially in Chapter 4), so here we alert you only to a few additional things that you should keep in mind as you plan a mixed-methods research project.

Identifying Research Questions and Hypotheses

Curious people tend to ask questions—*lots* of questions—and different questions can't necessarily all be addressed in the same way. Such multiple question-asking can give rise to mixed-methods research. In general, however, such questions should all be related to a single, overarching research problem.

As an example, we return to a study described in Chapter 7, one in which three groups of college professors—geographers, sociologists, and educational psychologists—studied maps in an effort to remember the maps' contents (J. E. Ormrod, Ormrod, Wagner, & McCallin, 1988). The general research problem could be phrased as a question:

Do geographers study and remember maps differently than nongeographers do?

Both quantitative data and qualitative data were potentially relevant to the problem: Quantitative data could reveal whether geographers tend to remember *more* map content than nongeographers, and qualitative data could reveal whether geographers study and remember maps in distinctly different ways than nongeographers do. In a sense, then, the research question could be broken down into two subproblems:

Do geographers remember more details of a new map than nongeographers do? (This question calls for quantitative data.)

Do geographers think about new maps in different ways than nongeographers do? (This question calls for qualitative data.)

The answer to the first (quantitative) question was *yes:* Geographers remember more details of a new map *if* the map is consistent with well-established geographical principles of how various land forms and human constructions are arranged on the Earth's surface. The answer to the second (qualitative) question was also *yes:* Geographers think about a new map differently than nongeographers do. In particular, geographers try to make sense of the arrangement of features in a map, whereas nongeographers are likely to engage in rote memorization as they study it. The answers to both subproblems, then, converged to answer the overall research question.

As you plan a mixed-methods study, we urge you to identify several separate subproblems or research questions to guide you in your investigation. Furthermore, if you conduct a study with two or more phases, one or two additional subproblems or questions may emerge as being important ones to address. Following are general frameworks you might consider in the *quantitative* questions you ask:

- To what extent do ___[certain kinds of people, animals, plants, inanimate objects]___ exhibit ___[certain kinds of behaviors or characteristics]___?
- Do _____ have more/less of _____ than _____ do?
- Is there a predictable correlation between _____ and _____?
- Does _____ have an effect on _____?

Meanwhile, your *qualitative* questions might take forms such as these:

- What is the general nature of ___[a certain group or phenomenon]___?
- How do people think or feel about _____?
- How do participants in the sample explain _____?

We also recommend one or more questions that require an *integration* of the study's quantitative and qualitative elements—perhaps questions along these lines:

- Do the quantitative data and qualitative data converge to support the conclusion that _____?
- Can the qualitative data help to explain and elaborate on the quantitative findings?
- Do the qualitative data suggest hypotheses that might be supported or disconfirmed by quantitative data?

The final question in the preceding list brings up the issue of *hypotheses.* Mixed-methods studies may or may not involve the testing of certain hypotheses. In some cases, one or more hypotheses may be posed in advance, presumably as a result of a review of related literature. In other cases—for instance, in the exploratory and multiphase iterative designs described previously—qualitative data collected early in the study might yield hypotheses that the researcher subsequently tests more systematically by collecting quantitative data.

Conducting the Literature Review

As is true for strictly quantitative and strictly qualitative designs, a mixed-methods researcher should conduct much of his or her literature review at the very beginning of the project. (Grounded theory studies are occasionally exceptions to this rule; see Chapter 9.) A review of the related literature can help the researcher pin down appropriate questions and hypotheses, suggest possible research designs, and reveal potentially helpful measurement instruments.

Especially in studies with two or more phases, additional visits to the library or its online databases may be useful midway through the research project. For example, in the first, qualitative phase of a two-phase exploratory study, you may unearth intriguing ideas about which you need to learn more so that you can better plan the second, quantitative phase. Or, in a two-phase explanatory study, your initial quantitative findings may necessitate a search for new literature that will assist you as you conduct the subsequent, qualitative phase.

Choosing One or More Appropriate Samples

In virtually any kind of research—whether it be quantitative, qualitative, or mixed-methods— the quality of the data obtained can be only as good as the quality of the sample(s) used. When the goal is to estimate what a relatively large population does, thinks, or feels, some form of *probability sampling* is called for—perhaps stratified random sampling or cluster sampling (see Chapter 6). Alternatively, a researcher might engage in *purposive sampling,* choosing particular participants who can provide certain desired perspectives on a topic or issues. Following are examples of the many forms that purposive sampling might take in a mixed-methods study (Collins, 2010):

- Choosing participants who will represent diverse attitudes or opinions, including some who hold extreme views
- Intentionally choosing seemingly "average" or "typical" individuals
- Choosing participants on the basis of certain prespecified characteristics relevant to the research problem (e.g., people who are over 65 and retired, or parents who have children with significant physical disabilities)
- In a later phase of a multiphase study, choosing participants who can best help to either support or cast doubt on conclusions drawn in an earlier phase

In some studies with two or more phases, the samples used in various phases should be connected, or *linked,* in some meaningful way. For example, a study might involve one of these strategies (Teddlie & Tashakkori, 2010):

- Choosing a large sample for a first, quantitative phase of a study and then selecting a subset of the sample for a subsequent, qualitative phase
- Choosing two samples that are related by biology, marriage, or some other connection relevant to the research problem (e.g., collecting data from parents in one phase and then collecting data from their children in a second phase)

Even when the focus of study is on nonhuman animal species, plants, or nonliving objects—rather than people—a researcher should identify samples that can truly yield the information the researcher seeks. And regardless of whom or what is being studied, a researcher should provide a reasonable rationale for the sampling technique(s) being used.

Addressing Validity Concerns

Whether conducting a qualitative, quantitative, or mixed-methods study, any researcher must ensure that its measurement techniques—even such simple techniques as counting or computing percentages—are valid indicators of the variables under investigation (see Chapter 4). In this chapter our focus is not on the validity of measurement instruments but rather on the validity of the overall research effort, including:

- Its *internal validity*—the extent to which the study enables defensible conclusions about cause-and-effect and other between-variable relationships
- Its *external validity*—the extent to which the study's results can be generalized to a larger population or broader context
- Its general *credibility* and *trustworthiness*—the extent to which other individuals perceive the study's findings to be convincing and worth taking seriously

All three of these ideas should look familiar, as we have previously discussed each of them in Chapter 4.

Additional validity issues come up in mixed-methods research, especially in relation to how a study's quantitative and qualitative components come together—or in some cases *don't* come together. Drawing on suggestions by Creswell (2010; Creswell & Plano Clark, 2011) and O'Cathain (2010), we urge you to consider and address questions such as the following whenever you conduct a mixed-methods study:

- Are the samples for the quantitative and qualitative aspects of the study the same or else sufficiently similar to justify comparisons between the quantitative and qualitative data?
- Are the quantitative and qualitative data equally relevant to the same or related topics and research question(s)?
- What personal or methodological biases might have differentially affected collection and interpretation of the quantitative data and of the qualitative data?

▓ Are quantitative sample sizes significantly larger than qualitative sample sizes? If so, what impact might the differing sample sizes have on the validity of conclusions?

▓ Can specific statements or artifacts from the qualitative element of the study be used to support or illustrate some of the quantitative results?

▓ Do the quantitative and qualitative data lead to the same or similar conclusions? If not, can discrepancies be reasonably resolved?

Special Ethical Considerations in Mixed-Methods Research

In conducting any mixed-methods research study, the usual ethical guidelines apply, including protection from harm, voluntary and informed consent, and participants' right to privacy regarding anything they might reveal about themselves. Furthermore, the researcher must obtain permission from the appropriate committee at his or her institution for any research involving human beings or nonhuman animals—from the internal review board (IRB) in the case of human participants, or otherwise from the institutional animal care and use committee (IACUC).

We alert you to two issues that can arise for mixed-methods studies in particular, and especially for studies with two or more phases—that is, in exploratory, explanatory, and multiphase iterative designs. First, when results of one phase in some way guide the implementation of a subsequent phase, the researcher may have to submit two or more complete proposals to the IRB or IACUC, one for each phase of the study. Alternatively, the researcher's first proposal might describe Phase 1 in detail and give a general overview of the intended procedure for later phases, followed by updated, more specific (but perhaps briefer) proposals for the later phases (Creswell & Plano Clark, 2011). Either way, securing permission for the entire study will require more effort than would be the case for a one-shot research study. Don't let this fact discourage you: A project with two or more phases may make a more substantial and enlightening contribution to your field than a shorter, more limited investigation could possibly do.

A second ethical issue arises in explanatory designs and some multiphase iterative designs, especially if the researcher wants to use the results of Phase 1 quantitative data to choose a subsample to interview in a later phase (Hesse-Biber, 2010). When participants respond in Phase 1— say, to a questionnaire about a potentially sensitive topic—they can reasonably expect that you won't be able to attach particular responses to particular people *unless you have explicitly told them otherwise during the informed consent process.* Yet in fact, you may very well want to use participants' responses in Phase 1 to identify an appropriate and informative subsample for your follow-up in a subsequent phase. You must plan for this eventuality before you implement Phase 1 and must describe your intentions in your IRB proposal and informed consent materials. One commonly used strategy is to give participants in Phase 1 data collection the option of participating— *voluntarily*—in a second, follow-up part of the study and providing a place to include their name and a telephone number or e-mail address so that you can contact them.

ANALYZING AND INTERPRETING MIXED-METHODS DATA

The final activity in any mixed-methods study is to analyze and then *interpret* the collected data. At this point in the book, this should hardly be news.

Unfortunately, there are no fixed procedures—no prescriptions, no recipes—for analyzing data in a mixed-methods study. Specific data analysis procedures depend on the design of the study, the kinds of data collected, and, of course, the nature of the research problem and its subproblems and questions.

One decision you must make early in the game—ideally, before you collect your data— regards whether you will (a) give qualitative data and quantitative data equal weight in drawing your conclusions or (b) give higher importance to one form of data over the other. You certainly can't disregard one set of data simply because you don't like what they tell you! But with an appropriate rationale, you might make one form of data secondary and subservient to the other form of data. For example, this might be the case if you were using people's qualitative responses in follow-up interviews to shed light on their earlier (quantitative) responses to questionnaire items.

In general, any data analysis will probably include at least three of the following four steps (Onwuegbuzie & Teddlie, 2003):[2]

1. *Condensing the data.*   As noted in Chapter 1, the human mind can think about only so much—and not *very* much—at any single point in time. Trying to consider every single data point separately as you look at your data . . . well, you just can't do it. Instead, you need to boil it down to more compact entities your mind can reasonably handle at once. Condensing quantitative data might involve calculating basic descriptive statistics, such as means or medians, standard deviations or ranges, or correlation coefficients. Condensing qualitative data might involve inspecting the overall data set to get preliminary ideas about general themes or potentially useful codes.

2. *Depicting general patterns in the data in ways that enable quick visual inspection.* For example, quantitative data might be presented in line graphs, bar graphs, or statistical tables. Qualitative data might be depicted as diagrams, matrices, or hierarchical taxonomies.

3. *Transforming qualitative data into quantitative entities (an optional step).* Occasionally mixed-methods researchers transform quantitative data into a qualitative form—say, a general narrative—but more typically the transformation is in the other direction. For example, as noted in Chapter 11, many qualitative researchers code discrete elements within a data set—perhaps participants' responses to interviews or perhaps works of literature undergoing content analysis—and then count instances of each code. Alternatively, a researcher might use rating scales to assign rough indicators of magnitude or intensity to discrete pieces of qualitative data (see Miles et al., 2014).

4. *Systematically comparing and integrating results from the two types of data.*   As noted previously, some mixed-methods researchers use data from one or more early phases to guide the planning and implementation of one or more subsequent phases; this is especially likely to be true for exploratory designs and multiphase iterative designs. Whether or not such preliminary data integration has occurred in an early phase, it *must* occur after all data have been collected and analyzed. Again, there are no prescriptions for integrating quantitative and qualitative findings; the only generalization we can make is: *It all depends.* Such a generalization certainly isn't helpful for novice researchers. But we can offer a few possible strategies you might consider (Bazeley, 2010; Creswell, 2012, 2014):

   - Create a two-column table—one column for quantitative findings and another for qualitative findings—that can reveal consistencies or inconsistencies in findings related to each subproblem or research question within the overall research problem.
   - Identify concrete examples within the qualitative data that *give meaning and depth* to the numbers.
   - After conducting both a quantitative paper-and-pencil survey and open-ended, qualitative interviews, count the number of times each theme appears in the interviews and then compare the frequency counts with the quantitative analysis of survey responses.
   - Divide participants into two or more groups based on certain demographic variables (e.g., age-group, gender, political party membership) and statistically compare the frequencies of various codes or themes within the qualitative data for each group.

But remember, you cannot stop with an integration of the quantitative and qualitative data; you must also *interpret* those data. Not only must you draw inferences from each form of

---

[2]Onwuegbuzie and Teddlie (2003) described seven discrete steps. We have consolidated their Steps 4, 5, 6, and 7 into a single Step 4.

data, but you must also draw inferences—meta-inferences, if you will—from the entire data set (Onwuegbuzie & Combs, 2010). Your final step must be to determine *what the data mean* relative to your research problem.

USING TECHNOLOGY

PRACTICAL APPLICATION Using Computer Software to Facilitate Mixed-Methods Data Analysis

We authors hope that at this point in the book we have convinced you of the importance of using one or more software packages to assist you in data analysis. Some software programs are especially suited for mixed-methods data analysis; examples include EthnoNotes, MAXQDA, NVivo, and QDA Miner. Such software programs typically enable a researcher to:

- Sift through and sort data that might be relevant to particular subproblems or research questions
- Convert qualitative data into simple quantitative data
- Create matrixes that summarize certain aspects of a data set
- Integrate and compare results from quantitative data and coded qualitative data
- Compare data obtained from various demographic groups

For more details on these and other software packages, we refer you to a comprehensive book chapter by Bazeley (2010).

PRACTICAL APPLICATION Deciding Whether to Use a Mixed-Methods Design

By its very nature, a mixed-methods study is more complex than either a solely qualitative or solely quantitative one. Other things being equal, it is likely to take more of the researcher's time and energy and may also require more resources. Is it, then, worth the trouble? The following checklist can help you answer this question.

✔ CHECKLIST

Pinning Down the Logistics and Feasibility of a Mixed-Methods Study

_____ 1. Can your research problem be better addressed with both quantitative and qualitative data than with only one form of data or the other? If so, explain how each kind of data will contribute to your inquiry.

_____

_____

_____ 2. Does your proposed project reflect a convergent, embedded, exploratory, explanatory, or multiphase iterative design? If so, which one? If not, describe the general nature and structure of your design.

_____

_____

_____ 3. What specific steps should you take to ensure that your proposed study has:
  - Internal validity: _____
  - External validity: _____
  - Credibility and trustworthiness: _____

_____ 4. Given your design, how much of your time is the study likely to take?

_____

_____

_____ 5. What specific research skills do you need to collect the data? Do you currently have these skills? If not, explain how you might reasonably acquire them.

_____

_____

_____ 6. What specific research skills do you need to analyze and interpret the data? Do you currently have these skills? If not, explain how you might reasonably acquire them.

_____

_____

_____ 7. What special resources do you need to complete the study?

_____

_____

_____ 8. Do you have the time, energy, skills, and resources to carry out the study as you have designed it? If not, how might you scale down your study so that you can still address your research problem? Alternatively, how might you revise your research problem so that you can reasonably address it, given the time, skills, and resources you have?

_____

_____

_____

_____

SYSTEMATIC REVIEWS OF QUALITATIVE AND MIXED-METHODS STUDIES

When a researcher wants to consolidate the results of many quantitative studies related to a particular research problem, the researcher might conduct a _meta-analysis_—a statistical analysis of all of the studies' individual statistical results—in order to discern general trends in the findings. But when a researcher wants to synthesize the results of many previous qualitative or mixed-methods studies, a statistical meta-analysis obviously isn't possible, at least not for most of the reported data.

A viable alternative for qualitative and mixed-methods studies is a systematic review, in which _research reports,_ rather than individual people or other individual entities, are the objects of study (Harden & Thomas, 2010; Petticrew & Roberts, 2006). The review is _systematic_ in the sense that a researcher identifies and implements an explicit, rigorous method for selecting and analyzing the reports. For example, the researcher is likely to:

  Conduct an extensive search for studies related to the research problem—for instance, by using certain keywords in appropriate online databases and then including all relevant juried qualitative and/or mixed-methods research reports (e.g., articles, dissertations, conference presentations) in the sample.

■ Evaluate the quality of each report (e.g., Were rigorous methods used to collect and analyze data? Are obvious researcher biases affecting conclusions?) and then possibly either exclude or give less credence to certain reports.
■ Code the contents of the reports for key ideas, concepts, themes, and/or theories.
■ Perform one or more meta-analyses of any statistical findings reported in the studies.

Aside from taking steps such as these, there is no single "best" way to conduct a systematic review. As is true for most qualitative and mixed-methods research, the specific strategies used depend on the nature of the research problem and the particular methodologies used in the individual studies included in the sample.

An example described by Harden and Thomas (2010) can illustrate what a systematic review might involve. In response to a request from the United Kingdom's Department of Health, these two researchers and several colleagues wanted to review current research regarding effective strategies for getting children to eat more healthfully. The research team identified their overall research problem and three more specific questions as follows:

What are the barriers to and facilitators of healthy eating?

■ Which interventions are effective in promoting healthy eating habits?
■ What are children's perspectives on, and experiences of, healthy eating?
■ What are the implications of Questions 1 and 2 for intervention development? (Harden & Thomas, 2010, p. 760)

In an extensive search of relevant research with children ages 4 to 10, the researchers located 33 studies that included both a treatment group and a control group to evaluate the effectiveness of an intervention designed to improve eating habits. They also found eight studies that examined children's perspectives about healthful eating. These 41 studies included a variety of research methodologies (e.g., experiments, surveys, interviews) and, in combination, yielded a large body of quantitative and qualitative data.

The "data" that the team initially analyzed were the verbatim contents of sections in the reports that were labeled either "results" or "findings." Analyses of these data involved three major steps:

1. Separately coding each line of the text for one or more possible meanings, sometimes using words that the study authors themselves had used
2. Grouping the Step 1 codes into more general descriptive themes and subthemes related to what children's understandings of healthy eating involved and what factors affected their food choices
3. Identifying six overall "analytical themes" (i.e., general conclusions) within the data that each addressed at least one of the team's research questions and either directly or indirectly had implications for intervention strategies (e.g., children like to make their own choices about food, children don't seriously consider the long-term consequences of poor eating habits)

The six analytical themes, in turn, became the focuses of subsequent qualitative and quantitative analyses. For example, the team examined various interventions to determine which ones best incorporated principles consistent with the analytical themes identified in Step 3. It then calculated *effect sizes*[3] for the interventions and asked the question: "Did interventions consistent with one or more of the identified analytical themes have a greater impact than other interventions?" The answer was *yes*, leading the research team to make some tentative recommendations for future policies and practices.

We have only skimmed the surface of mixed-methods research, but we have, we hope, given you food for thought about the appropriateness of mixed-methods approaches for your own research problems and questions. If you wish to delve into these approaches in greater depth, we urge you to consult one or more of the resources in the "For Further Reading" section at the end of the chapter.

---

[3]As noted in Chapter 8, an *effect size* is a statistical indicator of how much of an impact an experimental intervention has in comparison with outcomes for a control group or other comparison group.

✔ Check Your Understanding in the Pearson etext

Practice Thinking Like a Researcher

Practice Thinking Like a Researcher Activity 12.1: Planning Mixed-Methods Research
Practice Thinking Like a Researcher Activity 12.2: Selecting a Mixed-Methods Research Design
Practice Thinking Like a Researcher Activity 12.3: Conducting Mixed-Methods Research

A SAMPLE DISSERTATION

We conclude the chapter with an example of a mixed-methods study that used a two-phase, explanatory design. Laura Lara (who shortly thereafter became Laura Lara-Brady) conducted the study for her doctoral dissertation in educational psychology at the University of Northern Colorado (Lara, 2009). Her focus was on factors that might influence the college success of Latina/o students, especially those with Mexican American backgrounds. Phase 1 of her study involved the administration of three questionnaires; hence, it had a descriptive, quantitative nature. Phase 2 involved in-depth interviews with a small subsample of Phase 1 participants; it made use of methods common in qualitative phenomenological studies and content analysis.

In her dissertation, Lara expresses concern about "the relatively low numbers of Latina/os attending and graduating from higher education institutions" (p. 3). She then draws on related research literature to identify four potentially important factors in Latina/o students' college success—family, religion, other people's support, and motivation—and she ties these factors to theories of child development and ethnic identity. We pick up the dissertation at the beginning of Chapter III, in which she repeats the four research questions she first posed in Chapter I and then describes her methodology. Although most of the excerpts we present are from Chapter III, we also include a paragraph from Chapter IV to give you an idea of how Lara effectively integrates quantitative and qualitative results in interpreting her data.

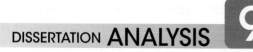

DISSERTATION ANALYSIS 9

	Comments

CHAPTER III

METHODOLOGY

The purpose of this mixed-method study is to identify the perceptions of predominantly Mexican American college students regarding their academic successes and challenges, with special attention to the role of parents, views of education, meaning of success, and the importance of religion. This chapter describes the *quantitative* procedure used to answer the following questions:

1. How are parenting, education, meaning of success, and religion associated with the academic achievement of predominantly Mexican American college students with low and high GPAs?

2. How is ethnic identity associated with the academic achievement of predominantly Mexican American college students?

The word "associated" in Questions 1 and 2 implies that the author will compute correlation coefficients, which she indeed does in the quantitative phase of her study.

This chapter also describes the *qualitative* procedure used to answer the following questions:

3. How do predominantly Mexican American college students describe aspects of family, religion, meaning of success, and motivation in terms of being protective factors and risk factors in their academic achievement?

4. Are there any additional protective or risk factors related to the academic achievement of predominantly Mexican American college students?

Both quantitative and qualitative research methods were employed to study the academic achievement of predominantly Mexican American college students. Although there are numerous types of mixed-method designs, I selected the Sequential Explanatory Design (Creswell, 2003; Tashakkori & Teddlie, 2003) due to its use of qualitative research to explain and interpret quantitative findings. The Sequential Explanatory Design is characterized by the collection and analysis of quantitative data followed by the collection and analysis of qualitative data. In this design, qualitative data are used to expand and provide depth of meaning to the experiences of diverse populations (Merchant & Dupuy, 1996).

[In the pages that follow, the author gives an advance organizer for the chapter, describes the participants in her study, and provides details about the three questionnaires administered in the study's quantitative part and the general protocol used in conducting follow-up qualitative interviews. Then, in a "Design/Procedure" section, she presents a rationale for using a Sequential Explanatory Design. We pick up the chapter where she begins to describe data collection.]

Quantitative Data Collection

The first phase of the study involved understanding participants' backgrounds, influences on academic achievement, and their level of Latina/o ethnic identity (exploration, resolution, affirmation). Potential participants received a link to complete the questionnaires via e-mail. After giving consent to participate in this study, participants were directed to the demographic questionnaire (Appendix A), Academic Factors Questionnaire (Appendix B), and the Ethnic Identity Scale (EIS) (Umaña-Taylor, Yazedjian, & Bámaca-Gómez, 2004) (Appendix C) online. The completion of all three questionnaires took approximately 30–40 minutes. All participants were invited to share their academic achievement stories.

To protect participants' confidentiality, questionnaire responses were separated from qualitative interview responses, and a separate online form asked participants' age, place of birth, languages spoken, as well as five demographic questions (ethnicity, generation, gender, GPA, and socioeconomic status). Consent forms and questionnaires were encrypted online and accessed only through a secure password by me, the lead researcher.

[In two subsequent paragraphs, the author describes how she statistically analyzed responses to the questionnaires.]

Notice that the research questions are slightly different—but clearly related—for the quantitative and qualitative aspects of the study.

Protective factors and risk factors are sometimes seen as moderating variables in cause-and-effect relationships (see Chapter 2). In this case, however, the author recognizes that her design does not allow for hard-and-fast conclusions about cause and effect, and so she chooses her words carefully.

Notice the use of e-mail for the quantitative phase of the study. This is quite appropriate for the population being studied here, as students at virtually all 4-year colleges and universities are quite accustomed to and comfortable with using e-mail for many school-related tasks. In earlier decades, however, such a procedure might have led to considerable bias in a researcher's sample.

Notice the precautions that the author takes to ensure confidentiality and participants' right to privacy.

Qualitative Data Collection

Participants who completed the questionnaires were asked to provide their contact information for a follow-up interview. Students who gave consent to participate in a follow-up interview were selected based on gender, ethnicity, and GPA. Interviews took approximately 40–60 minutes and explored issues of family life, views of success, motivation, and support given at home that impacted the academic achievement of predominantly Mexican American college students, as well as other factors related to participants' academic success. All participants were allowed to select a pseudonym or their own name during the interview. However, none chose a pseudonym.

Epoché. In order to understand the phenomenon exactly as participants experience it, the concept of epoché became central. Epoché evolves from the Greek word "check." Originated by Husserl, the epoché is the separation or "bracketing" of the researcher's biases, prejudices, and any preconceived ideas about the phenomenon being studied (Field & Morse, 1985; Stanghellini, 2005). The epoché allowed for each participant's experience to be considered as a single entity in and of itself. This perception of the phenomenon thus calls for looking, watching, and becoming aware without importing the researcher's judgment (Moustakas, 1994). As suggested by Moustakas (1994), researchers should engage in the epoché process before conducting each interview to minimize any biases. In this study, every attempt was made to bracket any prejudices and biases of the researcher by noting them in a journal, along with any expectations prior to and subsequent to each interview. For example, before each interview I would briefly describe my expectations and other ideas I had on my mind, such as having an expectation for students in the high GPA group to be more strongly supported by their families than were students in the low GPA group. By confronting my expectations, I tried to minimize their influences as I listened to and interpreted what the participants said.

Selecting interview participants. The goal of purposeful sampling is to understand a specific phenomenon, not to represent a population, by selecting information-rich cases for research (Creswell, 2003). Studying information-rich cases yields in-depth understanding of the phenomenon that gives insight into questions under study (Patton, 2002). One strategy of purposeful sampling that captures variations between cases studied is stratified purposeful sampling. Stratified purposeful sampling [uses] characteristics of specific subgroups to facilitate comparisons by selecting participants based on key dimensions (Patton, 1990). Potential cases are then divided into "strata" containing variations of the phenomenon. In this study, "strata" to be researched were participants' GPA. Ten participants (five students in each group) were chosen for follow-up interviews based on purposeful sampling [using participants'] GPAs.

[I]n the next three paragraphs, under the subhead "Phenomenology," the author describes using a phenomenological approach to focus on the "lived experiences of the participants" and to "find meaning in participants' actual experiences." [See Chapter 9 of this book for a more in-depth description of the phenomenological approach to qualitative research.]

Data analysis. Interview questions were aimed at expanding the responses gathered in the quantitative portion of the study, specifically responses gathered from the

Here the author briefly alludes to the sampling procedure she uses in her study's qualitative phase. Details follow a bit later, as you will see.

Epoché *is an important strategy for maximizing a researcher's objectivity in a phenomenological study (see Chapter 9).*

The author uses what we have, in this book, called purposive *sampling; she also engages in* stratified *sampling (see Chapter 6 for discussions of both purposive sampling and stratified sampling). In particular, the author intentionally selects students of Mexican American heritage (both genders), including some with high GPAs and some with low GPAs.*

Academic Factor Questionnaire. Interview questions were refined after the quantitative results were gathered (for a copy of the final interview questions, please refer to Appendix D). Interviews took approximately 40–60 minutes at a coffee shop across the street from the university. All interviews were recorded using a voice recorder and an external microphone and were later uploaded to the researcher's computer. Views of success, family life, motivation, and support given at home were explored as a basis for the interview. The focus of the interviews was to understand the contextual factors surrounding participants' academic success, as well as the differences between academically successful and non-academically successful students. All of the questions were open-ended, and I probed participants for clarification and detail. For consistency, all participants were given the same interview questions. Interviews were administered in English (although a Spanish version was available).

Qualitative data were transcribed in a personal computer using the software HyperTRANSCRIBE. This software allowed for easy transcription of MP3 audio files into a Microsoft Word document. After all interviews were collected, they were stored in the researcher's computer and transferred into HyperTRANSCRIBE for transcription into a Word document. Another researcher with expertise in educational psychology and I later conducted a content analysis of the interviews for triangulation (Campbell & Fiske, 1959; Creswell, 1998 . . .). The content analysis included both coding and theme analysis (Moustakas, 1994). Coding of the data consisted of looking at the content of the responses elicited by participants and arranging them with a color scheme in terms of frequency/repetition and theme. A thematic analysis followed, and it analyzed all components in participants' interviews to form a comprehensive picture of a collective experience. As a continuation of the content analysis, the second educational psychology researcher and I separately conducted a thematic exploration to ensure uniformity and validity of the results. Once patterns were established, we compared results and developed all patterns into themes to finally compare them with the quantitative analysis.

[In the remaining two paragraphs of the chapter, the author continues the discussion of triangulating the results and then describes strategies used to maintain participants' confidentiality and right to privacy.]

[We now jump way ahead to a section called "Interpretation of Final Analysis" in Chapter IV ("Results") in the author's dissertation. We include this paragraph to give you a flavor of how she pulled the quantitative and qualitative results into a single, integrated discussion.]

[S]tudents in the low and high GPA groups showed distinct views of success, family, religion, and motivation. Three of the strongest differences were view of education, view of religion, and academic preparation. Students in the high GPA group viewed education as a privilege and as something that had to be earned. One student in the high GPA group mentioned, "I don't get grades, I earn grades. I mean you just don't . . . you know what I mean? Teachers don't just hand things out. You get what you deserve." Students in the high GPA group also saw college as the next step in their lives: "I think it's just one of the next steps as far as being able to do something that I'm passionate about." One student in the low GPA group indicated, "Well I'm . . . I know it's cocky, and whatever, but I'm smarter than the good chunk of the students in my class, but

Notice the informal setting for the qualitative interviews. Such a setting might be more comfortable for participants, setting them at ease and enabling them to be more candid and expansive in their responses.

Notice the Spanish option here—presumably another strategy for making participants feel comfortable and at ease.

The author makes good use of technology to facilitate interview transcription and content analysis.

Notice how participants' qualitative responses give depth and meaning to the more abstract idea that perception of personal effort might be an important factor in high-GPA students' academic success.

because I don't put any effort into it, no one ever sees it." Students in the high GPA group viewed grades as the result of personal effort, while students in the low GPA group described seeing themselves as being already smart and not needing to work hard to prove it.

Note: Excerpt is from *A Mixed Method Study of Factors Associated With the Academic Achievement of Latina/o College Students From Predominantly Mexican American Backgrounds: A Strengths-Based Approach* (pp. 73–74, 86–89, 91–93, 145) by L. G. Lara, 2009, doctoral dissertation, University of Northern Colorado, Greeley (available through the online database ProQuest Dissertations & Theses: Full text; publication number 3397099). Reprinted with permission.

FOR FURTHER READING

Boland, A., Cherry, G., & Dickson, R. (2014). *Doing a systematic review: A student's guide.* London: Sage.

Bryman, A. (2006). Integrating quantitative and qualitative research: How is it done? *Qualitative Research, 6*(1), 97–113.

Cobb, P., Confrey, J., diSessa, A., Lehrer, R., & Schauble, L. (2003). Design experiments in educational research. *Educational Researcher, 32,* 9–13.

Creswell, J. W., & Plano Clark, V. L. (2011). *Designing and conducting mixed methods research* (2nd ed.). Thousand Oaks, CA: Sage.

Edmonds, W. A., & Kennedy, T. D. (2013). *An applied reference guide to research designs: Quantitative, qualitative, and mixed methods.* Thousand Oaks, CA: Sage.

Greene, J. C. (2007). *Mixed methods in social inquiry.* San Francisco: Jossey-Bass.

Hesse-Biber, S. N. (2010). *Mixed methods research: Merging theory with practice.* New York: Guilford Press.

Hulme, D., & Toye, J. (2006). The case for cross-disciplinary social science research on poverty, inequality and well-being. *The Journal of Development Studies, 42,* 1085–1107.

Johnson, R. B., & Onwuegbuzie, A. J. (2004). Mixed methods research: A research paradigm whose time has come. *Educational Researcher, 33*(7), 14–26.

Onwuegbuzie, A. J., & Johnson, R. B. (2006). The validity issue in mixed research. *Research in the Schools, 13*(1), 48–63.

Petticrew, M., & Roberts, H. (2006). *Systematic reviews in the social sciences: A practical guide.* Oxford, UK: Blackwell.

Plowright, D. (2011). *Using mixed methods: Frameworks for an integrated methodology.* London: Sage.

Tashakkori, A., & Teddlie, C. (Eds.). (2010). *Handbook of mixed methods in social and behavioral research* (2nd ed.). Thousand Oaks, CA: Sage.

Teddlie, C., & Tashakkori, A. (2009). *Foundations of mixed methods research: Integrating quantitative and qualitative approaches in the social and behavioral sciences.* Thousand Oaks, CA: Sage.

Teddlie, C., & Yu, F. (2007). Mixed methods sampling: A typology with examples. *Journal of Mixed-Methods Research, 1,* 77–100.

ANSWERS TO THE CONCEPTUAL ANALYSIS EXERCISE "Identifying Mixed-Methods Research Designs":

1. This is an *exploratory design:* Qualitative data from the case studies (Phase 1) is used to create quantitative checklist questions in Phase 2. The design might be depicted as QUAL→QUAN.

2. This can best be categorized as an *embedded design:* The rating-scale responses yield quantitative data; the responses to the open-ended questions yield qualitative data that help to explain why participants responded to particular rating-scale items as they did. Because qualitative data are collected for only 10% of the rating-scale items and appear to carry less weight than the quantitative data, this design might be symbolized as QUAN(qual).

3. This is an *explanatory design:* The initial questionnaire yields quantitative data regarding apparently popular and unpopular individuals, and the subsequent interviews yield qualitative data that might shed light on why certain individuals are well-liked and disliked. The design might be depicted as QUAN→QUAL.

4. This is a *multiphase iterative design* with three phases. In Phase 1, the program is administered and quantitative data (GPAs) are collected for program participants and nonparticipants. In Phase 2, qualitative data are collected from unstructured interviews to gain insights about how the program might be improved. In Phase 3, the revised program is offered, and once again quantitative data are collected to determine the program's effectiveness. The design might be depicted as QUAN→QUAL→QUAN.

Chapter 13

Planning and Preparing a Final Research Report

Ultimately, what you put on paper and how you put it there reveals your knowledge, the quality of your thinking, and your standards of excellence with greater clarity than anything else you do.

Learning Outcomes

13.1 Describe several essential components of a good research report, including discussions of (a) the research problem, (b) method(s) used, (c) obtained data and analyses of them, (d) interpretations of the data, (e) possible weaknesses of the study, and (f) relevance to a broader context.

13.2 Discuss various strategies for maintaining your academic integrity as you write a final report.

13.3 Explain the nature of possible front matter and end matter in a report.

13.4 Describe two or more distinctly different organizational schemes for a research report.

13.5 Identify effective strategies for (a) writing a good report within a reasonable time frame and (b) critiquing a first draft.

13.6 Explain possible means by which you can present your research findings to people who are unlikely to read an unpublished research report.

Bringing a research effort to its rightful conclusion involves writing a report that is faithful to the data but also finds meaning in those data. The research report is a straightforward document that sets forth clearly and precisely what the researcher has done to resolve the research problem. Like the research proposal, it makes no pretense at being a fine work of literature. It must, however, be organized and easy to understand, so that readers can quickly grasp what the researcher has done and found. It must also be flawless in its sentence and paragraph structures, punctuation, and spelling. The research document one writes is a clear reflection of one's scholarship as a researcher, and for this reason it is often used as a culminating measure of a student's educational achievements.

GETTING STARTED

If you are writing a thesis or dissertation, be sure to check first with your university's graduate school office to ascertain whether it has a prescribed set of guidelines for writing theses. Check such matters as paper quality, width of margins, size and style of font, and heading format. What is permitted at one institution may be unacceptable at another. Ask whether your university has a style manual for writing research documents or whether it recommends that you adhere to a particular published style manual.

University guidelines aside, different disciplines tend to adhere to different styles in research reports; for example, psychologists typically use American Psychological Association (APA) style, whereas historians tend to use Chicago style. Differences among the styles are

TABLE 13.1 ■
Commonly Used Styles
in Research Reports

Style	Manual	Online Assistance
APA Style: American Psychological Association	American Psychological Association (APA). (2010). *Publication manual of the American Psychological Association* (6th ed.). Washington, DC: Author. *Also see:* American Psychological Association. (2012). *APA style guide to electronic references* (6th ed.). Washington, DC: Author.	apastyle.org psychwww.com/resource/apacrib.htm
Chicago Style: University of Chicago	*Chicago manual of style* (16th ed.). (2010). Chicago: University of Chicago Press.	chicagomanualofstyle.org
CSE Style: Council of Science Editors	Council of Science Editors. (2006). *Scientific style and format: The CSE manual for authors, editors, and publishers* (7th ed.). Reston, VA: Author.	Many university libraries and writing centers provide on-line assistance; search the Internet for "CSE style"
MLA Style: Modern Language Association	Modern Language Association. (2008). *MLA style manual and guide to scholarly publishing* (3rd ed.). New York: Author.	mla.org/style

most noticeable in the formats used for citations and reference lists. For example, the dissertation near the end of Chapter 8 includes citations within parentheses, consistent with APA style. In contrast, the dissertation near the end of Chapter 10 uses footnotes, consistent with Chicago style. Table 13.1 lists four commonly used styles, along with sources of information about each one.

USING TECHNOLOGY

Surfing the Internet for Writing Assistance

Many Internet websites offer assistance on the nitty-gritty details of different styles. The right-most column of Table 13.1 provides websites that are active as this book goes to press (helpful websites for CSE style are limited and spotty at best). Another strategy is to use a search engine such as Google or Bing and type such keywords as "style manuals," "MLA style," and the like in the search box; doing so will lead you to many potentially useful sites at universities and elsewhere.

Some websites offer more general suggestions for writers. A good example is the Online Writing Lab (OWL) at Purdue University (owl.english.purdue.edu). If you go to OWL's website and click on "Site Map," you can find links to discussions of a wide range of topics related to writing—for instance, how to write persuasively, how to enhance sentence clarity, when to use various pronouns and verb tenses, and in what circumstances to use hyphens. OWL also provides guidance on APA, Chicago, and MLA styles.

Learn by Looking

Perhaps the best way to understand and appreciate the nature of research reports—and to prepare yourself for writing one—is to look at existing reports. Any university library should have a collection of graduates' theses and dissertations on its shelves. You can find theses and dissertations from other universities in the ProQuest Dissertations & Theses database, an online resource to which many university libraries subscribe. Also, look once again at some of the research articles and reports you previously read for your literature review; these, too, might give you ideas about how to structure and write your own report.

Keep in mind that not all published research reports provide good models for novice researchers. Some, in fact, are poorly written. If you have trouble reading and understanding a report concerning a topic about which you have considerable knowledge, you might reasonably conclude that the report's author is *not* a writer whose style you want to emulate!

ESSENTIAL ELEMENTS OF A RESEARCH REPORT

Any research report should achieve six main objectives:

1. It should give readers a clear understanding of the research problem and why it merited an in-depth investigation.
2. It should describe exactly what methods were used in an attempt to resolve the research problem.
3. It should present the obtained data precisely and completely. The data presented in the report should substantiate all the interpretations and conclusions that will follow.
4. It should interpret the data for readers and demonstrate either how the data resolve the research problem or why they do *not* completely resolve the problem. A report that merely presents raw data and uninterpreted facts (in the form of tables, graphs, and other data-summary devices) is of little help to readers in deriving meaning from those data.
5. It should alert readers to possible weaknesses of the study (e.g., what its delimitations and limitations may have been, what assumptions and biases might have affected results and interpretations).
6. It should conclude by summarizing the findings and connecting them to contexts beyond the study itself—for example, relating them to current theories about the topic or drawing implications for future policies or practices.

In the following sections, we discuss each of these matters. Then, in a subsequent section, we remind you once again about the importance of being completely truthful and forthcoming about what you have accomplished.

Explanation of the Research Problem

Typically, the first section of a report provides a statement of the problem and any other information that readers will need to understand the problem. Readers should be able to comprehend *from the report alone* what the problem is and what its ramifications are. Readers should appreciate the setting in which the problem was conceived. In addition, readers should learn why, from both academic and practical standpoints, the study was an important one to conduct.

The beginning pages of any research report serve an essential purpose: to create a meeting of minds between the writer and readers of the report. Many research reports begin badly because their writers have not set forth the problem clearly and completely for readers. By not doing so, these writers get readers off to a confused start, which can create a cloudy haze that lingers as they read subsequent parts of the report. Any writer of a research report must keep in mind that readers are likely to know only those things that the writer has actually put on paper.

Thus, after a few introductory comments (perhaps a few sentences or paragraphs) that provide the background and a rationale for your study, your report should set forth clearly and unmistakably the problem you have investigated. Often, an appropriate subheading can draw readers' attention to the research problem. If the problem has been divided into subproblems, these should be presented following the statement of the problem and announced with proper subheadings. And, of course, any preliminary hypotheses should be clearly stated early in the report. By presenting the problem, its subproblems, and any hypotheses, you give readers a clear and complete understanding of the *principal thrust* of the research effort. Having this thrust in mind, readers will be in a better position to judge the merits of the research and understand interpretations of the data.

Also, you should define any terms that may have multiple meanings or in some other way might be ambiguous (see the section "Defining Terms" in Chapter 2). For a meeting of minds, it is imperative that you and your readers share a common understanding of key concepts around which the research effort has revolved.

The extent to which related literature is presented in an introductory section of the report depends on the nature of the report. In a journal article, the literature immediately relevant to the problem is summarized in the introductory paragraphs before the statement of the research problem. In a thesis or dissertation, only a few key works are identified in the first chapter, and the bulk of the related literature is reserved for a separate chapter.

Description of Methods

The general *design* of the study should be clear early in the report. In particular, the researcher should state whether qualitative or quantitative methods (or both) were used and what particular research traditions were followed—for example, whether the study was a longitudinal study, a survey, a single-group time-series study, a 2-by-2 factorial design, an ethnography, a grounded theory study, or some combination of approaches.

Almost without exception, a research report should include a specific section labeled "Methods," "Methodology," or something similar. The research setting, sample, assessment instruments, and procedures should be described with as much precision as possible. Ideally, readers should know—from this description alone—exactly what was done, to the point where readers could replicate the study and in most cases get similar results.

Description of the Data and Data Analyses

After readers fully understand what the problem was and the manner in which it was investigated, the next question is, "What is the evidence?" You have collected a large body of data. You have also analyzed the data in one or more ways, perhaps by performing appropriate statistical computations or perhaps by systematically coding interview responses. In most quantitative research reports, the obtained results are described in a single section appropriately called "Results" or "Findings," with interpretations to follow in a separate section. In some qualitative reports, however, the data and the researcher's interpretations of them are woven together in one or more topic-specific sections following the "Methods" section.

If you have performed one or more statistical analyses of the data, you should include your rationale for employing the particular statistical approach(es) you have used. It's important for readers to know not only that you used a particular technique but also *why* you used it. In fact, throughout the entire research process, you should keep in mind that, generally, the answer to the question *Why?* is just as important as the answer to the question *What?* One of the weakest links in many research reports is the failure to substantiate what one has done with a solid rationale as to why one has done it.

If you have not conducted any statistical analyses (as might be the case in a qualitative study), you should present your data in such a way that they speak for themselves. As previously mentioned in Chapter 4 and Chapter 9, qualitative researchers often engage in *thick description,* presenting the data in such detail that readers can see for themselves what kinds of observations have been made. One well-known ethnographer has generally taken this approach:

> In striking the delicate balance between providing too much detail and too little, I would rather err on the side of too much; conversely, between overanalyzing and underanalyzing data, I would rather say too little. (Wolcott, 1994, p. 350)

So that readers don't get lost in the data presentation, it is often helpful to begin the discussion of the data with an *advance organizer* in which you lay out the overall organization of your data presentation. We refer you back to the Guidelines section "Writing to Communicate" in Chapter 1 for a description of advance organizers.

Usually the data are presented *as they relate to the problem and its subproblems.* One logical approach is to devote a separate section (each with its own heading or subheading) to each subproblem and its pertinent quantitative and/or qualitative data. Present the subproblem, describe the results of data analyses related to the subproblem, and state whether and to what degree the results have adequately addressed the subproblem and supported any *a priori* hypotheses.

Yet you need not limit your discussion of results only to the problem and subproblems you have identified at the beginning of your report. In fact, if you have designed a rating-scale instrument to assess people's attitudes or beliefs regarding a particular issue, you should, if applicable, report the internal consistency reliability of the instrument (see the discussion of internal consistency reliability in Chapter 4, as well as the suggestion to "Check for consistency" in Chapter 6). If you have used two or more raters to code your data in some way, you should describe both the interrater reliability and the steps taken to maximize it (see the discussions of interrater reliability in Chapter 4 and Chapter 11). And in a later subsection in your "Results" section, you might describe additional findings of interest—for instance, unexpected gender differences in participants' performance or intriguing questionnaire responses that raised issues you had not initially considered.

The data should be presented thoroughly and, of course, accurately. In many cases, some of the data can be synthesized in tables, figures, and other concise presentations. A table is usually an arrangement of words, numbers, or combinations of these elements in a two-dimensional matrix for the purpose of exhibiting certain information in a compact and comprehensive form. A figure is any kind of graphic illustration other than a table; for instance, it might be a graph, chart, map, flowchart, photograph, or drawing. (Sometimes a picture really is worth a thousand words!) Many computer software programs can create tables and figures for you; for example, see Microsoft Word and Microsoft Excel (for tables and graphs), Inspiration (for flowcharts), and Maptitude or Mapland (for maps). All tables and figures should be specifically labeled (e.g., "Table 1," "Figure 3") and have captions that describe their contents, and you should refer to all of them in the text of your report. If you are writing a thesis or dissertation, most universities ask that you present tables and figures as soon after the in-text reference as possible; however, check with your own university's graduate school office for its own requirements about such things.[1]

Descriptions of data in quantitative studies are typically written in an objective, "scientific" style. Those in qualitative studies vary from the objective and aloof, on the one hand, to the more subjective and personal, on the other. Qualitative researchers frequently include dialogues and participants' statements to illustrate their findings. They may also use metaphors and analogies to make a point. We see a simple yet effective "anti-metaphor"—an example of what something was *not*—in Matthew McKenzie's (2003) dissertation about the Boston Marine Society, previously excerpted at length in Chapter 10:

> *No mere gentleman's club,* common work experiences defined the society as a community, set aside from the rest of the town. (McKenzie, 2003, p. 20; emphasis added)

Regardless of how you present the data, it is imperative that you present them in enough detail that they will support the conclusions you will draw. If the data are extensive and you choose to present them only in summary form in the main body of the report, you might present them in their entirety in an appendix; this strategy is especially common in qualitative research reports. In this way, anyone wishing to replicate the results of the research effort should be able to reach essentially the same conclusions.

Interpretation of the Data

All too frequently, researchers believe that, having once presented the facts and figures, they have done all that needs to be done. To display the data is certainly important, but as we have said so many times before, the *interpretation of the data* is the essence of research. Without inquiring into the intrinsic meaning of the data, no resolution of the research problem or its subproblems is possible.

In interpreting the data, however, you must be careful not to go *too* far beyond the data. Beginning researchers often lose sight of what they have actually found; they are so enthusiastic about their topic that they make extravagant claims and unwarranted inferences. As an example, one of us authors once sat on a doctoral dissertation committee for a student who had been

---

[1]When writing manuscripts for publication, tables and figures often appear at the end of the document, and a notation within the running text indicates where they should be inserted in the published version of the report. For more specific guidance, consult the "Instructions to Authors" guidelines for the journal or other publication in question; such instructions are often found in each issue of the publication or on the publisher's website.

studying the use of regional dialects in children's literature. Although the student drew many appropriate conclusions from her data, one of her conclusions was that literature that incorporates a regional dialect can help schoolchildren develop "an understanding and acceptance of sociocultural groups other than their own." The student had collected no data whatsoever about children who were reading such literature, let alone data specifically related to their understanding and acceptance of diverse sociocultural groups. The student's "conclusion" was, in reality, merely her strongly held conviction about the value of literature written in various dialects, and she should have presented it as such.

Be especially careful that you don't draw conclusions about causation or influence when the design of your study doesn't warrant such conclusions. A point we have previously made in several earlier chapters bears repeating one more time: *Correlation does not, in and of itself, indicate causation.* Certainly you can speculate that there *might* be a cause-and-effect relationship between two correlated variables, but you should never state or imply that there *definitely* is one. Make the speculative nature of your conclusion crystal clear, and back up your speculation with contemporary theory, other researchers' findings, or qualitative data in your own study. And stay away from words and phrases that imply a causal relationship—words and phrases such as *influence, affect, bring about, help children develop,* and *lead people to believe.* All of these inappropriately communicate that *one thing leads to another* in a causal manner.

And by all means, avoid the word *prove.* Research data rarely prove something beyond the shadow of a doubt. Remember, inferential statistics are based on probabilities: If a particular finding is statistically significant, it probably *wasn't* a fluke, a result that one might get strictly by chance two or three times in a thousand. Even so, it *might* be a fluke due strictly to the researcher's (unlucky) luck of the draw. A good researcher always makes this point clear to readers, possibly by saying something such as, "The results support the hypothesis that . . ." or "The significant difference in means for the two groups is consistent with the premise that. . . ."

Research is indeed an exciting quest, but researchers must never let their enthusiasm interfere with their objectivity in interpreting and drawing conclusions from the data. The answer to the research question should rest solidly and completely on its own empirical foundation.

Look the data steadfastly in the face. Report honestly what those data reveal to you. Ferret out every conclusion you have drawn, underscore it in red, and then be sure that the data in your tables, graphs, and other exhibits solidly support what those words underlined in red declare. That is good research.

What if the data *don't* support your predictions? Does this mean your hypotheses were wrong? Not necessarily. Look once again at your methodology and statistical analyses to see if you can identify one or more weaknesses in what you have done. Perhaps one of your measurement instruments had lower validity or reliability than you had anticipated and therefore was not yielding accurate and dependable measures of a critical variable in your study. Maybe you gave participants misleading instructions or asked them misleading questions. Perhaps your statistical analyses lacked power—maybe your sample was too small or your measures too unreliable—and so you made a Type II error.[2] You should report any weaknesses and flaws in your study that may have influenced its outcome.

At the same time, maybe your hypotheses *were* wrong. In the interest of advancing the frontiers of knowledge, you must be sufficiently objective to admit when your thinking was flawed and offer reasonable explanations for the results you obtained, perhaps in the form of alternative hypotheses that future research efforts might test.

In the final analysis, *the data must speak for themselves.* You are only their mouthpiece. You may not like what the data say. They may not confirm your fondest hopes or support your preconceived notions, but a researcher must be the servant of the scientific method. That method looks at evidence squarely and without prejudice; it reports candidly and precisely what the impersonal data affirm.

---

[2]A *Type II error* occurs when the probability is too high that an obtained result was simply due to chance (see the section "Making Errors in Hypothesis Testing" in Chapter 8).

Identification of Possible Weaknesses of the Study

Throughout a research report you must be upfront about any assumptions that may have influenced your methods, analyses, and interpretations. You must also alert readers to personal, social, political, or philosophical biases that may have limited your ability to study the research problem with complete objectivity. But acknowledging your biases involves first *consciously thinking about* what your biases might be—a process that qualitative researchers call *reflexivity* (see Chapter 9)—and then speculating on how these may have affected what you did, what data you collected, and how you interpreted your results.

Delimitations and limitations of the study should be clearly set forth as well. All who read the research report should know precisely how far the research effort extended and what its limits were. Into what relevant areas did the research effort not inquire? What aspects of the problem were not studied? What methodological flaws emerged during the project? Delimitations—what a researcher never intended to do—are typically stated near the beginning of the report. Limitations—weaknesses that may cast doubts on results and interpretations—can be mentioned wherever they are most relevant, but they definitely *should* be mentioned.

For guidance on pinning down such things, we refer you back to the sections "Stating Assumptions" and "Identifying Delimitations and Limitations" in Chapter 2, as well as to the section "Acknowledging the Role of Researcher-as-Instrument in Qualitative Research" in Chapter 11.

Summary and Connections to a Broader Context

Any research report should end by bringing closure to the interpretation of the data. In a thesis or dissertation, this discussion is often in a separate section or chapter, perhaps one titled "Summary, Conclusions, and Recommendations" or simply "Discussion."

In a final section, you should clearly summarize your findings and interpretations relative to the research problem and its subproblem. This is the place for looking backward, for distilling into a few paragraphs precisely what has been accomplished in each phase of the research activity. Readers should be able to see the entire research endeavor as through the wrong end of a telescope or set of binoculars: clearly, in miniature, with all significant aspects brought together in proper perspective.

In addition, you need to address the question *So what?* In what way does the study contribute to our collective knowledge about some aspect of our physical or biological world or of human experience? The connection(s) you make here might take one or more of several forms. You might compare your findings with other, previously reported research findings and point out similarities and dissimilarities. You might argue that your results either support or disconfirm an existing hypothesis or theory. You might draw implications for teaching, social services, medicine, animal welfare, or business. You might offer suggestions for how future research could further advance the frontiers of knowledge about your topic. And if you developed new strategies or assessment tools to study your problem, you might justifiably argue that they are, in and of themselves, valuable contributions to the research methodologies of your field.

Maintaining Your Academic Integrity

By academic integrity, we mean conducting and writing about research with utmost honesty and a desire to learn and convey the truth—and *nothing but* the truth—about a topic of investigation. In writing a research report, academic integrity includes all of the following:

- Appropriately crediting the words and ideas of other people (see the discussion of plagiarism in Chapter 3)
- Maintaining confidentiality and protecting participants' right to privacy (in some cases, this may require using pseudonyms or altering a few basic facts for certain participants, in which case you should specifically state that you have made these changes)
- Explicitly identifying any biases in your sample selection—for instance, by reporting low return rates in mailed surveys or high attrition (drop-out) rates in longitudinal studies

▨ Describing any participants you dropped from your research sample and explaining why you dropped them

▨ Describing the limitations of your measurement instruments—for instance, by reporting any evidence of poor validity or reliability

▨ Describing any procedures you may have used to fill in missing data points in order to increase the number of participants for which you could conduct various statistical analyses

▨ Providing a comprehensive report of your research findings, including those findings that do *not* support your hypotheses

▨ Explicitly identifying any potential confounding variables that may cast doubt on conclusions about cause-and-effect relationships

We must emphasize a point we have previously made in Chapter 4: *Researchers must report their findings in a complete and honest fashion, without misrepresenting what they have done or intentionally misleading others about the nature of their findings.* Only by being honest with one another can researchers truly advance the frontiers of knowledge. To misrepresent the facts or mislead readers in any other way—no matter how well-intentioned those actions might be—is to potentially lead a community of scholars astray in their quest for knowledge.

FRONT MATTER AND END MATTER

The topics described in the preceding section typically appear in the main body of a research report. But many lengthy research reports, including theses and dissertations, also contain front matter (content that precedes the introductory first chapter) and end matter (content that follows the final chapter). We now take a few pages to describe this material.

Preliminary Pages

The preliminary pages include all the introductory material that precedes the discussion of the research problem and study. The title page comes first; this also includes the author and, typically, a university affiliation and date. In a thesis or dissertation, a page for signatures of the faculty advisor and research committee also appears at the beginning. Next are an abstract, a page for the dedication (if any), an acknowledgment of indebtedness to individuals who have assisted in or in some other way supported the research, a table of contents, lists of any tables and figures, and, if desired, a preface.

In some instances, a copyright page is also included in the front matter. Copyright is the protection given by law to the authors of literary, dramatic, musical, artistic, and other intellectual works. In the United States, this is U.S. Code, Title 17. Under current U.S. law, which applies to works created on or after January 1, 1978, copyright protection lasts for 70 years following the author's death. A thesis or dissertation is protected by copyright law even if you do not register it with the United States Copyright Office. Nevertheless, registering it often provides reassurance and peace of mind. As this book goes to press early in 2014, the fee for filing a research report with the copyright office is either $35 or $65, depending on whether the application is filed electronically or on paper. You can get more information about U.S. copyright laws and procedures at the Copyright Office's website (copyright.gov).

The abstract provides a summary of the entire research effort in a paragraph or two. For a journal article, the length of the abstract is usually 100 to 250 words, depending on the journal. For a dissertation, the abstract should be 350 words or less. The abstract should include sufficient information about the research problem, methodology, results, and interpretations to give potential readers an idea as to whether the study addresses a topic of concern to them and thus merits their further attention. The abstract you write is likely to be included in one or more online databases (e.g., ProQuest Dissertations & Theses) available at many research libraries around the world. It is essential, therefore, that you take seriously the task of writing the abstract and describe your project as clearly, precisely, and succinctly as possible.

To get a sense of what abstracts entail, we urge you to look at numerous examples in professional journals and doctoral dissertations. As you peruse each example, ask yourself questions such as these:

- What was this research project intended to accomplish—in other words, what research problem did it set out to address?
- What was the general design and methodology of the study?
- What were the results, and what conclusions can reasonably be drawn from them?

Find several abstracts that enable you to answer all of these questions easily, and use those abstracts as models as you write your own abstract.

We cannot overemphasize the importance of writing a good abstract. It should summarize your project and findings clearly and succinctly—enough so that readers gain a concrete, stand-alone, take-away understanding of what you have done. But it should also pique readers' interest sufficiently that they follow up by reading your full research report. The more that other people read your report, the more that your research project and report will have an impact on your field and, as a result, will enhance the world's knowledge of your research topic.

A brief acknowledgments section graciously recognizes the assistance of those people through whose kindness the research effort has been possible. These individuals may include those who introduced you to data sources that helped you in your project or those who guided your study and gave counsel or support—perhaps an academic dissertation committee, a faithful typist and proofreader, and key family members. One hallmark of a true scholar is to say "Thank you" to those who have given their time and assistance to support one's efforts and aspirations. The acknowledgments page is the proper place for the expression of such indebtedness.

The remainder of the front matter indicates the content and organization of the text. Any lengthy research report should include a table of contents. The table of contents is a bird's-eye view of what the document contains, how it is organized, and on which page each section and subsection begins. Often following the main table of contents are two more specific ones, one for tables and another for figures that appear throughout the report.

Endnotes and Footnotes

Generally, endnotes (appearing at the end of the text) and footnotes (appearing at the bottoms of relevant pages within the text itself) are used for three purposes. First, depending on the style manual being followed, such notes may be used to indicate sources of information and ideas (e.g., see the footnotes in the sample dissertation at the end of Chapter 10). Second, endnotes and footnotes are occasionally used to acknowledge permission to quote or reproduce something from a copyrighted document. When you quote extensively or use a table or other graphic representation from a copyrighted work in a report you intend to publish or distribute widely, you must secure permission to reprint the material (in writing) from the copyright holder (typically the publisher or author). Immediately after including the material, you can indicate its original source in an endnote or footnote, followed by the words "Reprinted by permission" or other wording stipulated by the copyright holder.

A third important function of endnotes or footnotes is to supplement information in the text of the report with additional information that strengthens the discussion. This type of note should be used sparingly and should not be used to explain complicated concepts. Keep such notes short and to the point. If you find your endnotes or footnotes becoming overly long and involved, sharpen your ideas and integrate them into the body of the report.

Reference List

A reference list at the end of your report allows readers to locate and use the sources you have cited. For this reason, it is imperative that reference information be complete—it should include references for *all* of your citations—and accurate. The reference list is not a bibliography, however; that is, it should *not* include references that you have *not* specifically cited in your report. Tempting as it might be to list all of the many books, journal articles, and other resources you have perused in an effort to better understand your topic, resources that you don't specifically cite in your literature review or elsewhere have no place in your reference list.

Each entry in the reference list should contain information about the author, year of publication, title of the work, and publication information. To some extent, researchers in different academic disciplines format their reference lists differently, and you should follow the format that your institution or your discipline requires. Furthermore, you should apply that format consistently throughout your reference list. Most of the bibliographic software programs described in Chapter 3 (e.g., EndNote, RefWorks, Zotero) can quickly format your references in whatever style you need.

One widely used style in reference lists is that of the American Psychological Association (APA). APA style is described in detail in the association's *Publication Manual* (2010) and *APA Style Guide to Electronic References* (2012). The reference list in this book is an example of APA formatting. Following are key elements of each entry in an APA-formatted reference list.

Author In an APA-style reference list, the author's name appears with the surname first, followed by the author's first initial and any middle initials. When multiple authors are involved, the names are separated by commas. Commas are always used between the names (even between only two names), and an ampersand (&) is used before the last name in the list. Note, however, that, especially in the biological and medical sciences, some research articles have a large number of coauthors. In APA style, the first six authors are listed, followed by a 3-dot ellipses (. . .) and then the final author's name. For example, see the entry for Abraham and colleagues (1941) in this book's reference list.

Date of Publication After the names of one or more authors is the year of publication in parentheses, followed by a period. Magazines, newsletters, newspapers, and presentations also include the month and, if necessary to pin down the particular issue, the day.

Occasionally, a reference list includes two or more sources by the same author(s) in the same year. In such instances, lowercase letters *a, b,* and (if needed) subsequent alphabet letters follow the year inside the parentheses. For example, if you wanted to cite two sources written by sole author Deanna Kuhn in 2001—in this case, a journal article and a chapter in an edited book—you would list them in alphabetical order by title like this:

Kuhn, D. (2001a). How do people know? *Psychological Science, 12,* 1–8.

Kuhn, D. (2001b). Why development does (and does not) occur: Evidence from the domain of inductive reasoning. In J. L. McClelland & R. S. Siegler (Eds.), *Mechanisms of cognitive development: Behavioral and neural perspectives* (pp. 221–249). Mahwah, NJ: Erlbaum.

Any citations in the text would then be either "Kuhn, 2001a" or "Kuhn, 2001b."

Title of the Work In APA style, the title of the article, book, or other source follows the publication year. If you are referencing an article using APA style, the title of the article is *not* italicized, but the title of the journal in which it appears *is* (e.g., see the first Kuhn citation just listed). The title of a book is always italicized. So, too, is the title of a conference presentation or doctoral dissertation (e.g., see the entry for Laura Lara's dissertation in this book's reference list).

Be sure to pay attention to the rules for capitalization in whatever style manual you are using. Can you determine what APA's rules are from the entries in this book's reference list? As you should notice, the first word in a book, article, or presentation title is the only one capitalized unless (a) the word is a proper noun or proper adjective or (b) it follows a colon. In contrast, all major words of a journal title are capitalized.

Publication Information   For journal articles, publication information usually includes the volume number (which is italicized), issue, and page numbers. (If separate issues within each volume begin with sequentially numbered pages—for example, if the first issue of a particular volume ends on page 96 and the second issue begins on page 97—then the issue number can be omitted.) Publication information for a book includes the location and name of the publishing company or agency. In the case of a paper presented at a conference, the name of the conference and its location are provided.

Notice how such information is formatted in this book's reference list. All redundancy is eliminated; there are no extra words such as *volume, issue,* and *pages*. By their specific locations in a citation, readers understand their meaning. This practice eliminates many extra words; such a reduction means fewer manuscript pages, which translates into lower printing costs.

Notice, too, that references to a publisher are usually short and succinct; with a few idiosyncratic exceptions, they exclude such words as "Publishing Company" and "Publishers, Inc." These words add no new information and thus can be eliminated.

USING TECHNOLOGY

Referencing Sources Obtained on the Internet   Sources found on the Internet require additional information. Typically, this information includes either (a) the Internet address at which the document was found or (b) the Digital Object Identifier (DOI). In computer lingo, an Internet address is called a *Uniform Resource Locator,* or *URL* (see Chapter 3). For example, in APA style, a 2002 article by Amrein and Berliner in the online journal *Education Policy Analysis Archives* would be referenced using the following format:

> Amrein, A. L., & Berliner, D. C. (2002, March 28). High-stakes testing, uncertainty, and student learning. *Education Policy Analysis Archives, 10*(18), 1–71. Retrieved from epaa.asu.edu/ojs/article/view/297/423

A 2008 report written by Keeter and colleagues for the Pew Research Center would be referenced using this format:

> Keeter, S., Dimock, M., Christian, L., & Kennedy, C. (2008, January 31). *The impact of "cell-onlys" on public opinion polls: Ways of coping with a growing population segment.* Washington, DC: Pew Research Center. Retrieved from Pew Research Center for the People and the Press website: people-press.org/files/legacy-pdf/391.pdf

Whereas a document's Internet address can change over time, its Digital Object Identifier (DOI) should remain constant for the foreseeable future. As noted in Chapter 3, DOIs are a fairly recent development for Internet-based documents; hence, you are likely to see them only for documents posted since the year 2000, and only for *some* of those documents. DOIs are especially helpful when research reports and other scholarly works are available only in electronic form. For instance, they are used to identify journal articles that appear online before they appear in paper. Following is an example:

> Wiers, R. W., Eberl, C., Rinck, M., Becker, E. S., & Lindenmeyer, J. (2011). Retraining automatic action tendencies changes alcoholic patients' approach bias for alcohol and improves treatment outcome. *Psychological Science.* Advance online publication. dx.doi .org/10.1177/0956797611400615

People who see this entry in a reference list can track down the publication by typing the URL in an Internet browser or, alternatively, by going to the International DOI Foundation's website (doi.org) and then entering the article's DOI—in this instance, 10.1177/0956797611400615—in the "Submit" box.

Potential resources in a literature review take a wide variety of forms—books, articles, government reports, conference presentations, posters, videos, website pages, blog postings, and so on—and various style manuals have prescribed formats for each one of them. Thus, we strongly urge you to obtain an up-to-date version of the manual appropriate for your discipline and follow its prescriptions to the letter.

Note that URLs and DOIs can be quite lengthy—often so long that they spill over onto a second line on the page. If you need to split one up, you should do so before a period (.), a forward slash (/), or a hyphen (-) within the sequence of letters, numbers, and punctuation marks.

Appendix Content

Following the main report may be supplementary appendixes (sometimes instead pluralized as *appendices*) that might help readers understand the research study more completely but are not essential to readers' general comprehension of the study. A rule of thumb is that *material appearing in an appendix enables readers to go further in understanding the method and/or results if so desired.* For instance, an appendix might include informed consent letters, questionnaires and other measurement instruments, response sheets, field notes, statistical computations, or extensive data tables.

In reporting research, nothing is hidden. All of the data are laid out. The researcher's integrity is thereby preserved, and the results and conclusions of the study can be readily verified.

ORGANIZING A RESEARCH REPORT

Research reports for most quantitative studies are similar in their organizational format. After any necessary preliminary pages (e.g., title page, acknowledgments, table of contents), they typically have five major sections: an introduction (which includes the research problem, an explanation of its importance, assumptions, definitions of terms, etc.), a review of the related literature, a description of the methodology, a presentation of findings and specific interpretations (e.g., whether the data do or do not support any *a priori* hypotheses), and general conclusions (including implications and suggestions for future research). Reports of qualitative and mixed-methods studies are less predictable; their organizational schemes are apt to depend somewhat on the nature and design of the studies themselves. Virtually all research reports include a reference list. Appendixes are less common, although they are usually important components of dissertations and theses.

As illustrations, we present the outlines for two of the dissertations from which we have presented excerpts in previous chapters. The first is a traditional outline, used for a primarily quantitative, quasi-experimental study with an embedded qualitative component; the second is less traditional, used for a qualitative, grounded theory study. In the interest of space, we omit any subheadings that appear under the major headings within each chapter.

Effects of Training in Self-Generation on the Quality of Students' Questions, Class Notes and Examination Scores (Jackson, 1996)

Front Matter
Copyright Notice
Title Page
Signature Page
Abstract
Acknowledgments
Table of Contents
List of Tables
List of Figures

Body of the Report
Chapter I.   INTRODUCTION
                   Statement of the Problem
                   Purpose of the Study
                   Research Questions and Hypotheses
                   Limitations of the Study
                   Definitions and Terms
Chapter II.   REVIEW OF THE LITERATURE
                   Adjunct Questioning Research

Uncovering the Conceptual Representations of Students with Reading Disabilities (Zambo, 2003)

WRITING—AND FINISHING!—A REPORT

A final research report is precisely that—a *report*. You need to report on what you have done over the course of your research effort. In the process, you need to acquaint your readers with the problem, the data you brought to bear on the resolution of the problem, the means you used to gather those data, the ways in which you analyzed and interpreted the data, and the overall conclusions you reached.

Remember that your report is *you*. Whether or not you intend it to do so, a report can say a great deal about you to your mentors and professional colleagues—not only about your abilities as a researcher and scholar but also about your diligence in completing a project in a timely manner. In the following two practical applications, we offer strategies for writing a clear, coherent report and for completing your report within a reasonable timeframe.

PRACTICAL APPLICATION Writing Your Final Report

As you begin your final report, we urge you to revisit five of the Guidelines sections included in earlier chapters: "Writing to Communicate" and "Using the Tools in Word Processing Software" (both in Chapter 1), "Writing a Clear and Cohesive Literature Review" (in Chapter 3), and "Writing the First Draft" and "Revising Your Proposal" (both in Chapter 5). Most of the guidelines in these sections are as applicable to a final research report as they are to a research proposal or any other piece of scholarly writing. At the risk of repeating a few suggestions presented in those earlier Guidelines sections, we now offer some general recommendations to keep in mind as you sit down to write.

GUIDELINES Writing a Clear, Coherent Report

Writing a research report isn't just a matter of mindlessly putting on paper the things you have done and discovered in your research project. Rather, writing a good report involves actively, consciously striving to *communicate* what you have done. The following guidelines can greatly enhance the effectiveness with which you tell readers about your research project.

1. *Choose an appropriate style for your intended audience.* Most research reports use a somewhat formal and impersonal style. There are exceptions to this rule, however; for example, ethnographic researchers sometimes describe their findings in a personal, story-telling manner, and historical researchers often tell a story as well (see Chapter 10). Perusing research reports in your own academic discipline can give you a good sense of the writing style that is most prevalent (and thus most acceptable) in your field.

As briefly noted in Chapter 5, various disciplines and their preferred style manuals have different standards with regard to active versus passive voice. For example, the APA *Publication Manual* (2010) prefers that authors write in active voice (e.g., "A research assistant interviewed the participants," "Participants completed the survey") rather than *passive voice* (e.g., "The participants were interviewed by a research assistant," "Participants were given the survey").

Also, although writing in the third person was the preferred style throughout most of the 20th century (e.g., "The researcher analyzed the data"), increasingly researchers are using a first person style to describe their procedures (e.g., "I instructed participants" in the case of a single author, "We analyzed the data" in the case of multiple authors). Use of the third person can be ambiguous; for instance, if you talk about yourself as "the researcher," it may give some readers the impression that you didn't take part in your own study! Whichever style you choose, you should be consistent in using it throughout the report.

If you are writing a thesis or dissertation, consult with your university's graduate school office about its preferred or required style. If you are writing a manuscript for publication in a particular journal, look for "Instructions to Authors" guidelines in the journal itself or on the publisher's website.

2. *Create and follow a logical overall structure.* To facilitate readers' "journey" through your research report, you should create a logical, predictable structure for the report. You should also provide regular guideposts in the forms of headings, transitional words and paragraphs, and other means of helping readers follow your train of thought.

After you have written 10 or 20 pages of your report, go back and read your headings and subheadings and the paragraphs following each one. Do they form a logical whole? Do the various levels of heads accurately depict how different sections of text are interrelated? For instance, do they appropriately show that some sections are smaller subparts of other, larger sections? And overall, do the headings and text show a logical progression from one idea to the next? They should.

3. *Be clear and precise in your wording.* A research report must be crisp with clarity and precision. There is no place in it for "sort-of's" and "I-guess-so's." This is not the time for ambiguous or foggy terms or half-stated conclusions. Your report should present what you have thought, done, and learned in a straightforward manner. Show how your data resolve your subproblems and how the subproblems help to resolve the main problem. Lead your readers through your own thought processes step by step. Such tactics provide evidence that you have approached your entire research endeavor in a thoughtful, systematic manner.

4. *Use appropriate verb tenses.* In writing a final report, some novice researchers simply cut and paste large portions of their research proposals into their final reports, the unfortunate result sometimes being that the report describes what "will" be done when it already *has* been done. Attentiveness to such details as verb tenses is yet another sign of a good, conscientious researcher and writer. Past tense is most appropriate for describing things that have already happened. APA's *Publication Manual* suggests that simple past tense be used for things that occurred at a specific time (e.g., "Participants were randomly divided . . .") and present perfect tense be

used for actions and events that either happened over a lengthy period or are continuing into the present (e.g., "Theorists have suggested"). When drawing conclusions and suggesting implications, however, present tense is appropriate.

The grammar checker in your word processing software may enable you to check for inconsistencies in your use of active versus passive voice or past versus present tense. Exactly where you find such options in your program depends on whether you are using a PC or Macintosh computer and which version of a software program you are using. Our best advice is to search the Internet for instructions relative to your specific platform and software.

5. *Strive for as much objectivity and impartiality as possible in what you say and how you say it.*   Although it's probably inevitable that certain personal, theoretical, or philosophical biases will influence what you say, you should actively strive to avoid making judgments as much as you can. Even small changes in wording can make a difference. For example, when describing your findings in an ethnographic study, rather than saying, "Only one villager had ever graduated from high school," you might say, "One villager had graduated from high school" (Wolcott, 1994, pp. 352–353). And rather than saying, "Few pupils were at task," you might instead say, "Five pupils appeared to be engaged in the assignment" (Wolcott, 1994, p. 353). Such words as *only* and *few* can imply such meanings as "insufficient" or "disappointing"—value judgments that an impartial researcher tries to avoid.

6. *Regularly summarize what you have just said.*   After your lengthy and intensive involvement in your study, you are apt to have a keen understanding of your master plan and of the relationships and contributions of various components of the study to your overall research endeavor. Your entire research project—the problem, the data and their organization, the relationships and interrelationships—are likely to be crystal clear in your mind. Your readers, however, will not be so fortunate. As they proceed through your report, they may need to stop occasionally to consider and reconsider how a certain piece fits into the total investigation. Thus, especially in a lengthy research report such as a dissertation, you can help readers immensely by providing a brief summary at the close of each extended discussion.

A report that merely rambles on and on, going blindly forward from one topic to another, can lead to psychological numbness, bewilderment, and confusion. Frequent summaries help to minimize such reader disorientation.

7. *Submit a neat, clean final copy that strictly adheres to required formats.*   Your pages should be easy to read, with double-spaced lines and clean letters. In addition, you should format the text in a consistent manner, setting tabs for paragraph indents, bulleted lists, and the like, and setting the document's margins to control for line and page length. Most word processing software allows you to insert footnotes that will appear on the appropriate pages and to create tables that present numbers and text in perfect columns.

Check and double-check for spelling and grammatical errors. Keep an eye out for possible misuse of homonyms, such as using *their* when you mean *there* or using *affect* when you mean *effect* (see Chapter 5). Lack of attention to such details—some of which may seem trivial and picayune to you—can leave lasting impressions on others.

PRACTICAL APPLICATION   Developing a Writing Schedule

Make no mistake about it, writing a research report—especially writing one *well*—takes considerable time and effort. A research report isn't something you can whip up in a week or two. In the case of a lengthy report such as a dissertation, you should plan on taking not several days, not several weeks, but several *months* to complete the report-writing process.

We authors can recall too many sad cases in which aspiring doctoral students completed all the required coursework for their doctoral degrees, passed their written and oral comprehensive exams with flying colors, got approval for their dissertation projects, collected and analyzed their data, and then became "stuck" indefinitely in the process of writing their final dissertations. Some never got unstuck: They never finished their dissertations and therefore never received their doctoral degrees. Such a waste, we think, and so unnecessary!

To help you start *and finish* a lengthy research report—to grease your wheels and keep them greased so that you don't get stuck somewhere along the way—we offer two pieces of advice. First, *develop a reasonable writing schedule for yourself.* Second, *stick to it!* The guidelines that follow can help you do both of these things.

GUIDELINES Pinning Down and Adhering to a Workable Schedule

The suggestions we offer here have emerged from our own experiences in writing research reports and other lengthy documents, including our own doctoral dissertations—and also this textbook!

1. ***Identify small, easily accomplishable goals within the overall project.*** A lengthy research report will seem less overwhelming if you break it into small, manageable pieces. These pieces might have such labels as "revision of the methods section," "data analysis related to the first subproblem," "implications section," or "suggestions for future research." Make each piece small enough that you can complete it within a few days' time.

2. ***Write easier sections first.*** No rule says you have to write the sections of a research report in order, starting at the beginning and working your way to the end. Most researchers find it easier to write some parts than others. For instance, writing a Methods section can be fairly simple and straightforward. What were the general characteristics of your sample? How did you recruit human participants? What assessment instruments did you use? What procedures did you follow? And after you have conducted appropriate statistical analyses of quantitative data, creating one or more tables to summarize them should be a relatively easy task. Once you have completed easier parts of the report, you may begin to see a glimmer of light at the end of your report-writing tunnel and be reinvigorated to tackle more challenging sections.

3. ***Set reasonable target dates for achieving each goal.*** We strongly emphasize the word *reasonable* here. To get an idea of how much you can write in any given day or week, think about how long it has taken you to finish other lengthy writing projects. For instance, how long did it take you to complete your research proposal? How many pages could you write—and write *well*—in a day? (One of us authors has learned from experience that she can usually write only about 8 to 10 double-spaced manuscript pages a day. After that, she's essentially brain-dead and should wait until the following morning before she continues.)

Consider personal matters when you establish your schedule. Do you have a part-time or full-time job to consider? Do you have responsibilities to other family members that will take some of your time and energy? Have you built in adequate time for health and fitness, meals, shopping, home and car repairs, and occasional relaxation? You need to *get real* about how quickly you can complete various aspects of your writing project. Otherwise, you'll never stick to your schedule; you'll be doomed to failure even before you start.

4. ***Reward yourself each time you reach one of your goals.*** Give yourself a treat of some sort after you successfully finish each significant piece of your report. Watch a movie, read a magazine or short mystery novel, clean the house, play a few games on your computer, surf the Internet—whatever you need to do to get refreshed and ready to tackle the next task on your schedule.

5. ***Seek regular feedback.*** We've said it before and we'll say it again: Ask others to give you honest feedback about what you say and how clearly you say it. Honest feedback now can save you more serious criticism—and, we might add, it can save you considerable aggravation and heartache—later on.

6. ***Build time into your schedule for at least two or three revisions.*** Most research reports are reviewed by others before they ever see the light of day. A committee of university

faculty looks closely at any doctoral dissertation. An editorial review board carefully scrutinizes any manuscript submitted to a professional journal. A formal review process ensures that all approved research reports meet basic standards of scholarship, accuracy, and scientific rigor.

In the case of dissertations, *we have yet to see a report that has not had to undergo at least two revisions.* In fact, a doctoral student often completes four or five rewrites before defending a dissertation before a doctoral committee. Let's face it: You are very close to your research project and, at the end, are equally close to the report you have written about the project. So close, sometimes, that omissions, errors, and logical inconsistencies that may be blatantly obvious to others are not at all obvious to you. Furthermore, other people might have useful ideas about better ways to organize a discussion, suggestions about additional statistical analyses that may shed further light on the data, or new sources of literature that are potentially relevant to unexpected findings. The recommendations that others make, as well as the revisions that occur as a result of these recommendations, have one primary purpose: to make a research report the very best it can possibly be.

Furthermore, you must remember that any report bearing a stamp of approval from other individuals—whether that "stamp" takes the form of the signatures of a doctoral committee or acceptance for publication in a scholarly journal—reflects not only on the author of the report but also on those who have approved the report. A poorly written research report makes a lot of people look bad.

The final stages of the writing project, especially the revisions, may seem to go on interminably. But persist! You have expended a great deal of time and effort in conducting your research project, and perhaps others have devoted considerable time and effort to it as well. It is only by completing your report that your project will ultimately contribute to the world's knowledge about the topic you have studied.

PRACTICAL APPLICATION Critiquing a Final Research Report

Beck (1990) has developed a list of insightful questions that every researcher in the field of nursing should satisfactorily answer before submitting a final version of a quantitative research report. We have adapted her list of questions to create a checklist that can be applied to virtually any research report in any discipline. The checklist can both help you evaluate the reports you read and serve as a guide as you assess your own writing.

✓ CHECKLIST
Criteria for Critiquing a Research Report

STEP 1. THE PROBLEM

	YES	NO
Is the problem clearly and concisely stated?	___	___
Is the problem adequately narrowed down into a researchable problem?	___	___
Is the problem significant enough to warrant a formal research effort?	___	___
Is the relationship between the identified problem and previous research clearly described?	___	___

STEP 2. LITERATURE REVIEW

	YES	NO
Is the literature review logically organized?	___	___
Does the review provide a critique of the relevant studies?	___	___

	YES	NO
Are gaps in knowledge about the research problem identified?	_____	_____
Are important previous research studies relevant to the topic included in the literature review?	_____	_____
Are all cited works included in the reference list?	_____	_____
Are all works included in the reference list cited in the literature review or elsewhere in the report?	_____	_____

STEP 3. THEORETICAL OR CONCEPTUAL FRAMEWORK

Is the theoretical or conceptual framework clearly applicable to the problem (as opposed to being a "stretch" in which the framework is only marginally relevant to the problem)?	_____	_____
If a conceptual framework is used, are the concepts adequately defined, and are the relationships among these concepts clearly identified?	_____	_____

STEP 4. RESEARCH VARIABLES

Are any independent and dependent variables operationally defined?	_____	_____
Are any confounding variables present? If so, are they identified?	_____	_____

STEP 5. HYPOTHESES

Are hypotheses clear, testable, and specific?	_____	_____
Does each hypothesis describe a predicted relationship between two or more variables included in the hypothesis?	_____	_____
Do the hypotheses flow logically from the theoretical or conceptual framework?	_____	_____

STEP 6. SAMPLING

Is the sample size adequate?	_____	_____
Is the sample representative of the defined population?	_____	_____
Is the method for selecting the sample appropriate?	_____	_____
Is any sampling bias in the method acknowledged?	_____	_____
Are the criteria for selecting the sample clearly identified?	_____	_____

STEP 7. RESEARCH DESIGN

Is the research design clearly described?	_____	_____
Is the design appropriate for the research problem?	_____	_____
Does the research design address issues related to the internal and external validity of the study?	_____	_____

STEP 8. DATA COLLECTION METHODS

Are data collection methods appropriate for the study?	_____	_____
Are data collection instruments adequately described?	_____	_____
Do measurement tools have reasonable validity and reliability?	_____	_____

STEP 9. DATA ANALYSIS

Is the Results section clearly and logically organized?	_____	_____

	YES	NO
Are analyses appropriate for each set of quantitative and qualitative data? For example, is each analysis of quantitative data appropriate for the type of measurement scale (nominal, ordinal, interval, ratio) that the data reflect?	____	____
Are tables and figures clear and understandable?	____	____
Is each analysis relevant to answering the research question?	____	____

STEP 10. INTERPRETATION AND DISCUSSION OF THE FINDINGS

	YES	NO
Does the investigator clearly distinguish between actual findings and interpretations?	____	____
Are the interpretations based on the data obtained?	____	____
Are the findings discussed in relation to previous research and to the theoretical/conceptual framework?	____	____
Are all generalizations warranted and defended?	____	____
Are limitations of the results and interpretations identified?	____	____
Are implications of the results discussed?	____	____
Are recommendations for future research identified?	____	____
Are the conclusions justified?	____	____

BEYOND THE UNPUBLISHED RESEARCH REPORT: PRESENTING AND PUBLISHING

If you have completed an unpublished research report, such as a master's thesis or doctoral dissertation, consider this: In most cases, only a few people will ever read your report in its current form. If your research project has uncovered new information, new ideas, and new understandings that can make a significant contribution to the world's body of knowledge about a particular topic, we strongly urge you to seek a wider audience.

One easy way to gain a broader audience for a thesis or dissertation is to publish it in the online database ProQuest Dissertations & Theses: Full Text (proquest.com). In fact, some universities *require* doctoral students to submit their final dissertations to ProQuest. Two additional ways to get the word out about your study are conference presentations and journal articles.

Conference Presentations

Many researchers present their research findings at regional, national, or international conferences. Some conferences are annual or biennial meetings sponsored by societies related to particular academic disciplines (e.g., American Sociological Association, European Association for Research on Learning and Instruction, Modern Language Association). Others are more specific to particular interest areas (e.g., family violence, Piaget's theory of child development). The organizers of many of these conferences eagerly seek presentations (a.k.a. *papers*) from new researchers as well as from more experienced ones. Some conferences also include poster sessions, which (as the word *poster* implies) involve visual displays of research projects on large (perhaps 4-foot-by-6-foot) bulletin boards. Typically, one or more of each poster's authors is present at the poster session to describe the project undertaken and answer questions.

If you would like to present a paper or poster at a professional conference, you will probably need to submit a proposal several months in advance to the association or institution sponsoring the conference. These proposals are usually much shorter than the research proposals described in Chapter 5. Furthermore, their purpose is different: You are submitting a proposal to present a research project that you either (a) have already completed or (b) are currently conducting but will definitely have completed before the conference.

Proposals for paper and poster presentations are often only two or three pages in length. Their specific format varies considerably from one professional group to another, and we urge you to consult the *call for papers* that invites proposals for conference presentations. Regardless of the format, one thing is true for all of these proposals: They need to be written with the same clarity and academic rigor required for any research proposal or research report. Furthermore, they need to adhere faithfully to the guidelines that conference sponsors specify.

PRACTICAL APPLICATION Presenting Your Research at a Professional Conference

Many novice researchers find a conference presentation to be a highly anxiety-arousing experience. It's quite common to have some stage fright, especially when presenting a paper to a large audience. You might find it a bit reassuring to know that even many renowned and well-respected scholars still get nervous when they must speak in front of a large group of peers. Knowing that you're in good company won't make your public-speaking jitters go away, but it will at least help you realize that you're simply feeling as most people do in such a situation.

The best way to keep your nerves under control is to be well prepared for your paper or poster. Here we offer a few guidelines that can help you put your best foot forward—and thus can give you a confidence boost—in presenting your research project.

GUIDELINES Presenting an Effective Paper or Poster

Drawing on recommendations by Munter and Paradi (2009) and Nicol and Pexman (2010), as well as on our own experiences, we offer several suggestions for presenting papers and posters at professional conferences.

1. *Be concise and to the point.* If you give a paper, you are likely to have only 10 to 20 minutes to describe what you have done. If you present a poster, your text (including font size) and graphics should be sufficiently large that other people can readily see them from at least 3 feet away. In either situation, you won't have the time (in the case of a paper) or the space (in the case of a poster) to describe every detail of what you have done and learned. Instead, present those aspects of your project that are key to your audience's understanding of what you have accomplished, including:

- The title of your presentation, plus your name, affiliation, and contact information
- Your research problem and, if applicable, your hypotheses
- A general rationale and context for your study
- A general description of your design and methodology (including the nature and size of your sample)
- Results that are most central to your research problem and hypotheses
- Your interpretations of and conclusions from your data

Many posters also include a one-page abstract immediately after the title and author(s), plus a short list of cited references at the end.

2. *Prepare polished, professional-looking visuals in advance.* One widely used tool for both papers and posters is Microsoft PowerPoint, with which you can create a wide variety of eye-catching visuals—PowerPoint calls them *slides*—including bulleted lists, charts, and graphs. PowerPoint also allows you to incorporate photographs, scanned documents, and (in the case of paper presentations) short videos into your presentation. If you are presenting a paper, you simply hook up your laptop computer to an LCD (liquid crystal display) projector, which will probably be available at the front of the presentation room, and click on a mouse or wireless

clicker to advance to successive slides.[3] If you are presenting a poster, you print out the slides, either on individual sheets of paper or on a single large poster sheet. An Internet search of "poster presentation template" can give you numerous companies that can convert PowerPoint slides into a high-quality poster.

We urge you not to clutter up your presentation or poster with too many visual effects, such as distracting and irrelevant images and animations. However, simple images and animations—for instance, having individual bullet points "march" across the screen as you introduce them (which PowerPoint lets you do)—are quite appropriate and can catch and hold people's attention.

3. *Practice ahead of time, but don't overdo it.*   Especially if you are giving a paper, it's a good idea to rehearse it at least once, if only in order to time yourself to make sure you can keep your presentation to the prescribed time limit. It's helpful, too, to review your speaking notes within an hour or two of your presentation so that they are fresh in your mind. However, we do *not* recommend that you either read or memorize your presentation; by doing these things, you will come across as a mindless robot. Instead, you want to convey the impression that you know your project and subject matter *very well*—something you can do only if you talk somewhat extemporaneously about what you have done.

4. *Prepare handouts that summarize or complement your presentation.*   Handouts can take a variety of forms. For instance, your handout might provide small versions of your Power-Point slides. (In its "Print" feature, PowerPoint lets you specify how many slides you print on a single page; for readability's sake, we suggest three to six slides per page.) If your paper or poster is based on a manuscript you have submitted for possible publication, your handout might be a copy of the manuscript. Alternatively, you might direct interested audience members to a website at which they can download the paper or poster. And in some instances—this is most often the case when someone hasn't sufficiently planned ahead!—a presenter takes people's e-mail addresses and sends the desired materials after returning home.

5. *Anticipate and be prepared to answer questions.*   By their very nature, poster sessions give your audience a chance to ask questions, and most paper sessions also include time for audience members to ask questions. To the extent that you can do so, you should try to anticipate questions and bring any supplementary materials that might help you answer them. But you shouldn't expect that you will be able to answer every question someone might ask. It's quite acceptable—in fact, it's a sign of a candid and open-minded researcher—to respond to some questions by saying, "You raise a good point that I hadn't considered" or "Unfortunately, my study wasn't able to address that particular concern."

6. *Make connections with your audience, including connections you can follow up on after the conference.*   Regardless of whether you are presenting a paper or a poster, present *yourself* as someone who is approachable and eager to exchange ideas. Smile, make eye contact, and in other ways convey the message that you want to hear other people's ideas, concerns, and suggestions. And if you don't already have them, get business cards printed that include, at a minimum, your name, affiliation, and mailing and e-mail addresses.

Journal Articles

An even more effective way to disseminate your findings and interpretations—and certainly a more permanent one—is to submit a research report to an academic journal. The guidelines we have presented in this book should get you well on your way to writing a manuscript for submission to a research journal, but once again we urge you to *be concise*. As a rule, journal space is at a premium, so journal editors have little tolerance for researchers who say in 100 words what they could have said in 10.

---

[3]Most PC laptops have a standard outlet for hooking up to an LCD projector. In our experience, however, Macintosh laptops require special adaptors; check with your local Apple store to be sure you have the appropriate adaptor for your own laptop.

Before you submit a manuscript to a particular journal, read several recent issues of the journal to make sure it is the right place for your article. Determine whether the journal includes research reports, including reports about your general topic. Also look at the style of writing that is typical in the journal; you will want to use a similar style in any manuscript you submit. And (forgive us for saying this one more time) seek critical feedback from others about your manuscript, including from people who have published in that journal or similar ones, and use their suggestions to revise and strengthen what you have written.

Sharing Authorship

Whether you are presenting a paper at a conference or submitting a manuscript to a research journal, you must determine whether you should be sole author or share authorship with one or more other individuals. For example, when presenting or publishing reports based on master's theses or doctoral dissertations, students often share authorship with their major advisors and perhaps with one or two other faculty members as well.

A general rule of thumb is this: *Individuals who have made significant intellectual contributions to the work should share in its authorship.* Typically, any co-authors have been actively involved in the conceptualization, design, execution, and/or in-depth analysis of the research project. Multiple authors are usually listed in an order indicating which individuals have made the most substantial contributions.

People who have assisted with data collection, coding, computer programming, simple statistical analyses, typing, or minor editing—but who have not contributed *intellectually* to the work—usually don't warrant authorship (Elliott & Stern, 1997; McGue, 2000). Nor do people who have reviewed a paper or manuscript and given their suggestions for how the author(s) might improve it. Such minor contributions are more appropriately acknowledged in a footnote or endnote.

Sharing authorship with others who have contributed in important ways to your research project and listing co-authors in an order that acknowledges their relative contributions are two additional dimensions of the "honesty with professional colleagues" issue mentioned in the discussion of ethics in Chapter 4. Not only must researchers be honest with their colleagues about what they have done and what they have found, but they must also be honest about who has helped them with their research endeavors.

Responding to Reviewers' Critiques

Throughout the book we have offered many guidelines and checklists that, in one way or another, should strengthen either your project or your writing and thus, we hope, help you successfully present and publish your research. Yet not every proposal gets accepted for a conference presentation, and not every manuscript gets accepted for publication in a professional journal. Many proposals and manuscripts get rejected for good reasons. In some cases, however, conference program chairs and journal editors simply don't have the space for every good research project that comes their way.

Rejection letters are always disappointing, but we urge you not to let them discourage you. Typically program chairs and journal editors have had one or more people in the field review your submission, and they are apt to include the reviewers' comments when they give you the bad news. Put these reviews aside for a few days—at least long enough to let your frustration and disappointment dissipate a bit—and then try to look objectively and dispassionately at what the reviewers have had to say. Occasionally a reviewer will be unforgivably nasty, but more often reviewers will have constructive criticisms that can help you strengthen what you have written. You can then resubmit your proposal to another conference or send your manuscript to another journal.

You can take heart in the fact that even very experienced researchers occasionally get rejection letters. *Good* researchers constructively use negative reviews, perusing them closely for important ways in which they might strengthen their reports and make them the very best that they can be.

In general, we urge you to *persist* in your efforts to get out the word—and to as broad an audience as possible—about what you have done!

A CLOSING THOUGHT

As you prepare to write your research report, you might do well to read one or more books on effective writing. One classic source is Strunk and White's *The Elements of Style* (e.g., 2009); you can find many others in the "For Further Reading" sections in this chapter and in Chapter 1.

In general, keep your thoughts and statements clear, precise, and concise. Look closely at your choices of nouns, verbs, and adjectives. Avoid exaggerated and unwarranted claims. Stick to the facts. Report them accurately but, in so doing, enliven your prose with variety in sentence structure and sentence length.

More do's and don'ts at this point are probably "TMI"—too much information. We leave you with this last thought. Distilled into a brief stanza by an anonymous hand is a broad guideline for all of your writing. Follow it.

> The written word
> Should be clean as bone:
> Clear as light,
> Firm as stone;
> Two words are not
> As good as one.

✔ Check Your Understanding in the Pearson etext

Practice Thinking Like a Researcher

Practice Thinking Like a Researcher Activity 13.1: Outlining a Research Report
Practice Thinking Like a Researcher Activity 13.2: Critiquing a Research Report
Practice Thinking Like a Researcher Activity 13.3: Determining Authorship

FOR FURTHER READING

American Psychological Association (APA). (2010). *Publication manual of the American Psychological Association* (6th ed.). Washington, DC: Author.

American Psychological Association. (2010). *Concise rules of APA style* (6th ed.). Washington, DC: Author.

American Psychological Association. (2012). *APA style guide to electronic references* (6th ed.). Washington, DC: Author.

Barzun, J. (2001). *Simple and direct: A rhetoric for writers* (4th ed.). New York: HarperCollins.

Boice, R. (1993). Writing blocks and tacit knowledge. *Journal of Higher Education, 64*(1), 19–54.

Booth, W. C., Colomb, G. G., & Williams, J. M. (2008). *The craft of research* (3rd ed.). Chicago: University of Chicago Press.

Chicago manual of style (16th ed.). (2010). Chicago: University of Chicago Press.

Cone, J. D., & Foster, S. L. (2006). *Dissertations and theses from start to finish: Psychology and related fields* (2nd ed.). Washington, DC: American Psychological Association.

Council of Science Editors. (2006). *Scientific style and format: The CSE manual for authors, editors, and publishers* (7th ed.). Reston, VA: Author.

Dahlberg, B., Wittink, M. N., & Gallo, J. J. (2010). Funding and publishing integrated studies: Writing effective mixed methods manuscripts and grant proposals. In A. Tashakkori & C. Teddlie (Eds.), *Mixed methods in social & behavioral research* (2nd ed., pp. 775–802). Thousand Oaks, CA: Sage.

Day, R. A., & Gastel, B. (2006). *How to write and publish a scientific paper* (6th ed.). Westport, CT: Greenwood.

Day, R. A., & Sakaduski, N. (2011). *Scientific English: A guide for scientists and other professionals* (3rd ed.). Santa Barbara, CA: ABC-CLIO.

Gopen, G. D., & Swan, J. A. (1990). The science of scientific writing. *American Scientist, 78,* 550–558.

Greene, A. E. (2013). *Writing science in plain English.* Chicago: University of Chicago Press.

Hacker, D., & Sommers, N. (2007). *A writer's reference* (7th ed.). New York: Bedford/St. Martin's.

Hacker, D., & Sommers, N. (2012). *Rules for writers* (7th ed.). New York: Bedford/St. Martin's.

Lunenburg, F. C., & Irby, B. J. (2008). *Writing a successful thesis or dissertation.* Thousand Oaks, CA: Corwin.

Madigan, R., Johnson, S., & Linton, P. (1995). The language of style: APA style as epistemology. *American Psychologist, 50,* 428–436.

Matthews, J. R., & Matthews, R. W. (2008). *Successful scientific writing: A step-by-step guide for the biological and medical sciences* (3rd ed.). Cambridge, England: Cambridge University Press.

McGue, M. (2000). Authorship and intellectual property. In B. D. Sales & S. Folkman (Eds.), *Ethics in research with human participants* (pp. 75–95). Washington, DC: American Psychological Association.

McQuain, J. (1996). *Power of language: Getting the most out of your words.* Boston: Houghton Mifflin.

Meloy, J. M. (2001). *Writing the qualitative dissertation: Understanding by doing* (2nd ed.). Hillsdale, NJ: Erlbaum.

Miles, M. B., Huberman, A. M., & Saldaña, J. (2014). *Qualitative data analysis: A methods sourcebook* (3rd ed.). Los Angeles: Sage. [See Chapter 12.]

Modern Language Association. (2008). *MLA style manual and guide to scholarly publishing* (3rd ed.). New York: Author.

Munter, M., & Paradi, D. (2012). *Guide to PowerPoint 2010.* Upper Saddle River, NJ: Pearson.

Nicol, A. A. M., & Pexman, P. M. (2010). *Presenting your findings: A practical guide for creating figures, posters, and presentations* (6th ed.). Washington, DC: American Psychological Association.

Rocco, T. S., & Hatcher, T. (Eds.). (2011). *The handbook of scholarly writing and publishing.* San Francisco, CA: Jossey-Bass.

Seely, J. (2013). *Oxford guide to effective writing and speaking: How to communicate clearly* (3rd ed.). Oxford, England: Oxford University Press.

U.S. Government Printing Office. (2008). *Style manual* (30th ed.). Washington, DC: Author.

Wolcott, H. F. (2009). *Writing up qualitative research* (3rd ed.). Thousand Oaks, CA: Sage.

Appendix A
Using a Spreadsheet:
Microsoft Excel

USING TECHNOLOGY

On the surface, an electronic spreadsheet looks like nothing more than a table with innumerable rows and columns. But the typical features of spreadsheet software enable you to do many things with the data you put in the table. For example, you can recode your data, reorganize it in various ways, and perform simple calculations on subsets of data that you designate.

Here we look at one widely used spreadsheet, Microsoft Excel. We should point out that Excel's format may differ slightly depending on whether it is used with Microsoft Windows or a Macintosh operating system. Also, each new update of Excel tends to be slightly different from its predecessor in appearance and function. We are basing this discussion on the 2008 version of Excel for Macintosh computers.

USING EXCEL TO KEEP TRACK OF LITERATURE RESOURCES

In any literature review, you are likely to draw on a variety of resources, probably including books, journal articles, and Internet websites. You need to keep track of and report different information about each kind of resource. For a book, you need to know the author(s) or editor(s), title, publication date, publisher, and the publisher's location; in order to find the book in the library stacks, you also need its call number. For a journal article, you need to know the author(s), titles of both the article and the journal, publication date, volume number (and perhaps issue number), and page numbers. The information you need for an Internet website is apt to vary depending on the nature of its content, but at a minimum you need to record either (a) the Internet address (Uniform Resource Locator, or URL) and date on which you retrieved the document or (b) for many documents posted since 2000, the document's Digital Object Identifier (DOI).

Let's organize such information with Excel by going to the "File" menu and creating a "New Workbook." An empty two-dimensional table appears on the screen, with tabs labeled "Sheet 1" and "+" at the very bottom. We'll use Sheet 1 to keep track of books. By clicking on the top left-hand cell in the table, we can insert the word "BOOKS" in uppercase letters. Then, by hitting the *down* arrow key on the keyboard, we move to the cell just below, where we insert the words "Authors/Editors" (never mind for now that the words may appear to spill over into the second column—appearances to the contrary, all words typed in any single cell remain in that cell). Then, we hit the *right* arrow key on the keyboard, move to the cell to the right, and insert the word "Title." We continue moving to the right four more times, inserting the words and phrases "Date," "Call Number," "Publisher," and "Pub. Loc." (short for "Publisher's Location"). The words and phrases we have just entered in Row 2 will be our headings for the columns. At this point some of our headings might be too long for the cells, so let's do two things. First, let's go to the "File" menu and then to "Page Setup" and click on "Landscape" and "OK." By doing this, we turn the page sideways and give ourselves more room across the page. Then, let's move the cursor to the very top of the screen, where we see alphabet letters labeling the columns. If we move the cursor to the line separating the A and B columns, a cross-with-arrow-points icon appears. By clicking on the mouse at this point, we can drag the line to the right to make the "Authors/Editors" column wider. We can do the same thing for the other columns as well, in each case adjusting column width to accommodate the column heading or kind of information we expect to insert in the column cells. To make our headings more visible, we'll also put them in boldface by highlighting those cells and going to the "Format" menu, then "Cells," and then "Font" and clicking on "Bold" and "OK." With such steps we've set up our list for keeping track of books.

Now let's click on the "+" tab at the very bottom of the page. Doing so gives us "Sheet 2," where we can follow a similar procedure for journal articles. Again let's set up the page in *landscape* mode. In Row 1 we can insert "ARTICLES"; then, in the first six cells of Row 2, we can insert the headings "Authors," "Article Title," "Journal Title," "Date," "Vol/Iss" (for "volume and issue"), and "Pp." (for "page numbers"). As we did on Sheet 1, we can adjust the column widths and bold-face our headings. If we create a Sheet 3 for Internet websites, we need columns labeled "Address" and "Date Retrieved," plus possibly additional columns in which to insert names of authors or organizations, titles, posting dates, DOIs (if available), and other pertinent information.

Our workbook of three spreadsheets is now ready for us to enter information about our various library and Internet resources. We can print out the sheets and add the necessary information in pen or pencil; better still, we can take a laptop or tablet computer with us to the library and insert the information directly into a computer document. Figure A.1 shows how the three spreadsheets might look for a few resources on the topic of schizophrenia. Notice that some of the entries (e.g., some book titles) are too long for the column width. No matter, because the entries *are* recorded in their entirety in the spreadsheet document, and clicking on their particular cells will bring them into full view. Notice, too, that the entries in the "Address" column for the WEBSITES spreadsheet are in colored font rather than in black font; they would be in blue font in the spreadsheet itself. When you type an Internet address into a cell, Excel automatically makes it a *hyperlink:* If your computer is currently online and you click on the cell, your computer will take you to that website.

BOOKS					
Authors/Editors	**Title**	**Date**	**Call Number**	**Publisher**	**Pub. Loc.**
Noll, R.	Encyclopedia of Schizophrenia and Other Psychotic Di	2007	RC514 .N63 2007	Facts on File	New York
Walker, E. F. (Ed.)	Schizophrenia: A Life-Course Developmental Perspec	1991	RC514 .S3342 19	Academic Pre	San Diego
Frith, C., & Johnston	Schizophrenia: A Very Short Introduction	2003	RC514 .F755 200	Oxford U. Pre	Oxford, Er

ARTICLES					
Authors	**Article Title**	**Journal Title**	**Date**	**Vol/Iss**	**Pp.**
Lublin, H.,& Eberhard, J.	Content versus delivery: Challenges	European Neuropsychopharm	2008	18(Suppl 3)	v–vi
Tabarés-Seisdedos,R.	Neurocognitive and clinical predictors	Journal of Affective Disorders	2008	109(3)	286–299
Schwab, S. G., & Wilden	Research on causes for schizophrenia	Schizophrenia Research	2008	102(1–3)	29–30

WEBSITES					
Address	**Date Ret'd**	**Author/Org.**	**Title**	**Date Posted**	**Other Info.**
www.nimh.nih.gov/health/to	9/15/08	NIMH/	Schizophrenia	4/2/08	
www.nim.nih.gov/medlineplu	9/17/08	NIM/NIH	Schizophrenia	no date	
www.schizophrenia.com/diac	9/18/08	NARSAD	Schizophrenia sympt	no date	

FIGURE A.1 ■ Using Excel to Keep Track of Library and Internet Resources

USING EXCEL TO RECORD AND RECODE DATA

As you have seen in the preceding section, the data you enter in the cells of an electronic spreadsheet can take a variety of forms—for instance, as text, numbers, and dates. Thus, you can use a spreadsheet to keep track of the information you collect from a qualitative study (provided that the text entries are relatively short), a quantitative study, or a mixed-methods design.

For illustrative purposes, we'll use hypothetical data from a descriptive quantitative study. We return to the four rating-scale items for risk taking presented in Chapter 6:

		Not at All True		Somewhat True		Very True
11.	I would prefer to teach in a way that is familiar to me rather than trying a teaching strategy that I would have to learn how to do.	1	2	3	4	5
16.	I like trying new approaches to teaching, even if I occasionally find they don't work very well.	1	2	3	4	5
39.	I would choose to teach something I knew I could do, rather than a topic I haven't taught before.	1	2	3	5	5
51.	I sometimes change my plan in the middle of a lesson if I see an opportunity to practice teaching skills I haven't yet mastered.	1	2	3	4	5

As you may recall from our discussion in that chapter, the researchers included these items in a longer list of items designed to assess a variety of traits in college education majors who were completing their teaching internship year (Middleton, Ormrod, & Abrams, 2007). Let's consider how we might create a spreadsheet to enter the data for participants' responses to the entire survey. The general convention is to assign each *row* in the spreadsheet to a particular participant and to assign each *column* to a particular variable assessed for each participant. In this research project, Middleton and his colleagues included several demographic variables (e.g., age, gender), supervisor ratings of teacher effectiveness, and participants' responses to 69 rating-scale items designed to measure several personality and motivational characteristics. For simplicity's sake, we'll limit ourselves to the four rating-scale items just presented plus four additional rating-scale items designed to measure perfectionism, as follows:

		Not at All True		Somewhat True		Very True
19.	It is very important that I always appear to be "on top of things."	1	2	3	4	5
27.	It does not bother me if I occasionally make mistakes in the classroom.	1	2	3	4	5
38.	I do not want people to see me teaching unless I am very good at it.	1	2	3	4	5
60.	I always try to present a picture of perfection in my teaching.	1	2	3	4	5

We'll create a spreadsheet for a sample of 10 hypothetical respondents to the questionnaire and their responses to the four risk-taking and four perfectionism items (see Figure A.2). Note that the labels "RISK-TAKING" and "PERFECTIONISM" are only in cells B1 and F1, respectively, but because cells to their immediate right are blank, we see the content of these cells in their entirety.

Can we combine a person's responses to the four risk-taking items to create an overall risk-taking score and, similarly, combine responses to the four perfectionism items to create an overall perfectionism score? Not necessarily—it depends on whether the responses yield ordinal or interval data (see the section "Types of Measurement Scales" in Chapter 4 and the Practical Application "Using Checklists, Rating Scales, and Rubrics" in Chapter 6). But for purposes of

FIGURE A.2 ■
Hypothetical Data for
10 People Responding
to Eight Rating-Scale
Items Related to Risk
Taking and Perfectionism

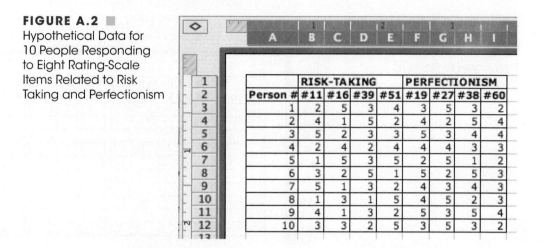

Person #	RISK-TAKING				PERFECTIONISM			
	#11	#16	#39	#51	#19	#27	#38	#60
1	2	5	3	4	3	5	3	2
2	4	1	5	2	4	2	5	4
3	5	2	3	3	5	3	4	4
4	2	4	2	4	4	4	3	3
5	1	5	3	5	2	5	1	2
6	3	2	5	1	5	2	5	3
7	5	1	3	2	4	3	4	3
8	1	3	1	5	4	5	2	3
9	4	1	3	2	5	3	5	4
10	3	3	2	5	3	5	3	2

our example, let's say that the eight rating-scale items just presented *do* yield interval data. Even so, we can't just add up the numbers to get total scores. If you look at the wordings for the eight items, you should notice that the self-descriptions in Items 16 and 51 are indicative of high risk taking but the self-descriptions in Items 11 and 39 are indicative of *low* risk taking. Similarly, Items 19, 38, and 60 reflect a desire for perfection, but Item 27 reflects comfort with *im*perfection. In order to have responses to all items for a particular characteristic reflect a high degree of that characteristic, we need to reverse, or *recode,* people's responses to Items 11, 39, and 27, changing 1s into 5s, 2s into 4s, 4s into 2s, and 5s into 1s, but leaving 3s as they are. Thus, in their recoded forms, higher-number responses to these three items would indicate high rather than low risk taking or perfectionism. The following simple formula makes this conversion for us:

$$6 - \text{Original response} = \text{Recoded response}$$

For example, if we want to recode a response of 5, then

$$6 - 5 = 1$$

Similarly, if we want to recode a response of 2, then

$$6 - 2 = 4$$

In Column J of our spreadsheet, we will make a new column, which we'll label "Rev11" (for "Reverse of Response to #11"). We're going to use a *formula* to create the values in this column. In particular, let's click on the first cell below our "Rev11" column heading (this is the cell for Person #1). We type an equals sign (=), followed by a 6 and a minus sign. Before doing anything else, we move the cursor to the cell containing Person #1's response to Item #11 (where we see a response of "2" for the item) and click on that cell. What we see in the Rev11 cell for Person #1 is the following:

$$= 6 - \text{B3}$$

We immediately press the Enter or Return button on the keyboard—we must press this button before we do anything else—and Excel executes the formula to give us the desired value of 4. Now here's the cool part: We can click on the cell in which we've just entered a formula, "copy" its contents, and then "paste" the contents into the nine cells immediately below in the same column. What appears in each cell is the result of the same calculation *using the appropriate value for each person in our sample.* For example, Person #2's response of "4" has been recoded as "2," and Person #3's response of "5" has been recoded as "1."

Items 39 and 27 need to be recoded as well. Let's label Columns K and L "Rev39" and "Rev27" (for Items 39 and 27, respectively) and use the same procedure we used in the "Rev11" column. This time, however, after typing "=6−" in the cell below the new column heading, we click on the cell immediately below the heading "#39" or "#27," depending on which item responses we're recoding. The spreadsheet with the three new columns is shown in Figure A.3.

We are now ready to compute overall scores for our risk-taking and perfectionism items. Let's create yet another column in the spreadsheet and label it "RtScore" (for "Risk-Taking Score").

Person #	Risk Taking Items				Perf'ism Items				Rev11	Rev39	Rev27
	#11	#16	#39	#51	#19	#27	#38	#60			
1	2	5	3	4	3	5	3	2	4	3	1
2	4	1	5	2	4	2	5	4	2	1	4
3	5	2	3	3	5	3	4	4	1	3	3
4	2	4	2	4	4	4	3	3	4	4	2
5	1	5	3	5	2	5	1	2	5	3	1
6	3	2	5	1	5	2	5	3	3	1	4
7	5	1	3	2	4	3	4	3	1	3	3
8	1	3	1	5	4	5	2	3	5	5	1
9	4	1	3	2	5	3	5	4	2	3	3
10	3	3	2	5	3	5	3	2	3	4	1

We can again use the *formula* tool, this time adding together each person's responses in the #16, #51, Rev11, and Rev39 columns. We take the following steps:

1. Click on Person #1's cell in the new column.
2. Hit the equals sign key (=) on the keyboard.
3. Click on the first cell below the "#16" label.
4. Hit the plus sign key (+) on the keyboard.
5. Click on the first cell below the "#51" label.
6. Hit the plus sign key (+) on the keyboard.
7. Click on the first cell below the "Rev11" label.
8. Hit the plus sign key (+) on the keyboard.
9. Click on the first cell below the "Rev39" label.

At this point, the entry in the cell you're creating should look like this:

$$= C3 + E3 + J3 + K3$$

Immediately hit the Enter or Return button and—*voila!*—the value 16 should appear. Now copy the contents of this cell into the nine cells below it in the column, and you'll see totals ranging from 6 to 18 for the risk-taking items.

We can follow essentially the same procedure to create a total (which we'll call "PerfScore") for the perfectionism items, this time using the values in the #19, #38, #60, and Rev27 columns. The results of our calculations are shown in Figure A.4.

Person #	Risk Taking Items				Perf'ism Items				Rev11	Rev39	Rev27	RtScore	PerfScore
	#11	#16	#39	#51	#19	#27	#38	#60					
1	2	5	3	4	3	5	3	2	4	3	1	16	9
2	4	1	5	2	4	2	5	4	2	1	4	6	17
3	5	2	3	3	5	3	4	4	1	3	3	9	16
4	2	4	2	4	4	4	3	3	4	4	2	16	12
5	1	5	3	5	2	5	1	2	5	3	1	18	6
6	3	2	5	1	5	2	5	3	3	1	4	7	17
7	5	1	3	2	4	3	4	3	1	3	3	7	14
8	1	3	1	5	4	5	2	3	5	5	1	18	10
9	4	1	3	2	5	3	5	4	2	3	3	8	17
10	3	3	2	5	3	5	3	2	3	4	1	15	9

FIGURE A.4 ▥ Adding Two Columns with Overall Scores for Risk Taking and Perfectionism

REORGANIZING DATA IN EXCEL

An additional feature of virtually all spreadsheets is an ability to organize the data by one or more variables. Our current spreadsheet for responses to risk-taking and perfectionism items is organized by person number. But perhaps, instead, we want to organize it by risk-taking score, with the greatest risk takers listed first and the relatively nonrisk-taking people listed last. We first need to use the cursor to highlight all of the data we want to reorganize—in this case, the 10 rows and 14 columns of numbers. We move the cursor to the leftmost cell in the third row (for Person #1), hold the mouse button down, drag the cursor down and to the right until the 140 cells with numbers are all highlighted, and then release the mouse button so that those 140 cells remain highlighted. At this point we move the cursor to the "Data" menu and select "Sort." A box appears in which we can sort by several variables in order of priority, but in this situation we want to sort only by risk-taking score. We type "RtScore" in the first box and, because we want to have the high risk takers appear at the top, we click "Descending" (for descending order). When we click on the "OK" button, the data rearrange themselves, with Persons #5 and #8 (with risk-taking scores of 18) appearing first and Person #2 (with a risk-taking score of 6) appearing last.

A *word of caution,* however. Be sure that you highlight *all* of the data columns in your spreadsheet before hitting the "OK" button. If you highlight only some of them (or perhaps only one or two), you will reorganize the data *only* in those columns, leaving the data in other columns untouched. The result will be a scrambled mess, with some numbers for, say, Person #8 moving to a new row and others staying where they were originally.

The *sort* tool isn't limited to numerical data. For example, let's return to the spreadsheets we created for the books, journal articles, and websites in our literature review. We could easily sort our books by call number or our journal articles alphabetically by journal title, thereby making our search for them in the library stacks more efficient.

USING EXCEL TO PERFORM SIMPLE STATISTICAL ANALYSES

When we used formulas to recode some item responses and to compute overall scores for risk taking and perfectionism, we were using the *function* feature of Excel. Many functions are available in Excel, including numerous preprogrammed statistical analyses. For example, let's say that we want to compute basic descriptive statistics for the risk-taking and perfectionism scores for our hypothetical sample of 10 people. We begin by typing the labels "Mean," "SD" (for "Standard Deviation"), and "Corr" (for "Correlation") in Column A in the three cells immediately below our data set. This step isn't required to complete our mission, but it helps us keep track of which statistics we're putting in which cells.

The procedure we follow next depends somewhat on the particular version of Excel we are using. In Excel 2008 for Macintosh, we now click on the cell representing the intersection of the "Mean" row and the "RtScore" column, then go to the "Insert" pull-down menu at the top of the screen and click on "Function." An equals sign (=) appears in the table cell we've selected and a function box appears on the screen; this box includes many possible calculations we might perform. In the function box, we scroll down to "AVERAGE" (we may possibly have to scroll a long way until we reach the category "Statistical") and *double*-click on AVERAGE. At this point we need to tell Excel *which* numbers—which in this case Excel calls "arguments"—to use in calculating the average (mean). The bottom portion of the function box presents two places where we can indicate the range of numbers we want to use in calculating the mean; for the mean, we want to use only the first of these two places. Excel may also "suggest" one or more table cells with a colored box; if it doesn't, we can create a box by clicking on one of the cells in our spreadsheet. Then, by clicking on various sides and/or corners of the box and dragging the box in appropriate directions, we can capture the numbers to be averaged—and *only* those numbers—at which point we again hit the Enter or Return button on the keyboard. In the example here, we capture the 10 RtScore values for our 10 people, and the mean risk-taking score (12) for our sample appears in the designated cell. We follow a similar procedure for the "PerfScore" column to obtain a mean Perfectionism score (12.7).

We do essentially the same thing to obtain a standard deviation for our two sets of scores, this time clicking on the appropriate cells in the "SD" row of our spreadsheet and double-clicking "STDEV" in the right-hand column in the function box. This procedure gives us standard deviations of 4.9889 and 4.056545 for the Risk-Taking and Perfectionism scores, respectively.

Finally, let's calculate a Pearson product-moment correlation coefficient between the Risk-Taking and Perfectionism scores. This calculation requires a slightly different procedure. We must first click on the cell where we want the r value to appear, so let's use the cell representing the intersection of the "Corr" row and the "PerfScore" column. We choose the function feature as we did for means and standard deviations, then double-click on "CORREL." At this point a box appears that asks for "Array1" and "Array2." With the Array1 sub-box highlighted, we highlight the 10 data cells in the "RtScore" column of the spreadsheet (we must be sure *not* to highlight the mean and standard deviation we've already calculated). We then move the cursor to the Array2 sub-box, click on it, and then highlight the 10 data cells in the "PerfScore" column of the spreadsheet. What we will see in the two sub-boxes are the following:

M3:M12

N3:N12

We immediately hit the Enter or Return key, and a correlation coefficient of -0.91139 appears. In our hypothetical data set, then, risk taking and perfectionism are strongly and negatively correlated.

The statistics we've just calculated include more decimal places than we need and communicate a precision that isn't warranted from such a small sample size. We can limit the number of decimal places to 2 by going to the "Format" menu, then to "Cells," then to "Number," and then, under "Category," to "Number" again. Our final calculations are shown in Figure A.5, along with the data as previously reorganized by the "Sort" function.

You can find other simple statistical tests in Excel, including t-tests and chi-square (χ^2) tests. For more sophisticated analyses, however, you will need statistical software such as SPSS, described in Appendix B.

		Risk Taking Items				Perf'ism Items								
	Person #	#11	#16	#39	#51	#19	#27	#38	#60	Rev11	Rev39	Rev27	RtScore	PerfScore
	5	1	5	3	5	2	5	1	2	5	3	1	18	6
	8	1	3	1	5	4	5	2	3	5	5	1	18	10
	1	2	5	3	4	3	5	3	2	4	3	1	16	9
	4	2	4	2	4	4	4	3	3	4	4	2	16	12
	10	3	3	2	5	3	5	3	2	3	4	1	15	9
	3	5	2	3	3	5	3	4	4	1	3	3	9	16
	9	4	1	3	2	5	3	5	4	2	3	3	8	17
	6	3	2	5	1	5	2	5	3	3	1	4	7	17
	7	5	1	3	2	4	3	4	3	1	3	3	7	14
	2	4	1	5	2	4	2	5	4	2	1	4	6	17
Mean													12	12.7
SD													4.99	4.06
Corr														-0.91

FIGURE A.5 The Data Set as Reorganized, with Descriptive Statistics Calculated

Appendix B
Using SPSS

USING TECHNOLOGY

A complete explanation of how to use SPSS—short for Statistical Package for the Social Sciences—is well beyond the scope of a short appendix. However, a brief explanation of some of the basics can get you started. The version of SPSS we describe is PASW Statistics Student Version 18.0 for Macintosh.

CREATING A DATA SET

When you open SPSS, you will see a two-dimensional table that looks very much like a spreadsheet. Each row in the table designates a specific individual (human participant, animal subject, artifact, etc.) in your data set. Each column designates a specific variable in the data set. Once filled in, this table will provide the basis for your data analyses.

As an example, we use data from a pilot study that Dinah Jackson conducted in preparation for her dissertation study (1996; excerpts from her dissertation appear in Chapter 1 and Chapter 13). The data include the following information for 15 students in a college psychology class: (a) their gender; (b) their scores on three exams administered during the semester; (c) the total of the three exam scores; (d) the quantity of class notes (i.e., number of pages) they took during the semester; and (e) the quality of their class notes. The last of these variables—quality of notes—is based on content analyses of students' notes; the numbers are proportions of notes that reflect an integration of two or more ideas rather than a single, isolated fact. In Jackson's study, better-integrated notes (reflected in higher proportions, such as .406 or .496) were theorized to facilitate better learning—and thus to be of better quality—than relatively non-integrated notes (reflected in lower numbers, such as .166 or .040). Jackson's pilot data are shown in Figure B.1.

Notice that the seven columns in the table in Figure B.1 have short labels that tell us what each variable is. To insert such labels, we go down to the bottom of the screen, where there are two "buttons" called "Data View" and "Variable View." If we click on "Variable View," we get another table, which looks like Figure B.2. In this table, we have entered information about each of the variables in the data set. Here the variables are the rows (rather than the columns, as they are in the "Data" table), and the things we want to say about the variables are the columns. To keep our discussion simple, we describe only some of these columns:

- *Name.*   In this column we identify the label that will appear for each variable in the "Data View" table. Labels can include alphabet letters, numbers, and a few other meaningful symbols (e.g., "$").
- *Type.*   In this column we identify the type of data each variable represents, perhaps a number (numerical data), a letter string, a dollar amount, a date, or something else altogether.
- *Decimals.*   In this column we specify an upper limit on the number of digits that will appear to the right of a decimal point.
- *Label.*   In this column we identify the labels that the variables will have when we create a table or graph—perhaps one to be included in a dissertation or research report.

FIGURE B.1 ▧
The "Data" Table

	Gender	Exam1	Exam2	Exam3	TotalExam	NoteQuan	NoteQual	var
1	1	35.00	36.50	33.50	105.00	31	.315	
2	2	39.50	41.00	41.50	122.00	28	.384	
3	1	45.00	45.50	39.00	129.50	37	.381	
4	1	34.50	33.00	29.00	96.50	31	.251	
5	2	31.00	43.00	37.00	111.00	42	.305	
6	2	38.00	30.25	32.00	100.25	27	.190	
7	2	40.50	43.00	42.00	125.50	43	.350	
8	1	44.00	45.00	43.00	132.00	26	.166	
9		43.00	38.00	40.00	121.00	52	.406	
10	1	38.00	32.00	30.00	100.00	33	.208	
11	1	43.00	47.00	44.00	134.00	43	.496	
12	2	43.50	34.75	41.00	119.25	24	.201	
13	2	45.00	43.00	42.00	130.00	50	.321	
14	1	39.50	44.00	43.00	126.50	23	.179	
15	2	40.00	36.00	33.00	109.00	14	.040	
16								

Data View   Variable View

	Name	Type	Width	Decimals	Label	Values	Missing	Columns	Align	Measure	Role
1	Gender	Numeric	8	0	Gender	{1, Male}...	None	8	≣ Right	♣ Nominal	↘ Input
2	Exam1	Numeric	8	2	Exam 1 Score	None	None	8	≣ Right	⬦ Scale	↘ Input
3	Exam2	Numeric	8	2	Exam 2 Score	None	None	8	≣ Right	⬦ Scale	↘ Input
4	Exam3	Numeric	8	2	Exam 3 Score	None	None	8	≣ Right	⬦ Scale	↘ Input
5	TotalExam	Numeric	8	2	Exam Score Total	None	None	8	≣ Right	⬦ Scale	↘ Input
6	NoteQuan	Numeric	8	0	Quantity of No...	None	None	8	≣ Right	⬦ Scale	↘ Input
7	NoteQual	Numeric	8	3	Quality of Notes	None	None	8	≣ Right	⬦ Scale	↘ Input
8											
9											

Data View   Variable View

FIGURE B.2 ▧ The "Variables" Table

▧ *Values.*   In this column we can identify any labels we want to give to particular values of a variable. For example, one of our variables is gender, a nominal scale. If we click on this "values" cell in the "Gender" row, a little button appears at the right side of the cell. We click on the button, and a box appears that allows us to tell the computer that a value of 1 means "Male" and a value of 2 means "Female." In Figure B.3, we show this box midway through the process: We've already told the software that a value of 1 means "Male," and we're in the process of telling it that 2 means "Female." After we have finished doing so, we click on "Add" and then on "OK" to say that we have labeled all possible values of the "Gender" variable.

▧ *Measure.*   In this column, we specify whether each variable reflects a nominal scale or an ordinal scale; the category "ordinal scale" also encompasses interval and ratio scales. (You can find descriptions of the four kinds of scales in either Chapter 4 or Chapter 8.) As you can see in Figure B.2, our sample data set consists of one variable (Gender) on a nominal scale and six variables that are on interval or ratio scales—hence, also on an ordinal scale, which in the Variables table is simply called "scale."

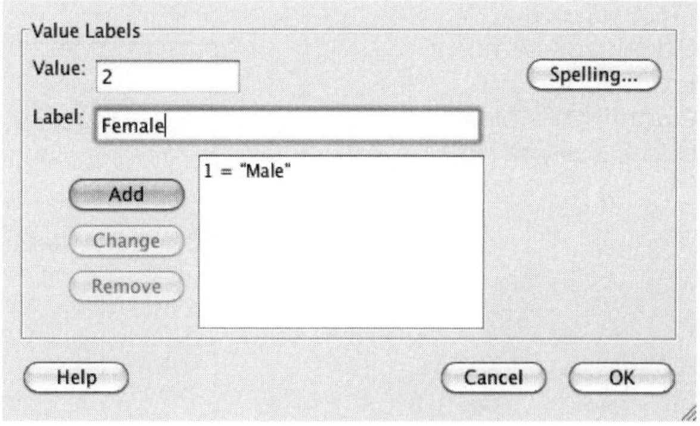

FIGURE B.3 ▨ The "Value Labels" Box for the "Variable View" Table

Value Labels

Value: 2

Label: Female

Spelling...

Add
Change
Remove

1 = "Male"

Help   Cancel   OK

COMPUTING BASIC DESCRIPTIVE STATISTICS

Now that we have our data set, let's conduct some simple analyses. First, let's compute basic descriptive statistics for six of the seven variables (computing a mean and standard deviation for the "Gender" variable would yield meaningless numbers). We move the cursor to the word "Analyze" at the top of the screen and click on the mouse. A pull-down menu appears, and we move the cursor down until the term "Descriptive Statistics" is highlighted, at which point another menu appears to its right. We click on "Descriptives" in the right-hand box. A new box appears in front of our data set. This box contains two smaller boxes, with all seven of our variables listed in the left box. To calculate descriptive statistics for the last six variables, we want to move them into the right box. We do this by highlighting each one and then clicking the right-arrow button between the two boxes. After we've moved the six variables, we click on the "OK" button (see Figure B.4). At this point, a table appears that lists the number of observations (N), minimum and maximum values, mean, and standard deviation for each variable. The final row in the table, "Valid N (listwise)," simply means that SPSS found all 15 numbers for each variable to be appropriate ones; in other words, it didn't omit any scores in doing the calculations.

Now let's suppose that we want to see how overall exam performance (Exam Score Total), quantity of notes (Quantity of Notes), and quality of notes (Quality of Notes) are intercorrelated. To do this, we can calculate Pearson r correlation coefficients for each possible pairing of these three variables. Once again, we go up to "Analyze" at the top of the screen and click on the mouse. When the pull-down menu appears, we move the cursor down until the word "Correlate" is highlighted, then move the cursor to the right to highlight "Bivariate," and then click on the mouse. Once again, the two-box box appears, and we must move the three variables we want to analyze to the right box and then click on "OK." We now have a table that gives us the intercorrelations among these variables, which we can print out by going to the "File" pull-down menu and then to "Print" (see Figure B.5). The first number in each cell of the table tells us the Pearson r for a particular pair of variables (this number is 1 when a variable is correlated with itself), and the third number tells us the number of people for whom the r has been calculated. The middle number tells us the probability (p) that we would obtain an r that high if the two variables were

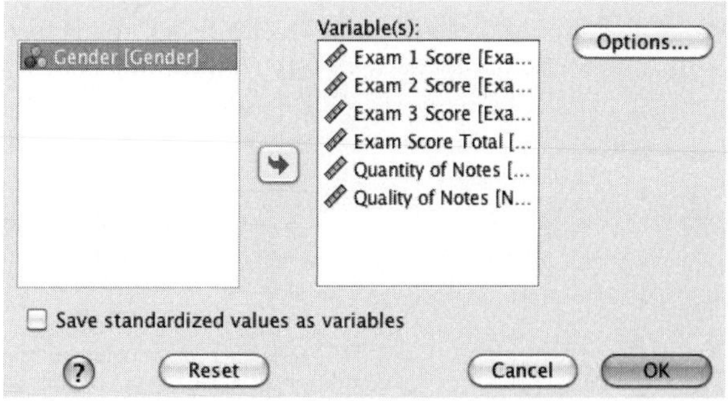

FIGURE B.4 ▨
Identifying Variables for Which We Want Basic Descriptive Statistics to Be Calculated

Gender [Gender]

Variable(s):
Exam 1 Score [Exa...
Exam 2 Score [Exa...
Exam 3 Score [Exa...
Exam Score Total [...
Quantity of Notes [...
Quality of Notes [N...

Options...

☐ Save standardized values as variables

(?)   Reset   Cancel   OK

FIGURE B.5 ▨
Correlations Among
Exam Score Total,
Quantity of Notes,
and Quality of Notes

Correlations

		Exam Score Total	Quantity of Notes	Quality of Notes
Exam Score Total	Pearson Correlation	1	.323	.425
	Sig. (2–tailed)		.241	.114
	N	15	15	15
Quantity of Notes	Pearson Correlation	.323	1	.777**
	Sig. (2–tailed)	.241		.001
	N	15	15	15
Quality of Notes	Pearson Correlation	.425	.777**	1
	Sig. (2–tailed)	.114	.001	
	N	15	15	15

**. Correlation is significant at the 0.01 level (2–tailed).

not correlated in the overall population from which the sample has been drawn. (For a review of *p* values, see the section "Testing Hypotheses" in Chapter 8.)

The table in Figure B.5 marks with two asterisks (**) all *r*s that are significant at an α level of .01. But we don't necessarily have to use that alpha level. Imagine, instead, that we decide to use a significance level (α) of 0.05 for all of our analyses. Any *p* value in the table that is *smaller* than 0.05 indicates that the variables probably *are* correlated in the population from which our sample has been drawn. For example, the correlations between Exam Score Total and the Quantity and Quality of Notes are .323 and .425, respectively. Although these correlations are in the low-to-moderate range, the *p* values associated with them (.241 and .114) tell us that we might get correlations this high *simply by chance* when the two variables are actually unrelated in the overall population. (With a much larger sample size, such correlations would be statistically significant. Our small sample size may be leading us to make Type I errors here.) Now let's look at the correlation between Quantity of Notes and Quality of Notes. This correlation is .777, which has an associated probability of 0.001. This *r* is statistically significant: Students who take more notes also take better notes. We must be careful, however, that we don't conclude that the correlation necessarily indicates a causal relationship: Taking more notes doesn't necessarily cause a student to take better ones, nor does taking better ones cause a student to take more of them. Remember, correlational data alone *never* allows us to draw clear-cut conclusions about cause-and-effect relationships.

COMPUTING INFERENTIAL STATISTICS

In the preceding section we already ventured into inferential statistics a bit. When we looked at the probabilities that our correlation coefficients occurred by chance for a set of possibly unrelated variables, we were drawing inferences. But now let's do so intentionally. Let's see if there are any gender differences in the test performance of males and females. To find out, we need to perform a *t*-test between the two groups. Once again, we go up to "Analyze," and this time we highlight "Compare Means" and then "Independent Samples T Test."[1] A box similar to that shown in Figure B.4 appears, but this one has three boxes within it. We move our dependent variable (Exam Score Total) into the "Test Variable(s)" box and our independent variable (Gender) into the "Grouping Variable" box. Next, we click on the "Define Groups" button and tell the

---

[1]As noted in Table 8.5 in Chapter 8, a *t*-test can take either of two basic forms. An *independent-samples* *t*-test enables a comparison of means for two separate, independent groups. For instance, an independent-samples *t*-test enables a comparison of males versus females, as in the example presented here. In contrast, a *dependent-samples* *t*-test—also known as a *paired samples* *t*-test—enables a comparison of means for a single group of individuals or, instead, for two related groups. For example, a researcher might obtain measures of two characteristics of a single group of students or, alternatively, might obtain measures of one particular characteristic both for a group of fathers and for their first-born sons.

Group Statistics

	Gender	N	Mean	Std. Deviation	Std. Error Mean
Exam Score Total	Male	7	117.6429	16.38524	6.19304
	Female	8	117.2500	9.76418	3.45216

Independent Samples Test

		Levene's Test for Equality of Variances		t-test for Equality of Means						
									95% Confidence Interval of the Difference	
		F	Sig.	t	df	Sig. (2–tailed)	Mean Difference	Std. Error Difference	Lower	Upper
Exam Score Total	Equal variances assumed	8.335	.013	.057	13	.955	.39286	6.85139	–14.40868	15.19439
	Equal variances not assumed			.055	9.520	.957	.39286	7.09022	–15.51373	16.29945

FIGURE B.6 ▨ Computing *t* to Determine if Males and Females Have Different Total Exam Scores

computer that a value of "1" puts a person in Group 1 (the males) and a value of "2" puts a person in Group 2 (the females). We click on the "Continue" button and then click on "OK." We get tables that provide descriptive statistics for the two groups, information about whether the variances of the two groups are equivalent, and results of *t*-tests (see Figure B.6). The program has calculated two *t*s, one based on the assumption of equal variances and another based on the assumption of unequal variances. Given the unequal variances for the two groups (the *F* value for Levene's test has a probability of .013), we'll look at the second *t*, which is .055. This value indicates that the two groups are probably not different in their overall exam performance (the *p* value is .957). (You can find explanations for the other numbers in this table in many statistics textbooks or through an Internet search.)

We have room for one final statistical analysis. Let's say we want to know whether the students performed differently on the three exams they took during the semester. To compare three means for the same group of students, we would ideally want to conduct a repeated-measures analysis of variance. Unfortunately, the version of SPSS we are using here performs only between-subjects ANOVAs, so we will have to settle for three paired-samples *t*-tests.

To conduct our *t*-tests, we go back up to "Analyze," move the cursor down to highlight "Compare Means," and then move it to the right to highlight "Paired-Samples T Tests." We release the mouse button. Once again, we see a two-box box, but in this one the second box includes three columns labeled "Pair," "Variable 1," and "Variable 2." When we click on Exam 1 in the left box and then click on the arrow, and then subsequently do the same thing for Exam 2, we get an Exam 1–Exam 2 pair in the right box. In a similar manner, we can form Exam1–Exam 3 and Exam 2–Exam 3 pairs. We now have three pairs of variables in the right-hand box. We click on "OK" and print out the three tables that the analysis generates (Figure B.7). The first table gives us descriptive statistics; we've seen most of these before, but the column for standard error of the mean is new. We also see Pearson *r*s for the three pairs. We are most interested in the *t* values for three pairs of exam scores, which are shown in the seventh column in the bottom table. None of these *t*s is statistically significant at our significance level of .05 (see the rightmost column), although the Exam 1–Exam 3 pair comes close, with a *p* value of .087.

We have merely scratched the surface of what SPSS can offer. We have ignored some of the values in the statistical tables we've presented. And we haven't even touched on SPSS's graphing capabilities. We urge you to explore SPSS for yourself to discover the many analyses it can perform and the many graphical displays it can create.

Paired Samples Statistics

		Mean	N	Std. Deviation	Std. Error Mean
Pair 1	Exam 1 Score	39.9667	15	4.15102	1.07179
	Exam 2 Score	39.4667	15	5.42388	1.40044
Pair 2	Exam 1 Score	39.9667	15	4.15102	1.07179
	Exam 3 Score	38.0000	15	5.15128	1.33006
Pair 3	Exam 2 Score	39.4667	15	5.42388	1.40044
	Exam 3 Score	38.0000	15	5.15128	1.33006

Paired Samples Correlations

		N	Correlation	Sig.
Pair 1	Exam 1 Score & Exam 2 Score	15	.388	.153
Pair 2	Exam 1 Score & Exam 3 Score	15	.622	.013
Pair 3	Exam 2 Score & Exam 3 Score	15	.814	.000

Paired Samples Test

		Paired Differences					t	df	Sig. (2–tailed)
					95% Confidence Interval of the Difference				
		Mean	Std. Deviation	Std. Error Mean	Lower	Upper			
Pair 1	Exam 1 Score – Exam 2 Score	.50000	5.40089	1.39450	-2.49091	3.49091	.359	14	.725
Pair 2	Exam 1 Score – Exam 3 Score	1.96667	4.14241	1.06956	-.32732	4.26065	1.839	14	.087
Pair 3	Exam 2 Score – Exam 3 Score	1.46667	3.23329	.83483	-.32387	3.25720	1.757	14	.101

FIGURE B.7 ▨ Computing ts to Determine if Students Performed Differently on the Three Exams

Glossary

abduction In scientific inquiry, a theory-building process in which a researcher begins with the facts known about a phenomenon and then brainstorms ideas about a plausible best explanation for the phenomenon.

abstract In a research report, a brief summary of the purpose, methods, and findings of a research project, along with general conclusions drawn from the project.

academic integrity Honesty and responsible behavior in scholarly activities; includes ensuring the privacy and well-being of research participants, accurately portraying findings and weaknesses of one's research, and appropriately crediting the works of others.

acknowledgments In a research report, a section that recognizes other individuals who have provided noteworthy assistance to the research endeavor.

advance organizer Introduction to a discussion that provides an overall organizational scheme for the discussion.

alpha (α) In statistical analysis, a predetermined probability level at which a researcher can reject a null hypothesis; also known as a *significance level.*

applied research Research that has immediate relevance to current procedures or policies and can inform decision making about practical problems.

assumption In a research study, a premise that is taken for granted without confirmatory evidence.

baseline data Measures of a dependent variable taken before any experimental treatment or intervention has been administered.

basic research Research intended to advance theoretical conceptualizations about a particular topic.

bias In a research study, any source of influence that may distort the data obtained or conclusions drawn.

case study Qualitative research design in which a single individual, program, or event is studied in depth for a defined period of time.

checklist List of characteristics that may or may not be evident in an individual performance or product; can be used to quantify the overall quality of the performance or product.

cohort-sequential study Descriptive quantitative study in which participants in (a) two or more age-groups are followed over a lengthy period, (b) data are collected at two or more times, and (c) developmental trends for the various age-groups are compared.

comparative-historical research Historical research in which the histories of two or more societies or cultures are compared, with the goal of identifying similarities, differences, and patterns that might reflect cause-and-effect relationships.

confidence interval Statistically computed range within which a population parameter probably lies; also known as an *interval estimate.*

confirmation bias Tendency to seek information that confirms rather than discredits one's current beliefs.

confounding variable Unexamined variable that is or might be correlated with both an independent variable and a dependent variable; must be controlled if conclusions about cause-and-effect relationships are desired.

constant comparative method Strategy in qualitative research in which a researcher moves back and forth between data collection and data analysis.

construct validity Extent to which a measurement instrument accurately measures a characteristic that cannot be directly observed but is assumed to exist based on patterns in people's behavior (such a characteristic is a *construct*).

constructivism Philosophical perspective based on the idea that any understandings of physical or psychological phenomena are inevitably only human creations and beliefs; that is, researchers *construct* understandings that can never reflect "true" reality (if such a reality exists).

content analysis Qualitative research design in which a body of material is systematically examined in order to detect general patterns, themes, or biases; the material typically involves some form of human communication.

content validity Extent to which a measurement instrument includes a representative sample of the content domain being measured; most often used for measures of academic achievement.

continuous variable Variable that has an infinite number of possible values falling along a continuum.

control group Group of people in a research study who are given either no experimental treatment or a *placebo* treatment that is unlikely to have an effect on the dependent variable(s) of interest.

convergent design Mixed-methods design in which a researcher collects both quantitative and qualitative data in parallel, usually at the same time and with respect to the same general research problem; similar weight is given to the two types of data, with the hope that they will yield consistent or complementary findings.

copyright Legal right of the creator of an intellectual or artistic work to have exclusive use of that work unless the creator explicitly grants permission for someone else to use it.

correlation Extent to which two variables are associated, such that when one variable increases, the other either increases or decreases somewhat predictably.

correlation coefficient Statistic that indicates the strength and direction of an association between two variables.

correlational study Descriptive quantitative study that explores possible relationships among two or more variables.

criteria for admissibility of the data Criteria used to determine whether individual pieces of data warrant inclusion in a researcher's overall data set.

criterion validity Extent to which the results of a measurement instrument correlate with the results of a measure of a presumably related characteristic; also known as *predictive validity* if the related characteristic is assessed at a future point in time.

critical thinking Process of evaluating the accuracy, credibility, and worth of information and lines of reasoning.

cross-sectional study Descriptive quantitative study in which participants from two or more age-groups are sampled and the groups' characteristics or behaviors compared.

deductive logic Reasoning process in which a researcher begins with one or more premises ("givens") and then identifies conclusions that can undisputedly be drawn from the premise(s).

dependent variable Variable in a quantitative research study that is hypothesized to be influenced by an independent variable; hence, its value *depends* on the value of the independent variable.

descriptive research Research that enables researchers to draw conclusions about the current state of affairs regarding a situation or issue but not about cause-and-effect relationships.

descriptive statistics Statistics that summarize the nature of a particular set of numerical data (e.g., means, standard deviations, correlation coefficients).

Digital Object Identifier (DOI) Unique, permanent number assigned to a document posted on the Internet; enables one to find the document even if its exact location (URL) changes over time.

discrete variable Variable that has a finite and usually small number of possible values.

discriminant sampling In a grounded theory study, a follow-up to theoretical sampling in which a researcher identifies one or more data sources that might help substantiate an emerging theory of the phenomenon under investigation.

DOI *See* Digital Object Identifier (DOI).

double-blind experiment Experiment in which neither participants nor research associates (e.g., those who administer interventions or analyze qualitative data) are aware of any participant's membership in a particular treatment or control group.

effect size (ES) Statistically determined estimate of the strength of a relationship between two variables (e.g., the degree to which an intervention has an effect on a dependent variable, or the strength of a correlation between two variables).

electronic spreadsheet Software program that enables a researcher to enter and then manipulate data in a two-dimensional table.

embedded design Mixed-methods design in which a researcher collects both quantitative and qualitative data in parallel, usually at the same time and with respect to the same general research problem; one form of data is given higher priority, with the other form serving in a secondary, supplementary role.

emergent design In qualitative research, a strategy in which data collected early in the investigation influence the methods that are subsequently used and the kinds of data that are subsequently collected.

end matter In a research report, content that follows the final section or chapter (e.g., reference list, appendixes).

endnote Brief note at the end of a written document that communicates further information about a particular statement within the document.

equivalent forms reliability Extent to which two different versions of the same measurement instrument (e.g., "Form A" and "Form B") yield similar results.

ethnography Qualitative research design in which a researcher looks in depth at a cultural group in its natural setting.

ex post facto design Quantitative research design in which a researcher identifies existing conditions or previously occurring events in people's lives and then collects data to investigate a possible relationship between these factors and subsequent characteristics or behaviors.

experimental design Quantitative research design that enables conclusions about cause-and-effect relationships; involves both (a) manipulation of one or more variables to determine their possible effects on one or more other, dependent variables; and (b) control of additional variables that might otherwise have an impact on the dependent variables.

experimental group Group of people in a research study who are given a particular experimental intervention in order to observe the intervention's possible effect on one or more dependent variables; also known as a *treatment group.*

explanatory design Two-phase mixed-methods design in which quantitative data collection is followed by the collection of qualitative information that can help clarify the meanings of the quantitative findings.

exploratory design Two-phase mixed-methods design in which qualitative data are collected in an effort to inform the planning and implementation of subsequent quantitative data collection.

external evidence In historical research, evidence that a document is genuine rather than counterfeit; also called *external criticism.*

external validity Extent to which the results of a research study are applicable to other contexts, especially in real-world situations.

face validity Extent to which, on the surface, a measurement instrument *looks like* it is measuring a particular characteristic.

factorial design Quantitative research design that examines the possible effects of two or more independent variables and possible ways they might interact in their influences.

figure Graphic illustration of certain concepts, phenomena, or statistical findings.

five-number summary Method of describing variability in which five numbers are reported: the lowest and highest numbers in the distribution, Quartile 1 (25th percentile), the median, and Quartile 3 (75th percentile).

focus group Small group of people who are assembled and asked to express their perspectives about a particular issue.

footnote Brief note at the bottom of a page that communicates further information about a particular statement on the page.

front matter In a research report, content that precedes the introductory text (e.g., title, abstract, table of contents).

gatekeeper In an ethnographic study, a person who can smooth the way for a researcher's entrance into a particular cultural group.

geometric mean Measure of central tendency appropriate for a data set reflecting growth or deceleration; calculated by multiplying all data points and then finding the Nth root of the product.

grounded theory study Qualitative research design in which a researcher collects data relevant to a research problem and uses them to develop a new theory about a particular phenomenon.

Hawthorne effect Phenomenon in which participants in a research project change their behavior simply because they know they are being exposed to an experimental intervention.

historical research Research study in which the focus is on trends in and meanings of certain historical events.

hypothesis Proposed explanation for an observed phenomenon; typically made on the basis of an existing theory or previous observations.

independent variable Variable in a quantitative research study that is hypothesized to have an influence on one or more other variables; in many cases, is directly manipulated by the researcher.

inductive reasoning Reasoning process in which a researcher begins with multiple specific observations about a particular phenomenon and then makes broader generalizations about the phenomenon.

inferential statistics Statistics that enable inference-drawing about large populations from sample data.

informed consent Practice of both (a) informing participants (or, if applicable, their legal guardians) about the nature of a research study and (b) obtaining written permission for participation.

informed consent form Form that describes the nature of a research project and of one's participation in it; required for many studies involving human beings.

institutional animal care and use committee (IACUC) Committee at a research institution that scrutinizes proposals for studies involving nonhuman animals; its primary role is to determine and minimize the extent to which the studies might cause unnecessary suffering, distress, or death.

instrumentation bias Characteristic of a measurement instrument or procedure that consistently and differentially slants the obtained results in a particular direction.

insubstantial phenomenon Phenomenon that has no clear-cut basis in the physical world (e.g., an opinion, feeling, or underlying personality characteristic).

interlibrary loan Multilibrary alliance through which one can gain access to books and additional sources at libraries other than one's own.

internal consistency reliability Extent to which all of the items in a single measurement instrument yield similar results.

internal evidence In historical research, evidence that helps a researcher impose meaning on a document that contains ambiguous or otherwise puzzling information or statements; also called *internal criticism.*

internal review board (IRB) Committee at a research institution that scrutinizes proposals for studies involving human participants; its primary role is to ensure that the studies will not expose participants to undue harm or in some other way violate basic ethical standards.

internal validity Extent to which a research design and its implementation enable accurate conclusions about cause-and-effect and other relationships among variables studied in a research project.

interquartile range Measure of variability reflecting the difference between Quartile 1 (25th percentile) and Quartile 3 (75th percentile).

interrater reliability Extent to which two or more individuals evaluating the same product or performance make identical or similar judgments.

interval estimate Statistically computed range within which a population parameter probably lies; also known as a *confidence interval.*

interval scale Numerical scale that reflects equal units of measurement, but with an arbitrary zero point (i.e., the number 0 does *not* indicate total absence of the characteristic being measured).

IQ score Standard score with a mean of 100 and a standard deviation of 15.

juried research report Research report that has been judged by respected colleagues in one's field and deemed to be of sufficient quality and importance to warrant presentation or publication; also known as a *refereed* report.

key informant In an ethnographic study or similar qualitative design, a person who can provide especially useful information and insights and possibly also facilitate contacts with other helpful individuals.

keywords Words or short phrases used to locate relevant sources in a database or on the Internet.

kurtosis Parameter of a symmetrical distribution that reflects the degree to which the distribution is unusually pointy or flat, such that the percentages within each portion of the distribution are notably different from those in the normal distribution.

leptokurtic distribution Distribution in which a greater percentage of data points are clustered near the mean than is true for a normal distribution; in its graphic representation, it appears more "pointy" at the middle than a normal distribution does.

Likert scale Numerical continuum on which a particular characteristic might be judged and quantified; also known as a *rating scale.*

list server Internet-based mailing list to which people can subscribe in order to get ongoing messages, newsletters, and other postings related to a particular topic.

longitudinal study Descriptive quantitative study in which participants are followed over a lengthy period, with data being collected at two or more times.

matched pairs Pairs of people who are quite similar with respect to certain characteristics that might possibly have an effect on a dependent variable (e.g., gender, age, grade-point-average); used as a strategy for controlling for possible confounding variables in a study.

mean Measure of central tendency based on the arithmetic (i.e., mathematical) average of all data points related to a particular variable; in everyday language, known simply as an *average.*

measurement Limiting of data related to a phenomenon so that they can be interpreted and compared to a particular qualitative or quantitative standard; a systematic method of assigning numerical values or categories to data so that they can be analyzed and interpreted with some degree of objectivity.

median Measure of central tendency based on the exact midpoint of a distribution of data points related to a particular variable.

mediating variable Variable in a quantitative research study that is influenced by an independent variable and then, in turn, influences a dependent variable; can help explain why the independent variable has a certain effect on the dependent variable.

memos In qualitative research, a researcher's notes-to-self about preliminary interpretations of data being collected.

meta-analysis Statistical procedure in which statistical analyses from many previous quantitative studies become the "data" to be analyzed as a whole; useful in determining the degree to which previous studies about a topic have yielded consistent results.

mixed-methods research Research that includes elements of both quantitative and qualitative research.

mode Measure of central tendency based on the most frequently occurring number in a data set related to a particular variable.

moderating variable Contextual variable in a quantitative research study that influences the nature and strength of a cause-and-effect relationship between two other variables.

multiphase iterative design Mixed-methods design that includes three or more phases; earlier phases inform conceptualization and implementation of subsequent phases.

multitrait–multimethod approach Strategy in which two or more different characteristics are each measured using two or more different techniques; useful in determining the validity of each technique.

narrative research In historical research, a research strategy in which a researcher interviews people who have previously participated in one or more events under investigation; also called *oral history.*

negative correlation Relationship between two variables in which one variable tends to decrease as the other variable increases, reflecting an inverse relationship.

negatively skewed distribution Distribution in which data points lower than the median (midpoint) have greater variability than do data points higher than the median.

nominal scale Use of numbers or verbal labels to assign each piece of data to one of two or more categories.

nonjuried research report Research report that has not been screened for quality or accuracy by one or more experts; also known as a *nonrefereed* report.

nonparametric statistics Statistical procedures that are not based on any assumptions about the nature of the population from which one or more samples have been drawn; available only for relatively simple statistical questions (e.g., questions related to central tendency or correlation).

nonprobability sampling Sample selection process in which some members of a population have a greater chance of being selected than others.

normal distribution (normal curve) Theoretical pattern that many research variables approximate, in which most data points are in the middle range and only a few lie at the extremes; also known as a *bell curve.*

norm-referenced score Score that indicates where each individual is positioned in a distribution relative to other members of the person's norm group.

novelty effect Phenomenon in a research study in which participants' behavior changes not as the result of a specific experimental intervention, but rather as a result of the fact that the environment has changed in a noticeable way.

null hypothesis Hypothesis postulating that a statistically significant result is due entirely to chance.

observation study Descriptive quantitative study in which observations focus on specific, predetermined behaviors and are systematically quantified in some manner.

online database In academic research, an Internet-based resource containing general information about thousands of scholarly works; is easily searchable with the use of appropriate keywords or other relevant information (e.g., author, journal title, publication date).

operational definition Definition of a characteristic or variable in a research study in terms of how it will be identified or measured (e.g., an operational definition of *intelligence* might be participants' performance on an IQ test).

oral history In historical research, a research strategy in which a researcher interviews people who have previously participated in one or more events under investigation; also called *narrative research.*

ordinal scale Numerical scale in which assigned numbers reflect only the rank-ordering of various pieces of data with respect to a particular variable; does not legitimately allow addition or subtraction of two or more data points.

parameter Numerical characteristic of a specific, entire population that summarizes a certain aspect of its distribution (e.g., its central tendency or variability).

parametric statistics Statistical procedures based on certain assumptions about the nature of the population from which one or more samples have been drawn; two common assumptions are (a) that the data reflect an interval or ratio scale and (b) that the data approximate a normal distribution.

participant observation In some ethnographic studies, an approach in which researchers immerse themselves in the daily lives of the people they are studying.

pdf *See* portable document format (pdf).

percentile *See* percentile rank (percentile).

percentile rank (percentile) Norm-referenced score indicating the percentage of peers in a norm group getting a raw score less than or equal to a particular person's raw score.

periodical Publication for which new issues come out on a regular basis (e.g., a newspaper, magazine, or professional journal).

phenomenological study Qualitative research design in which a researcher tries to understand people's perceptions and perspectives relative to a particular situation.

pilot study Brief exploratory investigation to determine the feasibility and validity of procedures, measurement instruments, or methods of analysis that might be useful in a subsequent, more in-depth research study.

placebo In an experimental study, a treatment that is presumed to have little or no effect on a dependent variable of interest.

plagiarism Misrepresentation of another person's work as being one's own.

platykurtic distribution Distribution in which a greater percentage of data points are located near the extremes than is true for a normal distribution; in its graphic representation, it appears flatter at the middle than a normal distribution does.

point estimate Single statistic that is used as a reasonable estimate of the corresponding population parameter.

portable document format (pdf) Electronic document that captures both the content and format of a printed document or static computer file.

positive correlation Relationship between two variables in which one variable tends to increase as the other variable increases.

positively skewed distribution Distribution in which data points higher than the median (midpoint) have greater variability than do data points lower than the median.

positivism Philosophical perspective based on the idea that with appropriate techniques, scientists can objectively uncover absolute facts about cause-and-effect relationships in the physical world and in human experience.

postpositivism Philosophical perspective based on the ideas that (a) progress toward an accurate understanding of a phenomenon is likely to be gradual and probabilistic and (b) a truly complete understanding of the phenomenon may ultimately be impossible.

power Degree to which a statistical test maximizes the likelihood of correctly rejecting an incorrect null hypothesis and thus minimizes the chances of making a Type II error.

practical significance Degree to which findings related to a research intervention are useful in real-world procedures and practices; often involves a cost-benefit analysis.

pragmatism Philosophical perspective based on the idea that absolute "truths" about certain phenomena *and* people's constructed beliefs about those phenomena are both legitimate objects of study; also known as *realism.*

pre-experimental design Primitive quantitative research design in which either (a) the independent "variable" has only one value (and hence doesn't vary) or (b) members of two or more treatment and/or control groups have not been selected randomly; useful only for forming tentative hypotheses that require further testing.

primary data Data that directly emerge or emanate from an unobservable phenomenon.

primary source In historical research, a data source that emerged when or soon after a particular event occurred.

probability sampling Sample selection process in which each member of a population has an equal chance of being chosen.

qualitative research Research yielding information that cannot be easily reduced to numbers; typically involves an in-depth examination of a complex phenomenon.

quantitative research Research yielding information that is inherently numerical in nature or can be easily reduced to numbers.

quasi-experimental design Quantitative research design in which an independent variable is manipulated in order to determine its possible effect on another (dependent) variable, but without total control of additional variables that might have an impact on the dependent variable.

range Measure of variability calculated by subtracting the lowest-value data point from the highest-value data point.

rating scale Numerical continuum on which a particular characteristic might be judged and quantified; also known as a *Likert scale.*

ratio scale Numerical scale that reflects equal units of measurement and a true zero point that indicates total absence of the characteristic being measured.

raw score Number of questions correctly answered or number of points accumulated that a research participant earns on a measurement instrument.

reactivity General phenomenon in which people's behavior changes once they know they are being observed.

realism Philosophical perspective based on the idea that absolute "truths" about certain phenomena *and* people's constructed beliefs about those phenomena are both legitimate objects of study; also known as *pragmatism.*

reflexivity In qualitative research, a researcher's conscious attempt to (a) identify personal, social, political, or philosophical biases that might influence data collection and interpretation and then (b) take steps to minimize such influences.

reliability Extent to which a measurement instrument yields consistent information about the characteristic(s) being assessed.

repeated-measures design Quantitative research design in which all participants are exposed to all experimental treatments and any control conditions; enables control of confounding individual-difference variables; also known as a *within-subjects design.*

research Process of systematically collecting, analyzing, and interpreting data in order to enhance understanding of a particular phenomenon.

research design General structure that guides data collection and analysis in order to address a research problem.

research methodology General approach a researcher takes in carrying out a research project (e.g., a particular quantitative or qualitative research design).

research tool Specific mechanism or strategy a researcher uses to collect, manipulate, or interpret data.

respondent validation Qualitative research strategy in which a researcher seeks validation from study participants about conclusions and interpretations drawn from collected data.

response bias Tendency for people to make inaccurate statements (often inadvertently) in their responses to questions in interviews or on questionnaires.

response rate Percentage of people agreeing to participate in a survey.

return rate Percentage of people completing and submitting questionnaires that they have received via mail or e-mail.

robustness In statistics, degree to which a statistical procedure yields generally valid results even when the data violate one or more basic assumptions on which the procedure rests.

rubric Two-dimensional table that includes (a) two or more characteristics on one dimension and (b) concrete criteria for rating them on the other dimension; useful in numerically measuring characteristics of a multifaceted performance or product.

sample Subset of a population of people, another biological species, or inanimate objects; data collected from this subset used to draw conclusions about the population from which it has come.

sampling bias Any factor that causes a researcher to inadvertently obtain a nonrepresentative sample of the population being studied.

scales Categories of measurement that ultimately dictate the statistical procedures (if any) that can be used in processing numerical data. *See also* interval scale, nominal scale, ordinal scale, ratio scale.

scatter plot Two-dimensional graphic representation of the relationship between two variables, with each dot on the graph representing a particular participant; also known as a *scattergram.*

scientific method General approach to learning about a phenomenon in which a researcher (a) identifies a currently unanswered problem (or question), (b) systematically plans and implements data collection relevant to the problem, and then (c) analyzes and interprets the data in an effort to resolve the problem.

search engine Program that enables one to identify Internet websites relevant to a particular topic (e.g., Google, Bing, or Yahoo!).

secondary data Data obtained from one or more people's descriptions or interpretations of primary data related to an unobservable phenomenon.

secondary source In historical research, a data source that emerged at some point subsequent to an event; typically reflects the assumptions and biases of its author(s).

semistructured interview Interview in which a researcher asks predetermined questions but also asks individually tailored follow-up questions in order to gain clarity regarding certain responses.

significance level Probability that a statistically significant result might be due to chance alone; when determined in advance as the criterion for rejecting a null hypothesis, it is also known as *alpha (α).*

single-subject design Quantitative research design in which just a single individual is exposed to all experimental treatments and any control conditions.

skewed distribution Nonsymmetrical distribution of a research variable in which data points on one side extend much further from the median (midpoint) than do data points on the other side.

sociogram Graphic depiction of people's interpersonal links within a group.

sociometric matrix Two-dimensional table that represents how members of a group view one another with respect to a particular characteristic (e.g., likeability or trustworthiness).

standard deviation Measure of variability in which (1) each data point is squared, (2) the sum of the squares is calculated, (3) this sum is divided by the total number of data points, and (4) the square root of the obtained result is calculated; is a frequently used value in parametric statistics.

standard error of the mean Standard deviation for a distribution of sample means; indicates how much a sample mean is likely to vary from one sample to another when all samples are the same size and randomly drawn from the same population.

standard score Norm-referenced score that indicates how far a person's performance is from the mean of a distribution in terms of standard deviation units.

standardization Extent to which a measurement instrument or procedure involves similar content, format, administration procedures, and scoring criteria for all participants in a research study.

stanine Standard score with a mean of 5 and a standard deviation of 2; always reported as a whole number between 1 and 9.

statistic Number computed for a sample that has been drawn from a larger population; intended to provide an estimate of a parameter of the overall population.

statistical regression Phenomenon in which research participants who are identified as being at extreme ends of a distribution at one time tend to be closer to the mean at a subsequent time; is often the result of imprecise measurement of a characteristic at either or both times.

statistical significance Situation in which a statistical result meets or surpasses a predetermined significance level and hence the null hypothesis can be rejected.

statistics Academic discipline comprised of computational procedures for finding patterns in numerical data; alternatively, two or more numbers intended to provide estimates of population parameters based on data collected from a sample of that population.

structured interview Interview in which a researcher predetermines all of the questions to be asked.

subproblem In research, a component of a research problem that is researchable in its own right; sometimes called a *research question*.

substantial phenomenon Phenomenon that can be directly observed in the physical world.

survey research Descriptive quantitative study in which a large number of people are asked questions and their responses tabulated in an effort to identify general patterns or trends in a certain population.

systematic review Research study in which results of many previous qualitative and/or mixed-methods research reports become the objects of investigation; potentially relevant reports are systematically analyzed for their quality, and contents of high-quality reports are coded in an effort to identify key ideas and themes.

table Two-dimensional matrix in which words and/or numbers are displayed for the purpose of summarizing certain ideas or showing certain patterns or relationships.

table of contents List of major sections and subsections in a written document.

table of random numbers Large two-dimensional list of numbers that can guide random selection of population members to be included in a research sample.

table of specifications Two-dimensional grid that lists both the specific topics and the specific behaviors that reflect achievement in a particular content domain, with individual cells indicating the relative importance of each topic-behavior combination.

test–retest reliability Extent to which a measurement instrument yields similar results for each individual over a short time interval.

theoretical sampling In a grounded theory study, a strategy of choosing data sources that are most likely to help a researcher develop a theory of the phenomenon under investigation.

theory Integrated set of concepts and principles developed to explain a particular phenomenon.

thick description Qualitative research strategy in which an observed situation is described in enough detail that readers can construct some of their own interpretations.

treatment In an experimental study, an experimenter-controlled intervention hypothesized to have an effect on one or more dependent variables.

treatment group Group of people in a research study who are given a particular experimental intervention in order to observe the intervention's possible effect on one or more dependent variables; also known as an *experimental group*.

triangulation Collection and comparison of multiple kinds of data, with the goal of finding consistencies or inconsistencies among them.

Type I error Error in statistical decision making in which a null hypothesis that is true is inappropriately rejected; also called an *alpha error*.

Type II error Error in statistical decision making in which an incorrect null hypothesis is inappropriately retained; also called a *beta error*.

Uniform Resource Locator (URL) Specific Internet address at which a particular resource or document can be found (e.g., "www.google.com" or "www.census.gov").

unobtrusive measure Means of assessing research participants' behaviors in such a way that the participants are unaware that they are being observed.

URL *See* Uniform Resource Locator (URL).

validity [in measurement] Extent to which a measurement instrument accurately measures the characteristic it is intended to measure and enables justifiable inferences about that characteristic.

variable In a research project, any quality or characteristic of interest that has two or more possible values.

variance Measure of variability equal to the square of the standard deviation; is a frequently used value in parametric statistics.

web page Document posted on the Internet relative to a specific topic; often includes links to other relevant pages.

within-subjects design Quantitative research design in which all participants are exposed to all experimental treatments and any control conditions; enables control of confounding individual-difference variables; also known as a *repeated-measures design*.

within-subjects variable Independent variable that is systematically varied for each participant in a research study, such that all participants are exposed to all experimental treatments and any control conditions.

Z-score Standard score with a mean of 0 and a standard deviation of 1.

References

Abraham, E. P., Chain, E., Fletcher, C. M., Gardner, A. D., Heatley, N. G., Jennings, M. A., . . . Florey, H. W. (1941). Further observations on penicillin. *Lancet, 2,* 177–188.

Allen, E. M. (1960, November). Why are research grant applications disapproved? *Science, 132,* 1532–1534.

Altheide, D. L., & Johnson, J. M. (1994). Criteria for assessing interpretive validity in qualitative research. In N. K. Denzin & Y. S. Lincoln (Eds.), *Handbook of qualitative research* (pp. 485–499). Thousand Oaks, CA: Sage.

American Psychological Association. (2010). *Publication manual of the American Psychological Association* (6th ed.). Washington, DC: Author.

American Psychological Association. (2012). *APA style guide to electronic references* (6th ed.). Washington, DC: Author.

Anderson, C. A., Lindsay, J. J., & Bushman, B. J. (1999). Research in the psychological laboratory: Truth or triviality? *Current Directions in Psychological Science, 8,* 3–9.

Anderson, T., & Shattuck, J. (2012). Design-based research: A decade of progress in education research? *Educational Researcher, 41,* 16–25.

Bandura, A. (1997). *Self-efficacy: The exercise of control.* New York: Freeman.

Bartholomew, D. J. (2004). *Measuring intelligence: Facts and fallacies.* Cambridge, England: Cambridge University Press.

Bazeley, P. (2010). Computer-assisted integration of mixed methods data sources and analyses. In A. Tashakkori & C. Teddlie (Eds.), *Mixed methods in social & behavioral research* (2nd ed., pp. 431–467). Thousand Oaks, CA: Sage.

Beck, C. T. (1990, January–February). The research critique: General criteria for evaluating a research report. *Journal of Gynecology and Neonatal Nursing, 19,* 18–22.

Becker, H. S. (1970). Whose side are we on? In W. J. Filstead (Ed.), *Qualitative methodology* (pp. 15–26). Chicago: Markham.

Bender, G. (2001). Resisting dominance? The study of a marginalized masculinity and its construction within high school walls. In J. N. Burstyn, G. Bender, R. Casella, H. W. Gordon, D. P. Guerra, K. V. Luschen, . . . K. M. Williams, *Preventing violence in schools: A challenge to American democracy* (pp. 61–77). Mahwah, NJ: Erlbaum.

Bergman, M. M. (2010). Hermeneutic content analysis: Textual and audiovisual analyses within a mixed methods framework. In A. Tashakkori & C. Teddlie (Eds.), *Mixed methods in social & behavioral research* (2nd ed., pp. 379–396). Thousand Oaks, CA: Sage.

Bransford, J. D., Brown, A. L., & Cocking, R. R. (Eds.). (2000). *How people learn: Brain, mind, experience, and school* (expanded ed.). Washington, DC: National Academy Press.

Breisach, E. (1994). *Historiography: Ancient, medieval, and modern* (2nd ed.). Chicago: University of Chicago Press.

Brown, A. L. (1992). Design experiments: Theoretical and methodological challenges in creating complex interventions in classroom settings. *The Journal of the Learning Sciences, 2,* 141–178.

Bryman, A. (2006). Integrating quantitative and qualitative research: How is it done? *Qualitative Research, 6*(1), 97–113.

Campbell, D. T., & Fiske, D. W. (1959). Convergent and discriminant validation by the multitrait-multimethod matrix. *Psychological Bulletin, 56,* 81–105.

Campbell, D. T., & Russo, M. J. (2001). *Social measurement.* Thousand Oaks, CA: Sage.

Campbell, D. T., & Stanley, J. C. (1963). Experimental and quasi-experimental designs for research on teaching. In N. L. Gage (Ed.), *Handbook of research on teaching* (pp. 171–246). Chicago: Rand McNally.

Cepeda, N. J., Vul, E., Rohrer, D., Wixted, J. T., & Pashler, H. (2008). Spacing effects in learning: A temporal ridgeline of optimal retention. *Psychological Science, 19,* 1095–1102.

Chain, E., Florey, H. W., Gardner, A. D., Heatley, N. G., Jennings, M. A., Orr-Ewing, J., . . . Sanders, A. G. (1940). Penicillin as a chemotherapeutic agent. *Lancet, 2,* 226.

Chandler, J. L. S. (2014). *Learning from the collusions, collisions, and contentions with White privilege experienced in the United States by White mothers of sons and daughters whose race is not White.* Doctoral dissertation, Cardinal Stritch University, Milwaukee, WI (available through the online database ProQuest Dissertations & Theses: Full text; publication number 3614469).

Charmaz, K. (2000). Grounded theory: Objective and constructivist methods. In N. K. Denzin & Y. S. Lincoln (Eds.), *Handbook of qualitative research* (2nd ed., pp. 509–535). Thousand Oaks, CA: Sage.

Charmaz, K. (2002). Qualitative interviewing and grounded theory analysis. In J. F. Gubrium & J. A. Holstein (Eds.), *Handbook of interview research: Context and method.* Thousand Oaks, CA: Sage.

Charmaz, K. (2014). *Constructing grounded theory* (2nd ed.). Thousand Oaks, CA: Sage.

Chatterjee, B. B., & Srivastava, A. K. (1982). A systematic method for drawing sociograms. *Perspectives in Psychological Researches, 5*(1), 1–6.

Chicago manual of style (16th ed.). (2010). Chicago: University of Chicago Press.

Chipman, S. F. (2005). Research on the women and mathematics issue: A personal case history. In A. M. Gallagher & J. C. Kaufman (Eds.), *Gender differences in mathematics: An integrative psychological approach* (pp. 1–24). Cambridge, England: Cambridge University Press.

Cizek, G. J. (2003). *Detecting and preventing classroom cheating: Promoting integrity in assessment.* Thousand Oaks, CA: Corwin Press.

Cobb, P., Confrey, J., diSessa, A., Lehrer, R., & Schauble, L. (2003). Design experiments in educational research. *Educational Researcher, 32,* 9–13.

Coghill, R. D. (1944). Penicillin: Science's Cinderella. The background of penicillin production. *Chemical and Engineering News, 22,* 588–593.

Coghill, R. D., & Koch, R. S. (1945). Penicillin: A wartime accomplishment. *Chemical and Engineering News, 23,* 2310.

Cole, D. B., & Ormrod, J. E. (1995). Effectiveness of teaching pedagogical content knowledge through summer geography institutes. *Journal of Geography, 94,* 427–433.

Collins, K. M. T. (2010). Advanced sampling designs in mixed research: Current practices and emerging trends in the social and behavioral sciences. In A. Tashakkori & C. Teddlie (Eds.), *Mixed methods in social & behavioral research* (2nd ed., pp. 353–377). Thousand Oaks, CA: Sage.

Corbin, J., & Strauss, A. C. (2008). *Basics of qualitative research: Techniques and procedures for developing grounded theory* (3rd ed.). Thousand Oaks, CA: Sage.

Cowan, N. (2010). The magical mystery four: How is working memory capacity limited, and why? *Current Directions in Psychological Science, 19,* 51–57.

Creswell, J. W. (2010). Mapping the landscape of mixed methods research. In A. Tashakkori & C. Teddlie (Eds.), *Mixed methods in social & behavioral research* (2nd ed., pp. 45–68). Thousand Oaks, CA: Sage.

373

Creswell, J. W. (2012). *Educational research: Planning, conducting, and evaluating quantitative and qualitative research* (4th ed.). Upper Saddle River, NJ: Pearson.

Creswell, J. W. (2013). *Qualitative inquiry and research design: Choosing among five approaches* (3rd ed.). Thousand Oaks, CA: Sage.

Creswell, J. W. (2014). *Research design: Qualitative, quantitative, and mixed methods approaches* (4th ed.). Thousand Oaks, CA: Sage.

Creswell, J. W., & Plano Clark, V. L. (2011). *Designing and conducting mixed methods research* (2nd ed.). Thousand Oaks, CA: Sage.

Cuca, J. M., & McLoughlin, W. J. (1987, May). Why clinical research grant applications fare poorly in review and how to recover. In *Preparing a research grant application to the National Institutes of Health: Selected articles* (a bulletin from the research branch of the Department of Health and Human Services). Washington, DC: Department of Health and Human Services. (Reprinted from *Clinical Investigation, 5,* pp. 55–58, 1987.)

Cumming, G. (2014). The new statistics: Why and how. *Psychological Science, 25,* 7–29.

Dahlberg, B., Wittink, M. N., & Gallo, J. J. (2010). Funding and publishing integrated studies: Writing effective mixed methods manuscripts and grant proposals. In A. Tashakkori & C. Teddlie (Eds.), *Mixed methods in social & behavioral research* (2nd ed., pp. 775–802). Thousand Oaks, CA: Sage.

Davitz, J. R., & Davitz, L. L. (1996). *Evaluating research proposals: A guide for the behavioral sciences.* Upper Saddle River, NJ: Prentice Hall.

Deaver, C. M., Miltenberger, R. G., & Stricker, J. M. (2001). Functional analysis and treatment of hair twirling in a young child. *Journal of Applied Behavior Analysis, 34,* 535–538.

Do, S. L., & Schallert, D. L. (2004). Emotions and classroom talk: Toward a model of the role of affect in students' experiences of classroom discussions. *Journal of Educational Psychology, 96,* 619–634.

Dowson, M., & McInerney, D. M. (2001). Psychological parameters of students' social and work avoidance goals: A qualitative investigation. *Journal of Educational Psychology, 93,* 35–42.

Efron, S. E., & Ravid, R. (2013). *Action research in education: A practice guide.* New York: Guilford Press.

Eisner, E. W. (1998). *The enlightened eye: Qualitative inquiry and the enhancement of educational practice.* Upper Saddle River, NJ: Merrill/Prentice Hall.

Elliott, D., & Stern, J. E. (Eds.). (1997). *Research ethics: A reader.* Hanover, NH: University Press of New England.

Ferguson, D. L., & Rosales-Ruiz, J. (2001). Loading the problem loader: The effects of target training and shaping on trailer-loading behavior of horses. *Journal of Applied Behavior Analysis, 34,* 409–424.

Fidler, F., & Cumming, G. (2013). Effect size estimation and confidence intervals. In

J. A. Schinka & W. F. Velicer (Eds.), *Handbook of psychology: Vol. 2. Research methods in psychology* (2nd ed., pp. 142–163). Hoboken, NJ: Wiley.

Forbes, M. L., Ormrod, J. E., Bernardi, J. D., Taylor, S. L., & Jackson, D. L. (1999, April). *Children's conceptions of space, as reflected in maps of their hometown.* Paper presented at the American Educational Research Association, Montreal.

Fossey, D. (1983). *Gorillas in the mist.* Boston: Houghton Mifflin.

Freeman, L. C. (2004). *The development of social network analysis: A study in the sociology of science.* North Charleston, SC: BookSurge, LLC.

Gall, M. D., Gall, J. P., & Borg, W. R. (2007). *Educational research: An introduction* (8th ed.). Upper Saddle River, NJ: Merrill/Pearson Education.

Garson, G. D. (2013). *Grounded theory.* Asheboro, NC: Statistical Publishing Associates.

Gay, L. R., Mills, G. E., & Airasian, P. (2012). *Educational research: Competencies for analysis and application* (10th ed.). Upper Saddle River, NJ: Pearson.

Glaser, B. G. (1978). *Theoretical sensitivity: Advances in the methodology of grounded theory.* New York: Sociology Press.

Glaser, B. G. (1992). *Basics of grounded theory analysis.* Mill Valley, CA: Sociology Press.

Glaser, B. G., & Strauss, A. (1967). *The discovery of grounded theory.* Chicago: Aldine.

Good, R. (1993). More guidelines for reviewing research. *Journal of Research in Science Teaching, 30*(1), 1–2.

Goodall, J. (1986). *The chimpanzees of Gombe: Patterns of behavior.* Cambridge, MA: Harvard University Press.

Gorard, S. (2010). Research design, as independent of methods. In A. Tashakkori & C. Teddlie (Eds.), *Mixed methods in social & behavioral research* (2nd ed., pp. 237–251). Thousand Oaks, CA: Sage.

Gosling, S. D., Vazire, S., Srivastava, S., & John, O. P. (2004). Should we trust Web-based studies? A comparative analysis of six preconceptions about Internet questionnaires. *American Psychologist, 59,* 93–104.

Gould, S. J. (1985, June). The median isn't the message. *Discover, 6,* 40–42.

Greene, J. C., Caracelli, V. J., & Graham, W. F. (1989). Toward a conceptual framework for mixed-method evaluation designs. *Educational Evaluation and Policy Analysis, 11,* 255–274.

Halpern, D. F. (1998). Teaching critical thinking for transfer across domains. *American Psychologist, 53,* 449–455.

Halpern, D. F. (2008). Is intelligence critical thinking? Why we need a new definition of intelligence. In P. C. Kyllonen, R. D. Roberts, & L. Stankov (Eds.), *Extending intelligence: Enhancement and new constructs* (pp. 349–370). New York: Erlbaum/Taylor & Francis.

Harden, A., & Thomas, J. (2010). Mixed methods and systematic reviews: Examples and emerging issues. In A. Tashakkori & C. Teddlie (Eds.), *Mixed methods in social & behavioral research*

(2nd ed., pp. 749–774). Thousand Oaks, CA: Sage.

Harwell, M. R., & Gatti, G. G. (2001). Rescaling ordinal data to interval data in educational research. *Review of Educational Research, 71,* 105–131.

Haskins, L., & Jeffrey, K. (1990). *Understanding quantitative history.* New York: McGraw-Hill.

Heather, P. (2009). *Empires and barbarians: The fall of Rome and the birth of Europe.* New York: Oxford University Press.

Heck, A., Collins, J., & Peterson, L. (2001). Decreasing children's risk taking on the playground. *Journal of Applied Behavior Analysis, 34,* 349–352.

Heine, S. J. (2007). Culture and motivation: What motivates people to act in the ways that they do? In S. Kitayama & D. Cohen (Eds.), *Handbook of cultural psychology* (pp. 714–733). New York: Guilford.

Hesse-Biber, S. N. (2010). *Mixed methods research: Merging theory with practice.* New York: Guilford.

Holmbeck, G. N. (1997). Toward terminological, conceptual, and statistical clarity in the study of mediators and moderators: Examples from the child-clinical and pediatric psychology literatures. *Journal of Consulting and Clinical Psychology, 65,* 599–610.

Howe, K., & Eisenhardt, M. (1990). Standards for qualitative (and quantitative) research: A prolegomenon. *Educational Researcher, 19*(4), 2–9.

Jaccard, J., & Jacoby, J. (2010). *Theory construction and model-building skills.* New York: Guilford.

Jackson, D. L. (1996). *Effects of training in self-generation on the quality of students' questions, class notes and examination scores.* Unpublished doctoral dissertation, University of Northern Colorado, Greeley.

Johnson, B. (2001). Toward a new classification of nonexperimental quantitative research. *Educational Researcher, 30*(2), 3–13.

Johnson, R. B., & Onwuegbuzie, A. J. (2004). Mixed methods research: A research paradigm whose time has come. *Educational Researcher, 33*(7), 14–26.

Kahn, P. G. K., & Pompea, S. M. (1978, October 19). Nautiloid growth rhythms and dynamical evolution of the Earth-moon system. *Nature, 275,* 606–611.

Karabenick, S. A., Woolley, M. E., Friedel, J. M., Ammon, B. V., Blazevski, J. B., Bonney, C. R., . . . Kelly, K. L. (2007). Cognitive processing of self-report items in educational research: Do they think what we mean? *Educational Psychologist, 42,* 139–151.

Kearns, K. C. (1994). *Dublin tenement life.* Dublin, Ireland: Gill & MacMillan.

Keeter, S., Dimock, M., Christian, L., & Kennedy, C. (2008, January 31). *The impact of "cell-onlys" on public opinion polls: Ways of coping with a growing population segment.* Washington, DC: Pew Research Center. Retrieved from Pew Research Center for the People and the Press website: http://people-press.org/files/legacy-pdf/391.pdf

Kellogg, R. T. (1994). *The psychology of writing.* New York: Oxford University Press.

Kim-Cohen, J., Moffitt, T. E., Caspi, A., & Taylor, A. (2004). Genetic and environmental processes in young children's resilience and vulnerability to socioeconomic deprivation. *Child Development, 75,* 651–668.

Kime, N. (2008). Children's eating behaviours: The importance of the family setting. *Area, 40,* 315–322.

Kinnick, V. (1989). *Learning fetal monitoring under three conditions of concept teaching.* Unpublished doctoral dissertation, University of Colorado, Boulder.

Kontos, S. (1999). Preschool teachers' talk, roles, and activity settings during free play. *Early Childhood Research Quarterly, 14*(3), 363–382.

Kozinets, R. V. (2010). *Netnography: Doing ethnographic research online.* London: Sage.

Krathwohl, D. R. (1993). *Methods of educational and social science research: An integrated approach.* White Plains, NY: Longman.

Kraut, R., Olson, J., Banaji, M., Bruckman, A., Cohen, J., & Couper, M. (2004). Psychological research online: Report of Board of Scientific Affairs' Advisory Group on the Conduct of Research on the Internet. *American Psychologist, 59,* 105–117.

Krueger, R. A., & Casey, M. A. (2009). *Focus groups: A practical guide for applied research* (4th ed.). Thousand Oaks, CA: Sage.

Kuhn, D. (1995). Microgenetic study of change: What has it told us? *Psychological Science, 6,* 133–139.

Kvale, S., & Brinkmann, S. (2009). *InterViews: Learning the craft of qualitative research interviewing* (2nd ed.). Thousand Oaks, CA: Sage.

Lara, L. G. (2009). *A mixed method study of factors associated with the academic achievement of Latina/o college students from predominantly Mexican American backgrounds: A strengths-based approach.* Doctoral dissertation, University of Northern Colorado, Greeley. (Available through the online database ProQuest Dissertations & Theses: Full Text; publication number 3397099)

Lauer, J. M., & Asher, J. W. (1988). *Composition research: Empirical designs.* New York: Oxford University Press.

Laursen, B., Bukowski, W. M., Aunola, K., & Nurmi, J.-E. (2007). Friendship moderates prospective associations between social isolation and adjustment problems in young children. *Child Development, 78,* 1395–1404.

Leavenworth, P. S. (1998). *"The best title that Indians can claime . . .": Native agency and consent in the transferal of Penacook-Pawtucket land in the seventeenth century.* Unpublished master's thesis, University of New Hampshire, Durham.

Leung, C. Y. Y. (2012). *The immigration experiences, acculturation, and parenting of Chinese immigrant mothers.* Unpublished doctoral dissertation, University of Maryland, Baltimore County.

Lincoln, Y. S., & Guba, E. G. (1985). *Naturalistic inquiry.* Thousand Oaks, CA: Sage.

Lippa, R. A. (2002). *Gender, nature, and nurture.* Mahwah, NJ: Erlbaum.

Lipsey, M. W. (1990). *Design sensitivity: Statistical power for experimental research.* Newbury Park, CA: Sage.

Loftus, E. F., & Palmer, J. C. (1974). Reconstruction of automobile destruction: An example of the interaction between language and memory. *Journal of Verbal Learning and Verbal Behavior, 13,* 585–589.

Lowes, J. L. (1927). *The road to Xanadu.* Boston: Houghton Mifflin.

Lowes, J. L. (1955). *The road to Xanadu: A study in the ways of the imagination* (Rev. ed.). Boston: Houghton Mifflin.

Lundeberg, M., & Mohan, L. (2009). Context matters: Gender and cross-cultural differences in confidence. In D. J. Hacker, J. Dunlosky, & A. C. Graesser (Eds.), *Handbook of metacognition in education* (pp. 221–239). New York: Routledge.

Malthus, T. R. (1963). *An essay on the principle of population; or, a view of its past and present effects on human happiness, with an inquiry into our prospects respecting the future removal or mitigation of the evils which it occasions.* Homewood, IL: Irwin. (Original work published 1826)

Mandler, J. M. (2007). On the origins of the conceptual system. *American Psychologist, 62,* 741–751.

Marius, R. (1989). *A short guide to writing about history.* New York: HarperCollins.

Marsh, H. W., Gerlach, E., Trautwein, U., Lüdtke, O., & Brettschneider, W.-D. (2007). Longitudinal study of preadolescent sport self-concept and performance: Reciprocal effects and causal ordering. *Child Development, 78,* 1640–1656.

Martin, V. B., & Gynnild, A. (Eds.). (2011). *Grounded theory: The philosophy, method, and work of Barney Glaser.* Boca Raton, FL: BrownWalker Press.

Maurois, A. (1959). *The life of Alexander Fleming: Discoverer of penicillin.* New York: E. P. Dutton.

Maxwell, J. A., & Mittapalli, K. (2010). Realism as a stance for mixed methods research. In A. Tashakkori & C. Teddlie (Eds.), *Mixed methods in social & behavioral research* (2nd ed., pp. 145–167). Thousand Oaks, CA: Sage.

McCallin, R. C. (1988). *Knowledge application orientation, cognitive structure, and achievement.* Unpublished doctoral dissertation, University of Northern Colorado, Greeley.

McCaslin, M., Vega, R. I., Anderson, E. E., Calderon, C. N., & Labistre, A. M. (2011). Tabletalk: Navigating and negotiating in small-group learning. In D. M. McInerney, R. A. Walker, & G. A. D. Liem (Eds.), *Sociocultural theories of learning and motivation: Looking back, looking forward* (pp. 191–222). Charlotte, NC: Information Age.

McCloskey, M. (1983). Naive theories of motion. In D. Gentner & A. L. Stevens (Eds.), *Mental models* (pp. 299–324). Hillsdale, NJ: Erlbaum.

McCrea, S. M., Liberman, N., Trope, Y., & Sherman, S. J. (2008). Construal level and procrastination. *Psychological Science, 19,* 1308–1314.

McGibbon, E., Peter, E., & Gallop, R. (2010). An institutional ethnography of nurses' stress. *Qualitative Health Research, 20,* 1353–1378.

McGraw, K. O., Tew, M. D., & Williams, J. E. (2000). The integrity of Web-delivered experiments: Can you trust the data? *Psychological Science, 11,* 502–506.

McGrew, K. S., Flanagan, D. P., Zeith, T. Z., & Vanderwood, M. (1997). Beyond *g*: The impact of *Gf-Gc* specific cognitive abilities research on the future use and interpretation of intelligence tests in the schools. *School Psychology Review, 26,* 189–210.

McGue, M. (2000). Authorship and intellectual property. In B. D. Sales & S. Folkman (Eds.), *Ethics in research with human participants* (pp. 75–95). Washington, DC: American Psychological Association.

McKenzie, M. G. (2003). *Vocational science and the politics of independence: The Boston Marine Society, 1754–1812.* Unpublished doctoral dissertation, University of New Hampshire, Durham.

Medawar, P. B. (1979). *Advice to a young scientist.* New York: Harper & Row.

Mehan, H. (1979). *Social organization in the classroom.* Cambridge, MA: Harvard University Press.

Mehan, H., & Wood, H. (1975). *The reality of ethnomethodology.* New York: Wiley.

Merten, D. E. (2011). Being there awhile: An ethnographic perspective on popularity. In A. H. N. Cillessen, D. Schwartz, & L. Mayeux (Eds.), *Popularity in the peer system* (pp. 57–76). New York: Guilford Press.

Mertler, C. A. (2012). *Action research: Improving schools and empowering educators* (3rd ed.). Thousand Oaks, CA: Sage.

Middleton, M., Ormrod, J. E., & Abrams, E. (2007, April). Motivation, cognition, and social support: Achievement goals and preservice teacher apprenticeship. In M. Middleton & M. A. Duggan (Chairs), *Motivation of teachers as learners of the teaching craft.* Symposium presented at the American Educational Research Association, Chicago.

Milch-Reich, S., Campbell, S. B., Pelham, W. E., Jr., Connelly, L. M., & Geva, D. (1999). Developmental and individual differences in children's on-line representations of dynamic social events. *Child Development, 70,* 413–431.

Miles, M. B., Huberman, A. M., & Saldaña, J. (2014). *Qualitative data analysis: A methods sourcebook* (3rd ed.). Los Angeles: Sage.

Miller, G. A. (1956). The magical number seven, plus or minus two: Some limits on our capacity for processing information. *Psychological Review, 63,* 81–97.

Miller, S. M., Nelson, M. W., & Moore, M. T. (1998). Caught in the paradigm gap: Qualitative researchers' lived experience and the politics of epistemology. *American Educational Research Journal, 35,* 377–416.

Mills, G. E. (2014). *Action research: A guide for the teacher researcher* (5th ed.). Upper Saddle River, NJ: Pearson.

Mitchell, G. (2012). Revisiting truth or triviality: The external validity of research in the psychological laboratory. *Perspectives on Psychological Science, 7,* 109–117.

Mitchell, K. J. (1998). *Childhood sexual abuse and family functioning linked with eating and substance misuse: Mediated structural models.* Unpublished doctoral dissertation, University of Rhode Island, Kingston.

Morelli, G. A., & Rothbaum, F. (2007). Situating the child in context: Attachment relationships and self-regulation in different cultures. In S. Kitayama & D. Cohen (Eds.), *Handbook of cultural psychology* (pp. 500–527). New York: Guilford.

Munter, M., & Paradi, D. (2009). *Guide to PowerPoint.* Upper Saddle River, NJ: Pearson/ Prentice Hall.

Murphy, K. R., Myors, B., & Wolach, A. (2009). *Statistical power analysis: A simple and general model for traditional and modern hypothesis tests* (3rd ed.). New York: Routledge.

Nelson, S. K., Kushlev, K., English, T., Dunn, E. W., & Lyubomirsky, S. (2013). In defense of parenthood: Children are associated with more joy than misery. *Psychological Science, 24,* 3–10.

Neuman, W. L. (2011). *Social research methods: Qualitative and quantitative approaches* (7th ed.). Boston: Allyn & Bacon.

Nicholls, M. E. R., Orr, C. A., Okubo, M., & Loftus, A. (2006). Satisfaction guaranteed: The effect of spatial biases on responses to Likert scales. *Psychological Science, 17,* 1027–1028.

Nichols, J. D. (1998). Multiple perspectives of collaborative research. *International Journal of Educational Reform, 7,* 150–157.

Nicol, A. A. M., & Pexman, P. M. (2010). *Presenting your findings: A practical guide for creating figures, posters, and presentations* (6th ed.). Washington, DC: American Psychological Association.

Nussbaum, E. M. (2008). Collaborative discourse, argumentation, and learning: Preface and literature review. *Contemporary Educational Psychology, 33,* 345–359.

O'Cathain, A. (2010). Assessing the quality of mixed methods research: Toward a comprehensive framework. In A. Tashakkori & C. Teddlie (Eds.), *Mixed methods in social & behavioral research* (2nd ed., pp. 531–555). Thousand Oaks, CA: Sage.

Onwuegbuzie, A. J., & Combs, J. P. (2010). Emergent data analysis techniques in mixed methods research: A synthesis. In A. Tashakkori & C. Teddlie (Eds.), *Mixed methods in social & behavioral research* (2nd ed., pp. 397–430). Thousand Oaks, CA: Sage.

Onwuegbuzie, A. J., & Leech, N. L. (2005). Taking the "Q" out of research: Teaching research methodology courses without the divide between quantitative and qualitative paradigms. *Quality and Quantity, 39,* 267–296.

Onwuegbuzie, A. J., & Teddlie, C. (2003). A framework for analyzing data in mixed methods research. In A. Tashakkori & C. Teddlie (Eds.), *Handbook of mixed methods in social and behavioral research* (pp. 351–383). Thousand Oaks, CA: Sage.

Ormrod, J. E. (2011). *Our minds, our memories.* Boston: Allyn & Bacon/Pearson.

Ormrod, J. E. (2012). *Human learning* (6th ed.). Upper Saddle River, NJ: Pearson.

Ormrod, J. E., Ormrod, R. K., Wagner, E. D., & McCallin, R. C. (1988). Reconceptualizing map learning. *American Journal of Psychology, 101,* 425–433.

Ormrod, R. K. (1974). *Adaptation in cultural ecosystems: Early 19th century Jamaica.* Unpublished doctoral dissertation, The Pennsylvania State University, University Park.

Ormrod, R. K., & Trahan, R. G. (1982). Can signs help visitors control their own behavior? *Trends, 19*(4), 25–27.

Peterson, C. (2009). Minimally sufficient research. *Perspectives on Psychological Science, 4,* 7–9.

Petticrew, M., & Roberts, H. (2006). *Systematic reviews in the social sciences: A practical guide.* Oxford, UK: Blackwell.

Polkinghorne, D. E. (1989). Phenomenological research methods. In R. S. Valle & S. Halling (Eds.), *Existential-phenomenological perspectives in psychology* (pp. 41–60). New York: Plenum.

Rakison, D. H., & Oakes, L. M. (Eds.). (2003). *Early category and concept development: Making sense of the blooming, buzzing confusion.* Oxford, England: Oxford University Press.

Ramirez, I. L. (2001). *The relation of acculturation, criminal history, and social integration of Mexican American and non-Mexican students to assaults on intimate partners.* Unpublished doctoral dissertation, University of New Hampshire, Durham.

Rogelberg, S. G., & Luong, A. (1998). Nonresponse to mailed surveys: A review and guide. *Current Directions in Psychological Science, 7,* 60–65.

Sales, B. D., & Folkman, S. (Eds.). (2000). *Ethics in research with human participants.* Washington, DC: American Psychological Association.

Schram, T. H. (2006). *Conceptualizing and proposing qualitative research* (2nd ed.). Upper Saddle River, NJ: Merrill/Prentice Hall.

Schuman, H. (1967). Economic development and individual change: A social-psychological study of the Comilla Experiment in Pakistan. *Occasional Papers in International Affairs, No. 15.* Cambridge, MA: Harvard University, Center for International Affairs.

Schunk, D. H., & Pajares, F. (2005). Competence perceptions and academic functioning. In A. J. Elliot & C. S. Dweck (Eds.), *Handbook of competence and motivation* (pp. 85–104). New York: Guilford Press.

Schwarz, N. (1999). Self-reports: How the questions shape the answers. *American Psychologist, 54,* 93–105.

Scott, K. M., McGee, M. A., Wells, J. E., & Oakley Browne, M. A. (2008). Obesity and mental disorders in the adult general population. *Journal of Psychosomatic Research, 64,* 97–105.

Scott-Jones, D. (2000). Recruitment of research participants. In B. D. Sales & S. Folkman (Eds.), *Ethics in research with human participants* (pp. 27–34). Washington, DC: American Psychological Association.

Senders, V. L. (1958). *Measurement and statistics: A basic text emphasizing behavioral science.* New York: Oxford University Press.

Shaklee, J. M. (1998). *Elementary children's epistemological beliefs and understandings of science in the context of computer-mediated video conferencing with scientists.* Unpublished doctoral dissertation, University of Northern Colorado, Greeley.

Shanahan, T. (2004). Overcoming the dominance of communication: Writing to think and to learn. In T. L. Jetton & J. A. Dole (Eds.), *Adolescent literacy research and practice* (pp. 59–74). New York: Guilford.

Shank, G. D. (2006). *Qualitative research: A personal skills approach* (2nd ed.). Upper Saddle River, NJ: Pearson.

Shavinina, L. V., & Ferrari, M. (2004). Extracognitive facets of developing high ability: Introduction to some important issues. In L. V. Shavinina & M. Ferrari (Eds.), *Beyond knowledge: Extracognitive aspects of developing high ability* (pp. 3–13). Mahwah, NJ: Erlbaum.

Sheehan, K. B. (2001, January). E-mail survey response rates: A review. *Journal of Computer-Mediated Communication, 6* (2). Retrieved from http://jcmc.indiana.edu/vol6/issue2/sheehan.html

Sieber, J. E. (2000). Planning research: Basic ethical decision-making. In B. D. Sales & S. Folkman (Eds.), *Ethics in research with human participants* (pp. 13–26). Washington, DC: American Psychological Association.

Silverman, D. (1993). *Interpreting qualitative data: Methods for analysing talk, text and interaction.* London: Sage.

Silverman, D., Masland, R., Saunders, M. G., & Schwab, R. S. (1970, June). Irreversible coma associated with electrocerebral silence. *Neurology, 20,* 525–533.

Skagert, K., Dellve, L., Eklöf, M., Pousette, A., & Ahlborg, G. (2008). Leaders' strategies for dealing with their own and their subordinates' stress in public human service organisations. *Applied Ergonomics, 39,* 803–811.

Smith, R. M. (1999). *Academic engagement of high school students with significant disabilities: A competence-oriented interpretation.* Unpublished doctoral dissertation, Syracuse University, Syracuse, New York.

Solomon, R. I. (1949). An extension of control group design. *Psychological Bulletin, 46,* 137–150.

Sowell, E. R., Thompson, P. M., Holmes, C. J., Jernigan, T. L., & Toga, A. W. (1999). *In vivo* evidence for post-adolescent brain maturation in frontal and striatal regions. *Nature Neuroscience, 2,* 859–861.

Steiner, E. (1988). *Methodology of theory building.* Sydney, Australia: Educology Research Associates.

Stevens, S. S. (1946, June 7). On the theory of scales of measurement. *Science, 103,* 677–680.

Strauss, A., & Corbin, J. (1990). *Basics of qualitative research: Grounded theory procedures and techniques.* Thousand Oaks, CA: Sage.

Strunk, W., Jr., & White, E. B. (2009). *The elements of style* (50th anniversary ed.). New York: Pearson/ Longman.

Survey Research Center, Institute for Social Research at the University of Michigan. (1976). *Interviewer's manual* (Rev. ed.). Ann Arbor: Author.

Teddlie, C., & Tashakkori, A. (2010). Overview of contemporary issues in mixed methods research. In A. Tashakkori & C. Teddlie (Eds.), *Mixed methods in social & behavioral research* (2nd ed., pp. 1–41). Thousand Oaks, CA: Sage.

Tesch, R. (1994). The contribution of a qualitative method: Phenomenological research. In M. Langenbach, C. Vaughn, & L. Aagaard (Eds.), *An introduction to educational research* (pp. 143–157). Boston: Allyn & Bacon.

Thompson, B. (2008). *Foundations of behavioral statistics.* New York: Guilford.

Thompson, K. R. (2006). Axiomatic theories of intentional systems: Methodology of theory construction. *Scientific Inquiry Journal, 7*(1), 13–24.

Thrailkill, N. J. (1996). *Imagery-evoking and attention-attracting material as facilitators of learning from a lecture.* Unpublished doctoral dissertation, University of Northern Colorado, Greeley.

Toynbee, A. (1939–1961). *A study of history* (12 vols.). London: Oxford University Press, Royal Institute of International Affairs.

Trahan, R. G. (1978). *Social science research: Rocky Mountain National Park* (Contract agreement PX 1520-8-A529). Greeley, CO: Author.

Tyler, K. M., Uqdah, A. L., Dillihunt, M. L., Beatty-Hazelbaker, R., Connor, T., Gadson, N., . . . Stevens, R. (2008). Cultural discontinuity: Toward a quantitative investigation of a major hypothesis in education. *Educational Researcher, 37,* 280–297.

Uziel, L. (2010). Rethinking social desirability scales: From impression management to interpersonally oriented self-control. *Perspectives on Psychological Science, 5,* 243–263.

Walton, D. N. (2003). *Ethical argumentation.* New York: Lexington Books.

Ward, C., Bochner, S., & Furnham, A. (2001). *The psychology of culture shock* (2nd ed.). London: Routledge.

Wasserman, S., & Faust, K. (1994). *Social network analysis: Methods and applications.* Cambridge, England: Cambridge University Press.

Wennick, A., Lundqvist, A., & Hallström, I. (2009). Everyday experience of families three years after diagnosis of Type 1 diabetes in children: A research paper. *Journal of Pediatric Nursing, 24,* 222–230.

Wheelan, C. (2013). *Naked statistics: Stripping the dread from the data.* New York: Norton.

Witt, E., & Best, J. (April 21, 2008). *How different are people who don't respond to pollsters?* Washington, DC: Pew Research Center. Retrieved from http://pewresearch.org/pubs/807/

Wolcott, H. F. (1994). *Transforming qualitative data: Description, analysis, and interpretation.* Thousand Oaks, CA: Sage.

Wong, P. T. P. (n.d.). *How to write a research proposal.* Retrieved from http://www.meaning.ca/archives/archive/art_how_to_write_P_Wong.htm

Zambo, D. (2003). *Uncovering the conceptual representations of students with reading disabilities.* Unpublished doctoral dissertation, Arizona State University, Tempe.

Index